# Probability Theory and Stochastic Modeling with Applications

# Probability Theory and Stochastic Modeling with Applications

Editors

**Francisco German Badía**
**María D. Berrade**

MDPI

Basel • Beijing • Wuhan • Barcelona • Belgrade • Novi Sad • Cluj • Manchester

*Editors*
Francisco German Badía
Department of Statistics
University of Zaragoza
Zaragoza, Spain

María D. Berrade
Department of Statistics
University of Zaragoza
Zaragoza, Spain

*Editorial Office*
MDPI
St. Alban-Anlage 66
4052 Basel, Switzerland

This is a reprint of articles from the Special Issue published online in the open access journal *Mathematics* (ISSN 2227-7390) (available at: https://www.mdpi.com/si/mathematics/Probab_Theory_Stoch_Modeling).

For citation purposes, cite each article independently as indicated on the article page online and as indicated below:

| Lastname, A.A.; Lastname, B.B. Article Title. *Journal Name* **Year**, *Volume Number*, Page Range. |
|---|

**ISBN 978-3-0365-8852-0 (Hbk)**
**ISBN 978-3-0365-8853-7 (PDF)**
**doi.org/10.3390/books978-3-0365-8853-7**

# Contents

**About the Editors** . . . . . . . . . . . . . . . . . . . . . . . . . . . . . . . . . . . . . . . . . . . . vii

**Francisco Germán Badía and María D. Berrade**
Special Issue "Probability Theory and Stochastic Modeling with Applications"
Reprinted from: *Mathematics* **2023**, *11*, 3196, doi:10.3390/math11143196 . . . . . . . . . . . . . . . 1

**Shuxia Jiang, Nian Liu and Yuanyuan Liu**
A Wavelet-Based Computational Framework for a Block-Structured Markov Chain with a Continuous Phase Variable
Reprinted from: *Mathematics* **2023**, *11*, 1587, doi:10.3390/math11071587 . . . . . . . . . . . . . . . 5

**Huda M Alshanbari, Zubair Ahmad, Hazem Al-Mofleh, Clement Boateng Ampadu and Saima K. Khosa**
A New Probabilistic Approach: Estimation and Monte Carlo Simulation with Applications to Time-to-Event Data
Reprinted from: *Mathematics* **2023**, *11*, 1583, doi:10.3390/math11071583 . . . . . . . . . . . . . . . 23

**Zhengu Zhang and Sheldon M. Ross**
Finding the Best Dueler
Reprinted from: *Mathematics* **2023**, *11*, 1568, doi:10.3390/math11071568 . . . . . . . . . . . . . . . 53

**Antonia Oya**
RKHS Representations for Augmented Quaternion Random Signals: Application to Detection Problems
Reprinted from: *Mathematics* **2022**, *10*, 4432, doi:10.3390/math10234432 . . . . . . . . . . . . . . . 65

**Beatris Adriana Escobedo-Trujillo, Javier Garrido-Meléndez, Gerardo Alcalá and J. D. Revuelta-Acosta**
Optimal Control with Partially Observed Regime Switching: Discounted and Average Payoffs
Reprinted from: *Mathematics* **2022**, *10*, 2073, doi:10.3390/math10122073 . . . . . . . . . . . . . . . 81

**Alfonso García-Pérez**
On Robustness for Spatio-Temporal Data
Reprinted from: *Mathematics* **2022**, *10*, 1785, doi:10.3390/math10101785 . . . . . . . . . . . . . . . 109

**Jesica Escobar and Alexander Poznyak**
Robust Parametric Identification for ARMAX Models with Non-Gaussian and Coloured Noise: A Survey
Reprinted from: *Mathematics* **2022**, *10*, 1291, doi:10.3390/math10081291 . . . . . . . . . . . . . . . 127

**Agustín G. Nogales**
On Consistency of the Bayes Estimator of the Density
Reprinted from: *Mathematics* **2022**, *10*, 636, doi:10.3390/math10040636 . . . . . . . . . . . . . . . . 165

**Maria Chiara Pocelli, Manuel L. Esquível and Nadezhda P. Krasii**
Spectral Analysis for Comparing Bitcoin to Currencies and Assets
Reprinted from: *Mathematics* **2023**, *11*, 1775, doi:10.3390/math11081775 . . . . . . . . . . . . . . . 171

**Li-Peng Shao, Jia-Jia Chen, Lu-Wen Pan and Zi-Juan Yang**
A Credibility Theory-Based Robust Optimization Model to Hedge Price Uncertainty of DSO with Multiple Transactions
Reprinted from: *Mathematics* **2022**, *10*, 4420, doi:10.3390/math10234420 . . . . . . . . . . . . . . . 193

**José Clemente Jacinto Ferreira, Ana Paula Matias Gama, Luiz Paulo Fávero, Ricardo Goulart Serra, Patrícia Belfiore, Igor Pinheiro de Araújo Costa and Marcos dos Santos**
Economic Performance and Stock Market Integration in BRICS and G7 Countries: An Application with Quantile Panel Data and Random Coefficients Modeling
Reprinted from: *Mathematics* **2022**, *10*, 4013, doi:10.3390/math10214013 . . . . . . . . . . . . . . . **213**

**Gabriela M. Rodrigues, Edwin M. M. Ortega, Gauss M. Cordeiro and Roberto Vila**
Quantile Regression with a New Exponentiated Odd Log-Logistic Weibull Distribution
Reprinted from: *Mathematics* **2023**, *11*, 1518, doi:10.3390/math11061518 . . . . . . . . . . . . . . . **249**

**Francisco Germán Badía and María Dolores Berrade**
On the Residual Lifetime and Inactivity Time in Mixtures
Reprinted from: *Mathematics* **2022**, *10*, 2795, doi:10.3390/math10152795 . . . . . . . . . . . . . . . **269**

**Hyunju Lee, Ji Hwan Cha and Maxim Finkelstein**
A Preventive Replacement Policy for a System Subject to Bivariate Generalized Polya Failure Process
Reprinted from: *Mathematics* **2022**, *10*, 1833, doi:10.3390/math10111833 . . . . . . . . . . . . . . . **289**

**Zihui Zhang and Wenhao Gui**
Statistical Analysis of the Lifetime Distribution with Bathtub-Shaped Hazard Function under Lagged-Effect Step-Stress Model
Reprinted from: *Mathematics* **2022**, *10*, 674, doi:10.3390/math10050674 . . . . . . . . . . . . . . . . **305**

**Rigoberto Real-Miranda and José Daniel López-Barrientos**
A Geologic-Actuarial Approach for Insuring the Extraction Tasks of Non-Renewable Resources by One and Two Agents
Reprinted from: *Mathematics* **2022**, *10*, 2242, doi:10.3390/math10132242 . . . . . . . . . . . . . . . **329**

# About the Editors

**Francisco German Badía**

Francisco German Badía has been a tenured Professor with the Department of Statistics at the University of Zaragoza, Zaragoza, Spain, since 2003, where he received his Ph.D. degree in mathematics in 1997. He has been a visiting scholar at the Department of Statistics of Ewha Womans University, Seoul, Korea, four times. Prof. Badía researches probabilistic methods in approximation theory (the topic of his Ph.D. thesis), the reliability properties of mixtures, stochastic comparisons of counting processes, maintenance optimization, the aging properties of counting process observed in a random time and theoretical reliability and has published 42 papers in *JCR* journals, with 27 of them being published in the last ten years. In addition, 10 papers from the last decade appear in journals occupying the first quartile (Q1). The paper entitled "Optimal inspection and preventive maintenance of units with revealed and unrevealed failures" (2002) is among the most outstanding one, with 111 citations in Scopus. He has also supervised two post-doc students Ebrahim Salehi (from the University of Isfahan, Isfahan, Iran) and Hyunju Lee (from Ewha Womans University, Seoul, South Korea).

**María D. Berrade**

María D. Berrade is currently a tenured Professor of Statistics with the Department of Statistics at the University of Zaragoza, where she received her Ph.D. degree in mathematics in 1999. Prof. Berrade has been involved in 14 projects in the field of statistics resulting from competitive calls for proposals. She has authored and co-authored 28 publications indexed in Scopus. Her research interests include reliability analysis, aging classes, maintenance modeling, inspection policies and optimization. She usually supervises bachelor and master's theses for students in mathematics, engineering and social sciences.

mathematics

*Editorial*

# Special Issue "Probability Theory and Stochastic Modeling with Applications"

**Francisco Germán Badía * and María D. Berrade**

Department of Statistical Methods, University of Zaragoza, 50018 Zaragoza, Spain; berrade@unizar.es
* Correspondence: gbadia@unizar.es

This Special Issue (SI), titled "Probability Theory and Stochastic Modeling with Applications", is concerned with the theory and applications of stochastic models. It consists of sixteen papers, and we would like to thank all the authors for their positive answers to our call for papers for the SI, as well as for their efforts to provide a high-quality contribution. The outcome of each paper is also due to the reviewers, who helped the authors to clarify their research, detect mistakes or come up with new ideas following the review. Forty-two reviewers were involved in the revision of this SI, with between two and three working on each paper. Therefore, we would like to recognize their commitment to research improvement.

Among the papers with a theoretical approach to the SI's subject matter, that of S. Jiang, N. Liu and Y. Liu [1] focused on a theoretical analysis framework and computing issues regarding the steady probabilities in block-structured, discrete-time Markov chains. Their proposal extends previous results on quasi-birth-death processes.

The work of H. M. Alshanbari, Z. Ahmad, H. Al-Mofleh, C. B. Ampadu and S. K. Khosa [2] proposes a method to obtain new probability distributions that cover the gap in models that fit data sets with extreme values. This is a common problem in a number of areas, such as reliability/survival, finance or hydrology, where heavy-tailed distributions are required for goodness of fit. The major disadvantage of previous research is that a number of parameters must be introduced to the models to ensure they have enough flexibility to match extreme observations. The authors try to avoid this shortcoming, thus preventing estimation and re-parametrization problems.

Z. Zhang and S. Ross [3] present new research on dueling bandit problems with the objective of determining the best among a set of $n$ players with games involving two players. The authors aim to find the optimum policy that minimizes the expected number of games needed to find the best player. The proposed strategy outperforms other policies in the literature, and this superiority suggests its potential use for algorithm development in large-scale applications.

The paper [4] by A. Oya addresses the solution to a number of problems in signal processing by means of quaternion models, which have a higher capacity to manipulate multi-dimensional data than conventional kernel-based formulations. This research presents a general framework based on Hilbert space theory that simplifies the statistical treatment, resulting in a suitable approach to signal detection.

B. A. Escobedo-Trujillo, J. Garrido-Meléndez, G. Alcalá, and J. D. Revuelta-Acosta [5] deal with an optimal control problem with applications in car suspension systems and the accumulation of pollution caused by the consumption of gas, oil, etc. A number of assumptions prove the existence of optimal controls that can be useful in real life, according to the examples.

The research [6] carried out by A. García-Pérez is centered on robust statistics for handling spatio-temporal data. He presents a new estimator of the variogram used in prediction by kriging. When a random characteristic is measured at different locations and times, sample data are realizations of a random field and the variogram is the function that

**Citation:** Badía, F.G.; Berrade, M.D. Special Issue "Probability Theory and Stochastic Modeling with Applications". *Mathematics* **2023**, *11*, 3196. https://doi.org/10.3390/math11143196

Received: 5 July 2023
Accepted: 17 July 2023
Published: 21 July 2023

measures the dependence between observations. This is a valuable tool for the analysis of spatio-temporal phenomena such as temperature or precipitation, and the new estimators defined in this paper are less sensitive to outliers than previous ones. The objective of this investigation is, therefore, relevant to the analysis of climatic change and geostatistics, among others.

The work [7] of J. Escobar and A. Poznyak addresses the problem of parameter estimation in auto-regressive-moving average with exogenous input (ARMAX) models under non-Gaussian noise. The authors also provide a review of the significant literature on this subject. This type of time series is found in Econometrics studies.

The research [8] by A. G. Nogales focuses on Bayesian statistics, exploring the properties of the Bayes estimator of densities and sampling distributions. These estimators, which are provided by the posterior predictive distribution and density, respectively, are key to making inferences from the data. The Bayesian interpretation holds in many studies and is expected to become more widely used in the era of Big Data.

A second group of papers [9–11] is centered on the application of stochastic models in economics. M. C. Pocelli, M. L. Esquível, and N. P. Krasii [9] developed a spectral analysis to distinguish Bitcoin from some traditional currencies and gold. The particular volatility property of the former is highlighted.

L.-P. Shao, J.-J. Chen, L.-W. Pan and Z.-J. Yang [10] study the deregulated electricity market. Using fuzzy variables and robust optimization, the authors provide the electricity transaction policy under different expected costs so that the expectation of the risk-averse distribution system operator is fulfilled.

J.C.J. Ferreira, A.P. Matias Gama, L. P. Fávero, R. Goulart Serra, P. Belfiore, I. Pinheiro de Araújo Costa, and M. dos Santos [11] use quantile regression to explain the variability in economic growth over time in emerging and developed countries. They also analyze the significance of two explanatory variables, time and country, by means of random coefficient models.

Four papers [12–15] are devoted to reliability/survival: G. M. Rodrigues, E. M. M. Ortega, G. M. Cordeiro, and R. Vila [12] build a new quantile regression model to analyze the effect of covariates on the quantiles of the survival times. When compared to classical approaches, it presents several advantages and presents some of them as particular cases.

Two reliability measures, the residual lifetime and the inactivity time, are analyzed by F.G. Badía and M.D. Berrade [13]. The authors study their behaviour under changing risks when there are no observable covariates, using mixtures of distributions.

H. Lee, J.H. Cha and M. Finkelstein [14] present a preventive maintenance policy for a system with two dependent components. The authors model the real-life situation when non-failed components are severely affected by the failed ones. Thus, the reliability of the former is worse after repairing the failed units than before the failure. This is known as a worse-than-minimal repair.

Z. Zhang and W. Gui [15] deal with accelerated life testing. The authors consider a cumulative risk model, assuming that there is a lagged effect of increasing the stress level, rather than its being instantaneous. Their study involves a parameter estimation of the Chen distribution, which is more flexible than the exponential and Weibull models.

The last paper [16] by R. Real-Miranda and J.D. López-Barrientos is connected to both economics and reliability, as it is motivated by insurance in the extraction of non-renewable resources. The probability of ruin is key for actuaries; therefore, the cost and the time to failure have to be weighted. Stochastic dynamic programming is the basis of this research.

**Funding:** The work of both authors was supported by the Spanish Ministry of Science and Innovation under Project PID2021-123737NB-I00.

**Acknowledgments:** We would like to thank Helene Hu from the *Mathematics* Editorial Office for her friendly support and help in our task as guest editors. She has resolved all our concerns with kindness and efficacy.

**Conflicts of Interest:** The authors declare no conflict of interests.

## References

1. Jiang, S.; Liu, N.; Liu, Y. A Wavelet-Based Computational Framework for a Block-Structured Markov Chain with a Continuous Phase Variable. *Mathematics* **2023**, *11*, 1587. [CrossRef]
2. Alshanbari, H.; Ahmad, Z.; Al-Mofleh, H.; Ampadu, C.; Khosa, S. A New Probabilistic Approach: Estimation and Monte Carlo Simulation with Applications to Time-to-Event Data. *Mathematics* **2023**, *11*, 1583. [CrossRef]
3. Zhang, Z.; Ross, S. Finding the Best Dueler. *Mathematics* **2023**, *11*, 1568. [CrossRef]
4. Oya, A. RKHS Representations for Augmented Quaternion Random Signals: Application to Detection Problems. *Mathematics* **2022**, *10*, 4432. [CrossRef]
5. Escobedo-Trujillo, B.; Garrido-Meléndez, J.; Alcalá, G.; Revuelta-Acosta, J. Optimal Control with Partially Observed Regime Switching: Discounted and Average Payoffs. *Mathematics* **2022**, *10*, 2073. [CrossRef]
6. García-Pérez, A. On Robustness for Spatio-Temporal Data. *Mathematics* **2022**, *10*, 1785. [CrossRef]
7. Escobar, J.; Poznyak, A. Robust Parametric Identification for ARMAX Models with Non-Gaussian and Coloured Noise: A Survey. *Mathematics* **2022**, *10*, 1291. [CrossRef]
8. Nogales, A. On Consistency of the Bayes Estimator of the Density. *Mathematics* **2022**, *10*, 636. [CrossRef]
9. Pocelli, M.; Esquível, M.; Krasii, N. Spectral Analysis for Comparing Bitcoin to Currencies and Assets. *Mathematics* **2023**, *11*, 1775. [CrossRef]
10. Shao, L.-P.; Chen, J.-J.; Pan, L.-W.; Yang, Z.-J. A Credibility Theory-Based Robust Optimization Model to Hedge Price Uncertainty of DSO with Multiple Transactions. *Mathematics* **2022**, *10*, 4420. [CrossRef]
11. Ferreira, J.; Gama, A.; Fávero, L.; Serra, R.; Belfiore, P.; Costa, I.; Santos, M. Economic Performance and Stock Market Integration in BRICS and G7 Countries: An Application with Quantile Panel Data and Random Coefficients Modeling. *Mathematics* **2022**, *10*, 4013. [CrossRef]
12. Rodrigues, G.; Ortega, E.; Cordeiro, G.; Vila, R. Quantile Regression with a New Exponentiated Odd Log-Logistic Weibull Distribution. *Mathematics* **2023**, *11*, 1518. [CrossRef]
13. Badía, F.; Berrade, M. On the Residual Lifetime and Inactivity Time in Mixtures. *Mathematics* **2022**, *10*, 2795. [CrossRef]
14. Lee, H.; Cha, J.; Finkelstein, M. A Preventive Replacement Policy for a System Subject to Bivariate Generalized Polya Failure Process. *Mathematics* **2022**, *10*, 1833. [CrossRef]
15. Zhang, Z.; Gui, W. Statistical Analysis of the Lifetime Distribution with Bathtub-Shaped Hazard Function under Lagged-Effect Step-Stress Model. *Mathematics* **2022**, *10*, 674. [CrossRef]
16. Real-Miranda, R.; López-Barrientos, J. A Geologic-Actuarial Approach for Insuring the Extraction Tasks of Non-Renewable Resources by One and Two Agents. *Mathematics* **2022**, *10*, 2242. [CrossRef]

mathematics

MDPI

*Article*

# A Wavelet-Based Computational Framework for a Block-Structured Markov Chain with a Continuous Phase Variable

**Shuxia Jiang [1], Nian Liu [2] and Yuanyuan Liu [3,*]**

[1] School of Traffic and Logistics, Central South University of Forestry and Technology, Changsha 410004, China
[2] Department of Statistics and Probability, Michigan State University, East Lansing, MI 48824, USA
[3] School of Mathematics and Statistics, HNP-LAMA, New Campus, Central South University, Changsha 410083, China
* Correspondence: liuyy@csu.edu.cn

**Abstract:** We consider the computing issues of the steady probabilities for block-structured discrete-time Makrov chains that are of upper-Hessenberg or lower-Hessenberg transition kernels with a continuous phase set. An effective computational framework is proposed based on the wavelet transform, which extends and modifies the arguments in the literature for quasi-birth-death (QBD) processes. A numerical procedure is developed for computing the steady probabilities based on the fast discrete wavelet transform, and several examples are presented to illustrate its effectiveness.

**Keywords:** Markov chains; stationary distribution; wavelet transform; numerical algorithm

**MSC:** 60J10; 33F05

## 1. Introduction

Consider a two-dimensional block-structured discrete-time Markov chain (DTMC) $\{(L_n, X_n) : n \in \mathbb{N}\}$ on the state space $\mathbb{N} \times \mathbb{R}$, where $\mathbb{N}$ and $\mathbb{R}$ are sets of non-negative integers and real numbers, respectively. Denote by $\mathcal{B}(\mathbb{R})$ the Borel $\sigma$-field of the set $\mathbb{R}$. The transition probability law is time homogeneous and is characterized by the following transition kernel

$$P_{ij}(x, A) = \mathbb{P}\{(L_{n+1}, X_{n+1}) \in j \times A | (L_n, X_n) = (i, x)\},$$

where $i, j \in \mathbb{N}$, $x \in \mathbb{R}$ and $A \in \mathcal{B}(R)$. Recall that a two-dimensional function $F(x, A)$ is called a kernel if it is a measurable function in $x$ for each $A \in \mathcal{B}(R)$, and a non-negative measure on $\mathbb{R}$ for each $x \in \mathbb{R}$. When $A = (-\infty, y]$, we write $F(x, A)$ to be $F(x, y)$ for simplicity. Note that the kernel function $P_{ij}(x, y)$ is stochastic in the sense that $P_{ij}(x, \infty) := \lim_{y\to\infty} \sum_{j\geq 0} P_{ij}(x, y) = 1$ for all $i$ and all $x$. The level and phase of each state $(i, x)$ are respectively represented by the first component $i$ and the second component $x$. For any $i \geq 0$, define $\ell_i = \{(i, x) : x \in \mathbb{R}\}$ to be the $i$ level set. Then, the state space $E$ can be decomposed as $E = \bigcup_{i=0}^{\infty} \ell_i$. For $n \geq 1$, the corresponding $n$-step transition kernel is given by

$$P^n(i, x; j, A) = \sum_{k\in\mathbb{N}} \int_{\mathbb{R}} P^{n-1}(i, x; k, dz) P(k, z; j, A) = \mathbb{P}\{X_n \in j \times A | X_0 = (i, x)\}.$$

Two different types of block-structured discrete-time Markov chains are the focus of this paper. The first one is the discrete-time GI/M/1-type Markov chain, whose transition

**Citation:** Jiang, S.; Liu, N.; Liu, Y. A Wavelet-Based Computational Framework for a Block-Structured Markov Chain with a Continuous Phase Variable. *Mathematics* **2023**, *11*, 1587. https://doi.org/10.3390/math11071587

Academic Editors: Francisco German Badía and María D. Berrade

Received: 25 February 2023
Revised: 19 March 2023
Accepted: 20 March 2023
Published: 24 March 2023

kernel matrix $P_{GI}(x,y) := (P_{GI}(i,x;j,y))_{i,j\in\mathbb{N}}$ is level independent and has the following lower-Hessenberg block form:

$$P_{GI}(x,y) = \begin{pmatrix} B_0(x,y) & A_0(x,y) & 0 & 0 & \cdots \\ B_1(x,y) & A_1(x,y) & A_0(x,y) & 0 & \cdots \\ B_2(x,y) & A_2(x,y) & A_1(x,y) & A_0(x,y) & \cdots \\ B_3(x,y) & A_3(x,y) & A_2(x,y) & A_1(x,y) & \cdots \\ \vdots & \vdots & \vdots & \ddots & \ddots \end{pmatrix}. \tag{1}$$

The second one is the discrete-time M/G/1-type Markov chain, whose transition kernel matrix $P_M(x,y) := (P_M(i,x;j,y))_{i,j\in\mathbb{N}}$ is level independent and has the following upper-Hessenberg block form:

$$P_M(x,y) = \begin{pmatrix} B_0(x,y) & B_1(x,y) & B_2(x,y) & B_3(x,y) & \cdots \\ A_0(x,y) & A_1(x,y) & A_2(x,y) & A_3(x,y) & \cdots \\ 0 & A_0(x,y) & A_1(x,y) & A_2(x,y) & \cdots \\ 0 & 0 & A_0(x,y) & A_1(x,y) & \cdots \\ \vdots & \vdots & \vdots & \vdots & \ddots \end{pmatrix}, \tag{2}$$

These block-structured Markov chains are of the special features that the transition of the level is skip-free to the right or skip-free to the left, respectively.

Tweedie [1] proposed the GI/M/1-type Markov chain with a continuous phase set and demonstrated that the positive recurrent GI/M/1-type Markov chain is of the operator-geometric stationary distribution. Thus, Tweedie [1] extended the well-known results for the GI/M/1-type Markov chain with a finite phase set, which was derived by Neuts [2]. Tweedie's finding was later applied by Breuer [3] to investigate the stationary distribution for the embedded GI/G/k queue with a Lebsegue-dominated inter-arrival time distribution. A positive recurrent tridiagonal block-structured quasi-birth-death (QBD) process with a continuous phase set, as well as a computational framework of its stationary distribution, are investigated by Nielsen and Ramaswami [4]. They also demonstrated the motivation for investigating a model with a continuous phase set. The computational framework was recently extended and improved by Jiang et al. [5] by incorporating the wavelet transform approach.

The GI/M/1-type and M/G/1-type Markov chains with a finite phase set were investigated systematically by Neuts in 1981 [2] and 1989 [6], respectively. Effective solver tools for solving the stationary distribution for these chains were developed by Bini et al. in [7], based on the algorithms collected in [8]. It is known that the matrices $R$ and $G$ are key matrices for solving stationary distributions for GI/M/1-type and M/G/1-type Markov chains, respectively. Since $R$ and $G$ are closely connected by Ramaswami dual and Bright dual, the computation of matrix $R$ for GI/M/1-type chains can be reduced to the computation of matrix $G$ for M/G/1-type Markov chains ([9–12]). Several effective algorithms have been developed to compute the matrix $G$, such as functional iteration, Newton iteration, invariant subspace method, cyclic reduction and Ramaswami Reduction. Please refer to [13] for a detailed description of the algorithms.

As far as we know, the following two issues are still not well addressed in the literature:

(i) For a positive recurrent GI/M/1-type Markov chain with a continuous phase set, numerical algorithms for computing the stationary distribution are missing, although the theoretical framework has been established in [1],

(ii) M/G/1-type Markov chains are of the same importance as GI/M/1-type Markov chains. However, both the theoretical and computational framework are missing for M/G/1-type Markov chains with a continuous phase set.

The current research is motivated to investigate the above two issues. This paper is organized into six sections. We provide an overview of DTMCs on a general state space and the wavelet series expansion in two dimensions in Section 2. The GI/M/1-type Markov chains are introduced in Section 3, most of which are well known in the literature [1], except for the computational analysis. The analysis of stationary distributions for M/G/1-type Markov chains is performed in Section 4. Numerical experiments, including a brief description of numerical algorithms and two illustrative examples, are presented in Section 5. Comparisons among different algorithms are executed with respect to the accuracy and speed of calculation. Conclusions are presented in Section 6. Please refer to Table A1 for a summary of frequently used notations.

## 2. Preliminaries

### 2.1. Basics about DTMCs on a General State Space

We present some basic concepts for DTMCs on a general state space. Please refer to [14] for more details.

Let $\Phi_n$ be a DTMC on a general state space $E$ endowed with the countably generated $\sigma$-field $\mathcal{B}(E)$. Define $\tau_A = \{n \geq 1 : \Phi_n \in A\}$ to be the first return time on $A$. For a non-negative nontrivial measure $\psi$, the chain $\Phi_n$ is called $\psi$-irreducible if there exits a non-negative nontrivial measure $\varphi$, such that $\Phi_n$ is $\varphi$-irreducible, i.e.,

$$L(x, A) := P\{\tau_A < \infty | \Phi_0 = x\} > 0$$

for any $A \in \mathcal{B}(E)$, $\varphi(A) > 0$ and any $x \in A$, and $\psi$ is a maximal irreducible measure with respect to $\varphi$. A set $A \in \mathcal{B}(E)$ is called a Harris recurrent if $L(x, A) = 1$ for all $x \in A$. The chain $\Phi_n$ is called a Harris recurrent if it is $\psi$-irreducible and every set in $\mathcal{B}_+(E) := \{A \in \mathcal{B}(E) : \psi(A) > 0\}$ is Harris recurrent. A Harris recurrent chain has an unique invariant measure $\Pi$ such that

$$\Pi(A) = \int_E \Pi(dx) P(x, A).$$

A Harris recurrent chain with a finite $\Pi(E)$ is said to be Harris positive recurrent. If $\Phi_n$ is Harris positive recurrent and aperiodic, then

$$\Pi(A) = \lim_{n \to \infty} P^n(x, A),$$

which implies that the limit of the transition kernel exists independently of the initial state $(i, x)$. In this case, $\Pi(A)$ is called the invariant probability measure or the stationary probability distribution.

We now introduce the censored Markov chain, which will be used later to deal with the invariant probability distributions for block-structured Harris positive recurrent chains. Let $A$ be a non-empty subset in $\mathcal{B}(E)$. Let $\theta_k$ be the $kth$ time that $\Phi_n$ successively visits a state in $A$, i.e., $\theta_0 = \inf\{m \geq 0 : \Phi_m \in A\}$ and $\theta_{k+1} = \inf\{m \geq \theta_k + 1 : \Phi_m \in A\}$. The censored Markov chain $\Phi^A = \{\Phi_k^A, k \geq 0\}$ on $A$ is defined by $\Phi_k^A = \Phi_{\theta_k}, k \geq 0$, whose one-step transition kernel is denoted by $P^A(x, B)$, $x \in E, B \in \mathcal{B}(E)$. Define

$$_A P^n(x, B) = P\{\Phi_n \in B, \Phi_m \notin A, 1 \leq m \leq n \mid \Phi_0 = x\},$$

and

$$U_A(x, B) = \sum_{n=1}^{\infty} {}_A P^n(x, B).$$

When starting with $\Phi_0 = x \in A$ and $B \subseteq A$, the censored chain $\Phi^A$ evolves according to the transition law

$$P^A(x, B) = U_A(x, B) = P\{\Phi_{\tau_A} \in B \mid \Phi_0 = x\}.$$

### 2.2. Basics about Wavelet in Two Dimensions

This section is concerned on some basics about the wavelet, most of which is taken from [5] directly. Please refer to [15,16] for more details about the wavelet analysis.

Respectively denote the *scaling function* and the *wavelet function* by $\phi$ and $\psi$. For all $j \in \mathbb{Z}$, let $\phi_{j,n}(x) = 2^{-j/2}\phi(2^{-j}(x - 2^j n))$ and $\psi_{j,n}(x) = 2^{-j/2}\psi(2^{-j}(x - 2^j n))$. Define three wavelets

$$W^{(1)}(x_1, x_2) = \phi(x_1)\psi(x_2), \; W^{(2)}(x_1, x_2) = \psi(x_1)\phi(x_2), \; W^{(3)}(x_1, x_2) = \psi(x_1)\psi(x_2),$$

and for all $j$ in $\mathbb{Z}$,

$$W^{(k)}_{j,n_1,n_2}(x_1, x_2) = \frac{1}{2^j} W^{(k)}\left(\frac{x_1 - 2^j n_1}{2^j}, \frac{x_2 - 2^j n_2}{2^j}\right), n_1, n_2 \in \mathbb{Z}, \; 1 \le k \le 3.$$

Now, we consider the wavelet series expansion of a two-dimensional function. For each $i \in \mathbb{Z}$, define column vectors $\boldsymbol{\phi}_i(x) = [\phi_{i,n}(x) : n \in \mathbb{Z}]$, $\boldsymbol{\psi}_i(x) = [\psi_{i,n}(x) : n \in \mathbb{Z}]$, and $\zeta_i(x) = [\phi_i^T(x), \psi_i^T(x)]^T$. By Lemma 3.1 in [5], any function $u(x, y) \in \boldsymbol{L}^2(\mathbb{R}^2)$ can be expanded as follows

$$u(x, y) = \boldsymbol{\zeta}^T(x)\overline{U}\boldsymbol{\zeta}(y), \tag{3}$$

where $\boldsymbol{\zeta}(x) = [\zeta_i(x) : i \in \mathbb{Z}]$ is a column vector, the diagonal blocks of $\overline{U}$ are written as

$$\overline{U}_i = \begin{bmatrix} 0 & \overline{U}_i^{(1)} \\ \overline{U}_i^{(3)} & \overline{U}_i^{(3)} \end{bmatrix}$$

with $(\overline{U}_i^{(k)})_{m,n} =< u, W^{(k)}_{i,m,n} >$.

Let $U(x, y)$ be a kernel function whose density function is assumed to exist and is denoted by $u(x, y) := \frac{\partial U(x,y)}{\partial y}$. On the one hand, by performing (3) for the density of the kernel function $U(x, y)$, which is referred to as the wavelet transform (WT), we can find the matrix $\overline{U}$, also known as the associated matrix of $U(x, y)$. On the other hand, for a given associated matrix $\overline{U}$, we can find the density function $u(x, y)$ by performing (3) in the other side, which is called the inverse wavelet transform (IWT).

As you will see in the following sections, it is crucial to deal with the convolution operations of the transition kernels in order to investigate the stationary distributions. The wavelet transform is introduced to transform these convolution operations into matrix operations by expanding the kernels using the wavelet series. For any $A \in \mathcal{B}(\mathcal{E})$, define the convolution $C_1 * C_2$ of two kernel functions $C_1(x, y)$ and $C_2(x, y)$ by

$$C_1 * C_2(x, A) = \int_{\mathbb{R}} C_1(x, dz)C_2(z, A),$$

and define $C_1^{(k)}(x, y)$ recursively by

$$C_1^{(k)}(x, y) = \int_{\mathbb{R}} C_1^{(k-1)}(x, dz)C_1(z, y) = \int_{\mathbb{R}} C_1(x, dz)C_1^{(k-1)}(z, y),$$

where $C_1^{(0)}(x, x) = 1$ and $C_1^{(0)}(x, y) = 0$ for any $y \neq x$. If $\nu$ is a signed measure on $E$, we write

$$\nu * C_1(A) = \int_E \nu(dx)C_1(x, A).$$

In order to expand the kernel functions through the wavelet transform, we need the following assumption and theorem, which are both taken from [5].

**Assumption 1.** *All the kernel functions $B_i(x,y)$ and $A_i(x,y)$, $i \geq -1$ belong to $\sum_H$, where $H \subset \mathbb{R}$ is of finite Lebesgue measure, and $\sum_H$ is the set of kernel functions $U(x,y)$ having a density function $u(x,y)$ equaling to zeros outside of $H \times H$.*

**Theorem 1** ([5]). *Let $\{F_k(x,y), k \geq 1\}$ be a sequence of kernel functions in $\sum_H$. Denote their density functions by $\{f_k(x,y), k \geq 1\}$, and their associated matrices by $\{\bar{F}_k, k \geq 1\}$.*

*(i) For any fixed $n$, the convolution kernel function $F_1 * F_2 * \cdots * F_n(x,y)$ is also in $\sum_H$, and its associated matrix is $\prod_{k=1}^n \bar{F}_k$;*

*(ii) For any fixed $n$, the additive kernel function $(F_1 + F_2 + \cdots + F_n)(x,y)$ is also in $\sum_H$ and its associated matrix is $\sum_{k=1}^n \bar{F}_k$;*

*(iii) If $f_n(x,y)$ converges to $f(x,y)$, then the kernel function $F(x,y) := \int_{-\infty}^{y} f(x,y)dy$ is also in $\sum_H$, and its associated matrix is $\bar{F} = \lim_{n\to\infty} \bar{F}_n$.*

## 3. *GI/M/1*-Type Markov Chains

Consider a GI/M/1-type Markov chain $(L_n, X_n)$, whose transition law $P$ given by (1) satisfies that for any $C \in \mathcal{B}(\mathbb{R})$

$$P(i,x;j,\mathbb{R}) = 0, \;\; j > i+1,$$

$$P(i,x;j,C) = A_{i-j+1}(x,C), \;\; i \geq j-1, j \geq 1,$$

$$P(i,x;0,C) = B_i(x,C), \;\; i \geq 0.$$

Define the kernel $R(x,C)$ to be the expected number of visits to $(i+1) \times C$, starting from $(i,x)$ under the taboo set of $\bigcup_{k=0}^{i} \ell_k$. From [1], we know that the censored Markov chain $(L_n, X_n)^{\ell_0}$ of the GI/M/1-type Markov chain on the zero level set $\ell_0$ has the following transition kernel

$$P_{GI}^{\ell_0}(x,C) = \sum_{k=0}^{\infty} R^{(k)} * B_k(x,C).$$

The following theorem is taken from [1], which characterizes the invariant probability measure for GI/M/1-type Markov chains with a continuous phase set.

**Theorem 2** ([1]). *Suppose that the GI/M/1-type Markov Chain $(L_n, X_n)$ with a continuous phase set is $\Psi$-irreducible and Harris positive recurrent. Then, its unique stationary probability measure $\Pi$, decomposed by $\Pi(A) = (\Pi_0(A), \Pi_1(A), \Pi_2(A), \cdots)$, satisfies the following recursive formula*

$$\Pi_k(A) = \Pi_0 * R^{(k)}(A),$$

*where the kernel $R(x,A)$ is the minimal non-negative solution of the following equation*

$$R(x,A) = \sum_{i=0}^{\infty} R^{(i)} * A_i(x,A),$$

*and $\Pi_0(A)$ is uniquely determined by*

$$\Pi_0 * P_{GI}^{\ell_0}(x,A) = \Pi_0(A), \quad \sum_{k=0}^{\infty} \Pi_0 * R^{(k)}(x,E) = 1.$$

Applying Theorem 2 and Theorem 1, we can obtain the following theorem directly.

**Theorem 3.** *Suppose that the GI/M/1-type Markov Chain $(L_n, X_n)$ with a continuous phase set is $\psi$-irreducible and Harris positive recurrent and that Assumption 1 holds.*

*(i) The kernels $P_{GI}^{\ell_0}(x,y)$ and $R(x,y)$ are in $\sum_H$, whose associated matrices are, respectively, denoted by $\bar{P}_{GI}^{\ell_0}$, $\bar{R}$ and $\bar{B}_k$.*

*(ii) The invariant probability measure $\Pi_k$ is in $\sum_H$. Let $\bar{\Pi}_k$ be the associated row vector of $\Pi_k(y)$, i.e., $\pi_k(y) = \bar{\Pi}_k \zeta(y)$, where $\pi_k(y)$ is the density of $\Pi_k(y)$, and $\zeta(y)$ is defined in Section 2.2. Then, we have*

$$\bar{\Pi}_k = \bar{\Pi}_0 \bar{R}^{(k)},$$

*and*

$$\bar{\Pi}_0 \bar{P}_{GI}^{\ell_0} = \bar{\Pi}_0, \quad \bar{\Pi}_0 (I - \bar{R})^{-1}\mathbf{1} = 1,$$

*where $\bar{P}_{GI}^{\ell_0} = \sum_{k=0}^{\infty} \bar{R}^{(k)} \bar{B}_k$ and $\mathbf{1}$ is the vector of 1's with an appropriate dimension.*

## 4. *M/G/*1-Type Markov Chains

In this section, we consider a M/G/1-type Markov Chain $(L_n, X_n)$, whose transition law $P$, given by (1), satisfies that for any $C \in \mathcal{B}(\mathbb{R})$

$$P(i, x; j, C) = 0, \quad \text{for } j < i - 1, i \geq 1,$$

$$P(0, x; j, C) = B_j(x, C),$$

$$P(i, x; j, C) = A_{j-i+1}(x, C), \quad \text{for } j \geq i - 1, i \geq 1.$$

Define $\tau_{\ell_i} = \inf\{n \geq 1 : L_n \in \ell_i\}$ to be the first return time to the level set $\ell_i$ for any $i \geq 0$. For any $x \in \mathbb{R}$ and any $A \in \mathcal{B}(\mathbb{R})$, define the following kernel function

$$G(x, A) = P\Big\{\tau_{\ell_i} < \infty, X_{\tau_{\ell_i}} \in A \mid L_0 = i + 1, X_0 = x\Big\},$$

which is independent of $i$ due to the level independent structure of the chain. The first result is about the kernel $G(x, A)$, which plays a key role in analyzing M/G/1-type Markov chains.

**Theorem 4.** *Suppose that the M/G/1-type Markov chain $(L_n, X_n)$ is $\psi$-irreducible. For any $A \in \mathcal{B}(\mathbb{R})$, the kernel $G(x, A)$ is the minimal nonnegative solution of the following equation*

$$G(x, A) = \sum_{i=0}^{\infty} A_i * G^{(i)}(x, A), \tag{4}$$

*where $G^{(i)}(x, A)$ is the i-fold convolution of the kernel $G(x, A)$ itself.*

**Proof.** We first show that the kernel $G(x, A)$ is a solution of Equation (4).

By conditioning on the state of the first transition, the kernel $G(x, A)$ can be decomposed as follows

$$\begin{aligned} G(x, A) &= \int_{\mathbb{R}} \sum_{i \in \mathbb{N}} [P\{L_1 = i, X_1 \in dy \mid L_0 = 1, X_0 = x\} \\ &\quad \times P\Big\{\tau_{\ell_0} < \infty, X_{\tau_{\ell_0}} \in A \mid L_0 = i, X_0 = y\Big\}\Big] \\ &= \int_{\mathbb{R}} \sum_{i \in \mathbb{N}} A_i(x, dy) P\Big\{\tau_{\ell_0} < \infty, X_{\tau_{\ell_0}} \in A \mid L_0 = i, X_0 = y\Big\}. \end{aligned} \tag{5}$$

We will use the inductive arguments to show

$$G^{(i)}(y, A) = P\Big\{\tau_{\ell_0} < \infty, X_{\tau_{\ell_0}} \in A \mid L_0 = i, X_0 = y\Big\}, i \geq 1. \tag{6}$$

Since the chain is level independent, when $i = 1$, we have

$$G^{(1)}(y, A) = G(y, A) = P\Big\{\tau_{\ell_k} < \infty, X_{\tau_{\ell_k}} \in A \mid L_0 = k + 1, X_0 = y\Big\}$$

for any $k \geq 0$. Suppose that $G^{(n)}$ satisfies

$$G^{(n)}(y, A) = P\Big\{\tau_{\ell_0} < \infty, X_{\tau_{\ell_0}} \in A \mid L_0 = n, X_0 = y\Big\}.$$

By conditioning on the state of the first hitting on level $\ell_n$ and using the strong Markov property, we have

$$\begin{aligned}
&P\Big\{\tau_{\ell_0} < \infty, X_{\tau_{\ell_0}} \in A \mid L_0 = n+1, X_0 = y\Big\} \\
&= \int_{\mathbb{R}} P\Big\{\tau_{\ell_n} < \infty, X_{\tau_{\ell_n}} \in dx \mid L_0 = n+1, X_0 = y\Big\} P\Big\{\tau_{\ell_0} < \infty, X_{\tau_{\ell_0}} \in A \mid L_{\tau_{\ell_n}} = n, X_{\tau_{\ell_n}} = x\Big\} \\
&= \int_{\mathbb{R}} P\Big\{\tau_{\ell_n} < \infty, X_{\tau_{\ell_n}} \in dx \mid L_0 = n+1, X_0 = y\Big\} P\Big\{\tau_{\ell_0} < \infty, X_{\tau_{\ell_0}} \in A \mid L_0 = n, X_0 = x\Big\} \\
&= \int_{\mathbb{R}} G^{(1)}(y, dx) G^{(n)}(x, A) \\
&= G^{(n+1)}(y, A).
\end{aligned}$$

Substituting (6) into (5), we have

$$G(x, A) = \int_{\mathbb{R}} \sum_{i=0}^{\infty} A_i(x, dy) G^{(i)}(y, A) = \sum_{i=0}^{\infty} A_i * G^{(i)}(y, A),$$

where we exchange the order between integration and summation by Fubini theorem.

Next we demonstrate that $G(x, A)$ is the minimal non-negative solution of (4). We divide the proof into two steps.

We first define a sequence of kernels $\{T_N(x, A), N \geq 1\}$ by setting $T_0(x, A) = 0$, and

$$T_{N+1}(x, A) = \sum_{i=0}^{\infty} A_i * T_N^{(i)}(x, A), \quad N \geq 0.$$

Let $\hat{G}(x, A)$ be any solution of Equation (4). Obviously, $\hat{G}(x, A) \geq 0 = T_0(x, A)$. Suppose that $T_{N-1}(x, A) \leq \hat{G}(x, A)$, then $T_{N-1}^{(i)}(x, A) \leq \hat{G}^{(i)}(x, A)$ for $i \geq 1$. Moreover, we have

$$T_N(x, A) = \sum_{i=0}^{\infty} A_i * T_{N-1}^{(i)}(x, A) \leq \sum_{i=0}^{\infty} A_i * \hat{G}^{(i)}(x, A) = \hat{G}(x, A). \tag{7}$$

Similarly, if we assume inductively that $T_{N-1}(x, A) \leq T_N(x, A)$ , we have

$$T_N(x, A) = \sum_{i=0}^{\infty} A_i * T_{N-1}^{(i)}(x, A) \leq \sum_{i=0}^{\infty} A_i * T_N^{(i)}(x, A) = T_{N+1}(x, A),$$

and so $T_N(x, A)$ is monotonically increasing in $N$. Hence, the limit $T_*(x, A) := \lim_{N \to \infty} \uparrow T_N(x, A)$ exists. Further, we have

$$T_N^{(k)}(x, A) \uparrow T_*^{(k)}(x, A),\ k \geq 1,$$

By taking the limit of both sides of Equation (6) and using the dominated convergence theorem, we know that the kernel $T_*(x, A)$ is a solution of (4), i.e.,

$$T_*(x, A) = \sum_{i=0}^{\infty} A_i * T_*^{(i)}(x, A),$$

We further have that $T_*(x, A)$ is the minimal solution since $T_*(x, A) \leq \hat{G}(x, A)$.

Next, we need to prove that $T_*(x,A) = G(x,A)$. Define

$$G_N(x,A) = P\Big\{\tau_{\ell_0} \le N, X_{\tau_{\ell_0}} \in A \mid L_0 = 1, X_0 = x\Big\},\ N \ge 1.$$

Obviously, we know that $G_N(x,A) \uparrow G(x,A)$. By conditioning on the state of the first transition, we have

$$\begin{aligned} G_{N+1}(x,A) &= \int_{\mathbb{R}} \sum_{i=0}^{N} P\Big\{\tau_{\ell_0} \le N, X_{\tau_{\ell_0}} \in A \mid L_0 = i, X_0 = y\Big\} \\ &\times\ P\{L_1 = i, X_1 \in dy \mid L_0 = 1, X_0 = x\}. \end{aligned} \tag{8}$$

Denote

$$M_N^{(i)}(y,A) = P\Big\{\tau_{\ell_0} \le N, X_{\tau_{\ell_0}} \in A \mid L_0 = i, X_0 = y\Big\}.$$

By conditioning on the state of the first return time to level $\ell_{i-1}$ and repeating the same arguments, we have

$$\begin{aligned} M_N^{(i)}(y,A) &\le \int_{\mathbb{R}} P\Big\{\tau_{\ell_{i-1}} \le N, X_{\tau_{\ell_{i-1}}} \in dx \mid L_0 = i, X_0 = y\Big\} M_N^{(i-1)}(x,A) \\ &= G_N^{(1)} * M_N^{(i-1)}(y,A) \\ &\le G_N^{(2)} * M_N^{(i-2)}(y,A) \\ &\le \cdots \\ &\le G_N^{(i-1)} * M_N^{(1)}(y,A) \\ &= G_N^{(i)}(y,A). \end{aligned} \tag{9}$$

By (8) and (9), we can deduce that

$$\begin{aligned} G_{N+1}(x,A) &\le \int_{\mathbb{R}} \sum_{i=0}^{N} A_i(x,dy) G_N^{(i)}(y,A) \\ &\le \int_{\mathbb{R}} \sum_{i=0}^{\infty} A_i(x,dy) G_N^{(i)}(y,A) \\ &= \sum_{i=0}^{\infty} A_i * G_N^{(i)}(x,A) \end{aligned}$$

Finally, note that $G_1(x,A) = A_0(x,A) = T_1(x,A)$, and so from (6), we have by induction $G_N(x,A) \le T_N(x,A)$. Taking the limit as $N \to \infty$ gives $G(x,A) \le T_*(x,A)$, as required. □

In the following, we will investigate numerical computing issues of the invariant probability distribution for M/G/1-type chains. The key point is to set up the Ramaswami algorithm, a well-known result for M/G/1-type chains with finite phases, for the M/G/1-type chains with continuous phases.

**Theorem 5.** *Suppose that the M/G/1-type Markov chain $(L_n, X_n)$ is $\psi$-irreducible and Harris positive recurrent. Let the unique invariant probability measure be $\Pi$ with $\Pi(C) = (\Pi_0(C), \Pi_1(C), \Pi_2(C), \dots)$, $C \in \mathcal{B}(\mathbb{R})$. Then, the measure $\Pi$ satisfies the following recursive formula*

$$\Pi_k(C) = \Pi_0 * \hat{B}_k(C) + \sum_{i=1}^{k} \Pi_i * \hat{A}_{k+1-i}(C), \tag{10}$$

*where*

$$\hat{B}_k(x,C) = \sum_{i=k}^{\infty} B_i * G^{(i-k)}(x,C),\ \ k \in \mathbb{N},$$

$$\hat{A}_m(x,C) = \sum_{i=m}^{\infty} A_i * G^{(i-m)}(x,C), \;\; 1 \le m \le k, \tag{11}$$

*and* $\Pi_0$ *is a unique solution of the equation* $\Pi_0(C) = \Pi_0 * \hat{B}_0(C)$.

**Proof.** By (6), we know that for any $v \ge 1$ and $i \ge 0$, the kernel function $G^{(v)}(x,C)$ is the probability that the Markov chain first returns to level $\ell_i$ by hitting the state $(i,C)$, given that it starts from the state $(i+v,x)$. The transition kernel function of the Markov chain embedded at epochs of visits to the set $A = \bigcup_{m=0}^{\infty} \ell_m$ is given by

$$P^A(x,C) = \begin{pmatrix} B_0(x,C) & B_1(x,C) & \dots & B_{k-1}(x,C) & \hat{B}_k(x,C) \\ A_0(x,C) & A_1(x,C) & \dots & A_{k-1}(x,C) & \hat{A}_k(x,C) \\ 0 & A_0(x,C) & \dots & A_{k-2}(x,C) & \hat{A}_{k-1}(x,C) \\ \vdots & \vdots & & \vdots & \vdots \\ 0 & 0 & \dots & A_0(x,C) & \hat{A}_1(x,C) \end{pmatrix}.$$

We now explain how to determine the transition kernel $P^A(x,C)$. The first $k$ block columns of the kernel function $P^A(x,C)$ are the same as those of $P(x,C)$, since the chain $(L_n, X_n)$ can only move down by one level at a time. As for the $(k+1)$th (i.e., last) block column of $P^A(x,C)$, its first entry is as follows.

$$\begin{aligned} \hat{B}_k(x,C) &= P\{(L_1,X_1)^A \in k \times C \mid (L_0,X_0)^A = (0,x)\} \\ &= P\{L_1 = k, X_1 \in C \mid L_0 = 0, X_0 = x\} \\ &\quad + \sum_{i=k+1}^{\infty} \int_{\mathbb{R}} [P\{L_1 = i, X_1 \in dy \mid L_0 = 0, X_0 = x\} \\ &\quad \times P\{\tau_{\ell_k} < \infty, X_{\tau_{\ell_k}} \in C \mid L_1 = i, X_1 = y\}] \\ &= B_k(x,C) + \sum_{i=k+1}^{\infty} B_i * G^{(i-k)}(x,C) \\ &= \sum_{i=k}^{\infty} B_i * G^{(i-k)}(x,C). \end{aligned}$$

The equality (11) can be proved in a similar way.

Since this chain $(L_n, X_n)$ is $\psi$-irreducible and a Harris positive recurrent, for $\forall x \in X, M \subseteq E$, starting from $x$, the set $M$ will almost certainly be returned infinitely, and so is the censored Markov chain $(L_n, X_n)^A$. Thus, $(L_n, X_n)^A$ is also $\psi$-irreducible and a Harris positive recurrent. Let $\Pi^A(C) = (\Pi_0^A(C), \Pi_1^A(C), \dots, \Pi_k^A(C))$ be the unique invariant probability measure of $(L_n, X_n)^A$.

Next, we will demonstrate that $(\Pi_0(C), \Pi_1(C), \dots, \Pi_k(C))$ is also an invariant measure of the censored chain $\Phi_n^A$. Define the measure $\Pi^\circ$ by

$$\Pi_i^\circ(C) := \int_{\mathbb{R}} \Pi_i^A(dx) U_A(x, i \times C), \;\; i \in N.$$

By Propostion 10.4.8 in [14], we know that

$$\Pi_i^A(C) = \Pi_i^\circ(C), \;\; 0 \le i \le k \tag{12}$$

and that $\Pi^\circ$ is invariant measure for $(L_n, X_n)$. Since $(L_n, X_n)$ is assumed to be a Harris positive recurrent, the invariant measure is unique up to a constant. This shows that $\Pi^\circ(C) = c\Pi(C)$ for some constant $c$, from which and (12), and we have

$$\Pi_i^A(C) = c\Pi_i(C), \text{ for } 0 \le i \le k.$$

Since $\sum_{i=0}^{k} \Pi_i^A(-\infty,\infty) = 1$, we can obtain

$$c = \frac{1}{\sum_{i=0}^{k} \Pi_i(-\infty,\infty)}.$$

Thus, we have proved that $(\Pi_0, \Pi_1, \Pi_2, \ldots, \Pi_k)$ is an invariant measure of $\Phi^A$. Taking into account the last block equation of $\Pi^A(C) = \Pi * P^A(C)$, we have

$$\Pi_k(y) = \Pi_0 * \hat{B}_k(y) + \sum_{i=1}^{k} \Pi_i * \hat{A}_{k+1-i}(y), \ \ k \geq 1. \tag{13}$$

This proves (10).

To determine $\Pi_0(C)$, we reset $A = \ell_0$ and consider the censored chain $(L_n, X_n)^A$, whose transition kernel is given by

$$P^{\ell_0}(x, C) = \hat{B}_0(x, C).$$

By (13), we know that $\Pi_0(C) = \Pi_0 * \hat{B}_0(C)$. □

Applying Theorem 5 and performing the wavelet series expansion, we can obtain the following theorem directly.

**Theorem 6.** *Suppose that the M/G/1-type Markov chain $(L_n, X_n)$ is $\psi$-irreducible and Harris positive recurrent and that Assumption 1 holds.*

*(i) The kernels $G(x,y)$, $\bar{A}_k(x,y)$ and $\bar{B}_k(x,y)$ are in $\sum_H$, whose associated matrices satisfies that*

$$\bar{\bar{B}}_k = \sum_{i=k}^{\infty} B_i \bar{G}^{i-k}, \ \ \bar{\bar{A}}_k = \sum_{i=k}^{\infty} A_i \bar{G}^{i-k}.$$

*(ii) The invariant probability measure $\Pi_k$ is in $\sum_H$. Let $\bar{\Pi}_k$ be the associated row vector of $\Pi_k(y)$. Then, the associated matrices satisfy*

$$\bar{\Pi}_k = \left[\bar{\Pi}_0 \bar{\bar{B}}_k + \sum_{i=1}^{k-1} \bar{\Pi}_i \bar{\bar{A}}_{k+1-i}\right] \left(I - \bar{\bar{A}}_1\right)^{-1}, \ \ k \geq 1, \tag{14}$$

*where $\bar{\Pi}_0 = \bar{\Pi}_0 \bar{\bar{B}}_0$.*

**Remark 1.** *(i) We note that the entries in the associated matrices of a kernel function may be negative. Hence, the associated transition kernel matrices $\bar{A}_k'$s and $\bar{B}_k'$s cannot construct a stochastic transition matrix.*

*(ii) We now consider numerical algorithms for computing the associated matrix $\bar{G}$. In the literature, several known algorithms, including the functional iteration ([17,18]), Newton iteration ([19]), invariant subspace method ([20]), cyclic reduction ([21]) and Ramaswami Reduction ([22]), have been developed to solve the G-matrix for M/G/1-type chains with a finite phase. For a collection of these algorithms, please refer to [13]. Similar to what we did in Theorems 4 and 5, we can set up the corresponding algorithms for $\bar{G}$ by modifying these algorithms from the finite phase to the general phase. We omit the details in order to avoid tedious presentations.*

## 5. Numerical Experiments

### 5.1. Discrete Wavelet Transforms

We need to perform discrete wavelet transforms for numerical experiments. Without a loss of generality, we assume that the phase space is taken to be $\mathbb{R}$. In the following, we only give a simple presentation of the computation framework; please refer to Section 5 in [5] for more details.

We first consider numerical issues of the M/G/1-type Markov chain with a continuous phase, which are divided into the following steps:

Step 1: Choose appropriate real numbers $\underline{y}$, $\overline{y}$ and positive integer $N$. Then, evenly sample $N$ points from the truncated phase space $[\underline{y}, \overline{y}]$. Performing the DWT in Algorithm 5.1 in [5] to kernels $A_i(x,y)$ and $B_i(x,y)$ produces the associated sample matrices $(A_i)_{asm}$ and $(B_i)_{asm}$.

Step 2: Solve the the associated sample matrix $G_{asm}$ through the algorithms listed in (ii) of Remark 1, such as functional iteration, Newton iteration, invariant subspace method, cyclic reduction and Ramaswami Reduction.

Step 3: Solve the associated sample invariant probability vector $\Pi_{asm}$ using Theorem 6.

Step 4: Performing the IDWT in Algorithm 5.2 in [5] to the matrix of $G_{asm}$ and the vector $\Pi_{asm}$ produces the kernels $G(x,y)$ and $\Pi(x)$.

Now, we consider numerical issues of GI/M/1-type Markov chains with the continuous phase, which are also divided into four steps. The first step and the last step are the same as that for the M/G/1-type Markov chains. In Step 3, we solve the associated sample invariant probability vector $\Pi_{asm}$ based on Theorem 3. For Step 2, we use the Ramaswami dual to solve the associated sample matrix $R_{asm}$. It is known that the Ramaswami dual [11] enables us to compute the matrix $R$ for a GI/M/1-type chain with a finite phase in terms of computing the matrix $G$ for a dual M/G/1-type Markov chain. Note that the Ramaswami dual can be modified and extended to the case of M/G/1-type and GI/M/1-type chains with a continuous phase.

### 5.2. Illustration with Examples

#### 5.2.1. Example 1: An $M/G/1$-Type Chain

The Markov chain in this example is modified from Example 2 in [5] by extending the tri-diagonal structure to the more general upper-Hessenberg setting.

Denote by $S_i, i \geq 0$ the arrival times of a Poisson process with parameter $\lambda$. Let $S_0 = 0$. Define a sequence of i.i.d. random variables $V(S_n), n \geqslant 0$, which are distributed with

$$\mathbb{P}\{V(S_n) = j\} = p_j, \quad j \geq -1,$$

where $p_j'$s are non-negative constants such that $\sum_{j=-1}^{\infty} p_j = 1$. We define

$$L(t) = \begin{cases} L(S_0) = L(0), & \text{if} \quad 0 = S_0 \leqslant t < S_1, \\ \max\{0, L(S_{n-1}) + j\}, & \text{if } V(S_n) = j, S_n \leqslant t < S_{n+1}, \end{cases} \tag{15}$$

$$Y(t) = \begin{cases} Y(S_k) + (t - S_k), & \text{if } V(S_k) = \ell, S_k \leqslant t < S_{k+1}, \\ t - S_k, & \text{if } V(S_k) = -1, S_k \leqslant t < S_{k+1}, \end{cases} \tag{16}$$

where $n \geq 1, j \geq -1, k \geq 0, \ell \geq 0$.

Let $L_n = L(S_n)$ and $Y_n = Y(S_{n+1} - 0)$, then $(L_n, Y_n)$ is a M/G/1-type chain, whose phase space is $\mathbb{R}_+$. Its transition kernels are derived as

$$\begin{aligned} A_0(x,y) &= p_{-1}(1 - e^{-\lambda y}), \text{ for all } x, y, \\ A_{j+1}(x,y) &= \begin{cases} 0, & \text{if} \quad y < x; \\ p_j\left[1 - e^{-\lambda(y-x)}\right], & \text{if} \quad y \geqslant x, \end{cases} \quad \text{if} \quad j \geq 0. \end{aligned} \tag{17}$$

and finally

$$B_0(x,y) = A_0(x,y) + A_1(x,y), \quad B_i(x,y) = A_{i+1}(x,y), i \geq 1. \tag{18}$$

The marginal invariant probability measures for the $M/G/1$-type chain $(L_n, Y_n)$ has analytical expressions, as follows:

$$\begin{aligned} {}_L\Pi_0 &= \frac{p_{-1}-\sum_{n=0}^{\infty} n p_n}{p_{-1}}, \\ {}_L\Pi_k &= \frac{{}_L\pi_0(\sum_{n=k}^{\infty} p_n)+\sum_{i=1}^{k-1}\sum_{j=0}^{\infty} {}_L\pi_i p_{k-i+j}}{p_{-1}}, \\ {}_P\Pi(y) &= \begin{cases} 0, & \text{if} \quad y < 0 \\ 1-e^{-\lambda p_{-1} y}, & \text{if} \quad y \geqslant 0, \end{cases} \end{aligned} \tag{19}$$

where ${}_L\Pi_k$ and ${}_P\Pi(y)$ are, respectively, the level and phase marginal invariant probability measures.

Take $p_{-1} = \frac{1}{2}$, $p_k = (\frac{1}{3})^{k+1}$, $k \geq 0$. From (19), we can have the following exact value of the marginal level stationary probabilities

$${}_L\Pi_0 = \frac{1}{2}, \ {}_L\Pi_k = \frac{1}{4}(\frac{2}{3})^k, \ k \geq 1.$$

Evenly take 256 samples on $[0, 45]$ as values of $x$ and 256 samples on $[0, 50]$ as values of $y$, and choose the Haar wavelet for the wavelet transform. Figure 1 presents the numerical solutions of kernel functions $G(x, y)$. The marginal distributions are obtained numerically based on the $G_{asm}$ solved by functional iteration. The numerical solutions for level marginal distribution and phase marginal distribution are, respectively, shown in Figures 2 and 3, together with the corresponding analytical solutions. For each method used to derive $G_{asm}$, we calculate its mean absolute error defined as $\frac{1}{K+1}\sum_{k=0}^{K} |{}_L\Pi_k - {}_L\hat{\Pi}_k|$, where $K = 500$ and ${}_L\hat{\Pi}_k$ is the numerical solution of the marginal level stationary probability at level $k$. (We take $K = 500$ because values of ${}_L\Pi_k$ when $k > 500$ are small enough to be considered as negligible.) In this example, different methods of solving matrix G lead to the same numerical solutions of level and phase marginal distributions. According to Figure 4, performances of various methods are similar in the sense of accuracy and computational time.

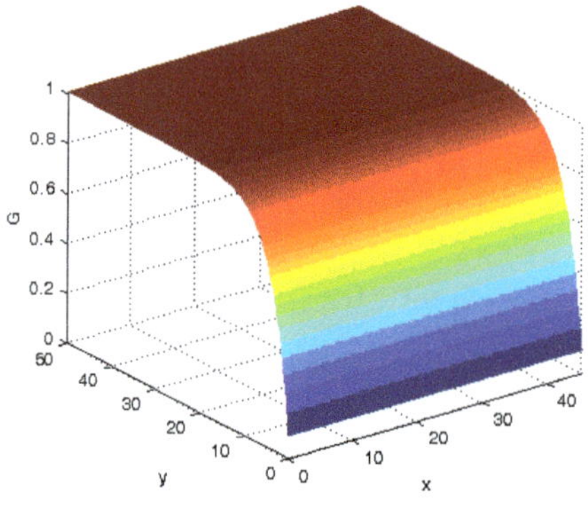


**Figure 1.** Numerical solution of kernel function $G(x, y)$.

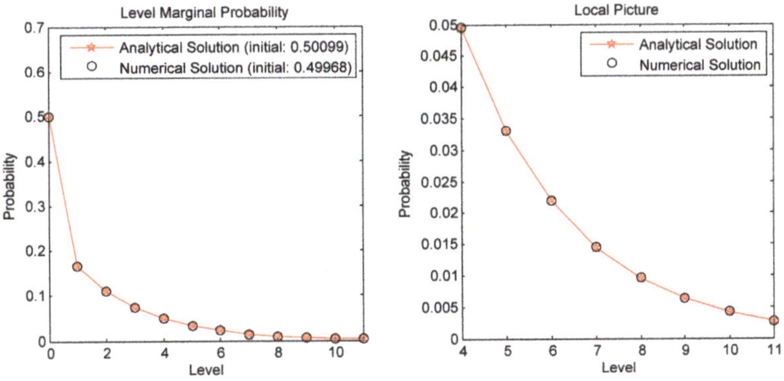


**Figure 2.** Level marginal invariant probability distribution ${}_L\Pi_k$.

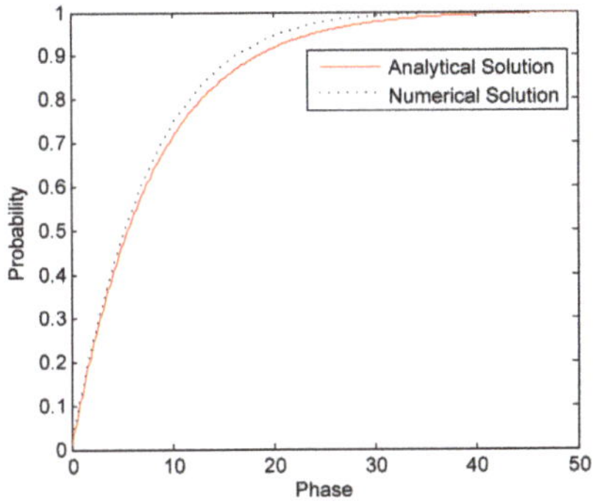


**Figure 3.** Phase marginal invariant probability distribution ${}_P\Pi(y)$.

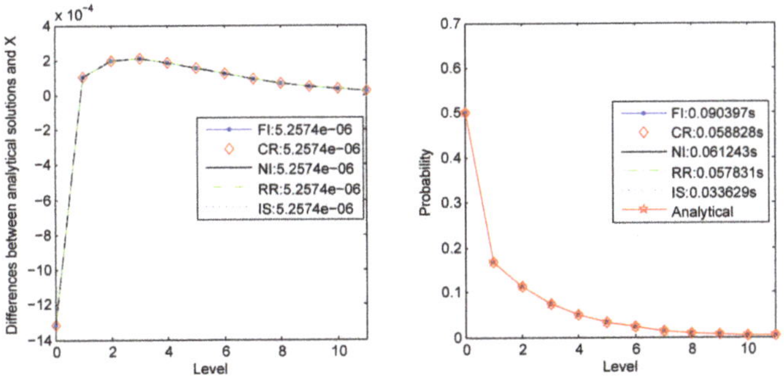


**Figure 4.** Difference among methods on level marginal invariant probability distribution ${}_L\Pi_k$. The legend of the first plot includes mean absolute errors, and the legend of the second plot includes computational times. (FI: functional iteration, CR: cyclic reduction, NI: Newton iteration, RR: Ramaswami Reduction and IS: invariant subspace)

#### 5.2.2. Example 2: A $GI/M/1$-Type Chain

Consider a first-come first-served single server $GI/G/1$ queuing system, which was considered by [1] for the theoretical analysis of the invariant probability distribution. Here, we consider the computational issue. In this $GI/G/1$ queue, the service times and interarrival times are distributed with general distribution functions $S(x)$ and $F(x)$. We assume that both the mean arrival interval $\lambda = \int_0^\infty t dF(t)$ and the mean service time $\mu_0 := \int_0^\infty t dS(t)$ are finite.

Let $L_n$ be the number of customers right before the arrival time of the $n$th customer and let $X_n$ be the remaining service time just after the $n$th arrival. Let $Z_n$ be the departure time of the $n$th customer, and let $X(t)$ be the remaining service time at time $t$ of a customer who is receiving the service. Write

$$D_n^t(x,y) = P\{Z_n \le t < Z_{n+1}, X(t) \le y | X(0) = x\}.$$

Then, $(L_n, X_n), n \ge 1$ is a GI/M/1-type Markov chain with discrete levels and continuous phases, whose transition probabilities are given by (1) with (see [1])

$$A_n(x,y) = \int_0^\infty D_n^t(x,y)dF(t), \tag{20}$$

$$B_n(x,y) = \left(\sum_{j=n+1}^{\infty} A_j(x,\infty)\right) S(y). \tag{21}$$

From [1], we know that if $\lambda > \mu_0$, then $(L_n, X_n)$ has an invariant probability measure $\Pi_j$ with

$$\Pi_k(\cdot) = d\int_0^\infty dS(x) R^{(k)}(x,\cdot)$$

where the constant $d$ is given by

$$d = 1 + \left(\int_0^\infty \left[\sum_{n=0}^{\infty} F^{n*}(x)\right] dS(x)\right) \left[\exp \sum_{n=1}^{\infty} \left(1 - \int_0^\infty [1 - F^{n*}(x)] dS^{*n}(x)\right)/n\right].$$

To illustrate our algorithm, we would like to compare numerical solutions for the level of marginal distribution with its analytical value. For numerical calculation, let $F(t)$ be uniformly distributed in the interval $(0,1]$, i.e., $F(t) \sim U(0,1)$, and let the service time be exponentially distributed with parameter $\mu$, i.e., $S(t) \sim \exp(\mu)$. Then we have, for $n \ge 1$

$$D_n^t(x,y) = \begin{cases} \frac{\mu^{n-1}(t-x)^{n-1}}{(n-1)!}(e^{-\mu(t-x)} - e^{-\mu(t-x+y)}), & t \ge x, \\ 0, & t < x, \end{cases}$$

and, for $n = 0$

$$D_0^t(x,y) = I_{[0,y]}(x-t).$$

The kernels $A_n(x,y)$ and $B_n(x,y)$ are calculated as follows. For $n \ge 1$, by (20)

$$\begin{aligned} A_n(x,y) &= \int_x^1 \frac{\mu^{n-1}(t-x)^{n-1}}{(n-1)!}\left(e^{-\mu(t-x)} - e^{-\mu(t-x+y)}\right)dt \\ &= \frac{1-e^{-\mu y}}{\mu}\int_0^{1-x} \frac{\mu^n}{(n-1)!} t^{n-1} e^{-\mu t} dt. \end{aligned}$$

For $0 \le x \le 1, y \ge x$

$$A_0(x,y) = \int_{x-y}^{x} 1dt = \int_0^x 1dt = x,$$

and for $0 \le x \le 1, y < x$

$$A_0(x,y) = \int_{x-y}^{x} 1dt = y.$$

For $n \ge 0$, by (21) we have

$$B_n(x,y) = (1-e^{-\mu y}) \cdot \int_0^{1-x} \left[1 - \sum_{j=0}^{n-1} e^{-\mu t}\frac{(\mu t)^j}{j!}\right] dt.$$

Since $\lambda = 1/2$ and $E[S] = \mu_0 = \frac{1}{\mu}$, the queuing system is stable if

$$\rho = \frac{1/\lambda}{1/E[S]} = \frac{E[S]}{\lambda} = \frac{2}{\mu} < 1.$$

It is well known that the level marginal invariant probability distribution is

$$_L\Pi_j = c^j(1-c),$$

where $c$ is the solution of $\int_0^\infty e^{-\mu t(1-c)} dF(t) = c$ on the interval $[0,1]$. Since $F \sim U(0,1)$, then

$$e^{(c-1)\mu} - 1 = c(c-1)\mu.$$

For numerical experiments, we take $\mu = 4.7$. The constant $c$ is solved to be approximately 0.2885. The exact marginal level distribution $_L\Pi$ can be obtained. On the other hand, we can perform the numerical algorithm in the previous section to approximate $_L\Pi$. We may then compare the numerical results to the analytical results, and provide a verification of the algorithm afterward. Here, we do not consider the marginal phase distribution, since its closed form cannot be obtained.

Evenly take 256 samples on $[0,1]$ as values of $x$ and 256 samples on $[0,1.5]$ as values of $y$, and choose the Haar wavelet for a wavelet transform. The numerical solutions of kernel functions $G(x,y)$ and $R(x,y)$ are shown in Figure 5. The level marginal distribution of this queuing system could be computed by a previous algorithm. We show the numerical solutions using $G_{asm}$ solved by functional iteration, together with the analytical solutions in Figure 6. Among the five numerical methods mentioned in (ii) of Remark 1, we note that the method of the invariant subspace does not work during the run of the algorithm, which may be caused by the fact that some matrices are not invertible. With numerical solutions of marginal invariant probability distributions for the level and phase, we can further estimate the mean and variance of the queue length and the remaining service time, which are listed in Table 1. This implies practical uses of invariant probability distributions.

Since we are not able to obtain analytical solutions of marginal invariant probability distributions for the phase, only the analytical mean and variance for the level are presented in Table 1. When using the Ramaswami reduction, the mean queue length is the most accurate among four methods, but the variance of the queue length is not close to the analytical variance. However, the mean and variance solved using the functional iteration are both relatively accurate.

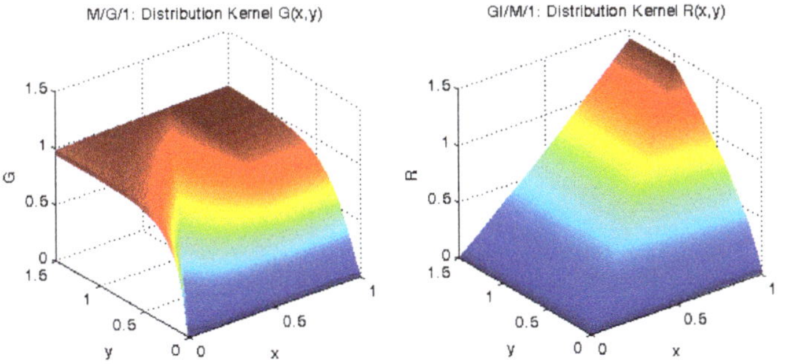


**Figure 5.** Numerical solutions of kernel functions. The right picture is about the kernel $R(x,y)$, and the left is about its dual kernel $G(x,y)$.

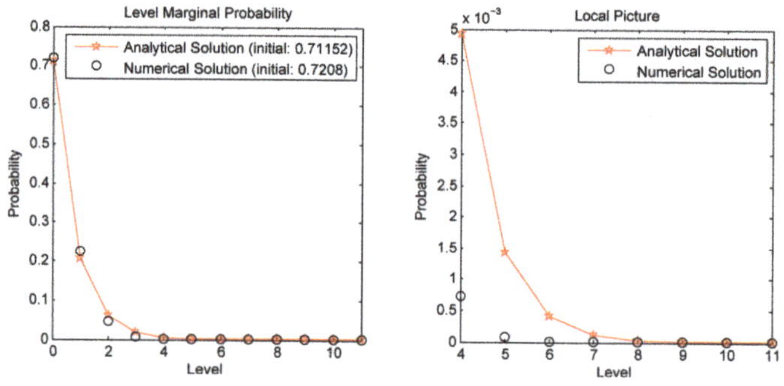


**Figure 6.** Level marginal invariant probability distribution ${}_L\Pi_k$.

We compare properties of the other four methods according to their mean absolute errors and speeds of computation. From Figure 7 and Table 1, the functional iteration performs the best among all the four methods, since it is the fastest and also the most accurate. When we raise the sample size from 256 to 512, it takes 20.98 s to solve $G_{asm}$ using a functional iteration. The computational times of the cyclic reduction, Newton iteration and Ramaswami reduction are 116.35 s, 1997.53 s and 2191.45 s, respectively. The differences between the mean absolute errors of numerical solutions and the errors when using a sample size of 256, however, are only around $10^{-4}$.

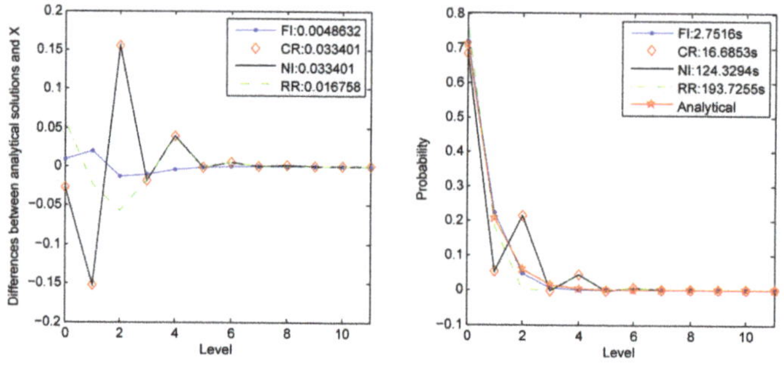


**Figure 7.** Difference among methods on level marginal invariant probability distribution ${}_L\Pi_k$. The legend of the first plot includes mean absolute errors, and the legend of the second plot includes computational times. (FI: functional iteration, CR: cyclic reduction, NI: Newton iteration and RR: Ramaswami Reduction).

**Table 1.** Mean and variance of level and phase.

| | Queue Length (Level) | | Remaining Service Time (Phase) | |
|---|---|---|---|---|
| **Method** | **Mean** | **Variance** | **Mean** | **Variance** |
| FI | 0.3415 | 0.3680 | 0.3125 | 0.1127 |
| CR | 0.6964 | 1.3918 | 0.3345 | 0.1255 |
| NI | 0.6964 | 1.3918 | 0.3345 | 0.1255 |
| RR | 0.3911 | 0.9596 | 0.4385 | 0.1641 |
| Analytical | 0.4054 | 0.5698 | - | - |

## 6. Conclusions

For invariant probability measures of Harris positive recurrent $GI/M/1$-type or $M/G/1$-type Markov chains with discrete levels and a general phase set, we establish wavelet-based computational frameworks in this paper. A theoretical analysis framework is also established for $M/G/1$-type Markov chains. These results extend the known findings in [4,5] for QBD processes to the current more general block-structured Markov chains. Numerical experiments support the effectiveness of our numerical algorithms based on DTWC. An interesting observation in Example 2 is that among the adopted five algorithms for $G$-matrix, the functional iteration performs the best, but the invariant subspace may fail.

For future research, it is interesting to consider block-structured continuous-time Markov processes with discrete levels and continuous phases. In this case, the processes should be presented in terms of the extended generators. It is expected that the research is more challenging when setting up these models and preforming the theoretical and numerical analysis of their invariant probability measures.

**Author Contributions:** Methodology, Y.L.; Software, S.J.; Writing—original draft, S.J., Y.L. and N.L.; Writing—review and editing, Y.L and N.L.; Visualization, S.J. and N.L.; Funding acquisition, Y.L. All authors have read and agreed to the published version of the manuscript.

**Funding:** This research was funded in part by the National Natural Science Foundation of China (Grants No. 11971486).

**Data Availability Statement:** No data is used in this study.

**Conflicts of Interest:** The authors declare no conflict of interest.

## Appendix A

**Table A1.** Summary of frequently used notations.

| Notation | Description |
|---|---|
| $E$ | State space of a Markov chain |
| $\ell_i$ | The $i$ level set of Markov chain $\{(L_n, X_n) : n \in \mathbb{N}\}$ |
| $\tau_{\ell_i}$ | The first return time to the level set $\ell_i$ |
| $P_{GI}(\cdot,\cdot)$ | Transition kernel matrix of $GI/M/1$-type Markov chain |
| $P_M(\cdot,\cdot)$ | Transition kernel matrix of $M/G/1$-type Markov chain |
| $P^A(\cdot,\cdot)$ | One-step transition kernel of a censored Markov chain on set $A$ |
| $\Pi$ | Invariant probability measure |
| $\overline{U}$ | Associated matrix of kernel function $U(x,y)$ |
| $\Sigma_H$ | Set of kernel functions having a density function equaling to zeros outside of $H \times H$ |

## References

1. Tweedie, R.L. Operator-geometric stationary distributions for Markov chains, with application to queueing models. *Adv. Appl. Probab.* **1982**, *14*, 368–391. [CrossRef]
2. Neuts, M.F. *Matrix-Geometric Solutions in Stochastic Models: An Algorithmic Approach*; Johns Hopkins University Press: Baltimore, MD, USA, 1981.
3. Breuer, L. Transient and stationary distributions for the GI/G/k Queue with Lebesgue-dominated inter-arrival time distribution. *Queueing Syst.* **2003**, *45*, 47–57. [CrossRef]
4. Nielsen, B.F.; Ramaswami, V. *A Computational Framework for a Quasi Birth and Death Process with a Continuous Phase Variable*; Ramaswami, V., Wirth, P., Eds.; ITC 15; Elsevier: Amsterdam, The Netherlands, 1997; pp. 477–486.
5. Jiang, S.; Latouche, G.; Liu, Y. Wavelet transform for quasi-birth-death process with a continuous phase set. *Appl. Math. Comput.* **2015**, *252*, 354–376. [CrossRef]
6. Neuts, M.F. *Structured Stochastic Matrices of M/G/1 Type and Their Applications*; Marcel Dekker: New York, NY, USA, 1989.
7. Bini, D.A.; Meini, B.; Steffé, S.; Van Houdt, B. Structured Markov chains solver: Software tools. In Proceedings of the SMCTOOLS, Pisa, Italy, 10 October 2006.
8. Bini, D.A.; Meini, B.; Steffé, S.; Van Houdt, B. Structured Markov chains solver: Algorithms. In Proceedings of SMCTOOLS, Pisa, Italy, 10 October 2006.
9. Bright, L.W. *Matrix-Analytic Methods in Applied Probability*; The University of Adelaide: Adelaide, Australia, 1996.
10. Ramaswami, V. Nonlinear matrix equations in applied probability-solution techniques and open problems. *Siam Rev.* **1988**, *30*, 256–263. [CrossRef]
11. Ramaswami, V. A duality theorem for the matrix paradigms in aueueing theory. *Commun. Stat. Stoch. Model.* **1990**, *6*, 151–161. [CrossRef]

12. Taylor, P.G.; Van Houdt, B. On The dual relationship between Markov chains of GI/M/1 and M/G/1 type. *Adv. Appl. Probab.* **2010**, *42*, 210–225. [CrossRef]
13. Bini, D.A.; Latouche, G.; Meini, B. *Numerical Methods for Structured Markov Chains*; Oxford University Press: New York, NY, USA, 2005.
14. Meyn, S.P.; Tweedie, R.L. *Markov Chains And Stochastic Stability*, 2nd ed.; Cambridge University Press: Cambridge, UK, 2009.
15. Stéphane, M. *A Wavelet Tour of Signal Processing*; Academic Press: New York, NY, USA, 2009.
16. Daubechies, I. Orthonormal base of compactly supported wavelets. *Commun. Pure Appl. Math.* **1988**, *41*, 909–996. [CrossRef]
17. Favati, P.; Meini, B. Relaxed functional iteration techniques for the numerical solution of M/G/1 type Markov chains. *Bit Numer. Math.* **1998**, *38*, 510–526. [CrossRef]
18. Favati, P.; Meini, B. On functional iteration methods for solving nonlinear matrix equations arising in queueing problems. *IMA J. Numer. Anal.* **1999**, *19*, 39–49. [CrossRef]
19. Latouche, G. Newton's iteration for non-linear equations in Markov chains. *IMA J. Numer. Anal.* **1994**, *14*, 583–598. [CrossRef]
20. Akar, N.; Sohraby, K. An invariant subspace approach in M/G/1 and G/M/1 type Markov chains. *Stoch. Model.* **1997**, *13*, 381–416. [CrossRef]
21. Bini, D.A.; Meini, B. *On Cyclic Reduction Applied to a Class of Toeplitz-like Matrices Arising in Queueing Problems, Computations with Markov Chains*; Springer: Boston, MA, USA, 1995.
22. Ramaswami, V. The generality of Quasi Birth-and-Death processes. In *Advances in Matrix Analytic Methods for Stochastic Models*; Alfa, A.S., Chakravarthy, S.R., Eds.; Notable Publications: Branchburg, NJ, USA, 1998; pp. 93–113.

mathematics

MDPI

Article

# A New Probabilistic Approach: Estimation and Monte Carlo Simulation with Applications to Time-to-Event Data

**Huda M. Alshanbari [1], Zubair Ahmad [2,*], Hazem Al-Mofleh [3], Clement Boateng Ampadu [4] and Saima K. Khosa [5]**

1 Department of Mathematical Sciences, College of Science, Princess Nourah bint Abdulrahman University, P.O. Box 84428, Riyadh 11671, Saudi Arabia
2 Department of Statistics, Quaid-i-Azam University, Islamabad 44000, Pakistan
3 Department of Mathematics, Tafila Technical University, Tafila 66110, Jordan
4 Independent Researcher, 31 Carrolton Road, Boston, MA 02132, USA
5 Department of Mathematics and Statistics, University of Saskatchewan, Saskatoon, SK S7N 5E5, Canada
* Correspondence: zahmad@stat.qau.edu.pk

**Abstract:** In this paper, we propose a useful method without adding any extra parameters to obtain new probability distributions. The proposed family is a combination of the two existing families of distributions and is called a weighted sine-*G* family. A two-parameter special member of the weighted sine-*G* family, using the Weibull distribution as a baseline model, is considered and investigated in detail. Some distributional properties of the weighted sine-*G* family are derived. Different estimation methods are considered to estimate the parameters of the special model of the weighted sine-*G* family. Furthermore, simulation studies based on these different methods are also provided. Finally, the applicability and usefulness of the weighted sine-*G* family are demonstrated by analyzing two data sets taken from the engineering sector.

**Keywords:** Weibull model; trigonometric function; family of distributions; simulation; statistical modeling; engineering data

**MSC:** 62N01; 62N02

**Citation:** Alshanbari, H.M.; Ahmad, Z.; Al-Mofleh, H.; Ampadu, C.B.; Khosa, S.K. A New Probabilistic Approach: Estimation and Monte Carlo Simulation with Applications to Time-to-Event Data. *Mathematics* **2023**, *11*, 1583. https://doi.org/10.3390/math11071583

Academic Editors: Francisco German Badía, María D. Berrade and Manuel Alberto M. Ferreira

Received: 24 January 2023
Revised: 11 March 2023
Accepted: 20 March 2023
Published: 24 March 2023



## 1. Introduction

A challenging work for researchers is to look for flexible probability models to cater to the analysis of various types of data that possess extreme observations, such as (i) Reliability data [1], (ii) healthcare data [2], (iii) financial data [3], (iv) hydrological data [4], (v) time-to-event data [5–7], and (vi) lifetime data analysis [8,9], etc. However, the traditional distribution does not provide the best fit for the data sets, as it has extreme observations. Based on the available literature, we know that the heavy-tailed (HT) distributions have proven to be substantial for the data sets that possess extreme observations. Unfortunately, there are only a few probability models that possess HT characteristics. Therefore, researchers are always in search of new probability distributions that possess HT characteristics.

To improve the flexibility of the existing models, new methods have been suggested; see the truncated burr *XG* family [10], Fréchet Topp Leone-*G* family [11], shifted Gompertz-*G* family [12], Teissier-*G* family [13], and Gudermannian-generated family [14], among others. Thanks to these methods, they have significantly improved the fitting power of the existing distributions. However, there are certain deficiencies/problems associated with these methods, for instance, these methods involve from one to five or more additional parameters. This fact leads to estimation difficulties and re-parametrization problems. To avoid the re-parametrization problem, researchers are focusing on generating new methods without adding extra parameters. In this regard, Kumar et al. [15] suggested a useful method using a trigonometric function, namely, a sine-$G$ family. Let $X$ have a sine-$G$ family with a cumulative distribution function (CDF) $K(x;\boldsymbol{\vartheta})$, if it is given by

$$K(x;\boldsymbol{\vartheta}) = \sin\left(\frac{\pi}{2}G(x;\boldsymbol{\vartheta})\right), \qquad x \in \mathbb{R}, \tag{1}$$

where $\boldsymbol{\vartheta}$ is a parameter vector and $G(x;\boldsymbol{\vartheta})$ is a baseline CDF with respect to Equation (1). Since $G(x;\boldsymbol{\vartheta})$ is a baseline CDF, it must obey the following properties:

- $G(x;\boldsymbol{\vartheta})$ is a non-decreasing function.
- The maximum of $G(x;\boldsymbol{\vartheta})$ is when $x = \infty : G(\infty;\boldsymbol{\vartheta}) = 1$.
- The minimum of $G(x;\boldsymbol{\vartheta})$ is when $x = -\infty : G(-\infty;\boldsymbol{\vartheta}) = 0$.

For more contributed work using the sine function, we refer interested readers to [16–23]. Ahmad et al. [24] produced further efforts by proposing another method without any additional parameters. They used the T-$X$ method to generate a weighted T-$X$ (WT-$X$) family. For detailed information about the T-$X$ method, we refer to [25]. The CDF $F(x;\boldsymbol{\vartheta})$ of the WT-$X$ method is

$$F(x;\boldsymbol{\vartheta}) = 1 - \frac{[1 - K(x;\boldsymbol{\vartheta})]}{e^{K(x;\boldsymbol{\vartheta})}}, \qquad x \in \mathbb{R}, \tag{2}$$

where $K(x;\boldsymbol{\vartheta})$ is a baseline CDF with respect to Equation (2).

To bring further flexibility to the sine-$G$ and WT-$X$ methods, we propose another useful approach that possesses the HT characteristics. The proposed approach is obtained by following the spirit of the WT-$X$ method along with the sine-$G$ family. The proposed method may be called a weighted sine-$G$ (WS-$G$) family of distributions. The key features of the WS-$G$ method are (i) it has no extra parameters and (ii) it provides a useful alternative to the sine-$G$ and WT-$X$ methods, with possible different aims in terms of modeling.

Suppose $X$ has the WS-$G$ distributions with parameter vector $\boldsymbol{\vartheta}$, then, the CDF $F(x;\boldsymbol{\vartheta})$ of $X$ is

$$F(x;\boldsymbol{\vartheta}) = 1 - \frac{\left[1 - \sin\left(\frac{\pi}{2}G(x;\boldsymbol{\vartheta})\right)\right]}{e^{\sin\left(\frac{\pi}{2}G(x;\boldsymbol{\vartheta})\right)}}, \qquad x \in \mathbb{R}, \tag{3}$$

with PDF

$$f(x;\boldsymbol{\vartheta}) = \left(\frac{\pi}{2}\right)\frac{g(x;\boldsymbol{\vartheta})\cos\left(\frac{\pi}{2}G(x;\boldsymbol{\vartheta})\right)}{e^{\sin\left(\frac{\pi}{2}G(x;\boldsymbol{\vartheta})\right)}}\left[2 - \sin\left(\frac{\pi}{2}G(x;\boldsymbol{\vartheta})\right)\right], \qquad x \in \mathbb{R}, \tag{4}$$

where $\frac{d}{dx}G(x;\boldsymbol{\vartheta}) = g(x;\boldsymbol{\vartheta})$.

Furthermore, the survival function (SF) $S(x;\boldsymbol{\vartheta}) = 1 - F(x;\boldsymbol{\vartheta})$, hazard function (HF) $\frac{f(x;\boldsymbol{\vartheta})}{1-F(x;\boldsymbol{\vartheta})}$, and cumulative HF (CHF) $H(x;\boldsymbol{\vartheta}) = -\log[1 - F(x;\boldsymbol{\vartheta})]$ are, respectively, given by

$$S(x;\boldsymbol{\vartheta}) = \frac{\left[1 - \sin\left(\frac{\pi}{2}G(x;\boldsymbol{\vartheta})\right)\right]}{e^{\sin\left(\frac{\pi}{2}G(x;\boldsymbol{\vartheta})\right)}}, \qquad x \in \mathbb{R}, \tag{5}$$

$$h(x;\boldsymbol{\vartheta}) = \left(\frac{\pi}{2}\right)\frac{g(x;\boldsymbol{\vartheta})\cos\left(\frac{\pi}{2}G(x;\boldsymbol{\vartheta})\right)}{\left[1 - \sin\left(\frac{\pi}{2}G(x;\boldsymbol{\vartheta})\right)\right]}\left[2 - \sin\left(\frac{\pi}{2}G(x;\boldsymbol{\vartheta})\right)\right], \qquad x \in \mathbb{R}, \tag{6}$$

and

$$H(x;\boldsymbol{\vartheta}) = -\log\left(\frac{\left[1 - \sin\left(\frac{\pi}{2}G(x;\boldsymbol{\vartheta})\right)\right]}{e^{\sin\left(\frac{\pi}{2}G(x;\boldsymbol{\vartheta})\right)}}\right), \qquad x \in \mathbb{R}. \tag{7}$$

The WS-$G$ method has certain advantages while implementing it in practice. The advantages of the WS-$G$ method are given by

- Since the WS-$G$ method has no additional parameters, it may reduce the estimation problems.
- Due to no additional parameters, the WS-$G$ method avoids the re-parametrization problems.
- The WS-$G$ method possesses heavy-tailed (HT) characteristics; see Section 3.

Besides the above advantages, the WS-$G$ method also has certain limitations. The limitations of the WS-$G$ method are

- Due to the complicated form of the PDF of the WS-$G$ method, more computational efforts are required to derive its distributional properties.
- Since the quantile function of the WS-$G$ method is not in an explicit form, the computer software must be implemented to generate random numbers from the WS-$G$ distributions.

Based on the WS-$G$ method, we study an updated form of the Weibull distribution, namely, a weighted sine-Weibull (WS-Weibull) distribution. Some basic functions of the WS-Weibull model are obtained in Section 2. Visual behaviors of the PDF of the WS-Weibull distribution are also presented. Some distributional properties of the WS-$G$ method are discussed in Section 3. Section 4 is devoted to estimate the parameters of the WS-Weibull distribution using different estimation methods. The applicability of the WS-Weibull distribution is shown in Section 5. Some concluding remarks are presented in Section 6.

## 2. Special Model

This section offers some basic functions of a special member (i.e., WS-Weibull distribution) of the WS-$G$ method with support $(0, \infty)$. Furthermore, the behaviors of the WS-Weibull distribution are also presented.

### 2.1. The WS-Weibull Distribution

Suppose $X$ has the Weibull model with support $(0, \infty)$; then, its CDF $G(x; \boldsymbol{\vartheta})$ is given by

$$G(x; \boldsymbol{\vartheta}) = 1 - e^{-\lambda x^{\delta}}, \qquad x \geq 0, \delta, \lambda \in \mathbb{R}^{+}, \tag{8}$$

with PDF

$$g(x; \boldsymbol{\vartheta}) = \delta \lambda x^{\delta - 1} e^{-\lambda x^{\delta}}, \qquad x > 0,$$

where $\boldsymbol{\vartheta} = (\delta, \lambda)^{\top}$. Using $G(x; \boldsymbol{\vartheta}) = 1 - e^{-\lambda x^{\delta}}$ in Equation (3), we define the CDF of the WS-Weibull model. Suppose $X$ has the WS-Weibull model, then, its CDF $F(x; \boldsymbol{\vartheta})$ is

$$F(x; \boldsymbol{\vartheta}) = 1 - \frac{\left[1 - \sin\left(\frac{\pi}{2}\left(1 - e^{-\lambda x^{\delta}}\right)\right)\right]}{e^{\sin\left(\frac{\pi}{2}\left(1 - e^{-\lambda x^{\delta}}\right)\right)}}, \qquad x \geq 0, \tag{9}$$

with PDF

$$f(x; \boldsymbol{\vartheta}) = \frac{\delta \lambda \pi x^{\delta - 1} e^{-\lambda x^{\delta}} \cos\left(\frac{\pi}{2}\left(1 - e^{-\lambda x^{\delta}}\right)\right)}{2 e^{\sin\left(\frac{\pi}{2}\left(1 - e^{-\lambda x^{\delta}}\right)\right)}} \left[2 - \sin\left(\frac{\pi}{2}\left(1 - e^{-\lambda x^{\delta}}\right)\right)\right]. \tag{10}$$

For different values of $\delta$ and $\lambda$, Figure 1 offers different plots: $f(x; \boldsymbol{\vartheta})$ (WS-Weibull), $g(x; \boldsymbol{\vartheta})$ (Weibull), and $k(x; \boldsymbol{\vartheta})$ (sin-Weibull) distributions. Figure 1 shows that the shapes of $f(x; \boldsymbol{\vartheta})$, $g(x; \boldsymbol{\vartheta})$ and $k(x; \boldsymbol{\vartheta})$ have different forms such as right-skewed, symmetrical, left-skewed, and decreasing.

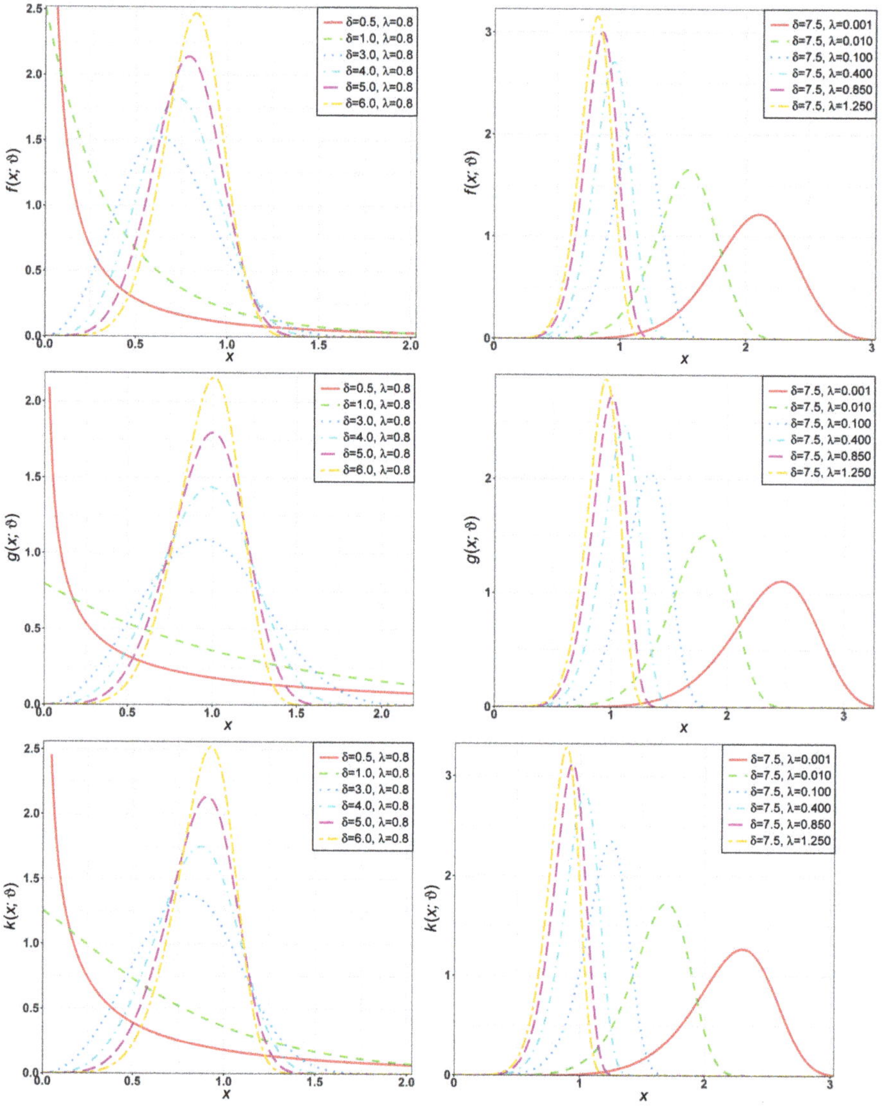


**Figure 1.** Plots of $f(x;\boldsymbol{\vartheta})$ of the WS-Weibull distribution for different values of $\delta$ and $\lambda$.

Table 1 shows the summation formula exact values for the PDFs of the WS-Weibull, Weibull, and sin-Weibull distributions for different values of $x$, $\delta$, and $\lambda$ at truncated $N$ terms. From Table 1 and Figure 1, it can be concluded that the PDF value of the WS-Weibull distribution is less than the PDF values of the Weibull and sin-Weibull distributions for the same $x$, $\delta$ and $\lambda$. These results are calculated by using R software (version 4.2.2).

Furthermore, the SF, CHF, and HF of the WS-Weibull distribution are

$$S(x;\boldsymbol{\vartheta}) = \frac{\left[1-\sin\left(\frac{\pi}{2}\left(1-e^{-\lambda x^{\delta}}\right)\right)\right]}{e^{\sin\left(\frac{\pi}{2}\left(1-e^{-\lambda x^{\delta}}\right)\right)}}, \tag{11}$$

$$H(x;\boldsymbol{\vartheta}) = -\log\left(\frac{\left[1-\sin\left(\frac{\pi}{2}\left(1-e^{-\lambda x^{\delta}}\right)\right)\right]}{e^{\sin\left(\frac{\pi}{2}\left(1-e^{-\lambda x^{\delta}}\right)\right)}}\right), \tag{12}$$

and

$$h(x;\boldsymbol{\vartheta}) = \frac{\delta\lambda\pi x^{\delta-1}e^{-\lambda x^{\delta}}\cos\left(\frac{\pi}{2}\left(1-e^{-\lambda x^{\delta}}\right)\right)}{2\left[1-\sin\left(\frac{\pi}{2}\left(1-e^{-\lambda x^{\delta}}\right)\right)\right]}\left[2-\sin\left(\frac{\pi}{2}\left(1-e^{-\lambda x^{\delta}}\right)\right)\right], \tag{13}$$

respectively.

**Table 1.** The summation formula and the exact value for the PDFs of WS-Weibull, Weibull, and sin-Weibull distributions for different values of $x$, $\delta$, and $\lambda$ at truncated $N$ terms.

| $x$ | $\delta$ | $\lambda$ | $N$ | WS-Weibull | | sin-Weibull | | Weibull |
|---|---|---|---|---|---|---|---|---|
| | | | | Summation | Exact Value | Summation | Exact Value | Exact Value |
| 0.5 | 0.8 | 1.2 | 2 | 0.4090627 | | 0.6170058 | | |
| | | | 4 | 0.3950064 | 0.3946863 | 0.6167320 | 0.6167320 | 0.5535454 |
| | | | 10 | 0.3946863 | | 0.6167320 | | |
| | | 2.2 | 2 | 0.1841287 | | 0.3880394 | | |
| | | | 4 | 0.1718327 | 0.1714237 | 0.3855453 | 0.3855445 | 0.5714233 |
| | | | 10 | 0.1714237 | | 0.3855445 | | |
| | 1.5 | 1.2 | 2 | 1.0064660 | | 1.1198750 | | |
| | | | 4 | 0.9908311 | 0.9906327 | 1.1198280 | 1.1198280 | 0.8327257 |
| | | | 10 | 0.9906327 | | 1.1198280 | | |
| | | 2.2 | 2 | 0.6842317 | | 1.1132750 | | |
| | | | 4 | 0.6566751 | 0.6559729 | 1.1124090 | 1.1124090 | 1.0720057 |
| | | | 10 | 0.6559729 | | 1.1124090 | | |
| 1.0 | 0.8 | 1.2 | 2 | 0.1009522 | | 0.2080368 | | |
| | | | 4 | 0.0945207 | 0.0943092 | 0.2069571 | 0.2069568 | 0.2891464 |
| | | | 10 | 0.0943092 | | 0.2069568 | | |
| | | 2.2 | 2 | 0.0230105 | | 0.0560985 | | |
| | | | 4 | 0.0201815 | 0.0201114 | 0.0530495 | 0.0530471 | 0.1950136 |
| | | | 10 | 0.0201114 | | 0.0530471 | | |
| | 1.5 | 1.2 | 2 | 0.1892854 | | 0.3900691 | | |
| | | | 4 | 0.1772264 | 0.1768297 | 0.3880446 | 0.3880440 | 0.5421496 |
| | | | 10 | 0.1768297 | | 0.3880440 | | |
| | | 2.2 | 2 | 0.0431448 | | 0.1051847 | | |
| | | | 4 | 0.0378403 | 0.0377088 | 0.0994678 | 0.0994634 | 0.3656504 |
| | | | 10 | 0.0377088 | | 0.0994634 | | |
| 2.5 | 0.8 | 1.2 | 2 | 0.0058948 | | 0.0145537 | | |
| | | | 4 | 0.0049978 | 0.0049798 | 0.0133140 | 0.0133129 | 0.0657602 |
| | | | 10 | 0.0049798 | | 0.0133129 | | |
| | | 2.2 | 2 | 0.0003286 | | 0.0008248 | | |
| | | | 4 | 0.0001409 | 0.0001402 | 0.0003815 | 0.0003809 | 0.0150408 |
| | | | 10 | 0.0001402 | | 0.0003809 | | |
| | 1.5 | 1.2 | 2 | 0.0005063 | | 0.0012709 | | |
| | | | 4 | 0.0001970 | 0.0001960 | 0.0005335 | 0.0005326 | 0.0247858 |
| | | | 10 | 0.0001960 | | 0.0005326 | | |
| | | 2.2 | 2 | 0.0000110 | | 0.0000277 | | |
| | | | 4 | 0.0000001 | 0.0000001 | 0.0000004 | 0.0000004 | 0.0008725 |
| | | | 10 | 0.0000001 | | 0.0000004 | | |

Figure 2 displays HF plots for the WS-Weibull distribution for various $\delta$ and $\lambda$ values; it can be observed that the HF shapes of the WS-Weibull distribution can be increasing, decreasing, and unimodal.

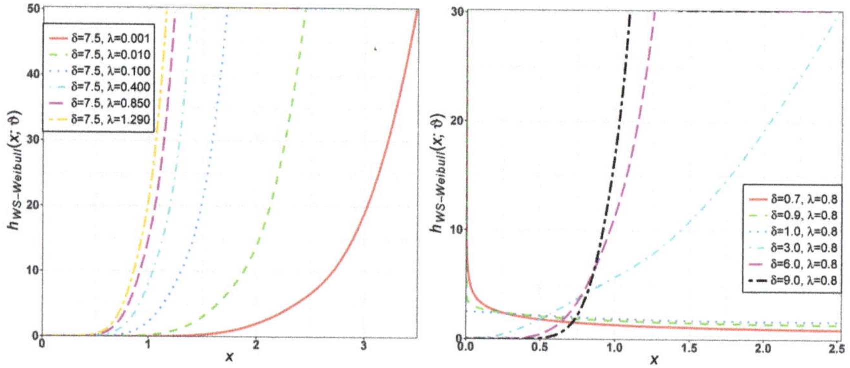


**Figure 2.** Plots of $h_{WS-Weibull}(x;\boldsymbol{\vartheta})$ of the WS-Weibull distribution for different values of $\delta$ and $\lambda$.

### 2.2. *The Behaviors of the PDF and HF of the WS-Weibull Model*

Here, we discuss the behaviors of the PDF and HF of the WS-Weibull distribution. The behaviors of the PDF of the WS-Weibull distribution when $x \to 0$ and $x \to \infty$ are, respectively, given by

$$\lim_{x\to 0} f(x;\boldsymbol{\vartheta}) = \begin{cases} \infty & \text{if } \delta < 1, \\ \pi\lambda & \text{if } \delta = 1, \\ 0 & \text{if } \delta > 1, \end{cases}$$

and

$$\lim_{x\to\infty} f(x;\boldsymbol{\vartheta}) = 0.$$

Similarly, the behavior of the HF defined in Equation (13) when $x \to 0$ and $x \to \infty$ are, respectively, given by

$$\lim_{x\to 0} h_{WS-Weibull}(x;\boldsymbol{\vartheta}) = \begin{cases} \infty & \text{if } \delta < 1, \\ \pi\lambda & \text{if } \delta = 1, \\ 0 & \text{if } \delta > 1, \end{cases}$$

and

$$\lim_{x\to\infty} h_{WS-Weibull}(x;\boldsymbol{\vartheta}) = \begin{cases} 0 & \text{if } \delta < 1, \\ 2\lambda & \text{if } \delta = 1, \\ \infty & \text{if } \delta > 1. \end{cases}$$

Now, we compare the behaviors of the HF of the Weibull, sin-Weibull (as a special case from the family in Equation (1)), and WS-Weibull distributions. The behavior of the HF of the Weibull distribution when $x \to 0$ and $x \to \infty$ are, respectively, given by

$$\lim_{x\to 0} h_{Weibull}(x;\delta,\lambda) = \begin{cases} \infty & \text{if } \delta < 1, \\ \lambda & \text{if } \delta = 1, \\ 0 & \text{if } \delta > 1, \end{cases}$$

and

$$\lim_{x\to\infty} h_{Weibull}(x;\delta,\lambda) = \begin{cases} 0 & \text{if } \delta < 1, \\ \lambda & \text{if } \delta = 1, \\ \infty & \text{if } \delta > 1. \end{cases}$$

Now, the behavior of the HF of the sin-Weibull distribution when $x \to 0$ and $x \to \infty$ are, respectively, given by

$$\lim_{x\to 0} h_{\sin-Weibull}(x;\delta,\lambda) = \begin{cases} \infty & \text{if } \delta < 1, \\ \frac{\pi\lambda}{2} & \text{if } \delta = 1, \\ 0 & \text{if } \delta > 1, \end{cases}$$

and

$$\lim_{x\to \infty} h_{\sin-Weibull}(x;\delta,\lambda) = \begin{cases} 0 & \text{if } \delta < 1, \\ 2\lambda & \text{if } \delta = 1, \\ \infty & \text{if } \delta > 1. \end{cases}$$

From the above results, we can conclude that the HF behaviors of these distributions are roughly similar.

Table 2 displays the summary of the HF limits for the WS-Weibull, Weibull, and sin-Weibull distributions. From the above mathematical results and numerical illustration in Table 2, we can conclude that the HF behaviors of these distributions are roughly similar.

**Table 2.** The summary of the HF limits for the WS-Weibull, Weibull, and sin-Weibull distributions.

| **Distributions** | **Limit as $x \to 0$** | | | **Limit as $x \to \infty$** | | |
|---|---|---|---|---|---|---|
| | $\delta < 1$ | $\delta = 1$ | $\delta > 1$ | $\delta < 1$ | $\delta = 1$ | $\delta > 1$ |
| WS-Weibull | $\infty$ | $\pi\lambda$ | 0 | 0 | $2\lambda$ | $\infty$ |
| Weibull | $\infty$ | $\lambda$ | 0 | 0 | $\lambda$ | $\infty$ |
| sin-Weibull | $\infty$ | $\frac{\pi}{2}\lambda$ | 0 | 0 | $2\lambda$ | $\infty$ |

## 3. Distributional Properties

Here, we give some distributional properties associated with the proposed method.

### 3.1. Expansion for the CDF

Using the power series representation for $\sin(x)$ and $e^x$, we can write the CDF as

$$F(x;\boldsymbol{\vartheta}) = 1 - \frac{1 - \sum_{n=0}^{\infty}(-1)^n \frac{\left(\frac{\pi}{2}G(x;\boldsymbol{\vartheta})\right)^{2n+1}}{(2n+1)!}}{\sum_{n=0}^{\infty} \frac{\left(\sin\left(\frac{\pi}{2}G(x;\boldsymbol{\vartheta})\right)\right)^n}{n!}}.$$

### 3.2. Expansion for the PDF

Using the power series representation for $\sin(x)$, $\cos(x)$, and $e^x$ we can write the PDF as

$$f(x;\boldsymbol{\vartheta}) = \frac{\pi}{2} g(x;\vartheta) \frac{\sum_{n=0}^{\infty} \frac{(-1)^n \left(\frac{\pi}{2}G(x;\vartheta)\right)^{2n}}{2n!}}{\sum_{n=0}^{\infty} \frac{\left(\sin\left(\frac{\pi}{2}G(x;\vartheta)\right)\right)^n}{n!}} \left(2 - \sum_{n=0}^{\infty}(-1)^n \frac{\left(\frac{\pi}{2}G(x;\vartheta)\right)^{2n+1}}{(2n+1)!}\right).$$

### 3.3. Quantile Function

We solve for $Q(p)$ in the following, where $0 < p < 1$,

$$p = 1 - \frac{1 - \sin\left(\frac{\pi}{2}G(Q(p))\right)}{e^{\sin\left(\frac{\pi}{2}G(Q(p))\right)}}.$$

After some algebraic manipulations, we arrive at

$$Q(p) = G^{-1}\left[-\frac{2}{\pi}\sin^{-1}(1 - W_{-1}((1-p)e))\right],$$

where $W_{-1}(\cdot)$ is the negative branch of the Lambert function.

### 3.4. Moment-Generating Function

The moment-generating function is defined as

$$M_X(t) = \sum_{r=0}^{\infty} \frac{t^r}{r!} \int_0^{\infty} x^r f(x)dx.$$

For the given family of distributions, we have

$$M_X(t) = \frac{\pi}{2} \sum_{r=0}^{\infty} \frac{t^r}{r!} \int_0^{\infty} x^r g(x;\vartheta) \frac{\sum_{n=0}^{\infty} \frac{(-1)^n \left(\frac{\pi}{2}G(x;\vartheta)\right)^{2n}}{2n!}}{\sum_{n=0}^{\infty} \frac{\left(\sin\left(\frac{\pi}{2}G(x;\vartheta)\right)\right)^n}{n!}} \times \left(2 - \sum_{n=0}^{\infty} (-1)^n \frac{\left(\frac{\pi}{2}G(x;\vartheta)\right)^{2n+1}}{(2n+1)!}\right) dx.$$

### 3.5. Incomplete Moments

The incomplete moments are defined by

$$M_r(x) = \int_0^x x^r f(x)dx.$$

For the given distribution, we have

$$M_r(x) = \frac{\pi}{2} \int_0^x x^r g(x;\vartheta) \frac{\sum_{n=0}^{\infty} \frac{(-1)^n \left(\frac{\pi}{2}G(x;\vartheta)\right)^{2n}}{2n!}}{\sum_{n=0}^{\infty} \frac{\left(\sin\left(\frac{\pi}{2}G(x;\vartheta)\right)\right)^n}{n!}} \times \left(2 - \sum_{n=0}^{\infty} (-1)^n \frac{\left(\frac{\pi}{2}G(x;\vartheta)\right)^{2n+1}}{(2n+1)!}\right) dx.$$

### 3.6. The $r^{th}$ Non-Central Moment

The $r^{th}$ non-central moment is defined as

$$\mu'_r = \int_0^{\infty} x^r f(x)dx.$$

For the proposed family, we have

$$\mu_r' = \frac{\pi}{2}\int_0^{\infty} x^r g(x;\vartheta)\frac{\sum_{n=0}^{\infty}\frac{(-1)^n\left(\frac{\pi}{2}G(x;\vartheta)\right)^{2n}}{2n!}}{\sum_{n=0}^{\infty}\frac{\left(\sin\left(\frac{\pi}{2}G(x;\vartheta)\right)\right)^{n}}{n!}}\left(2-\sum_{n=0}^{\infty}(-1)^n\frac{\left(\frac{\pi}{2}G(x;\vartheta)\right)^{2n+1}}{(2n+1)!}\right)dx.$$

Now, we compute the above integral numerically. Table 3 displays the summation formula and the numerical integration (NI) values for the $r^{th}$ non-central moments of the WS-Weibull, Weibull, and sin-Weibull distributions for different values of $r$, $\delta$, and $\lambda$ at truncated $N$ terms. From the given results in Table 3, it can be concluded that the $r^{th}$ non-central moments of the WS-Weibull distribution is less than the $r^{th}$ non-central moments of the Weibull and sin-Weibull distributions for the same $r$, $\delta$, and $\lambda$.

**Table 3.** The summation formula and the numerical integration values for the $r^{th}$ non-central moments of the WS-Weibull, Weibull, and sin-Weibull distributions for different values of $r$, $\delta$, and $\lambda$ at truncated $N$ terms.

| $r$ | $\delta$ | $\lambda$ | $N$ | WS-Weibull | | sin-Weibull | | Weibull |
|---|---|---|---|---|---|---|---|---|
| | | | | **Summation** | **NI** | **Summation** | **NI** | **Exact Integration** |
| 1.0 | 0.8 | 1.2 | 2 | 0.2712448 | | 0.4416135 | | |
| | | | 4 | 0.2560016 | 0.2556559 | 0.4294283 | 0.4294168 | 0.9020998 |
| | | | 10 | 0.2556559 | | 0.4294168 | | |
| | | 2.2 | 2 | 0.1271481 | | 0.2070096 | | |
| | | | 4 | 0.1200027 | 0.1198406 | 0.2012978 | 0.2012924 | 0.4228660 |
| | | | 10 | 0.1198406 | | 0.2012924 | | |
| | 1.5 | 1.2 | 2 | 0.4124430 | | 0.5530663 | | |
| | | | 4 | 0.3983605 | 0.3980281 | 0.5457003 | 0.5456939 | 0.7994250 |
| | | | 10 | 0.3980281 | | 0.5456939 | | |
| | | 2.2 | 2 | 0.2753402 | | 0.3692180 | | |
| | | | 4 | 0.2659389 | 0.2657171 | 0.3643006 | 0.3642963 | 0.5336831 |
| | | | 10 | 0.2657171 | | 0.3642963 | | |
| 2.0 | 0.8 | 1.2 | 2 | 0.2331464 | | 0.4881900 | | |
| | | | 4 | 0.2027422 | 0.2022463 | 0.4433054 | 0.4432577 | 2.1067990 |
| | | | 10 | 0.2022463 | | 0.4432577 | | |
| | | 2.2 | 2 | 0.0512301 | | 0.1072717 | | |
| | | | 4 | 0.0445493 | 0.0444403 | 0.0974091 | 0.0973986 | 0.4629345 |
| | | | 10 | 0.0444403 | | 0.0973986 | | |
| | 1.5 | 1.2 | 2 | 0.2609388 | | 0.4347446 | | |
| | | | 4 | 0.2453182 | 0.2449682 | 0.4215772 | 0.4215647 | 0.9336954 |
| | | | 10 | 0.2449682 | | 0.4215647 | | |
| | | 2.2 | 2 | 0.1162921 | | 0.1937518 | | |
| | | | 4 | 0.1093305 | 0.1091745 | 0.1878835 | 0.1878779 | 0.4161181 |
| | | | 10 | 0.1091745 | | 0.1878779 | | |
| 3.0 | 0.8 | 1.2 | 2 | 0.4160335 | | 0.9762510 | | |
| | | | 4 | 0.3061227 | 0.3051022 | 0.7563797 | 0.7561286 | 8.3717721 |
| | | | 10 | 0.3051022 | | 0.7561286 | | |
| | | 2.2 | 2 | 0.0428522 | | 0.1005556 | | |
| | | | 4 | 0.0315312 | 0.0314261 | 0.0779084 | 0.0778826 | 0.8623072 |
| | | | 10 | 0.0314261 | | 0.0778826 | | |
| | 1.5 | 1.2 | 2 | 0.2236855 | | 0.4328695 | | |
| | | | 4 | 0.2024038 | 0.2019931 | 0.4071599 | 0.4071336 | 1.3888889 |
| | | | 10 | 0.2019931 | | 0.4071336 | | |
| | | 2.2 | 2 | 0.0665511 | | 0.1287876 | | |
| | | | 4 | 0.0602193 | 0.0600971 | 0.1211385 | 0.1211307 | 0.4132231 |
| | | | 10 | 0.0600971 | | 0.1211307 | | |

### 3.7. Rényi Entropy

The Rényi entropy of a random variable $X$ is a measure of the variation of uncertainty. It is defined by

$$I_v(X) = (1-v)^{-1}\log\left(\int_{-\infty}^{\infty} f(x)^v dx\right), \quad v > 0 \text{ and } v \neq 1.$$

Using the WS-Weibull density, we obtain

$$f(x;\boldsymbol{\vartheta})^v = \left(\frac{\delta\lambda\pi}{2}\right)^v \frac{x^{v(\delta-1)}e^{-\lambda v x^\delta}\left(\cos\left(\frac{\pi}{2}\left(1-e^{-\lambda x^\delta}\right)\right)\right)^v}{e^{v\sin\left(\frac{\pi}{2}\left(1-e^{-\lambda x^\delta}\right)\right)}}\left[2-\sin\left(\frac{\pi}{2}\left(1-e^{-\lambda x^\delta}\right)\right)\right]^v.$$

Then, the Rényi entropy of the WS-Weibull density takes the form

$$I_v(X) = (1-v)^{-1}\log\left\{\left(\frac{\delta\lambda\pi}{2}\right)^v \int_0^{\infty} \frac{x^{v(\delta-1)}e^{-\lambda v x^\delta}\left(\cos\left(\frac{\pi}{2}\left(1-e^{-\lambda x^\delta}\right)\right)\right)^v}{e^{v\sin\left(\frac{\pi}{2}\left(1-e^{-\lambda x^\delta}\right)\right)}} \times\left[2-\sin\left(\frac{\pi}{2}\left(1-e^{-\lambda x^\delta}\right)\right)\right]^v dx\right\}.$$

Table 4 displays the summation formula and the NI values for the Rényi entropy of the WS-Weibull, Weibull, and sin-Weibull distributions for different values of $v$, $\delta$, and $\lambda$ at truncated $N$ terms. From Table 4, we can observe that the values of the Rényi entropy for the WS-Weibull distribution is less than the Rényi values of the Weibull and sin-Weibull distributions for the same $v$, $\delta$, and $\lambda$.

**Table 4.** The summation formula and the numerical integration values for the Rényi entropy of WS-Weibull, Weibull, and sin-Weibull distributions for different values of $v$, $\delta$, and $\lambda$ at truncated $N$ terms.

| $v$ | $\delta$ | $\lambda$ | N | WS-Weibull | | sin-Weibull | | Weibull |
|---|---|---|---|---|---|---|---|---|
| | | | | Summation | NI | Summation | NI | Exact Value |
| 0.5 | 0.8 | 1.2 | 2 | 0.3572427 | | 0.7321667 | | |
| | | | 4 | 0.2645767 | 0.2631333 | 0.6566993 | 0.6564579 | 1.4347754 |
| | | | 10 | 0.2631333 | | 0.6564579 | | |
| | | 2.2 | 2 | −0.4004269 | | −0.0255028 | | |
| | | | 4 | −0.4930927 | −0.4945364 | −0.1009705 | −0.1012118 | 0.6771066 |
| | | | 10 | −0.4945364 | | −0.1012118 | | |
| | 1.5 | 1.2 | 2 | 0.3055993 | | 0.4904644 | | |
| | | | 4 | 0.2511143 | 0.2501745 | 0.4488667 | 0.4487522 | 0.8705198 |
| | | | 10 | 0.2501745 | | 0.4487522 | | |
| | | 2.2 | 2 | −0.0984913 | | 0.0863738 | | |
| | | | 4 | −0.1529758 | −0.1539160 | 0.0447768 | 0.0446617 | 0.4664292 |
| | | | 10 | −0.1539160 | | 0.0446617 | | |
| 2.0 | 0.8 | 1.2 | 2 | −1.0818547 | | −0.3444082 | | |
| | | | 4 | −1.0767934 | −1.0767260 | −0.3439980 | −0.3439978 | 0.3118210 |
| | | | 10 | −1.0767261 | | −0.3439978 | | |
| | | 2.2 | 2 | −1.8395245 | | −1.1020779 | | |
| | | | 4 | −1.8344632 | −1.8343958 | −1.1016677 | −1.1016675 | −0.4458487 |
| | | | 10 | −1.8343958 | | −1.1016675 | | |
| | 1.5 | 1.2 | 2 | −0.2044980 | | 0.1123635 | | |
| | | | 4 | −0.1918153 | −0.1916098 | 0.1136098 | 0.1136103 | 0.5103751 |
| | | | 10 | −0.1916098 | | 0.1136103 | | |
| | | 2.2 | 2 | −0.6085886 | | −0.2917271 | | |
| | | | 4 | −0.5959058 | −0.5957003 | −0.2904808 | −0.2904803 | 0.1062845 |
| | | | 10 | −0.5957004 | | −0.2904803 | | |

**Table 4.** *Cont.*

| $v$ | $\delta$ | $\lambda$ | $N$ | WS-Weibull | | sin-Weibull | | Weibull |
|---|---|---|---|---|---|---|---|---|
| | | | | Summation | NI | Summation | NI | Exact Value |
| 4.0 | 0.8 | 1.2 | 2 | −1.7438683 | | −0.9049445 | | |
| | | | 4 | −1.7437275 | −1.7437268 | −0.9049410 | −0.9049410 | −0.3185747 |
| | | | 10 | −1.7437268 | | −0.9049410 | | |
| | | 2.2 | 2 | -2.5015382 | | −1.6626142 | | |
| | | | 4 | -2.5013973 | -2.5013966 | −1.6626107 | −1.6626107 | −1.0762445 |
| | | | 10 | -2.5013966 | | −1.6626107 | | |
| | 1.5 | 1.2 | 2 | −0.3274484 | | 0.0083556 | | |
| | | | 4 | −0.3237034 | −0.3236696 | 0.0085064 | 0.0085064 | 0.3971834 |
| | | | 10 | −0.3236696 | | 0.0085064 | | |
| | | 2.2 | 2 | −0.7315390 | | −0.3957349 | | |
| | | | 4 | −0.7277940 | −0.7277602 | −0.3955842 | −0.3955842 | −0.0069071 |
| | | | 10 | −0.7277602 | | −0.3955842 | | |

### *3.8. The HT Characteristics of the WS-G Method*

Here, we provide a complete mathematical description to derive the HT characteristics of the WS-G method.

#### 3.8.1. The Regularly Varying Characteristics of the WS-G Method

The regularly varying characteristics (RVC) play an important role in defining HT distributions. This subsection offers the RVC of the WS-G method. Using Karamata's theorem [26], in terms of SF $S(x;\boldsymbol{\vartheta})$, we have

**Theorem 1.** *Suppose $\bar{K}(x;\boldsymbol{\vartheta}) = 1 - K(x;\boldsymbol{\vartheta})$ represents the SF of a regularly varying function (RVF), then $S(x;\boldsymbol{\vartheta}) = 1 - F(x;\boldsymbol{\vartheta})$ also represents the SF of a RVF.*

**Proof.** Assume $\lim_{x\to\infty} \frac{\bar{K}(tx;\boldsymbol{\vartheta})}{\bar{K}(x;\boldsymbol{\vartheta})} = \tau(t)$ is a finite and nonzero function $\forall\ t > 0$. Then, by incorporating the expression in Equation (5), we have

$$\frac{S(tx;\boldsymbol{\vartheta})}{S(x;\boldsymbol{\vartheta})} = \frac{\left[1-\sin\left(\frac{\pi}{2}G(tx;\boldsymbol{\vartheta})\right)\right]}{e^{\sin\left(\frac{\pi}{2}G(tx;\boldsymbol{\vartheta})\right)}} \times \frac{e^{\sin\left(\frac{\pi}{2}G(x;\boldsymbol{\vartheta})\right)}}{\left[1-\sin\left(\frac{\pi}{2}G(x;\boldsymbol{\vartheta})\right)\right]},$$

$$\frac{S(tx;\boldsymbol{\vartheta})}{S(x;\boldsymbol{\vartheta})} = \frac{\left[1-\sin\left(\frac{\pi}{2}G(tx;\boldsymbol{\vartheta})\right)\right]}{\left[1-\sin\left(\frac{\pi}{2}G(x;\boldsymbol{\vartheta})\right)\right]} \times \frac{e^{\sin\left(\frac{\pi}{2}G(x;\boldsymbol{\vartheta})\right)}}{e^{\sin\left(\frac{\pi}{2}G(tx;\boldsymbol{\vartheta})\right)}},$$

$$\frac{S(tx;\boldsymbol{\vartheta})}{S(x;\boldsymbol{\vartheta})} = \frac{\left[1-K(tx;\boldsymbol{\vartheta})\right]}{\left[1-K(x;\boldsymbol{\vartheta})\right]} \times \frac{e^{\sin\left(\frac{\pi}{2}G(x;\boldsymbol{\vartheta})\right)}}{e^{\sin\left(\frac{\pi}{2}G(tx;\boldsymbol{\vartheta})\right)}}. \tag{14}$$

Applying $\lim_{x\to\infty}$ on both sides of Equation (14), we obtain

$$\lim_{x\to\infty}\frac{S(tx;\boldsymbol{\vartheta})}{S(x;\boldsymbol{\vartheta})} = \lim_{x\to\infty}\frac{\left[1-K(tx;\boldsymbol{\vartheta})\right]}{\left[1-K(x;\boldsymbol{\vartheta})\right]} \times \frac{e^{\sin\left(\frac{\pi}{2}G(x;\boldsymbol{\vartheta})\right)}}{e^{\sin\left(\frac{\pi}{2}G(tx;\boldsymbol{\vartheta})\right)}},$$

$$\lim_{x\to\infty}\frac{S(tx;\boldsymbol{\vartheta})}{S(x;\boldsymbol{\vartheta})} = \tau(t) \times \frac{e^{\sin\left(\frac{\pi}{2}G(\infty;\boldsymbol{\vartheta})\right)}}{e^{\sin\left(\frac{\pi}{2}G(t\infty;\boldsymbol{\vartheta})\right)}}. \tag{15}$$

As we mentioned earlier, $G(\infty;\boldsymbol{\vartheta}) = 1$. Thus, from Equation (15), we obtain

$$\lim_{x\to\infty}\frac{S(tx;\boldsymbol{\vartheta})}{S(x;\boldsymbol{\vartheta})} = \tau(t) \times \frac{e^{\sin\left(\frac{\pi}{2}\right)}}{e^{\sin\left(\frac{\pi}{2}\right)}},$$

$$\lim_{x\to\infty}\frac{S(tx;\boldsymbol{\vartheta})}{S(x;\boldsymbol{\vartheta})} = \tau(t). \tag{16}$$

The expression in Equation (16) is finite and nonzero $\forall\ t > 0$. Therefore, $S(x;\boldsymbol{\vartheta})$ is an RVF. $\square$

3.8.2. The Regular Variational Result

Suppose $X$ possesses the power law behavior, then, we have

$$\bar{K}(x;\boldsymbol{\vartheta}) = 1 - K(x;\boldsymbol{\vartheta}) = \mathbb{P}(X > x) \sim x^{-\sigma}.$$

By implementing the results of Karamata's characterization theorem, we can write $S(x;\boldsymbol{\vartheta})$ as

$$S(x;\boldsymbol{\vartheta}) = x^{-\sigma} L(x),$$

where $L(x)$ is a slowly varying function (SVF). Note that

$$S(x;\boldsymbol{\vartheta}) = \frac{[1 - K(x;\boldsymbol{\vartheta})]}{e^{\sin\left(\frac{\pi}{2} G(tx;\boldsymbol{\vartheta})\right)}} \tag{17}$$

Since $1 - K(x;\boldsymbol{\vartheta}) \sim x^{-\sigma}$, from Equation (17), we obtain

$$S(x;\boldsymbol{\vartheta}) = \frac{x^{-\sigma}}{e^{1-x^{-\sigma}}},$$

$$S(x;\boldsymbol{\vartheta}) = x^{-\sigma} L(x),$$

where $L(x) = \frac{1}{e^{1-x^{-\sigma}}}$.

Now, if we demonstrated that $L(x)$ is a SVF, the RVC of the WS-G method derived above is true. In order to demonstrate that $L(x)$ is a SVF, we must show that

$$\lim_{x\to\infty} \frac{L(tx)}{L(x)} = 1, \quad \forall\, t > 0. \tag{18}$$

Now, we use

$$\frac{L(tx)}{L(x)} = \frac{\frac{1}{e^{1-(tx)^{-\sigma}}}}{\frac{1}{e^{1-x^{-\sigma}}}},$$

$$\frac{L(tx)}{L(x)} = \frac{e^{1-x^{-\sigma}}}{e^{1-(tx)^{-\sigma}}}. \tag{19}$$

Appling $\lim_{x\to\infty}$ on both sides of Equation (19), we obtain

$$\lim_{x\to\infty} \frac{L(tx)}{L(x)} = \lim_{x\to\infty} \frac{e^{1-x^{-\sigma}}}{e^{1-(tx)^{-\sigma}}},$$

$$\lim_{x\to\infty} \frac{L(tx)}{L(x)} = 1.$$

## 4. Eight Estimation Methods for the WS-Weibull Parameters

Eight estimation methods have been opted for in this section to estimate the WS-Weibull parameters, namely, the weighted least-squares (WLSE), ordinary least-squares (OLSE), maximum likelihood (MLE), the maximum product of spacing (MPSE), Cramér-von Mises (CVME), Anderson-Darling (ADE), right-tail Anderson-Darling (RADE), and percentile estimator (PCE).

*4.1. Maximum Likelihood*

Suppose that $x_1, x_2, ..., x_n$ are given values of a random sample of size $n$ from the WS-Weibull distribution with parameters $\delta$ and $\lambda$. The log-likelihood function for the WS-Weibull model with PDF in (10) is given by

$$\begin{aligned}\ell(\boldsymbol{\vartheta}) =& n\log\left(\frac{\pi}{2}\right) + n\log(\delta\lambda) - \lambda\sum_{i=1}^{n} x_i^{\delta} + \sum_{i=1}^{n}\log\left(2 - \sin\left(\frac{\pi}{2}\left(1 - e^{-\lambda x_i^{\delta}}\right)\right)\right)\\ &+ (\delta - 1)\sum_{i=1}^{n}\log(x_i) - \sum_{i=1}^{n}\sin\left(\frac{\pi}{2}\left(1 - e^{-\lambda x_i^{\delta}}\right)\right)\\ &+ \sum_{i=1}^{n}\log\left(\cos\left(\frac{\pi}{2}\left(1 - e^{-\lambda x_i^{\delta}}\right)\right)\right),\end{aligned} \tag{20}$$

where $\boldsymbol{\vartheta} = (\delta, \lambda)^{\top}$. The function provided in Equation (20) can be numerically solved by using the Newton–Raphson method (iteration method). The partial derivatives of Equation (9) with respect to the parameters $\delta$ and $\lambda$ are

$$\begin{aligned}\frac{\partial\ell}{\partial\delta} =& \frac{n}{\delta} - \lambda\sum_{i=1}^{n} x_i^{\delta}\log(x_i) - \frac{\pi}{2}\lambda\sum_{i=1}^{n} x_i^{\delta}\log(x_i)e^{-\lambda x_i^{\delta}}\tan\left(\frac{\pi}{2}\left(1 - e^{-\lambda x_i^{\delta}}\right)\right)\\ &- \frac{\pi}{2}\lambda\sum_{i=1}^{n} x_i^{\delta}\log(x_i)e^{-\lambda x_i^{\delta}}\cos\left(\frac{\pi}{2}\left(1 - e^{-\lambda x_i^{\delta}}\right)\right) + \sum_{i=1}^{n}\log(x_i)\\ &- \frac{\pi}{2}\lambda\sum_{i=1}^{n}\frac{x_i^{\delta}\log(x_i)e^{-\lambda x_i^{\delta}}\cos\left(\frac{\pi}{2}\left(1 - e^{-\lambda x_i^{\delta}}\right)\right)}{2 - \sin\left(\frac{\pi}{2}\left(1 - e^{-\lambda x_i^{\delta}}\right)\right)},\end{aligned}$$

and

$$\begin{aligned}\frac{\partial\ell}{\partial\lambda} =& \frac{n}{\lambda} - \frac{\pi}{2}\sum_{i=1}^{n} x_i^{\delta}e^{-\lambda x_i^{\delta}}\cos\left(\frac{\pi}{2}\left(1 - e^{-\lambda x_i^{\delta}}\right)\right) - \frac{\pi}{2}\sum_{i=1}^{n} x_i^{\delta}e^{-\lambda x_i^{\delta}}\tan\left(\frac{\pi}{2}\left(1 - e^{-\lambda x_i^{\delta}}\right)\right)\\ &- \frac{\pi}{2}\sum_{i=1}^{n}\frac{x_i^{\delta}e^{-\lambda x_i^{\delta}}\cos\left(\frac{\pi}{2}\left(1 - e^{-\lambda x_i^{\delta}}\right)\right)}{2 - \sin\left(\frac{\pi}{2}\left(1 - e^{-\lambda x_i^{\delta}}\right)\right)} - \sum_{i=1}^{n} x_i^{\delta}.\end{aligned}$$

By setting $\frac{\partial\ell}{\partial\delta} = 0$ and $\frac{\partial\ell}{\partial\lambda} = 0$, one can solve them numerically to obtain the MLEs of the parameters $\delta$ and $\lambda$.

*4.2. Ordinary and Weighted Least-Squares*

The OLSE of the WS-Weibull parameters can be obtained by minimizing the following function with respect to $\delta$ and $\lambda$,

$$V(\delta, \lambda) = \sum_{i=1}^{n}\left[F(x_i|\delta, \lambda) - \frac{i}{n+1}\right]^2.$$

Further, the OLSE of the WS-Weibull parameters can also be obtained by solving the non-linear equation

$$\sum_{i=1}^{n}\left[F(x_i|\delta, \lambda) - \frac{i}{n+1}\right]\Delta_s(x_i|\delta, \lambda) = 0, \quad s = 1, 2,$$

where

$$\begin{aligned}\Delta_1(x_{(i)}|\delta,\lambda) =& \frac{\partial}{\partial\delta}F(x_{(i)}|\delta,\lambda)\\ =&\lambda\frac{\pi}{2}x_{(i)}^{\delta}\log(x_{(i)})\cos\left(\frac{\pi}{2}\left(1-e^{-\lambda x_{(i)}^{\delta}}\right)\right)e^{-\lambda x_{(i)}^{\delta}-\sin\left(\frac{\pi}{2}\left(1-e^{-\lambda x_{(i)}^{\delta}}\right)\right)}\\ &\times\left[2-\sin\left(\frac{\pi}{2}\left(1-e^{-\lambda x_{(i)}^{\delta}}\right)\right)\right],\end{aligned} \tag{21}$$

and

$$\begin{aligned}\Delta_2(x_{(i)}|\delta,\lambda) =& \frac{\partial}{\partial\lambda}F(x_{(i)}|\delta,\lambda)\\ =&\frac{\pi}{2}x_{(i)}^{\delta}\cos\left(\frac{\pi}{2}\left(1-e^{-\lambda x_{(i)}^{\delta}}\right)\right)e^{-\lambda x_{(i)}^{\delta}-\sin\left(\frac{\pi}{2}\left(1-e^{-\lambda x_{(i)}^{\delta}}\right)\right)}\\ &\times\left[2-\sin\left(\frac{\pi}{2}\left(1-e^{-\lambda x_{(i)}^{\delta}}\right)\right)\right].\end{aligned} \tag{22}$$

The WLSE of the WS-Weibull parameters are obtained by minimizing the following

$$W(\delta,\lambda)=\sum_{i=1}^{n}\frac{(n+1)^2(n+2)}{i(n-i+1)}\left[F(x_i|\delta,\lambda)-\frac{i}{n+1}\right]^2,$$

with respect to $\delta$ and $\lambda$. Moreover, the WLSE can also be obtained by solving the non-linear equation

$$\sum_{i=1}^{n}\frac{(n+1)^2(n+2)}{i(n-i+1)}\left[F(x_i|\delta,\lambda)-\frac{i}{n+1}\right]\Delta_s(x_i)=0,\quad s=1,2,$$

where $\Delta_1(\cdot|\delta,\lambda)$ and $\Delta_2(\cdot|\delta,\lambda)$ are, respectively, defined in Equations (21) and (22).

### 4.3. Maximum Product of Spacing

The MPSE is considered an alternative to the maximum likelihood method. Let $D_i(\delta,\lambda)=F\left(x_{(i)}|\delta,\lambda\right)-F\left(x_{(i-1)}|\delta,\lambda\right)$, for $i=1,2,\ldots,n+1$, be the uniform spacing of a random sample from the WS-Weibull model, where $F\left(x_{(0)}|\delta,\lambda\right)=0$, $F\left(x_{(n+1)}|\delta,\lambda\right)=1$ and $\sum_{i=1}^{n+1}D_i(\delta,\lambda)=1$. The MPSE of the WS-Weibull parameters can be obtained by maximizing the "geometric mean of the spacing"

$$G(\delta,\lambda)=\left[\prod_{i=1}^{n+1}D_i(\delta,\lambda)\right]^{\frac{1}{n+1}},$$

with respect to $\delta$ and $\lambda$, or by maximizing the "logarithm of the geometric mean" of sample-spacings given by

$$H(\delta,\lambda)=\frac{1}{n+1}\sum_{i=1}^{n+1}\log D_i(\delta,\lambda).$$

Moreover, the MPSE can be obtained by solving the following nonlinear expression

$$\frac{1}{n+1}\sum_{i=1}^{n+1}\frac{1}{D_i(\delta,\lambda)}\left[\Delta_s(x_{(i)}|\delta,\lambda)-\Delta_s(x_{(i-1)}|\delta,\lambda)\right]=0,\quad s=1,2,$$

where $\Delta_1(\cdot|\delta,\lambda)$ and $\Delta_2(\cdot|\delta,\lambda)$ are defined in Equation (21) and Equation (22), respectively.

*4.4. Cramér-Von Mises Estimation Approach*

The CVME of the WS-Weibull parameters is obtained by minimizing

$$C(\delta,\lambda) = -\frac{1}{12n} + \sum_{i=1}^{n}\left[F(x_i|\delta,\lambda) - \frac{2i-1}{2n}\right]^2,$$

with respect to $\delta$ and $\lambda$. Moreover, the CVME can be numerically obtained by solving the following non-linear equation

$$\sum_{i=1}^{n}\left[F(x_i|\delta,\lambda) - \frac{2i-1}{2n}\right]\Delta_s(x_i|\delta,\lambda) = 0, \quad s = 1,2,$$

where $\Delta_1(\cdot|\delta,\lambda)$ and $\Delta_2(\cdot|\delta,\lambda)$ are, respectively, presented in Equations (21) and (22).

*4.5. Anderson–Darling and Right-Tail Anderson-Darling*

Suppose that $x_{(1)}, x_{(2)}, \ldots, x_{(n)}$ is the ordered random sample from $F(x|\delta,\lambda)$ of the WS-Weibull model. The ADE of the WS-Weibull parameters can be obtained by minimizing

$$A(\delta,\lambda) = -n - \frac{1}{n}\sum_{i=1}^{n}(2i-1)[\log F(x_i|\delta,\lambda) + \log S(x_i|\delta,\lambda)],$$

or by solving the non-linear equation

$$\sum_{i=1}^{n}(2i-1)\left[\frac{\Delta_s(x_i)}{F(x_i|\delta,\lambda)} - \frac{\Delta_i(x_{n+1-i})}{S(x_{n+1-i}|\delta,\lambda)}\right] = 0, \quad s = 1,2,$$

Moreover, the RADEs of the WS-Weibull parameters can be obtained by minimizing

$$R(\delta,\lambda) = \frac{n}{2} - 2\sum_{i=1}^{n}F(x_{i:n}|\delta,\lambda) - \frac{1}{n}\sum_{i=1}^{n}(2i-1)\log S(x_{n+1-i:n}|\delta,\lambda),$$

with respect to $\delta$ and $\lambda$, which are equivalent by solving the non-linear equations

$$-2\sum_{i=1}^{n}\Delta_s(x_{i:n}|\delta,\lambda) + \frac{1}{n}\sum_{i=1}^{n}(2i-1)\frac{\Delta_s(x_{n+1-i:n}|\delta,\lambda)}{S(x_{n+1-i:n}|\delta,\lambda)} = 0, \; s = 1,2,$$

where $\Delta_1(\cdot|\delta,\lambda)$ and $\Delta_2(\cdot|\delta,\lambda)$ are presented in Equation (21) and Equation (22), respectively.

*4.6. Percentile*

From (8), the PCE of the parameters of WS-Weibull model can be obtained by minimizing the following function

$$P(p|\delta,\lambda) = \sum_{i=1}^{n}\left[x_{(i)} - \left(-\frac{1}{\lambda}\log\left[1 - \frac{2}{\pi}\sin^{-1}(1 - W_{-1}((1-p)e))\right]\right)^{1/\delta}\right]^2,$$

with respect to $\delta$ and $\lambda$, where $0 < p < 1$.

*4.7. Simulation Study*

In order to explore the performances of the estimators of the WS-Weibull distribution, we consider some detailed simulation studies. The performances of the estimators are judged by considering several statistical tools. These tools include

- The absolute value of biases given by

$$|\mathrm{Bias}(\widehat{\boldsymbol{\vartheta}})| = \frac{1}{N}\sum_{i=1}^{N}|\widehat{\boldsymbol{\vartheta}} - \boldsymbol{\vartheta}|.$$

- The mean square error of the estimates given by

$$MSE\left(\widehat{\boldsymbol{\vartheta}}\right) = \frac{1}{N}\sum_{i=1}^{N}(\widehat{\boldsymbol{\vartheta}} - \boldsymbol{\vartheta})^2.$$

- The mean relative estimates

$$MRE = \left(\widehat{\boldsymbol{\vartheta}}\right) = \frac{1}{N}\sum_{i=1}^{N}|\widehat{\boldsymbol{\vartheta}} - \boldsymbol{\vartheta}|/\boldsymbol{\vartheta}.$$

The values of the estimators are calculated for different samples of sizes, say $n = \{30, 80, 120, 200, 350\}$, taken from the WS-Weibull model. We use `R` codes throughout the simulations with the `nlminb` function within the `stats` package [27].

The simulation studies are carried out for the following parameter combinations: $\delta = \{0.45, 0.75, 1.50, 4.00\}$ and $\lambda = \{0.50, 1.00, 1.75, 3.00\}$. For each setting, the process is repeated $N = 5000$ times and the average values of $|Bias|$, $MSE$, and $MRE$ for $\delta$ and $\lambda$ are obtained. To save space, four out of sixteen simulated outcomes are reported in Tables 5–8. The numbers in each row have superscripts giving the ranks of the estimates of all methods, and the $\sum Ranks$ is the partial sum of the ranks. Furthermore, Figures 3–6 display the heatmaps of the $|Bias|$, $MSE$, and $MRE$ for the $\delta$ and $\lambda$ of the simulation results.

Table 9 gives the partial and overall ranks of the estimates, thus indicating that the MPSEs outperform all other estimates for the WS-Weibull model distribution, with an overall score of 117.5.

**Table 5.** Simulation results for $\boldsymbol{\vartheta} = (\delta = 0.45, \lambda = 0.50)^{\intercal}$.

| $n$ | Est. | Est. Par. | WLSE | OLSE | MLE | MPSE | CVME | ADE | RADE | PCE |
|---|---|---|---|---|---|---|---|---|---|---|
| 30 | $\lvert BIAS\rvert$ | $\hat{\delta}$ | $0.05995^{\{4\}}$ | $0.06450^{\{6\}}$ | $0.05682^{\{3\}}$ | $0.05619^{\{1\}}$ | $0.06912^{\{7\}}$ | $0.05653^{\{2\}}$ | $0.06200^{\{5\}}$ | $0.13974^{\{8\}}$ |
| | | $\hat{\lambda}$ | $0.08844^{\{4\}}$ | $0.09183^{\{6\}}$ | $0.08879^{\{5\}}$ | $0.07678^{\{1\}}$ | $0.10129^{\{7\}}$ | $0.08676^{\{2\}}$ | $0.08707^{\{3\}}$ | $0.12877^{\{8\}}$ |
| | MSE | $\hat{\delta}$ | $0.00602^{\{4\}}$ | $0.00688^{\{6\}}$ | $0.00560^{\{3\}}$ | $0.00472^{\{1\}}$ | $0.00846^{\{7\}}$ | $0.00533^{\{2\}}$ | $0.00660^{\{5\}}$ | $0.02904^{\{8\}}$ |
| | | $\hat{\lambda}$ | $0.01418^{\{5\}}$ | $0.01533^{\{6\}}$ | $0.01395^{\{4\}}$ | $0.00947^{\{1\}}$ | $0.01996^{\{7\}}$ | $0.01316^{\{2\}}$ | $0.01324^{\{3\}}$ | $0.02630^{\{8\}}$ |
| | MRE | $\hat{\delta}$ | $0.13322^{\{4\}}$ | $0.14334^{\{6\}}$ | $0.12627^{\{3\}}$ | $0.12487^{\{1\}}$ | $0.15361^{\{7\}}$ | $0.12562^{\{2\}}$ | $0.13777^{\{5\}}$ | $0.31052^{\{8\}}$ |
| | | $\hat{\lambda}$ | $0.17688^{\{4\}}$ | $0.18366^{\{6\}}$ | $0.17758^{\{5\}}$ | $0.15356^{\{1\}}$ | $0.20259^{\{7\}}$ | $0.17352^{\{2\}}$ | $0.17415^{\{3\}}$ | $0.25754^{\{8\}}$ |
| | $\sum Ranks$ | | $25^{\{5\}}$ | $36^{\{6\}}$ | $23^{\{3\}}$ | $6^{\{1\}}$ | $42^{\{7\}}$ | $12^{\{2\}}$ | $24^{\{4\}}$ | $48^{\{8\}}$ |
| 80 | $\lvert BIAS\rvert$ | $\hat{\delta}$ | $0.03464^{\{4\}}$ | $0.03822^{\{6\}}$ | $0.03195^{\{1\}}$ | $0.03310^{\{2\}}$ | $0.03910^{\{7\}}$ | $0.03377^{\{3\}}$ | $0.03631^{\{5\}}$ | $0.10987^{\{8\}}$ |
| | | $\hat{\lambda}$ | $0.05339^{\{5\}}$ | $0.05558^{\{6\}}$ | $0.05247^{\{2\}}$ | $0.04897^{\{1\}}$ | $0.05771^{\{7\}}$ | $0.05269^{\{4\}}$ | $0.05253^{\{3\}}$ | $0.11998^{\{8\}}$ |
| | MSE | $\hat{\delta}$ | $0.00192^{\{4\}}$ | $0.00232^{\{6\}}$ | $0.00165^{\{1\}}$ | $0.00166^{\{2\}}$ | $0.00249^{\{7\}}$ | $0.00182^{\{3\}}$ | $0.00212^{\{5\}}$ | $0.01895^{\{8\}}$ |
| | | $\hat{\lambda}$ | $0.00492^{\{5\}}$ | $0.00541^{\{6\}}$ | $0.00457^{\{2\}}$ | $0.00378^{\{1\}}$ | $0.00598^{\{7\}}$ | $0.00468^{\{4\}}$ | $0.00460^{\{3\}}$ | $0.02945^{\{8\}}$ |
| | MRE | $\hat{\delta}$ | $0.07698^{\{4\}}$ | $0.08494^{\{6\}}$ | $0.07100^{\{1\}}$ | $0.07355^{\{2\}}$ | $0.08688^{\{7\}}$ | $0.07504^{\{3\}}$ | $0.08068^{\{5\}}$ | $0.24415^{\{8\}}$ |
| | | $\hat{\lambda}$ | $0.10679^{\{5\}}$ | $0.11117^{\{6\}}$ | $0.10493^{\{2\}}$ | $0.09794^{\{1\}}$ | $0.11542^{\{7\}}$ | $0.10538^{\{4\}}$ | $0.10505^{\{3\}}$ | $0.23997^{\{8\}}$ |
| | $\sum Ranks$ | | $27^{\{5\}}$ | $36^{\{6\}}$ | $9^{\{1.5\}}$ | $9^{\{1.5\}}$ | $42^{\{7\}}$ | $21^{\{3\}}$ | $24^{\{4\}}$ | $48^{\{8\}}$ |
| 120 | $\lvert BIAS\rvert$ | $\hat{\delta}$ | $0.02861^{\{4\}}$ | $0.03150^{\{6\}}$ | $0.02625^{\{1\}}$ | $0.02709^{\{2\}}$ | $0.03195^{\{7\}}$ | $0.02796^{\{3\}}$ | $0.02994^{\{5\}}$ | $0.09873^{\{8\}}$ |
| | | $\hat{\lambda}$ | $0.04350^{\{5\}}$ | $0.04567^{\{6\}}$ | $0.04224^{\{2\}}$ | $0.04037^{\{1\}}$ | $0.04672^{\{7\}}$ | $0.04320^{\{4\}}$ | $0.04294^{\{3\}}$ | $0.11737^{\{8\}}$ |
| | MSE | $\hat{\delta}$ | $0.00131^{\{4\}}$ | $0.00158^{\{6\}}$ | $0.00112^{\{1\}}$ | $0.00113^{\{2\}}$ | $0.00165^{\{7\}}$ | $0.00124^{\{3\}}$ | $0.00145^{\{5\}}$ | $0.01581^{\{8\}}$ |
| | | $\hat{\lambda}$ | $0.00304^{\{5\}}$ | $0.00333^{\{6\}}$ | $0.00288^{\{2\}}$ | $0.00255^{\{1\}}$ | $0.00354^{\{7\}}$ | $0.00297^{\{4\}}$ | $0.00296^{\{3\}}$ | $0.03116^{\{8\}}$ |
| | MRE | $\hat{\delta}$ | $0.06358^{\{4\}}$ | $0.06999^{\{6\}}$ | $0.05834^{\{1\}}$ | $0.06019^{\{2\}}$ | $0.07099^{\{7\}}$ | $0.06212^{\{3\}}$ | $0.06653^{\{5\}}$ | $0.21941^{\{8\}}$ |
| | | $\hat{\lambda}$ | $0.08699^{\{5\}}$ | $0.09135^{\{6\}}$ | $0.08447^{\{2\}}$ | $0.08073^{\{1\}}$ | $0.09345^{\{7\}}$ | $0.08639^{\{4\}}$ | $0.08588^{\{3\}}$ | $0.23474^{\{8\}}$ |
| | $\sum Ranks$ | | $27^{\{5\}}$ | $36^{\{6\}}$ | $9^{\{1.5\}}$ | $9^{\{1.5\}}$ | $42^{\{7\}}$ | $21^{\{3\}}$ | $24^{\{4\}}$ | $48^{\{8\}}$ |

**Table 5.** *Cont.*

| $n$ | Est. | Est. Par. | WLSE | OLSE | MLE | MPSE | CVME | ADE | RADE | PCE |
|---|---|---|---|---|---|---|---|---|---|---|
| 200 | $\lvert BIAS\rvert$ | $\hat{\delta}$ | $0.02157^{\{4\}}$ | $0.02409^{\{6\}}$ | $0.01990^{\{1\}}$ | $0.02058^{\{2\}}$ | $0.02430^{\{7\}}$ | $0.02128^{\{3\}}$ | $0.02262^{\{5\}}$ | $0.08542^{\{8\}}$ |
| | | $\hat{\lambda}$ | $0.03250^{\{5\}}$ | $0.03426^{\{6\}}$ | $0.03147^{\{2\}}$ | $0.03055^{\{1\}}$ | $0.03475^{\{7\}}$ | $0.03224^{\{4\}}$ | $0.03205^{\{3\}}$ | $0.10781^{\{8\}}$ |
| | MSE | $\hat{\delta}$ | $0.00073^{\{4\}}$ | $0.00091^{\{6\}}$ | $0.00062^{\{1\}}$ | $0.00065^{\{2\}}$ | $0.00094^{\{7\}}$ | $0.00071^{\{3\}}$ | $0.00081^{\{5\}}$ | $0.01231^{\{8\}}$ |
| | | $\hat{\lambda}$ | $0.00168^{\{5\}}$ | $0.00187^{\{6\}}$ | $0.00158^{\{2\}}$ | $0.00146^{\{1\}}$ | $0.00194^{\{7\}}$ | $0.00165^{\{4\}}$ | $0.00163^{\{3\}}$ | $0.02986^{\{8\}}$ |
| | MRE | $\hat{\delta}$ | $0.04793^{\{4\}}$ | $0.05353^{\{6\}}$ | $0.04422^{\{1\}}$ | $0.04574^{\{2\}}$ | $0.05399^{\{7\}}$ | $0.04728^{\{3\}}$ | $0.05027^{\{5\}}$ | $0.18983^{\{8\}}$ |
| | | $\hat{\lambda}$ | $0.06501^{\{5\}}$ | $0.06852^{\{6\}}$ | $0.06294^{\{2\}}$ | $0.06111^{\{1\}}$ | $0.06950^{\{7\}}$ | $0.06449^{\{4\}}$ | $0.06410^{\{3\}}$ | $0.21563^{\{8\}}$ |
| | $\sum Ranks$ | | $27^{\{5\}}$ | $36^{\{6\}}$ | $9^{\{1.5\}}$ | $9^{\{1.5\}}$ | $42^{\{7\}}$ | $21^{\{3\}}$ | $24^{\{4\}}$ | $48^{\{8\}}$ |
| 350 | $\lvert BIAS\rvert$ | $\hat{\delta}$ | $0.01625^{\{4\}}$ | $0.01819^{\{6\}}$ | $0.01503^{\{1\}}$ | $0.01551^{\{2\}}$ | $0.01826^{\{7\}}$ | $0.01614^{\{3\}}$ | $0.01703^{\{5\}}$ | $0.07426^{\{8\}}$ |
| | | $\hat{\lambda}$ | $0.02426^{\{5\}}$ | $0.02557^{\{6\}}$ | $0.02364^{\{2\}}$ | $0.02330^{\{1\}}$ | $0.02577^{\{7\}}$ | $0.02418^{\{4\}}$ | $0.02399^{\{3\}}$ | $0.09992^{\{8\}}$ |
| | MSE | $\hat{\delta}$ | $0.00042^{\{4\}}$ | $0.00052^{\{6\}}$ | $0.00036^{\{1\}}$ | $0.00038^{\{2\}}$ | $0.00053^{\{7\}}$ | $0.00041^{\{3\}}$ | $0.00046^{\{5\}}$ | $0.00954^{\{8\}}$ |
| | | $\hat{\lambda}$ | $0.00096^{\{5\}}$ | $0.00106^{\{6\}}$ | $0.00091^{\{2\}}$ | $0.00086^{\{1\}}$ | $0.00109^{\{7\}}$ | $0.00095^{\{4\}}$ | $0.00094^{\{3\}}$ | $0.02750^{\{8\}}$ |
| | MRE | $\hat{\delta}$ | $0.03612^{\{4\}}$ | $0.04042^{\{6\}}$ | $0.03341^{\{1\}}$ | $0.03447^{\{2\}}$ | $0.04059^{\{7\}}$ | $0.03587^{\{3\}}$ | $0.03784^{\{5\}}$ | $0.16503^{\{8\}}$ |
| | | $\hat{\lambda}$ | $0.04853^{\{5\}}$ | $0.05114^{\{6\}}$ | $0.04729^{\{2\}}$ | $0.04660^{\{1\}}$ | $0.05154^{\{7\}}$ | $0.04836^{\{4\}}$ | $0.04797^{\{3\}}$ | $0.19983^{\{8\}}$ |
| | $\sum Ranks$ | | $27^{\{5\}}$ | $36^{\{6\}}$ | $9^{\{1.5\}}$ | $9^{\{1.5\}}$ | $42^{\{7\}}$ | $21^{\{3\}}$ | $24^{\{4\}}$ | $48^{\{8\}}$ |

**Table 6.** Simulation results for $\boldsymbol{\vartheta} = (\delta = 0.45, \lambda = 3.00)^{\intercal}$.

| $n$ | Est. | Est. Par. | WLSE | OLSE | MLE | MPSE | CVME | ADE | RADE | PCE |
|---|---|---|---|---|---|---|---|---|---|---|
| 30 | $\lvert BIAS\rvert$ | $\hat{\delta}$ | $0.05971^{\{4\}}$ | $0.06420^{\{6\}}$ | $0.05651^{\{3\}}$ | $0.05581^{\{1\}}$ | $0.06864^{\{7\}}$ | $0.05621^{\{2\}}$ | $0.06158^{\{5\}}$ | $0.13667^{\{8\}}$ |
| | | $\hat{\lambda}$ | $1.12196^{\{5\}}$ | $1.21709^{\{6\}}$ | $1.08373^{\{3\}}$ | $0.84246^{\{1\}}$ | $1.51324^{\{7\}}$ | $1.01079^{\{2\}}$ | $1.11567^{\{4\}}$ | $1.63339^{\{8\}}$ |
| | MSE | $\hat{\delta}$ | $0.00609^{\{4\}}$ | $0.00693^{\{6\}}$ | $0.00556^{\{3\}}$ | $0.00466^{\{1\}}$ | $0.00850^{\{7\}}$ | $0.00525^{\{2\}}$ | $0.00658^{\{5\}}$ | $0.02832^{\{8\}}$ |
| | | $\hat{\lambda}$ | $4.22063^{\{5\}}$ | $5.49202^{\{6\}}$ | $3.15053^{\{3\}}$ | $1.31291^{\{1\}}$ | $10.36952^{\{8\}}$ | $2.49643^{\{2\}}$ | $4.12599^{\{4\}}$ | $9.25795^{\{7\}}$ |
| | MRE | $\hat{\delta}$ | $0.13270^{\{4\}}$ | $0.14267^{\{6\}}$ | $0.12557^{\{3\}}$ | $0.12401^{\{1\}}$ | $0.15252^{\{7\}}$ | $0.12491^{\{2\}}$ | $0.13685^{\{5\}}$ | $0.30370^{\{8\}}$ |
| | | $\hat{\lambda}$ | $0.37399^{\{5\}}$ | $0.40570^{\{6\}}$ | $0.36124^{\{3\}}$ | $0.28082^{\{1\}}$ | $0.50441^{\{7\}}$ | $0.33693^{\{2\}}$ | $0.37189^{\{4\}}$ | $0.54446^{\{8\}}$ |
| | $\sum Ranks$ | | $27^{\{4.5\}}$ | $36^{\{6\}}$ | $18^{\{3\}}$ | $6^{\{1\}}$ | $43^{\{7\}}$ | $12^{\{2\}}$ | $27^{\{4.5\}}$ | $47^{\{8\}}$ |
| 80 | $\lvert BIAS\rvert$ | $\hat{\delta}$ | $0.03402^{\{4\}}$ | $0.03796^{\{6\}}$ | $0.03160^{\{1\}}$ | $0.03287^{\{2\}}$ | $0.03885^{\{7\}}$ | $0.03293^{\{3\}}$ | $0.03535^{\{5\}}$ | $0.11267^{\{8\}}$ |
| | | $\hat{\lambda}$ | $0.57172^{\{4\}}$ | $0.64569^{\{6\}}$ | $0.53441^{\{2\}}$ | $0.48778^{\{1\}}$ | $0.69673^{\{7\}}$ | $0.54880^{\{3\}}$ | $0.57223^{\{5\}}$ | $0.79479^{\{8\}}$ |
| | MSE | $\hat{\delta}$ | $0.00188^{\{4\}}$ | $0.00232^{\{6\}}$ | $0.00163^{\{1.5\}}$ | $0.00163^{\{1.5\}}$ | $0.00251^{\{7\}}$ | $0.00176^{\{3\}}$ | $0.00204^{\{5\}}$ | $0.02171^{\{8\}}$ |
| | | $\hat{\lambda}$ | $0.61772^{\{5\}}$ | $0.80634^{\{6\}}$ | $0.51857^{\{2\}}$ | $0.36839^{\{1\}}$ | $1.00380^{\{7\}}$ | $0.54497^{\{3\}}$ | $0.60290^{\{4\}}$ | $1.00973^{\{8\}}$ |
| | MRE | $\hat{\delta}$ | $0.07559^{\{4\}}$ | $0.08435^{\{6\}}$ | $0.07021^{\{1\}}$ | $0.07304^{\{2\}}$ | $0.08634^{\{7\}}$ | $0.07318^{\{3\}}$ | $0.07855^{\{5\}}$ | $0.25038^{\{8\}}$ |
| | | $\hat{\lambda}$ | $0.19057^{\{4\}}$ | $0.21523^{\{6\}}$ | $0.17814^{\{2\}}$ | $0.16259^{\{1\}}$ | $0.23224^{\{7\}}$ | $0.18293^{\{3\}}$ | $0.19074^{\{5\}}$ | $0.26493^{\{8\}}$ |
| | $\sum Ranks$ | | $25^{\{4\}}$ | $36^{\{6\}}$ | $9.5^{\{2\}}$ | $8.5^{\{1\}}$ | $42^{\{7\}}$ | $18^{\{3\}}$ | $29^{\{5\}}$ | $48^{\{8\}}$ |
| 120 | $\lvert BIAS\rvert$ | $\hat{\delta}$ | $0.02747^{\{4\}}$ | $0.03039^{\{6\}}$ | $0.02559^{\{1\}}$ | $0.02655^{\{2\}}$ | $0.03090^{\{7\}}$ | $0.02686^{\{3\}}$ | $0.02865^{\{5\}}$ | $0.10426^{\{8\}}$ |
| | | $\hat{\lambda}$ | $0.44990^{\{4\}}$ | $0.50301^{\{6\}}$ | $0.41951^{\{2\}}$ | $0.39811^{\{1\}}$ | $0.52717^{\{7\}}$ | $0.43823^{\{3\}}$ | $0.45485^{\{5\}}$ | $0.70458^{\{8\}}$ |
| | MSE | $\hat{\delta}$ | $0.00121^{\{4\}}$ | $0.00147^{\{6\}}$ | $0.00107^{\{1\}}$ | $0.00108^{\{2\}}$ | $0.00155^{\{7\}}$ | $0.00116^{\{3\}}$ | $0.00134^{\{5\}}$ | $0.01861^{\{8\}}$ |
| | | $\hat{\lambda}$ | $0.36433^{\{4\}}$ | $0.45494^{\{6\}}$ | $0.31850^{\{2\}}$ | $0.25459^{\{1\}}$ | $0.52517^{\{7\}}$ | $0.34239^{\{3\}}$ | $0.37420^{\{5\}}$ | $0.76800^{\{8\}}$ |
| | MRE | $\hat{\delta}$ | $0.06105^{\{4\}}$ | $0.06754^{\{6\}}$ | $0.05686^{\{1\}}$ | $0.05900^{\{2\}}$ | $0.06866^{\{7\}}$ | $0.05969^{\{3\}}$ | $0.06367^{\{5\}}$ | $0.23169^{\{8\}}$ |
| | | $\hat{\lambda}$ | $0.14997^{\{4\}}$ | $0.16767^{\{6\}}$ | $0.13984^{\{2\}}$ | $0.13270^{\{1\}}$ | $0.17572^{\{7\}}$ | $0.14608^{\{3\}}$ | $0.15162^{\{5\}}$ | $0.23486^{\{8\}}$ |
| | $\sum Ranks$ | | $24^{\{4\}}$ | $36^{\{6\}}$ | $9^{\{1.5\}}$ | $9^{\{1.5\}}$ | $42^{\{7\}}$ | $18^{\{3\}}$ | $30^{\{5\}}$ | $48^{\{8\}}$ |
| 200 | $\lvert BIAS\rvert$ | $\hat{\delta}$ | $0.02204^{\{4\}}$ | $0.02465^{\{6\}}$ | $0.02002^{\{1\}}$ | $0.02099^{\{2\}}$ | $0.02480^{\{7\}}$ | $0.02159^{\{3\}}$ | $0.02250^{\{5\}}$ | $0.08845^{\{8\}}$ |
| | | $\hat{\lambda}$ | $0.35292^{\{5\}}$ | $0.39916^{\{6\}}$ | $0.31828^{\{2\}}$ | $0.31005^{\{1\}}$ | $0.41017^{\{7\}}$ | $0.34345^{\{3\}}$ | $0.34659^{\{4\}}$ | $0.57534^{\{8\}}$ |
| | MSE | $\hat{\delta}$ | $0.00077^{\{4\}}$ | $0.00096^{\{6\}}$ | $0.00064^{\{1\}}$ | $0.00067^{\{2\}}$ | $0.00099^{\{7\}}$ | $0.00074^{\{3\}}$ | $0.00082^{\{5\}}$ | $0.01333^{\{8\}}$ |
| | | $\hat{\lambda}$ | $0.21230^{\{5\}}$ | $0.27196^{\{6\}}$ | $0.17276^{\{2\}}$ | $0.15367^{\{1\}}$ | $0.29665^{\{7\}}$ | $0.19999^{\{3\}}$ | $0.20515^{\{4\}}$ | $0.49874^{\{8\}}$ |
| | MRE | $\hat{\delta}$ | $0.04898^{\{4\}}$ | $0.05478^{\{6\}}$ | $0.04449^{\{1\}}$ | $0.04665^{\{2\}}$ | $0.05511^{\{7\}}$ | $0.04798^{\{3\}}$ | $0.05001^{\{5\}}$ | $0.19655^{\{8\}}$ |
| | | $\hat{\lambda}$ | $0.11764^{\{5\}}$ | $0.13305^{\{6\}}$ | $0.10609^{\{2\}}$ | $0.10335^{\{1\}}$ | $0.13672^{\{7\}}$ | $0.11448^{\{3\}}$ | $0.11553^{\{4\}}$ | $0.19178^{\{8\}}$ |
| | $\sum Ranks$ | | $27^{\{4.5\}}$ | $36^{\{6\}}$ | $9^{\{1.5\}}$ | $9^{\{1.5\}}$ | $42^{\{7\}}$ | $18^{\{3\}}$ | $27^{\{4.5\}}$ | $48^{\{8\}}$ |
| 350 | $\lvert BIAS\rvert$ | $\hat{\delta}$ | $0.01603^{\{4\}}$ | $0.01790^{\{6\}}$ | $0.01472^{\{1\}}$ | $0.01516^{\{2\}}$ | $0.01798^{\{7\}}$ | $0.01583^{\{3\}}$ | $0.01670^{\{5\}}$ | $0.07556^{\{8\}}$ |
| | | $\hat{\lambda}$ | $0.25736^{\{5\}}$ | $0.29045^{\{6\}}$ | $0.23334^{\{2\}}$ | $0.22047^{\{1\}}$ | $0.29502^{\{7\}}$ | $0.25314^{\{3\}}$ | $0.25613^{\{4\}}$ | $0.45532^{\{8\}}$ |
| | MSE | $\hat{\delta}$ | $0.00041^{\{4\}}$ | $0.00051^{\{6\}}$ | $0.00034^{\{1\}}$ | $0.00036^{\{2\}}$ | $0.00052^{\{7\}}$ | $0.00040^{\{3\}}$ | $0.00044^{\{5\}}$ | $0.00980^{\{8\}}$ |
| | | $\hat{\lambda}$ | $0.10852^{\{5\}}$ | $0.13908^{\{6\}}$ | $0.08890^{\{2\}}$ | $0.08355^{\{1\}}$ | $0.14606^{\{7\}}$ | $0.10417^{\{3\}}$ | $0.10831^{\{4\}}$ | $0.30891^{\{8\}}$ |
| | MRE | $\hat{\delta}$ | $0.03563^{\{4\}}$ | $0.03978^{\{6\}}$ | $0.03271^{\{1\}}$ | $0.03369^{\{2\}}$ | $0.03995^{\{7\}}$ | $0.03517^{\{3\}}$ | $0.03712^{\{5\}}$ | $0.16791^{\{8\}}$ |
| | | $\hat{\lambda}$ | $0.08579^{\{5\}}$ | $0.09682^{\{6\}}$ | $0.07778^{\{2\}}$ | $0.07349^{\{1\}}$ | $0.09834^{\{7\}}$ | $0.08438^{\{3\}}$ | $0.08538^{\{4\}}$ | $0.15177^{\{8\}}$ |
| | $\sum Ranks$ | | $27^{\{4.5\}}$ | $36^{\{6\}}$ | $9^{\{1.5\}}$ | $9^{\{1.5\}}$ | $42^{\{7\}}$ | $18^{\{3\}}$ | $27^{\{4.5\}}$ | $48^{\{8\}}$ |

**Table 7.** Simulation results for $\boldsymbol{\vartheta} = (\delta = 0.75, \lambda = 0.50)^{\intercal}$.

| $n$ | Est. | Est. Par. | WLSE | OLSE | MLE | MPSE | CVME | ADE | RADE | PCE |
|---|---|---|---|---|---|---|---|---|---|---|
| 30 | $\|BIAS\|$ | $\hat{\delta}$ | 0.09871$^{\{4\}}$ | 0.10640$^{\{6\}}$ | 0.09417$^{\{3\}}$ | 0.09199$^{\{1\}}$ | 0.11374$^{\{7\}}$ | 0.09328$^{\{2\}}$ | 0.10185$^{\{5\}}$ | 0.16592$^{\{8\}}$ |
| | | $\hat{\lambda}$ | 0.09056$^{\{4\}}$ | 0.09400$^{\{7\}}$ | 0.09115$^{\{5\}}$ | 0.07839$^{\{1\}}$ | 0.10412$^{\{8\}}$ | 0.08816$^{\{2\}}$ | 0.08853$^{\{3\}}$ | 0.09283$^{\{6\}}$ |
| | MSE | $\hat{\delta}$ | 0.01668$^{\{4\}}$ | 0.01937$^{\{6\}}$ | 0.01524$^{\{3\}}$ | 0.01283$^{\{1\}}$ | 0.02362$^{\{7\}}$ | 0.01442$^{\{2\}}$ | 0.01768$^{\{5\}}$ | 0.04375$^{\{8\}}$ |
| | | $\hat{\lambda}$ | 0.01595$^{\{6\}}$ | 0.01825$^{\{7\}}$ | 0.01529$^{\{5\}}$ | 0.01017$^{\{1\}}$ | 0.02430$^{\{8\}}$ | 0.01422$^{\{2\}}$ | 0.01442$^{\{3\}}$ | 0.01468$^{\{4\}}$ |
| | MRE | $\hat{\delta}$ | 0.13161$^{\{4\}}$ | 0.14186$^{\{6\}}$ | 0.12556$^{\{3\}}$ | 0.12265$^{\{1\}}$ | 0.15166$^{\{7\}}$ | 0.12437$^{\{2\}}$ | 0.13580$^{\{5\}}$ | 0.22122$^{\{8\}}$ |
| | | $\hat{\lambda}$ | 0.18112$^{\{4\}}$ | 0.18800$^{\{7\}}$ | 0.18230$^{\{5\}}$ | 0.15677$^{\{1\}}$ | 0.20825$^{\{8\}}$ | 0.17631$^{\{2\}}$ | 0.17705$^{\{3\}}$ | 0.18565$^{\{6\}}$ |
| | $\sum$ *Ranks* | | 26$^{\{5\}}$ | 39$^{\{6\}}$ | 24$^{\{3.5\}}$ | 6$^{\{1\}}$ | 45$^{\{8\}}$ | 12$^{\{2\}}$ | 24$^{\{3.5\}}$ | 40$^{\{7\}}$ |
| 80 | $\|BIAS\|$ | $\hat{\delta}$ | 0.05830$^{\{4\}}$ | 0.06451$^{\{6\}}$ | 0.05363$^{\{1\}}$ | 0.05486$^{\{2\}}$ | 0.06619$^{\{7\}}$ | 0.05670$^{\{3\}}$ | 0.06013$^{\{5\}}$ | 0.11911$^{\{8\}}$ |
| | | $\hat{\lambda}$ | 0.05319$^{\{5\}}$ | 0.05535$^{\{6\}}$ | 0.05218$^{\{2\}}$ | 0.04890$^{\{1\}}$ | 0.05732$^{\{7\}}$ | 0.05259$^{\{3.5\}}$ | 0.05259$^{\{3.5\}}$ | 0.06567$^{\{8\}}$ |
| | MSE | $\hat{\delta}$ | 0.00544$^{\{4\}}$ | 0.00663$^{\{6\}}$ | 0.00471$^{\{2\}}$ | 0.00462$^{\{1\}}$ | 0.00719$^{\{7\}}$ | 0.00513$^{\{3\}}$ | 0.00591$^{\{5\}}$ | 0.02320$^{\{8\}}$ |
| | | $\hat{\lambda}$ | 0.00468$^{\{5\}}$ | 0.00510$^{\{6\}}$ | 0.00449$^{\{2\}}$ | 0.00378$^{\{1\}}$ | 0.00560$^{\{7\}}$ | 0.00455$^{\{3\}}$ | 0.00456$^{\{4\}}$ | 0.00782$^{\{8\}}$ |
| | MRE | $\hat{\delta}$ | 0.07774$^{\{4\}}$ | 0.08602$^{\{6\}}$ | 0.07150$^{\{1\}}$ | 0.07315$^{\{2\}}$ | 0.08825$^{\{7\}}$ | 0.07561$^{\{3\}}$ | 0.08017$^{\{5\}}$ | 0.15881$^{\{8\}}$ |
| | | $\hat{\lambda}$ | 0.10637$^{\{5\}}$ | 0.11070$^{\{6\}}$ | 0.10437$^{\{2\}}$ | 0.09780$^{\{1\}}$ | 0.11464$^{\{7\}}$ | 0.10519$^{\{4\}}$ | 0.10517$^{\{3\}}$ | 0.13135$^{\{8\}}$ |
| | $\sum$ *Ranks* | | 27$^{\{5\}}$ | 36$^{\{6\}}$ | 10$^{\{2\}}$ | 8$^{\{1\}}$ | 42$^{\{7\}}$ | 19.5$^{\{3\}}$ | 25.5$^{\{4\}}$ | 48$^{\{8\}}$ |
| 120 | $\|BIAS\|$ | $\hat{\delta}$ | 0.04696$^{\{4\}}$ | 0.05194$^{\{6\}}$ | 0.04361$^{\{1\}}$ | 0.04479$^{\{2\}}$ | 0.05282$^{\{7\}}$ | 0.04612$^{\{3\}}$ | 0.04939$^{\{5\}}$ | 0.10186$^{\{8\}}$ |
| | | $\hat{\lambda}$ | 0.04386$^{\{5\}}$ | 0.04606$^{\{6\}}$ | 0.04274$^{\{2\}}$ | 0.04059$^{\{1\}}$ | 0.04722$^{\{7\}}$ | 0.04351$^{\{4\}}$ | 0.04341$^{\{3\}}$ | 0.05651$^{\{8\}}$ |
| | MSE | $\hat{\delta}$ | 0.00349$^{\{4\}}$ | 0.00428$^{\{6\}}$ | 0.00301$^{\{1\}}$ | 0.00304$^{\{2\}}$ | 0.00451$^{\{7\}}$ | 0.00334$^{\{3\}}$ | 0.00387$^{\{5\}}$ | 0.01717$^{\{8\}}$ |
| | | $\hat{\lambda}$ | 0.00310$^{\{5\}}$ | 0.00340$^{\{6\}}$ | 0.00299$^{\{2\}}$ | 0.00261$^{\{1\}}$ | 0.00363$^{\{7\}}$ | 0.00303$^{\{3.5\}}$ | 0.00303$^{\{3.5\}}$ | 0.00589$^{\{8\}}$ |
| | MRE | $\hat{\delta}$ | 0.06262$^{\{4\}}$ | 0.06925$^{\{6\}}$ | 0.05814$^{\{1\}}$ | 0.05973$^{\{2\}}$ | 0.07043$^{\{7\}}$ | 0.06149$^{\{3\}}$ | 0.06586$^{\{5\}}$ | 0.13582$^{\{8\}}$ |
| | | $\hat{\lambda}$ | 0.08773$^{\{5\}}$ | 0.09212$^{\{6\}}$ | 0.08547$^{\{2\}}$ | 0.08117$^{\{1\}}$ | 0.09444$^{\{7\}}$ | 0.08703$^{\{4\}}$ | 0.08683$^{\{3\}}$ | 0.11303$^{\{8\}}$ |
| | $\sum$ *Ranks* | | 27$^{\{5\}}$ | 36$^{\{6\}}$ | 9$^{\{1.5\}}$ | 9$^{\{1.5\}}$ | 42$^{\{7\}}$ | 20.5$^{\{3\}}$ | 24.5$^{\{4\}}$ | 48$^{\{8\}}$ |
| 200 | $\|BIAS\|$ | $\hat{\delta}$ | 0.03643$^{\{4\}}$ | 0.04049$^{\{6\}}$ | 0.03307$^{\{1\}}$ | 0.03426$^{\{2\}}$ | 0.04082$^{\{7\}}$ | 0.03593$^{\{3\}}$ | 0.03793$^{\{5\}}$ | 0.08370$^{\{8\}}$ |
| | | $\hat{\lambda}$ | 0.03296$^{\{5\}}$ | 0.03447$^{\{6\}}$ | 0.03222$^{\{2\}}$ | 0.03115$^{\{1\}}$ | 0.03499$^{\{7\}}$ | 0.03278$^{\{4\}}$ | 0.03263$^{\{3\}}$ | 0.04497$^{\{8\}}$ |
| | MSE | $\hat{\delta}$ | 0.00209$^{\{4\}}$ | 0.00258$^{\{6\}}$ | 0.00176$^{\{1\}}$ | 0.00180$^{\{2\}}$ | 0.00266$^{\{7\}}$ | 0.00203$^{\{3\}}$ | 0.00230$^{\{5\}}$ | 0.01152$^{\{8\}}$ |
| | | $\hat{\lambda}$ | 0.00173$^{\{5\}}$ | 0.00190$^{\{6\}}$ | 0.00165$^{\{2\}}$ | 0.00152$^{\{1\}}$ | 0.00197$^{\{7\}}$ | 0.00171$^{\{4\}}$ | 0.00169$^{\{3\}}$ | 0.00375$^{\{8\}}$ |
| | MRE | $\hat{\delta}$ | 0.04857$^{\{4\}}$ | 0.05399$^{\{6\}}$ | 0.04409$^{\{1\}}$ | 0.04568$^{\{2\}}$ | 0.05443$^{\{7\}}$ | 0.04791$^{\{3\}}$ | 0.05058$^{\{5\}}$ | 0.11160$^{\{8\}}$ |
| | | $\hat{\lambda}$ | 0.06592$^{\{5\}}$ | 0.06895$^{\{6\}}$ | 0.06445$^{\{2\}}$ | 0.06230$^{\{1\}}$ | 0.06999$^{\{7\}}$ | 0.06557$^{\{4\}}$ | 0.06525$^{\{3\}}$ | 0.08995$^{\{8\}}$ |
| | $\sum$ *Ranks* | | 27$^{\{5\}}$ | 36$^{\{6\}}$ | 9$^{\{1.5\}}$ | 9$^{\{1.5\}}$ | 42$^{\{7\}}$ | 21$^{\{3\}}$ | 24$^{\{4\}}$ | 48$^{\{8\}}$ |
| 350 | $\|BIAS\|$ | $\hat{\delta}$ | 0.02723$^{\{4\}}$ | 0.03035$^{\{6\}}$ | 0.02505$^{\{1\}}$ | 0.02571$^{\{2\}}$ | 0.03051$^{\{7\}}$ | 0.02704$^{\{3\}}$ | 0.02837$^{\{5\}}$ | 0.06672$^{\{8\}}$ |
| | | $\hat{\lambda}$ | 0.02468$^{\{5\}}$ | 0.02597$^{\{6\}}$ | 0.02395$^{\{2\}}$ | 0.02366$^{\{1\}}$ | 0.02613$^{\{7\}}$ | 0.02460$^{\{4\}}$ | 0.02448$^{\{3\}}$ | 0.03502$^{\{8\}}$ |
| | MSE | $\hat{\delta}$ | 0.00116$^{\{4\}}$ | 0.00145$^{\{6\}}$ | 0.00099$^{\{1\}}$ | 0.00102$^{\{2\}}$ | 0.00148$^{\{7\}}$ | 0.00114$^{\{3\}}$ | 0.00126$^{\{5\}}$ | 0.00720$^{\{8\}}$ |
| | | $\hat{\lambda}$ | 0.00097$^{\{5\}}$ | 0.00107$^{\{6\}}$ | 0.00091$^{\{2\}}$ | 0.00088$^{\{1\}}$ | 0.00109$^{\{7\}}$ | 0.00096$^{\{4\}}$ | 0.00095$^{\{3\}}$ | 0.00213$^{\{8\}}$ |
| | MRE | $\hat{\delta}$ | 0.03631$^{\{4\}}$ | 0.04046$^{\{6\}}$ | 0.03340$^{\{1\}}$ | 0.03428$^{\{2\}}$ | 0.04068$^{\{7\}}$ | 0.03606$^{\{3\}}$ | 0.03783$^{\{5\}}$ | 0.08897$^{\{8\}}$ |
| | | $\hat{\lambda}$ | 0.04937$^{\{5\}}$ | 0.05193$^{\{6\}}$ | 0.04791$^{\{2\}}$ | 0.04732$^{\{1\}}$ | 0.05227$^{\{7\}}$ | 0.04921$^{\{4\}}$ | 0.04896$^{\{3\}}$ | 0.07005$^{\{8\}}$ |
| | $\sum$ *Ranks* | | 27$^{\{5\}}$ | 36$^{\{6\}}$ | 9$^{\{1.5\}}$ | 9$^{\{1.5\}}$ | 42$^{\{7\}}$ | 21$^{\{3\}}$ | 24$^{\{4\}}$ | 48$^{\{8\}}$ |

**Table 8.** Simulation results for $\boldsymbol{\vartheta} = (\delta = 4.00, \lambda = 3.00)^{\intercal}$.

| $n$ | Est. | Est. Par. | WLSE | OLSE | MLE | MPSE | CVME | ADE | RADE | PCE |
|---|---|---|---|---|---|---|---|---|---|---|
| 30 | $\|BIAS\|$ | $\hat{\delta}$ | 0.52826$^{\{5\}}$ | 0.57159$^{\{7\}}$ | 0.49972$^{\{3\}}$ | 0.49193$^{\{2\}}$ | 0.61053$^{\{8\}}$ | 0.50005$^{\{4\}}$ | 0.55036$^{\{6\}}$ | 0.47654$^{\{1\}}$ |
| | | $\hat{\lambda}$ | 1.11327$^{\{6\}}$ | 1.20970$^{\{7\}}$ | 1.07414$^{\{4\}}$ | 0.82845$^{\{1\}}$ | 1.50679$^{\{8\}}$ | 1.01227$^{\{3\}}$ | 1.09974$^{\{5\}}$ | 0.85244$^{\{2\}}$ |
| | MSE | $\hat{\delta}$ | 0.47263$^{\{5\}}$ | 0.54656$^{\{7\}}$ | 0.42643$^{\{4\}}$ | 0.36760$^{\{2\}}$ | 0.66271$^{\{8\}}$ | 0.41285$^{\{3\}}$ | 0.51336$^{\{6\}}$ | 0.35080$^{\{1\}}$ |
| | | $\hat{\lambda}$ | 4.47860$^{\{6\}}$ | 5.30036$^{\{7\}}$ | 2.98339$^{\{4\}}$ | 1.22399$^{\{1\}}$ | 10.16763$^{\{8\}}$ | 2.43795$^{\{3\}}$ | 3.46274$^{\{5\}}$ | 1.44294$^{\{2\}}$ |
| | MRE | $\hat{\delta}$ | 0.13207$^{\{5\}}$ | 0.14290$^{\{7\}}$ | 0.12493$^{\{3\}}$ | 0.12298$^{\{2\}}$ | 0.15263$^{\{8\}}$ | 0.12501$^{\{4\}}$ | 0.13759$^{\{6\}}$ | 0.11914$^{\{1\}}$ |
| | | $\hat{\lambda}$ | 0.37109$^{\{6\}}$ | 0.40323$^{\{7\}}$ | 0.35805$^{\{4\}}$ | 0.27615$^{\{1\}}$ | 0.50226$^{\{8\}}$ | 0.33742$^{\{3\}}$ | 0.36658$^{\{5\}}$ | 0.28415$^{\{2\}}$ |
| | $\sum$ *Ranks* | | 33$^{\{5.5\}}$ | 42$^{\{7\}}$ | 22$^{\{4\}}$ | 9$^{\{1.5\}}$ | 48$^{\{8\}}$ | 20$^{\{3\}}$ | 33$^{\{5.5\}}$ | 9$^{\{1.5\}}$ |

**Table 8.** *Cont.*

| $n$ | Est. | Est. Par. | WLSE | OLSE | MLE | MPSE | CVME | ADE | RADE | PCE |
|---|---|---|---|---|---|---|---|---|---|---|
| 80 | $\lvert BIAS \rvert$ | $\hat{\delta}$ | $0.31405^{\{5\}}$ | $0.34365^{\{7\}}$ | $0.29344^{\{2\}}$ | $0.29929^{\{3\}}$ | $0.35267^{\{8\}}$ | $0.30589^{\{4\}}$ | $0.32689^{\{6\}}$ | $0.28668^{\{1\}}$ |
| | | $\hat{\lambda}$ | $0.58521^{\{5\}}$ | $0.64431^{\{7\}}$ | $0.54668^{\{3\}}$ | $0.49869^{\{2\}}$ | $0.69457^{\{8\}}$ | $0.56545^{\{4\}}$ | $0.58551^{\{6\}}$ | $0.49536^{\{1\}}$ |
| | MSE | $\hat{\delta}$ | $0.16033^{\{5\}}$ | $0.19008^{\{7\}}$ | $0.14142^{\{3\}}$ | $0.13794^{\{2\}}$ | $0.20551^{\{8\}}$ | $0.15127^{\{4\}}$ | $0.17565^{\{6\}}$ | $0.12673^{\{1\}}$ |
| | | $\hat{\lambda}$ | $0.65356^{\{5\}}$ | $0.80065^{\{7\}}$ | $0.56111^{\{3\}}$ | $0.38873^{\{1\}}$ | $0.99591^{\{8\}}$ | $0.58436^{\{4\}}$ | $0.65407^{\{6\}}$ | $0.40210^{\{2\}}$ |
| | MRE | $\hat{\delta}$ | $0.07851^{\{5\}}$ | $0.08591^{\{7\}}$ | $0.07336^{\{2\}}$ | $0.07482^{\{3\}}$ | $0.08817^{\{8\}}$ | $0.07647^{\{4\}}$ | $0.08172^{\{6\}}$ | $0.07167^{\{1\}}$ |
| | | $\hat{\lambda}$ | $0.19507^{\{5\}}$ | $0.21477^{\{7\}}$ | $0.18223^{\{3\}}$ | $0.16623^{\{2\}}$ | $0.23152^{\{8\}}$ | $0.18848^{\{4\}}$ | $0.19517^{\{6\}}$ | $0.16512^{\{1\}}$ |
| | $\sum Ranks$ | | $30^{\{5\}}$ | $42^{\{7\}}$ | $16^{\{3\}}$ | $13^{\{2\}}$ | $48^{\{8\}}$ | $24^{\{4\}}$ | $36^{\{6\}}$ | $7^{\{1\}}$ |
| 120 | $\lvert BIAS \rvert$ | $\hat{\delta}$ | $0.24785^{\{5\}}$ | $0.27563^{\{7\}}$ | $0.22778^{\{1\}}$ | $0.23683^{\{3\}}$ | $0.27983^{\{8\}}$ | $0.24208^{\{4\}}$ | $0.25873^{\{6\}}$ | $0.23191^{\{2\}}$ |
| | | $\hat{\lambda}$ | $0.46276^{\{6\}}$ | $0.51714^{\{7\}}$ | $0.42345^{\{3\}}$ | $0.40160^{\{1\}}$ | $0.54292^{\{8\}}$ | $0.45070^{\{4\}}$ | $0.45972^{\{5\}}$ | $0.40345^{\{2\}}$ |
| | MSE | $\hat{\delta}$ | $0.09895^{\{5\}}$ | $0.12081^{\{7\}}$ | $0.08373^{\{2\}}$ | $0.08601^{\{3\}}$ | $0.12657^{\{8\}}$ | $0.09418^{\{4\}}$ | $0.10699^{\{6\}}$ | $0.08253^{\{1\}}$ |
| | | $\hat{\lambda}$ | $0.38541^{\{6\}}$ | $0.47566^{\{7\}}$ | $0.32147^{\{3\}}$ | $0.25482^{\{1\}}$ | $0.54743^{\{8\}}$ | $0.35719^{\{4\}}$ | $0.38073^{\{5\}}$ | $0.25766^{\{2\}}$ |
| | MRE | $\hat{\delta}$ | $0.06196^{\{5\}}$ | $0.06891^{\{7\}}$ | $0.05695^{\{1\}}$ | $0.05921^{\{3\}}$ | $0.06996^{\{8\}}$ | $0.06052^{\{4\}}$ | $0.06468^{\{6\}}$ | $0.05798^{\{2\}}$ |
| | | $\hat{\lambda}$ | $0.15425^{\{6\}}$ | $0.17238^{\{7\}}$ | $0.14115^{\{3\}}$ | $0.13387^{\{1\}}$ | $0.18097^{\{8\}}$ | $0.15023^{\{4\}}$ | $0.15324^{\{5\}}$ | $0.13448^{\{2\}}$ |
| | $\sum Ranks$ | | $33^{\{5.5\}}$ | $42^{\{7\}}$ | $13^{\{3\}}$ | $12^{\{2\}}$ | $48^{\{8\}}$ | $24^{\{4\}}$ | $33^{\{5.5\}}$ | $11^{\{1\}}$ |
| 200 | $\lvert BIAS \rvert$ | $\hat{\delta}$ | $0.19032^{\{5\}}$ | $0.21310^{\{7\}}$ | $0.17553^{\{1\}}$ | $0.18020^{\{3\}}$ | $0.21485^{\{8\}}$ | $0.18778^{\{4\}}$ | $0.20132^{\{6\}}$ | $0.17810^{\{2\}}$ |
| | | $\hat{\lambda}$ | $0.34904^{\{5\}}$ | $0.39646^{\{7\}}$ | $0.32026^{\{3\}}$ | $0.30712^{\{1\}}$ | $0.40727^{\{8\}}$ | $0.34387^{\{4\}}$ | $0.35187^{\{6\}}$ | $0.31010^{\{2\}}$ |
| | MSE | $\hat{\delta}$ | $0.05734^{\{5\}}$ | $0.07127^{\{7\}}$ | $0.04936^{\{1\}}$ | $0.05018^{\{3\}}$ | $0.07360^{\{8\}}$ | $0.05576^{\{4\}}$ | $0.06396^{\{6\}}$ | $0.04942^{\{2\}}$ |
| | | $\hat{\lambda}$ | $0.20823^{\{5\}}$ | $0.26525^{\{7\}}$ | $0.17626^{\{3\}}$ | $0.15069^{\{1\}}$ | $0.28980^{\{8\}}$ | $0.19912^{\{4\}}$ | $0.21183^{\{6\}}$ | $0.15211^{\{2\}}$ |
| | MRE | $\hat{\delta}$ | $0.04758^{\{5\}}$ | $0.05327^{\{7\}}$ | $0.04388^{\{1\}}$ | $0.04505^{\{3\}}$ | $0.05371^{\{8\}}$ | $0.04694^{\{4\}}$ | $0.05033^{\{6\}}$ | $0.04453^{\{2\}}$ |
| | | $\hat{\lambda}$ | $0.11635^{\{5\}}$ | $0.13215^{\{7\}}$ | $0.10675^{\{3\}}$ | $0.10237^{\{1\}}$ | $0.13576^{\{8\}}$ | $0.11462^{\{4\}}$ | $0.11729^{\{6\}}$ | $0.10337^{\{2\}}$ |
| | $\sum Ranks$ | | $30^{\{5\}}$ | $42^{\{7\}}$ | $12^{\{2\}}$ | $12^{\{2\}}$ | $48^{\{8\}}$ | $24^{\{4\}}$ | $36^{\{6\}}$ | $12^{\{2\}}$ |
| 350 | $\lvert BIAS \rvert$ | $\hat{\delta}$ | $0.14365^{\{5\}}$ | $0.16163^{\{7\}}$ | $0.13133^{\{1\}}$ | $0.13467^{\{3\}}$ | $0.16271^{\{8\}}$ | $0.14229^{\{4\}}$ | $0.15007^{\{6\}}$ | $0.13357^{\{2\}}$ |
| | | $\hat{\lambda}$ | $0.26016^{\{6\}}$ | $0.29563^{\{7\}}$ | $0.23584^{\{3\}}$ | $0.22725^{\{1\}}$ | $0.30114^{\{8\}}$ | $0.25688^{\{4\}}$ | $0.25873^{\{5\}}$ | $0.23506^{\{2\}}$ |
| | MSE | $\hat{\delta}$ | $0.03327^{\{5\}}$ | $0.04177^{\{7\}}$ | $0.02804^{\{2\}}$ | $0.02876^{\{3\}}$ | $0.04261^{\{8\}}$ | $0.03259^{\{4\}}$ | $0.03626^{\{6\}}$ | $0.02789^{\{1\}}$ |
| | | $\hat{\lambda}$ | $0.11087^{\{6\}}$ | $0.14275^{\{7\}}$ | $0.09219^{\{3\}}$ | $0.08504^{\{1\}}$ | $0.15033^{\{8\}}$ | $0.10750^{\{4\}}$ | $0.10999^{\{5\}}$ | $0.08680^{\{2\}}$ |
| | MRE | $\hat{\delta}$ | $0.03591^{\{5\}}$ | $0.04041^{\{7\}}$ | $0.03283^{\{1\}}$ | $0.03367^{\{3\}}$ | $0.04068^{\{8\}}$ | $0.03557^{\{4\}}$ | $0.03752^{\{6\}}$ | $0.03339^{\{2\}}$ |
| | | $\hat{\lambda}$ | $0.08672^{\{6\}}$ | $0.09854^{\{7\}}$ | $0.07861^{\{3\}}$ | $0.07575^{\{1\}}$ | $0.10038^{\{8\}}$ | $0.08563^{\{4\}}$ | $0.08624^{\{5\}}$ | $0.07835^{\{2\}}$ |
| | $\sum Ranks$ | | $33^{\{5.5\}}$ | $42^{\{7\}}$ | $13^{\{3\}}$ | $12^{\{2\}}$ | $48^{\{8\}}$ | $24^{\{4\}}$ | $33^{\{5.5\}}$ | $11^{\{1\}}$ |

**Table 9.** Partial and overall ranks of the classical estimation methods for several parametric values.

| $\boldsymbol{\vartheta}^{\top}$ | $n$ | WLSE | OLSE | MLE | MPSE | CVME | ADE | RADE | PCE |
|---|---|---|---|---|---|---|---|---|---|
| | 30 | 5 | 6 | 3 | 1 | 7 | 2 | 4 | 8 |
| | 80 | 5 | 6 | 1.5 | 1.5 | 7 | 3 | 4 | 8 |
| $(\delta = 0.45, \lambda = 0.50)$ | 120 | 5 | 6 | 1.5 | 1.5 | 7 | 3 | 4 | 8 |
| | 200 | 5 | 6 | 1.5 | 1.5 | 7 | 3 | 4 | 8 |
| | 350 | 5 | 6 | 1.5 | 1.5 | 7 | 3 | 4 | 8 |
| | 30 | 5 | 7 | 3 | 1 | 8 | 2 | 4 | 6 |
| | 80 | 5 | 6 | 2 | 1 | 8 | 3 | 4 | 7 |
| $(\delta = 0.45, \lambda = 1.00)$ | 120 | 5 | 6 | 1.5 | 1.5 | 7 | 3 | 4 | 8 |
| | 200 | 5 | 6 | 1.5 | 1.5 | 7 | 3 | 4 | 8 |
| | 350 | 5 | 6 | 1 | 2 | 7 | 3 | 4 | 8 |
| | 30 | 5 | 7 | 3 | 1 | 8 | 2 | 4 | 6 |
| | 80 | 4.5 | 6 | 2 | 1 | 8 | 3 | 4.5 | 7 |
| $(\delta = 0.45, \lambda = 1.75)$ | 120 | 4.5 | 6 | 2 | 1 | 7.5 | 3 | 4.5 | 7.5 |
| | 200 | 5 | 6 | 1.5 | 1.5 | 7.5 | 3 | 4 | 7.5 |
| | 350 | 5 | 6 | 1.5 | 1.5 | 7.5 | 3 | 4 | 7.5 |

**Table 9.** *Cont.*

| $\vartheta^{\top}$ | $n$ | WLSE | OLSE | MLE | MPSE | CVME | ADE | RADE | PCE |
|---|---|---|---|---|---|---|---|---|---|
| ($\delta = 0.45, \lambda = 3.00$) | 30 | 4.5 | 6 | 3 | 1 | 7 | 2 | 4.5 | 8 |
| | 80 | 4 | 6 | 2 | 1 | 7 | 3 | 5 | 8 |
| | 120 | 4 | 6 | 1.5 | 1.5 | 7 | 3 | 5 | 8 |
| | 200 | 4.5 | 6 | 1.5 | 1.5 | 7 | 3 | 4.5 | 8 |
| | 350 | 4.5 | 6 | 1.5 | 1.5 | 7 | 3 | 4.5 | 8 |
| ($\delta = 0.75, \lambda = 0.50$) | 30 | 5 | 6 | 3.5 | 1 | 8 | 2 | 3.5 | 7 |
| | 80 | 5 | 6 | 2 | 1 | 7 | 3 | 4 | 8 |
| | 120 | 5 | 6 | 1.5 | 1.5 | 7 | 3 | 4 | 8 |
| | 200 | 5 | 6 | 1.5 | 1.5 | 7 | 3 | 4 | 8 |
| | 350 | 5 | 6 | 1.5 | 1.5 | 7 | 3 | 4 | 8 |
| ($\delta = 0.75, \lambda = 1.00$) | 30 | 5.5 | 7 | 3 | 1 | 8 | 2 | 4 | 5.5 |
| | 80 | 5.5 | 7 | 2 | 1 | 8 | 3 | 4 | 5.5 |
| | 120 | 5 | 7 | 2 | 1 | 8 | 3 | 5 | 5 |
| | 200 | 5 | 7 | 2 | 1 | 8 | 3 | 4 | 6 |
| | 350 | 5 | 7 | 1.5 | 1.5 | 8 | 3 | 4 | 6 |
| ($\delta = 0.75, \lambda = 1.75$) | 30 | 5 | 7 | 3 | 1 | 8 | 2 | 4 | 6 |
| | 80 | 4.5 | 6 | 2 | 1 | 8 | 3 | 4.5 | 7 |
| | 120 | 4.5 | 6 | 1.5 | 1.5 | 8 | 3 | 4.5 | 7 |
| | 200 | 4.5 | 6 | 1.5 | 1.5 | 8 | 3 | 4.5 | 7 |
| | 350 | 4.5 | 6 | 1.5 | 1.5 | 7 | 3 | 4.5 | 8 |
| ($\delta = 0.75, \lambda = 3.00$) | 30 | 5 | 6 | 3 | 1 | 8 | 2 | 4 | 7 |
| | 80 | 4.5 | 6 | 1.5 | 1.5 | 7 | 3 | 4.5 | 8 |
| | 120 | 4 | 6 | 1.5 | 1.5 | 7 | 3 | 5 | 8 |
| | 200 | 4 | 6 | 1.5 | 1.5 | 7 | 3 | 5 | 8 |
| | 350 | 4 | 6 | 1.5 | 1.5 | 7 | 3 | 5 | 8 |
| ($\delta = 1.50, \lambda = 0.50$) | 30 | 6 | 7 | 4 | 1 | 8 | 2 | 5 | 3 |
| | 80 | 6 | 7 | 2 | 1 | 8 | 3 | 5 | 4 |
| | 120 | 5.5 | 7 | 2 | 1 | 8 | 3 | 4 | 5.5 |
| | 200 | 5.5 | 7 | 2 | 1 | 8 | 3 | 4 | 5.5 |
| | 350 | 5 | 7 | 1.5 | 1.5 | 8 | 3 | 4 | 6 |
| ($\delta = 1.50, \lambda = 1.00$) | 30 | 6 | 7 | 3 | 1 | 8 | 2 | 5 | 4 |
| | 80 | 5 | 7 | 2 | 1 | 8 | 3 | 5 | 5 |
| | 120 | 5 | 7 | 2 | 1 | 8 | 3 | 5 | 5 |
| | 200 | 5 | 7 | 1.5 | 1.5 | 8 | 3 | 4 | 6 |
| | 350 | 5 | 7 | 1.5 | 1.5 | 8 | 3 | 4 | 6 |
| ($\delta = 1.50, \lambda = 1.75$) | 30 | 5.5 | 7 | 3 | 1 | 8 | 2 | 5.5 | 4 |
| | 80 | 4.5 | 7 | 1.5 | 1.5 | 8 | 3 | 4.5 | 6 |
| | 120 | 4.5 | 7 | 1.5 | 1.5 | 8 | 3 | 4.5 | 6 |
| | 200 | 4.5 | 6 | 1.5 | 1.5 | 8 | 3 | 4.5 | 7 |
| | 350 | 5 | 6 | 1.5 | 1.5 | 8 | 3 | 4 | 7 |
| ($\delta = 1.50, \lambda = 3.00$) | 30 | 5.5 | 7 | 3 | 1 | 8 | 2 | 5.5 | 4 |
| | 80 | 4 | 6.5 | 2 | 1 | 8 | 3 | 5 | 6.5 |
| | 120 | 4 | 6.5 | 1.5 | 1.5 | 8 | 3 | 5 | 6.5 |
| | 200 | 4 | 6 | 1.5 | 1.5 | 8 | 3 | 5 | 7 |
| | 350 | 4 | 6 | 1.5 | 1.5 | 8 | 3 | 5 | 7 |
| ($\delta = 4.00, \lambda = 0.50$) | 30 | 5 | 7 | 5 | 2 | 8 | 3 | 5 | 1 |
| | 80 | 6 | 7 | 3 | 2 | 8 | 4 | 5 | 1 |
| | 120 | 6 | 7 | 3 | 2 | 8 | 4 | 5 | 1 |
| | 200 | 6 | 7 | 2 | 2 | 8 | 4 | 5 | 2 |
| | 350 | 6 | 7 | 2 | 1 | 8 | 4 | 5 | 3 |

**Table 9.** *Cont.*

| $\boldsymbol{\vartheta}^{\mathsf{T}}$ | $n$ | WLSE | OLSE | MLE | MPSE | CVME | ADE | RADE | PCE |
|---|---|---|---|---|---|---|---|---|---|
| | 30 | 6 | 7 | 4 | 1 | 8 | 3 | 5 | 2 |
| | 80 | 6 | 7 | 3 | 1.5 | 8 | 4 | 5 | 1.5 |
| $(\delta = 4.00, \lambda = 1.00)$ | 120 | 5.5 | 7 | 2 | 3 | 8 | 4 | 5.5 | 1 |
| | 200 | 6 | 7 | 1 | 2 | 8 | 4 | 5 | 3 |
| | 350 | 6 | 7 | 1 | 2 | 8 | 4 | 5 | 3 |
| | 30 | 6 | 7 | 4 | 2 | 8 | 3 | 5 | 1 |
| | 80 | 5.5 | 7 | 3 | 2 | 8 | 4 | 5.5 | 1 |
| $(\delta = 4.00, \lambda = 1.75)$ | 120 | 5.5 | 7 | 2.5 | 2.5 | 8 | 4 | 5.5 | 1 |
| | 200 | 6 | 7 | 2 | 3 | 8 | 4 | 5 | 1 |
| | 350 | 5.5 | 7 | 2 | 3 | 8 | 4 | 5.5 | 1 |
| | 30 | 5.5 | 7 | 4 | 1.5 | 8 | 3 | 5.5 | 1.5 |
| | 80 | 5 | 7 | 3 | 2 | 8 | 4 | 6 | 1 |
| $(\delta = 4.00, \lambda = 3.00)$ | 120 | 5.5 | 7 | 3 | 2 | 8 | 4 | 5.5 | 1 |
| | 200 | 5 | 7 | 2 | 2 | 8 | 4 | 6 | 2 |
| | 350 | 5.5 | 7 | 3 | 2 | 8 | 4 | 5.5 | 1 |
| $\sum$ **Ranks** | | **404** | **523** | **171** | **117.5** | **616.5** | **244** | **369.5** | **434.5** |
| **Overall Rank** | | **5** | **7** | **2** | **1** | **8** | **3** | **4** | **6** |

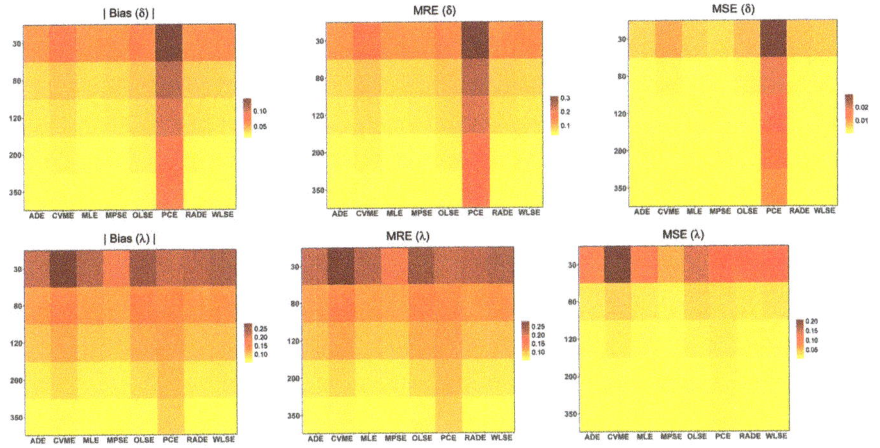


**Figure 3.** The heatmaps of the simulated biases, MSE and MRE of the eight simulation methods for $\delta = 0.45$ and $\lambda = 1.00$.

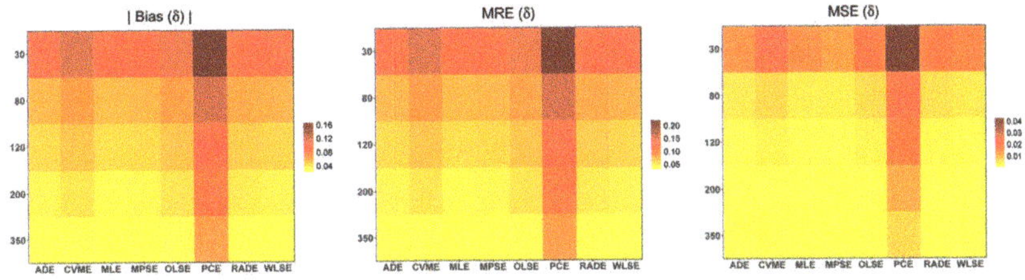


**Figure 4.** *Cont.*

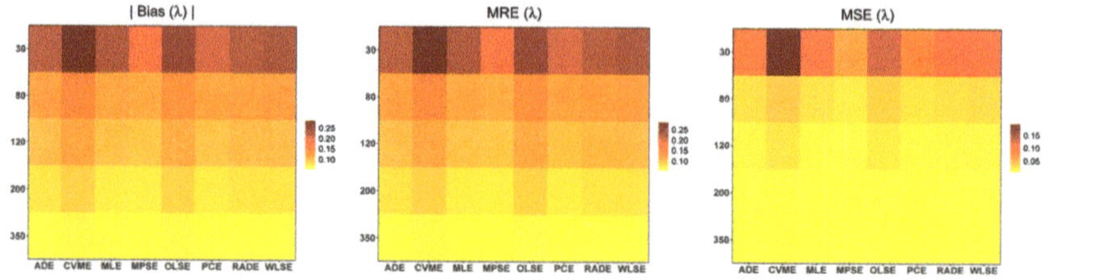


**Figure 4.** The heatmaps of the simulated biases, MSE and MRE of the eight simulation methods for $\delta = 0.75$ and $\lambda = 1.00$.

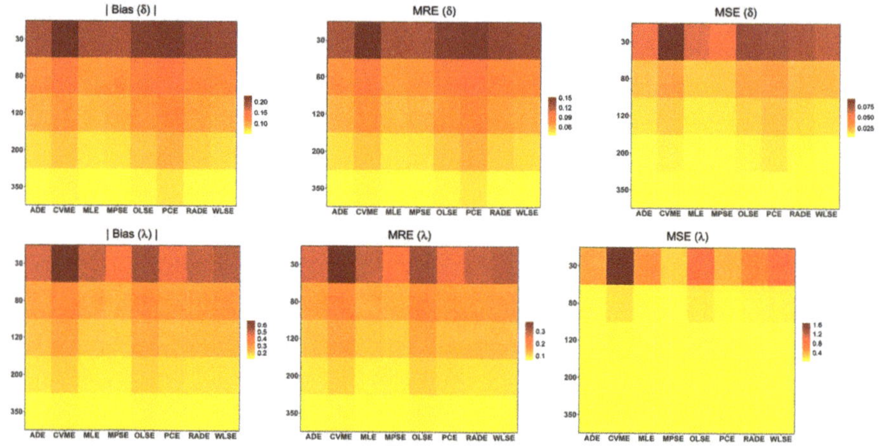


**Figure 5.** The heatmaps of the simulated biases, MSE and MRE, of the eight simulation methods for $\delta = 1.50$ and $\lambda = 1.75$.

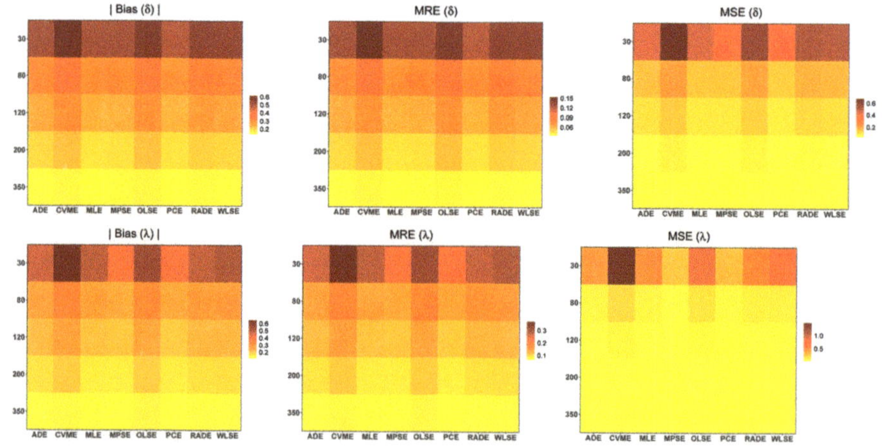


**Figure 6.** The heatmaps of the simulated biases, MSE and MRE, of the eight simulation methods for $\delta = 4.00$ and $\lambda = 1.75$.

## 5. Data Modeling

In this section, we carry out the practical evaluation of the WS-Weibull model. This fact is shown by choosing two data sets from the engineering sector. Both the data sets represent the failure times of the electronic components.

Using the failure time data sets, we compare the results of the WS-Weibull model with three other different well-known variants of the Weibull model. These models are given by the (i) exponentiated Weibull (for short "E-Weibull"), distribution, (ii) new exponential cosine Weibull (for short "NEC-Weibull") distribution, and (iii) logarithmic Weibull (for short "L-Weibull") distribution. The CDFs of the above-competing probability modes are expressed, respectively, by

$$G(x;\theta,\boldsymbol{\vartheta}) = \left(1 - e^{-\lambda x^{\delta}}\right)^{\theta}, \qquad x \geq 0, \theta > 0,$$

$$G(x;\beta,\boldsymbol{\vartheta}) = 1 - \cos\left(\frac{\pi}{2}\left[\frac{1 - e^{-\lambda x^{\delta}}}{1 - (1-\beta)e^{-\lambda x^{\delta}}}\right]\right), \qquad x \geq 0, \beta > 0,$$

and

$$G(x;\alpha,\phi,\boldsymbol{\vartheta}) = 1 - \left(1 - \frac{\phi\left(1 - e^{-\lambda x^{\delta}}\right)}{\phi - \log\left[1 - e^{-\lambda x^{\delta}}\right]}\right)^{\alpha}, \qquad x \geq 0, \alpha, \phi > 0.$$

The comparison of the WS-Weibull, E-Weibull, NEC-Weibull, and L-Weibull distributions is made using four different selection criteria. The selection criteria are chosen with the aim of figuring out the most suitable model for the failure time data set. The selection criteria are given by

- Akaike information criterion:
  The Akaike information criterion (AIC) is a useful method for evaluating how close/well a model fits the given data. It provides estimates of the relative amount of information lost by a given probability model. Therefore, a model that loses less information is a mark of the best fitting. It is calculated as

$$2k - 2\ell.$$

- Consistent Akaike information criterion:
  The consistent Akaike information criterion (CAIC) is another useful tool for comparing the quality of the model fitting. It is obtained as

$$\frac{2nk}{n-k-1} - 2\ell.$$

- Bayesian information criterion:
  The Bayesian information criterion (BIC) is another statistical criterion for choosing the best model among a set of competing models. Generally, a model with lower BIC is preferred. The value of the BIC is obtained as

$$k\log(n) - 2\ell.$$

- Hannan Quinn information criterion:
  Another model-fitting criterion is the Hannan-Quinn information criterion (HQIC). It also measures the goodness of fit of a given probability model. The HQIC is obtained as

$$2k\log[\log(n)] - 2\ell.$$

The numerical values of the above selection criteria are computed with the help of computer software called `R-package` using the BFGS method.

### *5.1. Data 1*

The first data set has fifty observations and represents the failure times of 50 (in weeks) components. These data were originally reported by [28]. Later on, numerous authors analyzed this data set; see [29–31].

Corresponding to the first failure times data, some basic description measures are skewness = 2.306048, kurtosis = 9.408282, range = 48.092, minimum = 0.013, maximum = 48.105, mean = 7.821, median = 5.320, variance = 84.75597, standard deviation = 9.2063, 1*st* quartile = 1.390, and 3*rd* quartile = 10.043; the size of the data, say $n$, is 50. A visual description of the first failure times data set is presented in Figure 7.

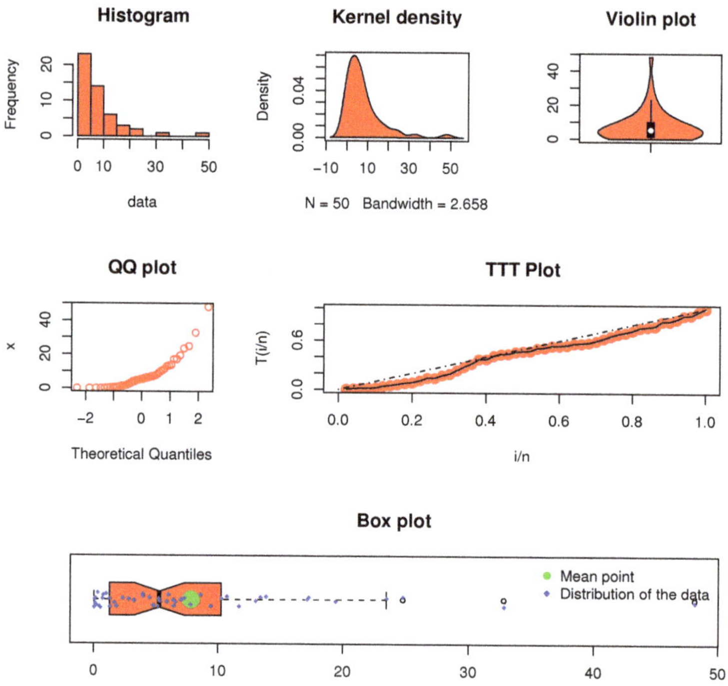


**Figure 7.** Visual description of the first failure times data set.

After analyzing the first data set, the values of $\hat{\delta}_{MLE}, \hat{\lambda}_{MLE}, \hat{\theta}_{MLE}, \hat{\alpha}_{MLE},$, and $\hat{\beta}_{MLE}$ are presented in Table 10. A visual display of the profiles of the LLF of $\hat{\delta}_{MLE}$ and $\hat{\lambda}_{MLE}$ of the WS-Weibull distribution is presented in Figure 8. The plots in Figure 8 reveal a unique solution of the MLEs of the WS-Weibull distribution.

**Table 10.** Using the first failure times data, the values of $\hat{\delta}_{MLE}, \hat{\lambda}_{MLE}, \hat{\theta}_{MLE}, \hat{\Phi}_{MLE}, \hat{\alpha}_{MLE}$, and $\hat{\beta}_{MLE}$ of the fitted distributions.

| Models | $\hat{\delta}_{MLE}$ | $\hat{\lambda}_{MLE}$ | $\hat{\theta}_{MLE}$ | $\hat{\Phi}_{MLE}$ | $\hat{\alpha}_{MLE}$ | $\hat{\beta}_{MLE}$ |
|---|---|---|---|---|---|---|
| WS-Weibull | 0.84861 | 0.06628 | - | - | - | - |
| E-Weibull | 0.32947 | 1.39376 | 5.28710 | - | - | - |
| L-Weibull | 0.55268 | 0.55492 | - | 0.48751 | 1.22066 | - |
| NEC-Weibull | 0.42927 | 1.03216 | - | - | - | 2.96768 |

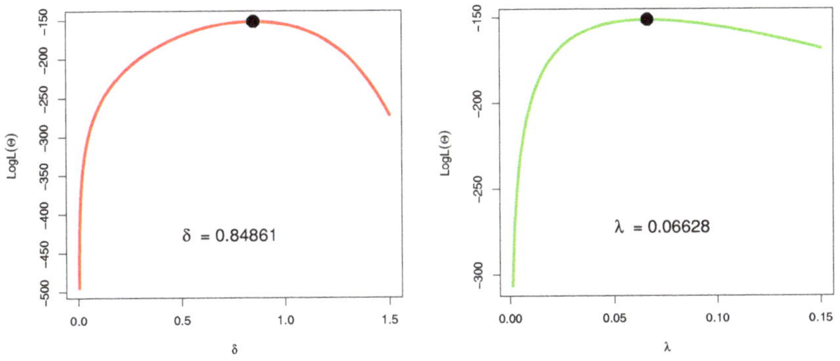


**Figure 8.** The profiles of the LLF of $\hat{\delta}_{MLE}$ and $\hat{\lambda}_{MLE}$ of WS-Weibull using the first failure times data.

Table 11 provides the values of the selection criteria of the WS-Weibull and other competing probability models. From the numerical description of fitted models in Table 11, it can be observed that the WS-Weibull is the best probability model for analyzing the failure data set. The second-best suitable model is the L-Weibull distribution. Whereas, the third-best model is the NEC-Weibull distribution.

After the numerical comparison of the WS-Weibull distribution and other variants of the Weibull distribution presented in Table 11, we also provide a visual illustration of the WS-Weibull distribution. For the visual comparison using the first failure times data, we select the plots of the fitted CDF, SF, PDF, quantile-quantile (QQ), and probability-probability (PP); see Figure 9. The visual description in Figure 9 reveals that the WS-Weibull distribution closely follows the first failure times data.

**Table 11.** For the first failure times data, the values of selection criteria of the competing distributions.

| Models | AIC | CAIC | BIC | HQIC |
| --- | --- | --- | --- | --- |
| WS-Weibull | 306.28000 | 306.53530 | 310.10400 | 307.73620 |
| E-Weibull | 315.68840 | 316.21010 | 321.42440 | 317.87270 |
| L-Weibull | 309.23860 | 310.12750 | 316.88670 | 312.15110 |
| NEC-Weibull | 310.05400 | 310.57570 | 315.79000 | 312.23830 |

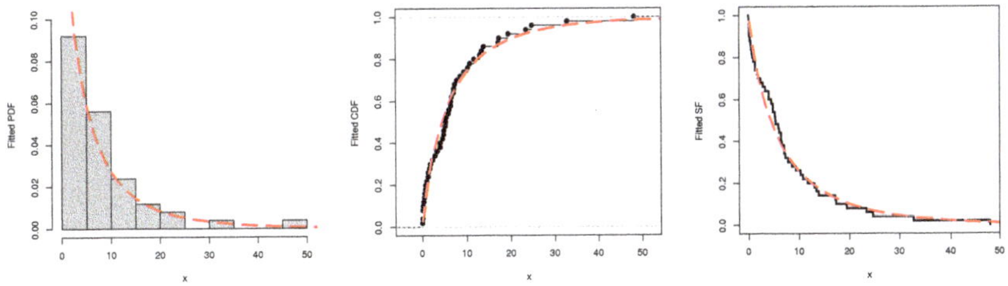


**Figure 9.** *Cont.*

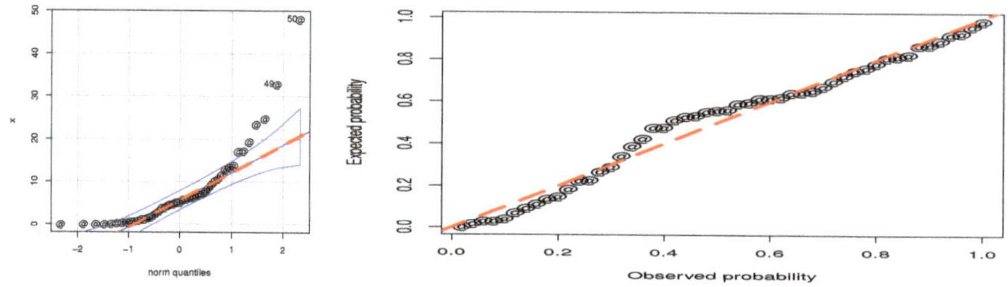


**Figure 9.** A visual illustration of the WS-Weibull distribution using the first failure times data.

*5.2. Data 2*

The second failure times data set also consists of fifty observations and represents the failure times of 50 (per 1000 h) components. These data were also originally reported by [28].

Linked to the second failure times data, the basic description measures are given by skewness = 1.416739, kurtosis = 4.084622, range = 15.044, minimum = 0.0360, maximum = 15.0800 mean = 3.3430, median = 1.4140, variance = 17.48477, standard deviation = 4.181479, 1*st* quartile = 0.2075, 3*rd* quartile = 4.4988, and $n = 50$. A visual description of the second failure time data set is provided in Figure 10.

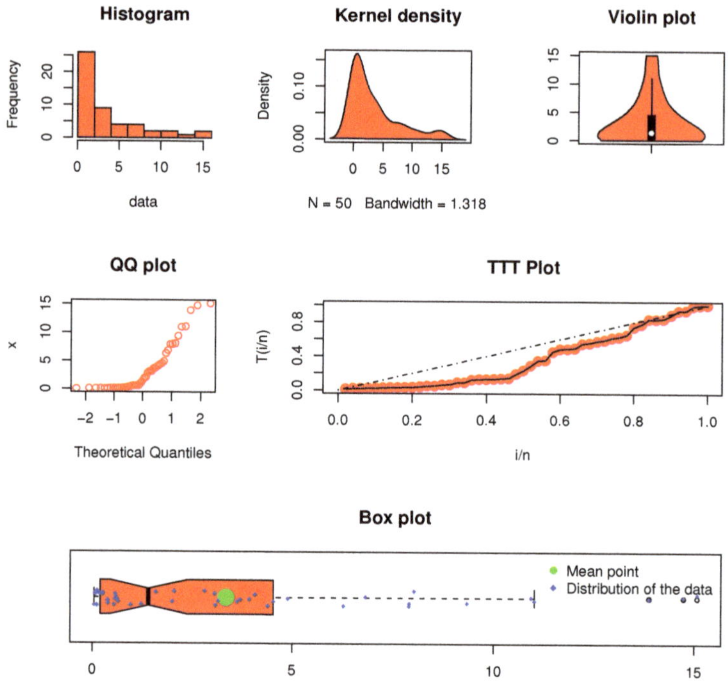


**Figure 10.** Visual description of the second failure times data set.

Corresponding to the second failure times data set, the numerical values of the MLEs $(\hat{\delta}_{MLE}, \hat{\lambda}_{MLE}, \hat{\theta}_{MLE}, \hat{\alpha}_{MLE}, \hat{\beta}_{MLE})$ are presented in Table 12. Furthermore, a visual display of the profiles of the LLF of $\hat{\delta}_{MLE}$ and $\hat{\lambda}_{MLE}$ of the WS-Weibull model is provided in Figure 11.

The plots of the profiles of the LLF in Figure 11 confirm a unique solution of $\hat{\delta}_{MLE}$ and $\hat{\lambda}_{MLE}$.

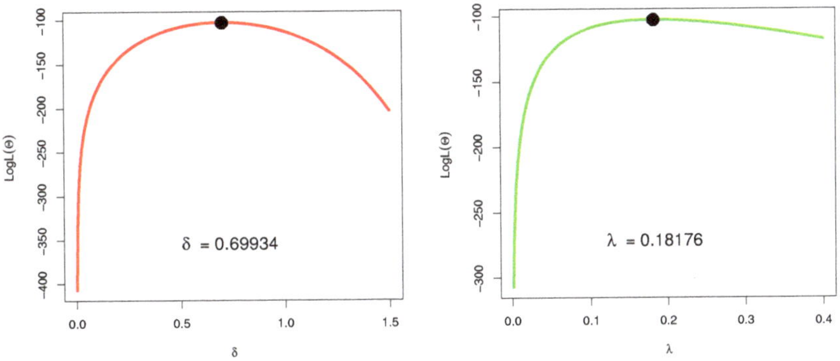


**Figure 11.** The profiles of the LLF of $\hat{\delta}_{MLE}$ and $\hat{\lambda}_{MLE}$ of WS-Weibull using the second failure times data.

Corresponding to the second failure times data, the values of the selection criteria of the WS-Weibull and other competing probability models are presented in Table 13. From Table 13, again, it can be observed that the WS-Weibull is the best probability model for analyzing the engineering data set.

In addition to the numerical comparison of the WS-Weibull distribution and other variants of the Weibull distribution, we show the performances of the WS-Weibull distribution visually. For the visual illustration of the WS-Weibull distribution, again we plotted the empirical CDF, SF, PDF, QQ , and PP; see Figure 12. Based on the visual description of the WS-Weibull distribution in Figure 12, we can observe that the WS-Weibull distribution closely fits the second failure times data.

**Table 12.** Using the second failure times data, the values of $\hat{\delta}_{MLE}, \hat{\lambda}_{MLE}, \hat{\theta}_{MLE}, \hat{\phi}_{MLE}, \hat{\alpha}_{MLE}$, and $\hat{\beta}_{MLE}$ of the fitted distributions.

| Models | $\hat{\delta}_{MLE}$ | $\hat{\lambda}_{MLE}$ | $\hat{\theta}_{MLE}$ | $\hat{\phi}_{MLE}$ | $\hat{\alpha}_{MLE}$ | $\hat{\beta}_{MLE}$ |
|---|---|---|---|---|---|---|
| WS-Weibull | 0.69934 | 0.18176 | - | - | - | - |
| E-Weibull | 0.53984 | 0.76136 | 1.37903 | - | - | - |
| L-Weibull | 0.10962 | 0.64226 | - | 5.09788 | 8.88077 | - |
| NEC-Weibull | 0.52723 | 0.57884 | - | - | - | 0.69887 |

**Table 13.** For the second failure time data, the values of selection criteria of the competing distributions.

| Models | AIC | CAIC | BIC | HQIC |
|---|---|---|---|---|
| WS-Weibull | 208.60920 | 209.86460 | 213.43330 | 211.06550 |
| E-Weibull | 210.90750 | 211.42920 | 216.64350 | 213.09180 |
| L-Weibull | 212.46140 | 213.35030 | 220.10950 | 215.37390 |
| NEC-Weibull | 210.69880 | 211.22050 | 216.43490 | 212.88310 |

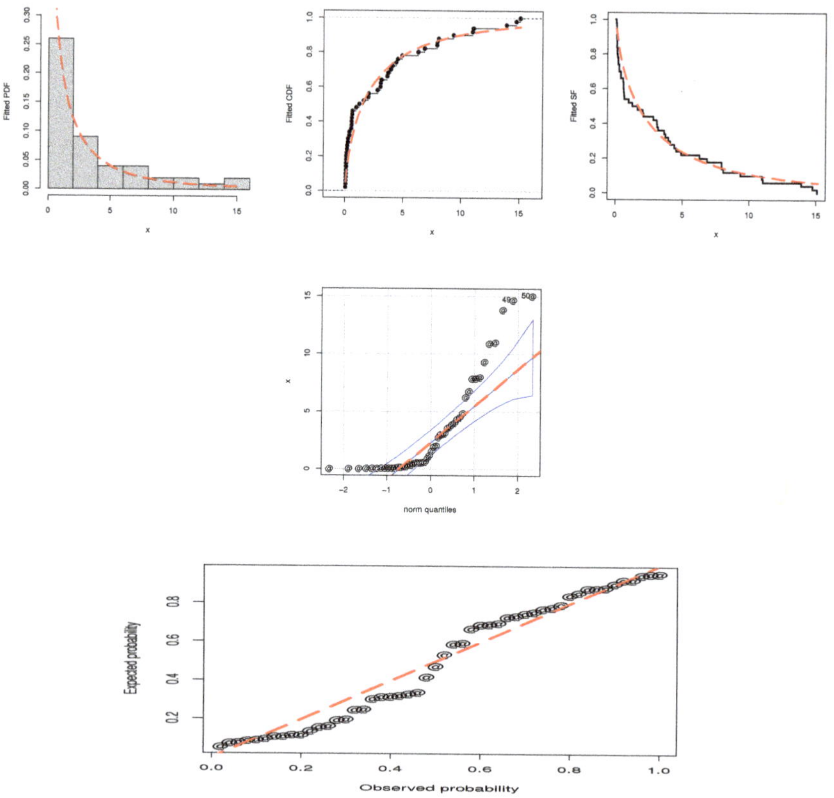


**Figure 12.** A visual illustration of the WS-Weibull distribution using the second failure times data.

## 6. Concluding Remarks

In recent times, the introduction of new families of distributions by using the trigonometric function has received great attention, especially thanks to the distributional flexibility in terms of modeling a wide variety of real data in applied sectors. In this study, we explore a new natural combination of sine-$G$ and WT-$X$ approaches. This combination led to a new method for generating new probability models named a weighted sine-$G$ method. Thanks to the weighted sine-$G$ method, it increases the distributional flexibility of the existing models without adding any new parameters. Certain distributional properties of the WS-$G$ distributions are obtained. Based on the WS-$G$ method, a new probability model, called the weighted sine-Weibull distribution, was studied. Eight different methods were implemented to estimate the parameters of the WS-Weibull distribution. After presenting distributional properties and simulation studies, we checked the practical ability of the WS-Weibull distribution by considering two engineering data sets. The practical applications demonstrate that the WS-Weibull distribution outperforms some well-established variants of the Weibull distribution.

**Author Contributions:** Conceptualization, H.M.A., Z.A. and C.B.A.; Methodology, H.M.A., Z.A. and C.B.A.; Software, H.M.A., Z.A., H.A.-M. and S.K.K.; Validation, Z.A. and H.A.-M.; Formal analysis, H.M.A., H.A.-M. and S.K.K.; Data curation, H.M.A. and Z.A.; Writing—original draft, H.M.A., Z.A., H.A.-M., C.B.A. and S.K.K.; Visualization, H.A.-M. All authors have read and agreed to the published version of the manuscript.

**Funding:** This research was funded by Princess Nourah bint Abdulrahman University Researchers Supporting Project number (PNURSP2023R 299), Princess Nourah bint Abdulrahman University, Riyadh, Saudi Arabia.

**Data Availability Statement:** The data sets are available from the corresponding author upon request.

**Conflicts of Interest:** The authors declare no conflict of interest.

## References

1. Sindhu, T.N.; Atangana, A. Reliability analysis incorporating exponentiated inverse Weibull distribution and inverse power law. *Qual. Reliab. Eng. Int.* **2021**, *37*, 2399–2422. [CrossRef]
2. Liu, X.; Ahmad, Z.; Gemeay, A.M.; Abdulrahman, A.T.; Hafez, E.H.; Khalil, N. Modeling the survival times of the COVID-19 patients with a new statistical model: A case study from China. *PLoS ONE* **2021**, *16*, e0254999. [CrossRef]
3. Shen, Z.; Alrumayh, A.; Ahmad, Z.; Abu-Shanab, R.; Al-Mutairi, M.; Aldallal, R. A new generalized rayleigh distribution with analysis to big data of an online community. *Alex. Eng. J.* **2022**, *61*, 11523–11535 [CrossRef]
4. Moccia, B.; Mineo, C.; Ridolfi, E.; Russo, F.; Napolitano, F. Probability distributions of daily rainfall extremes in Lazio and Sicily, Italy, and design rainfall inferences. *J. Hydrol. Reg. Stud.* **2021**, *33*, 100771. [CrossRef]
5. Chen, P.; Ye, Z.S. Estimation of field reliability based on aggregate lifetime data. *Technometrics* **2017**, *59*, 115–125. [CrossRef]
6. Xu, A.; Zhou, S.; Tang, Y. A unified model for system reliability evaluation under dynamic operating conditions. *IEEE Trans. Reliab.* **2019**, *70*, 65–72. [CrossRef]
7. Zhang, L.; Xu, A.; An L.; Li, M. Bayesian inference of system reliability for multicomponent stress-strength model under Marshall-Olkin Weibull distribution. *Systems* **2022**, *10*, 196. [CrossRef]
8. Luo, C.; Shen, L.; Xu, A. Modelling and estimation of system reliability under dynamic operating environments and lifetime ordering constraints. *Reliab. Eng. Syst. Saf.* **2022**, *218*, 108136. [CrossRef]
9. Zhuang, L.; Xu, A.; Wang, X.L. A prognostic driven predictive maintenance framework based on Bayesian deep learning. *Reliab. Eng. Syst. Saf.* **2023**, *234*, 109181. [CrossRef]
10. Bantan, R.A.; Chesneau, C.; Jamal, F.; Elbatal, I.; Elgarhy, M. The truncated burr XG family of distributions: Properties and applications to actuarial and financial data. *Entropy* **2021**, *23*, 1088. [CrossRef]
11. Reyad, H.; Korkmaz, M.C.; Afify, A.Z.; Hamedani, G.G.; Othman, S. The Fréchet Topp Leone-G family of distributions: Properties, characterizations and applications. *Ann. Data Sci.* **2021**, *8*, 345–366. [CrossRef]
12. Eghwerido, J.T.; Agu, F.I. The shifted Gompertz-G family of distributions: Properties and applications. *Math. Slovaca* **2021**, *71*, 1291–1308. [CrossRef]
13. Eghwerido, J.T.; Nzei, L.C.; Omotoye, A.E.; Agu, F.I. The Teissier-G family of distributions: Properties and applications. *Math. Slovaca* **2022**, *72*, 1301–1318. [CrossRef]
14. Altun, E.; Alizadeh, M.; Yousof, H.M.; Hamedani, G.G. The Gudermannian generated family of distributions with characterizations, regression models and applications. *Stud. Sci. Math. Hung.* **2022**, *59*, 93–115. [CrossRef]
15. Kumar, D.; Singh, U.; Singh, S.K. A new distribution using sine function-its application to bladder cancer patients' data. *J. Stat. Appl. Probab.* **2015**, *4*, 417.
16. Mahmood, Z.; Chesneau, C.; Tahir, M.H. A new sine-G family of distributions: Properties and applications. *Bull. Comput. Appl. Math.* **2019**, *7*, 53–81.
17. Al-Babtain, A.A.; Elbatal, I.; Chesneau, C.; Elgarhy, M. Sine Topp-Leone-G family of distributions: Theory and applications. *Open Phys.* **2020**, *18*, 574–593. [CrossRef]
18. Jamal, F.; Chesneau, C.; Aidi, K. The sine extended odd Fréchet-G family of distribution with applications to complete and censored data. *Math. Slovaca* **2021**, *71*, 961–982. [CrossRef]
19. Jamal, F.; Chesneau, C.; Bouali, D.L.; Ul Hassan, M. Beyond the Sin-G family: The transformed Sin-G family. *PLoS ONE* **2021**, *16*, e0250790. [CrossRef]
20. Tomy, L.; Chesneau, C. The Sine Modified Lindley Distribution. Mathematical and Computational. *Applications* **2021**, *26*, 81.
21. Sakthivel, K.M.; Dhivakar, K. Transmuted Sine-Dagum Distribution and its Properties. *Reliab. Theory Appl.* **2021**, *16*, 150–166.
22. Muhammad, M.; Alshanbari, H.M.; Alanzi, A.R.; Liu, L.; Sami, W.; Chesneau, C.; Jamal, F. A new generator of probability models: The exponentiated sine-G family for lifetime studies. *Entropy* **2021**, *23*, 1394. [CrossRef] [PubMed]
23. Rajkumar, J.; Sakthivel, K.M. A New Method of Generating Marshall–Olkin Sine–G Family and Its Applications in Survival Analysis. *Lobachevskii J. Math.* **2022**, *43*, 463–472. [CrossRef]
24. Ahmad, Z.; Mahmoudi, E.; Dey, S.; Khosa, S.K. Modeling vehicle insurance loss data using a new member of TX family of distributions. *J. Stat. Theory Appl.* **2020**, *19*, 133–147. [CrossRef]
25. Alzaatreh, A.; Lee, C.; Famoye, F. A new method for generating families of continuous distributions. *Metron* **2013**, *71*, 63–79. [CrossRef]
26. Seneta, E. Karamata's characterization theorem, feller and regular variation in probability theory. *PUblications L'Institut Math.* **2002**, *71*, 79–89. [CrossRef]
27. R Core Team. *R: A Language and Environment for Statistical Computing*; R Foundation for Statistical Computing: Vienna, Austria, 2022. Available online: https://www.R-project.org/(accessed on 31 October 2022).

28. Murthy, D.; Xie, M.; Jiang, R. *Weibull Models*; Wiley series in probability and statistics; John Wiley and Sons: Trenton, NJ, USA, 2004.
29. de Andrade, T.A.; Bourguignon, M.; Cordeiro, G.M. The exponentiated generalized extended exponential distribution. *J. Data Sci.* **2016**, *14*, 393–413. [CrossRef]
30. Gomes-Silva, F.; de Andrade, T.A.N.; Bourguignon, M. Ristić-Balakrishnan extended exponential distribution. Acta Scientiarum. *Technology* **2018**, *40*, e34963.
31. Tharshan, R.; Wijekoon, P. A modification of the Quasi Lindley distribution. *Open J. Stat.* **2021**, *11*, 369–392. [CrossRef]

mathematics

MDPI

Article

# Finding the Best Dueler

Zhengu Zhang † and Sheldon M. Ross *,†

Department of Industrial and Systems Engineering, University of Southern California, Los Angeles, CA 90089, USA; zhan892@usc.edu
* Correspondence: smross@usc.edu
† These authors contributed equally to this work.

**Abstract:** Consider a set of $n$ players. We suppose that each game involves two players, that there is some unknown player who wins each game it plays with a probability greater than $1/2$, and that our objective is to determine this best player. Under the requirement that the policy employed guarantees a correct choice with a probability of at least some specified value, we look for a policy that has a relatively small expected number of games played before decision. We consider this problem both under the assumption that the best player wins each game with a probability of at least some specified value $p_0 > 1/2$, and under a Bayesian assumption that the probability that player $i$ wins a game against player $j$ is $\frac{v_i}{v_i+v_j}$, where $v_1, \ldots, v_n$ are the unknown values of $n$ independent and identically distributed exponential random variables. In the former case, we propose a policy where chosen pairs play a match that ends when one of them has had a specified number of wins more than the other; in the latter case, we propose a Thompson sampling type rule.

**Keywords:** best arm identification; dueling bandit

**MSC:** 90-10; 62L99

## 1. Introduction

Consider a set of $n$ players, numbered $1, \ldots, n$. Suppose that each game played involves two players, and that a game between $i$ and $j$ is won by $i$ with some unknown probability $p_{i,j} = 1 - p_{j,i}$. Assuming that there is an unknown player $i^*$ such that $p_{i^*,j} > 1/2$, $j \neq i^*$, our objective is to identify player $i^*$. To do so, at each stage, we choose two of the players to play a game, with the winner of the game being noted. With a policy being a rule for determining whether to stop and make a choice as to which is the best player (namely, which player is $i^*$) or to choose a pair to play the next game, we want to find a policy that, with probability at least $1 - \delta$, makes the correct choice, while at the same time minimizing the expected number of games that need be played before a choice is made. We do this both under the Cordorcet assumption that $p_{i^*,j} \geq 0.5 + \epsilon$, $j \neq i^*$, where $\epsilon \in (0, 0.5)$ is a known number, as well as under a Bayesian model that makes the Bradley–Terry–Luce [1,2] assumption that $P_{i,j} = \frac{v_i}{v_i+v_j}$, where $v_1, \ldots, v_n$ are the unknown values of $n$ independent exponential random variables with a mean of 1.

Our problem is closely related to the multi-arm bandit problem, where the objective is to find the best arm. In the conventional stochastic setting, the learner is asked to sample a single arm at each stage and receive a real-valued feedback generated from the unknown distribution associated with the sampled arm. There is a variety of works addressing the identification of the best arm (see, for instance, [3–6]). However, in many scenarios, such as search engine and online recommendation, it is often difficult to obtain explicit and reliable feedback regarding a single arm, as the feedback often shows the preference of the user among a list of options (e.g., 'A looks better than B'). A more appropriate framework, known as dueling bandit, utilizes the pairwise comparison as actions and learns through pairwise preference. Though most dueling bandit algorithms focused on minimizing the

**Citation:** Zhang, Z.; Ross, S.M. Finding the Best Dueler. *Mathematics* **2023**, *11*, 1568. https://doi.org/10.3390/math11071568

Academic Editors: Francisco German Badía and María D. Berrade

Received: 2 February 2023
Revised: 16 March 2023
Accepted: 19 March 2023
Published: 23 March 2023

cumulative regret [7–9], many recent works (such as [10–12]) were developed under various notions of the best arm.

In Section 2, we look at the Condorcet winner setting. We propose two policies that use a knockout tournament structure to successively eliminate players. We suppose that, in each round, players still in contention are randomly paired and play a match, where a round $j$ match ends when one of them has $m_j$ more wins than the other. The match winners move on to the next round and the losers are eliminated from contention. The winner of the final match is then chosen as being the best. We show how to determine the critical numbers $m_j$ so as to guarantee that the probability that $i^*$ is the chosen player is at least $1-\delta$. We also consider a modification of this rule such that if in a round $j$ match there has not been a winner after $n_j$ games, then that match is ended and both of its participants are eliminated. We present upper bounds on the mean number of games needed by these policies as well as numerical evidence that these rules outperform others in the literature.

In Section 3, we turn our attention to the Bradley–Terry–Luce model. We propose a randomized policy whose logic uses a Thompson sampling approach to determine how to choose the next pair. To utilize this policy, we show how to effectively simulate from the posterior joint distribution of the player's values and how to effectively use simulation to determine the posterior probability that a given player has the largest value.

Conclusions are presented in the final section.

## 2. The Condorcet Winner Model

In this section, we make the Condorcet assumption that there is an unknown player $i^*$ such that $p_{i^*,j} \geq p_0 = 0.5 + \epsilon,\ j \neq i^*$, where $\epsilon \in (0, 0.5)$ is a known number. Let $k$ be the positive integer for which $2^{k-1} < n \leq 2^k$. Our policy utilizes a knockout tournament structure as follows.

**Knockout Tournament Framework**

- Initialization: all players are alive
- For round $t = 1, 2, \ldots, k$
  - If the number of alive players is odd, one of the players is randomly selected and given a bye. The others are randomly paired up.
  - If the number of alive players is even, randomly pair up these players.
  - Each pair then plays a match, consisting of a series of games. Depending on the match rules, at some point one of the players is declared the winner of the match.
  - The match winners along with the player given a bye, if there was such a player, remain alive and move on to the next round. The match losers are eliminated.
- Claim the winner of the match in round $k$ as the best dueler.

In the following two sections, we will present two ways of determining the winner for each match. Note that players who receive a bye in some rounds automatically advance to the next round.

### 2.1. A Gambler's Ruin Rule

Adopting the framework above, we propose a Gambler's Ruin Rule (GRR) to determine the winner of each match. Let $r_0 = \frac{p_0}{1-p_0} = \frac{1+2\epsilon}{1-2\epsilon}$, let $k$ be the positive integer for which $2^{k-1} < n \leq 2^k$, let $m_t^* = \log_{r_0}(2^t/\delta) = \frac{\ln(2^t/\delta)}{\ln(r_0)}$, and let $m_t = \text{ceil}(m_t^*)$, $t \geq 1$, where $\text{ceil}(a)$, called the ceiling of $a$, is the smallest integer at least as large as $a$.

**Gambler's Ruin Rule**

- In round $t$, each pair plays a sequence of games until one of them has achieved $m_t$ more wins than the other, with the one with more wins being declared the winner.

**Lemma 1.** *GRR identifies the best dueler $i^*$ with probability at least $1-\delta$.*

**Proof.** Given that $i^*$ successfully proceeds to round $t$, the probability that $i^*$ is eliminated in round $t$, denoted by $P_t$, can be upper bounded by using the gambler's ruin probability

$$P_t \leq \frac{1 - r_0^{m_t}}{1 - r_0^{2m_t}} = \frac{1}{1 + r_0^{m_t}} < \frac{1}{r_0^{m_t^*}} = \frac{\delta}{2^t}$$

To win the tournament, $i^*$ needs to win all $k$ rounds. Hence,

$$\begin{aligned} P(i^* \text{ is eliminated}) &= P(\cup_{t=1}^{k} \{i^* \text{ is eliminated at round } t\}) \\ &\leq \sum_{t=1}^{k} P(i^* \text{ is eliminated at round } t) \\ &< \sum_{t=1}^{k} P_t \\ &< \delta \end{aligned}$$

which indicates that the probability of finding the best arm is at least $1 - \delta$. □

Next, we show how to upper bound the expected number of games played when using GRR.

Let $N_m(p)$ be the total number of games for a match between players A and B, which ends when one of the players is ahead by $m$, where $p$ is the probability that player B wins each game. The following Lemma shows that $E[N_m(p)]$ is a unimodal function that is maximized when $p = 0.5$.

**Lemma 2.** *The expected number of plays until one of the players is ahead by $m$ is a decreasing function of $p$ when $p \geq 1/2$.*

**Proof.** Suppose that $p \neq 1/2$, and let $r = p/(1-p)$. We first show that $E[N_m(p)]$ is a decreasing function of $p$ for $p > 1/2$. Let, for $i \geq 1$, $X_i = 1$ if player A wins game $i$ and let it be $-1$ otherwise. Then, Wald's equation gives that

$$\begin{aligned} E[N_m(p)](2p-1) &= E[\sum_{i=1}^{N_m(p)} X_i] \\ &= \frac{m}{1+r^m} - \frac{mr^m}{1+r^m} \end{aligned}$$

where the final equality used the gambler's ruin probability

$$P(\sum_{i=1}^{N_m(p)} X_i = m) = \frac{1 - r^m}{1 - r^{2m}} = \frac{1}{1 + r^m}$$

Because $2p - 1 = \frac{r-1}{r+1}$, the preceding gives

$$E[N_m(p)] = m \frac{r+1}{r-1} \frac{r^m - 1}{r^m + 1}$$

As $r$ is an increasing function of $p$, it suffices to show that $f(r) \equiv \frac{r+1}{r-1}\frac{r^m-1}{r^m+1}$ is a decreasing function of $r$ when $r > 1$. Now,

$$\begin{aligned} f'(r) = & \frac{\left(r^m-1+m(r+1)r^{m-1}\right)(r-1)(r^m+1)}{(r-1)^2(r^m+1)^2} \\ & -\frac{\left(r^m+1+(r-1)mr^{m-1}\right)(r+1)(r^m-1)}{(r-1)^2(r^m+1)^2} \\ = & \frac{2mr^{m+1}-2mr^{m-1}-2r^{2m}+2}{(r-1)^2(r^m+1)^2} \end{aligned}$$

Let $g(r) = mr^{m+1} - mr^{m-1} - r^{2m} + 1$. It suffices to show that $g(r) < 0$ for all $r > 1$. Now,

$$\begin{aligned} g(r) &= (r^2-1)mr^{m-1} - r^{2m} + 1 \\ &= (r^2-1)mr^{m-1} - (r^2-1)(\sum_{i=0}^{m-1} r^{2i}) \\ &= (r^2-1)(mr^{m-1} - \sum_{i=0}^{m-1} r^{2i}) \end{aligned}$$

By the arithmetic and geometric means' inequality,

$$\frac{\sum_{i=0}^{m-1} r^{2i}}{m} \geq \sqrt[m]{\prod_{i=0}^{m-1} r^{2i}} = r^{m-1}$$

Thus,

$$g(r) \leq (r^2-1)(mr^{m-1} - mr^{m-1}) = 0$$

Hence, $E[N_m(p)]$ decreases in $p$ when $p > 1/2$. Because $E[N_m(p)]$ is a continuous function of $p$ that is symmetric about $1/2$, it follows that its maximal value occurs when $p = 1/2$, which completes the proof. □

**Corollary 1.** $E[N_m(p) \leq m^2$.

**Proof.** This follows as it is well known that $E[N_m(1/2)] = m^2$. □

Now, let $G_t$ be the number of games played in round $t$, and let $G = \sum_{j=1}^k G_t$ be the total number of games played. As Lemma 2 implies that $E[X_m] \leq m^2$, we see that $E[G] \leq \sum_{t=1}^k 2^{k-t} m_t^2$. This upper bound can be improved by using that the $m^2$ upper bound can be decreased if the best player is involved in the match. Indeed, it follows from Lemma 2 that the mean number of games in a match involving the best player ,which ends when one of the players is ahead by $m$, is upper bounded by

$$b(m) = m\,\frac{r_0+1}{r_0-1}\frac{r_0^m-1}{r_0^m+1}.$$

**Proposition 1.**

$$E[\textit{number of plays}] \leq \sum_{t=1}^k 2^{k-t} m_t^2 - \sum_{t=1}^k (m_t^2 - b(m_t)) \prod_{s=1}^{j-1} \frac{r_0^{m_t}}{1+r_0^{m_t}}$$

**Proof.** Let $R$ be the number of rounds played by the best player. Conditioning on whether the best player plays in round $t$ yields that

$$\begin{aligned} E[G_t] &\leq (2^{k-t}-1)m_t^2 + P(R \geq t)b(m_t) + P(R < t)m_t^2 \\ &= 2^{k-t}m_t^2 - P(R \geq t)(m_t^2 - b(m_t)) \end{aligned}$$

and the result follows because the proof of Lemma 1 implies that $P(R \geq t) \geq \prod_{s=1}^{t-1} \frac{r_0^{m_s}}{1+r_0^{m_s}}$.
□

**Remark 1.** *The upper bound of Proposition 1 is attained when* $n = 2^k$, $p_{i^*,j} = p_0$, $j \neq i$, *and* $p_{i,j} = 0.5, i, j \neq i^*$.

Of other methods considered in the literature, the closest to ours is the rule proposed in [13]. (Other rules, such as those of [12,14], deal with more specific models that typically assume, among other things, that there is a ranking of the players such that the probability that a higher ranked player will win a game against a lower ranked one is at least 0.5. In addition, numerical results cited in [13] indicate that its rule tends to outperform the others.)

Although the rule of [13], like GRR, uses a knockout tournament structure that eliminates half the remaining players in each round, it differs in two ways from GRR. The first is in how a match is decided, with the rule in [13] having a match consisting of a fixed odd number $g$ of games and then letting the winner of the match be the one with more wins. The second way is that $g$ is fixed and does not depend on the round. We now argue that the GRR way of deciding the winner of a match is superior.

Let the m-rule be the rule where each match, in any round, is decided when one of the players has $m$ more wins than the other, and let the g-rule be one where each match consists of $g$ games. To compare these, let $L_1(m, p)$ and $L_2(g, p)$ be the probabilities that the better player would lose a match when using an m-rule and when using a g-rule, when the better player wins each game with probability $p$. (Thus, $L_2(g, p) = P(\text{Bin}(g, p) < (g+1)/2)$, where $\text{Bin}(g, p)$ is a binomial random variable with parameters $(g, p)$.) The following table gives some values for these quantities when $p = 0.6$.

Thus, for instance, if $p_0 = 0.6$, then the use of the g-rule with $g = 77$ would result in each match being 77 games and have a resulting success probability of about $1 - k \times 0.0376$. On the other hand, use of the m-rule with $m = 8$ would lead to the same success probability, with the mean number of games in a match between $i$ and $j$ having a value that ranges between 8 and $m^2 = 64$ as $|P_{i,j} - 0.5|$ ranges from 0.5 to 0. On the other hand, if one wanted a larger success probability, then a g-rule with $g = 93$ and the m-rule with $m = 9$ both would result in a success probability of approximately $1 - k \times 0.02536$, with the g-rule requiring 93 games per match, and the m-rule requiring a mean number of games per match ranging from 9 to a maximum of 81.

The GRR rule modifies the m-rule by allowing a different value of $m$ in each round. Because the number of matches in each round decreases exponentially, it seems intuitive to have shorter matches in earlier rounds, which is what GRR does. For instance, in the case where $k = 5$ and $P_{i^*,j} = 0.6$, $j \neq i$ and $P_{i,j} = 0.5, i, j \neq i^*$, Table 1 indicates that if $m_t = 11, t \leq k$, then the probability of an incorrect choice is approximately 0.057, with the mean number of games needed being 3422.31. On the other hand, the mean number of games needed in this case by the GRR rule with $\delta = 0.057$ is 3093.72 (The means are computed by using Proposition 1).

The next section considers a modification of the GRR rule.

**Table 1.** Comparison of match win probabilities for g- and m-rules when $p = 0.6$.

| $m$ | $L_1(m, 0.6)$ | $g$ | $L_2(g, 0.6)$ |
|---|---|---|---|
| 8 | 0.0376 | 77 | 0.0376 |
| 9 | 0.02535 | 93 | 0.02537 |
| 10 | 0.01704 | 109 | 0.01724 |
| 11 | 0.0114 | 125 | 0.0118 |
| 15 | 0.00228 | 197 | 0.00226 |

### 2.2. Modified Gambler's Ruin Rule

One underlying drawback of GRR is that it may play too many games between two suboptimal arms to determine which seems better. In such cases, one might consider eliminating both arms as none of them show the potential to be best. Therefore, we can often improve GRR by limiting the number of games in each match, and drop both arms if none of them can win the match by the end. The resulting rule, called the Modified Gambler's Ruin Rule (MGRR), is as follows.

**Modified Gambler's Ruin Rule**

- Let $w_t^* = \frac{1}{4\epsilon}\ln(2^t/\delta)$, let $w_t = \text{ceil}(w_t^*)$, and let $n_t = \text{ceil}(3w_t^*/\epsilon)$, $t \geq 1$. In round $t$, play each pair until either one is ahead by $w_t$, with the leader being the winner, or until the total number of games reaches $n_t$, in which case both arms are eliminated.

  As a preparation of showing the strength of MGRR, we need the following Lemma.

**Lemma 3.** *For* $0 \leq x \leq 1$

$$\frac{1-x}{1+x} \leq e^{-2x}.$$

**Proof.** Let $f(x) = (1-x)e^{2x} - (1+x)$. It suffices to show that $f(x) \leq 0$ for $0 \leq x \leq 1$. Now,

$$\begin{aligned} f'(x) &= e^{2x} - 2xe^{2x} - 1 \\ f''(x) &= -4xe^{2x} \end{aligned}$$

Since $f''(x) \leq 0$, it follows that $f'(x)$ is decreasing, which, since $f'(0) = 0$, shows that $f(x)$ is decreasing. Hence, $f(x) \leq f(0) = 0$. □

**Lemma 4.** *MGRR identifies the best arm* $i^*$ *with probability at least* $1 - \delta$.

**Proof.** Given that the best player successfully advances to round $t$ and that she wins each game played in round $t$ with probability $a$, let $P_t(a)$ denote the conditional probability that the best player is eliminated in round $t$. Let $X_i, i \geq 1$ be independent Bernoulli random variables such that

$$X_i = \begin{cases} 1 & \text{with probability } a \\ -1 & \text{with probability } 1-a \end{cases}$$

and let $S_r(a) = \sum_{i=1}^{r} X_i$, $r \geq 1$. Then,

$$\begin{aligned} P_t(a) &= P(S_r(a) \text{ hits } -w_t \text{ before } w_t \cup S_r(a) \text{ does not hit } w_t \text{ within } n_t \text{ steps}) \\ &\leq P(S_r(a) \text{ hits } -w_t \text{ before } w_t) + P(S_r(a) \text{ does not hit } w_t \text{ within } n_t \text{ steps}) \\ &\leq P(S_r(a) \text{ hits } -w_t \text{ before } w_t) + P(S_{n_t}(a) < w_t) \end{aligned}$$

Because $a \geq p_0 = 1/2 + \epsilon$ and both terms on the right side of the preceding inequality are decreasing in $a$, we have that

$$\begin{aligned} P(S_r(a) \text{ hits } -w_t \text{ before } w_t) &\leq (1/r_0)^{w_t} \\ &\leq (\frac{1-2\epsilon}{1+2\epsilon})^{\frac{1}{4\epsilon}\ln(2^t/\delta)} \\ &\leq e^{-\ln(2^{t+1}/\delta)} \\ &= \frac{\delta}{2^{t+1}} \end{aligned}$$

where the second inequality follows by Lemma 4. In addition,

$$\begin{aligned} P(S_{n_t}(a) < w_t) &\leq P(S_{n_t}(p_0) < w_t) \\ &= P(S_{n_t}(p_0)) - 2n_t\epsilon < w_t - 2n_t\epsilon) \\ &\leq \exp(-\frac{(w_t - 2n_t\epsilon)^2}{2n_t}) \\ &\leq \exp(-\frac{25}{24}\ln(2^{t+1}/\delta)) \\ &< \exp(-\ln(2^{t+1}/\delta)) \\ &= \frac{\delta}{2^{t+1}} \end{aligned}$$

where the third inequality uses Azuma inequality (see [15]). Hence, $P_t(a) \leq \frac{\delta}{2^t}$, which shows that the conditional probability that the best player is eliminated in round $t$ given that she advances to that round is at most $\frac{\delta}{2^t}$. However, by the same argument as in Lemma 1, this shows that the probability that the best arm is identified is at least $1 - \delta$. □

**Remark 2.**

- *Since the number of games is upper bounded in each match, we are able to derive the upper bound of the total number of games when using MGRR:*

$$\begin{aligned} \textit{number of game} &\leq \sum_{t=1}^{k} 2^{k-t} X_t \\ &= \frac{3}{4\epsilon^2}\sum_{t=1}^{k} 2^{k-t}(\ln 2^{t+1} + \ln\frac{1}{\delta}) \\ &= \frac{3n}{4\epsilon^2}\sum_{t=1}^{k} \frac{\ln 2^{t+1} + \ln\frac{1}{\delta}}{2^t} \\ &< \frac{3n}{4\epsilon^2}(4 + \ln\frac{1}{\delta}) \\ &= O(\frac{n\ln\frac{1}{\delta}}{\epsilon^2}) \end{aligned}$$

- *There is basically no downside in using MGRR as opposed to GRR. Although $w_t^* > m_t^*$, the difference is usually small and often $w_t = m_t$. To see this, note that*

$$\frac{w_t^*}{m_t^*} = \frac{\ln(\frac{1+2\epsilon}{1-2\epsilon})}{4\epsilon} \tag{1}$$

*Since* $\frac{1+2\epsilon}{1-2\epsilon} - 1 = \frac{4\epsilon}{1-2\epsilon}$*, the Taylor series expansion of* $f(x) = \ln(x)$ *about* 1 *gives that*

$$\ln(\frac{1+2\epsilon}{1-2\epsilon}) \approx \frac{4\epsilon}{1-2\epsilon} - (\frac{4\epsilon}{1-2\epsilon})^2/2 + (\frac{4\epsilon}{1-2\epsilon})^3/3$$

*For an illustration, suppose* $\epsilon = 0.05$, $\delta = 0.01$. *Then,* $w_3^* = 33.42, m_3^* = 33.31, n_3 = 2006$, *so* $w_3 = m_3 = 34$. *Now, if* $P_{i,j} = 1/2$, *then the mean and variance of the number of games needed between players i and j until one is up by m is* $m^2$ *and* $2m^2(m^2-1)/3$ *(see [16] for the variance formula). Letting* $N_{GRR}$ *and* $N_{MGRR}$ *be the number of round 3 games such a match would take when using GRR and when using MGRR, it follows that the mean and standard deviation of* $N_{GRR}$ *are* 1156 *and* 943.46. *Hence, as* $N_{MGRR} = \min(N_{GRR}, 2006)$, *it follows that MGRR stops the match when the number of games played is roughly one standard deviation above the mean of* $N_{GRR}$, *which should result in a reasonable decrease in the mean number of games needed. (For instance, if X is exponential with mean* 1, *then* $E[\min(X,2)] = 1 - e{-}2 = 0.865$.*)*

- *The validity of* $w_t^* > m_t^*$ *follows from (1) upon using Lemma 3.*

The following Table 2 compares the performances of GRR and MGRR when $p_{i^*,j} = p_0$, $p_{i,j} = 0.5, i^* \neq i \neq j$, and $n = 2^k$.

**Table 2.** Mean number of games needed by GRR and MGRR.

| $\epsilon = 0.1$, $\delta = 0.05$ | $k = 2$ | $k = 3$ | $k = 4$ | $k = 5$ |
|---|---|---|---|---|
| GRR | 203.18 | 591.48 | 1482.14 | 3415.14 |
| MGRR | 196.82 | 565.21 | 1378.99 | 3112.67 |
| $k = 3$, $\delta = 0.05$ | $\epsilon = 0.05$ | $\epsilon = 0.1$ | $\epsilon = 0.2$ | $\epsilon = 0.3$ |
| GRR | 2240.49 | 591.48 | 153.51 | 61.40 |
| MGRR | 2156.00 | 563.03 | 148.96 | 75.65 |

## 3. The Bradley–Terry–Luce Bayesian Model

Suppose now that player $i$ has an unknown associated value $v_i$, and that a game between players $i$ and $j$ is won by $i$ with probability $\frac{v_i}{v_i+v_j}$. Furthermore, suppose that $v_1, \ldots, v_n$ are the values of $n$ independent exponential random variables $V_1, \ldots, V_n$ having a mean of 1. As before, our objective is to identify player $i^*$, where $i^* = \operatorname{argmax} v_i$. However, because we are assuming a prior distribution on the values, we now require that the posterior probability that our decision is correct is at least $1 - \delta$. That is, if C is the event that we made the correct choice, then we require that our rule is such that $P(C|\text{all data}) \geq 1 - \delta$. Subject to this constraint, we want the expected number of games played to be relatively small. Because we want to finish as soon as possible and we require that the posterior probability that we have made the correct decision is at least $1 - \delta$, it is clearly optimal to stop as soon as there is some $r$ for which $P(V_r = \max_j V_j|\text{all data}) \geq 1 - \delta$. More precisely, if $w_{i,j}$ is the number of times that $i$ has beaten $j$, then we should stop and declare for $r$ if $P(V_r = \max_j V_j | w_{i,j}, i \neq j) \geq 1 - \delta$.

The rule we suggest for determining the pair to play the next game is a randomized policy that relates to the Thompson sampling approach used in bandit problems (see [17,18]). Letting $V_{(1)} > V_{(2)} > \ldots > V_{(n)}$ be the ordered values of $V_1, \ldots, V_n$, and $P_{i,j}, i \neq j$, be the posterior probability that $V_{(1)} = V_i, V_{(2)} = V_j$, then $i$ and $j$ are chosen to be the next pair with probability $P_{i,j} + P_{j,i}$. We can implement this rule by simulating a random vector $V_1^*, \ldots, V_n^*$ having the conditional distribution (given all data) of $V_1, \ldots, V_n$. If $V_i^*$ and $V_j^*$ are the two largest of $V_1^*, \ldots, V_n^*$ then $i$ and $j$ are chosen to play the next game. Because it is difficult to directly simulate from the posterior distribution of $V_1, \ldots, V_n$, we next develop a Markov chain Monte Carlo approach for doing so.

### 3.1. The Sampling Approach: MCMC

With $w_{i,j}$ denoting the current number of times player $i$ has beaten $j$, the conditional (e.g., posterior) density of $\mathbf{V} = (V_1, \ldots, V_n)$ is

$$f(x_1, \ldots, x_n) = Ce^{-\sum_i x_i} \prod_{i \neq j} \left( \frac{x_i}{x_i + x_j} \right)^{w_{i,j}} \tag{2}$$

for a normalization factor $C$.

As noted previously, we now want to simulate from the preceding distribution and let the next game be between the two indices whose simulated values are largest. However, because directly simulating $\mathbf{V}$ from (2) does not seem computationally feasible (for one thing, $C$ is difficult to compute), we utilize the Hasting–Metropolis algorithm (see [19]) to generate a Markov chain whose limiting distribution is given by (2). The Markov chain is defined as follows. When its current state is $\mathbf{x} = (x_1, \ldots, x_n)$, a coordinate that is equally like to be any of $1, \ldots, n$ is selected. If $i$ is selected, a random variable Y is generated from an exponential distribution with mean $x_i$, and if $Y = y$, then $\mathbf{y} = (x_1, \ldots, x_{i-1}, y, x_{i+1}, \ldots, x_n)$ is considered as the candidate next state. In other words, if we let $\mathbf{y} = (x_1, \ldots, x_{i-1}, y, x_{i+1}, \ldots, x_n)$, the density function for the candidate next state is

$$q(\mathbf{y}|\mathbf{x}) = \frac{1}{n} \frac{1}{x_i} e^{-y/x_i}$$

The next state of the Markov chain, call it $\mathbf{x}^*$, is such that

$$\mathbf{x}^* = \begin{cases} \mathbf{y} & \text{with probability } \alpha(\mathbf{x}, \mathbf{y}) \\ \mathbf{x} & \text{with probability } 1 - \alpha(\mathbf{x}, \mathbf{y}) \end{cases}$$

where

$$\alpha(\mathbf{x}, \mathbf{y}) = \min \left\{ \frac{f(\mathbf{y})}{f(\mathbf{x})} \frac{q(\mathbf{x}|\mathbf{y})}{q(\mathbf{y}|\mathbf{x})}, 1 \right\}$$

The limiting distribution of this Markov chain is the posterior distribution of $V_1, \ldots, V_n$. Consequently, we can approximately simulate from the posterior by generating a large number of states of the chain and then choosing the two largest indices of the final state to play the next game. However, as it probably makes little difference if we choose $i$ and $j$ to play the next game not with the exact posterior probability that these are the two arms with largest values but with a probability close to the exact one, in practice, we do not need to determine many states of the Markov chain. Indeed, it is not clear that using the exact probabilities would lead to improved results. (In practice, for $n \leq 10$, 100 states of the Markov chain should suffice.) Moreover, after choosing a pair and observing the result of their game, then because of the new posterior distribution, which given the result of the last game should not be much different from the previous one, the initial state of the Markov chain used to determine the next pair should be chosen to be the final state of the previous chain.

Whereas the preceding simulations can be used to estimate the probability that a given player is best, we do not recommend using it to determine when to stop. Indeed, if a player's probability of being best appears to have a reasonable chance of being as large as $1 - \delta$, we propose to use the method in the next subsection to estimate $P(V_r = \max_j V_j | \text{all data})$.

### 3.2. The Stopping Criteria: A Simulation Approach

In this subsection, we will present a simulation approach to estimate $P(V_r = \max_j V_j|$ all data). It follows from (2) that for $r = 1, \ldots, n$

$$P(V_r = \max_i V_i | w_{i,j}, i \neq j) = \frac{E[I\{V_r = \max_i V_i\} \prod_{i \neq j} (\frac{V_i}{V_i + V_j})^{w_{i,j}}]}{E[\prod_{i \neq j} (\frac{V_i}{V_i + V_j})^{w_{i,j}}]} \tag{3}$$

$$= \frac{E[\prod_{i \neq j} (\frac{V_i}{V_i + V_j})^{w_{i,j}} | V_r = \max_i V_i]}{nE[\prod_{i \neq j} (\frac{V_i}{V_i + V_j})^{w_{i,j}}]}$$

$$= K\, E[\prod_{i \neq j} (\frac{V_i}{V_i + V_j})^{w_{i,j}} | V_r = \max_i V_i], \tag{4}$$

where $V_1, \ldots, V_n$ are iid exponentials with rate 1.

Thus, we can use simulation to estimate $P_r \equiv P(V_r = \max_i V_i | w_{i,j}, i \neq j)$, $r = 1, \ldots, n$ as follows. In the $t$th simulation run, generate $n$ independent exponentials with rate 1, $V_1, \ldots, V_n$ and let $i^*$ be such that $V_{i^*} = \max_i V_i$. To estimate $E[\prod_{i \neq j} (\frac{V_i}{V_i + V_j})^{w_{i,j}} | V_r = \max_i V_i]$, let

$$X_j(r) = \begin{cases} V_j, & \text{if } j \neq i^*, j \neq r \\ V_{i^*}, & \text{if } j = r \\ V_r, & \text{if } j = i^* \end{cases}$$

and let $b_r^{(t)} = \prod_{i \neq j} (\frac{X_i(r)}{X_i(r) + X_j(r)})^{w_{i,j}}$. Perform the preceding for each $r = 1, \ldots, n$. If we conduct $m$ simulation runs, then the estimator of $P(V_r = \max_i V_i | w_{i,j}, i \neq j)$ is $\frac{\sum_{t=1}^m b_r^{(t)}}{\sum_{r=1}^n \sum_{t=1}^m b_r^{(t)}}$.

In practice, it turns out that the variance of $\prod_{i \neq j} (\frac{V_i}{V_i + V_j})^{w_{i,j}}$ is very large. While this might not make much difference when using the proposed policy, it makes simulation studies of the effectiveness of the procedure difficult. To ameliorate this difficulty, we suggest using the following importance sampling estimator, which in our numerical experiments tended to reduce the variance by over 30%.

An Importance Sampling Estimator

Suppose we are at a stage where every player has at least one win. Let $w_i = \sum_{j \neq i} w_{i,j}$ be the total number of wins of player $i$, and let $w = \sum_{i=1}^n w_i$ be the total number of games played. Further, let $Y_1, \ldots, Y_n$ be independent, with $Y_i$ being exponential with rate $\frac{w}{nw_i}$, $i = 1, \ldots, n$. Then, the importance sampling identity (see [19]) gives

$$E[I\{V_r = \max_i V_i\} \prod_{i \neq j} (\frac{V_i}{V_i + V_j})^{w_{i,j}}]$$

$$= (\prod_{i=1}^n \frac{nw_i}{w})\, E[I\{Y_r = \max_i Y_i\} \prod_{i \neq j} (\frac{Y_i}{Y_i + Y_j})^{w_{i,j}} \prod_{i=1}^n \exp((\frac{w}{nw_i} - 1)Y_i)] \tag{5}$$

Thus, each simulation run generates $Y_1, \ldots, Y_n$ and, for each $r = 1, \ldots, n$, yields an unbiased estimator of $E[I\{V_r = \max_i V_i\} \prod_{i \neq j} (\frac{V_i}{V_i + V_j})^{w_{i,j}}]$. In each run, all but one of these $n$ estimators will equal 0.

We now give numerical examples comparing the Thompson sampling rule with the MGRR rule. It is worth noting that the implementation of Thompson sampling rule does not require knowledge of $\epsilon$, which specifies the least gap between the best player and an arbitrary player. We consider two examples with 5 players, where in the first example we use fixed strength $v = (0.3, 0.5, 0.7, 0.9, 1.5)$ and in the second example we randomly generate strengths from exponential (1) for each replication—that is, all replications in the first example use the same strength vector, whereas in the second example each replication starts by simulating player strengths from an exponential with rate 1.

In all cases, when using the MGRR rule, we take $\epsilon = \frac{V_{(1)}}{V_{(1)}+V_{(2)}} - 1/2$. We run 100 iterations of MCMC to determine the next pair and we utilize importance sampling in estimating the probabilities that check for stopping. The results, using $\delta = 0.05$, are summarized in Tables 3 and 4. The standard deviation columns refers to the standard deviation of the estimator of the expected number of games until stopping.

**Table 3.** Numerical example of Thompson sampling rule where strengths v = (0.3, 0.5, 0.7, 0.9, 1.5). Replication = 5000.

| Method | Percentage of Correct | Mean Number of Games | Standard Deviation |
|---|---|---|---|
| MGRR | 0.99 | 115.612 | 1.39 |
| Thompson Sampling | 0.9886 | 98.9916 | 0.8671405 |

**Table 4.** Numerical example of Thompson sampling rule where strengths are randomly generated from exponential (1). Replication = 3000.

| Method | Percentage of Correct | Mean Number of Games | Standard Deviation |
|---|---|---|---|
| MGRR | 0.99 | 8520 | 354 |
| Thompson Sampling | 0.953 | 248.3 | 13.5 |

## 4. Conclusions

We have considered the problem of finding the best among a set of $n$ players when we learn about the player's skills by successively choosing a pair of players and having them play a game. Our objective is to find a policy that minimizes the expected number of games to find the best player, subject to the condition that the probability of a correct choice is at least some specified value.

In our first model, we suppose that it is known that one of the players, called the best, will win each game it plays with a probability of at least $1/2+\epsilon$, where $\epsilon$ is a known positive value. The policy we suggest is based on a knockout tournament structure, where we have pairs play a match, with the winner of the match remaining in contention and the loser being eliminated. Whereas other policies in the literature using a knockout tournament structure let a match consist of a fixed number of odd games, with the winner being the one with more wins, we let a match end when one of the players has won a fixed number of games more than the other. We argue that our sequential-type matches lead to superior results. We also show how to improve this policy by letting the number of games one must be ahead to win the match depend on the number of remaining players, and by allowing for the stopping of a match after a fixed number of games if neither player has won by then, with both players being eliminated in this case.

Our second model supposes that each player has an unknown value, and that a game between two players with values $v$ and $w$ is won by the player with value $v$ with probability $\frac{v}{v+w}$. Supposing that these values have a known exponential prior distribution, the objective is to minimize the expected number of games needed to identify the player with the largest value, subject to the condition that the posterior probability that our decision is correct is at least some specified value. We present a Thompson sampling type policy and give a simulation approach to estimate its resulting expected number of games needed. The simulation results give evidence of the strength of this policy. Additional numerical work is planned for future research.

**Author Contributions:** Investigation, Z.Z. and S.M.R.; Writing—review & editing, Z.Z. and S.M.R. All authors have read and agreed to the published version of the manuscript.

**Funding:** The second author's work was supported by, or in part, by the National Science Foundation under contract/grant CMMI2132759.

**Data Availability Statement:** Not applicable.

**Conflicts of Interest:** The authors declare no conflict of interest.

## References

1. Braley, R.A.; Terry, M.E. Rank analysis of incomplete block designs: I. the method of paired comparisons. *Biometrika* **1952**, *39*, 324–345.
2. Luce, R.D. *Individual Choice Behavior: A Theoretical Analysis*; Courier Corporation: North Chelmsford, MA, USA, 2012.
3. Audebert, J.Y.; Bubeck, S.; Munos, R. Best arm identification in multi-armed bandits. In Proceedings of the 23rd Annual Conference on Learning Theory (COLT 2010), Haifa, Israel, 27–29 June 2010; pp. 41–53.
4. Azizi, M.J.; Ross, S.M.; Zhang, Z. Choosing the Best Arm with Guaranteed Confidence. *J. Stat. Theory Pract.* **2022**, *16*, 71. [CrossRef]
5. Even-Dar, E.; Mannor, S.; Mansour, Y. Action elimination and stopping conditions for the multi-armed bandit and reinforcement learning problems. *J. Mach. Learn. Res.* **2006**, *7*, 1079–1105.
6. Jamieson, K.; Katariya, S.; Despande, A.; Novak, R. Sparse dueling bandits. In Proceedings of the 18th International Conference on Artificial Intelligence and Statistics (AISTATS 2015), San Diego, CA, USA, 9–12 May 2015; pp. 416–424.
7. Komiyama, J.; Honda, J.; Kashima, H.; Nakagawa, H. Regret lower bound and optimal algorithm in dueling bandit problem. In Proceedings of the 28th Conference on Learning Theory (COLT 2015), Paris, France, 3–6 July 2015; pp. 1141–1154.
8. Peköz, E.; Ross, S.M.; Zhang, Z. Dueling Bandits. *Prob. Eng. Inf. Sci.* **2022**, *36*, 264–275. [CrossRef]
9. Zoghi, M.; Whiteson, S.; Munos, R.; Rijke, M. Relative upper confidence bound for the k-armed bandit dueling problem. In Proceedings of the 31st International Conference on International Conference on Machine Learning (ICML'14), Beijing, China, 21–26 June 2014; pp. 10–18.
10. Jamieson, K.; Malloy, M.; Novak, R.; Bubeck, S. lilucb: An optimal exploration algorithm for multi-armed bandits. In Proceedings of the 27th Conference on Learning Theory (COLT 2014), Barcelona, Spain, 13–15 June 2014; pp. 423–439.
11. Szorenyi, B.; Busa-Fekete, R.; Paul, A.; Hullermeier, E. Online rank elicitation for Plackett-Luce: A dueling bandits approach. *Adv. Neural Inf. Process. Syst.* **2015**, *28*, 604–612.
12. Yue, Y.; Joachims, T. Beat the mean bandit. In Proceedings of the 28th International Conference on Machine Learning, ICML-11, Bellevue, WA, USA, 28 June–2 July 2011; pp. 241–248.
13. Mohajer, S.; Suh, C.; Elmahdy, A. Active learning for top-k rank aggregation from noisy comparisons. In Proceedings of the 34th International Conference on Machine Learning, Sydney, Australia, 6–11 August 2017; pp. 2488–2497.
14. Falahatgar, M.; Orlitski, A.; Pichapati, V.; Suresh, A.T. Maximum selection and ranking under noisy comparisosns. *arXiv* **2017**, arXiv:1705.05388.
15. Ross, S.M. *Stochastic Processes*, 2nd ed.; John Wiley: Hoboken, NJ, USA, 1996.
16. Andel, J.; Hudecova, S. Variance of the game duration in the gambler's ruin problem. *Stat. Probab. Lett.* **2012**, *82*, 1750–1754. [CrossRef]
17. Agrawal, S.; Goyal, N. Analysis of thompson sampling for the multi-armed bandit problem. In Proceedings of the 25th Annual Conference on Learning Theory, Edinburgh, UK, 25–27 June 2012; pp. 1–39.
18. Russo, D.; Van Roy, B.; Kazerouni, A.; Osband, I.; Wen, A. A tutorial on Thompson sampling. *arXiv* **2017**, arXiv:1707.02038.
19. Ross, S.M. *Simulation*, 6th ed.; Academic Press: Cambridge, MA, USA, 2023.

mathematics

MDPI

*Article*

# RKHS Representations for Augmented Quaternion Random Signals: Application to Detection Problems

**Antonia Oya**

Department of Statistics and Operations Research, University of Jaén, 23071 Jaén, Spain; aoya@ujaen.es

**Abstract:** The reproducing kernel Hilbert space (RKHS) methodology has shown to be a suitable tool for the resolution of a wide range of problems in statistical signal processing both in the real and complex domains. It relies on the idea of transforming the original functional data into an infinite series representation by projection onto an specific RKHS, which usually simplifies the statistical treatment without any loss of efficiency. Moreover, the advantages of quaternion algebra over real-valued three and four-dimensional vector algebra in the modelling of multidimensional data have been proven useful in much relatively recent research. This paper accordingly proposes a generic RKHS framework for the statistical analysis of augmented quaternion random vectors, which provide a complete description of their second order characteristics. It will allow us to exploit the full advantages of the RKHS theory in widely linear processing applications, such as signal detection. In particular, we address the detection of a quaternion signal disturbed by additive Gaussian noise and the discrimination between two quaternion Gaussian signals in continuous time.

**Keywords:** quaternion random signal; reproducing kernel Hilbert space; widely linear processing; detection problem

**MSC:** 6E22; 60H30

**Citation:** Oya, A. RKHS Representations for Augmented Quaternion Random Signals. Application to Detection Problems. *Mathematics* **2022**, *10*, 4432. https://doi.org/10.3390/math10234432

Academic Editors: Francisco German Badía and María D. Berrade

Received: 28 October 2022
Accepted: 21 November 2022
Published: 24 November 2022



## 1. Introduction

The importance of Hilbert space theory in statistical signal processing applications lies in the advantageous mathematical properties they gather, namely, the geometry of Hilbert spaces and the structure of function spaces [1]. Some recent and interesting applications of Hilbert space theory can be found in [2,3], to name a few. The characterization of random processes by means of the reproducing kernel Hilbert space (RKHS) approach has shown to be a suitable tool for the resolution of many statistical signal processing problems [4,5]. In the late 1950s, Parzen [6,7] was the one who initially suggested using RKHS methodology in statistical signal processing and time series analysis. More specifically, he provided a functional analysis perspective of random processes defined by second-order statistics and illustrated that the RKHS approach offers an elegant general framework for addressing a wide range of problems that involve inner product computations, for instance, least-squares estimation of random variables and signal detection problems. The underlying idea consisted of transforming via projections, in an specific RKHS, the original functional data into an infinite-dimensional series representation counterpart, which usually simplified the statistical treatment, with no loss of efficiency at all. Afterwards, in the 70s, Kailath showed the usefullness of RKHS formulation in the construction of likelihood ratios and the testing for nonsingularity for several detection problems [8–10]. More recently, a numerical evaluation of the inner product in an arbitrary RKHS in the real domain was proposed and then applied in the approximate representation of second-order stochastic processes by means of series expansions, as well as in the signal detection problem [11]. Although, the underlying RKHS theory in the complex domain has been developed by the mathematicians [12,13], the machine learning and signal processing communities have primarily focused on the case of real kernels [14,15]. However, more recent developments emphasized extending the use of kernel-based formulation towards more complex settings: the kernel-based approach for treating complex-valued random signals has drawing increasing interest in the area of statistical signal processing [16–18]. Likewise, matrix-valued kernels commonly known as operator-valued kernels have been also considered in recent studies, such as in [19–21], where Hilbert spaces of vector-valued functions with operator-valued reproducing kernels for multi-task learning are constructed.

Furthermore, recent higher dimensional kernel algorithms have considered mapping the input samples to quaternion functions because the quaternion domain facilitates the modelling of three- and four-dimensional signals. Comparing the quaternion model to the conventional kernel paradigm, which maps the input sample to a real function, the quaternion model's capacity to manipulate multi-dimensional data has shown beneficial when dealing with quadrivariate signals. This suggests that increasing the dimensionality of the feature space enhances the efficiency of general kernel algorithms [22] and also enables the learning of various nonlinear features contained in the data. In fact, quaternion random signals appear in a variety of fields such as vector-sensor signals, image processing, aerospace, just to name a few, in order to model physical effects where several random components are involved [23–26] among others. The great interest in quaternion signal processing is due to the advantages of quaternion algebra over real-valued four-dimensional vector algebra in the modelling of such data [27–29]. However, the suitable statistical processing for quaternion random signals includes all the necessary second order statistical information accounting for a possible improperness (noncircular) of quaternion processes. The augmented covariance matrix contains too complementary covariance matrices in order to exploit complete second order information. This approach is known as quaternion widely linear (WL) processing. The effectiveness of the WL processing method for estimation problems involving complex-valued and quaternion-valued data has been formally demonstrated [30,31]. Althought the existence of RKHSs, positive definite kernels and an extension of the Mercer's theorem in the quaternion domain are issues addressed in the existing research [22,32,33], the extension to the widely linear processing and the availability of an explicit expression of its inner product are, to our knowledge, still not addressed.

The challenge we face with quaternion random signals and the RKHS framework is to extend these ideas to the more general setting of WL processing by considering the augmented quaternion statistics in order to maximise the use of available statistical information and to exploit all the advantages of RKHS theory for second-order quaternion random signals. In this paper we present a general framework to obtain a novel RKHS for quaternion-valued signals with complete representation capabilities, since it allows us to represent any quaternion function. To every correlation function corresponds a RKHS for which this function is its reproducing kernel. So as a result, the closed linear span of a random signal and the RKHS specified by its correlation function are very closely related (there is, in fact, an isometric isomorphism). The essential underlying idea is that a natural connection between stochastic and deterministic functional analysis is provided by the RKHS framework. Thus, the RKHS can be seen as the natural Hilbert space associated with a random signal and its inner product can be used to express the solutions to a number of statistical signal processing problems. Our research focuses on how the WL approach can be used to construct an RKHS for augmented quaternion-valued random signals. The explicit description of a quaternion RKHS can allow us to propose general solutions to quaternion-valued signal processing problems in continuous-time following a WL processing, for instance, detection problems. These solutions generalise those previously introduced in the literature in particular cases, for example, under the assumption of circular (rotation-invariantly distributed) quaternion signals or for mean-square continuous quaternion signals [34,35]. In fact, we use this quaternion RKHS approach to deal with several problems of detection, as it is the detection of a deterministic signal disturbed by additive Gaussian noise and the discrimination between two quaternion Gaussian signals with unequal covariances in the continuous-time case.

In summary, the major contributions of this paper are three-fold:

1. From the augmented covariance matrix of a quaternion-valued signal, we construct the corresponding RKHS instead of designing quaternion-valued kernels that verify the necessary conditions for the associated quaternion reproducing kernel Hilbert space (QRKHS) to exist, as in [36].
2. First, we develop the properties of the RKHS associated with the correlation matrix of an augmented complex vector process and, second, we obtain an explicit expression of the widely QRKHS inner product that can effectively transform the functional quaternion data into a series representation simplifying their statistical treatment.
3. We show the potential applications of the widely QRKHS for quaternion-valued processes in signal processing problems such as signal detection.

The rest of the paper is organized as follows. Section 2 briefly outlines the basic characteristics of quaternion-valued random signals and, for the sake of completeness, introduces the key results from RKHS theory in the case of vector-valued functions, as this is the main mathematical tool employed in this paper. Section 3 presents a detailed description of the proposed RKHS for quaternion-valued random signals. In Section 4 the QRKHS approach is used to obtain solutions for several Gaussian signal detection problems and a numerical example is shown to illustrate the solution proposed for the detection of a quaternion deterministic signal disturbed by additive quaternion Gaussian noise. Finally, concluding remarks, limitations, and perspectives are given in Section 5.

## 2. Preliminaries and Motivations

Here, we summarize the notations employed throughout the paper and we review some quaternions and RKHS theory facts necessary for the development of the manuscript and in order to make the paper self-contained.

We denote matrices with boldfaced uppercase letters, column vectors with boldfaced lowercase letters, and scalar quantities with lightfaced lowercase letters. Quaternion (or complex) conjugate, transpose, and Hermitian (i.e., transpose and quaternion conjugate) are represented by superscripts $(\cdot)^*$, $(\cdot)^{\mathrm{T}}$ and $(\cdot)^{\mathrm{H}}$, respectively. Throughout this paper, all the random variables considered are assumed with zero-mean.

### 2.1. Quaternion Random Signals

Let $\{\mathrm{i}, \mathrm{j}, \mathrm{k}\}$ be the imaginary units satisfying:

$$\begin{aligned} \mathrm{i}^2 &= \mathrm{j}^2 = \mathrm{k}^2 = \mathrm{ijk} = -1 \\ \mathrm{ij} &= \mathrm{k} = -\mathrm{ji} \\ \mathrm{jk} &= \mathrm{i} = -\mathrm{kj} \\ \mathrm{ki} &= \mathrm{j} = -\mathrm{ik} \end{aligned}$$

A quaternion $q \in \mathbb{H}$ is defined as

$$q = a + \mathrm{i}b + \mathrm{j}c + \mathrm{k}d$$

where $a, b, c, d$ are four real numbers. Quaternions form a noncommutative normed division algebra $\mathbb{H}$, i.e., for $p, q \in \mathbb{H}$, $pq \neq qp$ in general. The conjugate of a quaternion $q$ is defined as $q^* = a - \mathrm{i}b - \mathrm{j}c - \mathrm{k}d$ and the norm of a quaternion is $\|q\| = \sqrt{qq^*} = \sqrt{q^*q} = \sqrt{a^2 + b^2 + c^2 + d^2}$. The involution of a quaternion $q$ over a pure unit quaternion $\eta$ (that is, $\eta^2 = -1$) is

$$q^\eta = \eta q \eta^{-1} = \eta q \eta^* = -\eta q \eta$$

There are three types of Hilbert spaces in $\mathbb{H}$ depending on how the vectors are multiplied by the scalars because of the non-commutativity in the quaternion domain: left, right, and two-sided [37]. This fact may entail some drawbacks, for example, the set of linear operators acting on a one-sided Hilbert space does not have a linear structure. However, by fixing an arbitrary Hilbert basis, it is possible to introduce a notion of two-sided multiplication. The definition of a right quaternionic Hilbert space is given as follows [38].

**Definition 1.** *A right quaternionic Hilbert space is a complete and separable vector space under right multiplication by quaternions,* $\mathbf{H}_q$*, with an inner product* $\langle \cdot, \cdot \rangle_{\mathbf{H}_q} : \mathbf{H}_q \times \mathbf{H}_q \to \mathbb{H}$ *satisfying the following properties, for* $\mathbf{f}, \mathbf{g}, \mathbf{h} \in \mathbf{H}_q$ *and* $v \in \mathbb{H}$

1. $\langle \mathbf{f}, \mathbf{g} \rangle^*_{\mathbf{H}_q} = \langle \mathbf{g}, \mathbf{f} \rangle_{\mathbf{H}_q}$
2. $\langle \mathbf{f}, \mathbf{g} + \mathbf{h} \rangle_{\mathbf{H}_q} = \langle \mathbf{f}, \mathbf{g} \rangle_{\mathbf{H}_q} + \langle \mathbf{f}, \mathbf{h} \rangle_{\mathbf{H}_q}$
3. $\langle \mathbf{f}, \mathbf{g}v \rangle_{\mathbf{H}_q} = \langle \mathbf{f}, \mathbf{g} \rangle_{\mathbf{H}_q} v$
4. $\langle \mathbf{f}v, \mathbf{g} \rangle_{\mathbf{H}_q} = v^* \langle \mathbf{f}, \mathbf{g} \rangle_{\mathbf{H}_q}$
5. $\|\mathbf{f}\|^2_{\mathbf{H}_q} = \langle \mathbf{f}, \mathbf{f} \rangle_{\mathbf{H}_q} > 0$ *unless* $\mathbf{f} = \mathbf{0}$.

Many of the well-known characteristics of complex Hilbert spaces are also present in quaternionic Hilbert spaces, such as the fact that every separable quaternionic Hilbert space has a basis. Once a Hilbert basis is fixed, any right quaternionic Hilbert space becomes a left quaternionic space and vice versa [38].

**Definition 2.** *A continuous-time quaternion random signal is a stochastic process* $q(t) \in \mathbb{H}$ *of the form*

$$q(t) = a(t) + \mathrm{i}b(t) + \mathrm{j}c(t) + \mathrm{k}d(t), \quad t \in T \tag{1}$$

*with* $T$ *a real set and* $a(t), b(t), c(t), d(t)$ *real stochastic processes.*

Likewise, we can use the following modified Cayley-Dickson representation [29]

$$q(t) = \alpha(t) + \mathrm{k}\beta(t) \tag{2}$$

where $\alpha(t) = a(t) + \mathrm{i}b(t) \in \mathbb{C}$ and $\beta(t) = d(t) + \mathrm{i}c(t) \in \mathbb{C}$ are complex signals in the plane spanned by $\{1, \mathrm{i}\}$.

We will denote the correlation function of $q(t)$ as $R_q(t,s) = E[q(t)q^*(s)]$. Moreover, $\mathcal{H}(q)$ denotes the closed span of all quaternion-linear combinations of finitely many random variables $q(t)$ and their limits in quadratic mean (q.m.).

Analogously to the complex case, a complete description of the second-order properties of a quaternion random signal $q(t)$ is attained by considering the augmented quaternion random vector as [27]

$$\boldsymbol{q}(t) = [q(t), q^{\mathrm{i}}(t), q^{\mathrm{j}}(t), q^{\mathrm{k}}(t)]^{\mathrm{T}} \tag{3}$$

This type of quaternion processing that takes into account the quaternion signal and its involutions over the three pure unit quaternions $\{\mathrm{i}, \mathrm{j}, \mathrm{k}\}$ is known as full-widely linear (FWL) processing. The relationship between the augmented quaternion vector (3) and the real random signals in (1) is given by

$$\boldsymbol{q}(t) = 2\mathbf{T}[a(t), b(t), c(t), d(t)]^{\mathrm{T}}$$

where

$$\mathbf{T} = \frac{1}{2}\begin{bmatrix} 1 & \mathrm{i} & \mathrm{j} & \mathrm{k} \\ 1 & \mathrm{i} & -\mathrm{j} & -\mathrm{k} \\ 1 & -\mathrm{i} & \mathrm{j} & -\mathrm{k} \\ 1 & -\mathrm{i} & -\mathrm{j} & \mathrm{k} \end{bmatrix}$$

is a unitary quaternion operator, i.e., $\mathbf{T}^{\mathrm{H}}\mathbf{T} = \mathbf{I}_4$. Thus, the augmented correlation matrix $\boldsymbol{R}_{\boldsymbol{q}}(t,s) = E[\boldsymbol{q}(t)\boldsymbol{q}^{\mathrm{H}}(s)]$ is of the form

$$\boldsymbol{R}_{\boldsymbol{q}}(t,s) = \begin{bmatrix} R_q(t,s) & R_{qq^{\mathrm{i}}}(t,s) & R_{qq^{\mathrm{j}}}(t,s) & R_{qq^{\mathrm{k}}}(t,s) \\ R^{\mathrm{i}}_{qq^{\mathrm{i}}}(t,s) & R^{\mathrm{i}}_q(t,s) & R^{\mathrm{i}}_{qq^{\mathrm{k}}}(t,s) & R^{\mathrm{i}}_{qq^{\mathrm{j}}}(t,s) \\ R^{\mathrm{j}}_{qq^{\mathrm{j}}}(t,s) & R^{\mathrm{j}}_{qq^{\mathrm{k}}}(t,s) & R^{\mathrm{j}}_q(t,s) & R^{\mathrm{j}}_{qq^{\mathrm{i}}}(t,s) \\ R^{\mathrm{k}}_{qq^{\mathrm{k}}}(t,s) & R^{\mathrm{k}}_{qq^{\mathrm{j}}}(t,s) & R^{\mathrm{k}}_{qq^{\mathrm{i}}}(t,s) & R^{\mathrm{k}}_q(t,s) \end{bmatrix} \tag{4}$$

with $R_{qq^{\mathrm{i}}}(t,s)$, $R_{qq^{\mathrm{j}}}(t,s)$ and $R_{qq^{\mathrm{k}}}(t,s)$ the three complementary correlation functions. Likewise, by using the modified Cayley-Dickson representation (2), the augmented quaternion vector $\boldsymbol{q}(t)$ can be expressed as

$$\boldsymbol{q}(t) = \sqrt{2}\mathbf{A}[\alpha(t), \beta(t), \alpha^*(t), \beta^*(t)]^{\mathrm{T}}$$

with $\mathbf{A}$ given by

$$\mathbf{A} = \frac{1}{\sqrt{2}} \begin{bmatrix} 1 & \mathrm{k} & 0 & 0 \\ 1 & -\mathrm{k} & 0 & 0 \\ 0 & 0 & 1 & -\mathrm{k} \\ 0 & 0 & 1 & \mathrm{k} \end{bmatrix} \tag{5}$$

$\mathbf{A}$ is a unitary (one-to-one) quaternion operator, i.e., $\mathbf{A}^{\mathrm{H}}\mathbf{A} = \mathbf{A}\mathbf{A}^{\mathrm{H}} = \mathbf{I}_4$, thus it preserves inner product (an isometry) [39]. Then, the augmented correlation matrix $\boldsymbol{R}_{\boldsymbol{q}}(t,s)$ can be obtained from the correlation matrix of $\boldsymbol{a}(t) = [\alpha(t), \beta(t), \alpha^*(t), \beta^*(t)]^{\mathrm{T}}$, i.e., $\boldsymbol{R}_{\boldsymbol{q}}(t,s) = 2\mathbf{A}\boldsymbol{R}_{\boldsymbol{a}}(t,s)\mathbf{A}^{\mathrm{H}}$, with $\boldsymbol{R}_{\boldsymbol{a}}$ the correlation matrix corresponding to the augmented complex random vector $\boldsymbol{a}(t)$.

### *2.2. Reproducing Kernel Hilbert Spaces*

Let $\mathbf{H}$ be an auxiliary Hilbert space of $m$-variate complex-valued functions defined on $T$, $\mathbf{f}(t) = [f^{(1)}(t), f^{(2)}(t), \ldots, f^{(m)}(t)]^{\mathrm{T}}$, with $f^{(i)} \in H$, $i = 1, 2, \ldots, m$, a complex Hilbert space with a computationally convenient norm (usually a $L_2$-space or a RKHS). Then, $\mathbf{H}$ is a Hilbert space under the inner product

$$\langle \mathbf{f}, \mathbf{g} \rangle_{\mathbf{H}} = \sum_{i=1}^{m} \langle f^{(i)}, g^{(i)} \rangle_H$$

**Definition 3.** *Let $\mathcal{H}$ be a linear space of functions on $T$. We say that $\mathcal{H}$ is a reproducing kernel Hilbert space (RKHS) of functions $\mathbf{f} : T \to \mathbf{H}$, when for any $\mathbf{y} \in \mathbf{H}$ and $s \in T$ the linear functional which maps $\mathbf{f} \in \mathcal{H}$ to $\langle \mathbf{f}(s), \mathbf{y} \rangle_{\mathbf{H}}$ is continuous on $\mathcal{H}$.*

According to the Riesz representation theorem [40], we obtain that, for every $s \in T$ and $\mathbf{y} \in \mathbf{H}$, there is a linear operator $\mathbf{K}_s : \mathbf{H} \to \mathcal{H}$ such that verifies the following reproducing property

$$\langle \mathbf{f}(s), \mathbf{y} \rangle_{\mathbf{H}} = \langle \mathbf{f}, \mathbf{K}_s \mathbf{y} \rangle_{\mathcal{H}} \tag{6}$$

Moreover, for every $t, s \in T$ we also introduce the linear operator $\mathbf{K}(t,s) : \mathbf{H} \to \mathbf{H}$ defined as follows

$$\mathbf{K}(t,s)\mathbf{f} := (\mathbf{K}_s \mathbf{f})(t)$$

for $\mathbf{f} \in \mathbf{H}$. Thus, the kernel $\mathbf{K}$ satisfies the following property, for every $\mathbf{f}, \mathbf{g} \in \mathbf{H}$

$$\langle \mathbf{K}(t,s)\mathbf{g}, \mathbf{f} \rangle_{\mathbf{H}} = \langle \mathbf{K}_s \mathbf{g}, \mathbf{K}_t \mathbf{f} \rangle_{\mathcal{H}}$$

Alternatively, a RKHS can be also defined by means of its reproducing kernel. To this end, let $\mathcal{L}(\mathbf{H})$ be the set of all the bounded linear operators from $\mathbf{H}$ to $\mathbf{H}$.

**Definition 4.** *An $\mathcal{L}(\mathbf{H})$-valued reproducing kernel is a function $\mathbf{K} : T \times T \to \mathcal{L}(\mathbf{H})$ such that $\mathbf{K}$ is self-adjoint and nonnegative-definite. For each $\mathcal{L}(\mathbf{H})$-valued reproducing kernel $\mathbf{K}$ on $T$, there exists a unique Hilbert space $\mathcal{H}$, called RKHS of $\mathbf{K}$, consisting of $\mathbf{H}$-valued functions on $T$ such that*

1. $\mathbf{K}(\cdot, s)\mathbf{f} \in \mathcal{H}$ *for all* $s \in T$ *and* $\mathbf{f} \in \mathbf{H}$, *and*
2. $\langle \mathbf{f}(s), \mathbf{g} \rangle_{\mathbf{H}} = \langle \mathbf{f}, \mathbf{K}(\cdot, s)\mathbf{g} \rangle_{\mathcal{H}}$ *for all* $\mathbf{f} \in \mathcal{H}$, $s \in T$, *and* $\mathbf{g} \in \mathbf{H}$

There exists a bijective correspondence between $\mathcal{L}(\mathbf{H})$-valued reproducing kernels and $\mathbf{H}$-valued RKHS which is central to the theory of vector-valued RKHS. In fact, for each $\mathbf{H}$-valued RKHS, there exists a unique $\mathcal{L}(\mathbf{H})$-valued reproducing kernel $\mathbf{K}$ on $T$ that satisfies the above conditions. For this reason, $\mathbf{K}$ is called the reproducing kernel of $\mathcal{H}$.

Moreover, the RKHS $\mathcal{H}$ can be spanned by the set $\{\mathbf{K}_s\mathbf{f} | s \in T, \mathbf{f} \in \mathbf{H}\}$. For $\mathbf{f} = \sum_{i=1}^{n} c_i \mathbf{K}_{t_i} \mathbf{y}_i$ and $\mathbf{g} = \sum_{j=1}^{n} d_j \mathbf{K}_{s_j} \mathbf{w}_j$ the inner product is of the form

$$\langle \mathbf{f}, \mathbf{g} \rangle_{\mathcal{H}} = \sum_{i,j=1}^{n} c_i d_j^* \langle \mathbf{y}_i, \mathbf{K}(t_i, s_j) \mathbf{w}_j \rangle_{\mathbf{H}}$$

According to the Mercer's theorem for quaternionic kernels [33] and the Quaternion Moore-Aronszajn theorem [32] the existence and uniqueness (up to an isomorphism) of quaternion valued reproducing kernel Hilbert spaces is guaranteed for any positive definite quaternion-valued kernel, i.e., there exists a unique quaternion Hilbert space of functions for which the positive definite kernel is a reproducing kernel. Furthermore, a Mercer's type series expansion can be extended to represent continuous quaternion-valued kernels. Therefore, we address the construction of a QRKHS associated with the augmented correlation function $\boldsymbol{R}_q(t, s)$ which allows us to exploit all the advantages of RKHS theory in the quaternion FWL processing and obtain unified solutions to the quaternion signal detection problems. Based on the RKHS theory of complex random vectors, discussed in the next section, and taking into account the representation of the augmented quaternion vector in terms of the complex vector $\boldsymbol{a}(t)$, we derive an explicit expression for the inner product corresponding to the QRKHS.

## 3. Quaternion RKHS Representation in WL Processing

### *3.1. RKHS Representation for Complex Random Vectors*

Following the procedure developed in [6] for real stochastic processes, we apply the concepts of RKHS theory described in the previous section in the context of random signal processing by considering the correlation matrix of a complex vector stochastic process as the kernel. To do so, let $\mathbf{x}(t) = [x^{(1)}(t), x^{(2)}(t), \ldots, x^{(m)}(t)]^{\mathrm{T}}$, $t \in T$, be a $m$-variate second-order complex-valued random signal defined on the probability space $(\Omega, \mathcal{A}, \mathcal{P})$, and with correlation matrix $\mathbf{R}(t, s)$, whose elements are $R^{(l,p)}(t, s) = E[x^{(l)}(t) x^{(p)*}(s)]$, $t, s \in T; l, p = 1, 2, \ldots, m$.

**Theorem 1.** *Let $\mathbf{H}$ be an auxiliary Hilbert space of m-variate complex-valued functions $\mathbf{f}$ defined on $T$. Assume that $\mathbf{R}(t, s)$ belongs to the direct product Hilbert space $\mathbf{H} \otimes \mathbf{H}$ and define the correlation operator $\mathbf{R}$ on $\mathbf{H}$ as*

$$(\mathbf{R}\mathbf{f})^{(i)}(t) = \langle \mathbf{R}^{(i)}(t, \cdot), \mathbf{f} \rangle_{\mathbf{H}} = \sum_{j=1}^{m} \langle R^{(i,j)}(t, \cdot), f^{(j)} \rangle_{H}, \quad i = 1, 2, \ldots, m$$

*where $\mathbf{R}^{(i)}(t, s)$ denotes the i-th row of $\mathbf{R}(t, s)$, $i = 1, \ldots, m$. Then $\mathbf{R}$ is a linear, self-adjoint, non-negative definite, and completely continuous operator of $\mathbf{H}$ into itself.*

**Proof.** Note that $\mathbf{R}$ is well defined and, for all $\mathbf{f} \in \mathbf{H}$, $\mathbf{Rf} \in \mathbf{H}$. Furthermore, $\mathbf{R}$ is self-adjoint and non-negative definite since $\mathbf{R}(t,s)$ is a correlation matrix and $\mathbf{R}(t,s) = \mathbf{R}^{\mathrm{H}}(s,t)$. Now, from the fact that $\|\mathbf{R}\|_{\mathbf{H}\otimes\mathbf{H}} = M < \infty$ and the Cauchy-Schwarz inequality follows

$$\langle \mathbf{Rf}, \mathbf{g} \rangle_{\mathbf{H}} = \sum_{j=1}^{m} \langle (\mathbf{Rf})^{(j)}, g^{(j)} \rangle_{H} \leq M \|\mathbf{f}\|_{\mathbf{H}} \|\mathbf{g}\|_{\mathbf{H}} < \infty$$

for all $\mathbf{f}, \mathbf{g} \in \mathbf{H}$. Thus, $\mathbf{R}$ is a bounded operator. Finally, a bounded linear operator between normed spaces is always continuous [41] [Theorem 4.42]. □

From this theorem $\mathbf{R}$ is an $\mathcal{L}(\mathbf{H})$-valued reproducing kernel and therefore, there exists a unique RKHS generated by $\mathbf{R}(t,s)$, $\mathcal{H}(\mathbf{R})$. Moreover, $\mathbf{R}$ is a trace class operator, i.e.,

$$\sum_{n=1}^{\infty} \langle \mathbf{R}(t,\cdot)\mathbf{f}_n, \mathbf{R}(\cdot,t)\mathbf{f}_n \rangle_{\mathcal{H}(\mathbf{R})} = \sum_{n=1}^{\infty} \langle \mathbf{R}(t,t)\mathbf{f}_n, \mathbf{f}_n \rangle_{\mathbf{H}} < \infty$$

by using the reproducing property (6) in $\mathcal{H}(\mathbf{R})$ and with $\{\mathbf{f}_n\}_n$ a basis for $\mathbf{H}$. It follows from the spectral theory of completely continuous operators that the set of eigenvalues of $\mathbf{R}$ is an infinite sequence of positive real numbers converging to zero. In order to obtain a concrete structure, let $\nu_n$ and $\boldsymbol{\rho}_n$ be the eigenvalues and orthonormal eigenfunctions of $\mathbf{R}$ in $\mathbf{H}$, then the kernel enjoys a representation as follows [40]

$$\mathbf{R}(t,s) = \sum_{n=1}^{\infty} \nu_n \boldsymbol{\rho}_n(t) \boldsymbol{\rho}_n^H(s) \tag{7}$$

which converges in $\mathbf{H} \otimes \mathbf{H}$ and $\|\mathbf{R}\|^2_{\mathbf{H}\otimes\mathbf{H}} = \sum_{n=1}^{\infty} \nu_n^2 < \infty$. When the convergence of the series expansion in (7) is pointwise in $t,s \in T$, for instance if $\mathbf{R}(t,s)$ is continuous, then the RKHS generated by $\mathbf{R}(t,s)$, denoted by $\mathcal{H}(\mathbf{R})$, can be spanned by the set $\{\sqrt{\nu_n}\boldsymbol{\rho}_n(t)\}$ and the reproducing inner product can be obtained as follows

$$\langle \mathbf{f}, \mathbf{g} \rangle_{\mathbf{R}} = \sum_{n=1}^{\infty} \frac{1}{\nu_n} \langle \mathbf{f}, \boldsymbol{\rho}_n \rangle_{\mathbf{H}} \langle \boldsymbol{\rho}_n, \mathbf{g} \rangle_{\mathbf{H}} \tag{8}$$

for $\mathbf{f}(t) = \sum_{n=1}^{\infty} \langle \mathbf{f}, \boldsymbol{\rho}_n \rangle_{\mathbf{H}} \boldsymbol{\rho}_n(t)$ and $\mathbf{g}(t) = \sum_{n=1}^{\infty} \langle \mathbf{g}, \boldsymbol{\rho}_n \rangle_{\mathbf{H}} \boldsymbol{\rho}_n(t)$.

Let $\mathbf{H}(\mathbf{x})$ be the Hilbert space spanned by the variables of the complex-valued random vector $\mathbf{x}(t)$. Hence, if $\mathbf{f} \in \mathbf{H}$, the notation $\langle \mathbf{x}, \mathbf{f} \rangle_{\mathbf{H}}$ is an element of $\mathbf{H}(\mathbf{x})$ such that $E[\langle \mathbf{x}, \mathbf{f} \rangle_{\mathbf{H}}] = 0$ and $E[\langle \mathbf{x}, \mathbf{f} \rangle_{\mathbf{H}} \langle \mathbf{x}, \mathbf{g} \rangle^*_{\mathbf{H}}] = \langle \mathbf{Rf}, \mathbf{g} \rangle_{\mathbf{H}}$, with $\mathbf{f}, \mathbf{g} \in \mathbf{H}$. Similarly, if $\mathbf{f} \in \mathcal{H}(\mathbf{R})$, $\langle \mathbf{x}, \mathbf{f} \rangle_{\mathbf{R}}$ denotes a random variable in $\mathbf{H}(\mathbf{x})$ that can be expressed as follows

$$\langle \mathbf{x}, \mathbf{f} \rangle_{\mathbf{R}} = \sum_{n=1}^{\infty} \frac{1}{\nu_n} \langle \mathbf{x}, \boldsymbol{\rho}_n \rangle_{\mathbf{H}} \langle \boldsymbol{\rho}_n, \mathbf{f} \rangle_{\mathbf{H}}$$

By denoting $x_n = \langle \mathbf{x}, \boldsymbol{\rho}_n \rangle_{\mathbf{H}}$, it can proved that they are uncorrelated random variables and verify $E[x_n x_n^*] = \nu_n$. Thus, if the convergence of the series expansion in (7) is absolute in $t,s \in T$ the following series representation for $\mathbf{x}(t)$ can be deduced

$$\mathbf{x}(t) = \sum_{n=1}^{\infty} x_n \boldsymbol{\rho}_n(t), \quad t \in T$$

which is the projection of $\mathbf{x}(t)$ onto the subspace of $\mathbf{H}(\mathbf{x})$ spanned by the random variables $\{x_n/\sqrt{\nu_n}\}$.

### 3.2. Quaternion RKHS Representation

Based on the results on RKHSs for complex vector processes described above we derive a RKHS for augmented quaternion random processes (3). To do this, let us consider the augmented complex random vector $\boldsymbol{a}(t) = [\alpha(t), \beta(t), \alpha^*(t), \beta^*(t)]^{\mathrm{T}}$ with correlation matrix $\boldsymbol{R_a}(t,s)$, which is obtained from the Cayley-Dickson representation (2). Assume that $\boldsymbol{R_a}(t,s)$ belongs to the direct product Hilbert space $\mathbf{H} \otimes \mathbf{H}$ and denote by $\nu_n$ and $\boldsymbol{\rho}_n(t)$ the eigenvalues and orthonormal eigenfunctions of $\boldsymbol{R_a}$ in $\mathbf{H}$, respectively. It can be easily proved that $\boldsymbol{\rho}_n(t)$ are of the form

$$\boldsymbol{\rho}_n(t) = [\rho_n^{(1)}(t), \rho_n^{(2)}(t), \rho_n^{(1)^*}(t), \rho_n^{(2)^*}(t)]^{\mathrm{T}}$$

and $\langle \boldsymbol{\rho}_n, \boldsymbol{\rho}_m \rangle_{\mathbf{H}} = 2Re\langle \rho_n^{(1)}, \rho_m^{(1)} \rangle_H + 2Re\langle \rho_n^{(2)}, \rho_m^{(2)} \rangle_H = \delta_{nm}$. Then, $\boldsymbol{R_a}(t,s)$ can be represented by the series expansion of (7) and the RKHS associated can be spanned by $\{\sqrt{\nu_n}\boldsymbol{\rho}_n(t)\}$ with the inner product given in (8). Since the augmented correlation matrix (4) is related to $\boldsymbol{R_a}(t,s)$ by the equality $\boldsymbol{R_q}(t,s) = 2\mathbf{A}\boldsymbol{R_a}(t,s)\mathbf{A}^{\mathrm{H}}$, the eigenvalues and eigenfunctions of $\boldsymbol{R_q}$ are of the form

$$\lambda_n = 2\nu_n, \qquad \boldsymbol{\phi}_n(t) = \mathbf{A}\boldsymbol{\rho}_n(t)$$

with $\mathbf{A}$ given in (5). Let $\mathbf{H}_q$ be some coefficient or auxiliary right quaternionic Hilbert space with a computationally convenient norm (e.g., a $\mathbf{L}_2$ space) with $\langle \cdot, \cdot \rangle_{\mathbf{H}_q}$ its inner product. Assume that the augmented correlation matrix $\boldsymbol{R_q}$ belongs to the direct product Hilbert space $\mathbf{H}_q \otimes \mathbf{H}_q$. Let $\mathbf{H}_*$ be the subspace of $\mathbf{H}_q$ which contains the augmented quaternion functions, i.e., $\mathbf{H}_*$ is the image of $\mathbf{H}$ under the unitary map with matrix $\mathbf{A}$, $\mathbf{A}\underline{\mathbf{f}} \in \mathbf{H}_* \subseteq \mathbf{H}_q$, with $\underline{\mathbf{f}} \in \mathbf{H}$. It is isomorphic to $\mathbf{H}$ and widely linear with the product by scalar

$$\mathbf{f}(t)q = [f(t)q, f^{\mathrm{i}}(t)q^{\mathrm{i}}, f^{\mathrm{j}}(t)q^{\mathrm{j}}, f^{\mathrm{k}}(t)q^{\mathrm{k}}]^{\mathrm{T}} = [f(t)q, (f(t)q)^{\mathrm{i}}, (f(t)q)^{\mathrm{j}}, (f(t)q)^{\mathrm{k}}]^{\mathrm{T}} \in \mathbf{H}_*$$

for $\mathbf{f} = [f, f^{\mathrm{i}}, f^{\mathrm{j}}, f^{\mathrm{k}}]^{\mathrm{T}} \in \mathbf{H}_*$, $q \in \mathbb{H}$. This isomorphism allows us to obtain the following representation for the augmented correlation matrix from the series expansion (7) for $\boldsymbol{R_a}(t,s)$

$$\boldsymbol{R_q}(t,s) = \sum_{n=1}^{\infty} \lambda_n \boldsymbol{\phi}_n(t)\boldsymbol{\phi}_n^H(s) \tag{9}$$

which converges in $\mathbf{H}_* \otimes \mathbf{H}_*$. In particular, the eigenfunctions corresponding to the augmented correlation matrix belong to this subspace, $\boldsymbol{\phi}_n \in \mathbf{H}_*$, and are orthonormal, $\langle \boldsymbol{\phi}_n, \boldsymbol{\phi}_m \rangle_{\mathbf{H}_q} = \langle \mathbf{A}\boldsymbol{\rho}_n, \mathbf{A}\boldsymbol{\rho}_m \rangle_{\mathbf{H}_q} = \langle \boldsymbol{\rho}_n, \boldsymbol{\rho}_m \rangle_{\mathbf{H}} = \delta_{nm}$.

Thus, a RKHS generated by $\boldsymbol{R_q}(t,s)$, denoted by $\mathcal{H}(\boldsymbol{R_q})$, can be defined as the span of the set of the eigenfunctions, i.e., it consists of all augmented quaternion functions $\mathbf{f} \in \mathbf{H}_* \subseteq \mathbf{H}_q$ for which

$$\sum_{n=1}^{\infty} \frac{1}{\lambda_n} |\langle \mathbf{f}, \boldsymbol{\phi}_n \rangle_{\mathbf{H}_q}|^2 < \infty$$

Then, the reproducing kernel inner product of two augmented quaternion functions in $\mathcal{H}(\boldsymbol{R_q})$ can be expressed as shown

$$\langle \mathbf{f}, \mathbf{g} \rangle_{\boldsymbol{R_q}} = \sum_{n=1}^{\infty} \frac{1}{\lambda_n} \langle \mathbf{f}, \boldsymbol{\phi}_n \rangle_{\mathbf{H}_q} \langle \boldsymbol{\phi}_n, \mathbf{g} \rangle_{\mathbf{H}_q} \tag{10}$$

**Theorem 2.** *The expression given by Equation* (10) *defines an inner product on $\mathcal{H}(\boldsymbol{R_q})$, is well-defined and verifies the reproducing property* (6).

**Proof.** First, we prove that (10) really defines an inner product on $\mathcal{H}(\boldsymbol{R_q})$. In fact, by using the properties of $\langle \cdot, \cdot \rangle_{\mathbf{H}_q}$ as an inner product in $\mathbf{H}_q$, it is easy to check that (10) satisfies for $\mathbf{f}, \mathbf{g}, \mathbf{h} \in \mathcal{H}(\boldsymbol{R_q})$ and $v \in \mathbb{H}$ the following properties

(i) $\langle \mathbf{f}, \mathbf{g} \rangle^*_{\mathbf{R}_q} = \sum_{n=1}^{\infty} \frac{1}{\lambda_n} \langle \boldsymbol{\phi}_n, \mathbf{g}, \rangle^*_{\mathbf{H}_q} \langle \mathbf{f}, \boldsymbol{\phi}_n \rangle^*_{\mathbf{H}_q} = \langle \mathbf{g}, \mathbf{f} \rangle_{\mathbf{R}_q}$

(ii) $\langle \mathbf{f}, \mathbf{g} + \mathbf{h} \rangle_{\mathbf{R}_q} = \sum_{n=1}^{\infty} \frac{1}{\lambda_n} \langle \mathbf{f}, \boldsymbol{\phi}_n \rangle_{\mathbf{H}_q} (\langle \boldsymbol{\phi}_n, \mathbf{g} \rangle_{\mathbf{H}_q} + \langle \boldsymbol{\phi}_n, \mathbf{h} \rangle_{\mathbf{H}_q}) = \langle \mathbf{f}, \mathbf{g} \rangle_{\mathbf{R}_q} + \langle \mathbf{f}, \mathbf{h} \rangle_{\mathbf{R}_q}$

(iii) $\langle \mathbf{f}, \mathbf{g} v \rangle_{\mathbf{R}_q} = \sum_{n=1}^{\infty} \frac{1}{\lambda_n} \langle \mathbf{f}, \boldsymbol{\phi}_n \rangle_{\mathbf{H}_q} \langle \boldsymbol{\phi}_n, \mathbf{g} \rangle_{\mathbf{H}_q} v = \langle \mathbf{f}, \mathbf{g} \rangle_{\mathbf{R}_q} v$

(iv) $\langle \mathbf{f} v, \mathbf{g} \rangle_{\mathbf{R}_q} = \langle \mathbf{g}, \mathbf{f} v \rangle^*_{\mathbf{R}_q} = v^* \langle \mathbf{f}, \mathbf{g} \rangle_{\mathbf{R}_q}$

(v) $\|\mathbf{f}\|^2_{\mathbf{R}_q} = \langle \mathbf{f}, \mathbf{f} \rangle_{\mathbf{R}_q} = \sum_{n=1}^{\infty} \frac{1}{\lambda_n} |\langle \mathbf{f}, \boldsymbol{\phi}_n \rangle_{\mathbf{H}_q}|^2 > 0$ unless $\mathbf{f} = \mathbf{0}$.

Now, note that $\boldsymbol{R}_q(\cdot, s)\mathbf{f} \in \mathcal{H}(\boldsymbol{R}_q)$, for all $s \in T$ and $\mathbf{f} \in \mathbf{H}_*$, since

$$\sum_{n=1}^{\infty} \frac{1}{\lambda_n} |\langle \boldsymbol{R}_q(\cdot, s)\mathbf{f}, \boldsymbol{\phi}_n \rangle_{\mathbf{H}_q}|^2 = \sum_{n=1}^{\infty} \frac{1}{\nu_n} |\langle \boldsymbol{R}_a(\cdot, s)\underline{\mathbf{f}}, \boldsymbol{\rho}_n \rangle_{\mathbf{H}}|^2 < \infty$$

where $\mathbf{f} = \mathbf{A}\underline{\mathbf{f}}$ for $\underline{\mathbf{f}} \in \mathbf{H}$ and $\boldsymbol{R}_q(\cdot, s)\mathbf{f} = 2\mathbf{A}\boldsymbol{R}_a(\cdot, s)\underline{\mathbf{f}} \in \mathbf{H}_*$. Finally, Equation (10) satisfies the reproducing property for $\mathbf{f} \in H(\boldsymbol{R}_q)$ and $\mathbf{g} \in \mathbf{H}_*$ as demonstrated below

$$\begin{aligned}
\langle \mathbf{f}, \boldsymbol{R}_q(\cdot, s)\mathbf{g} \rangle_{\boldsymbol{R}_q} &= \sum_{n=1}^{\infty} \frac{1}{\lambda_n} \langle \mathbf{f}, \boldsymbol{\phi}_n \rangle_{\mathbf{H}_q} \langle \boldsymbol{\phi}_n, \boldsymbol{R}_q(\cdot, s)\mathbf{g} \rangle_{\mathbf{H}_q} \\
&= \sum_{n=1}^{\infty} \frac{1}{\nu_n} \langle \underline{\mathbf{f}}, \boldsymbol{\rho}_n \rangle_{\mathbf{H}} \langle \boldsymbol{\rho}_n, \boldsymbol{R}_a(\cdot, s)\underline{\mathbf{g}} \rangle_{\mathbf{H}} \\
&= \langle \underline{\mathbf{f}}, \boldsymbol{R}_a(\cdot, s)\underline{\mathbf{g}} \rangle_{\boldsymbol{R}_a} = \langle \underline{\mathbf{f}}(s), \underline{\mathbf{g}} \rangle_{\mathbf{H}} \\
&= \langle \mathbf{f}(s), \mathbf{g} \rangle_{\mathbf{H}_q}
\end{aligned}$$

with $\mathbf{f} = \mathbf{A}\underline{\mathbf{f}}$ and $\mathbf{g} = \mathbf{A}\underline{\mathbf{g}}$, $\underline{\mathbf{f}}, \underline{\mathbf{g}} \in \mathbf{H}$, and by using the fact that the inner product in $\mathcal{H}(\boldsymbol{R}_a)$ verifies the reproducing property. □

In a similar way to the complex case, we define the random variables

$$q_n = \langle \boldsymbol{q}, \boldsymbol{\phi}_n \rangle_{\mathbf{H}_q} = \sqrt{2} \langle \boldsymbol{a}, \boldsymbol{\rho}_n \rangle_{\mathbf{H}} \tag{11}$$

with $\langle \boldsymbol{a}, \boldsymbol{\rho}_n \rangle_{\mathbf{H}} = 2Re\langle \alpha, \rho_n^{(1)} \rangle_H + 2Re\langle \beta, \rho_n^{(2)} \rangle_H$ real-valued uncorrelated random variables. Thus, $q_n$ are real-valued uncorrelated random variables, $E[q_n q_m] = \lambda_n \delta_{nm}$, and they allow us to obtain the following series representation

$$\boldsymbol{q}(t) = \sum_{n=1}^{\infty} q_n \boldsymbol{\phi}_n(t), \quad t \in T \tag{12}$$

In the following examples, some interesting representations for quaternion random processes are deduced as particular cases of those obtained in this section by developing the RKHS theory in the field of WL processing.

#### 3.2.1. Example 1: Karhunen-Loéve-Type Representation

Firstly, let $q(t)$, $t \in [0, I]$, be a continuous in quadratic mean quaternion random signal. Consider $H = L_2[0, T]$, the space of square integrable functions and let $\mathbf{H}$ be the space of vector functions $\mathbf{f} = [f^{(1)}, f^{(2)}, f^{(3)}, f^{(4)}]^{\mathrm{T}}$ such that $\|\mathbf{f}\|_{\mathbf{H}} = \sum_{i=1}^{4} \|f^{(i)}\|_2^2 < \infty$. Let $\nu_n$ and $\boldsymbol{\rho}_n(t)$ be the eigenvalues and eigenfunctions of the integral operator $\boldsymbol{R}_a$ defined on $\mathbf{H}$ as follows

$$(\boldsymbol{R}_a \mathbf{f})(t) = \int_0^I \boldsymbol{R}_a(t, s)\mathbf{f}(s) ds$$

then, a Karhunen-Loéve-type expansion (12) can be deduced for the augmented quaternion vector $\boldsymbol{q}(t)$ with the random variables

$$q_n = \int_0^I \boldsymbol{\phi}_n^{\mathrm{H}}(t) \boldsymbol{q}(t) dt = \sqrt{2} \int_0^I \boldsymbol{\rho}_n^{\mathrm{H}}(t) \boldsymbol{a}(t) dt$$

This Karhunen-Loéve-type representation was proposed in [28] for a quaternion signal in continuous-time based on augmented statistics and was applied to the problems of estimation and detection.

3.2.2. Example 2: Gaussian Quaternion Signal plus Wiener Noise Representation

Now, let us consider the quaternion random process given by

$$q(t) = \int_0^t s(\tau)d\tau + w(t), \quad t \in [0, I]$$

with $s(t)$ a Gaussian, continuous in quadratic mean, quaternion signal with correlation function $L$, and $w(t)$ a $\mathbb{Q}$-proper (i.e., the three complementary correlation functions vanish) standard Wiener process, with correlation function $R$. Moreover, $s(t)$ and $w(t)$ are independent.

Let $\boldsymbol{L_a}$ and $\boldsymbol{R_a}$ be the correlation matrices corresponding to the complex random vectors obtained from the Cayley-Dickson representation of $s(t)$ and $w(t)$, respectively. In this case, $\boldsymbol{R_a}(t,s) = \min\{t,s\}\mathbf{I}_4$ and $\mathbf{H} = H(\boldsymbol{R_a})$ its associated RKHS which consists of complex functions $\mathbf{f} = [f^{(1)}, f^{(2)}, f^{(3)}, f^{(4)}]^{\mathrm{T}}$, with first derivate $\mathbf{f}'$ satisfying that

$$\int_0^I \mathbf{f}'^{\mathrm{H}}(t)\mathbf{f}'(t)dt < \infty$$

Denote by

$$\boldsymbol{K_a}(t,s) = \int_0^s \int_0^t \boldsymbol{L_a}(u,v)dudv$$

then, the kernel $\boldsymbol{K_a}$ belongs to the direct product space $H(\boldsymbol{R_a}) \otimes H(\boldsymbol{R_a})$. Let $\nu_n$ and $\boldsymbol{\rho}_n$ be its eigenvalues and eigenfunctions, respectively. The following series representation can be obtained for the augmented vector $\boldsymbol{q}(t)$

$$\boldsymbol{q}(t) = \sum_{n=1}^{\infty} \left( \int_0^t \mathbf{A}\boldsymbol{\phi}_n(u)du \right) q_n, \quad t \in [0, I]$$

where the random coefficients are given by

$$q_n = \sqrt{2} \int_0^I \boldsymbol{\phi}_n^{\mathrm{H}}(t)d\boldsymbol{a}(t)$$

and $\boldsymbol{\phi}_n(t)$ are the eigenfunctions of $\boldsymbol{L_a}$, i.e., $\boldsymbol{\rho}_n(t) = \int_0^t \boldsymbol{\phi}_n(u)du$. A similar series expansion was obtained by [42] for real signals and is especially useful in the problems of estimating and detecting a Gaussian signal in additive white Gaussian noise.

## 4. Application to Detection Problems in the Quaternion Domain

### *4.1. Detection of Quaternion Deterministic Signals in Quaternion Gaussian Noise*

The first issue we tackle is how to detect a quaternion deterministic signal that has been corrupted by quaternion additive Gaussian noise. A coordinate-free representation of the augmented quaternion noise based on the QRKHS associated with its augmented correlation function will allow us to obtain a log-likelihood ratio expression which unifies a variety of formulas for the optimum detection statistic (for instance, in terms of series expansions, solutions to integral equations, etc.). Specifically, the detection problem is formulated as follows

$$\begin{array}{l} \mathcal{H}_0 : y(t) = q(t), \quad t \in [0, I] \\ \mathcal{H}_1 : y(t) = s(t) + q(t), \quad t \in [0, I] \end{array} \tag{13}$$

with $s(t)$ a quaternion continuous completely known signal and $q(t)$ a quaternion mean-square continuous Gaussian noise. $\mathcal{P}_0$ and $\mathcal{P}_1$ stand for the probability measures corresponding to the null and alternative hypotheses, respectively. Different signal and noise representations can be used to derive a number of likelihood ratio formulas. In accordance with Grenander's Theorem [43] a method for determining likelihood ratios for continuous-time observation models entails first reducing the observation signal to an equivalent sequence, followed by determining the limit of the likelihood ratio for the truncated sequence. For this purpose, our approach considers the random coefficients obtained from the QRKHS representation of the observation quaternion random signal. Then, using calculations involving RKHS inner products, we compute the log-likelihood ratio to obtain a suitable detector expression.

**Theorem 3.** *Suppose that $\mathbf{s}(t)$ belongs to $H(\boldsymbol{R}_q)$, then the detection problem (13) is not singular ($\mathcal{P}_0 \equiv \mathcal{P}_1$) and the log-likelihood ratio test is as follows*

$$\log \frac{d\mathcal{P}_1}{d\mathcal{P}_0}(y) = \langle \boldsymbol{y}, \boldsymbol{s} \rangle_{\boldsymbol{R}_q} - \frac{1}{2}||\boldsymbol{s}||^2_{\boldsymbol{R}_q} \tag{14}$$

**Proof.** From (12) and the fact that $\mathbf{s}(t) \in H(\boldsymbol{R}_q)$ we can replace the continuous-time problem (13) by the following discrete one

$$\begin{aligned} &\mathcal{H}_0 : y_n = q_n, \quad n = 1, 2, \ldots \\ &\mathcal{H}_1 : y_n = s_n + q_n, \quad n = 1, 2, \ldots \end{aligned}$$

with $q_n$ given in (11) and $s_n = \langle \boldsymbol{s}, \boldsymbol{\phi}_n \rangle_{\mathbf{H}_q}$. Consequently, applying the Grenander's Theorem [43] to the discrete detection problem above we obtain that $\mathcal{P}_0 \equiv \mathcal{P}_1$ since $\sum_{n=1}^{\infty} \frac{|s_n|^2}{\lambda_n} = ||\boldsymbol{s}||^2_{\boldsymbol{R}_q} < \infty$ and

$$\log \frac{d\mathcal{P}_1}{d\mathcal{P}_0}(y) = \sum_{n=1}^{\infty} \frac{y_n s_n}{\lambda_n} - \frac{1}{2} \sum_{n=1}^{\infty} \frac{|s_n|^2}{\lambda_n}$$

Taking into account that $\langle \boldsymbol{y}, \boldsymbol{s} \rangle_{\boldsymbol{R}_q} = \sum_{n=1}^{\infty} \frac{1}{\lambda_n} \langle \mathbf{y}, \boldsymbol{\phi}_n \rangle_{\mathbf{H}_q} \langle \boldsymbol{\phi}_n, \mathbf{s} \rangle_{\mathbf{H}_q} = \sum_{n=1}^{\infty} \frac{y_n s_n}{\lambda_n}$ we prove (14). □

*4.2. Discrimination between Two Quaternion Gaussian Signals*

The second detection problem we study is the discrimination problem between two quaternion random signals which is formulated by the following hypotheses pair

$$\begin{aligned} &\mathcal{H}_0 : y(t) = q_1(t), \quad t \in [0, I] \\ &\mathcal{H}_1 : y(t) = q_2(t), \quad t \in [0, I] \end{aligned} \tag{15}$$

where $q_i(t)$, $i = 1, 2$, are Gaussian, continuous in quadratic mean, quaternion signals with correlation functions $R_i(t, s)$, respectively. $\mathcal{P}_0$ and $\mathcal{P}_1$ stand for the probability measures corresponding to the null and alternative hypotheses, respectively, and verify that $\mathcal{P}_0 \equiv \mathcal{P}_1$, that is, the detection problem (15) is not singular. Let $\boldsymbol{a}_i(t)$, $i = 1, 2$, be the complex random vectors associated with the Cayley-Dickson representation of $q_i(t)$, $i = 1, 2$, respectively. Let $\nu_n$ and $\boldsymbol{\rho}_n$ be the eigenvalues and eigenfunctions of operator $\mathbf{R}_{\mathbf{a}_1}$ on the RKHS $H(\mathbf{R}_{\mathbf{a}_2})$. Then the log-likelihood ratio for the underlying hypothesis test problem is provided in the following theorem.

**Theorem 4.** *The log-likelihood ratio test corresponding to (15) can be expressed as follows*

$$\log \frac{d\mathcal{P}_1}{d\mathcal{P}_0}(y) = \frac{1}{2} \sum_{n=1}^{\infty} \log \nu_n + \frac{1}{2} \sum_{n=1}^{\infty} \frac{1 - \nu_n}{\nu_n} y_n^* y_n \tag{16}$$

*where the uncorrelated random variables $y_n = \sqrt{2} \langle \boldsymbol{a}_1, \nu_n \boldsymbol{\rho}_n \rangle_{\mathbf{R}_{\mathbf{a}_1}}$, under $\mathcal{H}_0$ and $y_n = \sqrt{2} \langle \boldsymbol{a}_2, \boldsymbol{\rho}_n \rangle_{\mathbf{R}_{\mathbf{a}_2}}$, under $\mathcal{H}_1$.*

**Proof.** From the conditions of nonsingularity required we obtain that $\mathbf{R}_{\mathbf{a}_2} - \mathbf{R}_{\mathbf{a}_1} \in H(\mathbf{R}_{\mathbf{a}_2}) \otimes H(\mathbf{R}_{\mathbf{a}_2})$ and that $\mathbf{R}_{\mathbf{a}_2}$ dominates to $\mathbf{R}_{\mathbf{a}_1}$, that is, $\mathbf{R}_{\mathbf{a}_2} - \mathbf{R}_{\mathbf{a}_1}$ is a correlation matrix too [1]. On the other hand, $\mathbf{R}_{\mathbf{a}_2}$ is Hilbert-Schmidt on $\mathbf{L}_2[0, I]$ since $\mathbf{R}_{\mathbf{a}_2}(t, s)$ is a continuous function on $[0, I] \otimes [0, I]$. Thus, there exists an isomorphism between $H(\mathbf{R}_{\mathbf{a}_2})$ and $\mathbf{L}_2[0, I]$ [44], so $\rho_n = \mathcal{R}_{\mathbf{a}_2}^{1/2} \boldsymbol{\psi}_n$ with $\boldsymbol{\psi}_n \in \mathbf{L}_2[0, I]$. Using the series expansion (12) for the observation quaternion signal $y(t)$ with $\mathbf{H} = H(\mathbf{R}_{\mathbf{a}_2})$

$$\boldsymbol{y}(t) = \sum_{n=1}^{\infty} y_n \left( \mathbf{A} \mathcal{R}_{\mathbf{a}_2}^{1/2} \boldsymbol{\psi}_n \right)(t), \quad t \in T$$

we get the following equivalent problem in terms of the random coefficients $y_n$

$$\begin{aligned} \mathcal{H}_0 &: y_n = \sqrt{2} \langle \boldsymbol{a}_1, \nu_n \boldsymbol{\rho}_n \rangle_{\mathbf{R}_{\mathbf{a}_1}} \rightsquigarrow N(0, 2\nu_n), \quad n = 1, 2, \ldots \\ \mathcal{H}_1 &: y_n = \sqrt{2} \langle \boldsymbol{a}_2, \boldsymbol{\rho}_n \rangle_{\mathbf{R}_{\mathbf{a}_2}} \rightsquigarrow N(0, 2), \quad n = 1, 2, \ldots \end{aligned}$$

Then [10] the log-likelihood ratio for $y_1, y_2, \ldots$ is given by (16). □

### 4.3. Numerical Example

We consider the model (13) with the following quaternion signal to show the performance of the proposed detector (14)

$$s(t) = \frac{1}{\pi^2} \cos \pi t + \mathrm{i} \frac{1}{\pi^2} \cos \pi t + \mathrm{j} \frac{1}{\pi^2} \cos \pi t + \mathrm{k} \frac{1}{\pi^2} \cos \pi t, \quad t \in [0, 1]$$

and the quaternion noise $q(t) = \sqrt{2} x(t) e^{\mathrm{i}\theta} + \mathrm{k} \sqrt{2} x(t) e^{\mathrm{i}\theta}$, with $x(t)$ the zero-mean Wiener real process and $\theta$ an standard Normal random variable, independent of $x(t)$. Moreover, we consider $H = L_2[0, 1]$, the space of square integrable complex functions. Figure 1 shows the detection probability $P = 1 - \psi(\psi^{-1}(1 - \alpha) - d)$ ($\psi$ denotes the cumulative probability distribution function of a $N(0, 1)$ random variable) in relation to the false-alarm probability $\alpha$ by using the Neyman-Pearson criterion, in terms of the signal-to-noise ratio

$$d^2 = ||s||_{\mathbf{R}_q}^2 = \sum_{n=1}^{\infty} \frac{1}{\lambda_n} |\langle s, \boldsymbol{\phi}_n \rangle_{\mathbf{H}_q}|^2$$

obtained with $n = 5$ (blue line) and $n = 10$ (red line) terms, respectively.

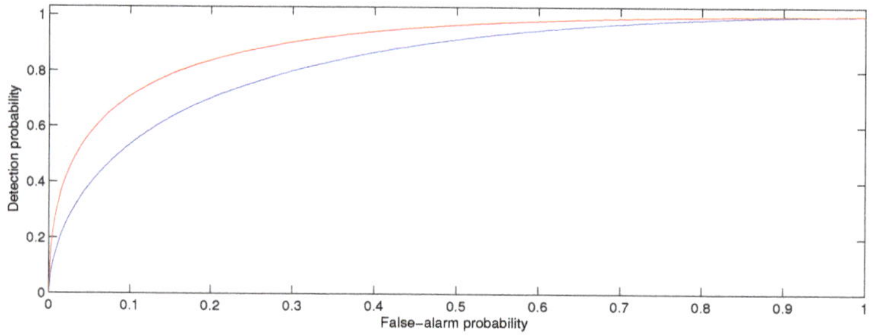


**Figure 1.** Detection probability versus the false-alarm probability.

## 5. Conclusions

A generic RKHS framework for the statistical analysis of augmented quaternion random vectors has been presented. First, we have developed the properties of the RKHS associated with the correlation matrix of an augmented complex vector process and, second, we have obtained an explicit expression of the widely QRKHS inner product that can effectively transform the functional quaternion data into a series representation simplifying their statistical treatment. This novel QRKHS has allowed us to exploit the full advantages of the RKHS theory to propose general solutions to WL processing problems in continuous-time, for instance, detection problems. These solutions have shown to generalise those previously introduced in the literature in particular cases, for example, under the assumption of proper (rotation-invariantly distributed) quaternion signals or for mean-square continuous quaternion signals [34,35]. In particular, the quaternion RKHS approach has been applied to deal with the detection of a deterministic signal disturbed by additive Gaussian noise and the discrimination between two quaternion Gaussian signals with unequal covariances in the continuous-time case. Note that, in practice, the determination of eigenvalues and eigenfunctions can be quite involved. However, it is possible to employ a numerical method of solution, such as the Rayleigh-Ritz method (see [45] for a detailed study about its practical application).

Further research related to other hypercomplex systems, such as the tessarines, will be explored in the future to study possible extensions of the results provided in this work.

**Funding:** This research was funded by I+D+i Project with reference number 1256911, under «Programa Operativo FEDER Andalucía 2014–2020», Junta de Andalucía, and the Project EI-FQM2-2021 of «Plan de Apoyo a la Investigación» of the University of Jaén, Spain.

**Institutional Review Board Statement:** Not applicable.

**Informed Consent Statement:** Not applicable.

**Data Availability Statement:** Not applicable.

**Conflicts of Interest:** The author declares no conflict of interest. The funders had no role in the design of the study: in the collection, analyses, or interpretation of data; in the writing of the manuscript, or in the decision to publish the results.

## Abbreviations

The following abbreviations are used in this manuscript:

| | |
|---|---|
| RKHS | Reproducing kernel Hilbert space |
| QRKHS | Quaternion reproducing kernel Hilbert space |
| WL | Widely linear |
| FWL | Full-widely linear |

## References


1. Aronszajn, N. Theory of reproducing kernels. *Trans. Amer. Math. Soc.* **1950**, *68*, 337–404. [CrossRef]
2. Liu, R.; Long, J.; Zhang, P.; Lake, R.E.; Gao, H.; Pappas, D.P.; Li, F. Efficient quantum state tomography with auxiliary Hilbert space. *arXiv* **2019**, arXiv:1908.00577.
3. Shafie, K.; Faridrohani, M.R.; Noorbaloochi, S.; Moradi Rekabdarkolaee, H. A global Bayes factor for observations on an infinite-dimensional Hilbert space. Applied to Signal Detection in fMRI. *Austrian J. Stat.* **2021**, *50*, 66–76. [CrossRef]
4. Small, C.G.; McLeish, D.L. *Hilbert Space Methods in Probability and Statistical Inference*; John Wiley and Sons: Hoboken, NJ, USA, 2011.
5. Berlinet, A.; Thomas-Agnan, C. *Reproducing Kernel Hilbert Spaces in Probability and Statistics*; Springer: Boston, MA, USA, 2012.
6. Parzen, E. Extraction and detection problems and reproducing kernel Hilbert space. *J. SIAM Control Ser. A* **1962**, *1*, 35–62. [CrossRef]
7. Parzen, E. Statistical inference on time series by Hilbert space methods. In *Proceedings of a Symposium on Time Series Analysis*; Rosenblatt, M., Ed.; Wiley: New York, NY, USA, 1963; pp. 253–382.
8. Kailath, T. An RKHS approach to detection and estimation problems-part I: Deterministic signals in Gaussian noise. *IEEE Trans. Inform. Theory* **1971**, *17*, 530–549. [CrossRef]
9. Kailath, T.; Duttweiler, D. An RKHS approach to detection and estimation problems-part III: Generalized innovations representations and a likelihood-ratio formula. *IEEE Trans. Inform. Theory* **1972**, *18*, 30–45. [CrossRef]
10. Kailath, T.; Weinert, H.L. An RKHS approach to detection and estimation problems-part II: Gaussian signal detection. *IEEE Trans. Inform. Theory* **1975**, *21*, 15–23. [CrossRef]
11. Oya, A.; Navarro-Moreno, J.; Ruiz-Molina, J.C. Numerical evaluation of Reproducing Kernel Hilbert Space inner products. *IEEE Trans. Signal Proc.* **2009**, *57*, 1227–1233. [CrossRef]
12. Kobayashi, H. Representations of Complex-Valued Vector Processes and Their Application to Estimation and Detection. Ph.D. Thesis, Department of Electrical Engineering, Princeton University, Princeton, NJ, USA, 1967.

13. Paulsen, V.I.; Raghupathi, M. *An Introduction to the Theory of Reproducing Kernel Hilbert Spaces*; Cambridge University Press: Cambridge, UK, 2016. [CrossRef]
14. Hofmann, T.; Scholkopf, B.; Smola, A.J. *A Review of Kernel Methods in Machine Learning*; Technical Report 156; Max Planck Institute for Biological Cybernetics: Tübingen, Baden-Württemberg, Germany, 2006. Available online: https://www.kyb.tuebingen.mpg.de/ (accessed on 2 February 2022).
15. Rojo-Álvarez, J.L.; Martínez-Ramón, M.; Muñoz-Marí, J.; Camps-Valls, G. Reproducing Kernel Hilbert Space Models for Signal Processing. In *Digital Signal Processing with Kernel Methods*; Wiley-IEEE Press: Hoboken, NJ, USA, 2018; pp. 241–279. [CrossRef]
16. Bouboulis, P.; Slavakis, K.; Theodoridis, S. Adaptive Learning in Complex Reproducing Kernel Hilbert Spaces employing Wirtinger's subgradients. *IEEE Trans. Neural Netw.* **2012**, *22*, 425–438. [CrossRef]
17. Bouboulis, P.; Theodoridis, S.; Mavroforakis, M. The augmented complex kernel LMS. *IEEE Trans. Signal Proc.* **2012**, *60*, 4962–4967. [CrossRef]
18. Boloix-Tortosa, R.; Murillo-Fuentes, J. J.; Santos, I.; Pérez-Cruz, F. Widely linear complex-valued kernel methods for regression. *IEEE Trans. Signal Proc.* **2017**, *65*, 5240–5248. [CrossRef]
19. Micchelli, C.A.; Pontil, M. Learning the kernel function via regularization. *J. Mach. Learn. Res.* **2005**, *6*, 1099–1125.
20. Carmeli, C.; De Vito, E.; Toigo, A. Vector valued Reproducing Kernel Hilbert Spaces of integrable functions and Mercer theorem. *Anal. Appl.* **2006**, *4*, 377–408. [CrossRef]
21. Kadri, H.; Duflos, E.; Preux, P.; Canu, S.; Rakotomamonjy, A.; Audiffren, J. Operator-valued kernels for learning from functional responde data. *J. Mach. Learn. Res.* **2015**, *16*, 1–54.
22. Tobar, F. A.; Mandic, D.P. The quaternion kernel least squares. In Proceedings of the IEEE International Conference on Acoustics, Speech and Signal Processing, Vancouver, BC, Canada, 26–30 May 2013; pp. 6128–6132.
23. Chen, B.; Liu, Q.; Sun, X.; Li, X.; Shu, H. Removing gaussian noise for color images by quaternion representation and optimisation of weights in non-local means filter. *IET Image Proc.* **2013**, *8*, 591–600. [CrossRef]
24. Tao, J.; Chang, W. Adaptive beamforming based on complex quaternion processes. *Math. Probl. Eng.* **2014**, *5*, 1–10. [CrossRef]
25. Bill, J.; Champagne, L.; Cox, B.; Bihl, T. Meta-Heuristic Optimization Methods for Quaternion-Valued Neural Networks. *Mathematics* **2021**, *9*, 938. [CrossRef]
26. Xia, Y.; Jahanchahi, C.; Mandic, D.P. Quaternion-valued echo state networks. *IEEE Trans. Neural Netw. Learn. Syst.* **2015**, *26*, 663–673. [PubMed]
27. Cheong Took, C.; Mandic, D.P. Augmented second-order statistics of quaternion random signals. *Signal Process* **2011**, *91*, 214–224. [CrossRef]
28. Navarro-Moreno, J.; Fernandez-Alcala, R.; Ruiz-Molina, J.C. A quaternion widely linear series expansion and its applications. *IEEE Signal Process Lett.* **2012**, *19*, 868–871. [CrossRef]
29. Vía, J.; Ramírez, D.; Santamaría, I. Properness and widely linear processing of quaternion random vectors. *IEEE Trans. Inform. Theory* **2010**, *56*, 3502–3515. [CrossRef]
30. Picinbono, B.; Chevalier, P. Widely linear estimation with complex data. *IEEE Trans. Signal Process* **1995**, *43*, 2030–2033. [CrossRef]
31. Nitta, T. A theoretical foundation for the widely linear processing of quaternion-valued data. *Appl. Math.* **2013**, *4*, 1616–1620. [CrossRef]
32. Tobar, F.A.; Mandic, D.P. Quaternion Reproducing Kernel Hilbert Spaces: Existence and uniqueness conditions. *IEEE Trans. Inform. Theory* **2014**, *60*, 5736–5749. [CrossRef]
33. Shilton, A. *Mercer's Theorem for Quaternionic Kernels*; Technical Report; Department of Electrical and Electronic Engineering, University Of Melbourne: Melbourne, Australia, 2007. Available online: http://www.ee.unimelb.edu.au/pgrad/apsh/publications/ (accessed on 8 December 2021).
34. Le Bihan, N.; Amblard, P.O. Detection and estimation of gaussian proper quaternion valued random processes. In Proceedings of the IMA Conference on Mathematics in Signal Process, The Royal Agricultural College, Cirencester, UK, 18–20 December 2006; pp. 23–26.
35. Navarro-Moreno, J.; Ruiz-Molina, J.C.; Oya, A.; Quesada-Rubio, J.M. Detection of continuous-time quaternion signals in additive noise. *EURASIP J. Adv. Signal Process* **2012**, *234*, 1–7. [CrossRef]
36. Tobar, F.A.; Mandic, D.P. Design of positive-definite quaternion kernels. *IEEE Signal Process Lett.* **2015**, *22*, 2117–2121. [CrossRef]
37. Thirulogasanthar, K.; Ali, S.T. General construction of reproducing kernels on a quaternionic Hilbert space. *Rev. Math. Phys.* **2017**, 29, 1750017 . [CrossRef]
38. Muraleetharan, B.; Thirulogasanthar, K. Berberian Extension and its S-spectra in a Quaternionic Hilbert Space. *Adv. Appl. Clifford Algebras.* **2020**, *30*, 1–18. [CrossRef]
39. Ghiloni, R.; Moretti, V.; Perotti, A. Continuous slice functional calculus in quaternionic Hilbert Spaces. *Rev. Math. Phys.* **2013**, 25, 1350006 . [CrossRef]
40. Riesz, F.; Nagy, B.S. *Functional Analysis*; Dover Publications: New York, NY, USA, 1990.
41. Friedman, A. *Foundations of Modern Analysis*; Dover Publications: New York, NY, USA, 1982.
42. Shepp, L. Radon-Nikodym derivatives of Gaussian measures. *Ann. Math. Stat.* **1966**, *37*, 321–354. [CrossRef]
43. Poor, H.V. *An Introduction to Signal Detection and Estimation*; Springer: New York, NY, USA, 1994.

44. Golosov, Y.I.; Tempelman, A.A. On the equivalence of measures corresponding to Gaussian vector-valued functions. *Dokl. Akad. Nauk SSSR* **1969**, *184*, 1271–1274.
45. Oya, A.; Navarro-Moreno, J.; Ruiz-Molina, J.C. Widely linear simulation of continuous-time complex-valued random signals. *IEEE Trans. Signal Process Lett.* **2011**, *18*, 513–516. [CrossRef]

*mathematics* MDPI

*Article*

# Optimal Control with Partially Observed Regime Switching: Discounted and Average Payoffs

**Beatris Adriana Escobedo-Trujillo [1,*], Javier Garrido-Meléndez [1], Gerardo Alcalá [2] and J. D. Revuelta-Acosta [1]**

1 Facultad de Ingeniería Campus Coatzacoalcos, Universidad Veracruzana, Coatzacoalcos 96535, Veracruz, Mexico; jgarrido@uv.mx (J.G.-M.); jrevuelta@uv.mx (J.D.R.-A.)
2 Centro de Investigación en Recursos Energéticos y Sustentables, Universidad Veracruzana, Coatzacoalcos 96535, Veracruz, Mexico; galcala@uv.mx
* Correspondence: bescobedo@uv.mx

**Abstract:** We consider an optimal control problem with the discounted and average payoff. The reward rate (or cost rate) can be unbounded from above and below, and a Markovian switching stochastic differential equation gives the state variable dynamic. Markovian switching is represented by a hidden continuous-time Markov chain that can only be observed in Gaussian white noise. Our general aim is to give conditions for the existence of optimal Markov stationary controls. This fact generalizes the conditions that ensure the existence of optimal control policies for optimal control problems completely observed. We use standard dynamic programming techniques and the method of hidden Markov model filtering to achieve our goals. As applications of our results, we study the discounted linear quadratic regulator (LQR) problem, the ergodic LQR problem for the modeled quarter-car suspension, the average LQR problem for the modeled quarter-car suspension with damp, and an explicit application for an optimal pollution control.

**Keywords:** ergodicity; filtering theory; hidden Markov models; partial observation; Wonham filter

**MSC:** 49N05; 49N10; 49N30; 49N90; 93C41

**Citation:** Escobedo-Trujillo, B.A.; Garrido-Meléndez, J.; Alcalá, G.; Revuelta-Acosta, J.D. Optimal Control with Partially Observed Regime Switching: Discounted and Average Payoffs. *Mathematics* **2022**, *10*, 2073. https://doi.org/10.3390/math10122073

Academic Editor: Panagiotis-Christos Vassiliou

Received: 18 May 2022
Accepted: 10 June 2022
Published: 15 June 2022



## 1. Introduction

In recent years, there has been more attention to a class of optimal control problems where the dynamic systems are governed means switching diffusions in which the switching is modeled by a continuous-time Markov chain ($\psi$) with unobservable hidden states (also known as partially observed optimal control problems). In these problems, an observable process $y$ whose outcomes are "influenced" by the outcomes of $\psi$ in a known way is assumed. Since $\psi$ cannot be observed directly, the goal is to learn about $\psi$ by observing $y$. Following the last mentioned, this article concerns with an optimal control problem with discounted and ergodic payoff in which the dynamic system $x(t)$ evolves according to a Markovian regime-switching diffusion $dx(t) = f(x(t), \psi(t))dt + \sigma(x(t), \psi(t))dW(t)$ for given continuous functions $f$ and $\sigma$. The reward rate is allowed to be unbounded from above and from below. In this paper, the Wonham filter to estimate the states of the Markov chain from the observable evolution of a given process ($y$) is used. As a result, the original system $x(t)$ is converted to a completely observable one $\overline{x}(t)$.

Our main results extend the dynamic programming technique to this family of stochastic optimal control problems with reward (or cost) rate per unit of time unbounded and Markovian regime-switching diffusions. The regime switching is modeled by a continuous-time Markov chain ($\psi$) with unobservable states. Early works include research on an optimal control problem with an ergodic payoff, considering that the dynamic system evolves according to Markovian switching diffusions. However, this diffusion does not depend on a hidden Markov chain [1]. Research on deriving the dynamic programming principle for a partially observed optimal control problem in which the dynamic system is governed by a discrete-time Markov control process taking values in a finite-dimensional space has also been proposed [2]. Finally, one paper studied the optimal control with Markovian switching that is completely observable and rewards rate unbounded [3]. As an application of our results, we study the discounted linear quadratic regulator (LQR) problem, the ergodic LQR problem for the modeled quarter-car suspension, the average (ergodic) LQR problem for the modeled quarter-car suspension with damp, and an explicit application for an optimal pollution control. Other applications with bounded payoff different from those studied in this work are found in [4–6].

The objective of the theory of controlled regime-switching diffusions is to model controlled diffusion systems whose dynamics are affected by discrete phenomena. In these systems, the discrete phenomena are modeled by a Markov chain in continuous time, whose states represent the discrete phenomenon involved. There is an extensive list of references dealing with the case of completely observable stochastic optimal control in which a switching diffusion governs the stochastic systems. A literature review includes the textbooks [7,8] and the papers [9–14], with several applications, including optimization portfolios, wireless communication systems, and wind turbines, among others.

Generally, to solve unobserved optimal control problems, where the dynamic systems are governed by a hidden Markovian switching diffusion, it is necessary to transform them into completely observed ones, which in our case is done using a Wonham filter.

This Wonham filter estimates the hidden state of the Markov chain from the observable evolution of the process $y$. When these estimates are replaced in the original system, this becomes a completely observable system [15,16] and ([17], Section 22.3). The numerical results for Wonham's filter are given in [18].

The paper is organized as follows: in Section 1, an introduction is given. In Section 2, the main assumptions are given. In this section, the partially observable system is converted into an observable system. The conditions to ensure the existence of optimal solutions for the optimal control problem with discounted payoff are given in Section 3. In Section 4, the conditions to ensure the existence of optimal solutions for the optimal control problem with average payoff are deduced. To illustrate our results, four applications are developed: an application on a linear quadratic regulator (LQR) with discounted payoff (Section 5); the development of a model of a quarter-car suspension LQR with an average payoff (Section 6); the study of an optimal control of a vehicle active suspension system with damp (Section 7); and an explicit application for an optimal pollution control (Section 8).

## 2. Formulation of the Problem

This work focuses on controlled hybrid stochastic differential Equations (HSDE) under partial observation. To explain this, first, we consider the stochastic differential equations of the form:

$$dx(t) = b(x(t), \psi(t), u(t))dt + \sigma(x(t), \psi(t))dW(t), \quad x(0) = x_0, \ \psi(0) = i, \tag{1}$$

where $b : \mathbb{R}^n \times E \times \mathcal{U} \to \mathbb{R}^n$ and $\sigma : \mathbb{R}^n \times E \to \mathbb{R}^{n\times d}$ in (1) depend on a finite state and time-continuous irreducible and aperiodic Markov chain $\psi(\cdot)$ taking values in $E = \{1, \ldots, N\}$. For all $i, j \in E$ the transition probabilities are given by:

$$\mathbb{P}(\psi(s+t)) = j \mid \psi(s) = i = \begin{cases} q_{ij}t + o(t), & \text{if } i \neq j, \\ 1 + q_{ii}t + o(t), & \end{cases}$$

where the constants $q_{ij} \geq 0$ are the transition rates from $i$ to $j$ and satisfy that $q_{ii}(x) = -\sum_{i\neq j} q_{ij}(x)$, the transition matrix is denoted by $Q = \{q_{ij}\}_{i,j=1,2,\ldots,N}$. The control component is $u(t) \in \mathcal{U}$ with $\mathcal{U}$ a compact set of $\mathbb{R}^m$, and $W$ is a $d$-dimensional standard Brownian motion independent of $\psi(\cdot)$. Throughout the work, it is considered that both the Markov chain $\psi(\cdot)$ and the Brownian motion $W$ are defined on a complete filtered probability space $(\Omega, \mathcal{F}, \mathbb{P}, \{\mathcal{F}_t\})$ that satisfies the usual conditions.

Until now, the switching diffusion (1) seems to be formulated as a classical switching diffusion, as in [11–14,19], among others. However, we propose that the process $\psi$ is a hidden Markov chain, i.e., at any given instant of time, the exact state of the Markov chain $\psi(\cdot)$ cannot be observed directly. Instead, we can only observe the process $y$ given by:

$$dy(t) = h(\psi(t))\mathrm{d}t + \sigma_0 \mathrm{d}B(t), \quad y(0) = 0, \tag{2}$$

whose dynamics depends on the value of $\psi(\cdot)$. In Equation (2), $h : E \to \mathbb{R}$ is a bounded function, whereas $B$ is a one-dimensional Brownian motion independent of $W$ and $\psi$, and $\sigma_0$ is a positive constant.

Under partial observation, the best way to work is through nonlinear filtering. This technique studies the conditional distribution of $\psi(t)$ given the observed data accumulated up to time $t$, namely:

$$\Psi_i(t) = \mathbb{P}(\psi(t) = i \mid \sigma_1(y(s),\ 0 \le s \le t)), \quad \forall i \in E, \tag{3}$$

where $\sigma_1(y(s),\ 0 \le s \le t))$ is the $\sigma_1$-algebra generated by the process $y(t)$ and $\sum_{i=1}^{N} \Psi_i(t) = 1$. Taking into account the following notation:

$$\begin{aligned} h^T(\Psi) &= (h(1), h(2), \ldots, h(N)), \\ \Psi^T(t) &= (\Psi_1(t), \ldots, \Psi_N(t)), \\ \mathrm{diag}(h) &= \mathrm{diag}(h(1), \ldots, h(N)), \end{aligned}$$

and using the Wonham filtering techniques, we know that the process $\Psi$ in (3) satisfies the following Equation (see for instance [15] or ([17], Section 22.3)):

$$\begin{aligned} \mathrm{d}\Psi(t) =& \Big[Q\Psi(t) - \sigma_0^{-2} h^T(\Psi(t))\Big(\mathrm{diag}(h) - h^T(\Psi(t)) I_N\Big)\Psi(t)\Big]\mathrm{d}t \\ &+\sigma_0^{-2}\Big(\mathrm{diag}(h) - h^T(\Psi(t)) I_N\Big)\Psi(t)\mathrm{d}y(t), \end{aligned} \tag{4}$$

where $I_N$ is the $N \times N$ identity matrix. If we introduce the process:

$$\mathrm{d}w_0(t) = \sigma_0^{-1}(\mathrm{d}y(t) - h^T(\Psi(t))dt),$$

then Equation (4) can be rewritten as:

$$\mathrm{d}\Psi(t) = Q\Psi(t)\mathrm{d}t + \sigma_0^{-1}\Big(\mathrm{diag}(h) - h^T(\Psi(t)) I_N\Big)\Psi(t)\mathrm{d}w_0(t). \tag{5}$$

**Remark 1.** *Note that the unique solution of (5) exists up to an explosion time $\tau$ (see, for instance [20]). However, $\tau = \infty$ a.s. since $\Psi_i(t) \le 1$ for all $t < \tau$ and $\forall i \in E$.*

At this point, we have defined the controlled HSDE with partial observation. To fulfill the objective of this work, that is, to solve an optimal control problem with the discounted and average payoff with partial observation, we will transform this problem into one with complete observation (see for instance [5,6,16]). First, we will establish the following notational convention.

For the coefficients $b : \mathbb{R}^n \times E \times \mathcal{U} \to \mathbb{R}^n$ and $\sigma : \mathbb{R}^n \times E \to \mathbb{R}^{n \times d}$

$$\begin{aligned} b(x(t), \psi(t), u(t)) &= (b_1(x(t), \psi(t), u(t)), \ldots, b_n(x(t), \psi(t), u(t))), \\ \sigma(x(t), \psi(t)) &= \{\sigma_{kl}(x(t), \psi(t))\}_{k=1,\ldots,n; l=1,\ldots,d}, \end{aligned}$$

we have their filtered estimates:

$$\overline{b}_k(x(t),\Psi(t),u(t)) = \sum_{i=1}^{N} \Psi_i(t) b_k(x(t),i,u(t)), \tag{6}$$

$$\overline{\sigma}_{kl}(x(t),\Psi(t)) = \sum_{i=1}^{N} \Psi_i(t) \sigma_{kl}(x(t),i), \tag{7}$$

and with equalities (6)–(7), we establish the new coefficients:

$$\overline{b}(x(t),\Psi(t),u(t)) = (\overline{b}_1(x(t),\Psi(t),u(t)),\ldots,\overline{b}_n(x(t),\Psi(t),u(t))),$$
$$\overline{\sigma}(x(t),\Psi(t)) = \{\overline{\sigma}_{kl}(x(t),\Psi(t))\}_{k=1,\ldots,n;l=1,\ldots,d}$$

With the use of above functions and Equation (1), we introduce the components of a new diffusion process as:

$$\mathrm{d}x_k(t) = \overline{b}_k(x(t),\Psi(t),u(t))\mathrm{d}t + \sum_{l=1}^{d} \overline{\sigma}_{kl}(x_k(t),\Psi(t))\mathrm{d}W_l(t), \quad x(0) = x_0, \tag{8}$$

and therefore, we obtain from (5) and (8) the following controlled system with complete observation:

$$\begin{cases} \mathrm{d}x(t) = \overline{b}(x(t),\Psi(t),u(t))\mathrm{d}t + \overline{\sigma}(x(t),\Psi(t))\mathrm{d}W(t), \\ \mathrm{d}\Psi(t) = Q\Psi(t)\mathrm{d}t + \sigma_0^{-1}(\mathrm{diag}(h) - h^T(\Psi(t))I_N)\Psi(t)\mathrm{d}w_0(t), \end{cases} \tag{9}$$

where $(x(t),\Psi(t)) \in \mathbb{R}^n \times S_N$ with:

$$S_N = \{\Psi = (\Psi_1,\ldots,\Psi_N) \in \mathbb{R}^N |\ \Psi_i(t) > 0,\ \sum_{i=1}^{N} \Psi_i(t) = 1\}.$$

Throughout this work, we will use the following Assumption 1.

**Assumption 1.**

(a) *The control set $\mathcal{U}$ is compact.*

(b) *$b : \mathbb{R}^n \times E \times \mathcal{U} \to \mathbb{R}^n$ is a continuous function that satisfies the Lipschitz continuous property on $x$ uniformly in $(i,u) \in E \times \mathcal{U}$, that is, there exists a constant $C_1 > 0$ such that:*

$$\max_{(i,u)\in E\times U} \|b(x,i,u) - b(y,i,u)\| \le C_1\|x-y\|.$$

(c) *There exists constants $C_2, C_3 > 0$ such that, $\sigma : \mathbb{R}^n \times E \to \mathbb{R}^{n\times d}$ satisfies:*

$$\|\sigma(x,i) - \sigma(y,i)\| \le C_2\|x-y\| \quad \text{and} \quad x^T\sigma(x,i)\sigma^T(x,i)x \ge C_3\|x\|^2$$

*for all $x,y \in \mathbb{R}^n$ and for all $i \in E$.*

(d) *There exists $C_4, C_5 > 0$ with:*

$$\|\sigma(x,i)\| \le C_4(1+\|x\|) \text{ and } \|b(x,i,u)\| \le C_5(1+\|x\|)$$

*for $i \in E$ and $u \in \mathcal{U}$.*

Under Assumption 1 and taking into account Remark 1, we know that the system (9) has a unique solution.

For $x \in \mathbb{R}^n$, we denote by $\nabla\nu_x$ and $\mathbb{H}_x$ the gradient and the Hessian matrix of $x$, respectively, and $\langle\cdot,\cdot\rangle$ the scalar product. For a sufficiently smooth real-valued function $\nu : \mathbb{R}^n \times \mathbb{R}^N \to \mathbb{R}$. Let:

$$\begin{aligned}\mathbb{L}^{u,\Psi}\nu(x,\Psi) \;&:=\; \left\langle \nabla\nu_x, \bar{b}(x,\Psi,u)\right\rangle + \frac{1}{2}Tr\left[(\mathbb{H}_x\nu)a(x,\Psi)\right] \\ &\quad + \langle\nabla\nu_\Psi, Q\Psi(t)\rangle + \frac{1}{2\sigma_0^2}Tr\left[(\mathbb{H}_\Psi\nu((x,\Psi)))A_2(\Psi(t))\right]\end{aligned}$$

with

$$a(x,\Psi) = \bar{\sigma}(x,\Psi)\bar{\sigma}(x,\Psi)^T,$$

$$A_2(\Psi(t)) = [\left(\text{diag}(h) - h^T(\Psi(t))I_N\right)\Psi(t)][\left(\text{diag}(h) - h^T(\Psi(t))I_N\right)\Psi(t)]^T,$$

the operator associated with Equation (9). In order to carry out the aim of this work, we define the control policies.

**Definition 1.** *A function of the form $u(t) := f(t, x(t), \Psi(t))$ for some measurable function $f : [0,\infty) \times \mathbb{R}^n \times S_N \to \mathcal{U}$, is called a Markov policy, whereas $u(t) := f(x(t), \Psi(t))$ for some measurable function $f : \mathbb{R}^n \times S_N \to \mathcal{U}$ is said to be a stationary Markov policy. The stationary Markov policies set is denote by $\mathbb{F}$.*

The following assumption represents a Lyapunov-like condition.

**Assumption 2.** *There exists a function $(w \geq 1) \in C^2(\mathbb{R}^n \times S_N)$, and constants $p \geq q > 0$, such that:*

*(i)* $\lim_{|x|\to\infty} w(x,\Psi) = +\infty$, *and*
*(ii)* $\mathbb{L}^{u,\Psi}w(x,\Psi) \leq -qw(x,\Psi) + p$ *for each $u \in \mathcal{U}$ and $(x,\Psi) \in \mathbb{R}^n \times S_N$.*

It is important to point out that since the $\psi(\cdot)$ is irreducible and aperiodic, we can ensure the existence of a unique invariant measure for the Markov–Feller process $(x^f(\cdot), \Psi(\cdot))$ (see [21,22]). Moreover, the Assumption 2 allows us to conclude that the Markov process $(x^f(\cdot), \Psi(\cdot))$, where $f \in \mathbb{F}$ is positive recurrent and there exists a unique invariant probability measure $\mu_f(dx,\Psi)$ for which is satisfied:

$$\mu_f(w) := \int_{\mathbb{R}^n \times S_N} w(x,\Psi)\mu_f(dx,d\Psi) < \infty. \tag{10}$$

Note that for every $f \in \mathbb{F}$, the measure $\mu_f$ belongs to the space defined as follows.

**Definition 2.** *The $w$-norm is defined as:*

$$\| \nu \|_w := \sup_{(x,\Psi)\in\mathbb{R}^n\times S_N} \frac{|\nu(x,\Psi)|}{w(x,\Psi)},$$

*where $\nu$ is the real-valued measurable function on $\mathbb{R}^n \times S_N$ and $w$ is the Lyapunov function given in Assumption 2. The normed linear space of real-valued measurable functions $\nu$ with finite $w$-norm is denoted by $\mathcal{B}_w(\mathbb{R}^n \times S_N)$. Moreover, the normed linear space of finite signed measures $\mu$ on $\mathbb{R}^n \times S_N$ such that:*

$$\| \mu \|_w := \int_{\mathbb{R}^n} w(x,\Psi) \mid \mu \mid (dx,d\Psi) < \infty,$$

*where $\mid \mu \mid$ is the total variation of $\mu$ is denoted by $\mathbb{M}_w(\mathbb{R}^n \times S_N)$.*

**Remark 2.** *For each $\nu \in \mathcal{B}_w(\mathbb{R}^n \times S_N)$ and $\mu \in \mathbb{M}_w(\mathbb{R}^n \times S_N)$, we get:*

$$\left|\int \nu(x,\Psi)\mu(dx,d\Psi)\right| \leq \| \nu \|_w \int w(x,\Psi) \mid \mu \mid (dx,d\Psi) = \| \nu \|_w \| \mu \|_w < \infty,$$

*that is, the integral* $\int v(x,\Psi)\mu(dx,\Psi)$ *is finite.*

The next result will be useful later.

**Lemma 1.** *The condition* $(ii)$ *in Assumption 2 implies that:*

$(a)$ $\mathbb{E}^{x,\Psi,f}[w(x(t),\Psi(t))] \leq e^{-qt}w(x,\Psi) + \frac{p}{q}(1-e^{-qt})$;

$(b)$ $\lim_{t\to\infty}\frac{1}{t}\mathbb{E}^{x,\Psi,f}[w(x(t),\Psi(t))] = 0$ *for all* $f \in \mathbb{F}$, $(x,\Psi) \in \mathbb{R}^n \times S_N$, *and* $t \geq 0$;

$(c)$ $\mu_f(w) \leq \frac{p}{q}$ *for all* $h \in \mathbb{F}$.

**Proof.** (a) After applying Dynkin's formula to the function $e^{qt}w$, we use case $(ii)$ of Assumption 2 to get:

$$\begin{aligned} \mathbb{E}^{x,\Psi,f}[e^{qt}w(x(t),\Psi(t))] &= w(x,\Psi_0) + \mathbb{E}^{x,\Psi,f}\left[\int_0^t e^{qs}[\mathbb{L}^{u,\Psi}w(x(s),\Psi(s)) + qw(x(s),\Psi(s))]ds\right] \\ &\leq w(x,\Psi_0) + \mathbb{E}^{x,\Psi,f}\left[\int_0^t e^{qs}p ds\right] \\ &\leq w(x,\Psi_0) + \frac{p}{q}(e^{qt}-1). \end{aligned} \tag{11}$$

Finally, if we multiply the inequality (12) by $e^{-qt}$, we obtain the result. To prove $(b)$, it is enough take the limit from the inequality (12). Integrating both sides of (12) with respect to the invariant probability $\mu_f$, we obtain $\mu_f(w) \leq e^{-qt}\mu_f(w) + \frac{p}{q}(1-e^{-qt})$, i.e., $\mu_f(w) \leq p/q$; thus, the result $(c)$ follows. □

In this work, the *reward rate* is a measurable function $r : \mathbb{R}^n \times E \times \mathcal{U} \to \mathbb{R}$ that satisfies the following conditions:

**Assumption 3.**

$(a)$ *The function* $r(x,i,u)$ *is continuous on* $\mathbb{R}^n \times E \times \mathcal{U}$; *moreover, for each* $R > 0$, *there exists a constant* $K(R) > 0$ *such that:*

$$\sup_{(i,u)\in E\times U} |r(x,i,u) - r(y,i,u)| \leq K(R)|x-y| \quad \text{for all} \quad |x|,|y| \leq R,$$

*i.e., r is locally Lipschitz in x uniformly with respect to* $i \in E$ *and* $u \in U$.

$(b)$ $r(\cdot,\cdot,u)$ *is in the normed linear space of real-valued functions* $\mathcal{B}_w(\mathbb{R}^n \times E)$ *uniformly in u; that is, there exists* $M > 0$ *such that for all* $(x,i) \in \mathbb{R}^n \times E$:

$$\sup_{u\in U} |r(x,i,u)| \leq Mw(x,i).$$

**Notation**. The rate reward $r : \mathbb{R}^n \times E \times \mathcal{U} \to \mathbb{R}$ is vector form is given by:

$$r^T(x,\Psi,u) = (r(x,1,u), r(x,2,u), \ldots, r(x,N,u)),$$

and its estimation is:

$$\bar{r}(x,\Psi(t),u) = \Psi^T(t)r(x,\Psi,u) = \sum_{i=1}^{N} \Psi_i(t)r(x,i,u). \tag{12}$$

Henceforth, for each stationary Markov policy $f \in \mathbb{F}$, we write:

$$\bar{r}(x,\Psi,f) := \bar{r}(x,\Psi,f(x,i)).$$

## 3. The Discounted Case

The objective of this section is to give conditions that guarantee the existence of discounted optimal policies for the $\alpha$-discounted payoff criterion we are concerned with.

**Definition 3.** *Let $r$ be as in Assumption 3 and $\alpha$ a positive constant. Given a stationary Markov policy $f \in \mathbb{F}$ and an initial state $x(0) = x, \Psi(0) = \Psi$, the total expected discount payoff (or discounted payoff, for short) is defined as:*

$$V_\alpha(x, \Psi, f) := \mathbb{E}^{x,\Psi,f}\Big[\int_0^\infty e^{-\alpha t}\bar{r}(x(t), \Psi(t), f)dt\Big].$$

Observe that the value function does not depend on the time at which the optimal control problem is studied to get the stationarity of the problem.

The following result shows a bound of the total expected discount payoff given in Definition 3. We will omit its proof because it is a direct consequence of Assumption 3 and inequality in Lemma 1a.

**Proposition 1.** *Suppose that Assumptions 2 and 3b hold. Then, for each $x$ in $\mathbb{R}^n$, $\Psi \in S_N$ and $f \in \mathbb{F}$ we have:*

$$\sup_{f\in\mathbb{F}} |V_\alpha(x, \Psi, f)| \leq M(\alpha)w(x, \Psi) \text{ with } M(\alpha) := M\frac{\alpha + d}{\alpha c}.$$

*implying that $\alpha$-discounted payoff $V_\alpha(\cdot, \cdot, f)$, belongs to the space $\mathcal{B}_w(\mathbb{R}^n \times S_N)$. Here, $q$ and $p$ are as in Assumption 2 and $M$ is the constant in Assumption 3b.*

**$\alpha$-discounted optimal problem.** The optimal control problem with discounted payoff consists of finding a policy $f^* \in \mathbb{F}$ such that:

$$V_\alpha^*(x, \Psi) = V_\alpha(x, \Psi, f^*) = \sup_{f\in\mathbb{F}} V_\alpha(x, \Psi, f). \tag{13}$$

The function $V_\alpha^*(x, \Psi)$ is referred to as *the optimal discount payoff*, whereas the policy $f^* \in \mathbb{F}$ is called *the discounted optimal*.

**Definition 4.** *We say that a function $v \in C^2(\mathbb{R}^n \times S_N) \cap \mathcal{B}_w(\mathbb{R}^n \times S_N)$, and a policy $f^* \in \mathbb{F}$ verify (are a solution of) the $\alpha$-*discounted payoff optimality equations *(or Hamilton–Jacobi–Bellman (HJB) equation) if, for every $x \in \mathbb{R}^n$ and $\Psi \in S_N$:*

$$\alpha v(x, \Psi) = \bar{r}(x, \Psi, f^*) + \mathbb{L}^{f^*,\Psi}v(x, \Psi) \tag{14}$$

$$= \sup_{f\in\mathbb{F}}\Big\{\bar{r}(x, \Psi, f) + \mathbb{L}^{f,\Psi}v(x, \Psi)\Big\}. \tag{15}$$

**Proposition 2.** *If Assumptions 1, 2, and 3 hold, then:*

*(a) There exists a function $v$ in $C^2(\mathbb{R}^n \times S_N) \cap \mathcal{B}_w(\mathbb{R}^n \times S_N)$ and a policy $f^* \in \mathbb{F}$, such that (14) and (15) hold.*

*(b) The function $v$ coincides with $V_\alpha^*(x, \Psi)$ in (13).*

*(c) A policy $f^* \in \mathbb{F}$ is an $\alpha$-discount optimal if and only if (14) and (15) are satisfied.*

**Proof.**

(a) Theorem 3.2 in [23] ensures that the value function $V_\alpha(x,\Psi)$ defined in (13) considering $\Psi \equiv 0$ is the unique solution of the HJB Equation (14) in $C^2(\mathbb{R}^n) \cap \mathcal{B}_w(\mathbb{R}^n)$. The existence of a function $v$ in $C^2(\mathbb{R}^n \times S_N) \cap \mathcal{B}_w(\mathbb{R}^n \times S_N)$ and a policy $f^* \in \mathbb{F}$, such that (14) and (15) hold, follows from Theorem 3.1 and 3.2 in [23] for each $\Psi \in S_N$ fixed.

(b) By Dynkin's formula for all $(x,\Psi) \in \mathbb{R}^n \times S_N$, $f \in \mathbb{F}$ and $t \geq 0$:

$$\mathbb{E}^{x,\Psi,f}[e^{-\alpha t}v(x(t),\Psi(t))] = v(x,\Psi) + \mathbb{E}^{x,\Psi,f}\left[\int_0^T \mathbb{L}^{f,\Psi}\left[e^{-\alpha t}v(x(t),\Psi(t))dt\right]\right. \tag{16}$$

Observe that:

$$\begin{aligned}\mathbb{L}^{f,\Psi}\left[e^{-\alpha t}v(x(t),\Psi(t))\right] &= -\alpha e^{-\alpha t}v(x,\Psi) \\ &+ e^{-\alpha t}\overline{b}(x,\Psi,f)v_x(x,\Psi) \\ &+ e^{-\alpha t}\frac{1}{2}Tr(a(x,\Psi))v_{xx}(x,\Psi) \\ &= e^{-\alpha t}[-\alpha v(x(t),\Psi(t)) + \mathbb{L}^{f,\Psi}v(x(t),\Psi(t))].\end{aligned}$$

Therefore, the right-hand member of (16) equals:

$$\mathbb{E}^{x,\Psi,f}[e^{-\alpha t}v(x(t),\Psi(t))] = v(x,\Psi) + \mathbb{E}^{x,\Psi,f}\left[e^{-\alpha t}(\mathbb{L}^{f,\Psi}v(x(t),\Psi(t)) - \alpha v(x(t),\Psi(t)))dt\right]$$

and from (15):

$$\mathbb{E}^{x,\Psi,f}[e^{-\alpha t}v(x(t),\Psi(t))] \leq v(x,\Psi) - \mathbb{E}^{x,\Psi,f}\left[\int_0^T e^{-\alpha t}\overline{r}(x(t),\Psi(t),f)dt\right].$$

This yields:

$$v(x,\Psi) \geq \mathbb{E}^{x,\Psi,f}\left[\int_0^t [e^{-\alpha t}\overline{r}(x(t),\Psi(t),f)dt\right] + \mathbb{E}^{x,\Psi,f}[e^{-\alpha t}v(x(t),\Psi(t))].$$

Now, as a consequence of $v$ is in $\mathcal{B}_w(\mathbb{R}^n \times S_N)$ and Lemma 1 (a),(b), we have that:

$$\begin{aligned}|\mathbb{E}^{x,\Psi,f}[e^{-\alpha t}v(x(t),\Psi(t))]| &\leq \mathbb{E}^{x,\Psi,f}[[e^{-\alpha t}\|v\|_w w(x(t),\Psi(t))] \\ &\leq e^{-\alpha t}\|v\|_w \mathbb{E}^{x,\Psi,f}w(x(t),\Psi(t)) \\ &\leq e^{-\alpha t}\|v\|_w\left[e^{-qT}w(x,\Psi) + \frac{p}{q}(1-e^{-qT})\right] \quad \text{(by Lemma 1(a))} \\ &\to 0 \quad \text{as} \quad t \to \infty.\end{aligned}$$

Therefore:

$$v(x,\Psi) \geq \mathbb{E}^{x,\Psi,f}\left[\int_0^\infty [e^{-\alpha s}\overline{r}(x(s),\Psi(s),f)ds\right] = V_\alpha(x,\Psi,f) \quad \text{for all } f \in \mathbb{F}.$$

Thus, $v(x,\Psi) \geq V_\alpha(x,\Psi,f)$. In particular, if we take $f^* \in \mathbb{F}$ satisfying (14) and proceed as above, we get:

$$v(x,\Psi) = V^*_\alpha(x,\Psi,f^*).$$

(c) *The if part.* Suppose that $f^* \in \mathbb{F}$ satisfies Equations (14) and (15). Then, proceeding as in part (b), we obtain that $f^* \in \mathbb{F}$ is an optimal policy.
*The only if part.* By mimic the same procedure of part (b), we can obtain that for any $f \in \mathbb{F}$ fixed:

$$\alpha V_\alpha(x,\Psi,f) = \overline{r}(x,\Psi,f) + \mathbb{L}^{f,\Psi}V_\alpha(x,\Psi,f); \quad \text{for all } x \in \mathbb{R}^n, \Psi \in S_N. \tag{17}$$

On the other hand, by part (b) we can assert that:

$$\alpha v(x,\Psi) = \sup_{f\in\mathbb{F}}\{\bar{r}(x,\Psi,f) + \mathbb{L}^{f,\Psi}v(x,\Psi)\}; \quad \text{for all } x\in\mathbb{R}^n, \Psi\in S_N. \tag{18}$$

Now let $f^*\in\mathbb{F}$ be an optimal policy, so that $V_\alpha(x,\Psi,f^*) = v(x,\Psi)$. Then, we get the result from (17) and (18).

□

**Remark 3.** *Briefly, Proposition 2 says that if the HJB-Equations (14) and (15) admit a solution $v\in C^2(\mathbb{R}^n\times S_N)\cap\mathcal{B}_w(\mathbb{R}^n\times S_N)$, then $v$ is the optimal discount payoff (13) to the switching Markovian stochastic control problem with a discounted payoff completely observed, and $f^*\in\mathbb{F}$ is an optimal stationary policy.*

## 4. Average Optimality Criteria

As in (10), let $\mu_f(\nu) := \int_{\mathbb{R}^n}\nu(x,\Psi)\mu_f(dx,\Psi)$ for every $\nu\in\mathcal{B}_w(\mathbb{R}^n\times S_N)$.

**Assumption 4.** *Let $(x(t),\Psi(t))$ be the solution of the hidden Markovian-switching diffusion (1)–(4). Then, we suppose that there exist positive constants C and $\delta$ such that:*

$$\sup_{f\in\mathbb{F}}|\mathbb{E}^{x,\Psi,f}[\nu(x(t),\Psi(t))] - \mu_f(\nu)| \le Ce^{-\delta t}\parallel\nu\parallel_w w(x,\Psi) \tag{19}$$

*for all $(x,\Psi)\in\mathbb{R}^n\times S_N$, $\nu\in\mathcal{B}_w(\mathbb{R}^n\times S_N)$, and $t\ge 0$. That is, we assume that the process $(x(t),\Psi(t))$ is uniformly $w$-*exponentially ergodic.

Next, we define the long-run average optimality criterion.

**Definition 5.** *For each $f\in\mathbb{M}$, $(x,\Psi)\in\mathbb{R}^n\times S_N$, and $T\ge 0$, let:*

$$J_T(x,\Psi,f) := \mathbb{E}^{x,\Psi,f}\Big[\int_0^T \bar{r}(t,x(t),\Psi(t),f)dt\Big]. \tag{20}$$

*The long-run expected average reward given the initial state $(x,\Psi)$ is:*

$$J(x,\Psi,f) := \liminf_{T\to\infty}\frac{1}{T}J_T(x,\Psi,f). \tag{21}$$

*The function:*

$$J^*(x,\Psi) := \sup_{f\in\mathbb{F}} J(x,\Psi,f) \quad \text{for all} \quad (x,\Psi)\in\mathbb{R}^n\times S_N$$

*is referred to as the optimal gain or the optimal average reward. If there is a policy $f^*\in\mathbb{F}$ for which $J(x,\Psi,f^*) = J^*(x,\Psi)$ for all $(x,\Psi)\in\mathbb{R}^n\times S_N$, then $f^*$ is called* average optimal.

**Remark 4.** *In some optimal control problems, the limit of $J_T(x,\Phi,f)/T$ as $T\to\infty$ might not exist. To avoid this difficulty, in optimal control problems, it defines the average payoff as a liminf as in (21), which be interpreted as the worst average payoff that is to be maximized.*

For each $f\in\mathbb{F}$, let:

$$J(f) := \mu_f(\bar{r}(\cdot,\Psi,f)) = \int_{\mathbb{R}^n}\bar{r}(x,\Psi,f)\mu_f(dx,d\Psi). \tag{22}$$

with $\mu_f$ as in (10). Now, observe that $J_T$ defined in (20) can be expressed as:

$$J_T(x,\Psi,f) = TJ(f) + \int_0^T[\mathbb{E}^{x,\Psi,f}\bar{r}(x(t),\Psi(t),f) - J(f)]dt, \tag{23}$$

therefore, multiplying (23) by $\frac{1}{T}$ and letting $T \to \infty$ we obtain, by (19):

$$J(x,\Psi,f) = \lim_{T\to\infty} \frac{1}{T} J_T(x,\Psi,f) = J(f) \text{ for all } (x,\Psi) \in \mathbb{R}^n \times S_N. \tag{24}$$

Moreover, by the definition (22) of $J(f)$, the Assumption 3b, and (10):

$$|J(f)| \le \int_{\mathbb{R}^n} |\ \bar{r}(x(t),\Psi(t),f)\ |\ \mu_f(dx,d\Psi) \le M \cdot \mu_f(w) < \infty \text{ for all } f \in \mathbb{F}.$$

Therefore, by Lemma 1c:

$$\sup_{f\in\mathbb{F}} |J(f)| \le M \cdot \mu_f(w) \le M \cdot \frac{p}{q}, \tag{25}$$

thus, the reward $J(f)$ is uniformly bounded on $\mathbb{F}$. From (24) and (25) we obtain that the following:

$$J^* := \sup_{f\in\mathbb{F}} J(f) = \sup_{f\in\mathbb{F}} J(x,\Phi,f) = J^*(x,\Phi) \text{ for all } (x,\Phi) \in \mathbb{R}^n \times S_N \tag{26}$$

has a finite value.

Thus, under the Assumptions 1, 2, and 4, it follows from (19) ($w$-exponential ergodicity) and (22) that the long-run expected average reward (21) coincides with the constant $J(f)$ for every $f \in \mathbb{F}$. Indeed, note that $J_T$ defined in (20) can be expressed as:

$$J_T(x,\Psi,f) = TJ(f) + \int_0^T [\mathbb{E}^{x,\Psi,f}\bar{r}(x(t),\Psi(t),f) - J(f)]dt.$$

**Definition 6.** *(a) A pair* $(J,v)$ *consisting of a constant* $J \in \mathbb{R}$ *and a function* $v \in C^2(\mathbb{R}^n \times S_N) \cap \mathcal{B}_w(\mathbb{R}^n \times S_N)$ *is said to be a solution of the* average reward HJB-equation *if:*

$$J = \max_{u\in U}[\bar{r}(x,\Psi,u) + \mathbb{L}^{u,\Psi} v(x,\Psi)] \text{ for all } (x,\Psi) \in \mathbb{R}^n \times S_N. \tag{27}$$

*(b) If a stationary policy* $f \in \mathbb{F}$ *attains the maximum in (27), that is:*

$$J = \bar{r}(x,\Psi,f) + \mathbb{L}^{f,\Psi} v(x,\Psi)] \text{ for all } (x,\Psi) \in \mathbb{R}^n \times S_N, \tag{28}$$

*then* $f$ *is called a* canonical policy.

The following theorem shows that if a policy satisfies the average reward HJB-equation, then it is an optimal average policy.

**Theorem 1.** *If Assumptions 1, 2, and 3 hold, then:*

(*i*) *The average reward HJB Equation (27) admits a unique solution* $(J,v)$, *with* $v \in C^2(\mathbb{R}^n \times S_N) \cap \mathcal{B}_w(\mathbb{R}^n \times S_N)$ *satisfying* $v(0,\Psi_0) = 0$ *for some* $\Psi_0 \in S_N$ *fixed.*
(*ii*) *There exists a canonical policy.*
(*iii*) *The constant* $J$ *in (27) equals* $J^*$ *in (26).*
(*iv*) *There exists a stationary average optimal policy.*

**Proof.** ($i$) The steps for the proof of this incise are essentially the same given in proof of Theorem 6.4 in [24]; thus, we omit the proof.

($ii$) Since $u \to r(\cdot,\cdot,u)$ and $u \to b(\cdot,\cdot,u)$ are continuous functions on the compact set $\mathcal{U}$, we obtain that $u \to \bar{r}(\cdot,\cdot,u) + \mathbb{L}^{u,\Psi} v(\cdot,\cdot)$ is a continuous function on $\mathcal{U}$; thus, the existence of a canonical policy $f \in \mathbb{F}$ follows from standard measurable selection theorems; see [25] (Theorem 12.2).

$(iii)$ Observe that, by (27):

$$J \geq \bar{r}(x, \Psi, u) + \mathbb{L}^{u,\Psi} v(x, \Psi) \ \text{ for all } (x, \Psi) \in \mathbb{R}^n \times S_N \text{ and } \ u \in U. \tag{29}$$

Therefore, for any $f \in \mathbb{F}$, using Dynkin's formula and (29) we obtain:

$$\begin{aligned} \mathbb{E}^{x,\Psi,f} v(x(t), \Psi(t)) &= v(x, \Psi) + \mathbb{E}^{x,\Psi,f}\Big( \int_0^t \mathbb{L}^{f,\Psi} h(x(s), \Psi(s)) ds \Big) \\ &\leq v(x, \Psi) + Jt - \mathbb{E}^{x,\Psi,f}\Big( \int_0^t \bar{r}(x(s), \Psi(s)) ds \Big). \end{aligned} \tag{30}$$

Thus, multiplying by $t^{-1}$ in (30) we have:

$$t^{-1} J_t(x, \Psi, f) \leq J + t^{-1} v(x, \Psi) - t^{-1} \mathbb{E}^{x,\Psi,f} v(x(t), \Psi(t)). \tag{31}$$

Consequently, letting $t \to \infty$ in (31), and using Lemma 1b and (24), we obtain:

$$J \geq J(f) \ \text{ for all } f \in \mathbb{F}.$$

To obtain the reverse inequality, similar arguments show that if:

$$J \leq \bar{r}(x, \Psi, u) + \mathbb{L}^{u,\Psi} v(x, \Psi) \ \text{ for all } \ (x, \Psi) \in \mathbb{R}^n \times S_N \text{ and } u \in U,$$

then $J \leq J(f)$ for all $f \in \mathbb{F}$. This last inequality together with (29) yields that if $f \in \mathbb{F}$ is a canonical policy, which satisfies (28), then we obtain that $J(f) = J$, and by (26):

$$J = J(f) = J^* = J^*(x, \Psi) \ \text{ for all } (x, \Psi) \in \mathbb{R}^n \times S_N. \tag{32}$$

$(iv)$ Similar arguments to those given in $(iii)$ lead us to that if $f \in \mathbb{F}$ is a canonical policy, then it is an average optimal. □

Theorem 1 indicates that if a policy satisfies the HJB Equation (27), then this policy is an optimal policy for the optimal control problem associated with the HJB equation. The difficulty with this approach is how to get a solution $(J^*, v, f)$ of the HJB equation. The most common form of the solve the HJB equation is based on variants on the *vanishing discount approach* (see [11,24,26] for details).

**Remark 5** ([1]). *In the optimality criteria known as bias optimality, overtaking optimality, sensitive discount optimality, and Blackwell optimality, the early returns and the asymptotic returns are both relevant; thus, to study them, we need first to analyze the discounted and average optimality criteria. These optimality criteria will be studied in future work.*

**Remark 6.**

- ***On Assumption 1*, ([7]**, *Theorems 3.17 and 3.18). The uniform Lipschitz and linear growth conditions of b and $\sigma$ ensure the existence and uniqueness of the global solution of the SDE with Markovian switching (1). The uniform Lipschitz condition* ($\max_{(i,u)\in E\times U} \|b(x,i,u) - b(y,i,u)\| \leq C_1\|x - y\|$, $\|\sigma(x,i) - \sigma(y,i)\| \leq C_2\|x - y\|$ *) imply that the change rates of the functions $b(x,i,u)$ and $\sigma(x,i)$ are minor or equal to the change rate of a linear function of $x$. This gives, in particular, the continuity of b and $\sigma$ in x for all $[t_0, \infty)$. Thus, the uniform Lipschitz condition excludes the functions b and $\sigma$ that are discontinuous concerning x. It is important to note that although a function let continuous, it does not guarantee that it satisfies the uniform Lipschitz condition; for example, the continuous function $sin(x^2)$ does not satisfy this condition. Uniform Lipschitz condition can be replaced by the local Lipschitz condition. In fact, the local Lipschitz condition allows us to include a great variety of functions, such as functions $v \in C^2(\mathbb{R}^n \times E)$. However, the linear growth condition (Assumption 1 (d)) also excludes some important functions, such as $b(x,i) = -|x|^2 x + i$. Assumption 1 (d) is quite* *standard but may be restrictive for some applications. As far as the results of this paper are concerned, the uniform Lipschitz condition may be replaced by the weaker condition:*

$$x^T b(x,i,u) + \frac{1}{2}||\sigma(x,i)||^2 \leq K(1+||x||^2), \text{ for all } (x,i) \in \mathbb{R}^n \times E, \quad (33)$$

*where K is a positive constant. This last condition allows us to include many functions as the coefficients b and $\sigma$. For example:*

$$b(x,i,u) = a(i)[x(t) - x^3(t)] + xg(u) \quad \sigma(x,i) = b(i)x^2(t)$$

*with $a(i), b(i) > 0$ such that $b^2(i) \leq 2a(i)$ and for some continuous function $g: U \to \mathbb{R}$ given. It is possible to check that a diffusion process with the parameters given above satisfies the local Lipschitz condition but the linear growth condition is not satisfied. On the other hand, note that:*

$$a(i)x[x - x^3] + x^2 g(u) + \frac{1}{2}b^2(i)x^4 \leq a(i)x^2 + x^2 g(u) \leq K(1+x^2)$$

*with $K = \max_{(i,u)\in E\times U}\{a(i) + g(u)\}$ and a compact control set U. That is, the condition (33) is fulfilled. Thus, ([7], Theorem 3.18) guarantees that the SDE with Markovian switching with these coefficients has a unique global solution on $[t_0, \infty)$.*

- ***On Assumption** 2, **(**[7], Theorem 5.2). This assumption guarantees the positive recurrence and the existence of an invariant measure $\mu_f(dx, \Psi)$ for the Markov–Feller process $(x(t), \Psi(t))$. Moreover, if this assumption holds together with the inequality $k(|x|^{\overline{p}}) \leq w(x,i)$ for positive numbers $k, \overline{p}, H$, then, the diffusion process (1) satisfies:*

$$limsup_{t\to\infty}\mathbb{E}|x(t)|^{\overline{p}} \leq H,$$

*that is, $x(t)$ is asymptotically bounded in $\overline{p}$th moment. Some Lyapunov functions are, for example:*

$$w(x,i) = k(i)|x|^{\overline{p}}, \; k(i) > 0, \; \overline{p} \geq 2, \; \forall\, (x,i) \in \mathbb{R}^n \times E, \quad (34)$$

*considering that the coefficients b and $\sigma$ in (1) satisfy the Lipschitz condition and:*

$$x^T b(x,i,u) + \frac{\overline{p}-1}{2}||\sigma(x,i)||^2 \leq B(i)||x||^2 + a, \quad (35)$$

*with $a > 0$, and $B(i)$ be constants. In fact, using the inequality $a^c b^{1-c} \leq ac + b(1-c)$ $\forall\, a,b \geq 0,\; c \in [0,1]$ and (35), we get:*

$$
\begin{aligned}
\mathbb{L}^{u,\psi}w(x,i) &= k(i)\overline{p}||x||^{\overline{p}-1}b(x,i,u)+\frac{1}{2}k(i)\overline{p}(\overline{p}-1)||\sigma(x,i)||^2|x|^{\overline{p}-2}+\sum_{j=i}^{N}q_{ij}k(j)||x||^{\overline{p}} \\
&= \overline{p}k(i)||x||^{\overline{p}-2}\Big\{x^Tb(x,i,u)+\frac{\overline{p}-1}{2}||\sigma(x,i)||^2\Big\}+\sum_{j=i}^{N}q_{ij}k(j)||x||^{\overline{p}} \\
&\leq \overline{p}k(i)||x||^{\overline{p}-2}\{B(i)||x||^2+a\}+\sum_{j=i}^{N}q_{ij}k(j)||x||^{\overline{p}} \\
&\leq (\overline{p}B(i)k(i)+\sum_{j=i}^{N}q_{ij}k(j))||x||^{\overline{p}}+a\overline{p}k(i)||x||^{\overline{p}-2} \\
&= (\overline{p}B(i)k(i)+\sum_{j=i}^{N}q_{ij}k(j))||x||^{\overline{p}} \\
&+ \Big[(a\overline{p}k(i))^{\overline{p}/2}\Big(\frac{2}{\lambda(i)}\Big)^{(\overline{p}-2)/2}\Big]^{2/\overline{p}}\Big[\frac{\lambda(i)}{2}||x||^{\overline{p}}\Big]^{(\overline{p}-2)/\overline{p}} \\
&\leq (\overline{p}B(i)k(i)+\sum_{j=i}^{N}q_{ij}k(j))||x||^{\overline{p}}+\frac{2}{\overline{p}}(a\overline{p}k(i))^{\overline{p}/2}\Big(\frac{2}{\lambda(i)}\Big)^{(\overline{p}-2)/2} \\
&+ \frac{\lambda(i)(\overline{p}-2)}{2\overline{p}}||x||^{p} \\
&\leq -\frac{\lambda(i)(\overline{p}+2)}{2\overline{p}}||x||^{\overline{p}}+\frac{2}{\overline{p}}(a\overline{p}k(i))^{\overline{p}/2}\Big(\frac{2}{\lambda(i)}\Big)^{(\overline{p}-2)/2}
\end{aligned}
\tag{36}
$$

*where $\lambda(i)=(\overline{p}B(i)k(i)+\sum_{j=i}^{N}q_{ij}k(j))$.*
*If we set:*

$$q:=\min_{i\in E}\Big[\frac{\lambda(i)(\overline{p}+2)}{2\overline{p}}\Big]\quad p:=\max_{i\in E}\Big[\frac{2}{\overline{p}}(a\overline{p}k(i))^{\overline{p}/2}\Big(\frac{2}{\lambda(i)}\Big)^{(\overline{p}-2)/2}\Big],$$

*then*

$$\mathbb{L}^{u,\psi}w(x,i)\quad\leq\quad -q||x||^{\overline{p}}+p\leq -qw(x,i)+p.$$

*Now, taking the Lyapunov function (34) we define:*

$$w(x,\Psi)=\sum_{i=1}^{N}\Psi_iw(x,i)=\sum_{i=1}^{N}\Psi_ik(i)||x||^{\overline{p}}.$$

*Considering that $w_x(x,\Psi)=\sum_{i=1}^{N}\Psi_ik(i)\overline{p}||x||^{\overline{p}-1}$, $w_{xx}(x,i)=\sum_{i=1}^{N}\Psi_ik(i)\overline{p}(\overline{p}-1)||x||^{\overline{p}-2}$, $\nabla w_{\Psi}(x,i)=[k(i),k(2),\dots,k(n)]||x||^{\overline{p}}$ and $w_{\Psi\Psi}(x,\Psi)=0$; a similar procedure to that given in (37) allows us to obtain that $W$ is also a Lyapunov function. That is:*

$$\mathbb{L}^{u,\Psi}w(x,\Psi)\quad\leq\quad -q||x||^{\overline{p}}+p\leq -qw(x,\Psi)+p.$$

- ***On Assumption** 3. This assumption allows us that the reward rate (or cost rate) can be unbounded from above and below. For the Lyapunov function $w(x,i)=k(i)|x|^{\overline{p}}$, a reward rate of the form:*

$$r(x,i,u)=k(i)|x|^{\overline{p}}+h(u)$$

*for some continuous function $h:U\to\mathbb{R}$ satisfies the Assumption 3. In fact:*

$$|r(x,i,u)|\leq k(i)|x|^{\overline{p}}+\max_{u\in U}h(u)\leq(k(i)+\max_{u\in U}h(u))|x|^{\overline{p}}=Mw(x,i)$$

*with* $M = \max_{i \in E}\{k(i) + \max_{u \in U}\}$ *and* $U$ *a compact set.*

- ***On Assumption 4***. *This assumption indicates asymptotic behavior of* $x(t)$ *when* $t$ *goes to infinite. Sufficient conditions for the* $w$*-exponentially ergodicity of the process* $(x(t), \psi(t))$ *can be seen in ([1], Theorem 2.8). In fact, in the proof of this theorem, Assumptions 1 and 2 are required. Note that, for the optimal control problem with discounted optimality criterion, the* $w$*-exponentially ergodicity of the process* $(x(t), \psi(t))$ *is not required. This assumption is only necessary to study the average reward optimality criterion.*

**Remark 7.** *In the following sections, our theoretical results are implemented in three applications. The dynamic system in the three applications evolves according to linear stochastic differential equations* $dx(t) = (A(i)x(t) + Bu(t))dt + \sigma dW(t)$, *namely, Assumption 1. The state numbers of the Markov chain is 2, that is,* $E = \{1,2\}$. *The payoff rate is of the form* $r(x,i,u) = x^T R(i)x + u^T Su$ *with* $x \in \mathbb{R}^2$ *and* $u \in \mathcal{U} := [0, a1] \times [0, a2]$, $a1, a2 > 0$. *Taking* $w(x,i) = x^T R(i)x + 1$ *we get:*

$$\begin{aligned} |r(x,i,u)| &= |x^T R(i)x| + |u^T Su| \\ &\leq |x^T R(i)x| + |u^T Su||x^T R(i)x + 1| \\ &= max_{u \in \mathcal{U}}(|u^T Su| + 1)|x^T R(i)x + 1| \\ &= M_2 w(x,i) \end{aligned}$$

*with* $M_2 = max_{u \in \mathcal{U}}(|u^T Su| + 1)$; *thus, Assumption 3 also holds. A few calculations allow us to obtain the Assumption 2 with* $w(x,\Psi) = \sum_{i=1}^2 \Psi_i(t) w(x,\psi(t)) = \sum_{i=1}^2 \Psi_i(t)(x^T R(\psi(t))x + 1)$. *In fact:*

$$\begin{aligned} \mathbb{L}^{u,\Psi} w(x,\Psi) &= x^2[2A(i)[\Psi_1 R(1) + \Psi_2 R(2)] + R(1)\sum_{i=1}^2 q_{i1}\Psi_i + R(2)\sum_{i=1}^2 q_{i2}\Psi_i] \\ &+ x[R(1)\sum_{i=1}^2 q_{i1}\Psi_i + R(2)\sum_{i=1}^2 q_{i2}\Psi_i] \\ &+ \sigma^2[\Psi_1 R(1) + \Psi_2 R(2)]. \end{aligned} \tag{37}$$

*Let* $0 < q < -[2A(i)[\Psi_1 R(1) + \Psi_2 R(2)] + R(1)\sum_{i=1}^2 q_{i1}\Psi_i + R(2)\sum_{i=1}^2 q_{i2}\Psi_i]$, *and rewrite* $\mathbb{L}^{u,\Psi} w(x,\Psi)$ *as:*

$$\mathbb{L}^{u,\Psi} w(x,\Psi) = -qw(x,\Psi) + l(x,i,u).$$

*where*

$$\begin{aligned} l(x,i,u) &:= qw(x,\Psi) + x^2[2A(i)[\Psi_1 R(1) + \Psi_2 R(2)] + R(1)\sum_{i=1}^2 q_{i1}\Psi_i + R(2)\sum_{i=1}^2 q_{i2}\Psi_i] \\ &+ x[R(1)\sum_{i=1}^2 q_{i1}\Psi_i + R(2)\sum_{i=1}^2 q_{i2}\Psi_i] \\ &+ \sigma^2[\Psi_1 R(1) + \Psi_2 R(2)] \\ &\leq p, \end{aligned} \tag{38}$$

*where the last inequality is obtained from fact that the function* $l(x.i.u)$ *is continuous on the compact set* $U$ *for all* $x \in \mathbb{R}$ *and that the term* $q + [2A(i)[\Psi_1 R(1) + \Psi_2 R(2)] + R(1)\sum_{i=1}^2 q_{i1}\Psi_i + R(2)\sum_{i=1}^2 q_{i2}\Psi_i]$ *is negative. Thus,* $\mathbb{L}^{u,\Psi} w(x,\Psi) = -qw(x,\Psi) + p$ *and Assumption 2b follows.*

## 5. Application 1: Discounted Linear Quadratic Regulator (LQR)

In this subsection, we consider the $\alpha$-discounted linear quadratic regulator. To this end, we suppose that the dynamic system evolves according to the linear stochastic differential equations:

$$dx(t) = (\overline{A}(\Psi(t))x(t) + Bu(t))dt + \sigma dW(t). \tag{39}$$

with $\overline{A}(\Psi(t)) := \sum_{i=1}^{N} A(i)\Psi_i(t)$, $A : E \to \mathbb{R}^{n\times n}$, $B \in \mathbb{R}^{n\times m}$, $W(\cdot)$ is a $m$-dimensional Brownian motion, and $\sigma$ is a positive constant. The expected cost is:

$$V_\alpha(x, \Psi, u) := \mathbb{E}^{u}_{x,\Psi}\left[\int_0^\infty e^{-\alpha s}\{x^T(s)\overline{D}(\Psi(s))x(s) + u^T\overline{R}(\Psi(s))u(s)\}ds\right].$$

where $\overline{D}(\Psi(t)) := \sum_{i=1}^{N} D(i)\Psi_i(t)$, $D : E \to \mathbb{R}^{n\times n}$, $\overline{R}(\Psi(t)) := \sum_{i=1}^{N} R(i)\Psi_i(t)$ and $R : E \to \mathbb{R}^{n\times n}$. The optimality equation or HJB-equation for the $\alpha$-discounted partially observed LQR-optimal control problem is:

$$\alpha v(x, \Psi) = \min_{u\in U}\{x\overline{D}(\Psi(t))x^T + u^T\overline{R}(\Psi(t))u + \mathcal{L}^u vs.(x, \Psi)\}, \tag{40}$$

where the infinitesimal generator for the process $(x(t), \Psi(t))$ applied to $v(x, \Psi) \in C^{2,2}$ $(\mathbb{R}^n \times S_N)$ is:

$$\begin{aligned}\mathbb{L}^u vs.(x, \Psi) = (\overline{A}(\Psi)x + Bu)v_x(x, \Psi) + \frac{1}{2}[Tr(\sigma\sigma^T)]v_{xx}(x, \psi) \\ + Q^T\Psi v_\Psi(x, \Psi, ) + \frac{1}{2}v_{\Psi\Psi}(x, \Psi, )Tr[A_2]\end{aligned} \tag{41}$$

where

$$A_2 = [\sigma_0^{-1}\left(\mathrm{diag}(h) - h^T(\Psi(t))I_N\right)\Psi(t)][\sigma_0^{-1}\left(\mathrm{diag}(h) - h^T(\Psi(t))I_N\right)\Psi(t)]^T. \tag{42}$$

Note that, by minimizing (40) with respect to $u$, we find that the optimal control is the form:

$$f^*(x, \Psi) = -\frac{\overline{R}^{-1}(\Psi)}{2}B^T v_x. \tag{43}$$

By Proposition 2, if there exist a function $v \in C^{2,2}(\mathbb{R}^n \times S_N) \cup \mathcal{B}_w(\mathbb{R}^n \times S_N)$ and a policy $f^* \in \mathbb{F}$ such that (14) and (15) hold, then $v$ coincides with the value function $v^*(x, \Psi) := \min_{u\in U} V_\alpha(x, \Psi, u)$ and $u(t) = f^*(x)$ is the $\alpha$-discount optimal policy. Thus, we propose that the function $v \in C^{2,2}(\mathbb{R}^n \times S_N) \cup \mathcal{B}_w(\mathbb{R}^n \times S_N)$ that solves the HJB-Equation (40) has the form:

$$v(x, \Psi) = x^T Kx + n(\Psi) + c, \tag{44}$$

where $n : S_N \to \mathbb{R}$ is a twice differentiable continuous function, $c$ is a constant, and $K$ is a positive definite matrix. Inserting the derivative of $v(x, \Psi)$ in (43) we get the optimal control:

$$f^*(x, \Psi) = -\overline{R}^{-1}(\Psi)B^T K^T x, \tag{45}$$

where the equality (40) holds if the matrix $K$ satisfies the algebraic Riccati equation:

$$\begin{aligned}\overline{A}^T(\Psi(t))K + K\overline{A}(\Psi(t)) - KB\overline{R}(\Psi(t))^{-1}B^T K \\ + \overline{D}(\Psi(t)) - \alpha K = 0,\end{aligned}$$

$$c = Tr[b(w(t))b^T(w(t))K]/\alpha$$

and $n(\cdot) \in \mathcal{C}^2(S_N)$ satisfies the partial differential equation:

$$Q^T\Psi(t)n'(\Psi(t)) + \frac{1}{2}Tr[A_2]n''(\Psi(t)) - \alpha n(\Psi(t)))I_n = 0, \ \forall \ \Psi(t) \in S_N,$$

where $A_2$ is as in (42), $I_N$ is the identity matrix of $N \times N$, and $n'$ and $n''$ are the gradient and the Hessian of the $n$, respectively.

**Simulation results.** In the following figures, we assume that the Markov chain $\psi(t)$ has two states, namely, $E = \{1,2\}$ and the dynamic system $x(t) \in \mathbb{R}^2$. We have computed the Wonham filter, the states of the dynamic system (39) $x(t) = [x_1(t), x_2(t)]^T$ with initial condition $x(0) = [10,15]^T$, the value function (44), and the optimal control (45) for the following data: $\sigma = 1$, $\sigma_0 = 1$, $\alpha = 0.01$, $h(1) = 1$, $h(2) = 2$, $\Psi_1(0) = 0.5$, $\Psi_2(0) = 0.5$, $R_1 = 1$, $R_2 = 2$:

$$A(1) = \begin{bmatrix} -5 & 1 \\ 0 & -10 \end{bmatrix}, \ A(2) = \begin{bmatrix} -10 & 1 \\ 0 & -10 \end{bmatrix},$$

$$D(1) = \begin{bmatrix} 1 & 0 \\ 0 & 1 \end{bmatrix}, \ D(2) = \begin{bmatrix} 2 & 0 \\ 0 & 3 \end{bmatrix},$$

and the transition matrix:

$$Q = \begin{bmatrix} -0.2 & 0.2 \\ 0.7 & -0.7 \end{bmatrix}.$$

To solve the Wonhan filter, we use the numerical method given in ([18], Section 8.4), considering that the Markov chain can only be observed through $dy(t) = h(\psi(t)) + \sigma_0 dB(t)$.

Figure 1 shows the solution of the filter Wonham equation and the states of the hidden Markov chain $\psi(t)$. As can be noted, in $t = 0.05$ s $\Psi_2(0.05) = \mathbb{P}(\psi(t) = 2 \mid y(s),$ $0 \leq s \leq 0.05) \geq \Psi_1(0.05)$, implying that the Markov chain with a higher probability to 0.5 is in state 2 in $t = 0.3$ ($\psi(0.3) = 2$). The evolution of the dynamic system (39) is given in Figure 2 (top); in this figure, we can note that the optimal control (45) moves the initial point $x(0) = [10,15]^T$ to the point $[0,0]^T$ in $t = 0.8$ s, indicating the good performance of the optimal control (45). The asymptotic behavior of the optimal control (45) is given in Figure 2 (bottom); this control stabilizes at zero around $t = 0.8$ s, since $x(t)$ also stabilizes at zero around $t = 0.8$ s.

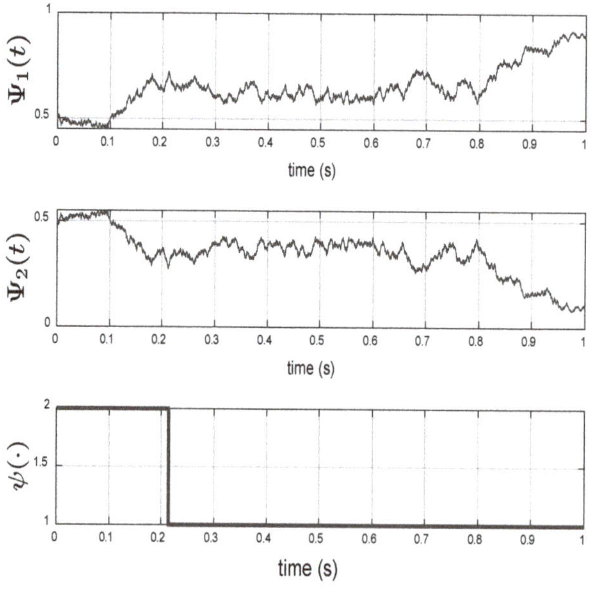


**Figure 1.** Wonham filter for the $\alpha$-discounted LQR.

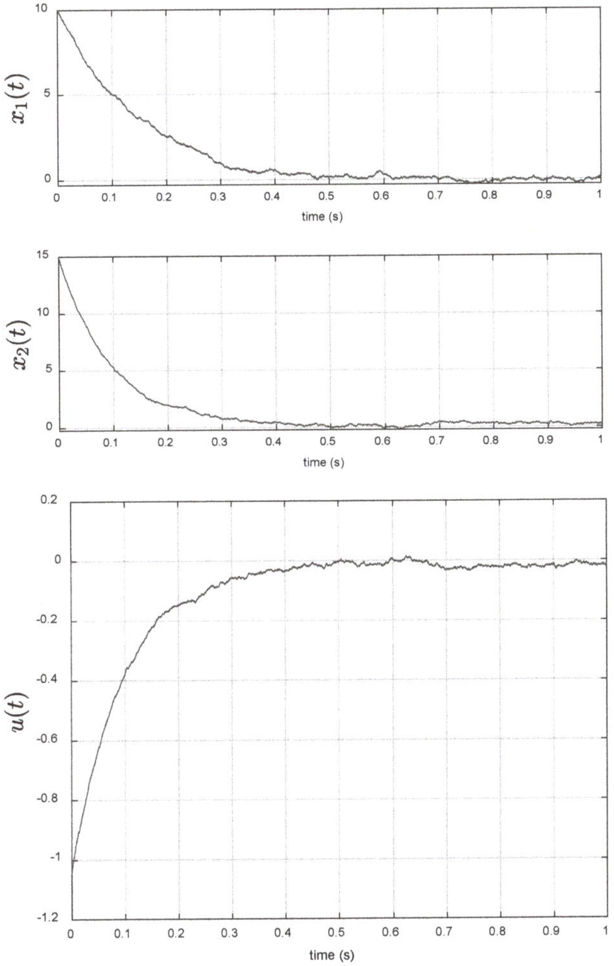


**Figure 2.** Asymptotic behavior of the state of dynamic system (**top**) and optimal control $\alpha$-discount LQR (**bottom**).

## 6. Application 2: Average LQR: Modeling of a Quarter-Car Suspension

In this section, the basic quarter-car suspension model analyzed in [27] is considered, see Figure 3. The parameters are: the sprung mass ($m_s$), the unsprung mass ($m_u$), the suspension spring constant ($k_s$), and the tire spring constant ($k$). Let $z_s, z_u$, and $z_r$ be the vertical displacements of the sprung mass, the unsprung mass, and the road profile, respectively. The equations of motion for this model are given by:

$$m_s z_s^{''}(t) = -k_s(z_s(t) - z_u(t)) - u(t), \tag{46}$$

$$m_u z_u^{''}(t) = k_s(z_s(t) - z_u(t)) - k(z_u(t) - z_r(t)) + u(t). \tag{47}$$

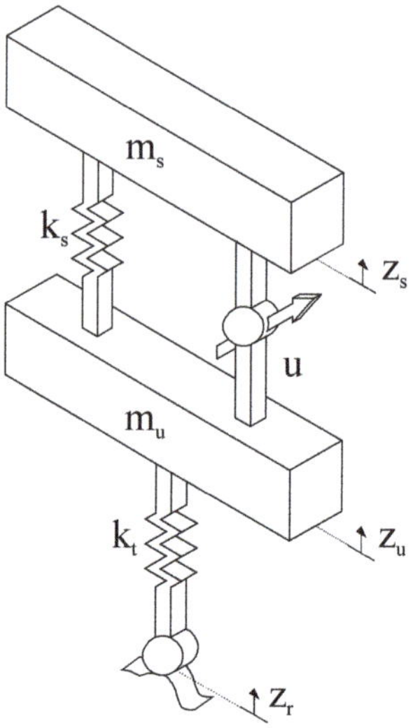


**Figure 3.** Schematic of a quarter-car suspension.

Now, defining $x_1(t) = z_s^{'}(t)$, $x_2(t) = z_u^{'}(t)$, $x_3(t) = z_s(t) - z_u(t)$, and $x_4(t) = z_u(t) - z_r$, the equations of motion (46) and (47) can be expressed in matrix form as:

$$dx(t) = (Ax(t) + Bu(t))dt + C_1 dz_r(t) \tag{48}$$

where $dx(t) = \begin{bmatrix} dx_1(t) \\ dx_2(t) \\ dx_3(t) \\ dx_4(t) \end{bmatrix}$, $A = \begin{bmatrix} 0 & 0 & \frac{k_s}{m_s} & 0 \\ 0 & 0 & \frac{k_s}{m_u} & \frac{k}{m_u} \\ 1 & -1 & 0 & 0 \\ 0 & 1 & 0 & 0 \end{bmatrix}$, $B = \begin{bmatrix} \frac{1}{m_s} \\ \frac{1}{m_s} \\ 0 \\ 0 \end{bmatrix}$, $C_1 = \begin{bmatrix} 0 \\ 0 \\ 0 \\ -1 \end{bmatrix}$, and in the time domain, the road profile, $z_r(t)$, can be represented as the output of a linear first-order filter to white noise as follows:

$$dz_r(t) = -a(\psi(t))Vz_r(t)dt + \sigma_2 dW_1(t),$$

where $V$ is the vehicle speed (assumed constant), $\sigma_2$ is a positive constant, and $a$ is the road roughness coefficient depending on the type of road. Here, we assume that $a$ depends on a hidden Markov chain, that is, $a(\psi(t))$ with $\psi(t) \in \{1, 2\}$. In our case, we consider that the dynamic system (48) evolves with additional white noise, that is:

$$dx(t) = (Ax(t) + Bu(t))dt + \sigma_1 dW(t) + C_1 dz_r(t) \tag{49}$$

The experts introduced the following performance index in order to trade off between the ride comfort and the handling while maintaining the constraint on suspension deflection:

$$\begin{aligned} J(x, \Psi, u) &= \lim_{T \to \infty} \frac{1}{T} \mathbb{E}^{x,\Psi,u} \left[ \int_0^T \left[ c_1 \frac{d^2 z_s}{d^2 t}^2 + c_2 [z_1(t) - z_u(t)]^2 \right. \right. \\ &+ \left. \left. c_3 [z_u(t) - z_r(t)]^2 + c_4 u(t)^2 \right] dt \right] \end{aligned} \tag{50}$$

Defining $y := \left[ \frac{d^2 z_s}{d^2 t}^2, [z_1(t) - z_u(t)]^2, [z_u(t) - z_r(t)]^2 \right]$, $C := diag(c_1, c_2, c_3)$, and $R := [c_4]$, we can rewrite (50) as:

$$J(x, \Psi, u) = \lim_{T \to \infty} \frac{1}{T} \mathbb{E}^{x,\Psi,u} \left[ \int_0^T yCy^T + u^T(t)Ru(t)dt \right] \tag{51}$$

Now, from the equations of motion in (46) and (47), note that $y = Mx + Nu$ with $M = \begin{bmatrix} 0 & 0 & \frac{k_s}{m_s} & 0 \\ 0 & 0 & 1 & 0 \\ 0 & 0 & 0 & 1 \end{bmatrix}$, and $N = \begin{bmatrix} -\frac{1}{m_s} \\ 0 \\ 0 \end{bmatrix}$. Thus, replacing this matrix form of $y$ in (51) we can rewrite (50) again as:

$$J(x, \Psi, u) = \lim_{T\to\infty} \frac{1}{T}\mathbb{E}^{x,\Psi,u}\Big[\int_0^T (x^T Q_1 x + 2x^T Q_2 u + u^T R_1 u)dt\Big] \tag{52}$$

where $Q_1 = M^T C M$, $Q_2 = M^T C N$, $R_1 = N^T C N + R$.

**The optimal control problem (OCP).** The OCP in this application consists of finding $u^* \in U$ such that it minimizes the performance index (52) considering that the dynamic system evolves according to the stochastic differential Equation (49).

In the dynamic programming technique, we need the infinitesimal generator $\mathcal{L}^u$ of the process $(x(t), \Psi(t))$ applied to $v(x, \Psi, z_r) \in C^{2,2,2}(\mathbb{R}^n \times S_N \times \mathbb{R})$; in this case, this generator is:

$$\begin{aligned} \mathcal{L}^u vs.(x, \Psi, z_r) = & -a(\Psi(t))v_{z_r}(x, \Psi, z_r) \\ & +(Ax + Bu)v_x(x, \Psi, z_r) \\ & +\mathcal{Q}^T \Psi v_\Psi(x, \Psi, z_r) \\ & +\frac{1}{2}Tr[\sigma_1\sigma_1^T]v_{xx}(x, \Psi, z_r). \\ & +\frac{1}{2}Tr[\sigma_2\sigma_2^T]v_{z_r z_r}(x, \Psi, z_r) \\ & +\frac{1}{2}v_{\Psi\Psi}(x, \Psi, z_r)Tr[A_2] \end{aligned} \tag{53}$$

where $A_2(\Psi(t)) = [\sigma_0^{-1}(\text{diag}(h) - h^T(\Psi(t))I_N)\Psi(t)][\sigma_0^{-1}(\text{diag}(h) - h^T(\Psi(t))I_N)\Psi(t)]^T$, whereas the Hamilton–Jacobi–Bellman Equation (or dynamic programming equation) associated with this problem is:

$$J = \max_{u\in U}[x^T Q_1 x + 2x^T Q_2 u + u^T R_1 u + \mathcal{L}^u vs.(x, \Psi, z_r)] \quad \text{for all} \quad (x, \Psi) \in \mathbb{R}^n \times S_N, \tag{54}$$

see [28] for more details.

**Proposition 3.** *Assume that $(x(t), z_r(t), \Psi(t))$ evolves according to (49). Then, the control that minimizes the long-run cost (52) is:*

$$f^*(x, \Psi, z_r) = -R_1^{-1}(Q_2^T + B^T K)^T x(t), \tag{55}$$

*whereas the corresponding function $v$ that solves the HJB Equation (54) is given by:*

$$v(x, \Psi, z_r) = x^T K x + g(z_r) + n(\Psi)$$

*where $K$ is a positive semi-definite matrix that satisfies the Ricatti differential equation*

$$\begin{aligned} K(A - BR_1^{-1}Q_2^T) + (A - BR_1^{-1}Q_2^T)K - KBR_1B^TP \\ (Q_1 - Q_2R_1^{-1}Q_2^T) = 0, \end{aligned} \tag{56}$$

*and $g(\cdot) \in C^2(\mathbb{R})$ satisfies the differential equation:*

$$a(\Psi)g'(z_r) + \frac{1}{2}\sigma_2^2 g''(z_r) = 0, \tag{57}$$

*and $n(\cdot) \in \mathcal{C}^2(S_N)$ satisfies the partial differential equation:*

$$Q^T \Psi n'(\Psi(t)) + \frac{1}{2} Tr[A_2] n''(\Psi) = 0, \tag{58}$$

*where $A_2$ is as in (41) and $n'$ and $n''$ denote the gradient and the Hessian of the $n$, respectively. The optimal cost is given by:*

$$J = Tr[\sigma_1 \sigma_1^T] K = J^*(x, \Psi) = \min_{u \in U} J(x, \Psi, u).$$

**Proof.** The HJB-equation for the partially observed LQR optimal control problem with $(x(t), \Psi(t))$ evolves according to (49) and finite cost (52) is (54), where $\mathcal{L}^u v(t, x, w, \Psi)$ is the infinitesimal generator given in (53). We are looking for a candidate solution $h \in \mathcal{C}^{2,2,2}(\mathbb{R}^n \times S_N \times \mathbb{R})$ to (54) in the form:

$$v(x, \Psi, z_r) = x^T K x + g(z_r) + n(\Psi), \tag{59}$$

for some continuous functions $g(\cdot) \in \mathcal{C}^2(\mathbb{R})$, $h(\cdot) \in \mathcal{C}^2(S_N)$ and $K$ a positive semi-definite matrix. We assume that $g''(z_r) > 0$ for all $z_r \in \mathbb{R}$ and $n''(\Psi)$ is positive definite, so that the function $(x, \Psi, z_r) \to v(x, \Psi, z_r)$ is convex.

Now, the function $u \in U \to 2x^T Q_2 u + u^T R_1 u + B u v_x$ is strictly convex on the compact set $U$, and thus, attains its minimum at:

$$f^*(x, \Psi, z_r) = -\frac{1}{2} R^{-1}[-2x^T Q_2 - B h_x] = -R_1^{-1}(Q_2^T + B^T K)^T x(t). \tag{60}$$

Inserting $f^*(x, \Psi, z_r)$ and the partial derivatives of $v$ with respect to $x$, $z_r$, and $\Psi$ in the HJB-Equation (54), we obtain:

$$\begin{aligned} J &= x^T Q_1 x + 2x^T Q_2(-R_1^{-1}(Q_2^T + B^T K)^T x) \\ &+ (-R_1^{-1}(Q_2^T + B^T K)^T x)^T R_1(-R_1^{-1}(Q_2^T + B^T K)^T x) \\ &- a(\Psi(t)) g'(z_r) + (Ax + B(-R_1^{-1}(Q_2^T + B^T K)^T x)) 2Kx + \mathcal{Q}^T \Psi h'(\Psi) + + Tr[\sigma_1 \sigma_1^T] K \\ &+ \frac{1}{2} Tr[\sigma_2 \sigma_2^T] g''(z_r) + \frac{1}{2} h''(\Psi) Tr[A_2]. \end{aligned} \tag{61}$$

For equality (61) to hold, it is necessary that the functions $g$ and $h$ satisfy (57) and (58), respectively, and the matrix $K$ satisfies the Ricatti differential Equation (56), whereas the constant $J = Tr[\sigma_1 \sigma_1^T] K$. Finally, from the Theorem 1, it follows that $f^*$ is an optimal Markovian control and the value function $J_T^*(t, x, w, \Psi)$ is equal to (59). That is:

$$J^*(x, \Psi) = \min_{u \in U} J(x, \Psi, u) = J = Tr[\sigma_1 \sigma_1^T] K.$$

□

**Simulation results.** To solve the Wonhan filter, we use the numerical method given in ([18], Section 8.4), considering that the Markov chain $\psi(t)$ has two states that can only be observed through $dy(t) = h(\psi(t)) + \sigma_0 dB(t)$. The following data were used: $\sigma_1 = 1$, $\sigma_2 = 1$, $\sigma_0 = 1$, $\alpha = 0.01$, $a(1) = 0.03$, $a(2) = 0.015$, $\Psi_1(0) = 0.5$, $\Psi_2(0) = 0.5$, $R = 1.0239 \times 10^{-5}$, $h(1) = -1$, $h(2) = 0.5$, $m_s = 329$ kg, $m_u = 51$ kg, $k_s = 4300$ N/m, $k = 210{,}000$ N/m, $V = 20$ m/s, $c_1 = 1$, $c_2 = c_3 = 1 \times 10^5$, $c_4 = 1 \times 10^{-6}$ and:

$$Q = \begin{bmatrix} -0.3 & 0.3 \\ 0.5 & -0.5 \end{bmatrix}.$$

The solution of the Wonham filter equation and the states of the hidden Markov chain $\psi(t)$ are shown in Figure 4. As can be noted, in $t = 1$ s, $\Psi_1(1) = \mathbb{P}(\psi(t) = 1 \mid y(s),$

$0 \leq s \leq 1) \geq \Psi_2(1)$, implying that the Markov Chain with a probability greater than 0.5 is in state 1 at $t = 1$.

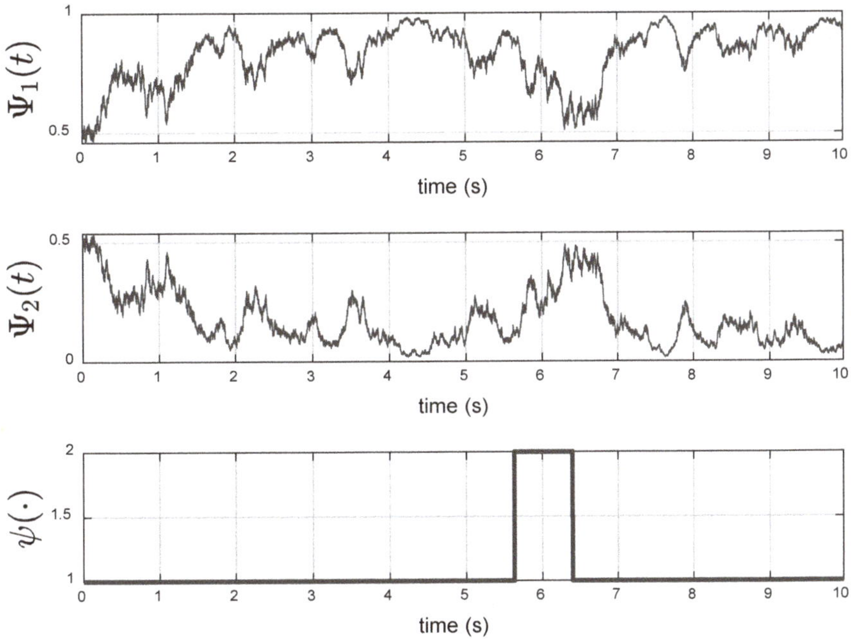


**Figure 4.** Wonham filter and hidden Markov chain (in $t$ = 1 s).

The asymptotic behavior of the optimal control (55) is given in Figure 5 (bottom). It is interesting to note that this control minimizes the magnitude of the sprung mass velocity, $x_1 = z_s^{'}$ and unsprung mass velocity, $x_2 = z_u^{'}$ after $t = 9$ s, see Figure 5 (top). This behavior implies that the magnitude of the sprung mass acceleration, $x_1 = z_s^{''}$ and unsprung mass acceleration $x_2 = z_u^{'}$ are also minimized, considering that the stochastic differential equation that models the road profile depends on a hidden Markov chain. These results agree with the obtained by authors in [27]. These authors mentioned that two important objectives of a suspension system are ride comfort and handling performance. The ride comfort requires that the car body be isolated from road disturbances as much as possible to provide a good feeling for passengers. In practice, we are looking to minimize the acceleration of the sprung mass.

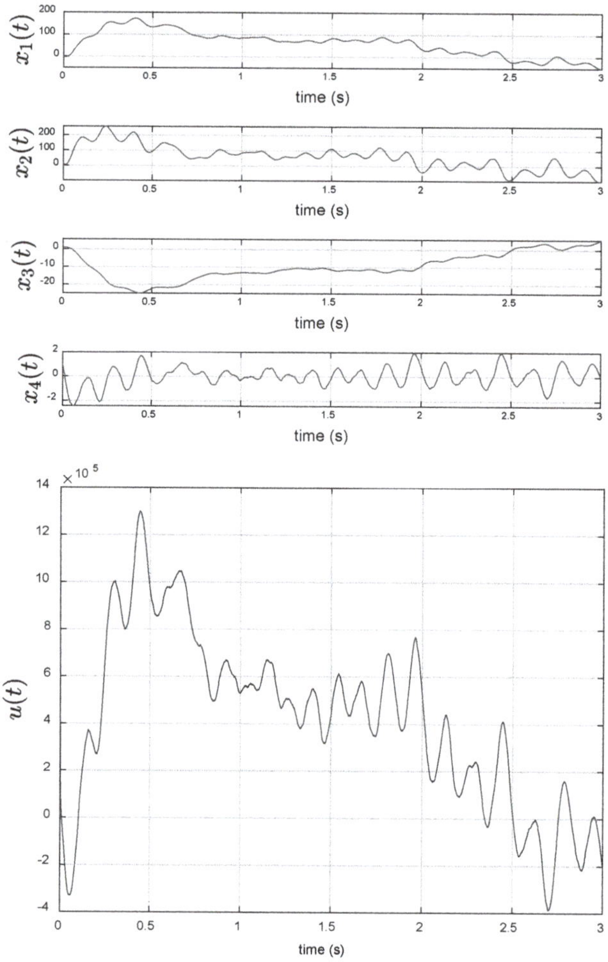


**Figure 5.** Asymptotic behavior of the state of dynamic system (**top**) and optimal control (**bottom**).

## 7. Application 3: Optimal Control of a Vehicle Active Suspension System with Damp

The model analyzed in this subsection is given in [29]. In this application, a damp $b_s$ is added to the quarter-car suspension given in Section 6, see Figure 6. The parameters in Figure 6 are: the sprung mass ($m_s$ ), the unsprung mass ($m_u$), the suspension spring constant ($k_s$ ), and the tire spring constant ($k$). Let $z_s, z_u$, and $r$ be the vertical displacements of the sprung mass, the unsprung mass, and the road disturbance, respectively. The equations of motion are given by:

$$m_s z_s''(t) = -k_s(z_s(t) - z_u(t)) + b_s(z_u' - z_s') + u(t), \quad (62)$$

$$m_u z_u''(t) = k_s(z_s(t) - z_u(t)) - k(r(t) - z_u(t)) - b_s(z_u' - z_s') - u(t). \quad (63)$$

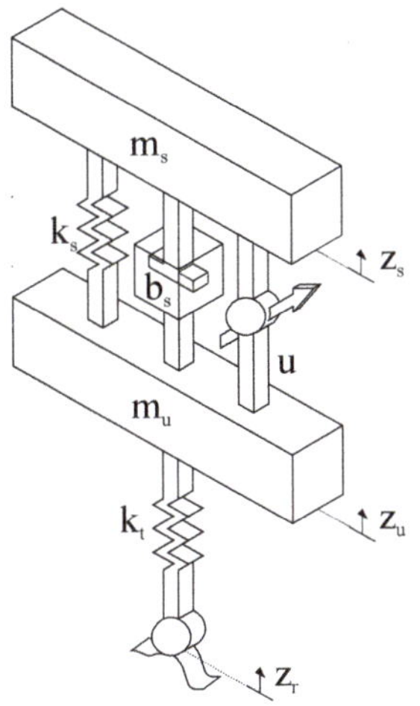


**Figure 6.** Quarter vehicle model of active suspension system.

Now, defining $x_1(t) = z_s(t)$, $x_2(t) = z_u(t)$, $x_3(t) = z_s'(t)$, and $x_4(t) = z_u'(t)$, the equations of motion in (62) and (63) can be expressed in matrix form as:

$$dx(t) = (Ax(t) + Bu(t))dt + Fr(t) \tag{64}$$

where $dx(t) = \begin{bmatrix} dx_1(t) \\ dx_2(t) \\ dx_3(t) \\ dx_4(t) \end{bmatrix}$, $A = \begin{bmatrix} 0 & 0 & 1 & 0 \\ 0 & 0 & 0 & 1 \\ -\frac{k_s}{m_s} & \frac{k_s}{m_s} & -\frac{k_s}{m_s} & \frac{k_s}{m_s} \\ \frac{k_s}{m_u} & -\frac{(k_s+k)}{m_u} & \frac{b_s}{m_u} & -\frac{b_s}{m_u} \end{bmatrix}$, $B = \begin{bmatrix} 0 \\ 0 \\ \frac{1}{m_s} \\ -\frac{1}{m_u} \end{bmatrix}$, $F = \begin{bmatrix} 0 \\ 0 \\ 0 \\ \frac{k}{m_u} \end{bmatrix}$, and we assume that the road profile $r(t)$ is represented by a function with hidden Markovian switchings:

$$r(t) = \begin{cases} a(\psi(t))\{1 - cos(8\pi t)\}, & \tau_p \leq t \leq \tau_{p+1} \\ 0 & otherwise \end{cases} \tag{65}$$

where $a(1) = 0.05$ (road bump height is 10 cm), $a(2) = 0.025$ (road bump height is 16 cm), and $\tau_p$, $p = 1, 2, \ldots$ are the random jump times of $\psi(t)$. In our case, we consider that the dynamic system (64) evolves with additional white noise, that is:

$$dx(t) = (Ax(t) + Bu(t) + Fr(t))dt + \sigma dW(t) \tag{66}$$

and we wish to minimize the discounted expected cost:

$$V_\alpha(x, \Psi, u) := \mathbb{E}^u_{x,\Psi}\left[\int_0^\infty e^{-\alpha s}\{x^T(s)Dx(s) + u^T(s)Ru(s)\}ds\right],$$

subject to (66) and (65). Considering the infinitesimal generator given in (53) with $z_r(t) \equiv r(t)$ and the Hamilton–Jacobi–Bellman equation associated as the following problem:

$$\alpha v(x, \Psi) = \max_{u \in U}[x^T Dx + u^T R_1 u + \mathcal{L}^u vs.(x, \Psi, r)] \quad \text{for all} \quad (x, \Psi) \in \mathbb{R}^n \times S_N,$$

similar arguments to these given in Sections 5 and 6 allow us to find the optimal control $f^*$ and the value function $v^*$ for this setting. In fact:

$$v^*(x, \Psi) = x^T Kx + n(\Psi) + g(r) + c,$$

where $n : S_N \to \mathbb{R}$ is a twice differentiable continuous function, $c$ is a constant, $g : \mathbb{R} \to \mathbb{R}$ is a twice differentiable continuous function, and $K$ is a positive definite matrix. Inserting the derivative of $v(x, \Psi)$ in (43), we get the optimal control:

$$f^*(x, \Psi) = -\overline{R}^{-1}(\Psi)B^T K^T x, \tag{67}$$

where the matrix $K$ satisfies the algebraic Riccati equation:

$$A^T K + KA - KBR^{-1}B^T K + D - \alpha K = 0,$$

$$c = Tr[\sigma\sigma^T K]/\alpha,$$

the function $g \in C^2(\mathbb{R})$ satisfies the differential equation:

$$a(\Psi(t))g'(r) + \alpha g(r) = 0,$$

and $n(\cdot) \in C^2(S_N)$ satisfies the partial differential equation:

$$Q^T\Psi(t)n'(\Psi(t)) + \frac{1}{2}Tr[A_2]n''(\Psi(t)) - \alpha n(\Psi(t)))I_4 = 0, \ \forall \ \Psi(t) \in S_N,$$

where $A_2$ is as in (42), $I_4$ is the identity matrix of $4 \times 4$, and $n^{'}$ and $n^{''}$ are the gradient and the Hessian of the $n$, respectively.

**Simulation results.** To solve the Wonhan filter, we use the numerical method given in ([18], Section 8.4) considering that the Markov chain $\psi(t)$ has two states and that can be only observed through $dy(t) = h(\psi(t)) + \sigma_0 dB(t)$. The following data were used: $\sigma = 1$, $\sigma_0 = 1$, $\alpha = 0.01$, $a(1) = 0.05$, $a(2) = 0.08$, $\Psi_1(0) = 0.4$, $\Psi_2(0) = 0.6$, $h(1) = 1, h(2) = 2$, $R = 1.0239 \times 10^{-5}$, $m_s = 300$ kg, $m_u = 60$ kg, $k_s = 1600$ N/m, $k = 190{,}000$ N/m, $b_s = 1000$ N/m, and:

$$Q = \begin{bmatrix} -0.2 & 0.2 \\ 0.4 & -0.4 \end{bmatrix}.$$

Figure 7 shows the solution of the Wonham filter equation and the states of the hidden Markov chain $\psi(t)$. As can be seen, in the time interval $[2, 4]$, $\Psi_1(1) = \mathbb{P}(\psi(t) = 1 \mid y(s),\ 0 \leq s \leq 1) \geq \Psi_2(1)$, implying that the Markov chain with a probability greater than 0.5 is in state 1.

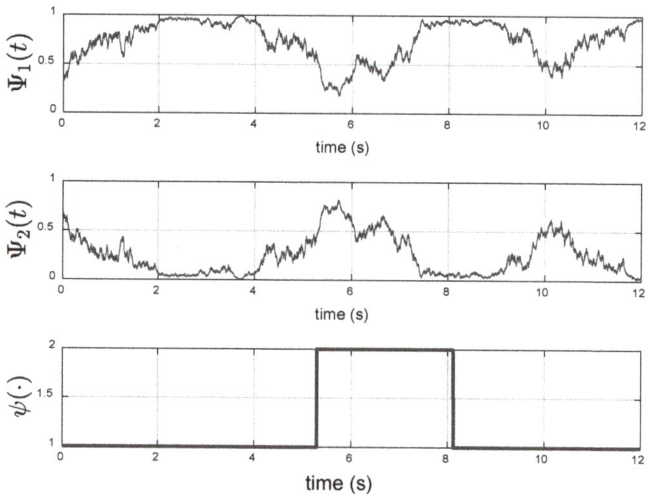


**Figure 7.** Wonham filter and hidden Markov chain (time interval [2, 4]).

The asymptotic behavior of the optimal control (67) is given in Figure 8 (bottom). It is interesting to note that this control minimizes the magnitude of the sprung mass, $x_1 = z_s$, and unsprung mass, $x_2 = z_u$, al well as their velocities, $x_3 = z_s^{'}$ and $x_4 = z_u^{'}$, after $t = 12$ s, see Figure 8 (top).

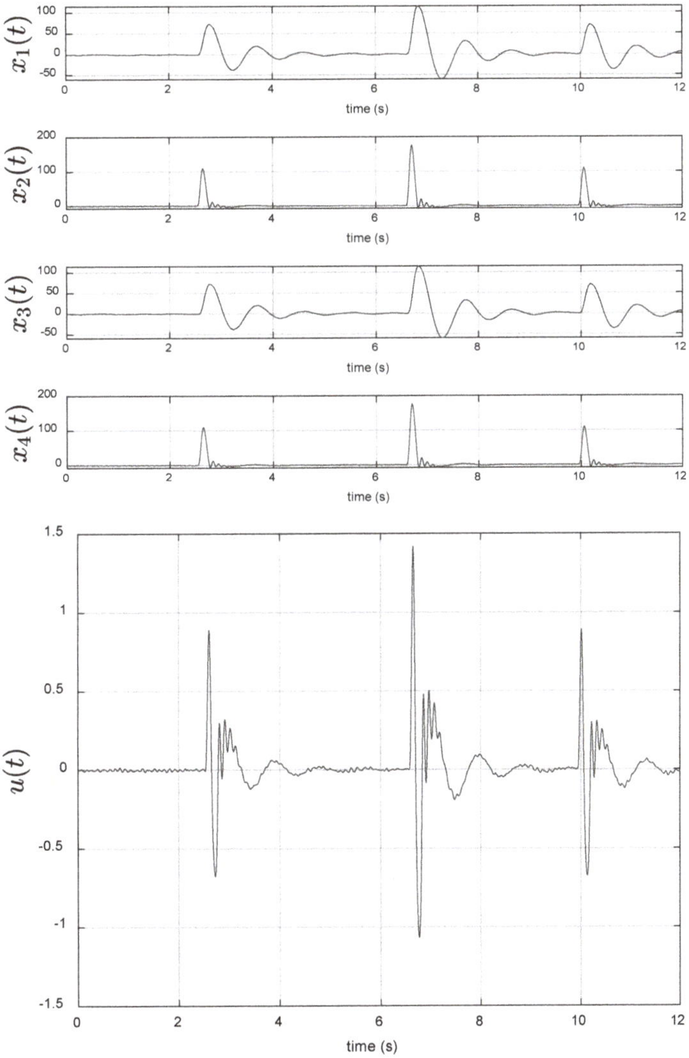


**Figure 8.** Asymptotic behavior of the state of the dynamic system (**top**) and optimal control (**bottom**).

## 8. Application 4: Optimal Pollution Control with Average Payoff

The application studies the pollution accumulation incurred by the consumption of a certain product, such as gas or petroleum, see [30]. The stock of pollution $x(\cdot)$ is governed by the controlled diffusion process:

$$dx(t) = [u(t) - \eta(\psi(t))x(t)]dt + kdW(t), \ x(0) = x > 0, \tag{68}$$

where $u(t)$ represents the pollution flow generated by an entity due to the consumption of the product, $\eta(\psi(t))$ represents the decay rate of pollution, chosen at each time by nature, and $k$ is a positive constant. We shall assume that $u(t) \in U = [0, \gamma]$ is bounded and the parameter $\gamma$ represents the consumption/production restriction. Let $\psi(t)$ be a Markov chain with two states $E = \{1, 2\}$ and a generator $Q$ given by:

$$\begin{pmatrix} q_{11} & q_{12} \\ q_{21} & q_{22} \end{pmatrix} = \begin{pmatrix} -\lambda_0 & \lambda_0 \\ \lambda_1 & -\lambda_1 \end{pmatrix}.$$

The reward rate $r : [0, \infty) \times E \times U \to \mathbb{R}$ in this example represents the social welfare and is defined as:

$$r(x, i, u) := F(u) - a(i)x, \ \forall \ (x, i, u) \in [0, \infty) \times E \times U, \tag{69}$$

where $F \in C^2(0, \infty) \cap C(0, \infty)$ and $D = a(i)x \in C([0, \infty) \times E)$ is the social utility of the consumption $u$ and the social disutility of the pollution $(x, i)$, respectively. We assume that the function $F$ in (69) satisfies:

$$\begin{cases} F'(u) > 0, \quad F''(u) < 0, \\ F'(\infty) = F(0) = 0, \quad F'(0+) = F(\infty) = \infty, \end{cases}$$

Clearly, (68) is a liner stochastic differential equation, and satisfies Assumption 1.

Now, we define the Banach space $\mathcal{B}_w(\mathbb{R} \times E)$ and use $w(x, i) := x + i$, $w(x, \Psi) = \sum_{i=1}^{2} \Psi_i w(x.i) = \Psi_1(x + 1) + \Psi_2(x + 2) = x + (1 - \Psi_1)$. Hence, $\lim_{x \to +\infty} w(x, \Psi) = +\infty$ and Assumption 2*i* holds. On the other hand, since the utility function $F(\cdot)$ is continuous on the compact interval $U = [0, \gamma]$, then:

$$|r(x, i, u)| = |F(u) - a(i)x| \leq (\max_{u \in [0,\gamma]} F(u) + \max_{i \in \{1,2\}} a(i))(x + i) = Mw(x, i)$$

where $M := \max_{u \in [0,\gamma]} F(u) + \max_{i \in \{1,2\}} a(i)$; thus, Assumption 3 holds. Note that:

$$\mathcal{L}^{u,\Psi} w(x, \Psi) = u - \eta(i)x - \lambda_0 \Psi_1 + \lambda_1(1 - \Psi_1), \quad \text{for all } x > 0.$$

Thus, taking $q := \max_{i \in E} \eta(i)$ and $p := \max_{u \in [0,\gamma]} u - (\lambda_0 - \lambda_1)\Psi_1$ we obtain:

$$\mathcal{L}^u w(x, \Psi) \leq -pw(x, \Psi) + q \quad \text{for all } x > 0.$$

Therefore, Assumption 2(ii) holds. It can be proven that the process (68) satisfies Assumption 2.6 in [1]; thus, by ([1], Theorem 2.8), $x(t)$ is exponentially ergodic (Assumption 4). In this application, we seek a policy $u$ that maximizes the long-run average welfare $J(x, i, f)$:

$$J(x, i, u) := \liminf_{T \to \infty} \frac{1}{T} \mathbb{E}^u_{x,i} \left[ \int_0^T [F(u) - a(i)x] \mathrm{d}t \right].$$

We propose $v(x, \Psi) = v(x) + h(\Psi)$, where $v \in C^2(\mathbb{R} \times E) \cap \mathcal{B}_w(\mathbb{R} \times E)$ and $h \in C^2(S_N)$ as a solution that verify the HJB Equation (27) associated with this pollution control problem. Simple calculations allow us to conclude that the policy on consumption/pollution takes the form:

$$u := f(x, \Psi) = \begin{cases} I(-v'(x)) & \text{if } F'(\gamma) < -v'(x), \\ \gamma & \text{if } F'(\gamma) \geq -v'(x). \end{cases}$$

where $I(-v'(x))$ is the inverse function of derivative $F'$, $f \in \mathbb{F}$.

## 9. Concluding Remarks

Under hypotheses such as uniform ellipticity in Assumption 1*c*, the Lyapunov-like conditions in Assumption 2, and the w-exponential ergodicity in (4) for the average criterion, this work shows the existence of optimal controls for the control problems with discounted and average payoffs, where the dynamic system evolves according to switching diffusion with hidden states. To conclude, we conjecture that the results obtained in this work still hold (with obvious changes) if the hidden Markov chain ($\psi$) in (1) is replaced with any other diffusion process. Furthermore, these results can be extended to constrained and unconstrained nonzero-sum stochastic differential games with additive structures, which will allow us to model a larger class of practical systems. This will be a topic in future works.

**Author Contributions:** Conceptualization, B.A.E.-T.; Formal analysis, B.A.E.-T. and J.G.-M.; Investigation, B.A.E.-T., J.G.-M. and G.A.; Methodology, B.A.E.-T., J.G.-M. and J.D.R.-A. All authors have read and agreed to the published version of the manuscript.

**Funding:** This research received no external funding.

**Institutional Review Board Statement:** Not applicable.

**Informed Consent Statement:** Not applicable.

**Data Availability Statement:** Not applicable.

**Conflicts of Interest:** The authors declare no conflict of interest.

## References

1. Escobedo-Trujillo, B.A.; Hernández-Lerma, O. Overtaking optimality for controlled Markov-modulated diffusions. *J. Optim.* **2011**, *61*, 1405–1426. [CrossRef]
2. Borkar, V.S. The value function in ergodic control of diffusion processes with partial observations. *Stoch. Stoch. Rep.* **1999**, *67*, 255–266. [CrossRef]
3. Borkar, V.S. Dynamic programming for ergodic control with partial observations. *Stoch. Process. Their Appl.* **2003**, *103*, 293–310. [CrossRef]
4. Rieder, U.; Bäuerle, N. Portfolio optimization with unobservable Markov-modulated drift Process. *J. Appl. Probab.* **2005**, 362–378. [CrossRef]
5. Tran, K. Optimal exploitation for hybrid systems of renewable resources under partial observation. *Nonlinear Anal. Hybrid Syst.* **2021**, *40*, 101013. [CrossRef]
6. Tran, K.; Yin, G. Stochastic competitive Lotka–Volterra ecosystems under partial observation: Feedback controls for permanence and extinction. *J. Frankl. Inst.* **2014**, *351*, 4039–4064. [CrossRef]
7. Mao, X.; Yuan, C. *Stochastic Differential Equations with Markovian Switching*; World Scientific Publishing Co.: London, UK, 2006. Available online: https://www.worldscientific.com/doi/pdf/10.1142/p473 (accessed on 20 March 2022). [CrossRef]
8. Yin, G.G.; Zhu, C. Hybrid Switching Diffusions. In *Stochastic Modelling and Applied Probability*; Properties and Applications; Springer: New York, NY, USA, 2010; Volume 63, p. xviii+395. [CrossRef]
9. Yin, G.; Mao, X.; Yuan, C.; Cao, D. Approximation methods for hybrid diffusion systems with state-dependent switching processes: numerical algorithms and existence and uniqueness of solutions. *SIAM J. Math. Anal.* **2009**, *41*, 2335–2352. [CrossRef]
10. Yu, L.; Zhang, Q.; Yin, G. Asset allocation for regime-switching market models under partial observation. *Dynam. Syst. Appl.* **2014**, *23*, 39–61.
11. Ghosh, M.K.; Arapostathis, A.; Marcus, S.I. Optimal control of switching diffusions with application to flexible manufacturing systems. *SIAM J. Control Optim.* **1993**, *31*, 1183–1204. [CrossRef]
12. Ghosh, M.K.; Marcus, S.I.; Arapostathis, A. Controlled switching diffusions as hybrid processes. In Proceedings of the International Hybrid Systems Workshop, New Brunswick, NJ, USA, 22–25 October 1995; Springer: Berlin/Heidelberg, Germany, 1995; pp. 64–75.
13. Zhang, X.; Zhu, Z.; Yuan, C. Asymptotic stability of the time-changed stochastic delay differential equations with Markovian switching. *Open Math.* **2021**, *19*, 614–628. [CrossRef]
14. Zhu, C.; Yin, G. Asymptotic properties of hybrid diffusion systems. *SIAM J. Control Optim.* **2007**, *46*, 1155–1179. [CrossRef]
15. Wonham, W.M. Some applications of stochastic differential equations to optimal nonlinear filtering. *J. SIAM Control Ser. A* **1965**, *2*, 347–369. [CrossRef]
16. Elliott, R.J.; Aggoun, L.; Moore, J.B. *Hidden Markov Models: Estimation and Control*; Springer: Berlin/Heidelberg, Germany, 1995.
17. Cohen, S.N.; Elliott, R.J. *Stochastic Calculus and Applications*, 2nd ed.; Probability and Its Applications; Springer: Cham, Switzerland, 2015; p. xxiii+666. [CrossRef]

18. Yin, G.; Zhang, Q. *Discrete-Time Markov Chains: Two-Time-Scale Methods and Applications*; Stochastic Modelling and Applied Probability; Springer: New York, NY, USA, 2006.
19. Yin, G.G.; Zhu, C. *Hybrid Switching Diffusions: Properties and Applications*; Springer Science & Business Media: Berlin/Heidelberg, Germany, 2009; Volume 63.
20. Protter, P.E. Stochastic integration and differential equations. In *Stochastic Modelling and Applied Probability*, 2nd ed.; Version 2.1, Corrected Third Printing; Springer: Berlin/Heidelberg, Germany, 2005; Volume 21, p. xiv+419. [CrossRef]
21. Chigansky, P. An ergodic theorem for filtering with applications to stability. *Syst. Control Lett.* **2006**, *55*, 908–917. [CrossRef]
22. Kunita, H. Asymptotic behavior of the nonlinear filtering errors of Markov processes. *J. Multivar. Anal.* **1971**, *1*, 365–393. [CrossRef]
23. Lu X.; Yin, G.; Guo, X. Infinite Horizon Controlled Diffusions with Randomly Varying and State-Dependent Discount Cost Rates. *J. Optim. Theory Appl.* **2017**, *172*, 535–553. [CrossRef]
24. Ghosh, M.K.; Arapostathis, A.; Marcus, S.I. Ergodic control of switching diffusions. *SIAM J. Contr. Optim* **1997**, *35*, 1962–1988. [CrossRef]
25. SchÄl, M. Conditions for optimality and for the limit of n-stage optimal policies to be optimal. *Z. Wahrs. Verw. Gerb.* **1975**, *32*, 179–196. [CrossRef]
26. Ghosh, M.K.; Marcus, S.I. Stochastic differential games with multiple modes. *Stoch. Anal. Appl.* **1998**, *16*, 91–105. [CrossRef]
27. Nguyen, L.H.; Seonghun, P.; Turnip, A.; Hong, K.S. Application of LQR Control Theory to the Design of Modified Skyhook Control Gains for Semi-Active Suspension Systems. In Proceedings of the ICROS-SICE International Joint Conference 2009, Fukuoka, Japan, 18–21 August 2009; pp. 4698–4703.
28. Escobedo-Trujillo, B.; Garrido-Meléndez, J. Stochastic LQR optimal control with white and colored noise: Dynamic programming technique. *Rev. Mex. Ing. Química* **2021**, *20*, 1111–1127. [CrossRef]
29. Maurya, V.K.; Bhangal, N.S. Optimal Control of Vehicle Active Suspension System. *J. Autom. Control. Eng.* **2018**, *6*, 1111–1127. [CrossRef]
30. Kawaguchi, K.; Morimoto, H. Long-run average welfare in a pollution accumulation model. *J. Econom. Dynam. Control* **2007**, *31*, 703–720. [CrossRef]

mathematics MDPI

Article

# On Robustness for Spatio-Temporal Data

**Alfonso García-Pérez**

Departamento de Estadística, I.O. y C.N., Universidad Nacional de Educación a Distancia (UNED), Senda del Rey 9, 28040 Madrid, Spain; agar-per@ccia.uned.es

**Abstract:** The spatio-temporal variogram is an important factor in spatio-temporal prediction through kriging, especially in fields such as environmental sustainability or climate change, where spatio-temporal data analysis is based on this concept. However, the traditional spatio-temporal variogram estimator, which is commonly employed for these purposes, is extremely sensitive to outliers. We approach this problem in two ways in the paper. First, new robust spatio-temporal variogram estimators are introduced, which are defined as $M$-estimators of an original data transformation. Second, we compare the classical estimate against a robust one, identifying spatio-temporal outliers in this way. To accomplish this, we use a multivariate scale-contaminated normal model to produce reliable approximations for the sample distribution of these new estimators. In addition, we define and study a new class of $M$-estimators in this paper, including real-world applications, in order to determine whether there are any significant differences in the spatio-temporal variogram between two temporal lags and, if so, whether we can reduce the number of lags considered in the spatio-temporal analysis.

**Keywords:** robust statistics; spatio-temporal outliers; von Mises expansions; saddlepoint approximations

**MSC:** 62F35; 62H11; 62E17

**Citation:** García-Pérez, A. On Robustness for Spatio-Temporal Data. *Mathematics* **2022**, *10*, 1785. https://doi.org/10.3390/math10101785

Academic Editors: Francisco German Badía and María D. Berrade

Received: 19 April 2022
Accepted: 18 May 2022
Published: 23 May 2022



## 1. Introduction

There exist several approaches for the treatment of spatio-temporal data. The most common approach is to assume that the data are a partial realization of a spatio-temporal random field $Z(\mathbf{s},t)$, $(\mathbf{s},t) \in D \times T$ (see, e.g., [1,2]). In this *superpopulation model* ([3], p. 8), we also assume that $D$ is a fixed subset of $\mathbb{R}^d$, $d \geq 1$ and $T \subset \mathbb{R}$; that is, we assume that a random variable $Z$, such as precipitation, temperature or atmospheric pollutant concentrations, is observed at some known fixed locations $\mathbf{s}$ and different time moments $t$, considering a *geostatistical* framework where the spatial observations are expected to be correlated with a decreasing correlation as the distance between locations increases.

We can conduct exploratory data analysis with spatio-temporal data, mainly through their visualization. However, it is more interesting to model the random field, allowing for inference of the model parameters and closed-form expressions (see [4]). As it is usually assumed that the data come from a joint Gaussian (i.e., normal) distribution, we are interested in estimating the parameters; that is, summaries of the first- and second-order characteristics. To make this feasible, we suppose that $Z(\mathbf{s},t)$ is intrinsically stationary in space and time; that is, its increments in space and time have a zero mean (possibly after a temporal trend has been removed) and have a variance that depends only on displacements in space and differences in time. With these assumptions, the parameter of interest is the spatio-temporal variogram of $Z$, defined as

$$2\,\gamma_z(\mathbf{h};\tau) = var(Z(\mathbf{s}+\mathbf{h};t+\tau) - Z(\mathbf{s};t)),$$

where $var$ is the variance of $Z$, $\mathbf{h}$ is a spatial lag, and $\tau$ is a temporal lag.

We also assume that $Z$ is spatially isotropic; that is, the variogram depends on the spatial lag $\mathbf{h}$ only through the Euclidean norm $\|\mathbf{h}\|$.

Furthermore, one of the most important problems in geostatistics is kriging prediction at new locations, for which the spatio-temporal variogram is required. Hence, the spatio-temporal variogram is the crucial parameter in geostatistics. However, the traditional spatio-temporal variogram estimator, which is commonly employed for these purposes, is extremely sensitive to outliers. Moreover, in a wide range of fields, such as geology, the environment, sustainability or climate change, detecting atypical observations is of special interest.

Considering these aims, we first define new robust estimators of the spatio-temporal variogram. Then, we obtain very accurate approximations for the sample distribution of these new estimators, and, with these, we finally identify spatio-temporal outliers.

The spatio-temporal variogram of $Z$ can also be written as

$$2\,\gamma_z(\mathbf{h};\tau) = E[(Z(\mathbf{s}+\mathbf{h};t+\tau) - Z(\mathbf{s};t))^2],$$

where $E$ denotes the mathematical expectation of $Z$.

To analyze $Z$, we consider observations of the random field $Z(\mathbf{s},t)$ at spatial locations $\{\mathbf{s}_i : i = 1,...,m\}$ and times $\{t_j : j = 1,...,T\}$, where $n = m \cdot T$ is the sample size.

In this situation, the spatio-temporal variogram is estimated using the classical method-of-moments estimator, also called the empirical spatio-temporal variogram (see [3,5,6]),

$$2\,\widehat{\gamma}_z(\mathbf{h};\tau) = \frac{1}{|N_{\mathbf{s}}(\mathbf{h})|}\frac{1}{|N_t(\tau)|}\sum_{\mathbf{s}_i,\mathbf{s}_k\in N_{\mathbf{s}}(\mathbf{h})}\;\sum_{t_j,t_l\in N_t(\tau)}(Z(\mathbf{s}_i;t_j) - Z(\mathbf{s}_k;t_l))^2,$$

where $N_{\mathbf{s}}(\mathbf{h})$ refers to the set containing all pairs of spatial locations with spatial lag $\mathbf{h}$, and $N_t(\tau)$ refers to the set containing all pairs of time points with time lag $\tau$. Furthermore, $|N(\cdot)|$ denotes the number of elements in the set $N(\cdot)$.

If we denote, by $n(\mathbf{h},\tau) = |N_{\mathbf{s}}(\mathbf{h})| \cdot |N_t(\tau)|$, the sample size considered in the estimator $2\,\widehat{\gamma}_z(\mathbf{h};\tau)$—that is, the number of pairs with spatio-temporal lag $(\mathbf{h},\tau)$—this estimator is a sample mean of $n(\mathbf{h},\tau)$ terms and, hence, sensitive to outliers in the terms.

In [7], robust estimators of the spatial variogram and accurate approximations for their distributions were obtained. In [8], these results were extended to the multivariate case, with robust estimators for the cross-variogram. In the first part of this paper, we extend these results by introducing a temporal component into the problem. This is achieved by defining new robust $M$-estimators of the spatio-temporal variogram and obtaining accurate approximations for their distributions, as well as for the classical one, $2\,\widehat{\gamma}_z(\mathbf{h};\tau)$. In the last part of this paper, we propose a method for identifying spatio-temporal outliers, also obtaining interesting properties of a new class of $M$-estimators.

The remainder of this paper is organized as follows: A spatio-temporal variogram $M$-estimator is proposed in Section 2, and an approximation to its distribution is obtained at the end of Section 3.2. The problem of independence of the transformed observations is addressed in Section 4. These results are applied in Section 5 to the empirical spatio-temporal variogram estimator. In Section 6, we introduce Huber's spatio-temporal variogram estimator and obtain an approximation to its distribution. An example is developed in Section 7. The question of whether some temporal lags can be dropped in the analysis is considered in Section 8. The problem of identifying spatio-temporal outliers is addressed in Section 9, where a new class of $M$-estimators is defined. The conclusions of the paper are presented in Section 10.

## 2. *M*-Estimators of the Spatio-Temporal Variogram

### 2.1. Underlying Model for Z

The common model assumption for spatio-temporal data $Z$ is a normal distribution. Nevertheless, this is a very strong assumption as, although most of the data will come from this model, it is very likely that some will not. For this reason, it is more realistic to assume a scale-contaminated normal distribution for the model (see, e.g., [9], p. 2):

$$(1-\epsilon)N(\mu,\sigma^2)+\epsilon N(\mu,g^2\sigma^2),$$

where $\epsilon \in (0,1)$ and $g>1$, with $\epsilon$ representing the proportion of outliers in the sample and $g$ denoting the quantity that contaminates them. For $\epsilon = 0$ or $g = 1$, this model is the normal distribution and, if $\epsilon > 0$ and $g > 1$, it is the $N(\mu,\sigma^2)$ in the central part but with heavier tails. In this way, we consider that the model for $Z$ is inside the class of scale contamination neighborhoods of the normal distribution, $\mathcal{P}_\epsilon(N) = \{F_\epsilon | F_\epsilon = (1-\epsilon)N(\mu,\sigma^2)+\epsilon N(\mu,g^2\sigma^2)\}$, one of the usual model classes considered in robustness studies ([9] p. 12 , [10,11] or [12] p. 870).

Although the main role in the question of the underlying model is played by the marginal distributions of $Z$, in order to complete the mathematical framework, we shall assume that these marginal distributions are obtained from the multivariate scale-contaminated normal distribution (see, e.g., [13], pp. 2, 220).

### 2.2. M-Estimators of the Spatio-Temporal Variogram

Let us consider the transformation

$$X_{ij} = (Z(\mathbf{s}_i+\mathbf{h};t_j+\tau) - Z(\mathbf{s}_i;t_j))^2 \quad \forall \mathbf{s}_i, t_j. \tag{1}$$

These new variables will be shortened, in some cases, by $X_u$, $u = 1,\ldots n$, considering them as a sample of a new variable $X = (Z(\mathbf{s}+\mathbf{h};t+\tau) - Z(\mathbf{s};t))^2$ defined from the lags of $Z$ in space and time. As the parameter of interest is now $2\,\gamma_z(\mathbf{h};\tau) = E[X]$, the problem of estimating the spatio-temporal variogram described in the previous section can be considered as the problem of estimating the expectation of the random variable $X$, obtained from the original $Z$ through this transformation.

This framework is especially suitable and useful in situations related to spatial or temporal data, where the initially dependent observations are separated by a spatial and/or temporal lag and where direct robust estimators, if they exist, are difficult to apply. Considering this mean (the spatio-temporal variogram) as a functional $T$ of the underlying distribution $F$,

$$T(F) = \int x dF(x),$$

where $F$ is the cumulative distribution function of $X$, and its classical method-of-moments estimator is the sample mean

$$T(F^*_{n(\mathbf{h},\tau)}) = \int x dF^*_{n(\mathbf{h},\tau)}(x) = \frac{1}{n(\mathbf{h},\tau)} \sum_{u=1}^{n(\mathbf{h},\tau)} X_u$$

of the transformed variables $X_u$, where $F^*_{n(\mathbf{h},\tau)}$ is the empirical cumulative distribution function. This approach—that is, expressing estimators as functionals of the empirical distribution function—is common and useful in robustness studies ([9,14]).

An important question here is how to choose the transformation (1) such that the new variables $X_u$ are independent in the new sample mean. We shall deal with this problem later. If we achieve this independence, obtaining robust estimators for the parameter $T(F)$ is an easy task with $M$-estimators and $\alpha$-trimmed means of the transformed variables $X_u$. With respect to the former, we can define a spatio-temporal $M$-estimator ([11]) $T_n$ for the parameter $T(F)$ (the spatio-temporal variogram) based on the transformed observations $X_u$ as a solution to the equation

$$\sum_{u=1}^{n} \psi(X_u, T_n) = 0, \tag{2}$$

assuming that $\psi(x,\theta)$ is monotonic decreasing in $\theta$ for all $x$. In fact, as $T_n$ is an estimator for a location problem, $\psi(x,\theta)$ is of the form $\psi(x-\theta)$, with $\psi(v)$ monotonically increasing in $v$. Now, we should control the local robustness of these $M$-estimators, through choosing different bounded score functions $\psi$ (see, e.g., refs. [9,15] for a background on robust methods and standard $M$-estimators.)

Hence, the idea that we propose in the paper is that, instead of considering a weird estimator for a strange parameter of the initial $Z$ distribution, we transform the original (and usually dependent) observations $Z_u$ into new data $X_u$ (independent under some conditions), obtaining, in this way, a natural parameter of the new variable (e.g., its mean), for which a manageable estimator (the sample mean) should be feasible. Then, standard techniques of robustification can be applied. The comparison between the traditional estimator (the empirical spatio-temporal variogram) and one of these robust $M$-estimators here introduced, both based on the observations $X_u$, is the well-known comparison between the sample mean and a robust $M$-estimator (see, e.g., [9,14]).

This idea was first successfully applied in [16] and has also been utilized in [7,8]. Furthermore, in the paper [17], this idea was used for the periodogram ordinates in the context of a time-series.

### 2.3. Distribution of Variables $X_u$

An important problem is to determine the distribution of this new variable $X$, from the original normal (or contaminated normal) distribution of $Z$, in order to later obtain the distribution of the robust estimators based on $X$.

If we consider a scale-contaminated normal model for the original observations $Z$, as the variable $Z(\mathbf{s}_i + \mathbf{h}; t_j + \tau) - Z(\mathbf{s}_i; t_j)$ follows a normal distribution with 0 mean and variance $2\gamma_z(\mathbf{h}; \tau)$. For each $\mathbf{s}_i, t_j$, the distribution of the transformed variables

$$X_{ij} = (Z(\mathbf{s}_i + \mathbf{h}; t_j + \tau) - Z(\mathbf{s}_i; t_j))^2$$

is the mixture

$$F = (1-\epsilon)\, 2\,\gamma_z(\mathbf{h};\tau)\,\chi_1^2 + \epsilon\, g^2\, 2\,\gamma_z(\mathbf{h};\tau)\,\chi_1^2 = (1-\epsilon)G + \epsilon H,$$

where $G = 2\gamma_z(\mathbf{h};\tau)\chi_1^2$ and $H = g^2 2\gamma_z(\mathbf{h};\tau)\chi_1^2$, where $\chi_1^2$ is a chi-square distribution with one degree of freedom, following a similar development to that followed in [7], Section 2.1.

## 3. Approximation to the Distribution of $M$-Estimators of the Spatio-Temporal Variogram

The distribution of these new robust $M$-estimators $T_n$, defined by (2), depends on the distribution of the new variables $X_u$ after the transformation. We obtain an approximation to the distribution of the robust estimators $T_n(X_1, \ldots, X_n)$ in two steps: in the first step, we consider a von Mises expansion (VOM) of the tail probability functional, which depends on another functional, for which we obtain a saddlepoint approximation (SAD) in the second step. The independence of the $X_u$ is now required.

### 3.1. von Mises Approximation

If $T_n(X_1, \ldots, X_n)$ is an estimator with associated functional $T$, and $F$ is the underlying model distribution of the observations $X_u$, we usually cannot express $T(F)$ explicitly; however, we can utilize a linearization based on the von Mises expansion, [18], at $G$ (called the pivotal distribution) as follows:

$$T(F) = T(G) + \int IF(x; T, G)dF(x) + O(||F-G||^2),$$

where $IF(\cdot; T, G)$ is the Hampel Influence Function; that is, the Gâteaux derivative of $T$ at $G$ in direction $\Delta_x$, the Dirac measure at $x$ (see [15,19,20]).

If we consider $T$ as the tail probability functional, $T(F) = P_{X_i \equiv F}\{T_n > a\}$, the Hampel Influence Function is now the Tail Area Influence Function TAIF ([21]), and the previous von Mises expansion is equal to

$$P_F\{T_n > a\} = P_G\{T_n > a\} + \int \mathrm{TAIF}(x;a;T_n,G)\,dF(x) + O\left(||F-G||^2\right),$$

from which we define the *von Mises approximation* (VOM)

$$P_F\{T_n > a\} \simeq P_G\{T_n > a\} + \int \mathrm{TAIF}(x;a;T_n,G)\,dF(x), \tag{3}$$

which will be accurate if the distributions $F$ and $G$ are close. In this case, we can use this approximation to compute the distribution of $T_n$ under the underlying model $F$ using a model $G$ in the class $\mathcal{P}_\epsilon(N)$.

In particular, if $F$ is the mixture $F = (1-\epsilon)G + \epsilon H$, the von Mises approximation will be

$$P_F\{T_n > a\} \simeq P_G\{T_n > a\} + \epsilon \int \mathrm{TAIF}(x;a;T_n,G)\,dH(x), \tag{4}$$

because

$$\int \mathrm{TAIF}(x;a;T_n,G)\,dF(x) = (1-\epsilon)\int \mathrm{TAIF}(x;a;T_n,G)\,dG(x)$$
$$+\epsilon \int \mathrm{TAIF}(x;a;T_n,G)\,dH(x) = (1-\epsilon)\cdot 0 + \epsilon \int \mathrm{TAIF}(x;a;T_n,G)\,dH(x).$$

### 3.2. Saddlepoint Approximation of the TAIF

The von Mises approximations (3) or (4) depend on the TAIF, which is the influence function of the tail probability functional. Daniels ([22], p. 94), using the Lugannani and Rice formula ([23]), gave the following saddlepoint approximation (SAD) for the tail probability of an $M$-estimator $T_n(X_1,\ldots,X_n)$ with score function $\psi$, assuming that $G$ is the underlying model for the $X_u$,

$$P_G\{T_n > a\} = 1 - \Phi(s) + \phi(s)\left[\frac{1}{r} - \frac{1}{s} + O(n^{-3/2})\right], \tag{5}$$

where $\Phi$ and $\phi$ are the cumulative and density functions of the standard normal distribution, and $s$ and $r$ are the functionals

$$s = \sqrt{-2nK(z_0,a)}\,,\; r_1 = z_0\sqrt{K''(z_0,a)}\,,\; r = \sqrt{n}\,r_1,$$

where

$$K(\lambda,a) = \log \int_{-\infty}^{\infty} e^{\lambda\psi(y,a)}\,dG(y)$$

is the cumulant generating function of the distribution $G$; $K''(\lambda,a)$ and $K'(\lambda,a)$ are the second and first partial derivatives of $K(\lambda,a)$ with respect to the first argument $\lambda$, respectively, and $z_0$ is the saddlepoint; that is, the functional solution of the *saddlepoint equation*

$$K'(z_0,a) = \int_{-\infty}^{\infty} e^{z_0\psi(y,a)}\,\psi(y,a)\,dG(y) = 0.$$

If, in approximation (5), we replace the model $G$ by the contaminated model $G_{\epsilon;x} = (1-\epsilon)G + \epsilon\Delta_x$ and obtain the derivative at $\epsilon = 0$, in all of the functionals involved in it, we obtain a saddlepoint approximation of the $\mathrm{TAIF}(x;a;T_n,G)$, (for details, see [24] pp. 402–404, [25] p. 77 or [9] p. 314), as

$$\mathrm{TAIF}(x;a;T_n,G) = \frac{\phi(s)}{r_1}\,n^{1/2}\left(\frac{e^{z_0\psi(x,a)}}{\int e^{z_0\psi(y,a)}dG(y)} - 1\right) + O(n^{-1/2}). \tag{6}$$

Replacing the SAD approximation (6) in the VOM approximation (3), we obtain the VOM + SAD approximation for the distribution of an $M$-estimator $T_n(X_1,\ldots,X_n)$ with score function $\psi$, at the model $F$, which is on the order of $O(n^{-1/2})$,

$$P_F\{T_n > a\} \simeq P_G\{T_n > a\} + \frac{\phi(s)}{r_1}\sqrt{n}\left(\frac{\int e^{z_0\psi(x,a)}dF(x)}{\int e^{z_0\psi(y,a)}dG(y)} - 1\right). \tag{7}$$

In the particular case that the transformed observations $X_u$ follow a mixture model $F = (1-\epsilon)G + \epsilon H$, the VOM+SAD approximation is

$$P_F\{T_n > a\} \simeq P_G\{T_n > a\} + \epsilon\,\frac{\phi(s)}{r_1}\sqrt{n}\left(\frac{\int e^{z_0\psi(x,a)}dH(x)}{\int e^{z_0\psi(y,a)}dG(y)} - 1\right). \tag{8}$$

**Remark 1.** *If the sample size is large and $T_n$ is asymptotically normal under $F$, we can approximate its distribution using the Central Limit Theorem, thereby, obtaining*

$$\begin{aligned} P_F\{T_n > a\} &\simeq P_F\{(T_n - E[T_n])/\sigma_{T_n} > (a - E[T_n])/\sigma_{T_n}\} \\ &= 1 - \Phi((a - E[T_n])/\sigma_{T_n}). \end{aligned}$$

*Alternatively, if $T_n$ is only asymptotically normal under $G$, we can approximate the leading terms of (7) and (8).*

**Remark 2.** *Approximations (7) and (8) are valid for any $M$-estimator with score function $\psi$ based on $X_u$ data, solution of (2). For spatio-temporal data, these $X_u$, which are transformations of the initial $Z_i$ observations, have different distributions than the $Y_s$ used in [7] for the estimation of the spatial variogram and also different from those used in [8] in the estimation of the cross-variogram.*

*In addition to the differences in the observations are the differences in the score functions. Here, for the spatio-temporal problem, $\psi$ will include the temporal dimension, which was not considered in the other two mentioned papers. However, the main difference is that, in [7], we obtained M-estimators for the spatial variogram, while here we obtained it for the spatio-temporal variogram. However, if the temporal dimension is removed (see Section 8), both estimators will agree. Hence, the estimators obtained here generalize those of the variogram (without temporal dimension) obtained there, as it should be.*

*This remark can be clearly observed in the example considered in Section 7, where we obtain seven different spatial variogram estimators (see Figure 6 for the classical and Figure 7 for the robust) at the seven different temporal lags considered—all of them obtained from the only one classical (Figure 4) or robust (Figure 5) three-dimensional spatio-temporal variogram estimator.*

## 4. Independence of the Transformed Variables $X_u$

As the locations $\mathbf{s}_i$ are fixed in advance, they can be considered as being equally spaced on a transect, as in [3], p. 32. Hence, we can match two contiguous $\mathbf{s}_i$ (for which the dependence of the $Z_i$ is supposed to be the strongest), such that $\mathbf{s}_i + \mathbf{h} = \mathbf{s}_{i+1}$. Under these conditions, with the same arguments as in [7], Section 2, it can be proved that, at each time $t_j$ and time lag $\tau$, the correlation between $\sqrt{X_{ij}} = Z(\mathbf{s}_i + \mathbf{h}; t_j + \tau) - Z(\mathbf{s}_i; t_j)$ and $\sqrt{X_{kj}} = Z(\mathbf{s}_k + \mathbf{h}; t_j + \tau) - Z(\mathbf{s}_k; t_j)$ is 0 if a linear semivariogram model can be accepted for all the initial $Z_u$ variables.

Moreover, following the ideas provided in [8] for the cross-variogram, if we can also accept a linear cross-variogram for each pair $(Z_i, Z_k)$ at any pair of time moments, assuming that all moments are equally spaced, the variables $\sqrt{X_{ij}} = Z(\mathbf{s}_i + \mathbf{h}; t_j + \tau) - Z(\mathbf{s}_i; t_j)$ and $\sqrt{X_{kl}} = Z(\mathbf{s}_k + \mathbf{h}; t_l + \tau) - Z(\mathbf{s}_k; t_l)$ will also be independent; then, so will all of the $X_u$, $u = 1,\ldots,n$, assuming that the vector $\mathbf{Z}$ of the observations is distributed as a multivariate (or contaminated) normal distribution.

Hence, to obtain the independence of the $X_u$, we must check that a linear semivariogram can be accepted for the $Z_u$ and a linear cross-variogram for each pair $(Z_i, Z_k)$.

This can easily be checked in a visual way with R and formally with the global test proposed in [7], Section 10.1. Furthermore, these linearity requirements should not be a serious problem, as we can move the spatial lag **h** and/or the time lag $\tau$ until linearized versions ([7], Section 9) of the variograms and cross-variograms can be accepted.

## 5. VOM + SAD Approximation of the Distribution of the Empirical Spatio-Temporal Estimator

As the classical method-of-moments estimator

$$2\,\widehat{\gamma}_z(\mathbf{h};\tau) = \frac{1}{n(\mathbf{h},\tau)} \sum_{u=1}^{n(\mathbf{h},\tau)} X_u$$

is an $M$-estimator and a solution of the equation

$$\sum_{u=1}^{n(\mathbf{h},\tau)} \psi(X_u, T_n) = 0$$

with the score function $\psi(v) = v$, we can use the results of Section 3 to obtain a VOM + SAD approximation for its distribution.

In the unrealistic case of no contamination—namely, if $Z \equiv N(\mu,\sigma^2)$ and so, $X_u \equiv 2\,\gamma_z(\mathbf{h};\tau)\,\chi_1^2$—the exact distribution of $2\,\widehat{\gamma}_z(\mathbf{h};\tau)$ is the tail of a $\chi^2$ distribution with $n(\mathbf{h},\tau)$ degrees of freedom,

$$P\{2\,\widehat{\gamma}_z(\mathbf{h};\tau) > a\} = P\left\{\chi^2_{n(\mathbf{h},\tau)} > \frac{a \cdot n(\mathbf{h},\tau)}{2\gamma_z(\mathbf{h};\tau)}\right\}.$$

Hence, using $G = 2\,\gamma_z(\mathbf{h};\tau)\,\chi_1^2$ as a pivotal distribution, the von Mises approximation (8) becomes

$$\begin{aligned} P_F\{2\,\widehat{\gamma}_z(\mathbf{h};\tau) > a\} \;\simeq\;& P\left\{\chi^2_{n(\mathbf{h},\tau)} > \frac{a \cdot n(\mathbf{h},\tau)}{2\gamma_z(\mathbf{h};\tau)}\right\} \\ &+\epsilon\,\frac{\phi(s)}{r_1}\sqrt{n(\mathbf{h},\tau)}\left(\frac{\int e^{z_0\psi(x,a)}dH(x)}{\int e^{z_0\psi(y,a)}dG(y)} - 1\right), \end{aligned} \tag{9}$$

considering a scale-contaminated normal distribution for the original observations $Z$, i.e., the following model for the $X_u$

$$F = (1-\epsilon)\,2\,\gamma_z(\mathbf{h};\tau)\,\chi_1^2 + \epsilon\,g^2\,2\,\gamma_z(\mathbf{h};\tau)\,\chi_1^2 = (1-\epsilon)G + \epsilon H,$$

where $G = 2\gamma_z(\mathbf{h};\tau)\chi_1^2$ and $H = g^2 2\gamma_z(\mathbf{h};\tau)\chi_1^2$; that is, where $G$ is a gamma distribution with parameters $(1/2, 1/(4\gamma_z(\mathbf{h};\tau)))$, and $H$ is a gamma distribution with parameters $(1/2, 1/(4g^2\gamma_z(\mathbf{h};\tau)))$.

In (9), the saddlepoint is

$$z_0 = \frac{1}{4\gamma_z(\mathbf{h};\tau)} - \frac{1}{2a},$$

and approximation (9) becomes

$$
\begin{aligned}
P_F\{2\widehat{\gamma}_z(\mathbf{h};\tau) > a\} \simeq \; & P\left\{\chi^2_{n(\mathbf{h},\tau)} > \frac{a\, n(\mathbf{h},\tau)}{2\gamma_z(\mathbf{h};\tau)}\right\} \\
& +\epsilon\sqrt{n(\mathbf{h},\tau)}\;\frac{2\gamma_z(\mathbf{h};\tau)}{\sqrt{\pi}(a-2\gamma_z(\mathbf{h};\tau))} \\
& \cdot\exp\left\{-\frac{n(\mathbf{h},\tau)}{2}\left(\frac{a}{2\gamma_z(\mathbf{h};\tau)}-1-\log\frac{a}{2\gamma_z(\mathbf{h};\tau)}\right)\right\} \\
& \cdot\left(\frac{\sqrt{2\gamma_z(\mathbf{h};\tau)}}{\sqrt{a-ag^2+2g^2\gamma_z(\mathbf{h};\tau)}}-1\right).
\end{aligned}
\tag{10}
$$

This approximation has the same accuracy as the VOM + SAD approximation obtained in [7] for Matheron's estimator because, in fact, the classical spatio-temporal estimator is a generalization of Matheron's estimator. For this reason, the lack of robustness of Matheron's estimator is also inherited in the empirical spatio-temporal estimator.

*Accuracy of the Approximation*

Let us observe that, if $\epsilon = 0$ or $g = 1$, the sum of the right-hand side of approximation (10) is zero. Moreover, we can observe the accuracy of this approximation with a simulation, as explained in the Supplementary Material.

With this simulation, we can see the quality of approximation (10) in Table 1 for several values of $a$, considering a sample size as small as $n(\mathbf{h},\tau) = 3$, $g = 1.1$ (i.e., 10% contamination in scale), $2\gamma_z(\mathbf{h};\tau) = 1.4$ and $\epsilon = 0.01$. The *exact* values were obtained with a simulation considering 100,000 samples.

**Table 1.** Tail probabilities for several values of $a$ and sample size $n(\mathbf{h},\tau) = 3$.

| $a$ | *Exact* | **Approximation** |
|---|---|---|
| 2.5 | 0.14714 | 0.148299 |
| 3.0 | 0.09308 | 0.093233 |
| 3.5 | 0.05577 | 0.058124 |
| 4.0 | 0.03548 | 0.036006 |
| 4.5 | 0.02089 | 0.022196 |
| 5.0 | 0.01313 | 0.013633 |

This VOM + SAD approximation is shown in Figure 1, as the dotted line, where the solid line shows the *exact* distribution.

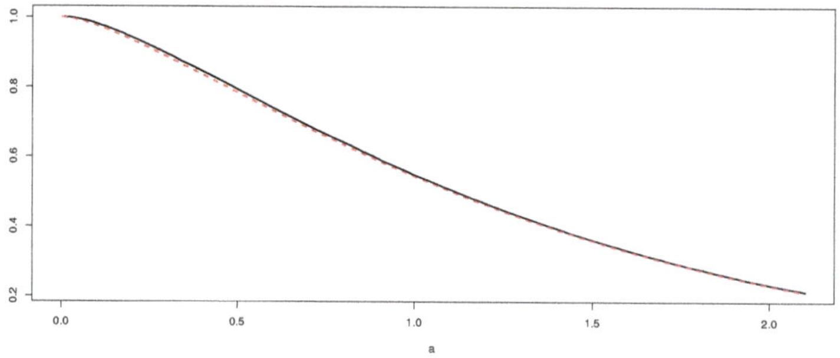


**Figure 1.** *Exact* and approximate tail probabilities for the empirical spatio-temporal estimator with $n(\mathbf{h},\tau) = 3$.

In Figure 2, we plot the VOM + SAD approximation with different contaminations: $\epsilon = 0.01$, $\epsilon = 0.05$, $\epsilon = 0.1$ and $\epsilon = 0.2$. We can see that, as the contamination percentage (i.e., the value of $\epsilon$) increases, the $p$-values and critical values are greatly affected, graphically indicating the lack of robustness of the classical spatio-temporal estimator.

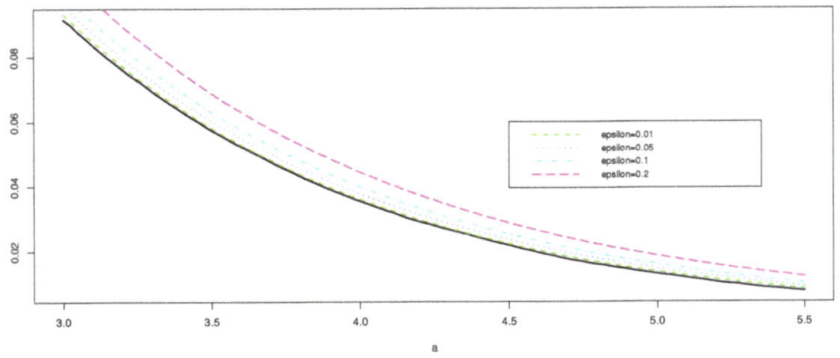


**Figure 2.** *Exact* and approximate tail probabilities of the empirical spatio-temporal estimator with contamination $\epsilon = 0.01$, $\epsilon = 0.05$, $\epsilon = 0.1$ and $\epsilon = 0.2$, with sample size $n(\mathbf{h}, \tau) = 3$.

The details of this and other computations, as well as the R functions ([26]) used in the paper, are available on the website https://www2.uned.es/pea-metodos-estadisticos-aplicados/spa-temp-variogram.htm as Supplementary Material (accessed on 18 April 2022).

## 6. Huber's Spatio-Temporal Variogram Estimator

We define the *Huber spatio-temporal variogram estimator* $2\,\widehat{\gamma}_H(\mathbf{h};\tau)$ as the $M$-estimator obtained from Equation (2) using, as the score function $\psi$, the Huber function $\psi_b(u) = \min\{b, \max\{u, -b\}\}$, where $b$ is the *tuning* constant.

This estimator is a generalization of the spatial Huber estimator for the spatial variogram defined in [7]. Here, the score function $\psi$ incorporates the time component, sometimes as spatial variograms at different time moments.

In the approximation proposed for the tail probability of Huber's spatio-temporal variogram estimator, we approximate the leading term using the Lugannani and Rice formula, [23], given in (5), and the second term using the integral of the saddlepoint approximation of the TAIF obtained in Section 3.2, assuming again a scale-contaminated normal model. The VOM + SAD approximation obtained in this way is

$$\begin{aligned} P_{X_i \equiv F}\{2\,\widehat{\gamma}_H(\mathbf{h};\tau) > a\} \;\simeq\;& 1 - \Phi(s) + \phi(s)\left[\frac{1}{r} - \frac{1}{s}\right] \\ &+ \epsilon\,\frac{\phi(s)}{r_1}\,\sqrt{n(\mathbf{h},\tau)}\left(\frac{\int e^{z_0 \psi_b(x-a)}\,dH(x)}{\int e^{z_0 \psi_b(y-a)}\,dG(y)} - 1\right), \end{aligned}$$

where the saddlepoint $z_0$ is obtained from the saddlepoint equation

$$\int e^{z_0 \psi_b(y-a)}\,\psi_b(y-a)\,dG(y) = 0.$$

Some applications of this estimator are given in the following example.

## 7. Example

For this example, we obtain the Huber spatio-temporal variogram estimator for the NOAA data set. This data set was introduced in [5] and refers to the daily weather data obtained by the US National Oceanic and Atmospheric Administration (NOAA) National Climatic Data Center.

In this data set, we considered the variable Tmax—the daily maximum temperature in degrees Fahrenheit. The classical spatio-temporal semivariogram for this variable is shown in Figure 2.17 of [5], p. 39. In Figure 3, we show the Huber spatio-temporal semivariogram estimator defined in this paper, considering the tuning constant $b = 1.345$.

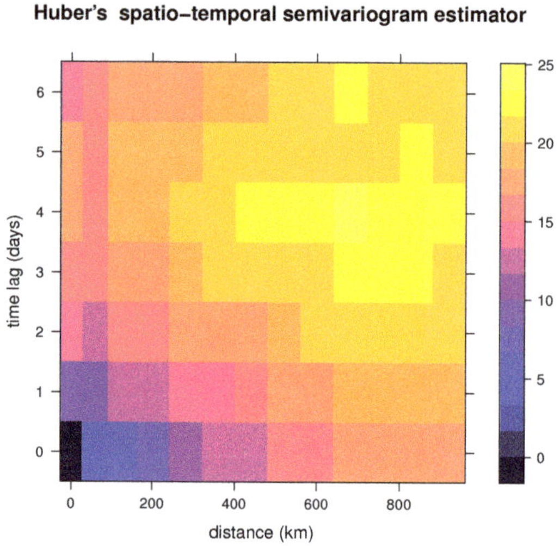


**Figure 3.** Huber's spatio-temporal semivariogram estimator (with tuning constant equal to 1.345) of daily Tmax from the NOAA data set for July 2003, computed using the estimator introduced in Section 6.

Three-dimensional representations of these classical and robust Huber's spatio-temporal semivariogram estimators are shown, respectively, in Figures 4 and 5.

Details of these computations are provided in the Supplementary Material.

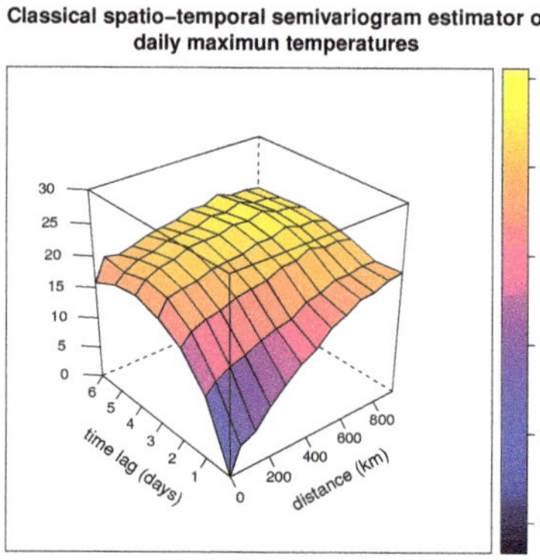


**Figure 4.** Three-dimensional picture of the classical spatio-temporal semivariogram estimator of the daily Tmax from the NOAA data for July 2003.

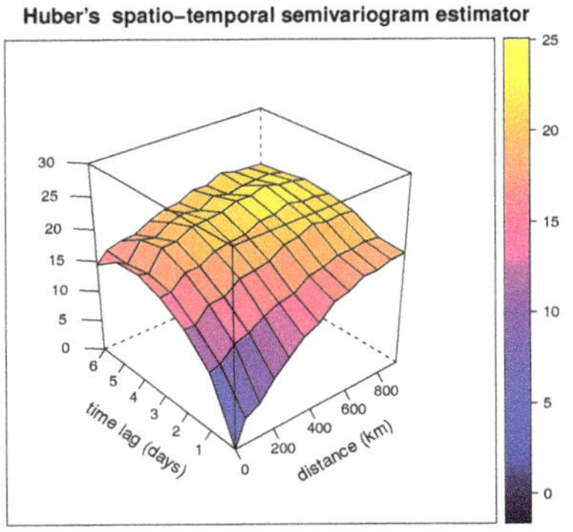


**Figure 5.** Three-dimensional picture of the Huber spatio-temporal semivariogram estimator (with a tuning constant equal to 1.345) of the daily Tmax from the NOAA data for July 2003 computed using the estimator introduced in Section 6.

## 8. Significant Time Dimension

We can see differences with respect to the selected temporal lags in Figures 6 and 7 for the classical and robust semivariogram estimators, respectively, obtained from the three-dimensional spatio-temporal variogram estimators by fixing the lags. These differences became smaller as we increased the time lag. If there were no significant differences between two of these semivariograms, we could group these two lags into one, thus, reducing the number of time lags considered.

Let us denote by $\gamma_z(\mathbf{h}, \tau_0)$ and $\gamma_z(\mathbf{h}, \tau)$ the semivariograms at lags $\tau_0$ and $\tau$ for a fixed spatial lag $\mathbf{h}$, having corresponding distributions $F_{\tau_0}$ and $F_\tau$. If we use approximation (7), considering the distributions $F = F_\tau$ and $G = F_{\tau_0}$, the VOM + SAD approximation of the distribution of the classical spatio-temporal estimator $T_n = 2\widehat{\gamma}_z(\mathbf{h}, \tau)$ at lag $\tau$ is

$$\begin{aligned} P_{F_\tau}\{T_n > a\} &\simeq P_{F_{\tau_0}}\{T_n > a\} + \frac{\phi(s)}{r_1}\sqrt{n(\mathbf{h},\tau_0)}\left(\frac{\int e^{z_0\psi(x,a)}dF_\tau(x)}{\int e^{z_0\psi(y,t)}dF_{\tau_0}(y)} - 1\right) \\ &= P\left\{\chi^2_{n(\mathbf{h},\tau_0)} > \frac{a\cdot n(\mathbf{h},\tau_0)}{2\gamma_z(\mathbf{h};\tau_0)}\right\} \\ &\quad + \sqrt{n(\mathbf{h},\tau_0)}\,\frac{2\gamma_z(\mathbf{h};\tau_0)}{\sqrt{\pi}(a - 2\gamma_z(\mathbf{h};\tau_0))} \\ &\quad \cdot \exp\left\{-\frac{n(\mathbf{h},\tau_0)}{2}\left(\frac{a}{2\gamma_z(\mathbf{h};\tau_0)} - 1 - \log\frac{a}{2\gamma_z(\mathbf{h};\tau_0)}\right)\right\} \\ &\quad \cdot \left(\exp\left\{-a\left(\frac{1}{4\gamma_z(\mathbf{h};\tau_0)} - \frac{1}{4\gamma_z(\mathbf{h};\tau)}\right)\right\}\frac{\sqrt{2\gamma_z(\mathbf{h};\tau)}}{\sqrt{2\gamma_z(\mathbf{h};\tau_0)}} - 1\right), \end{aligned}$$

where $n(\mathbf{h}, \tau_0)$ is the sample size used by $T_n$ at spatial lag $\mathbf{h}$ and temporal lag $\tau_0$.

In the same way as in a general testing problem, we test the null hypothesis $\theta = \theta_0$ against the alternative $\theta > \theta_0$ using a test statistic $S_n$, computing the tail probability $P_{\theta_0}\{S_n > s_n\}$, where $s_n$ is the observed value of $S_n$, and if this probability is small (large), we reject (accept) the null hypothesis. Here, we can test, for a fixed spatial lag $\mathbf{h}$, the null hypothesis of no significant change between two temporal lags $\tau_0$ and $\tau$—that is, $H_0$ : $\gamma_z(\mathbf{h}, \tau) = \gamma_z(\mathbf{h}, \tau_0)$, against $H_1 : \gamma_z(\mathbf{h}, \tau) > \gamma_z(\mathbf{h}, \tau_0)$—by computing the tail probability

$$P_{2\gamma_z(\mathbf{h},\tau_0)}\{2\widehat{\gamma}_z(\mathbf{h}, \tau) > 2\widehat{\gamma}_z(\mathbf{h}, \tau)^{obs.}\}.$$

A small value of this probability will discredit the null hypothesis and lead us to reject it, concluding that there exists a significant difference between the semivariograms at the lags

$\tau_0$ and $\tau$, suggesting that we must compute the (classical or robust) estimators in a separate way at these two lags. On the other hand, if we accept the null hypothesis, we shall group these two lags, thus, considering one less lag.

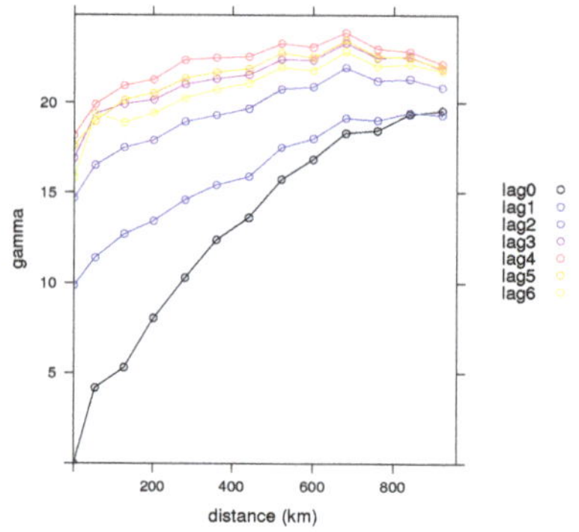


**Figure 6.** Classical semivariograms of the daily Tmax from the NOAA data with respect to the seven time lags considered.

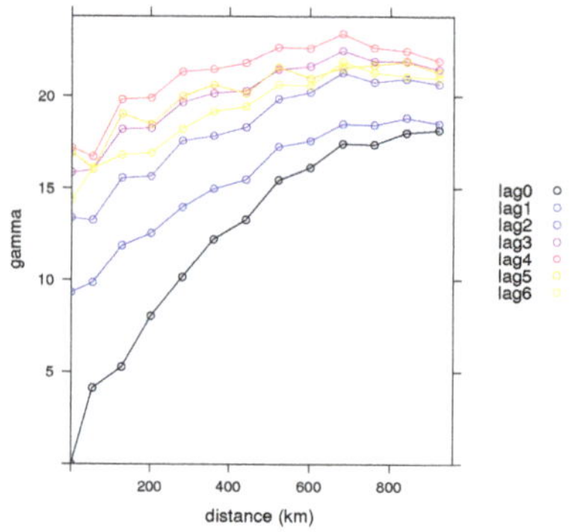


**Figure 7.** Huber's semivariograms (with tuning constant equal to 1.345) of the daily Tmax from the NOAA data with respect to the seven time lags considered.

For instance, in the previous example, considering the spatial lag **h** between 240 and 320, the previous probability between the starting moment and the first time lag or that between the first and second temporal lag, are both equal to 0, suggesting highly significant differences between these two pairs of lags (as can be appreciated in Figures 6 and 7).

On the other hand, the probability between time lags four and five is 0.9427521 and between the last two is 0.9737844, (for the spatial lag $240 < \mathbf{h} < 320$), leading us to accept the null hypothesis and suggesting that we can consider all of these observations in a single group for the computation of the spatio-temporal variogram estimator.

## 9. Identification of Spatio-Temporal Outliers

The second objective of this work is to identify spatio-temporal outliers. For this purpose, we calculated the VOM + SAD approximation of the distribution of the *Difference M-estimator*, an $M$-estimator that is essentially the difference between the classical method-of-moments estimator and the Huber estimator defined in Section 6. We chose this pair of estimators, as Huber's estimator minimizes the maximum asymptotic variance inside the class of contamination neighborhoods of the normal distribution—the class of models considered in the paper—and the mean is an extreme particular case of it (i.e., they are nested estimators). When this difference is significant at some pair of lags, we qualify this pair of lags as spatio-temporal outliers.

This $M$-estimator is completely defined in (12) below; however, we can also say that the Difference $M$-estimator is one of the estimators inside the class defined in the next section.

### 9.1. Average M-Estimators

$M$-estimators ([11]) are likely the most widely used robust estimators. Nevertheless, they are somewhat unpleasant to handle as they are defined in an implicit way, as a solution of an equation; in particular, the spatio-temporal $M$-estimator is a solution of Equation (2). Next, we define a new class of $M$-estimators, which is considered in this paper only for the case of location estimation.

**Definition 1.** *If $T_n$ is an M-estimator with score function $\psi$ and, thus, with M-functional $T(F)$ defined by*

$$\int \psi(x, T(F))\, dF(x) = 0,$$

*the Average M-estimator associated with $T_n$ is defined as*

$$T_n^a = \frac{1}{n} \sum_{i=1}^{n} \psi(X_i)$$

*with the associated functional*

$$T^a(F) = \int \psi(x)\, dF(x).$$

The Average $M$-estimator associated with the mean is exactly the mean and $\sum_{i=1}^{n} \psi_b(X_i)/n$ is the associated with the Huber estimator, $\psi_b$ being the Huber score function considered in Section 6.

An Average $M$-estimator is an $M$-estimator with score function $\psi(x, \theta) = \psi(x) - \theta$ because it is a solution of

$$\sum_{i=1}^{n} \psi(x_i, \theta) = 0;$$

that is,

$$\sum_{i=1}^{n} \psi(x_i) - n\theta = 0$$

or

$$T_n^a = \sum_{i=1}^{n} \psi(x_i)/n.$$

We summarize some of the main properties of this class of $M$-estimators in the following proposition.

**Proposition 1.** *(a) The Influence Function of a linear combination of estimators is the linear combination of their Influence Functions:*

*If $T = \sum_{j=1}^{q} w_j\, T_j$ is a linear combination of $q$ estimators with Influence Functions $\mathrm{IF}_j$, the Hampel Influence Function of $T$ is $\sum_{j=1}^{q} w_j\, \mathrm{IF}_j$.*

*(b) The linear combination of Average M-estimators is an M-estimator:*

*If $T = \sum_{j=1}^{q} w_j\, T_j^a$ is a linear combination of $q$ Average M-estimators with score functions $\psi_j(x_i) - \theta$, then $T$ is an M-estimator with score function*

$$\psi(x_i, \theta) = \left( \sum_{j=1}^{q} w_j\, \psi_j(x_i) \right) - \theta.$$

*(c) The Hampel Influence Function of an Average M-functional $T^a(F)$ is*

$$IF(x; T^a, F) = \psi(x) - T^a(F). \tag{11}$$

*(d) The robustness properties of an Average M-estimator are the same as those of the M-estimator from which it is defined.*
*(e) Any Average M-functional is a linear functional and is weakly continuous on the class of probability distributions on the Borel $\sigma$-algebra if $\psi$ is bounded.*
*(f) The asymptotic distribution of an Average M-estimator is normal with the mean being the associated functional and asymptotic variance*

$$(\psi(x) - T^a(F))^2/n.$$

**Proof.** The proof of (a) is straightforward due to the linearity properties of the limits (or derivatives) and because the Hampel Influence Function is defined as a limit.

To prove (b), we set up the equation

$$\sum_{i=1}^{n} \psi(X_i, T) = 0;$$

that is,

$$\sum_{i=1}^{n} \left( \sum_{j=1}^{q} w_j \, \psi_j(x_i) \right) - n\,T = 0$$

or

$$T = \left( \sum_{j=1}^{q} w_j \sum_{i=1}^{n} \psi_j(x_i)/n \right) = \left( \sum_{j=1}^{q} w_j T_j^a \right).$$

(c) The Hampel Influence Function of an Average $M$-functional $T^a(F)$

$$T^a(F) = \int \psi(y)\, dF(y)$$

is obtained first by contaminating the distribution

$$T^a(F_\epsilon) = (1-\epsilon) \int \psi(y)\, dF(y) + \epsilon\, \psi(x)$$

and then obtaining the derivative at $\epsilon = 0$,

$$IF(x; T^a, F) = \psi(x) - T^a(F).$$

(d) The infinitesimal robustness properties of an estimator, such as the gross-error sensitivity (B-robustness), local-shift sensitivity and rejection point, are based on its Influence Function which, in the case of $M$-estimators, depends on the behavior of their score functions. As the Influence Function of an Average $M$-estimator is the score function $\psi$ (shifted by $T^a(F)$) of the $M$-estimator from which it is defined, as obtained in (11), the robustness properties of both will be the same.

The same occurs with the global reliability (breakdown point) or with the qualitative robustness and its weak continuity, as highlighted in (e), which is true because of Lemma 2.1 in [9], p. 24.

The proof of (f) is obtained from the Central Limit Theorem, with the asymptotic variance of $M$-estimators equal to the square of the Influence Function ([9], p. 47). □

*9.2. Identification of Spatio-Temporal Outliers*

As the classical method-of-moments estimator $2\,\widehat{\gamma}_z(\mathbf{h};\tau)$ is the $M$-estimator associated with the score function $\psi(x) = x$ and the Huber spatio-temporal variogram estimator, $2\,\widehat{\gamma}_H(\mathbf{h};\tau)$ is the $M$-estimator associated with the score function $\psi_b(u) = \min\{b, \max\{u, -b\}\}$, where $b$ is the *tuning* constant, to evaluate the effect of contamination, we define the *Difference M-estimator* as a solution $T_n^{di}$ of the equation

$$\sum_{u=1}^{n} \psi_{di}(X_u, T_n^{di}) = 0, \tag{12}$$

where the score function in (12) is defined as $\psi_{di} = \psi - \psi_b$, which is plotted in Figure 8.

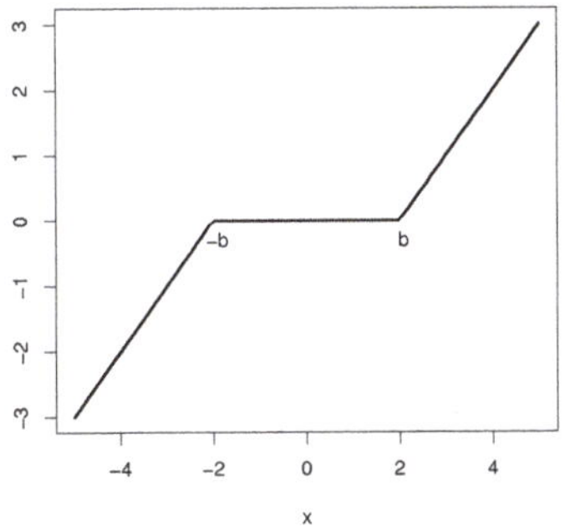


**Figure 8.** Score function defining the Difference $M$-estimator with tuning constant $b$.

The Difference $M$-estimator, completely defined from (12) as a general $M$-estimator, can be also considered as the difference of the Average $M$-estimators associated with the mean and the Huber estimator.

As it is an $M$-estimator, we can use the VOM + SAD approximation (8) for its distribution obtained above, $P_F\{T_n^{di} > a\}$, with $\psi_{di}$ being the score function.

As $2\,\widehat{\gamma}_Z(\mathbf{h};\tau)$ and $2\,\widehat{\gamma}_H(\mathbf{h};\tau)$ are sums of squares, and the latter is softer than the former, we should check for large positive values of the Difference $M$-estimator as spatio-temporal outliers. Hence, if the probability $P_F\{T_n^{di} > t_n^{di}\}$ for a pair of lags $(\mathbf{h},\tau)$ (where $t_n^{di}$ is the observed value of the Difference $M$-estimator), is significantly small, we conclude that $(\mathbf{h},\tau)$ is a spatio-temporal outlier.

**Example 1.** *Continuing with the example of Section 7, some of the differences between the classical spatio-temporal estimator and the Huber spatio-temporal estimator are small (e.g., 0.0000 and 0.0299), while others are large (e.g., 6.4689 and 6.6959). With the approximation of the Difference M-estimator, we obtain a table of tail probabilities (i.e., p-values for the test of significant differences), thus, allowing for the detection of spatio-temporal outliers.*

*The full table for the 91 pairs of lags considered in this paper is provided in the Supplementary Material. All 91 lags are shown in Figure 9 together with the highly significant spatio-temporal outliers (in red) and the doubtfully significant outliers (in blue).*

*From the figure, if we discard the doubtful outliers (in blue), we can conclude that some of spatio-temporal lag outliers are essentially only spatial outliers (at* $\mathbf{h} = 40$, $\mathbf{h} = 200$ *from the second temporal lag), while two of them are essentially only temporal outliers (*$\tau = 2$, $\tau = 6$*, from the distance lags* $\mathbf{h} = 40$ *to* $\mathbf{h} = 200$*; maybe* $\mathbf{h} = 280$*). The truly spatio-temporal outliers, in both components, are the intersection lags* $(\mathbf{h},\tau) = (40,2), (40,6), (200,2), (200,6)$.

*We remark that these spatio-temporal outliers are lag outliers (i.e., not observation coordinates); that is, they are outliers with respect to the variogram, where the observations are not the initial* $Z_i$ *but the transformed* $X_i$*. Nevertheless, they must be checked before kriging.*

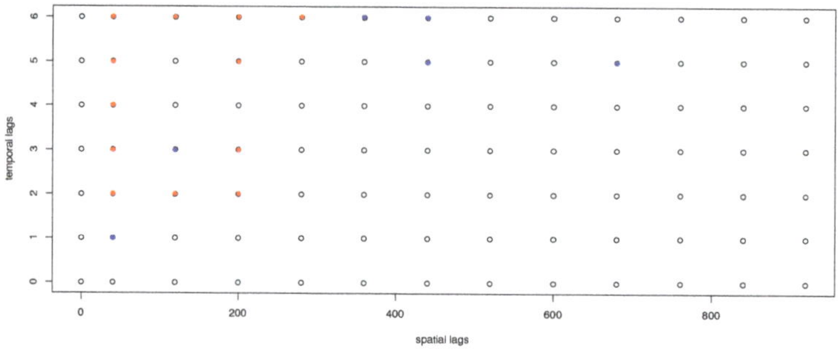


**Figure 9.** Highly significant spatio-temporal atypical lags (in red) and doubtfully significant (in blue) of the daily Tmax from the NOAA data.

## 10. Conclusions

In this paper, we proposed some robust estimators of the spatio-temporal variogram. We also obtained accurate approximations for their distributions. These were based on a von Mises expansion of the tail probability functional plus a saddlepoint approximation of the Tail Area Influence Function involved in the von Mises expansion. One of the advantages of these approximations is that they have a closed form, thus, allowing for easy interpretation of the elements that they involve, such as the sample size, contamination fraction, score function, temporal and spatial lags and so on.

These approximations are computed under a scale-contaminated normal model for the observations. One of the key points in obtaining these approximations is the transformation of the original variables into new independent variables. With the approximations obtained in this way, we can check, for instance, whether the common use of all the observations without temporal distinctions is valid or if the estimators must be computed for significantly different times. We also used these approximations to identify spatio-temporal outliers in the second part of the paper, defining a new class of $M$-estimators in the process.

**Supplementary Materials:** The following supporting information can be downloaded at: https://www.mdpi.com/article/10.3390/math10101785/s1.

**Funding:** This work was partially supported by grant PGC2018-095194-B-I00 from the Ministerio de Ciencia, Innovación y Universidades (Spain).

**Institutional Review Board Statement:** Not applicable.

**Informed Consent Statement:** Not applicable.

**Data Availability Statement:** Not applicable.

**Acknowledgments:** The author is very grateful to the referees for their kind and professional remarks.

**Conflicts of Interest:** The author declares no conflict of interest.

## References

1. Christakos, G. *Spatiotemporal Random Fields: Theory and Applications*, 2nd ed.; Elsevier: Amsterdam, The Netherlands, 2017.
2. Hristopulos, D.T. *Random Fields for Spatial Data Modeling: A Primer for Scientists and Engineers*; Springer Nature: Berlin, Germany, 2020.
3. Cressie, N.A.C. *Statistics for Spatial Data*; John Wiley & Sons: New York, NY, USA, 1993.
4. Chilès, J.P.; Delfiner, P. *Geostatistics: Modeling Spatial Uncertainty*, 2nd ed.; John Wiley & Sons: New York, NY, USA, 2012.
5. Wikle, C.K.; Zammit-Mangion, A.; Cressie, N. *Spatio-Temporal Statistics with R*; Chapman & Hall/CRC: London, UK, 2019.
6. Varouchakis, E.A.; Hristopulos, D.T. Comparison of spatiotemporal variogram functions based on a sparse dataset of groundwater level variations. *Spat. Stat.* **2019**, *34*, 1–18. [CrossRef]
7. García-Pérez, A. Saddlepoint approximations for the distribution of some robust estimators of the variogram. *Metrika* **2020**, *83*, 69–91. [CrossRef]
8. García-Pérez, A. New robust cross-variogram estimators and approximations for their distributions based on saddlepoint techniques. *Mathematics* **2021**, *9*, 762. [CrossRef]

9. Huber, P.J.; Ronchetti, E.M. *Robust Statistics*, 2nd ed.; John Wiley & Sons: New York, NY, USA, 2009.
10. Tukey, J.W. A survey of sampling from contaminated distributions. In *Contributions to Probability and Statistics: Essays in Honor of Harold Hotelling, Stanford Studies in Mathematics and Statistics*; Oklin, I., Ed.; Stanford University Press: Redwood City, CA, USA, 1960; Chaper 39, pp. 448–485.
11. Huber, P.J. Robust estimation of a location parameter. *Ann. Math. Stat.* **1964**, *35*, 73–101. https://www.jstor.org/stable/2238020. [CrossRef]
12. Ebner, B.; Henze, N. Tests for multivariate normality—A critical review with emphasis on weighted $L^2$-statistics. *Test* **2020**, *29*, 845–892. [CrossRef]
13. Kotz, S.; Balakrishnan, N.; Johnson, N.L. *Continuous Multivariate Distributions. Volume 1: Models and Applications*, 2nd ed.; John Wiley & Sons: New York, NY, USA, 2000.
14. Hampel, F.R.; Ronchetti, E.M.; Rousseeuw, P.J.; Syahel, W.A. *Robust Statistics: The Approach Based on Influence Functions*; John Wiley & Sons: New York, NY, USA, 1986.
15. Ronchetti, E. Accurate and robust inference. *Econom. Stat.* **2020**, *14*, 74–88. [CrossRef]
16. Cressie, N.; Hawkins, D.M. Robust estimation of the variogram: I. *Math. Geol.* **1980**, *12*, 115–125. [CrossRef]
17. La Vecchia, D.; Ronchetti, E. Saddlepoint approximations for short and long memory time series: A frequency domain approach. *J. Econom.* **2019**, *213*, 578–592. [CrossRef]
18. von Mises, R. On the asymptotic distribution of differentiable statistical functions. *Ann. Math. Stat.* **1947**, *18*, 309–348. [CrossRef]
19. Withers, C.S. Expansions for the distribution and quantiles of a regular functional of the empirical distribution with applications to nonparametric confidence intervals. *Ann. Stat.* **1983**, *11*, 577–587. [CrossRef]
20. Serfling, R.J. *Approximation Theorems of Mathematical Statistics*; John Wiley & Sons: New York, NY, USA, 1980.
21. Field, C.A.; Ronchetti, E. A tail area influence function and its application to testing. *Sequential Anal.* **1985**, *4*, 19–41. [CrossRef]
22. Daniels, H.E. Saddlepoint approximations for estimating equations. *Biometrika* **1983**, *70*, 89–96. [CrossRef]
23. Lugannani, R.; Rice, S. Saddle point approximation for the distribution of the sum of independent random variables. *Adv. Appl. Probab.* **1980**, *12*, 475–490. [CrossRef]
24. García-Pérez, A. Von Mises approximation of the critical value of a test. *Test* **2003**, *12*, 385–411. [CrossRef]
25. Jensen, J.L. *Saddlepoint Approximations*; Clarendon Press: Oxford, UK, 1995.
26. R Development Core Team. *A Language and Environment for Statistical Computing*; R Foundation for Statistical Computing: Viena, Austria, 2021. Available online: http://www.R-project.org (accessed on 18 April 2022).

mathematics MDPI

Article

# Robust Parametric Identification for ARMAX Models with Non-Gaussian and Coloured Noise: A Survey

Jesica Escobar [1,*,†] and Alexander Poznyak [2,†]

1 Instituto Politecnico Nacional ESIME Zacatenco, Unidad Profesional Adolfo Lopez Mateos, Av. IPN S/N, Mexico City 07738, Mexico
2 Department of Automatic Control, CINVESTAV-IPN A.P. 14-740, Mexico City 07000, Mexico; apoznyak@ctrl.cinvestav.mx
* Correspondence: jmescobar@esimez.mx
† These authors contributed equally to this work.

**Abstract:** In this paper the Cramer-Rao information bound for ARMAX (Auto-Regression-Moving-Average-Models-with-Exogenuos-inputs) under non-Gaussian noise is derived. It is shown that the direct application of the Least Squares Method (LSM) leads to incorrect (shifted) parameter estimates. This inconsistency can be corrected by the implementation of the parallel usage of the MLMW (Maximum Likelihood Method with Whitening) procedure, applied to all measurable variables of the model, and a nonlinear residual transformation using the information on the distribution density of a non-Gaussian noise, participating in Moving Average structure. The design of the corresponding parameter-estimator, realizing the suggested MLMW-procedure is discussed in details. It is shown that this method is asymptotically optimal, that is, reaches this information bound. If the noise distribution belongs to some given class, then the Huber approach (min-max version of MLM) may be effectively applied. A numerical example illustrates the suggested approach.

**Keywords:** parameter estimation; least squares method; whitening filter; Fisher information; maximum likelihood method; nonlinear residual transformation

**MSC:** 93E03; 93E10; 93E11; 93E24

**Citation:** Escobar, J.; Poznyak, A. Robust Parametric Identification for ARMAX Models with Non-Gaussian and Coloured Noise: A Survey. *Mathematics* **2022**, *10*, 1291. https://doi.org/10.3390/math10081291

Academic Editors: Alfonso Baños, Francisco German Badía and María D. Berrade

Received: 7 February 2022
Accepted: 29 March 2022
Published: 13 April 2022



## 1. Introduction

### 1.1. Road Map of This Survey

The topic of parameter identification in a large class of linear models with external noise acting on-line and perturbing the dynamics of an investigated system is addressed in this overview. The considered models are classified as ARMAX (auto-regression-moving average with exogenous inputs) and are commonly expressed in discrete-time format by recurrent linear stochastic difference equations. The class of distribution functions is supposed to be known a priori but not its exact analytical expression: such models contain "uncertainties" in their descriptions, which are associated with unknown parameters and probabilistic characteristics of external noise (perturbations): only a class of distribution functions is supposed to be known a priori but not its exact analytical expression. As a result, any identification technique that may be used in such a circumstance should be robust (resilient) with respect to existing uncertainty. The focus of this work is on a critical examination of robust parametric identification techniques, highlighting a gap in the current literature in which the vast majority of publications adopt the traditional assumption that external stochastic perturbations are independent and Gaussian (have a "normal distribution"). Only a few papers deal with a different non-standard assumption about the available stochastic characteristics of external noisy disturbances. Here, we expose readers to the underlying difficulties (mathematical and computational) and discuss a few distinct ways that have shown to be successful in the absence of available probabilistic data.

The structure of the paper is as follows:

- Review of publications:
  - It contains the descriptions of the important survey published in the 1970's–1990's (Åström, Becky, Ljung and Gunnarson, Billings among others).
  - Nongaussian noises have been studied by Huber, Tsypkin and Polyak.
- Problem formulation and model description:
  - The ARMAX model with correlated non-Gaussian noise, generated by a stable and non-minimal phase filter, is introduced.
- Some classes $\mathcal{P}_{3be}$ of noise p.d.f.:
  - In a rigorous mathematical manner several classes of random stationary sequences with different p.d.f. as an input of a forming filter are considered (all symmetric distributions non-singular in origin, all symmetric distributions with a bounded variance, all symmetric "approximately normal" distributions and "approximately uniform" distributions).
- Main assumptions:
  - These concern the martingale difference property with conditional bounder second moment for stochastic sequences in the input of the forming filter, stability and minimal-phase property for this filter, independent of this sequence with other measurable inputs).
- Regression representation format:
  - The extended regression form of the considered model is introduced.
- Main contribution of the paper:
  - The exact presentation of the main contribution of the paper.
- Why LSM does not work for the identification of ARMAX models with correlated noise:
  - A simple example exhibiting the lack of workability of this technique in the case of dynamic (autoregression) models is described in detail for a reader who is not actively involved in the least-squares method.
- Some other identification techniques:
  - Identification of non-stationary parameters and the Bayesian method, matrix forgetting factor and its adaptive version are reviewed.
- Regular observations and information inequality for observations with coloured noise:
  - the Cramér–Rao bound (CRB) and the Fisher information, characterising the maximal possible rate of estimation under the given information resource, are presented.
- Robust version of the maximum likelihood method with whitening (MLMW procedure):
  - This approach is demonstrated to reach the CRB bound, indicating that it is asymptotically the best among all identification procedures.
- Recurrent identification procedures with nonlinear residual transformations: static (regression) and dynamic (autoregression) models:
  - Within a specified noise p.d.f. class, it is proven that such a strategy with particular selection of nonlinear residual transformation is resilient (robust) optimum in achieving min–max error variance in CRB inequality.
- Instrumental variables ethod (IVM):
  - IV or total least-squares estimators is the method which also recommends to estimate parameters in the presence of coloured noises with a finite correlation.
- Joint parametric identification of ARMAX model and the forming filter:
  - The "generalised residual sequence" is introduced, which is shown to be asymptotically closed to the independent sequence acting in the input of the forming filter, which helps to resolve the identification problem in an extended parametric space.

    - Numerical example.
    - Discussion and conclusions.
- Appendix A and abbreviations:
    - This part offers proofs of some of the article's claims that appear to be significant from the authors' perspective, as well as a list of acronyms used throughout the work.

### 1.2. Review of the System Identification Literature

A mathematical model is a simplified mathematical structure connected to a component of reality and produced for a specific purpose of system analysis [1]. Differential equations, state space models and transfer functions are all examples of mathematical models of dynamic systems that are useful in a variety of fields [2]. System identification, which can be applied to nearly any system and give models that explain the system behaviour, is an alternative to modelling.

### 1.3. Classical Surveys on Identification

The least-squares method (LSM), as well as some of its variants, have been extensively researched in the past, according to the survey given by Åström [3]. The least squares, maximum likelihood, instrumental variables and tally principle are examples of these variety. Several approaches for the identification of dynamic systems using computer techniques, such as spectral analysis, certain gradient methods, quasi-linearization and stochastic approximations, were provided by Becky [4]. In the case of a time-varying situation, Ljung and Gunnarson investigated several methods for developing identification algorithms that could take into account the time-varying dynamics of systems as well as signals [5]. Some mean square expressions were examined in this study. In [6] by Billings, several methods for the nonlinear case were described; these algorithms were based on the functional expansion of Wiener and Volterra, block-oriented and bi-linear systems, structure detection and some catastrophe theory. System identification is a vast field of study, with a variety of methods based on the models to be estimated: linear, nonlinear, continuous, discrete, time-varying and so on. Ljung's survey [7] demonstrates that, despite the wide range of techniques, the field can be defined by a few key principles, such as data information, validation and model complexity and offers some basic principles and results, as well as a method for solving real-world problems. As it is mentioned by Ljung in [8], system identification is a well established research area, whose paradigms are most of the time based on classical statistical methods. Some recent techniques are based on kernel regularisation methods. The paper presented by Ljung presents some of the main ideas and results of kernel-based regularisation methods for system identification.

### 1.4. Identification under Correlated Noise Perturbations

In the measurements and modelling of dynamic systems [9], the unpredictability inherent in physical processes always creates inaccuracy. Stochastic processes make it possible to model these random events and create more realistic models [10]. It is commonly assumed that only white noise is presented in stochastic systems, however, there are also cases where the noise is correlated or "coloured". Coloured noise is prevalent in linear and pseudo-linear regression identification models, where one of the challenges is the presence of unknown inner variables and immeasurable noise components [11]. The stochastic gradient algorithm proved to be a useful technique for those cases. In situations where there are a lot of noisy sources, noise suppression is crucial. In many practical circumstances, coloured noise may be converted to white noise [12] by passing it through an invertible time-invariant linear ("whitening") filter. The existence of coloured noise typically leads to robust identification theory, which was first proposed by P. Huber [13] and Ya. Z. Tsypkin-B. Polyak [14] over fifty years ago. In [15], the basic principles of robust identification were presented, as well as the identification methods for auto regression with exogenous input (ARX) models. The suggested approach used a whitening procedure and a variant of the maximum likelihood method in parallel to conduct asymptotically the estimation of unknown parameters. The need of system identification has grown in some areas, such as robotics, due to the increasing interest in showing movement accuracy in the industry. The application of system identification in DC servomotors is widely used in robotics; in [16], a study on identifying two model structures, ARX and ARMAX, of the system to test and compare their performance on validation criterion is presented.

### *1.5. Identification of ARMAX and NARMAX Models*

For many years, the parameter estimation for autoregressive moving average exogenous input (ARMAX) models has been investigated [17,18]. The importance of parameter-bounding methods in the identification process is highlighted in [19] and stands for such models. These methods offer a radical alternative to compute parameter point estimates and covariances. They require constraints in an effectively deterministic model formulation instead of p.d.f. or mean and covariance for the noise and previous parameter estimations.

In the context of parameter-bounding identification, this study offers a preliminary assessment of certain typical tasks, such as experiment design, testing for outliers, tolerance prediction and worst-case control design. In [20], the parametrisation of ARMAX models was also discussed. The results reported in this work were aimed at developing a technique for modelling and fitting multivariable time-series data based on spatial approach and parametrisation, with tolerance for missing or incomplete data.

ARMAX models are widely used in industrial modelling nowadays [21–23]. For example, functional time series are the realisation of a stochastic process where each observation is a continuous function defined on a finite interval. These processes are commonly used in electricity markets and are gaining more importance as more market data become available and markets head toward continuous time-marginal pricing approaches. In [24], the authors propose a new functional forecasting method that attempts to generalise the standard seasonal ARMAX time-series model to the $L_2$ Hilbert space; the proposed approach is tested by forecasting the daily price profile of the Spanish and German electricity markets, and it is compared with other functional reference models. A physic-based ARMAX model of room temperature in office buildings was presented in [25], where thermodynamic equations are used to determine the structure and order of the model. In this study, extensive measurements over 109 days are used to develop and validate the model. This model can be used to predict the variations of the room temperature accurately in short-term, and long-term periods and has shown to be suitable for real-time fault detection and control applications.

Traditional stochastic information gradient methods for ARMAX identification have a lower computational cost, but its convergence speed is still low, in [26], a two-step algorithm based on gradient acceleration strategies is proposed to deal with this problem. When in the ARMAX process, the noises presented are additive; it is possible to introduce additional information to the estimation problem using nuisances variables to model the output noises (see [27]). Then, a regularised estimator suppresses the adverse effects of the noises and provides minimum variance estimates.

In [18], a technique for concurrently picking the order and identifying the parameters of an ARMAX model was explored, and it was also assessed by computational experiments. The technique presented in that work was based on reformulating the issue for a standard state space, then implementing a bank of Kalman filters, identifying the true model and utilizing multi-model partitioning theory to solve it. In the study presented by Correa and Poznyak in 2001 (see [28]), the problem of simultaneous robust state and parameter estimation for some class of MIMO non-linear systems under mixed uncertainties (unmodeled dynamics as well as observation noises) is presented. A switching gain robust "observer-identifier" is introduced to obtain the estimation. This is achieved by applying an observer to the so-called nominal extended system, obtained from the original system without any uncertainties and considering the parameters as additional constant states. As it was shown in general the extended systems, these can lose the global observability property, supposed to be valid for the original non-extended system, and a special procedure is needed to provide a good estimation process in this situation [29]. The suggested adaptive observer has the Luenberger-type observer structure with switching matrix gain that guarantees a good enough upper bound for the identification error performance index [30]. The Van der Monde generalised transformation is introduced to derive this bound which turns out to be "tight" (it is equal to zero in the absence of both noises and unmodeled dynamics). One approach for dealing with coloured noises is to utilise parameter estimate algorithms based on Kalman filters. The Kalman filter is frequently used for control and estimate (see [31]), and this technique may be thought of as Hammerstein–Wiener ARMAX models. An extended Kalman filter, or the unscented Kalman filter, can be implemented to extend this approach to the nonlinear situation. For the nonlinear autoregressive moving average with exogenous inputs (NARMAX) models, Kalman filters are a commonly used identification method. The off-line observer/Kalman filter presented in [32] was implemented as an identification method, since it has shown a good initial guess of the NARMAX model to reduce the on-line system identification process time, this method showed to be effective in the case of system faults and input failures. In the case of Hammerstein nonlinear systems with coloured noises, a maximum likelihood-based stochastic gradient algorithm was implemented in [33], where the unknown noises were replaced in the information vector by their estimates and through these, one can obtain the parameters. For multivariable Hammerstein controlled autoregressive moving average systems, an interactive maximum likelihood estimation method was implemented in [34]. In that paper, the logarithmic likelihood function over multiple parameter vectors is maximised; the proposed method overcomes the limit on an autoregressive model form with one parameter vector.

In this survey, we present a compendium of some of the existing literature regarding identification in ARMAX models and some of the techniques used in these type of models. We also obtain the Cramer–Rao information bound for ARMAX models with non-Gaussian noises and show that the maximum likelihood method with whitening procedure (MLMW) reaches this low bound, or in other words, is asymptotically optimal.

## 2. Problem Formulation

### 2.1. Robust Parametric Identification Model Description

Consider the following ARMAX (autoregression moving average exogenous input) model given by

$$y_n = \sum_{l=1}^{L} a_l y_{n-l} + \sum_{k=0}^{K} b_k w_{n-k} + \eta_n,\ n \geq 0, \tag{1}$$

where

- $\{y_n\} \in R^1$ is scalar sequence of available on-line state variables.
- $\{w_n\}$ is a measurable input sequence (deterministic or, in general, stochastic).
- $\{\eta_n\} \in R^1$ is a noise sequence (not available during the process) generated by the exogenous system

$$\eta_n + \sum_{s=1}^{K_2} d_{2,s}\eta_{n-s} = \xi_n + \sum_{s=1}^{K_1} d_{1,s}\xi_{n-s}, \tag{2}$$

which can be symbolically represented as the forming filter

$$\eta_n = H\left(q^{-1}\right)\xi_n \tag{3}$$

with the transition function

$$\left.\begin{array}{c} H\left(q^{-1}\right) = H_1\left(q^{-1}\right)/H_2\left(q^{-1}\right), \\ H_1\left(q^{-1}\right) = 1 + \sum\limits_{s=1}^{K_1} d_{2,s}q^{-s},\ H_2\left(q^{-1}\right) = 1 + \sum\limits_{s=1}^{K_2} d_{2,s}q^{-s} \\ q^{-1} \text{is the one-step delay operator acting as } y_{k-1} = q^{-1}y_k, \end{array}\right\} \tag{4}$$

- $\{\xi_n\}$ as an independent zero mean stationary sequence with the probability density function (p.d.f.) $p_\xi(x)$ which may be unknown but belonging to some given class $\mathcal{P}_\xi$ of p.d.f., that is,
$$p_\xi(x) \in \mathcal{P}_\xi\,.$$

### 2.2. *Some Classes $\mathcal{P}_\xi$ of p.d.f.*

All possible classes $\mathcal{P}_\xi$ of p.d.f., considered in practical applications, are related with a priori information on stationary generating sequence $\{\xi_n\}$. Here we present some of them which look natural from practical point of views.

- Class $\mathcal{P}_\xi^1$ (of all symmetric distributions non singular in the point $x = 0$):
$$\mathcal{P}_\xi^1 = \left\{p_\xi : \ p_\xi(0) \ge \frac{1}{2a} > 0\right\}. \tag{5}$$
We deal with this class if there is not any a priori information on a noise distribution $p_\xi$.
- Class $\mathcal{P}_\xi^2$ (of all symmetric distributions with a bounded variance):
$$\mathcal{P}_\xi^2 = \left\{p_\xi : \ \int\limits_{\mathbb{R}} x^2 p_\xi(x)ds \le \sigma^2 < \infty\right\}. \tag{6}$$
- Class $\mathcal{P}_\xi^3$ (of all symmetric "approximately normal" distributions):
$$\mathcal{P}_\xi^3 = \left\{p_\xi : p_\xi(x) = (1-\alpha)p_{\mathcal{N}(0,\sigma^2)}(x) + \alpha q(x)\right\}, \tag{7}$$
where $p_{\mathcal{N}(0,\sigma)}(x)$ is the centred Gaussian distribution density with the variance defined by $\sigma^2$ and $q(x)$ is another distribution density. The parameter $\alpha \in [0,1]$ characterises the level of the effect of a "dirty" distribution $q(x)$ to the basic Gaussian distribution $p_{\mathcal{N}(0,\sigma^2)}(x)$.
- Class $\mathcal{P}_\xi^4$ (of all symmetric "approximately uniform" distributions):
$$\mathcal{P}_\xi^4 = \{p_\xi : p_\xi(x) = (1-\alpha)p_{U(0,a)}(x) + \alpha q(x)\} \tag{8}$$
where
$$p_{U(0,a)}(x) := \frac{1}{2a}\chi(|x| \le a)$$
$$\chi(|x| \le a) = \begin{cases} 1 & \text{if} \quad |x| \le a \\ 0 & \text{if} \quad |x| > a \end{cases}$$
is the centred uniform distribution and $q(x)$ is one process with a different distribution density. The parameter $\alpha \in [0,1]$ characterises the level of the effect of a "dirty" distribution $q(x)$ to the basic one $p_{U(0,a)}(x)$.

### 2.3. *Main Assumptions*

1. All random variables $\{w_n, \xi_n\}$ are defined on the probability space $(\Omega, \mathcal{F}, P)$ with the $\sigma$-algebras flow $\mathcal{F}_n \subseteq \mathcal{F}_{n+1}$
$$\mathcal{F}_{n-1} = \sigma\big(y_{-l}, \dots, y_{-1}, \dots, y_{n-1}; w_0, \dots, w_n; \eta_{-K_2,\dots,}\eta_{n-1}; \xi_{-K_1,\dots,}\xi_{n-1}\big). \tag{9}$$
2. For all $n$
$$\mathrm{E}\{\xi_n \mid \mathcal{F}_{n-1}\} \overset{a.s.}{=} 0, \ \mathrm{E}\{\xi_n^2 \mid \mathcal{F}_{n-1}\} \overset{a.s.}{=} \sigma_\xi^2 < \infty. \tag{10}$$
3. The measurable input sequence $\{w_n\}_{n\ge 0}$ is of bounded power:
$$\mathrm{E}\{w_n^2 \mid \mathcal{F}_{n-1}\} \overset{a.s.}{=} \sigma_{w,n}^2 < \infty, \tag{11}$$

and is independent of $\{\xi_n\}$, i.e.,

$$\mathrm{E}\{w_n\xi_n \mid \mathcal{F}_{n-1}\} \overset{a.s.}{=} w_n\mathrm{E}\{\xi_n \mid \mathcal{F}_{n-1}\} \overset{a.s.}{=} 0. \tag{12}$$

4. It is assumed that the forming filter is stable and "minimal-phase", that is, both polynomials $H_1(q^{-1})$ and $H_2(q^{-1})$ are Hurwitz, i.e., have all roots inside of the unite circle in the complex plain.
5. The ARMAX plant (1) is stable: the polynomial

$$A(q^{-1}) = 1 - \sum_{l=1}^{L} a_l q^{-l} \tag{13}$$

is Hurwitz.

**Remark 1.** *As it follows from the assumptions above, the noise sequence admits to be non-Gaussian and correlated (coloured).*

### 2.4. Regression Format Representation

The system (1) can be represented in the, regression format as

$$y_n = z_n^{\top} c + \eta_n, \tag{14}$$

where the extended vector

$$c = (a_1, \ldots, a_L; b_0, \ldots, b_K)^{\top} \in R^{L+K+1}, \tag{15}$$

represents the collection of unknown parameters to be estimated, and the vector

$$z_n = (y_{n-1}, \ldots, y_{n-L}; w_n, \ldots, w_{n-K})^{\top} \in R^{L+K+1}, \tag{16}$$

is referred to as the generalised regression measurable (available on-line) input.

### 2.5. Robust Parametric Identification Problem Formulation

**Problem 1.** *We need to estimate the vector $c$ of unknown parameters based on available data $\{z_n\}$ and a priory knowledge of the p.d.f. class $\mathcal{P}_\xi$ of the stationary noise sequence $\{\xi_n\}$ in the input of the forming filter. Two possible cases may be considered:*

- *the parameters $(d_{1,s}, d_{2,s})$ of the forming filter $H(q^{-1})$ are known.*
- *The parameters $(d_{1,s}, d_{2,s})$ of the forming filter $H(q^{-1})$ are also unknown.*

### 2.6. Main Contribution of the Paper

- The Cramer–Rao information bound for ARMAX (autoregression moving average models with exogenous inputs) under non-Gaussian noises is derived.
- It is shown that the direct implementation of the least-squares method (LSM) leads to an incorrect (shifted) parameter estimation.
- This inconsistency can be corrected by the implementation of the parallel use of the MLMW (maximum likelihood method with whitening) procedure, applied to all measurable variables of the model, and a nonlinear residual transformation using the information on the distribution density of a non-Gaussian noise, participating in moving average structure.
- The design of the corresponding parameter estimator, realising the suggested MLMW procedure, containing a parallel on-line "whitening" process as well as a nonlinear residual transformation, is presented in detail.
- It is shown that the MLMW procedure attains the obtained information bound, and hence, is asymptotically optimal.

## 3. Why LSM Does Not Work for the Identification of ARMAX Models with Correlated Noise

The problem of LSM estimation and identification in ARMAX models has been widely studied in the past. The estimation of the noise-induced bias was presented, for example, in [35], where a unique structure of the ARMAX model was proposed, utilising extra outputs delay. Let us show in this section that for dynamic models (in particular for ARMA-models) the least-squares method (LSM) does not work properly, this means, it leads to biased estimates!

Consider the simplest stable ARMA model with the 1-step correlated noise given by

$$\left.\begin{array}{l} y_{n+1} = a y_n + \xi_n + d\xi_{n-1},\ y_0 \in \mathbb{R} \text{ is given}, \\ |a| < 1,\ d \in \mathbb{R},\ \mathrm{E}\{\xi_n\} = 0,\ \mathrm{E}\{\xi_n^2\} = \sigma^2 > 0 \end{array}\right\} \tag{17}$$

where $\{\xi_n\}$ is a sequence of independent random variables. Then, the LSM estimate, realising

$$a_n = \arg\min_{a \in \mathbb{R}} \sum_{t=1}^{n} (y_{t+1} - a y_t)^2,$$

is

$$a_n = \left[\sum_{t=1}^{n} y_t y_{t+1}\right]\left[\sum_{t=1}^{n} y_t^2\right]^{-1} \tag{18}$$

and under by the strong version of large number law (LNL) [36] it becomes

$$a_n \overset{a.s.}{=} \frac{\frac{1}{n}\sum\limits_{t=1}^{n} \mathrm{E}\{y_t y_{t+1}\}}{\frac{1}{n}\sum\limits_{t=1}^{n} \mathrm{E}\{y_t^2\}} + o_\omega(1),$$

$$o_\omega(1) \underset{n\to\infty}{\to} 0 \text{ (with Prob.1)}$$

or, equivalently,

$$a_n \overset{a.s.}{=} \frac{\frac{1}{n}\sum\limits_{t=1}^{n} \mathrm{E}\{y_t(a y_t + \xi_t + d\xi_{t-1})\}}{\frac{1}{n}\sum\limits_{t=1}^{n} \mathrm{E}\{y_t^2\}} + o_\omega(1) =$$

$$a\frac{\frac{1}{n}\sum\limits_{t=1}^{n} \mathrm{E}\{y_t(\xi_t + d\xi_{t-1})\}}{\frac{1}{n}\sum\limits_{t=1}^{n} \mathrm{E}\{y_t^2\}} + o_\omega(1) = a + d\frac{\frac{1}{n}\sum\limits_{t=1}^{n} \mathrm{E}\{y_t\xi_{t-1}\}}{\frac{1}{n}\sum\limits_{t=1}^{n} \mathrm{E}\{y_t^2\}} + o_\omega(1).$$

So, the corresponding identification error comes to be as

$$a_n - a \overset{a.s.}{=} d\frac{\frac{1}{n}\sum\limits_{t=1}^{n} \mathrm{E}\{y_t\xi_{t-1}\}}{\frac{1}{n}\sum\limits_{t=1}^{n} \mathrm{E}\{y_t^2\}} + o_\omega(1)$$

For stable models with $|a| < 1$ there exist limits

$$\lim_{n\to\infty} \mathrm{E}\{y_n\xi_{n-1}\} \text{ and } \lim_{n\to\infty} \mathrm{E}\{y_n^2\}$$

and hence, by the Kronecker lemma

$$a_n - a \overset{a.s.}{=} d\frac{\lim\limits_{n\to\infty} \mathrm{E}\{y_n\xi_{n-1}\}}{\lim\limits_{n\to\infty} \mathrm{E}\{y_n^2\}} + o_\omega(1) \tag{19}$$

Let us calculate these limits. From (17), it follows

$$\mathrm{E}\{y_{n+1}\xi_n\} = a\mathrm{E}\{y_n\xi_n\} + \mathrm{E}\{\xi_n^2\} + d\mathrm{E}\{\xi_{n-1}\xi_n\} = \sigma^2 \tag{20}$$

$$\begin{gathered}\mathrm{E}\{y_{n+1}^2\} = a^2\mathrm{E}\{y_n^2\} + \mathrm{E}\{\xi_n^2\} + d^2\mathrm{E}\{\xi_{n-1}^2\} + \\ 2a\mathrm{E}\{y_n\xi_n\} + 2ad\mathrm{E}\{y_n\xi_{n-1}\} + 2d\mathrm{E}\{\xi_{n-1}\xi_n\} = \\ a^2\mathrm{E}\{y_n^2\} + (1+d^2)\sigma^2 + 2ad\mathrm{E}\{y_n\xi_{n-1}\} = \\ a^2\mathrm{E}\{y_n^2\} + (1+d^2)\sigma^2 + 2ad\sigma^2\end{gathered} \tag{21}$$

Since, for the stable linear recursion

$$z_{n+1} = \bar{a}z_n + c, \ |\bar{a}| < 1$$

we have

$$\begin{gathered}z_{n+1} = \bar{a}z_n + c = \bar{a}(\bar{a}z_{n-1} + c) + c = \\ \bar{a}^2 z_{n-1} + c + \bar{a}c = \cdots = \bar{a}^n z_1 + c + \bar{a}c + \bar{a}^2 c + \cdots + \bar{a}^n c = \\ \bar{a}^n z_1 + c\left(\frac{1-\bar{a}^{n+1}}{1-\bar{a}}\right) \underset{n\to\infty}{\to} \frac{c}{1-\bar{a}}.\end{gathered}$$

Then, for (21), we get

$$\begin{gathered}\mathrm{E}\{y_n^2\} \to \frac{(1+d^2) + 2ad}{1-a^2}\sigma^2 = \\ \frac{(1-a^2) + (a^2 + 2ad + d^2)}{1-a^2}\sigma^2 = \left[1 + \frac{(a+d)^2}{1-a^2}\right]\sigma^2\end{gathered} \tag{22}$$

Substitute the obtained limits (20) and (22) into (19) leads to

$$\begin{gathered}a_n - a \overset{a.s.}{=} d\frac{\sigma^2}{\left[1 + \frac{(a+d)^2}{1-a^2}\right]\sigma^2} + o_\omega(1) = \\ d\frac{1}{1 + \frac{(a+d)^2}{1-a^2}} + o_\omega(1) \overset{a.s.}{\underset{n\to\infty}{\to}} d\frac{1}{1 + \frac{(a+d)^2}{1-a^2}}.\end{gathered}$$

The derivative calculation of the limit value with respect to $d$ then gives

$$\left(d\frac{1}{1 + \frac{(a+d)^2}{1-a^2}}\right)' = (a^2 - 1)\frac{d^2 - 1}{(d^2 + 2ad + 1)^2}$$

So, the extremal points are $d = \pm 1$, and hence,

$$\left(d\frac{1}{1 + \frac{(a+d)^2}{1-a^2}}\right)_{d=1} = \frac{1}{2} - \frac{1}{2}a, \ \left(d\frac{1}{1 + \frac{(a+d)^2}{1-a^2}}\right)_{d=-1} = -\frac{1}{2}a - \frac{1}{2}$$

These relations imply the following conclusion: the maximum bias of the LSM estimate is

$$\max_d \lim_{n\to\infty} |a_n - a| = \frac{1}{2}\max\{|1-a|; |1+a|\}$$

The illustrative graphic ($x := d$, $y := |a_n - a|$ for $a = 0.5$) is shown in Figure 1.

Conclusion: Be careful! The LS method does not work for identification of parameters of dynamic models with correlated noises!

As a result, certain unique approaches, distinct from LSM, must be developed.

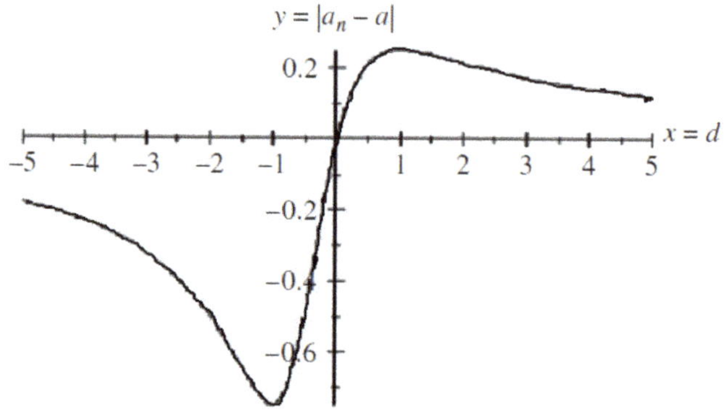


**Figure 1.** The bias dependence on the correlation coefficient $d$.

## 4. Some Other Identification Techniques

*Identification of Non-Stationary Parameters and Bayesian Method*

Some other parameter estimation/identification methods have been proposed for more complex situations. In [37], a combination of recursive version of the IV method with the matrix forgetting factor was presented for identification of time-varying parameters for ARMAX models, showing that the identification error in average has a bound dependent on the rate of the parameter variation, as well as on the variance of the noise. The version of IV method with adaptive matrix forgetting factor was studied in [38]. In some cases equation-error and output-error approaches have been used to deal with the problem where all the observed variables are corrupted by noise. The parameter bounding by the bounded equation error and the bounded errors in variables based on these approaches was studied in [39]. Bayesian parameter estimation and prediction of lineal-in-parameters models under the presence of coloured noise is addressed in [40], and it is based on a model called ARMAX. This model is a finite mixture of ARMAX elements with a common ARX part. This ARX part described a fixed deterministic input–output relationship: this model is estimated using a recursive quasi-Bayes algorithm that relies on a classical Bayesian solution without restriction on the MA component. The proposed model provides flexibility with respect to varying characteristics of the model noise. The measurement errors that affect data entries make the estimation problem more complicated. A solution to this problem was proposed in [41] by enhancing the ARMAX models by including some additive error terms on the output, and then developing a moving horizon estimator for the extended ARMAX model. The proposed method then models the measurement errors as nuisance variables and these are estimated simultaneously with the states, and the identifiability was achieved by regularising the LS cost with the $\ell_2$ norm of the nuisance variables, leading to an optimisation problem with an analytical solution. The nuisance variables have been recently used to model the output noise, as well as the potentially existing outliers (see [27]). These outliers are regularised with the $\ell_2$ norm for the estimation, and the regularised estimator suppresses the influence of the output noise and provides a minimum-variance estimate.

For the continuous-time case, the LSM with forgetting factor has been implemented for estimating constant and time-varying parameters ([42–44]). The proposed algorithms in [45] showed a good performance, but the bias, as in the discrete-time case, affects the estimation. The estimation algorithm was implemented for additive and multiplicative noises (see [46]), and in both scenarios, LSM is affected by the noise level, showing that is not the best method for stochastic systems, either in discrete or continuous time. To deal with the bias problem, a method combining the equivalent control with LSM was proposed, these two algorithms working in parallel reduce the bias in the estimation even in the presence of coloured noises (see [47]).

## 5. Regular Observations and Information Inequality for Observations with Coloured Noise

In estimation theory and statistics [48,49], the Cramér–Rao bound (CRB) expresses a lower bound on the variance of unbiased estimators $c_n$ of a deterministic (fixed, though unknown) parameter $c$, stating that the variance of any such estimator is at least as high as the inverse of the Fisher information (FIM) $\mathbb{I}_F^{-1}(c,n)$. Namely, for every unbiased estimator $c_n$ ($n$ is the number of available regular observations), an inequality of the type

$$\mathrm{Var}_c(c_n) \geq \mathbb{I}_F^{-1}(c,n) \tag{23}$$

for every $c$ in the parameter space $C$, it is called an information inequality, which plays a very important role in parameter estimation. The early works of Cramér (1946) [50] and Rao (1945) [51] introduced the Cramer–Rao inequality for regular density functions. Later, Vincze (1979) [52] and Khatri (1980) (see [53]) introduced information inequalities by imposing the regularity assumptions on a priori distribution rather than on the model. An unbiased estimator which achieves this lower bound is usually said to be (fully) efficient. This is a solution that achieves the lowest possible mean squared error among all unbiased methods, and therefore is the minimum variance unbiased (MVU) estimator. However, in some cases, there are no unbiased techniques that achieve this bound. This may occur either if for any unbiased estimator there exists another estimator with a strictly smaller variance, or if an MVU estimator exists but its variance is strictly greater than the inverse of the Fisher information. The Cramér–Rao bound (37) can also be used to bound the variance of biased estimators of given bias. In some cases, a biased approach can result in both a variance and a mean squared error that are below the unbiased Cramér–Rao lower bound.

Recall some important definitions.

### 5.1. Main Definitions and the Cramer–Rao Information Inequality

In a general case, the observable output sequence $\mathbf{y}_n := \{y_1, y_2, \ldots, y_n\}$ may be of a vector type $(y_t \in \mathbb{R}^L)$ containing the information on the parameter $c \in \mathbb{R}^N$. The function $p(\mathbf{y}_n \mid c)$, $c \in C \subseteq \mathbb{R}^N$ is called the joint density of the distribution of the vector $\mathbf{y}_n$. Any Borel function $c_n = c_n(\mathbf{y}_n) \in \mathbb{R}^N$ can be considered as an estimate of the parameter $c$.

**Definition 1.** *The vector-function*

$$m_n(c) = \mathrm{E}\{c_n\} = \int_{Y_n} c_n(\mathbf{y}_n) p(\mathbf{y}_n \mid c) d\mathbf{y}_n \in \mathbb{R}^N,$$
$$Y_n = \{\mathbf{y}_n \mid p(\mathbf{y}_n \mid c) > 0,\ c \in C\},$$

*is referred to as the averaged value of the estimate $c_n$, based on available observations $\mathbf{y}_n$;*

- *If $m_n(c) = c$, then the estimate $c_n$ is called unbiased and asymptotically unbiased if $\lim_{n\to\infty} m_n(c) = c$.*
- *The observations $\mathbf{y}_n$ are referred to be as regular on the class $C$ of parameters if*

$$\sup_{c\in C} \mathrm{E}\left\{\|\ln p(\mathbf{y}_n \mid c)\|^2\right\} = \sup_{c\in C} \int_{Y_n} \|\ln p(\mathbf{y}_n \mid c)\|^2 p(\mathbf{y}_n \mid c) d\mathbf{y}_n < \infty, \tag{24}$$

*and for any $c \in C$*

$$\begin{gathered}\mathbb{I}_F(c,n) = \mathrm{E}\{\nabla_c \ln p(\mathbf{y}_n \mid c) \nabla_c^\top \ln p(\mathbf{y}_n \mid c)\} = \\ \int_{Y_n} [\nabla_c \ln p(\mathbf{y}_n \mid c) \nabla_c^\top \ln p(\mathbf{y}_n \mid c)] p(\mathbf{y}_n \mid c) d\mathbf{y}_n > 0.\end{gathered} \tag{25}$$

- *The matrix $\mathbb{I}_F(c,n)$ is called the Fisher information matrix for the set of available observations $\mathbf{y}_n$.*

As it was mentioned in [54], when the Fisher information takes into account the stochastic complexity and the associated universal processes are derived for a class of parametric processes. The main condition required is that the maximum likelihood estimates satisfy the central limit theorems.

In some cases, the Fisher information matrix (FIM) is required to be non-singular (25) to guarantee the observability of the system (see [55]). The algebraic properties of FIM for stationary processes have been widely studied, for example there is a survey paper written by André Klein where this study is presented [56]. The FIM is necessary for the Cramer–Rao inequality; it is a basic tool for estimation theory in mathematical statistics, and in stationary processes is related to the solution of Stein equations. A procedure to compute the theoretical periodic autocovariance function in terms of the parameters of the periodic model for periodic autoregressive moving average models was presented in [57], where the necessary and sufficient condition for non-singular FIM of a periodic ARMA model was calculated. So, the Fisher information matrix for the Gaussian case in ARMAX processes has been previously studied. In [58], an algorithm composed by Chandrasekhar recursion equations at a vector-matrix level was proposed, where the recursions consist of derivatives based on appropriate differential rules that are applied to a state space model for a vector process. The recursions obtained were given in terms of expectations of derivatives of innovations.

**Theorem 1.** *Cramer–Rao information inequality. For any set $Y_n$ of regular observations, and for any estimate $c_n$ with differentiable averaged value function $m_n(c)$ the following inequality holds*

$$\begin{aligned} &\mathrm{E}\{(c_n - c)(c_n - c)^\top\} \geq \\ &[m_n(c) - c][m_n(c) - c]^\top + \nabla m_n(c)\mathbb{I}_F^{-1}(c,n)\nabla^\top m_n(c). \end{aligned} \tag{26}$$

**Corollary 1.** *For unbiased estimates satisfying $m_n(c) = c$, $\nabla m_n(c) = I_{n\times n}$, the Cramer–Rao inequality becomes*

$$\mathrm{E}\{(c_n - c)(c_n - c)^\top\} \geq \mathbb{I}_F^{-1}(c,n). \tag{27}$$

This inequality is widely used in discrete-time systems for various purposes. The posterior Cramer–Rao bound on the mean square error in tracking the bearing, bearing rate and power level of a narrowband source is developed in [59]. Their formulation used a lineal process model with additive noise and a general nonlinear measurement model, where the measurements are the sensor array data. This bound can be applied to multi-dimensional nonlinear and possibly non-Gaussian systems. In [60], the case of a singular conditional distribution of the one-step-ahead state vector given the present state was considered. The bound was evaluated for recursive estimation of slowly varying parameters of AR processes, tracking a slowly varying single cisoid in noise and tracking the parameters of a sinusoidal frequency with a sinusoidal phase modulation. A variation of the Cramer–Rao inequality is the Cramer–Rao–Frechet inequality, which has been applied for discrete-time nonlinear filtering. In [61], this inequality was reviewed and extended to track fitting, where it is shown that the inequality does not cause the limitations of the resolution of the track fits with a certain number of observations, and that the inequality remains valid even in irregular models supporting the similar improvement of resolution for realistic models.

### 5.2. Fisher Information Matrix Calculation

Using the Bayes formula

$$\begin{aligned} p(\mathbf{y}_n \mid c) &= p(y_n \mid \mathbf{y}_{n-1}; c)p(\mathbf{y}_{n-1} \mid c) = \\ \cdots &= \left[\prod_{k=1}^{n} p(y_k \mid \mathbf{y}_{k-1}; c)\right] p(y_0 \mid c), \end{aligned}$$

for the likelihood function $L_n(\mathbf{y}_n \mid c) = -\ln p(\mathbf{y}_n \mid c)$ we have the following representation:

$$L_n(\mathbf{y}_n \mid c) = -\ln p(\mathbf{y}_n \mid c) = -\sum_{k=1}^{n} \ln p(y_k \mid \mathbf{y}_{k-1}; c) - \ln p(y_0 \mid c). \tag{28}$$

Define also

$$u_t(c) = \nabla_c L_t(\mathbf{y}_t \mid c) - \nabla_c L_{t-1}(\mathbf{y}_{t-1} \mid c) = -\frac{\nabla_c p(y_t \mid \mathbf{y}_{t-1}; c)}{p(y_t \mid \mathbf{y}_{t-1}; c)} = -\nabla_c \ln p(y_t \mid \mathbf{y}_{t-1}; c),$$

which is a martingale difference, since $\mathrm{E}\{u_t(c) \mid \mathcal{F}_{t-1}\} \overset{a.s.}{=} 0$, and satisfies the property

$$\nabla_c u_t(c) = -\frac{\nabla_c^2 p(y_t \mid \mathbf{y}_{t-1}; c)}{p(y_t \mid \mathbf{y}_{t-1}; c)} + \frac{\nabla_c p(y_t \mid \mathbf{y}_{t-1}; c) \nabla_c^{\top} p(y_t \mid \mathbf{y}_{t-1}; c)}{p^2(y_t \mid \mathbf{y}_{t-1}; c)}. \tag{29}$$

For regular unbiased observations, the Fisher information matrix $\mathbb{I}_F(c, n)$ can be calculated as

$$\left.\begin{aligned} \mathbb{I}_F(c,n) &= \sum_{k=1}^{n} \mathrm{E}\{u_k u_k^{\top}\} = \sum_{k=1}^{n} \mathrm{E}\{\nabla_c u_k(c)\} = \\ &\mathrm{E}\left\{\sum_{k=1}^{n} \frac{\nabla_c p(y_k \mid \mathbf{y}_{k-1}; c) \nabla_c^{\top} p(y_k \mid \mathbf{y}_{k-1}; c)}{p^2(y_k \mid \mathbf{y}_{k-1}; c)}\right\} = \\ &\mathrm{E}\left\{\sum_{k=1}^{n} \nabla_c \ln p(y_k \mid \mathbf{y}_{k-1}; c) \nabla_c^{\top} \ln p(y_k \mid \mathbf{y}_{k-1}; c)\right\}. \end{aligned}\right\} \tag{30}$$

### *5.3. Asymptotic Cramer–Rao Inequality*

Multiplying both sides of (27) by $n$ we get

$$n\mathrm{E}\{(c_n - c)(c_n - c)^{\top}\} \geq \left(\frac{1}{n}\mathbb{I}_F(c,n)\right)^{-1}.$$

Taking $n \to \infty$ we get

$$\liminf_{n \to \infty} n\mathrm{E}\{(c_n - c)(c_n - c)^{\top}\} \geq \mathbb{I}_F^{-1}(c), \tag{31}$$

where

$$\mathbb{I}_F(c) := \limsup_{n \to \infty} \frac{1}{n}\mathbb{I}_F(c,n) = \limsup_{n \to \infty} \mathrm{E}\left\{\frac{1}{n}\sum_{k=1}^{n} u_k(c) u_k^{\top}(c)\right\} > 0.$$

**Remark 2.** *In view of (29) it follows*

$$\mathbb{I}_F(c) = \limsup_{n \to \infty} \frac{1}{n}\mathrm{E}\{\nabla_c^2 L_n(\mathbf{y}_t \mid c)\}. \tag{32}$$

### *5.4. Whitening Process for Stable and Minimal-Phase Forming Filters*

Although additive Gaussian white noise is widely used, in many research areas the present noises are non-Gaussian. In some cases, detectors are used to whiten the data and then the estimation/identification is performed (see for example [62]). In the presence of non-white noises, one of the most common methods to deal with this perturbation is a whitening filter. A transfer function of an estimated noise can be used to filter the input–output data of the system and presents a filtering-based recursive analogue of the LSM algorithm for the ARMAX model. In [63], it is shown that through data filtering one can obtain two identification models, the first one including the parameter of the system model and the second including the parameter of the noise model; this can lead to a more accurate parameter estimation. A whitening filter can be applied in coloured Gaussian noises when there is a residual white noise component present. The existence of a realisable whitening filter is demonstrated in [64].

The model (14) can be symbolically represented as

$$y_n = z_n^\top c + \eta_n = z_n^\top c + \frac{H_1(q)}{H_2(q)}\xi_n. \tag{33}$$

In view of the Assumption 4, the polynomials $H_1(q)$ and $H_2(q)$ are stable and, hence, we are able to apply the inverse operator $\frac{H_2(q)}{H_1(q)}$ to both sides of the model (33), obtaining

$$\begin{aligned} \tilde{y}_n &= \frac{H_2(q)}{H_1(q)}y_n,\ \tilde{y}_{-s} := 0,\ s = 0,1,\ldots,K_1, \\ \tilde{z}_n &= \frac{H_2(q)}{H_1(q)}z_n,\ \tilde{z}_{-s} := 0,\ s = 0,1,\ldots,K_1, \\ \tilde{\xi}_n &:= \frac{H_2(q)}{H_1(q)}\frac{H_1(q)}{H_2(q)}\xi_n \overset{a.s.}{=} \xi_n + O_\omega(\lambda^n),\ |\lambda| < 1, \end{aligned} \tag{34}$$

where $\lambda$ is one of the eigenvalues of the polynomials $H_1(q)$ and $H_2(q)$ which is most close to the unitary circle. The function $O_\omega(\lambda^n)$ is a random process, defined on $(\Omega, \mathcal{F}, P)$ and such that

$$0 \overset{a.s.}{<} \liminf_n O_\omega(\lambda^n)/\lambda^n \le \limsup_n O_\omega(\lambda^n)/\lambda^n \le \text{const}(\omega) \overset{a.s.}{<} \infty.$$

So, finally, after the "whitening process" (inverse operator) application we get

$$\tilde{y}_n = \tilde{z}_n^\top c + \tilde{\xi}_n. \tag{35}$$

**Remark 3.** *This means that on-line application of the "whitening process" to the initial model (33) permits considering the corresponding transformed model (34) which deals with "quasi" white noise $\tilde{\xi}_n$ exponentially quickly, tending to the exact white noise $\xi_n$, fulfilling*

$$\left\|\tilde{\xi}_n - \xi_n\right\| = O_\omega(\lambda^n) \overset{a.s.}{\to} 0$$

*when $n \to \infty$. This permits to represent (35) as*

$$\tilde{y}_n = \tilde{z}_n^\top c + \xi_n + O_\omega(\lambda^n). \tag{36}$$

### *5.5. Cramer–Rao Inequality for ARMAX Models with a Generating Noise from the Class $\mathcal{P}_\xi$ of p.d.f.*

**Theorem 2.** *The Cramer–Rao inequality (see [15]) in the form (31) is*

$$\left.\begin{aligned} \liminf_{n\to\infty} n\mathrm{E}\{(c_n - c)(c_n - c)^\top\} \ge \sup_{p_\xi \in \mathcal{P}_\xi} \mathbb{I}_F^{-1}(c) = \\ \sup_{p_\xi \in \mathcal{P}_\xi} \left(I_{F,\xi}(p_\xi)\mathcal{R}(p_\xi)\right)^{-1} \end{aligned}\right\} \tag{37}$$

*where*

$$\left.\begin{aligned} \mathcal{R}(p_\xi) &:= \limsup_{n\to\infty} \frac{1}{n}\sum_{k=1}^{n} \mathrm{E}\{\tilde{z}_k\tilde{z}_k^\top\}, \\ I_{F,\xi}(p_\xi) &= \mathrm{E}\left\{\left(\frac{\partial}{\partial \xi}\ln p_\xi(\xi(\omega))\right)^2\right\} = \int_{x\in\mathbb{R}^1} \frac{\left(\frac{\partial}{\partial x}p_\xi(x)\right)^2}{p_\xi(x)}dx. \end{aligned}\right\} \tag{38}$$

**Remark 4.** *In the regression case ($a_l = 0$, $l = 1,\ldots,L$) the matrix $\mathcal{R}$ (38) does not depend on $p_\xi$.*

Conclusion. According to the information inequality (37), the "best" (asymptotically optimum or efficient) estimate $c_n^*$ of the parameter $c \in C$ is the one that achieves equality in the (37). The inequality given by (37) implies that after $n$ regular observations $\mathbf{y}_n$ the covariance matrix of the estimation error $(c_n - c)$, which defines the quality of the estimation process, can not be less than the corresponding Fisher information matrix (25). In other words, the Fisher information matrix (25) will define the maximal possible quality of the identification process, which can not be improved by any other identification algorithm.

## 6. Robust Version of Maximum Likelihood Method with Whitening: MLMW Procedure

For parameter estimation and system modelling, the maximum likelihood technique is critical. The maximum of the likelihood function in Gaussian case is equivalent to minimising the least-squares cost function [65]. In this paper, a recursive maximum likelihood least-squares identification algorithm for systems with autoregressive moving average noises was derived. The maximum likelihood has been widely implemented under Gaussian perturbations, for example in [66], the Gaussian likelihood function was studied when data are generated by a high-order continuous-time ARMAX mode, and these data are observed as stocks and flows at different frequencies. The maximum likelihood method can be modified using the stochastic gradient; this modification was presented in [67], where this modification was proposed for ARMAX models. In this case, the modified algorithm can estimate unknown parameters and the unknown noise simultaneously, with less computational cost and better accuracy. Non-asymptotic deviations bounds for least-squared estimation in Gaussian AR processes have been recently studied (see [68]). The study relies on martingale concentration inequalities and tail bound for $\chi^2$-distributed variables; in the end, they provided a concentration bound for the sample covariance matrix of the process output.

### 6.1. *Whitening Method and Its Application*

The whitening method is commonly used to prevent the bias problem [69]. A modified version of direct whitening method, which is called MDWM, was proposed as an ARMA model parameter estimation technique in [70]. The proposed direct whitening method (DWM) provides the parameter estimates which make the prediction errors uncorrelated, in some cases this algorithms might fall at local minima and give parameter estimates. To deal with this problem, an MDWM which chooses the consistent estimates among a large number of DWM estimates can be implemented. Pre-whitening can be performed with first order differentiation of signals and/or the implementation of an inverse filter based on linear prediction, as it is shown in [71], where the whitening was the previous step in a cross-correlation method for identifying aircraft noise, showing that whitening can be successfully developed for real-time operation in the detection of correlation peaks. An iterative procedure for minimising and whitening the residual of the ARMAX model was presented in [72], since usually when the system is identified from input–output data in the time domain, it is assumed that the data is enough and the ARX model order is large enough. The results show that in the residual whitening method we can use an ARMAX model that includes the noise dynamics, instead of an ARX model, and the properties of the residual sequence, such as the orthogonal conditions, can convert to the optimal properties of the Kalman filter. The influence function is an analysis tool in robust statistics we used to formulate a recursive solution for ARMAX processes filtering in [73], in particular for a t-distribution noise. The filter was formulated as a maximum likelihood problem, where an influence function approximation was used to obtain a recursive solution to reduce computational load and facilitate the implementation.

Whitening techniques have also been implemented for noise cancellation, in [74] is the base for an approach to adaptive white noise cancellation based on adaptive control principles. In this case, the goal was to create a physical noise-reduced environment at the vicinity of noisy machinery for a stochastic machine noise. Another method implemented for filtering is signal smoothing when the data are generated (or represented) by an autoregressive moving average with exogenous inputs (ARMAX) model. In the case presented in [75], the original ARMAX recurrence relation is used and combined with a constrained LS optimisation to filter the system as well as the measurement noise components and estimate the desired signal in the form of a block-wise matrix formulation.

Whitening processes are a very useful pre-processing technique to deal with the presence of non-white noises, and the improve the estimation results regardless of the estimation algorithm used [76]. In [77], a residual whitening method enforces the properties of the Kalman filter for a finite set of data. This technique has been implemented in ARMAX models for the identification of inductor motor systems. The importance of the study and development of estimation/identification algorithms for ARMAX models with coloured noises relies on the importance of this model in various areas of study and its many applications. The identification of the ARMAX models allows the implementation of control techniques, such as the predictive control presented in [78], which is applied for the control of a pneumatic actuator based on an ARX model built by a neural network. There, the control showed a quick response and an accurate tracking. The estimation has been implemented for electromechanical modes and mode shapes for multiple synchrophasors (see [79]). Their approach was based on identifying the transfer function of the state space model of a linearised power system through the estimation of a multichannel ARMAX mode, and it was simulated using data from a reduced-order model of the Western Electricity Coordinating Council (WECC) system. The ARMAX model has been used to model an outlet temperature of the first-stage cyclone pre-heater in the cement firing system (see [80]). In that case, a Butterworth low-pas filter and normalized processing are used to process a cement firing system data, and the input variables modelled are selected by the Pearson correlation analysis. The parameters of the model were identified using a recursive maximum likelihood algorithm, and the results validated with a residual analysis method.

Econometrics is an area where the estimation/identification of ARMAX models (the integral version of the ARMAX model) has great importance (see [66,81,82]). The integration of macroeconomic indicators in the accuracy of throughput time-series forecasting model can be addressed using ARMAX models, as it is shown in [83]. There, the dynamic factors are extracted from external macroeconomic indicators influencing the observed throughput, and then a family of ARMAX models is generated based on derived factors. This model can be used to produce future forecasts. Some variations of the ARMAX model, such as the autoregressive moving average explanatory input model of the Koyck kind (KARMAX) are also used in econometrics. Another interesting application in econometrics is presented in [84], where it is shown how the recent deregulation of the electricity industry and reliance on competitive wholesale markets has generated significant volatility in wholesale electricity prices. Due to the importance of short-term price forecasts, an estimation and evaluation of the forecasting performance of four ARMAX–GARCH models for five MISO pricing hubs (Cinergy, First Energy, Illinois, Michigan and Minnesota) using hourly data from 1 June 2006 to 6 October 2007 is given. In this study, the importance of the patterns of the electricity price volatility is shown, as well as the volatility dynamics regulated by the states.

In [85], an identification algorithm is presented, where the debt management in indebted poor countries is studied, using data from the World Bank database from 1970 to 2018 based on the maximum likelihood method, and then comparing the results with prediction error and the instrumental variable methods.

### 6.2. Recurrent Robust Identification Procedures with Whitening and a Nonlinear Residual Transformation

Consider the following class of recurrent identification procedures [15] which may be applied to the transformed model (36):

$$\left.\begin{array}{c} c_n = c_{n-1} + \Gamma_n \tilde{z}_n \varphi(\tilde{y}_n - \tilde{z}_n^\top c_{n-1}) \\ c_0\text{—any given value} \\ \Gamma_n = \left( \sum\limits_{t=0}^{n} \tilde{z}_t \tilde{z}_t^\top \right)^{-1}, \ n \geq n_0 := \left\{ \min\limits_{k} \sum\limits_{t=0}^{k} \tilde{z}_t \tilde{z}_t^\top \right\} > 0. \end{array}\right\} \tag{39}$$

**Remark 5.** *Notice that $\Gamma_n$ in (39) can be calculated recursively (as in the least-square method)*

$$\Gamma_n = \Gamma_{n-1} - \frac{\Gamma_{n-1}\tilde{z}_n\tilde{z}_n^{\top}\Gamma_{n-1}}{1+\tilde{z}_n^{\top}\Gamma_{n-1}\tilde{z}_n},\ n \geq n_0, \tag{40}$$

*and possesses (in the accepted assumptions) the following property*

$$\begin{gathered} \Gamma_n \overset{a.s.}{\simeq} \frac{1}{n}\mathcal{R}^{-1} \\ \mathcal{R} = \lim_{n\to\infty} \frac{1}{n}\sum_{k=1}^{n} \mathrm{E}\{\tilde{z}_k^{\top}\tilde{z}_k\} > 0. \end{gathered} \tag{41}$$

**Theorem 3** ([15]). *If*

1. *$\xi_n$ is i.i.d. sequence with*

$$\mathrm{E}\{\xi_n\} = 0,\ \mathrm{E}\{\xi_n^2\} = \sigma^2 > 0,\ \mathrm{E}\{\xi_n^4\} = \mathrm{E}\{\xi_1^4\} < \infty.$$

2. *The nonlinear transformation $\varphi : \mathbb{R} \to \mathbb{R}$ satisfies the conditions*

$$x\psi(x) \geq \delta x^2,\ \delta > 0,\ \psi(0) = 0,\ S(x) \leq k_0 + k_1 x^2,$$

*with*

$$\psi(x) = \mathrm{E}\{\varphi(x+\xi_n)\},\ S(x) := \mathrm{E}\{\varphi^2(x+\xi_n)\},$$

*then*

$$\Delta_n = c_n - c \underset{n\to\infty}{\overset{a.s.}{\to}} 0. \tag{42}$$

Following to Lemma 13.7 in [36] and defining a new process $\{\tilde{\Delta}_n\}_{n\geq 0}$ as

$$\tilde{\Delta}_n = \left[1 - \frac{\psi'(0)}{n}\right]\tilde{\Delta}_{n-1} + \frac{1}{n}\mathcal{R}^{-1}\tilde{z}_n(o_\omega(1) + \zeta_n),\ \tilde{\Delta}_0 = \Delta_0, \tag{43}$$

we may formulate the following auxiliary result.

**Theorem 4** (on $\sqrt{n}$-equivalency). *Under the assumptions of Theorem 3, the process (42) is $\sqrt{n}$-equivalent to the process (43), that is,*

$$\sqrt{n}\left(\Delta_n - \tilde{\Delta}_n\right) \underset{n\to\infty}{\overset{a.s.}{\to}} 0. \tag{44}$$

The property of the asymptotic normality of the process $\{\sqrt{n}\Delta_n\}_{n\geq 0}$ helps us to estimate the exact rate of convergence (not only the order of convergence, but also its constant) of the identification procedure (39).

**Theorem 5** (on asymptotic normality). *Suppose that the conditions of Theorem 3 are fulfilled and, additionally,*

$$\psi(0) = 0,\ S(0) > 0,\ \psi'(0) > 1/2. \tag{45}$$

*Then, the process $\{\sqrt{n}\Delta_n\}_{n\geq 0}$ is asymptotically normal*

$$\sqrt{n}\Delta_n \underset{n\to\infty}{\overset{d}{\to}} \mathcal{N}(0, V), \tag{46}$$

*with the covariation matrix $V$, equal to*

$$V = \frac{S(0)}{2\psi'(0) - 1}\mathcal{R}^{-1}. \tag{47}$$

It results directly from Theorem 13.6 in [36].

**Remark 6.** *The matrix V defines the rate of the convergence of the procedure (39), that is*

$$\Delta_n \underset{n\to\infty}{\overset{d}{\to}} \mathcal{N}(0, n^{-1}V).$$

As it follows from (47), $V$ depends on a real noise density distribution $p_\xi$ (since $S(0)$, $\psi'(0)$ and $\mathcal{R}$ may be dependent on $p_\xi$) and on a nonlinear function $\varphi$ (through $S(0)$ and $\psi'(0)$). That's why, to emphasise this dependence, we use the notation

$$V = V(p_\xi, \varphi).$$

Following [13,14], let us introduce the main definition of this section.

**Definition 2.** *The pair of functions given by* $\left(p_\xi^*, \varphi^{**}\right)$ *define the estimating procedure (54) with the nonlinear residual transformation* $\varphi^*$*, which is robust with respect to a distribution* $p_\xi$*, belonging to a class* $\mathcal{P}_\xi$*, if for any admissible* $\varphi$*, satisfying the assumptions of Theorem 5, and any generating noise distribution* $p_\xi \in \mathcal{P}_\xi$ *the following "saddle-point" inequalities hold:*

$$V(p_\xi, \varphi^{**}) \le V\left(p_\xi^*, \varphi^{**}\right) \le V\left(\varphi, p_\xi^*\right). \tag{48}$$

*Here, both inequalities should be treated in a "matrix sense", that is,*

$$A = A^\top \le B = B^\top \text{ if } B - A \ge 0.$$

In other words:

- The distribution $p_\xi^*$ is the "worst" within the class $\mathcal{P}_\xi$.
- The nonlinear transformation $\varphi^{**}$ is "the best one" oriented on the "worst" noise with the distribution $p_\xi^*$.

This can be expressed mathematically as follows:

$$\left.\begin{aligned} \varphi^{**} &= \arg\inf_{\varphi} \sup_{p_\xi \in \mathcal{P}_\xi} V(p_\xi, \varphi), \\ p_\xi^* &= \arg \sup_{p_\xi \in \mathcal{P}_\xi} \inf_{\varphi} V(p_\xi, \varphi), \end{aligned}\right\} \tag{49}$$

so that

$$\inf_{\varphi} \sup_{p_\xi \in \mathcal{P}_\xi} V(p_\xi, \varphi) = \sup_{p_\xi \in \mathcal{P}_\xi} \inf_{\varphi} V(p_\xi, \varphi) := V^*. \tag{50}$$

According to (37), for any fixed $p_\xi \in \mathcal{P}_\xi$

$$\inf_{\varphi} V(p_\xi, \varphi) = \inf_{\varphi}\left(\frac{S(0)}{2\psi'(0) - 1}\mathcal{R}^{-1}\right) \ge \sup_{p_\xi \in \mathcal{P}_\xi} \left[I_{F,\xi}(p_\xi)\mathcal{R}(p_\xi)\right]^{-1} \tag{51}$$

**Lemma 1** ([15]). *The low bound in (51) coincides with the Cramer–Rao bound (37) and is achieved when the nonlinear function in (39) is*

$$\varphi^{**}(v) = -I_{F,\xi}^{-1}\left(p_\xi^*\right)\frac{d}{dv}\ln p_\xi^*(v) \tag{52}$$

*with*

$$p_\xi^* = \arg \sup_{p_\xi \in \mathcal{P}_\xi} \left[I_{F,\xi}(p_\xi)\mathcal{R}(p_\xi)\right]^{-1} \tag{53}$$

In other words, this lemma states that the nonlinear residual transformation $\varphi^{**}$ (52) is robust with respect to distributions $p_\xi \in \mathcal{P}_\xi$.

So, the asymptotically optimal recurrent robust identification procedure (39) for coloured noise perturbations in (33) is

$$\left.\begin{aligned} c_n &= c_{n-1} - \Gamma_n \tilde{z}_n I_{F,\xi}^{-1}\left(p_\xi^*\right) \frac{d}{dv} \ln p_\xi^*(v) \mid_{v=\tilde{y}_n - \tilde{z}_n^\top c_{n-1}} \\ \Gamma_n &= \Gamma_{n-1} - \frac{\Gamma_{n-1}\tilde{z}_n \tilde{z}_n^\top \Gamma_{n-1}}{1+\tilde{z}_n^\top \Gamma_{n-1}\tilde{z}_n},\ n \geq n_0, \end{aligned}\right\} \tag{54}$$

which in fact is the maximum likelihood recurrent procedure with the worst p.d.f. $p_\xi^*(v)$ on the given class $\mathcal{P}_\xi$.

**Remark 7.** *Notice that for the class of ARMAX models with coloured noises and regular observations, there does not exist any other algorithm providing, asymptotically, a rate of convergence better than the suggested procedure (54).*

As we can see, whitening is a pre-processing step in the estimation process which can be applied simultaneously with the identification procedure (54). In [86], this step was implemented in the blind source separation process, where a robust whitening is based on the eigenvalue decomposition of a positive definite linear combination of correlation matrices.

This problem can be addressed analysing the noise power spectra density. This has been implemented by identifying the noise power spectral density of interferometric detectors using parametric techniques (see [87]). This is an adaptive technique used to identify and to whiten data provided my the interferometric detectors. The least-squares lattice filter proved to be the best among the analysed filters. One of the applications for this technique was presented in [88] where it was implemented for gravitational data wave analysis. There, it is shown how it is possible to estimate the noise power spectral density of gravitational wave detectors using parametric techniques, and it also shows how is it possible to whiten the noise data before they pass the detection algorithms.

### 6.3. Particular Cases for Static (Regression) Models

Recall that for regression models ($a_l = 0, l = 1, \ldots, L$) the matrix $\mathcal{R}$ does not depend on p.d.f. $p_\xi$, and the relation (53) becomes

$$p_\xi^*(v) = \arg \sup_{p_\xi \in \mathcal{P}_\xi} \left[I_{F,\xi}(p_\xi)\right]^{-1} = \arg \inf_{p_\xi \in \mathcal{P}_\xi} I_{F,\xi}(p_\xi).$$

**Lemma 2.** *In the class* $\mathcal{P}_\xi^1 := \left\{p_\xi : \ p_\xi(0) \geq \frac{1}{2a} > 0\right\}$ *(5) the worth distribution density* $p_\xi^*(x)$ *is the Laplace p.d.f. given by*

$$p_\xi^*(x) = \arg \inf_{p_\xi \in \mathcal{P}_\xi^1} I_{F,\xi}(p_\xi) = \frac{1}{2a} \exp\left\{-\frac{|x|}{a}\right\}. \tag{55}$$

*See Figure 2.*

**Corollary 2.** *The robust on* $\mathcal{P}_\xi^1$ *version of the procedure (54) contains*

$$\varphi^{**}(x) = -I_{F,\xi}^{-1}\left(p_\xi^*\right) \frac{d}{dv} \ln p_\xi^*(v) = a \operatorname{sign}(x) \tag{56}$$

**Lemma 3.** *In the class* $\mathcal{P}_\xi^2 := \left\{p_\xi : \ \int_{\mathbb{R}} x^2 p_\xi(x) ds \leq \sigma^2 < \infty\right\}$ *(6), the worth distribution density* $p_\xi^*(x)$ *is the Laplace p.d.f. given by*

$$p^*_\xi(x) = \arg \inf_{p_\xi \in \mathcal{P}_2} I_F(p_\xi) = \frac{1}{\sqrt{2\pi}\sigma} \exp\left\{-\frac{x^2}{2\sigma^2}\right\}, \tag{57}$$

*that is, the worth on $\mathcal{P}^2_\xi$ distribution density is the Gaussian p.d.f. (57).*

**Corollary 3.** *The robust on $\mathcal{P}^2_\xi$ version of the procedure (54) contains*

$$\varphi^*(x) = -I_F^{-1}\left(p^*_\xi\right)\frac{d}{dv}\ln p^*_\xi(v) = x \tag{58}$$

*which means that the standard LSM algorithm with linear residual transformation is robust within the class $\mathcal{P}_2$.*

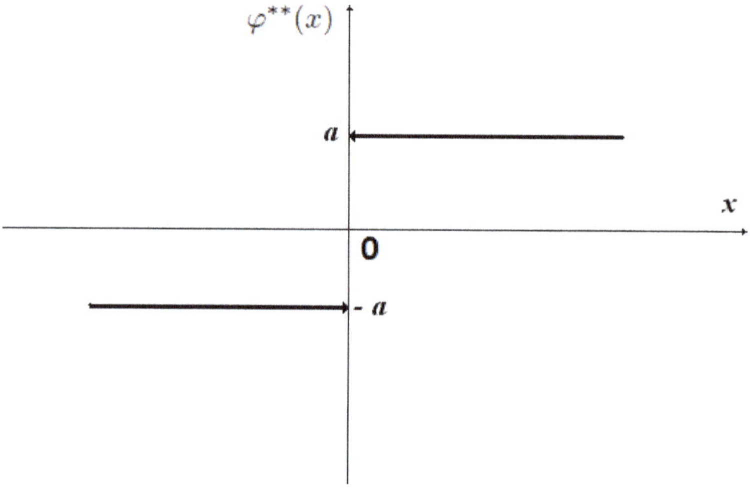


**Figure 2.** The nonlinear transformation $\varphi^{**}$ for the class $\mathcal{P}^1_\xi$.

**Lemma 4.** *In the class $\mathcal{P}^3_\xi := \left\{p_\xi : p_\xi(x) = (1-\alpha)p_{\mathcal{N}(0,\sigma^2)}(x) + \alpha q(x)\right\}$ (7) (of all symmetric "approximately normal" p.d.f.), the worth distribution density $p^*_\xi(x)$ is Gaussian p.d.f. within some zone $\Delta$ and the Laplace p.d.f. out of this zone:*

$$p^*_\xi(x) = \arg \inf_{p_\xi \in \mathcal{P}^3_\xi} I_{F,\xi}(p_\xi) = \left\{ \begin{array}{l} \frac{1-\alpha}{\sqrt{2\pi}\sigma}\exp\left\{-\frac{x^2}{2\sigma^2}\right\} \text{ for } |x| \le \Delta \\ \frac{1-\alpha}{\sqrt{2\pi}\sigma}\exp\left\{-\frac{\Delta|x|}{\sigma^2} + \frac{\Delta^2}{2\sigma^2}\right\} \text{ for } |x| > \Delta \end{array} \right. . \tag{59}$$

*The parameter $\alpha \in [0,1]$ characterises the level of the effect of a "dirty" distribution $q(x)$ to the basic one $p_{\mathcal{N}(0,\sigma)}(x)$, and $\Delta$ is a solution of the transcendent equation*

$$\frac{1}{1-\alpha} = \int_{-\Delta}^{\Delta} p_{\mathcal{N}(0,\sigma)}(x)dx + 2p_{\mathcal{N}(0,\sigma)}(\Delta)\frac{\sigma^2}{\Delta} \tag{60}$$

*that is, the worth on $\mathcal{P}^3_\xi$ distribution density is the Gaussian one for $|x| \le \Delta$ and the Laplace type for $|x| > \Delta$, (see Figure 3).*

**Corollary 4.** *The robust on $\mathcal{P}_\xi^3$ version of the procedure (54) contains*

$$\varphi^{**}(x) = -I_F^{-1}\left(p_\xi^*\right)\frac{d}{dv}\ln p_\xi^*(v) = \begin{cases} x \text{ for } |x| \le \Delta \\ \Delta \operatorname{sign}(x) \text{ for } |x| > \Delta \end{cases} \tag{61}$$

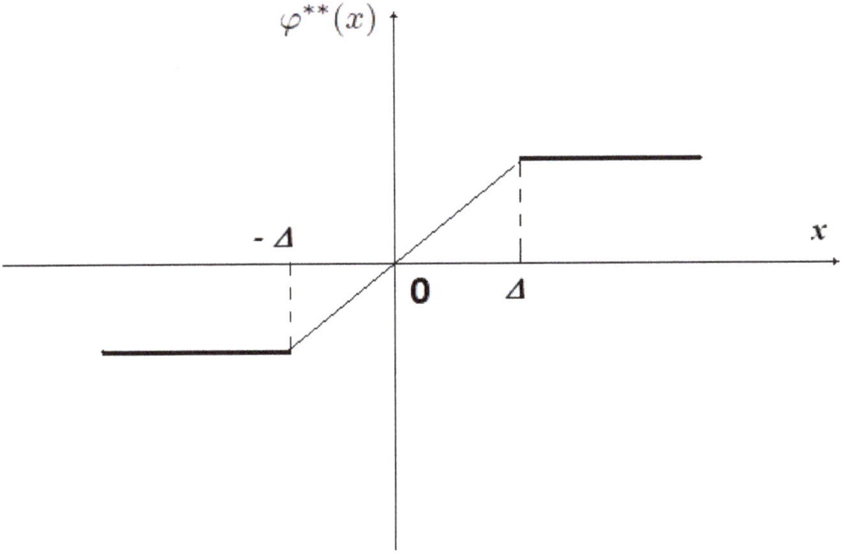


**Figure 3.** The nonlinear transformation $\varphi^{**}$ for the class $\mathcal{P}_\xi^3$.

**Lemma 5.** *In the class*

$$\mathcal{P}_\xi^4 = \left\{p_\xi : p_\xi(x) = (1-\alpha)p_{U(0,a)}(x) + \alpha q(x)\right\},$$
$$p_{U(0,a)}(x) := \tfrac{1}{2a}\chi(|x| \le a)$$

*(7) (of all symmetric "approximately uniform" distributions) the worth distribution density $p_\xi^*(x)$ is*

$$p_\xi^*(x) = \arg\inf_{p_\xi \in \mathcal{P}_\xi^4} I_{F,\xi}(p_\xi) = \begin{cases} \tfrac{1-\alpha}{2a} \text{ for } |x| \le a \\ \tfrac{1-\alpha}{2a}\exp\left\{-(1-\alpha)\tfrac{|x|-a}{\alpha a}\right\} \text{ for } |x| > a > 0 \end{cases}, \tag{62}$$

*that is, the worth on $\mathcal{P}_\xi^4$ distribution density is the uniform p.d.f. for $|x| \le a$ and the Laplace type for $|x| > a$.*

**Corollary 5.** *The robust on $\mathcal{P}_\xi^4$ version of the procedure (54) contains*

$$\varphi^{**}(x) = -I_F^{-1}\left(p_\xi^*\right)\frac{d}{dv}\ln p_\xi^*(v) = \begin{cases} 0 \text{ for } |x| \le a \\ \dfrac{1-\alpha}{\alpha a}\operatorname{sign}(x) \text{ for } |x| > a \end{cases} \tag{63}$$

*See Figure 4.*

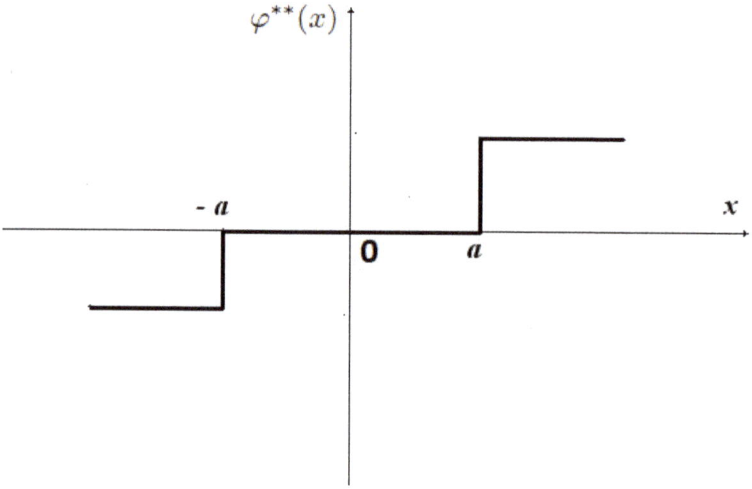


**Figure 4.** The nonlinear dead-zone transformation $\varphi^{**}$ for the class $\mathcal{P}_{\xi}^{4}$.

### 6.4. Robust Identification of Dynamic ARX Models

In the case of dynamic autoregression models (ARX model) where the generalised inputs are dependent on the state of the system, the matrix $\mathcal{R}$ depends on $p_\xi$, too, and therefore, we deal with the complete problem, namely, we need to calculate

$$\sup_{p_\xi \in \mathcal{P}} \left[ I_{F,}(p_\xi)\mathcal{R}(p_\xi) \right]^{-1} \tag{64}$$

For the ARX model (65) (for simplicity we put here $b_k = 0$, $(k = 0, \ldots, K)$, so $c_l = a_l$ $(l = 1, \ldots, L)$) the relation (36) becomes

$$\left.\begin{array}{r} \tilde{y}_n = a^\top \tilde{v}_n + \xi_n + O_\omega(\lambda^n) \\ a^\top = (a_1, \ldots, a_L), \tilde{v}_n^\top = (y_{n-1}, \ldots, y_{n-L}) \end{array}\right\} \tag{65}$$

Here we have

$$\frac{1}{n}\sum_{t=0}^{n} \mathrm{E}\{\tilde{v}_t \tilde{v}_t^\top\} \to \mathcal{R}(p_\xi)$$

where $\mathcal{R}(p_\xi)$ satisfies

$$\mathcal{R}(p_\xi) = A\mathcal{R}(p_\xi)A^\top + \sigma^2 \Xi_0 \tag{66}$$

with

$$A = \left\| \begin{array}{cccccc} a_0 & a_1 & \cdots & \cdots & a_{L_a} \\ 1 & 0 & \cdots & \cdots & 0 \\ 0 & 1 & 0 & \cdots & 0 \\ 0 & \cdots & \ddots & 0 & 0 \\ 0 & \cdots & 0 & 1 & 0 \end{array} \right\|, \quad \Xi_0 := \left\| \begin{array}{cccccc} 1 & 0 & \cdots & \cdots & 0 \\ 0 & 0 & \cdots & \cdots & 0 \\ 0 & 0 & 0 & \cdots & 0 \\ 0 & \cdots & \ddots & 0 & 0 \\ 0 & \cdots & 0 & 0 & 0 \end{array} \right\|$$

Obviously, $\mathcal{R}(p_\xi)$ can be represented as $\mathcal{R}(p_\xi) = \sigma^2 \mathcal{R}_0(p_\xi)$, where $\mathcal{R}_0$ is the solution of

$$\mathcal{R}_0(p_\xi) = A\mathcal{R}_0(p_\xi)A^\top + \Xi_0. \tag{67}$$

In this case, the problem (64) is reduced to

$$\sup_{p_\xi \in \mathcal{P}_\xi} \left[ \sigma^2(p_\xi) I_F(p_\xi) \right]^{-1}$$

or equivalently, to

$$\inf_{p_\xi \in \mathcal{P}_\xi} \left[\sigma^2(p_\xi) I_F(p_\xi)\right] \tag{68}$$

Consider now some classes $\mathcal{P}_\xi$ of a priory informative generating noise distributions and solutions of the problem (68) within these classes.

(1) Class $\mathcal{P}_\xi^{ARX-1}$ (containing among others the Gaussian distribution $p_{\mathcal{N}(0,\sigma_0^2)}(x)$).

**Lemma 6.** *For the class* $\mathcal{P}_\xi^{ARX-1}$

$$p_\xi^*(x) = \arg \inf_{p_\xi \in \mathcal{P}_1^{AR}} \left[\sigma^2(p_\xi) I_F(p_\xi)\right] = p_{\mathcal{N}(0,\sigma_0^2)}(x) \tag{69}$$

*that is, the worth on* $\mathcal{P}_\xi^{ARX-1}$ *p.d.f. is exactly that the Gaussian distribution* $p_{\mathcal{N}(0,\sigma_0^2)}(x)$.

**Proof.** Taking in (A1)

$$f(x) = x,\ \varphi(x) = p_\xi'(x)/p_\xi(x)$$

we get

$$\sigma^2 I_F(p_\xi) \geq \left(\int_{\mathbb{R}} x p_\xi'(x) dx\right)^2 = \left(\int_{\mathbb{R}} p_\xi(x) dx\right)^2 = 1$$

such that the equality is attained when $p_\xi'(x)/p_\xi(x) = \lambda x$, which leads to

$$p_\xi(x) = \frac{1}{\sqrt{2\pi/\lambda}} \exp\left\{-\frac{\lambda x^2}{2}\right\}$$

But since $I_F\left(p_{\mathcal{N}(0,\sigma_0^2)}\right) = \sigma_0^{-2}$ from the inequality above we get

$$\sigma^2(p_\xi) I_F(p_\xi) \geq 1 = \sigma_0^2 I_F\left(p_{\mathcal{N}(0,\sigma_0^2)}\right)$$

which means that $p_\xi^*(x) = p_{\mathcal{N}(0,\sigma_0^2)}(x)$. □

**Corollary 6.** *The robust on* $\mathcal{P}_\xi^{ARX-1}$ *version of the procedure (54) contains*

$$\varphi^{**}(x) = -I_F^{-1}\left(p_\xi^*\right) \frac{d}{dv} \ln p_\xi^*(v) = x.$$

(2) Class $\mathcal{P}_\xi^{ARX-2}$ (containing all centred distributions with a variance not less than a given value):

$$\mathcal{P}_\xi^{ARX-2} = \left\{p_\xi : \int_{\mathbb{R}} x^2 p_\xi(x) dx \geq \sigma_0^2\right\} \tag{70}$$

**Lemma 7.** *For the class* $\mathcal{P}_\xi^{ARX-2}$

$$p_\xi^*(x) = \arg \inf_{p_\xi \in \mathcal{P}_\xi^{ARX-2}} I_F(p_\xi) \tag{71}$$

*that is, the worth on $\mathcal{P}_{\xi}^{ARX-2}$ distribution density $p_{\xi}^{*}(x)$ coincides with the worth p.d.f. on the classes $\mathcal{P}_{\xi}^{i}$ $(i = 1, \ldots, 4)$ characterising distribution uncertainties (if additional information is available) for static regression models provided that*

$$\sigma^2\left(p_{\xi}^{*}(x)\right) = \sigma_0^2 \tag{72}$$

**Proof.** It follows directly from the inequality $\sigma^2(p_{\xi})I_F(p_{\xi}) \geq \sigma_0^2 I_F(p_{\xi})$. □

**Remark 8.** *Notice that all of the preceding analysis is based on the assumption that the transfer function (4) of the forming filter (3) is known a priory, allowing the parallel whitening process (34) to be applied and the information Cramer–Rao bound (37) to be reached, resulting in the asymptotically effective (the "best" ones) procedure, which is robust on given p.d.f. classes $\mathcal{P}_{\xi}$ of generating noises.*

Below, we look at a considerably more challenging scenario where the forming filter (3) is unknown a prior. In this situation, nobody can definitely achieve the information Cramer–Rao bound (37) and build an asymptotically successful parametric estimate technique in this circumstance. However, the problem can be handled utilising alternative techniques of identification.

## 7. Instrumental Variables Method for ARMAX Model with Finite Noise Correlation

### *7.1. About IVM*

Instrumental variables (IV) or total least-squares estimators is the method which also recommends to estimate parameters in the presence of white or coloured noises [89–91]. Even if the accuracy of the estimator for errors-in-variables models cannot be handled with a conventional analysis, the results produced by any of these estimators in practice demonstrate that their response can be well theoretically anticipated. The instrumental variables algorithms have been implemented for multivariable model forms, such as ARMAX models, dynamic adjustments with autoregressive errors and multivariable transfer functions (see [92]), where the IV algorithm provides asymptotically efficient estimation results and a low variance. The IV method can be adapted to work with the maximum likelihood method [93]. An analysis of the refined instrumental variable-approximate maximum likelihood (IVAML) method was presented. The proposed technique proved to be asymptotically efficient and to approach minimum variance estimation of the model parameters, even with a low sample size and low signal noise rations. An unified refined instrumental variable (RIV) approach was proposed in [94] for the estimation of discrete and continuous-time transfer functions. The estimator was based on the formulation of a pseudo-linear regression involving an optimal prefiltering process derived from a Box–Jenkins transfer function model. This method showed a reliable solution to the maximum likelihood optimisation equations, and the estimates are optimal in the maximum likelihood sense. The optimal refined instrumental variables for Box–Jenkins models has been studied on various occasions, for example in [95]. There, in contrast to the most common forms of the algorithm used in ARMAX models, a modification that facilitates the representation of the more general noise component of the Box–Jenkins model was proposed, and that could also be used as an adaptive filter and as a state variable feedback control. For the nonlinear case, the instrumental variable method has been used in particular for nonlinear Hammerstein models. The nonlinear recursive instrumental variables method has been used to deal with these models due to its simplicity in practical applications (see [96]). The recursive IV method also proves to be superior to the recursive LSM in terms of accuracy and convergence under the presence of coloured noises, and this is valid either for discrete or continuous-time [97].

Consider now the system (1) in the regression format

$$\left.\begin{aligned} y_n &= z_n^\top c + \eta_n, \\ c &= (a_1, \ldots, a_L; b_0, \ldots, b_K)^\top \in R^{L+K+1}, \\ z_n &= (y_{n-1}, \ldots, y_{n-L}; w_n, \ldots, w_{n-K})^\top \in R^{L+K+1} \end{aligned}\right\} \tag{73}$$

where the exogenous noise input $\eta_n$ has a finite correlation, that is, the transfer matrix of the forming filter has only the nominator:

$$H(q^{-1}) = H_1(q^{-1}) = 1 + \sum_{s=1}^{K_1} d_{2,s} q^{-s}, \; H_2(q^{-1}) = 1 \tag{74}$$

It is acknowledged that the parameters $d_{2,s}$ $(s = 1, \ldots, K_1)$ may be unknown a priory.

*7.2. Instrumental Variables and the System of Normal Equations*

Let $v_n \in R^{L+K+1}$ be an auxiliary vector variable (an instrumental variable) depending on information available up to time $n$. Considering the moments $t = 1, \ldots, n$ and multiplying both sides of (73) by $v_t$ we get the so-called system of "normal equations":

$$\left.\begin{aligned} v_1 y_1 &= v_1 z_1^\top c + v_1 \eta_1, \\ v_2 y_2 &= v_2 z_2^\top c + v_2 \eta_2, \\ &\vdots \\ v_n y_n &= v_n z_n^\top c + v_n \eta_n \end{aligned}\right\} \tag{75}$$

Summing these relations, after multiplying by $n^{-1}$, we obtain

$$n^{-1} \sum_{t=1}^{n} v_t y_t = \left( n^{-1} \sum_{t=1}^{n} v_t z_t^\top \right) c + n^{-1} \sum_{t=1}^{n} v_t \eta_t \tag{76}$$

Define the instrumental variable estimate $c_n^{IV}$ of the vector $c$ as a vector which in each time $n$ satisfies the relation

$$\sum_{t=1}^{n} v_t y_t = \left( \sum_{t=1}^{n} v_t z_t^\top \right) c_n^{IV}. \tag{77}$$

If the matrix $\left( \sum_{t=1}^{n} v_t z_t^\top \right)$ is invertible, that is, the matrix $\Gamma_n^{IV} := \left( \sum_{t=1}^{n} v_t z_t^\top \right)^{-1}$ exists (for all $n \geq n_0$), then $c_n^{IV}$ can be expressed as

$$c_n^{IV} = \Gamma_n^{IV} \sum_{t=1}^{n} v_t y_t, \tag{78}$$

or in the recurrent form

$$\left.\begin{aligned} c_n^{IV} &= c_{n-1}^{IV} + \Gamma_n^{IV} v_t \left( y_n - z_n^\top c_{n-1}^{IV} \right), \\ \Gamma_n^{IV} &= \Gamma_{n-1}^{IV} - \frac{\Gamma_{n-1}^{IV} v_n z_n^\top \Gamma_{n-1}^{IV}}{1 + z_n^\top \Gamma_{n-1}^{IV} v_n}, \; z_n^\top \Gamma_{n-1}^{IV} v_n \neq -1 \end{aligned}\right\} \tag{79}$$

**Remark 9.** *Notice that if $v_n = z_n$ the estimates $c_n^{IV}$ (77)–(79) coincide with LSM estimates.*

As it follows from (76) and (77), the estimation error $\delta_n = c_n^{IV} - c$ satisfies

$$-n^{-1} \sum_{t=1}^{n} v_t \eta_t = \left( n^{-1} \sum_{t=1}^{n} v_t z_t^\top \right) \delta_n \tag{80}$$

Under the main assumptions accepted above, in view of the strong large number law (see Theorem 8.10 in [36]), we have

$$n^{-1}\sum_{t=1}^{n} v_t y_t \overset{a.s.}{=} n^{-1}\sum_{t=1}^{n} \mathrm{E}\{v_t y_t\} + o_\omega(1),$$
$$n^{-1}\sum_{t=1}^{n} v_t z_t \overset{a.s.}{=} n^{-1}\sum_{t=1}^{n} \mathrm{E}\{v_t z_t\} + o_\omega(1),$$
$$n^{-1}\sum_{t=1}^{n} v_t \eta_t \overset{a.s.}{=} n^{-1}\sum_{t=1}^{n} \mathrm{E}\{v_t \eta_t\} + o_\omega(1)$$

$a.s.$ means almost sure or with probability 1.

and the relation (80) becomes

$$-n^{-1}\sum_{t=1}^{n} \mathrm{E}\{v_t \eta_t\} \overset{a.s.}{=} \left(n^{-1}\sum_{t=1}^{n} \mathrm{E}\{v_t z_t\}\right)\delta_n + o_\omega(1)$$

from which one may conclude that if

(1)

$$n^{-1}\sum_{t=1}^{n} \mathrm{E}\{v_t z_t\} \to \mathcal{R}_{IV}\,,\ \det \mathcal{R}_{IV} \neq 0; \tag{81}$$

(2)

$$n^{-1}\sum_{t=1}^{n} \mathrm{E}\{v_t \eta_t\} \to 0, \tag{82}$$

then the estimate $c_n^{IV}$ is asymptotically consistent with probability 1, namely, $\delta_n \overset{a.s.}{\to} 0$.

**Corollary 7.** *Evidently, the condition (82) holds if the instrumental variable $v_t$ and the external noise $\eta_t$ are not correlated:*

$$\mathrm{E}\{v_t \eta_t\} = 0 \textit{ for all } t = 1, \ldots$$

*So, in the example (17), instead of the LSM estimate (18) we need to use (see [98]) the IV estimate $c_n^{IV}$ (78) with $v_t = y_{t-k}$ $(k \geq 1)$ :*

$$a_n = \left[\sum_{t=1}^{n} y_{t-k} y_{t+1}\right]\left[\sum_{t=1}^{n} y_t y_{t-k}\right]^{-1} \overset{a.s.}{\to} a$$

*In general cases for the model (73) and (74) with a finite correlation ($\mathrm{E}\{\eta_t \eta_{t-k}\} = 0, k > K_1$) we may use the following IV estimate $c_n^{IV}$ with $v_t = z_{t-k}$ $(k \geq K_1)$ :*

$$\left.\begin{array}{c} c_n^{IV} = c_{n-1}^{IV} + \Gamma_n^{IV} z_{t-k}\left(y_n - z_n^{\intercal} c_{n-1}^{IV}\right), \\ \Gamma_n^{IV} = \Gamma_{n-1}^{IV} - \dfrac{\Gamma_{n-1}^{IV} z_{n-k} z_n^{\intercal} \Gamma_{n-1}^{IV}}{1 + z_n^{\intercal} \Gamma_{n-1}^{IV} z_{n-k}},\ z_n^{\intercal} \Gamma_{n-1}^{IV} z_{n-k} \neq -1. \end{array}\right\} \tag{83}$$

## 8. Joint Parametric Identification of ARMAX Model and the Forming Filter

Unfortunately, IVM identification algorithms cannot be applied in the situation when the correlation function of a coloured noise is not finite. Below, we treat exactly this case considering that the transfer function of a finite-dimensional forming filter is completely unknown, including both numerator and denominator parameters in (4). So, here our problem under the consideration is as follows: based on the available data (16) we need to construct an identification procedure, generating some parameter estimates $\hat{a}_{n,i}$ $(i = 1, \ldots, L)$, $\hat{b}_{n,i}$ $(i = 0, \ldots, K)$ ,$\hat{h}_{n,1i}$ $(i = 0, \ldots, K_1)$ and $\hat{h}_{n,2i}$ $(i = 1, \ldots, K_2)$ which asymptotically convergence with probability 1 (or almost sure) to the real values, namely,

$$\hat{a}_{n,i} \overset{a.s.}{\to} a_i,\ \hat{b}_{n,i} \overset{a.s.}{\to} b_i,\ \hat{h}_{n,1i} \overset{a.s.}{\to} h_{1,i},\ \hat{h}_{n,2i} \overset{a.s.}{\to} h_{2,i} \text{ when } n \to \infty. \tag{84}$$

## 8.1. An Equivalent ARMAX Representation

Multiplying (1) by $H_2(q) = 1 + \sum_{i=1}^{K_2} h_{2,i} q^i$ we obtain the corresponding ARMAX (autoregression with moving average noise term model)

$$\left(1 + \sum_{i=1}^{K_2} h_{2,i} q^i\right)\left(1 + \sum_{i=1}^{L} a_i q^i\right) y_n = \\ \left(1 + \sum_{i=1}^{K_2} h_{2,i} q^i\right)\left(\sum_{i=0}^{K} b_i q^i\right) u_n + \left(h_{1,0} + \sum_{i=1}^{K_1} h_{1,i} q^i\right)\xi_n$$

or, equivalently, in the "open format" (with $m_A := \max\{K_2, L\}$ and $m_B := \max\{K_2, K\}$)

$$\left.\begin{array}{c} \left(1 + \sum_{i=1}^{m_A} q^i \left[a_i \chi(i \le n_A) + h_{2,i} \chi(i \le n_{D_2}) \right.\right. \\ \left.\left. + \left(h_{2,i} \chi(i \le n_{D_2}) \sum_{j=1}^{m_A} a_j \chi(j \le n_A) q^j\right)\right]\right) y_n = \\ \left(b_0 + \sum_{i=1}^{M_B} q^i \left[b_i \chi(i \le M_B) + h_{2,i} \chi(i \le n_{D_2}) \sum_{j=0}^{M_B} b_j \chi(j \le n_B) q^j\right]\right) u_n \\ + \left(1 + \sum_{i=1}^{n_{D_1}} h_{1,i} q^i\right)\xi_n, \end{array}\right\} \tag{85}$$

where

$$\chi(\mathcal{A}) = \begin{cases} 1 & \text{if} \quad \text{the event } \mathcal{A} \text{ is valid} \\ 0 & \text{if} \quad \text{not} \end{cases}.$$

**Remark 10.** *Notice that since the polynomial $H_2(q)$ is stable, the reactions $\{y_\tau\}_{\tau=\overline{1,n}}$ of both difference Equations (4) and (85) on the same inputs $\{u_\tau\}_{\tau=\overline{-2m_B,n}}$ and $\{\xi_\tau\}_{0=\overline{-K_1,n}}$ are asymptotically closed, namely, the difference between these reactions tends to zero exponentially quickly with probability one. That is why to obtain the desired property (84), designing the identification procedure using the data of the model (4) can be realised based on data but generated by the ARMAX model (85) (see [99]).*

The ARMAX model (85) can be represented in the standard regression format (different from (14)) as

$$y_n = x_n^\top c + h_{1,0}\xi_n \tag{86}$$

with

$$x_n = \left(-y_{n-1}, \cdots, -y_{n-2m_A}; u_n, \cdots, u_{n-2m_B}; \xi_{n-1}, \cdots, \xi_{n-n_{K_1}}\right)^\top \in R^N \\ N := 2m_A + 2m_B + 1 + K_1 \tag{87}$$

and

$$c = \left(\tilde{a}_1, \cdots, \tilde{a}_{2m_A}, \tilde{b}_0, \cdots, \tilde{b}_{2m_B}, h_{1,1}, \ldots, h_{1,K_1}\right)^\top \in R^N, \tag{88}$$

containing the components

$$\left.\begin{array}{c} \tilde{a}_1 = a_1 + h_{2,1}, \\ \tilde{a}_i = a_i \chi(i \le n_L) + h_{2,i} \chi(i \le n_{K_2}) + \\ \sum_{k=1}^{m_A} h_{2,k} \chi(k \le n_{K_2}) a_{i-k} \chi(i-k \le L),\ i = 2, \ldots, 2m_A, \\ \tilde{b}_0 = b_0,\ \tilde{b}_i = b_i \chi(i \le m_B) + \\ \sum_{k=1}^{m_B} h_{2,k} \chi(k \le n_{K_2}) b_{i-k} \chi(i-k \le K),\ i = 1, \ldots, 2m_B. \end{array}\right\} \tag{89}$$

**Remark 11.** *Notice that the extended input vector $x_n$ is not completely available since it contains immeasurable components $\xi_{n-1}, \cdots, \xi_{n-n_{K_1}}$. This property is the main difference with the standard ARMAX model identification problem where the vector $x_n$ does not contain these immeasurable term.*

## 8.2. Auxiliary Residual Sequence

Now, let us define the "generalised residual sequence" given by the recursion relation

$$\varepsilon_n = y_n - \hat{x}_n^{\top} c_{n-1} \tag{90}$$

where the "extended vector" $\hat{x}_n \in R^{2m_A+2m_B+1+K_1}$ is defined as

$$\hat{x}_n = \left(-y_{n-1}, \cdots, -y_{n-2m_A}; u_n, \cdots, u_{n-2m_B}; \varepsilon_{n-1}, \cdots, \varepsilon_{n-n_{K_1}}\right)^{\top} \tag{91}$$

with $\varepsilon_{-1} = \cdots = \varepsilon_{-n_{D_1}} = 0$. Notice that the "extended vector" $\hat{x}_n$ is measurable on-line.

**Lemma 8** ([99]). *For $n \to \infty$*

$$\Delta_n = \varepsilon_n - \xi_n = O\left(\left|\lambda_{H_1}\right|^n\right) \overset{a.s.}{\to} 0, \tag{92}$$

*where $\lambda_{H_1}$ is the eigenvalue of the polynomial $H_1$ with minimal module $\left|\lambda_{H_1}\right| < 1$.*

From (A5) we get

$$y_n = \hat{x}_n^{\top} c - \sum_{i=1}^{n_{D_1}} h_{1,i}\Delta_{n-i} + h_{1,0}\xi_n = \hat{x}_n^{\top} c + h_{1,0}\xi_n + O\left(\left|\lambda_{H_1}\right|^n\right). \tag{93}$$

## 8.3. Identification Procedure

To estimate the extended vector $c$ from the relation (93) let us apply the least-squares method (LSM), defining the current estimate $\hat{c}_n$ as

$$\hat{c}_n = \left(\sum_{t=0}^{n} \hat{x}_t \hat{x}_t^{\top}\right)^{-1} \sum_{t=0}^{n} \hat{x}_t y_t,\ n \geq n_0 = \left\{\inf n: \sum_{t=t}^{n} \hat{x}_t \hat{x}_t^{\top} > 0\right\} \tag{94}$$

In the recurrent form, this estimate can be represented as in (39):

$$\left.\begin{array}{c} \hat{c}_n = \hat{c}_{n-1} + \Gamma_n \hat{x}_n \varphi(y_n - \hat{x}_n^{\top} \hat{c}_{n-1}), \\ \Gamma_n = \Gamma_{n-1} - \dfrac{\Gamma_{n-1}\hat{x}_n \hat{x}_n^{\top}\Gamma_{n-1}}{1 + \hat{x}_n^{\top}\Gamma_{n-1}\hat{x}_n},\ n \geq n_0 + 1, \\ \Gamma_{n_0}^{-1} := \sum\limits_{t=t}^{n_0} \hat{x}_t \hat{x}_t^{\top} \end{array}\right\} \tag{95}$$

Notice that taking $\Gamma_{n_0}^{-1}$ as

$$\Gamma_{n_0}^{-1} = \rho I_{N\times N} + \sum_{t=t}^{n_0} \hat{x}_t \hat{x}_t^{\top},\ 0 < \rho \ll 1, \tag{96}$$

we can select $n_0 = 0$, and the procedure (95) can be applied from the beginning of the process.

**Theorem 6** ([100]). *If*

(1) *the following "persistent excitation condition" (PEC) holds:*

$$\liminf_n \left(\frac{1}{n} \sum_{t=0}^{n} x_t x_t^{\top}\right) \overset{a.s.}{\geq} \nu I_{M\times M} \overset{a.s.}{>} 0,$$
$$M := 2m_A + 2m_B + 1 + D_1.$$

(2) *$\{\xi_n\}$ is a martingale difference sequence satisfying (10),*

*then, the LSM procedure (95) and (96) generates the sequence of the estimates $\{\hat{c}_n\}_{n\geq 0}$, which is asymptotically consistent with probability 1, that is, $\hat{c}_n \underset{n\to\infty}{\overset{a.s}{\to}} c$.*

### *8.4. Recuperation of the Model Parameters from the Obtained Current Estimates*

#### 8.4.1. Special Case When the Recuperation Process Can Be Realised Directly

When $K = 0$ and the gain parameter $b_0 \neq 0$ are a priori known, the system of algebraic Equations (89) becomes linear with respect to the unknown parameters $a_i(i = 0, \ldots, L)$ and $h_{2,i}\left(i = 0, \ldots, n_{K_2}\right)$, and may be resolved analytically without application of any numerical procedure.

#### 8.4.2. General Case Requiring the Application of Gradient Descent Method (GDM)

In view of (89), we can recuperate the parameters $a_i\left(i = \overline{0, L}\right)$, $b_i\ \left(i = \overline{0, K}\right)$ and $h_{2,i}$ $\left(i = 0, \ldots, n_{K_2}\right)$ for this purpose using the command Fsolve in Matlab or some numerical method such as GDM.

For example, if we consider the case when $K = L = n_{K_2} = m_A = m_B = 2$, the component relations from (89) become

$$\tilde{a}_1 = a_1 + h_{2,1},\ \tilde{a}_2 = a_2 + h_{2,2} + h_{2,1}a_1,$$
$$\tilde{a}_3 = h_{2,1}a_2 + h_{2,2}a_1,\ \tilde{a}_4 = h_{2,2}a_2,$$

$$\tilde{b}_0 = b_0,\ \tilde{b}_1 = b_1 + h_{2,1}b_0,$$
$$\tilde{b}_2 = b_2 + h_{2,1}b_1 + h_{2,2}b_0,$$
$$\tilde{b}_3 = h_{2,1}b_2 + h_{2,2}b_1,\ \tilde{b}_4 = h_{2,2}b_2.$$

Since this system is formed by nonlinear equations, and in some particular cases it is actually possible to solve the equations analytically, the gradient descent method (GDM) is implemented to estimate the values from the original system, taking the best average value from the estimated parameters. For this purpose, we define the following objective function:

$$F(a_1, a_2, b_1, h_{21}) = (a_1 + h_{21} - c_1)^2 +$$
$$(a_1 h_{21} + a_2 - c_2)^2 + (a_2 h_{21} - c_3)^2 +$$
$$(b_1 + h_{21} b_0 - c_5)^2 + (b_1 h_{21} - c_6)^2 \to \min$$

The original parameter can be recovered using some of the existing optimisation commands in Matlab, suc as Fsolve or optimvar, or some algorithms such as GDM mentioned previously, although some other optimisation techniques could be implemented (see [99]). The performance of Fsolve is good in second or third order systems; in these cases, the command can recover all the original parameters from the nonlinear system. In higher order systems, this method presents problems at recovering the original values, while gradient descent has a good performance with low- and high-order systems. In some cases, such as the example presented before, it is possible to recover the original values by a mathematical simplification. The main condition for a good estimation is that in the objective function one should have at least as many terms as variables to estimate, otherwise it is not possible to recover all the original values.

## 9. Numerical Example

The algorithms presented in the previous sections are illustrated with a numerical example.

### *Raised Cosine Distribution*

Consider the following system

$$y(k) = 0.85y(k-1) + 2u(k) + \eta(k),$$
$$\eta(k) = -0.3\eta(k-1) + \xi(k) + 0.8\xi(k-1),$$

with $\xi$ having the raised cosine distribution

$$p_\xi(v) = \frac{1}{2s}\left[1 + \cos\left(\frac{v-\mu}{s}\pi\right)\right],\ \mu > 0,\ s > 0,$$

which is a continuously differentiable function supported on the interval $[\mu - s, \mu + s]$. The system can be rewritten as follows

$$y(k) = z(k)^{\top}c + \eta(k),$$

with

$$z(k) = \begin{pmatrix} y(k-1) \\ u(k) \end{pmatrix}, \ c := \begin{pmatrix} 0.85 \\ 2 \end{pmatrix}.$$

The whitening process is then given by

$$\tilde{y}(k) = H(q^{-1})y(k), \ \tilde{z}(k) = H(q^{-1})z(k),$$

or in the extended form,

$$\begin{aligned} \tilde{y}(k) + 0.3\,\tilde{y}(k-1) = y(k) + 0.8y(k-1), \ \tilde{y}(0) = y(0), \\ \tilde{z}(k) + 0.3\,\tilde{z}(k-1) = z(k) + 0.8z(k-1), \ \tilde{z}(0) = z(0), \end{aligned}$$

where the "inverse filter" has the transfer function

$$H(q^{-1}) = \frac{1 + 0.8q^{-1}}{1 + 0.3q^{-1}}.$$

The recursive WLSM algorithm with the residual nonlinear transformation is given by

$$\begin{aligned} c_n = c_{n-1} - I_{F,\xi}^{-1}\Gamma_n\tilde{z}_n \frac{p_{\xi}'(v)}{p_{\xi}(v)}\Big|_{v=\tilde{y}_n - \tilde{z}_n^{\top}c_{n-1}} = \\ c_{n-1} + 2\pi I_{F,\xi}^{-1}\Gamma_n\tilde{z}_n \frac{\sin\left(\frac{v-\mu}{s}\pi\right)}{1+\cos\left(\frac{v-\mu}{s}\pi\right)}\Big|_{v=\tilde{y}_n - \tilde{z}_n^{\top}c_{n-1}} = \\ c_{n-1} + \frac{s}{\pi}\Gamma_n\tilde{z}_n \frac{\sin\left(\frac{\pi}{s}[\tilde{y}_n - \tilde{z}_n^{\top}c_{n-1} - \mu]\right)}{1+\cos\left(\frac{\pi}{s}[\tilde{y}_n - \tilde{z}_n^{\top}c_{n-1} - \mu]\right)}. \end{aligned} \tag{97}$$

Here, we have used that for the raised cosine distribution

$$I_{F,\xi} = 2\frac{\pi^2}{s}. \tag{98}$$

The initial conditions are $c(0) = 2$, $y(0) = 3$, $\Gamma(0) = 10^5$. The Figures 5 and 6 show the estimated parameters $a$ and $b$ using LSM and MLLM+ whitening with a nonlinear residual transformation.

In the Figures 5 and 6, one can see that in the LSM case the noise has a strong influence in the estimation results, while in the MLLM+ whitening, the noise influence is minimised in the estimated parameter, reducing the bias, which is the most common problem in parameter estimation using LSM under the presence of the correlated noises. The performance index of the estimated algorithm is illustrated in Figure 7; here, one can see that the MLLM+ whitening is a better option for parameter estimation in systems with coloured noises.

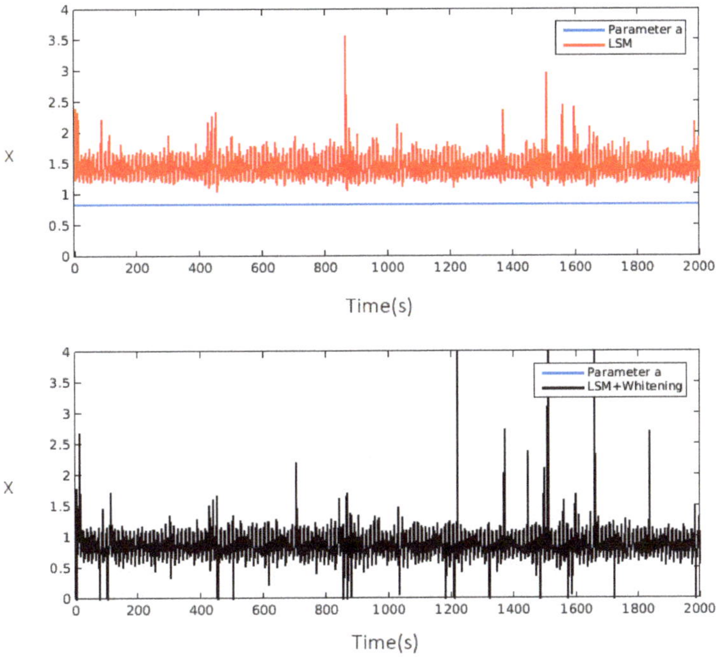


**Figure 5.** Parameter *a* and its estimated using LSM and LSM+ whitening (raised cosine distribution case).

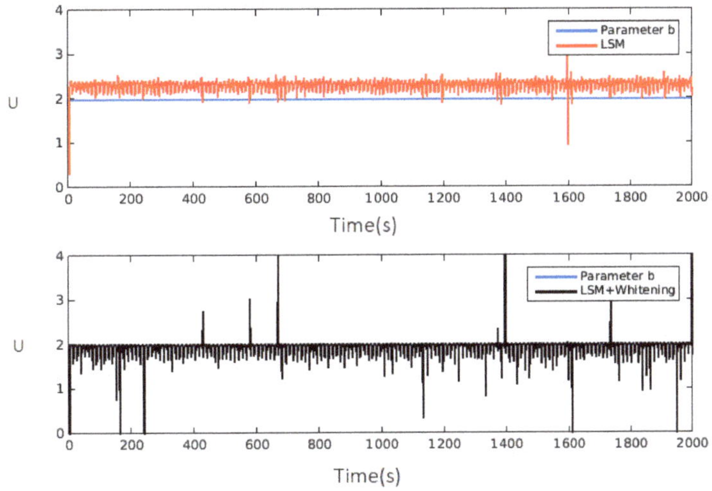


**Figure 6.** Parameter *b* and its estimated using LSM and LSM+ whitening (raised cosine distribution case).

In this case, the filter structure is known; a numerical example where the filter structure is unknown is presented in [99].

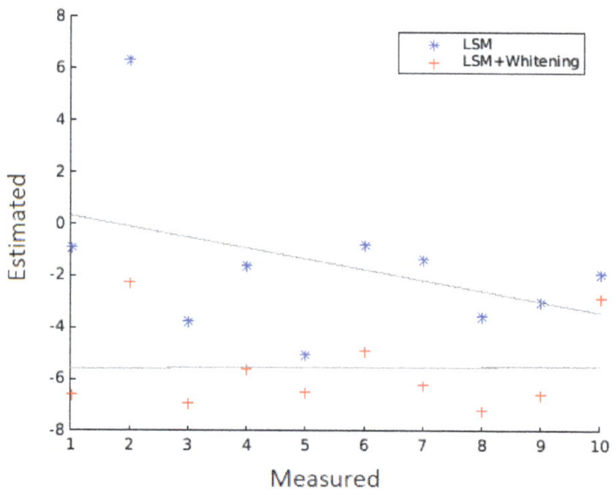


**Figure 7.** Performance indexes of the estimation algorithms implemented in a system with a raised cosine distribution.

## 10. Discussion

In this paper, we demonstrated that the traditional LSM algorithm failed to accurately estimate the parameters of ARX (dynamic) models when subjected to a coloured perturbation, and because of this, it is necessary to implement a different estimation strategy. For the identification issue under non-Gaussian and coloured noises, the Cramer–Rao inequality and the related Fisher information limits were explored, when the forming filter (the noise spectral function) is known a priori.

It was shown that a recurrent process, which employs both the whitening technique and the nonlinear residual transformation (operating in parallel), is the asymptotically effective (the "best") identification algorithm.

The main limitation of the proposed method is that in the case of having a partially unknown filter, the method cannot be implemented. In this case, there are two different identification methods that might be used:

- Instrumental variables method (IVM) for ARMAX models with a finite noise-correlation.
- The nonlinear residual transformation method for simultaneous parametric identification of the ARMAX model and the forming filter.

  Both techniques are not asymptotically effective, as they do not achieve the Cramer–Rao information limits.

In a future work, we plan to analyse the case in which the filter is partially known, or even unknown, and if it is possible to achieve the information limits that were previously mentioned.

## 11. Conclusions

In the present work, the limits for the Cramer–Rao inequality and the related Fisher information were explored under coloured noise perturbations, and we demonstrated that the whitening technique and the nonlinear residual transformation working in parallel generate an estimation sequence with the asymptotic convergence rate that proves to be the best identification algorithm for the case studied in this manuscript, reaching the Fisher information bound, which cannot be improved by any other estimation algorithm. The effectiveness of the suggested approach is illustrated by a numerical example with a non-Gaussian noise, having a raised cosine distribution.

**Author Contributions:** A.P. and J.E. conceived of the present idea. A.P. developed the theory and J.E. performed the computations and verified the analytical methods. All the authors discussed the results and contributed to the final manuscript. All authors have read and agreed to the published version of the manuscript.

**Funding:** This research received no external funding.

**Institutional Review Board Statement:** Not applicable.

**Informed Consent Statement:** Not applicable.

**Data Availability Statement:** Not applicable.

**Conflicts of Interest:** The authors declare no conflict of interest.

## Abbreviations

| | |
|---|---|
| ARX | Autoregressive model with exogenous variables |
| ARMAX | Autoregression moving average exogenous input |
| NARMAX | Nonlinear autoregression moving average exogenous input |
| LSM | Least-squares method |
| IVM | Instrumental variables method |
| LNL | Large number law |
| NARMAX | Nonlinear autoregressive moving average with |
| CRB | Cramer–Rao bound |
| FIM | Fisher information |
| MVU | Minimum variance unbiased |
| MLMW | Maximum likelihood method with whitening |
| DWM | Direct whitening method |
| WECC | Western Electricity Coordinating Council |
| KARMAX | Autoregressive moving average explanatory input model of the Koyck kind |
| IVAML | Instrumental variable approximate maximum likelihood |
| RIV | Refinen instrumental variables |
| GDM | Gradient descent method |

## Appendix A

*Appendix A.1. Proof of Lemma 2*

- By the Cauchy–Schwarz inequality

$$\left(\int_{\mathbb{R}^1} f\varphi p_\xi dx\right)^2 \le \left(\int_{\mathbb{R}^1} f^2 p_\xi dx\right)\left(\int_{\mathbb{R}^1} \varphi^2 p_\xi dx\right) \tag{A1}$$

valid for any p.d.f. $f, \varphi$, and any noise density distribution $p_\xi$ (for which the integrals have a sense), for $f := p'_\xi(x)/p_\xi(x)$, after integrating by parts it follows

$$I_{F,\xi}(p_\xi) \ge \left(\int_{\mathbb{R}^1} p_\xi(x) d\varphi(x)\right)^2 / \int_{\mathbb{R}^1} \varphi^2(x) p_\xi(x) dx, \tag{A2}$$

where the equality is attained when $p'_\xi(x)/p_\xi(x) = \lambda\varphi(x)$, $\lambda$ is any constant. Taking $\varphi(x) := \text{sign}(x)$ in (A2) and using the identity $[\text{sign}(x)]' = 2\delta(x)p_\xi(0)$ leads to

$$I_{F,\xi}(p_\xi) \ge 4p^2_\xi(0) \ge \frac{1}{a^2} \text{ for any } p_\xi \in \mathcal{P}_1, \tag{A3}$$

where the equality is attained when $p'_\xi(x)/p_\xi(x) = \lambda\text{sign}(x)$, or equivalently, for $p_\xi(x) = \frac{\lambda}{2}\exp\{-|x|/\lambda\}$. With $\lambda = a$ we have

$$p_\xi(x) = \frac{a}{2}\exp\{-|x|/a\} = p_\xi^*(x). \tag{A4}$$

So, $I_{F,\xi}(p_\xi^*) = \dfrac{1}{a^2}$ and the worst noise distribution within $\mathcal{P}_\xi^1$ is $p_\xi^*(x)$ (55).

*Appendix A.2. Proof of Lemma 3*

From (4), we have

$$\left.\begin{array}{l} y_n = x_n^\top c + h_{1,0}\xi_n = \hat{x}_n^\top c + c^\top(x_n - \hat{x}_n) + h_{1,0}\xi_n \\ \quad = \hat{x}_n^\top c + \sum\limits_{i=1}^{n_{K_1}} h_{1,i}(\xi_{n-i} - \varepsilon_{n-i}) + h_{1,0}\xi_n, \end{array}\right\} \tag{A5}$$

which implies the following recurrence

$$h_{2,0}\Delta_n + \sum_{i=1}^{n_{K_1}} h_{1,i}\Delta_{n-i} = H_1(q)\Delta_n = 0. \tag{A6}$$

Taking into account that the polynomial $H_1(q)$ is stable, we get (92).

*Appendix A.3. Proof of Lemma 4*

- Taking in (A2) $\varphi(x) = x$ for all $p_\xi \in \mathcal{P}_\xi^2$, we get

$$I_{F,\xi}(p_\xi) \geq 1/\int_{\mathbb{R}} x^2 p_\xi(x)dx \geq 1/\sigma^2, \tag{A7}$$

where the equality is attained when

$$p_\xi'(x)/p_\xi(x) = \lambda x,\ \lambda \text{ is any constant} \tag{A8}$$

or, equivalently, for

$$p_\xi(x) = \frac{1}{\sqrt{2\pi/\lambda}}\exp\left\{-\frac{\lambda x^2}{2}\right\} \tag{A9}$$

For $\lambda = \sigma^{-2}$ we have

$$p_\xi(x) = \frac{1}{\sqrt{2\pi}\sigma}\exp\left\{-\frac{x^2}{2\sigma^2}\right\} = p_\xi^*(x) \tag{A10}$$

implying

$$I_{F,\xi}(p_\xi) \geq 1/\int_{\mathbb{R}^1} x^2 p_\xi(x)dx \geq 1/\sigma^2 = I_F(p_\xi^*) \tag{A11}$$

So, the worst noise distribution within $\mathcal{P}_\xi^2$ is $p_\xi^*(x)$.

*Appendix A.4. Proof of Lemma 5*

- (without details). From (7) it follows

$$p_\xi(x) \geq (1-\alpha)p_{\mathcal{N}(0,\sigma^2)}(x) \tag{A12}$$

So, we need to solve the following variational problem:

$$\inf_{p_\xi : p_\xi \geq (1-\alpha)p_{N(0,\sigma^2)}} I_{F,\xi}(p_\xi) \tag{A13}$$

As it is shown in [14], its solution is (59).

## References


1. Bender, E. *An Introduction to Mathematical Modeling*; Dover Publications, Inc.: Mineola, NY, USA, 2012.
2. Hugues, G.; Liuping, W. *Identification of Continuous-Time Models from Sampled Data*; Springer: Berlin/Heidelberg, Germany, 2008.
3. Åström, K.J.; Eykhoff, P. System identification—A survey. *Automatica* **1971**, *7*, 123–162. [CrossRef]
4. Bekey, G.A. System Identification—An Introduction and a Survey. *Simulation* **1970**, *15*, 151–166. [CrossRef]
5. Ljung, L.; Gunnarsson, S. Adaptation and tracking in system identification—A survey. *Automatica* **1990**, *26*, 7–21. [CrossRef]
6. Billings, S.A. Identification of Nonlinear Systems—A Survey. In *Proceedings of the IEE Proceedings D-Control Theory and Applications*; IET: London, UK, 1980; Volume 127, pp. 272–285.
7. Ljung, L. Perspectives on system identification. *Annu. Rev. Control* **2010**, *34*, 1–12. [CrossRef]
8. Ljung, L.; Chen, T.; Mu, B. A shift in paradigm for system identification. *Int. J. Control* **2020**, *93*, 173–180. [CrossRef]
9. Tudor, C. *Procesos Estocásticos*; Sociedad Mexicana de Matemáticas: Ciudad de Mexico, Mexico, 1994.
10. Sobczyk, K. *Stochastic Differential Equations: With Applications to Physics and Engineering*; Springer Science and Business Media: Berlin/Heidelberg, Germany, 2013.
11. Feng, D.; Liu, P.X.; Liu, G. Auxiliary model based multi-innovation extended stochastic gradient parameter estimation with colored measurement noises. *Signal Process.* **2009**, *89*, 1883–1890.
12. Vo, B.-N.; Antonio Cantoni, K.L.T. *Filter Design with Time Domain Mask Constraints: Theory and Applications*; Springer Science and Business Media: Berlin/Heidelberg, Germany, 2013; Volume 56.
13. Huber, P. *Robustness and Designs: In "A Survey of Statistical Design and Linear Models"*; North-Holland Publishing Company: Amsterdam, The Netherlands, 1975.
14. Tsypkin, Y.; Polyak, B. Robust likelihood method. *Dyn. Syst. Math. Methods Oscil. Theory Gor'Kii State Univ.* **1977**, *12*, 22–46. (In Russian)
15. Poznyak, A.S. Robust identification under correlated and non-Gaussian noises: WMLLM procedure. *Autom. Remote Control* **2019**, *80*, 1628–1644. [CrossRef]
16. Mokhlis, S.E.; Sadki, S.; Bensassi, B. System identification of a dc servo motor using arx and armax models. In Proceedings of the 2019 International Conference on Systems of Collaboration Big Data, Internet of Things & Security (SysCoBIoTS), Granada, Spain, 22–25 October 2019; IEEE: Piscataway, NJ, USA, 2019; pp. 1–4.
17. AldemĞR, A.; Hapoğlu, H. Comparison of ARMAX Model Identification Results Based on Least Squares Method. *Int. J. Mod. Trends Eng. Res.* **2015**, *2*, 27–35.
18. Likothanassis, S.; Demiris, E. Armax model identification with unknown process order and time-varying parameters. In *Signal Analysis and Prediction*; Springer: Berlin/Heidelberg, Germany, 1998; pp. 175–184.
19. Norton, J. Identification of parameter bounds for ARMAX models from records with bounded noise. *Int. J. Control* **1987**, *45*, 375–390. [CrossRef]
20. Stoffer, D.S. Estimation and identification of space-time ARMAX models in the presence of missing data. *J. Am. Stat. Assoc.* **1986**, *81*, 762–772. [CrossRef]
21. Mei, L.; Li, H.; Zhou, Y.; Wang, W.; Xing, F. Substructural damage detection in shear structures via ARMAX model and optimal subpattern assignment distance. *Eng. Struct.* **2019**, *191*, 625–639. [CrossRef]
22. Ferkl, L.; Široký, J. Ceiling radiant cooling: Comparison of ARMAX and subspace identification modelling methods. *Build. Environ.* **2010**, *45*, 205–212. [CrossRef]
23. Rahmat, M.; Salim, S.N.S.; Sunar, N.; Faudzi, A.M.; Ismail, Z.H.; Huda, K. Identification and non-linear control strategy for industrial pneumatic actuator. *Int. J. Phys. Sci.* **2012**, *7*, 2565–2579. [CrossRef]
24. González, J.P.; San Roque, A.M.S.M.; Perez, E.A. Forecasting functional time series with a new Hilbertian ARMAX model: Application to electricity price forecasting. *IEEE Trans. Power Syst.* **2017**, *33*, 545–556. [CrossRef]
25. Wu, S.; Sun, J.Q. A physics-based linear parametric model of room temperature in office buildings. *Build. Environ.* **2012**, *50*, 1–9. [CrossRef]
26. Jing, S. Identification of an ARMAX model based on a momentum-accelerated multi-error stochastic information gradient algorithm. In Proceedings of the 2021 IEEE 10th Data Driven Control and Learning Systems Conference (DDCLS), Suzhou, China, 14–16 May 2021; IEEE: Piscataway, NJ, USA, 2021; pp. 1274–1278.
27. Le, Y.; Hui, G. Optimal Estimation for ARMAX Processes with Noisy Output. In Proceedings of the 2020 Chinese Automation Congress (CAC), Shanghai, China, 6–8 November 2020; IEEE: Piscataway, NJ, USA, 2020; pp. 5048–5051.
28. Correa Martinez, J.; Poznyak, A. Switching Structure Robust State and Parameter Estimator for MIMO Nonlinear Systems. *Int. J. Control* **2001**, *74*, 175–189. [CrossRef]
29. Shieh, L.; Bao, Y.; Chang, F. State-space self-tuning controllers for general multivariable stochastic systems. In Proceedings of the 1987 American Control Conference, Minneapolis, MN, USA, 10–12 June 1987; IEEE: Piscataway, NJ, USA, 1987; pp. 1280–1285.
30. Correa-Martínez, J.; Poznyak, A.S. Three electromechanical examples of robust switching structure state and parameter estimation. In Proceedings of the 38th IEEE Conference on Decision and Control, Phoenix, AZ, USA, 7–10 December 1999; pp. 3962–3963. [CrossRef]
31. Mazaheri, A.; Mansouri, M.; Shooredeli, M. Parameter estimation of Hammerstein-Wiener ARMAX systems using unscented Kalman filter. In Proceedings of the 2014 Second RSI/ISM International Conference on Robotics and Mechatronics (ICRoM), Tehran, Iran, 15–17 October 2014; IEEE: Piscataway, NJ, USA, 2014; pp. 298–303.

32. Tsai, J.S.-H.; Hsu, W.; Lin, L.; Guo, S.; Tann, J.W. A modified NARMAX model-based self-tuner with fault tolerance for unknown nonlinear stochastic hybrid systems with an input—Output direct feed-through term. *ISA Trans.* **2014**, *53*, 56–75. [CrossRef]
33. Pu, Y.; Chen, J. A novel maximum likelihood-based stochastic gradient algorithm for Hammerstein nonlinear systems with coloured noise. *Int. J. Model. Identif. Control* **2019**, *32*, 23–29. [CrossRef]
34. Wang, D.; Fan, Q.; Ma, Y. An interactive maximum likelihood estimation method for multivariable Hammerstein systems. *J. Frankl. Inst.* **2020**, *357*, 12986–13005. [CrossRef]
35. Zheng, W.X. On least-squares identification of ARMAX models. *IFAC Proc. Vol.* **2002**, *35*, 391–396. [CrossRef]
36. Poznyak, A.S. *Advanced Mathematical Tools for Automatic Control Engineers Volume 2: Stochastic Techniques*; Elsevier: Amsterdam, The Netherlands, 2009.
37. Medel-Juárez, J.; Poznyak., A. S. Identification of Non Stationary ARMA Models Based on Matrix Forgetting. 1999. Available online: http://repositoriodigital.ipn.mx/handle/123456789/15474 (accessed on 6 February 2022).
38. Poznyak, A.; Medel, J. Matrix Forgetting with Adaptation. *Int. J. Syst. Sci.* **1999**, *30*, 865–878. [CrossRef]
39. Cerone, V. Parameter bounds for armax models from records with bounded errors in variables. *Int. J. Control* **1993**, *57*, 225–235. [CrossRef]
40. He, L.; Kárný, M. Estimation and prediction with ARMMAX model: A mixture of ARMAX models with common ARX part. *Int. J. Adapt. Control Signal Process.* **2003**, *17*, 265–283. [CrossRef]
41. Yin, L.; Gao, H. Moving horizon estimation for ARMAX processes with additive output noise. *J. Frankl. Inst.* **2019**, *356*, 2090–2110. [CrossRef]
42. Moustakides, G.V. Study of the transient phase of the forgetting factor RLS. *IEEE Trans. Signal Process.* **1997**, *45*, 2468–2476. [CrossRef]
43. Paleologu, C.; Benesty, J.; Ciochina, S. A robust variable forgetting factor recursive least-squares algorithm for system identification. *IEEE Signal Process. Lett.* **2008**, *15*, 597–600. [CrossRef]
44. Zhang, H.; Zhang, S.; Yin, Y. Online sequential ELM algorithm with forgetting factor for real applications. *Neurocomputing* **2017**, *261*, 144–152. [CrossRef]
45. Escobar, J.; Poznyak, A.S. Time-varying matrix estimation in stochastic continuous-time models under coloured noise using LSM with forgetting factor. *Int. J. Syst. Sci.* **2011**, *42*, 2009–2020. [CrossRef]
46. Escobar, J. Time-varying parameter estimation under stochastic perturbations using LSM. *IMA J. Math. Control Inf.* **2012**, *29*, 35–258. [CrossRef]
47. Escobar, J.; Poznyak, A. Benefits of variable structure techniques for parameter estimation in stochastic systems using least squares method and instrumental variables. *Int. J. Adapt. Control Signal Process.* **2015**, *29*, 1038–1054. [CrossRef]
48. Taylor, J. The Cramer-Rao estimation error lower bound computation for deterministic nonlinear systems. *IEEE Trans. Autom. Control* **1979**, *24*, 343–344. [CrossRef]
49. Hodges, J.; Lehmann, E. Some applications of the Cramer-Rao inequality. In Proceedings of the Second Berkeley Symposium on Mathematical Statistics and Probability, Berkeley, CA, USA, 31 July–12 August 1950; University of California Press: Berkeley, CA, USA, 1951; pp. 13–22.
50. Cramér, H. A contribution to the theory of statistical estimation. *Scand. Actuar. J.* **1946**, *1946*, 85–94. [CrossRef]
51. Rao, C.R. Information and the accuracy attainable in the estimation of statistical parameters. *Reson. J. Sci. Educ.* **1945**, *20*, 78–90.
52. Vincze, I. On the Cramér-Fréchet-Rao inequality in the nonregular case. In *Contributions to Statistics, the J. Hajek Memorial*; Reidel: Dordrecht, The Netherlands; Boston, MA, USA, 1979; pp. 253–262.
53. Khatri, C. Unified treatment of Cramér-Rao bound for the nonregular density functions. *J. Stat. Plan. Inference* **1980**, *4*, 75–79. [CrossRef]
54. Rissanen, J. Fisher information and stochastic complexity. *IEEE Trans. Inf. Theory* **1996**, *42*, 40–47. [CrossRef]
55. Jauffret, C. Observability and Fisher information matrix in nonlinear regression. *IEEE Trans. Aerosp. Electron. Syst.* **2007**, *43*, 756–759. [CrossRef]
56. Klein, A. Matrix algebraic properties of the Fisher information matrix of stationary processes. *Entropy* **2014**, *16*, 2023–2055. [CrossRef]
57. Bentarzi, M.; Aknouche, A. Calculation of the Fisher information matrix for periodic ARMA models. *Commun. Stat. Methods* **2005**, *34*, 891–903. [CrossRef]
58. Klein, A.; Mélard, G. An algorithm for the exact Fisher information matrix of vector ARMAX time series. *Linear Algebra Its Appl.* **2014**, *446*, 1–24. [CrossRef]
59. Bell, K.L.; Van Trees, H.L. Posterior Cramer-Rao bound for tracking target bearing. In Proceedings of the 13th Annual Workshop on Adaptive Sensor Array Process, Puerta Vallarta, Mexico, 13–15 December 2005; Citeseer: Princeton, NJ, USA, 2005.
60. Tichavsky, P.; Muravchik, C.H.; Nehorai, A. Posterior Cramér-Rao bounds for discrete-time nonlinear filtering. *IEEE Trans. Signal Process.* **1998**, *46*, 1386–1396. [CrossRef]
61. Landi, G.; Landi, G.E. The Cramer—Rao Inequality to Improve the Resolution of the Least-Squares Method in Track Fitting. *Instruments* **2020**, *4*, 2. [CrossRef]
62. Efron, A.; Jeen, H. Detection in impulsive noise based on robust whitening. *IEEE Trans. Signal Process.* **1994**, *42*, 1572–1576. [CrossRef]

63. Liao, Y.; Wang, D.; Ding, F. Data filtering based recursive least squares parameter estimation for ARMAX models. In Proceedings of the 2009 WRI International Conference on Communications and Mobile Computing, Washington, DC, USA, 6–8 January 2009; IEEE: Piscataway, NJ, USA, 2009; Volume 1, pp. 331–335.
64. Collins, L. Realizable whitening filters and state-variable realizations. *Proc. IEEE* **1968**, *56*, 100–101. [CrossRef]
65. Wang, W.; Ding, F.; Dai, J. Maximum likelihood least squares identification for systems with autoregressive moving average noise. *Appl. Math. Model.* **2012**, *36*, 1842–1853. [CrossRef]
66. Zadrozny, P. Gaussian likelihood of continuous-time ARMAX models when data are stocks and flows at different frequencies. *Econom. Theory* **1988**, *4*, 108–124. [CrossRef]
67. Li, L.; Pu, Y.; Chen, J. Maximum Likelihood Parameter Estimation for ARMAX Models Based on Stochastic Gradient Algorithm. In Proceedings of the 2018 10th International Conference on Modelling, Identification and Control (ICMIC), Guiyang, China, 2–4 July 2018; IEEE: Piscataway, NJ, USA, 2018; pp. 1–6.
68. González, R.A.; Rojas, C.R. A Finite-Sample Deviation Bound for Stable Autoregressive Processes. In Proceedings of the 2nd Conference on Learning for Dynamics and Control, Berkeley, CA, USA, 10–11 June 2020; Bayen, A.M., Jadbabaie, A., Pappas, G., Parrilo, P.A., Recht, B., Tomlin, C., Zeilinger, M., Eds.; PMLR: Birmingham, UK, 2020; Volume 120, pp. 191–200.
69. Anderson, B.D.; Moore, J.B. State estimation via the whitening filter. In Proceedings of the Joint Automatic Control Conference, Ann Arbor, MI, USA, 26–28 June 1968; pp. 123–129.
70. Seong, S.M. A modified direct whitening method for ARMA model parameter estimation. In Proceedings of the 2007 International Conference on Control, Automation and Systems, Seoul, Korea, 17–20 October 2007; IEEE: Piscataway, NJ, USA, 2007; pp. 2639–2642.
71. Yamda, I.; Hayashi, N. Improvement of the performance of cross correlation method for identifying aircraft noise with pre-whitening of signals. *J. Acoust. Soc. Jpn. (E)* **1992**, *13*, 241–252. [CrossRef]
72. Kuo, C.H. An Iterative Procedure for Minimizing and Whitening the Residual of the ARMAX Model. *Mech. Tech. J.* **2010**, *3*, 1–6.
73. Ho, W.K.; Ling, K.V.; Vu, H.D.; Wang, X. Filtering of the ARMAX process with generalized t-distribution noise: The influence function approach. *Ind. Eng. Chem. Res.* **2014**, *53*, 7019–7028. [CrossRef]
74. Graupe, D.; Efron, A.J. An output-whitening approach to adaptive active noise cancellation. *IEEE Trans. Circuits Syst.* **1991**, *38*, 1306–1313. [CrossRef]
75. Roonizi, A.K. A new approach to ARMAX signals smoothing: Application to variable-Q ARMA filter design. *IEEE Trans. Signal Process.* **2019**, *67*, 4535–4544. [CrossRef]
76. Zheng, H.; Mita, A. Two-stage damage diagnosis based on the distance between ARMA models and pre-whitening filters. *Smart Mater. Struct.* **2007**, *16*, 1829. [CrossRef]
77. Kuo, C.H.; Yang, D.M. Residual Whitening Method for Identification of Induction Motor System. In *Proceedings of the 3rd International Conference on Intelligent Technologies and Engineering Systems (ICITES 2014)*; Springer: Berlin/Heidelberg, Germany, 2016, pp. 51–58.
78. Song, Q.; Liu, F. The direct approach to unified GPC based on ARMAX/CARIMA/CARMA model and application for pneumatic actuator control. In Proceedings of the First International Conference on Innovative Computing, Information and Control-Volume I (ICICIC'06), Beijing, China, 30 August–1 September 2006; IEEE: Piscataway, NJ, USA, 2006; Volume 1; pp. 336–339.
79. Dosiek, L.; Pierre, J.W. Estimating electromechanical modes and mode shapes using the multichannel ARMAX model. *IEEE Trans. Power Syst.* **2013**, *28*, 1950–1959. [CrossRef]
80. Chen, W.; Han, G.; Qiu, W.; Zheng, D. Modeling of outlet temperature of the first-stage cyclone preheater in cement firing system using data-driven ARMAX models. In Proceedings of the 2019 IEEE 3rd Advanced Information Management, Communicates, Electronic and Automation Control Conference (IMCEC), Chongqing, China, 11–13 October 2019; IEEE: Piscataway, NJ, USA, 2019; pp. 472–477.
81. Akal, M. Forecasting Turkey's tourism revenues by ARMAX model. *Tour. Manag.* **2004**, *25*, 565–580. [CrossRef]
82. Pan, B.; Wu, D.C.; Song, H. Forecasting hotel room demand using search engine data. *J. Hosp. Tour. Technol.* **2012**, *3*, 196–210. [CrossRef]
83. Intihar, M.; Kramberger, T.; Dragan, D. Container throughput forecasting using dynamic factor analysis and ARIMAX model. *Promet-Traffic Transp.* **2017**, *29*, 529–542. [CrossRef]
84. Hickey, E.; Loomis, D.G.; Mohammadi, H. Forecasting hourly electricity prices using ARMAX–GARCH models: An application to MISO hubs. *Energy Econ.* **2012**, *34*, 307–315. [CrossRef]
85. Ekhosuehi, V.U.; Omoregie, D.E. Inspecting debt servicing mechanism in Nigeria using ARMAX model of the Koyck-kind. *Oper. Res. Decis.* **2021**, *1*, 5–20.
86. Adel, B.; Cichocki, A. Robust whitening procedure in blind source separation context. *Electron. Lett.* **2000**, *36*, 2050–2051.
87. Cuoco, E.; Calamai, G.; Fabbroni, L.; Losurdo, G.; Mazzoni, M.; Stanga, R.; Vetrano, F. On-line power spectra identification and whitening for the noise in interferometric gravitational wave detectors. *Class. Quantum Gravity* **2001**, *18*, 1727–1751. [CrossRef]
88. Cuoco, E.; Losurdo, G.; Calamai, G.; Fabbroni, L.; Mazzoni, M.; Stanga, R.; Guidi, G.; Vetrano, F. Noise parametric identification and whitening for LIGO 40-m interferometer data. *Phys. Rev.* **2001**, *64*, 122022. [CrossRef]
89. Söderström, T.; Mahata, K. On instrumental variable and total least squares approaches for identification of noisy systems. *Int. J. Control* **2002**, *75*, 381–389. [CrossRef]
90. Bowden, R.J.; Turkington, D.A. *Instrumental Variables*; Cambridge University Press: Cambridge, UK, 1990.

91. Martens, E.P.; Pestman, W.R.; de Boer, A.; Belitser, S.V.; Klungel, O.H. Instrumental variables: Application and limitations. *Epidemiology* **2006**, *17*, 260–267. [CrossRef] [PubMed]
92. Jakeman, A.; Young, P. Refined instrumental variable methods of recursive time-series analysis Part II. Multivariable systems. *Int. J. Control* **1979**, *29*, 621–644. [CrossRef]
93. Young, P.; Jakeman, A. Refined instrumental variable methods of recursive time-series analysis Part III. Extensions. *Int. J. Control* **1980**, *31*, 741–764. [CrossRef]
94. Young, P.C. Refined instrumental variable estimation: Maximum likelihood optimization of a unified Box–Jenkins model. *Automatica* **2015**, *52*, 35–46. [CrossRef]
95. Wilson, E.D.; Clairon, Q.; Taylor, C.J. Non-minimal state-space polynomial form of the Kalman filter for a general noise model. *Electron. Lett.* **2018**, *54*, 204–206. [CrossRef]
96. Ma, L.; Liu, X. A nonlinear recursive instrumental variables identification method of Hammerstein ARMAX system. *Nonlinear Dyn.* **2015**, *79*, 1601–1613. [CrossRef]
97. Escobar, J.; Enqvist, M. Instrumental variables and LSM in continuous-time parameter estimation. *Esaim. Control Optim. Calc. Var.* **2017**, *23*, 427–442. [CrossRef]
98. Kazmin, S.; Poznyak, A. Recurrent estimates of ARX models with noises described by arma processes. *Autom. Remote Control* **1992**, *53*, 1549–1556.
99. Escobar, J.; Poznyak, A. Parametric identification of ARMAX models with unknown forming filters. *IMA J. Math. Control Inf.* **2021**, *39*, 171–184. [CrossRef]
100. Poznyak, A.S.; Tikhonov, S. Strong consistency of the extended least squares method with nonlinear error transformation. *Autom. Remote. Control* **1990**, *8*, 119–128.

mathematics

MDPI

*Article*

# On Consistency of the Bayes Estimator of the Density

**Agustín G. Nogales**

Departamento de Matemáticas, IMUEx, Universidad de Extremadura, 06006 Badajoz, Spain; nogales@unex.es

**Abstract:** Under mild conditions, strong consistency of the Bayes estimator of the density is proved. Moreover, the Bayes risk (for some common loss functions) of the Bayes estimator of the density (i.e., the posterior predictive density) goes to zero as the sample size goes to $\infty$. In passing, a similar result is obtained for the estimation of the sampling distribution.

**Keywords:** Bayesian density estimation; Bayesian estimation of the sampling distribution; posterior predictive distribution; consistency of the Bayes estimator

**MSC:** Primary: 62G07; 62G20; Secondary: 62F15

**Citation:** Nogales, A.G. On Consistency of the Bayes Estimator of the Density. *Mathematics* **2022**, *10*, 636. https://doi.org/10.3390/math10040636

Academic Editors: Francisco German Badía and María D. Berrade

Received: 2 February 2022
Accepted: 17 February 2022
Published: 18 February 2022



## 1. Introduction

In a statistical context, since the expression *the probability of an event* $A$ (usually denoted $P_\theta(A)$) depends on the unknown parameter, it is really a misuse of language. Before performing the experiment, this expression can be assigned a natural meaning from a Bayesian perspective as the prior predictive probability of $A$ since it is the prior mean of the probabilities $P_\theta(A)$. However, in accordance with Bayesian philosophy, once the experiment has been carried out and the value $\omega$ has been observed, a more appropriate estimate of $P_\theta(A)$ is the posterior predictive probability given $\omega$ of $A$. The author has recently proved ([1]) that not only is this the Bayes estimator of $P_\theta(A)$ but that the posterior predictive distribution (resp. the posterior predictive density) is the Bayes estimator of the sampling distribution $P_\theta$ (resp. the density $p_\theta$) for the squared variation total (resp. the squared $L^1$) loss function in the Bayesian experiment corresponding to an $n$-sized sample of the unknown distribution. It should be noted that the loss functions considered derive in a natural way from the commonly used squared error loss function when estimating a real function of the parameter.

The posterior predictive distribution is the cornerstone of Predictive Inference, which seeks to make inferences about a new unknown observation from a preceding random sample (see [2,3]). With that idea in mind, it has also been used in other areas such as model selection, testing for discordancy, goodness of fit, perturbation analysis, and classification (see additional fields of application in [1–5]). Furthermore, in [1], it has been presented as a solution for the Bayesian density estimation problem, giving several examples to illustrate the results and, in particular, to calculate a posterior predictive density. [3] provide many other examples of determining the posterior predictive distribution. But in practice, explicit evaluation of the posterior predictive distribution may be cumbersome, and its simulation may become preferable. The aforementioned work of [3] also constitutes a good reference for such simulation methods, and hence for the computation of the Bayes estimators of the density and the sampling distribution.

We would refer to the references cited in [1] for other statistical uses of the posterior predictive distribution and some useful ways to calculate it.

In this communication, we shall explore the asymptotic behaviour of the posterior predictive density as the Bayes estimator of the density, showing its strong consistency and that the Bayes risk goes to 0 as $n$ goes to $\infty$.

## 2. The Framework

Let

$$(\Omega, \mathcal{A}, \{P_\theta : \theta \in (\Theta, \mathcal{T}, Q)\})$$

be a Bayesian experiment (where $Q$ denotes de prior distribution on the parameter space $(\Theta, \mathcal{T})$), and consider the infinite product Bayesian experiment

$$(\Omega^{\mathbb{N}}, \mathcal{A}^{\mathbb{N}}, \{P_\theta^{\mathbb{N}} : \theta \in (\Theta, \mathcal{T}, Q)\})$$

corresponding to an infinite sample of the unknown distribution $P_\theta$. Let us write

$$I(\omega,\theta) := \omega, \quad J(\omega,\theta) := \theta, \quad I_n(\omega,\theta) := \omega_n \quad \text{and} \quad I_{(n)}(\omega) := \omega_{(n)} := (\omega_1, \ldots, \omega_n)$$

for integer $n$.

We suppose that $P^{\mathbb{N}}(\theta, A) := P_\theta^{\mathbb{N}}(A)$ is a Markov kernel. Let

$$\Pi_{\mathbb{N}} := P^{\mathbb{N}} \otimes Q$$

be the joint distribution of the parameter and the observations, i.e.,

$$\Pi_{\mathbb{N}}(A \times T) = \int_T P_\theta^{\mathbb{N}}(A)dQ(\theta), \quad A \in \mathcal{A}^{\mathbb{N}},\ T \in \mathcal{T}.$$

As $Q := \Pi_{\mathbb{N}}^J$ (i.e., the probability distribution of $J$ with respect to $\Pi_{\mathbb{N}}$), $P_\theta^{\mathbb{N}}$ is a version of the conditional distribution (regular conditional probability) $\Pi_{\mathbb{N}}^{I|J=\theta}$. Analogously, $P_\theta^n$ is a version of the conditional distribution $\Pi_{\mathbb{N}}^{I_{(n)}|J=\theta}$.

Let $\beta_{Q,\mathbb{N}}^* := \Pi_{\mathbb{N}}^I$, the prior predictive distribution in $\Omega^{\mathbb{N}}$ (so that $\beta_{Q,\mathbb{N}}^*(A)$ is the prior mean of the probabilities $P_\theta^{\mathbb{N}}(A)$). Similarly, write $\beta_{Q,n}^* := \Pi_{\mathbb{N}}^{I_{(n)}}$ for the prior predictive distribution in $\Omega^n$. So, the posterior distribution $P_{\omega,\mathbb{N}}^* := \Pi_{\mathbb{N}}^{J|I=\omega}$ given $\omega \in \Omega^{\mathbb{N}}$ satisfies

$$\Pi_{\mathbb{N}}(A \times T) = \int_T P_\theta^{\mathbb{N}}(A)dQ(\theta) = \int_A P_{\omega,\mathbb{N}}^*(T)d\beta_{Q,\mathbb{N}}^*(\omega), \quad A \in \mathcal{A}^{\mathbb{N}},\ T \in \mathcal{T}.$$

Denote by $P_{\omega_{(n)},n}^* := \Pi_{\mathbb{N}}^{J|I_{(n)}=\omega_{(n)}}$ for $\omega_{(n)} \in \Omega^n$ the posterior distribution given $\omega_{(n)} \in \Omega^n$.

Write $P_{\omega_{(n)},n}^{*\ P}$ for the posterior predictive distribution given $\omega_{(n)} \in \Omega^n$ defined for $A \in \mathcal{A}$ as

$$P_{\omega_{(n)},n}^{*\ P}(A) = \int_\Theta P_\theta(A)dP_{\omega_{(n)},n}^*(\theta).$$

So $P_{\omega_{(n)},n}^{*\ P}(A)$ is nothing but the posterior mean given $\omega_{(n)} \in \Omega^n$ of the probabilities $P_\theta(A)$.

In the dominated case, we can assume without loss of generality that the dominating measure $\mu$ is a probability measure (because of (1) below). We write $p_\theta = dP_\theta/d\mu$. The likelihood function $\mathcal{L}(\omega,\theta) := p_\theta(\omega)$ is assumed to be $\mathcal{A} \times \mathcal{T}$-measurable.

We have that, for all $n$ and every event $A \in \mathcal{A}$,

$$\begin{aligned} P_{\omega_{(n)},n}^{*\ P}(A) &= \int_\Theta P_\theta(A)dP_{\omega_{(n)},n}^*(\theta) = \int_\Theta \int_A p_\theta(\omega')d\mu(\omega')dP_{\omega_{(n)},n}^*(\theta) \\ &= \int_A \int_\Theta p_\theta(\omega')dP_{\omega_{(n)},n}^*(\theta)d\mu(\omega'), \end{aligned}$$

which proves that

$$p_{\omega_{(n)},n}^{*\ P}(\omega') := \int_\Theta p_\theta(\omega')dP_{\omega_{(n)},n}^*(\theta)$$

is a $\mu$-density of $P^{*\,P}_{\omega_{(n)},n}$ that we recognize as the posterior predictive density on $\Omega$ given $\omega_{(n)}$.

In the same way,

$$p^{*\,P}_{\omega,\mathbb{N}}(\omega') := \int_{\Theta} p_{\theta}(\omega')dP^{*}_{\omega,\mathbb{N}}(\theta)$$

is a $\mu$-density of $P^{*\,P}_{\omega,\mathbb{N}}$, the posterior predictive density on $\Omega$ given $\omega \in \Omega^{\mathbb{N}}$.

In the following, we will assume the following additional regularity conditions:

(i) $(\Omega, \mathcal{A})$ is a standard Borel space;
(ii) $\Theta$ is a Borel subset of a Polish space and $\mathcal{T}$ is its Borel $\sigma$-field;
(iii) $\{P_{\theta} \colon \theta \in \Theta\}$ is identifiable.

According to [1], the posterior predictive distribution $P^{*\,P}_{\omega_{(n)},n}$ (resp. the posterior predictive density $p^{*\,P}_{\omega_{(n)},n}$) is the Bayes estimator of the sampling distribution $P_{\theta}$ (resp. the density $p_{\theta}$) for the squared variation total (resp. the squared $L^1$) loss function in the product experiment $(\Omega^n, \mathcal{A}^n, \{P^n_{\theta} \colon \theta \in (\Theta, \mathcal{T}, Q)\})$. Analogously, the posterior predictive distribution $P^{*\,P}_{\omega,\mathbb{N}}$ (resp. the posterior predictive density $p^{*\,P}_{\omega,\mathbb{N}}$) is the Bayes estimator of the sampling distribution $P_{\theta}$ (resp. the density $p_{\theta}$) for the squared variation total (resp. the squared $L^1$) loss function in the product experiment $(\Omega^{\mathbb{N}}, \mathcal{A}^{\mathbb{N}}, \{P^{\mathbb{N}}_{\theta} \colon \theta \in (\Theta, \mathcal{T}, Q)\})$.

As a particular case of a well known result about the total variation distance between two probability measures and the $L^1$-distance between their densities, we have that

$$\sup_{A \in \mathcal{A}} \left| P^{*\,P}_{\omega_{(n)},n}(A) - P_{\theta}(A) \right| = \frac{1}{2} \int_{\Omega} \left| p^{*\,P}_{\omega_{(n)},n} - p_{\theta} \right| d\mu. \tag{1}$$

## 3. The Main Result

We ask whether the Bayes risk of the Bayes estimator $P^{*\,P}_{\omega_{(n)},n}$ of the sampling distribution $P_{\theta}$ goes to zero when $n \to \infty$, i.e., whether

$$\lim_{n} \int_{\Omega^{\mathbb{N}} \times \Theta} \sup_{A \in \mathcal{A}} \left| P^{*\,P}_{\omega_{(n)},n}(A) - P_{\theta}(A) \right|^2 d\Pi_{\mathbb{N}}(\omega, \theta) = 0.$$

In terms of densities, the question is whether the Bayes risk of the Bayes estimator $p^{*\,P}_{\omega_{(n)},n}$ of the density $p_{\theta}$ goes to zero when $n \to \infty$, i.e., whether

$$\lim_{n} \int_{\Omega^{\mathbb{N}} \times \Theta} \left( \int_{\Omega} \left| p^{*\,P}_{\omega_{(n)},n}(\omega') - p_{\theta}(\omega') \right| d\mu(\omega') \right)^2 d\Pi_{\mathbb{N}}(\omega, \theta) = 0.$$

Let us consider the auxiliary Bayesian experiment

$$(\Omega \times \Omega^{\mathbb{N}}, \mathcal{A} \times \mathcal{A}^{\mathbb{N}}, \{\mu \times P^{\mathbb{N}}_{\theta} \colon \theta \in (\Theta, \mathcal{T}, Q)\}).$$

For $\omega' \in \Omega$, $\omega \in \Omega^n$ and $\theta \in \Theta$, we will continue to write $I(\omega', \omega, \theta) = \omega$ and $J(\omega', \omega, \theta) = \theta$, and now we write $I'(\omega', \omega, \theta) = \omega'$.

The new prior predictive distribution is $\mu \times \beta^{*}_{Q,n}$ since

$$(\mu \times \Pi_{\mathbb{N}})^{(I', I_{(n)})}(A' \times A_{(n)}) = \mu(A') \cdot \beta^{*}_{Q,n}(A_{(n)}) = (\mu \times \beta^{*}_{Q,n})(A' \times A_{(n)}).$$

To compute the new posterior distributions, notice that

$$(\mu \times \Pi_{\mathbb{N}})(A' \times I^{-1}_{(n)}(A_{(n)}) \times T) =$$
$$\int_{A' \times I^{-1}_{(n)}(A_{(n)})} (\mu \times \Pi_{\mathbb{N}})^{J|(I', I_{(n)}) = (\omega', \omega_{(n)})}(T) d(\mu \times \Pi_{\mathbb{N}})^{(I', I_{(n)})}(\omega', \omega_{(n)}).$$

On the other hand,

$$(\mu \times \Pi_{\mathbb{N}})(A' \times I_{(n)}^{-1}(A_{(n)}) \times T) = \mu(A') \cdot \Pi_{\mathbb{N}}(I_{(n)}^{-1}(A_{(n)}) \times T) =$$

$$\mu(A') \cdot \int_{A_{(n)}} P^*_{\omega_{(n)},n}(T) d\beta^*_{Q,n}(\omega_{(n)}) = \int_{A' \times A_{(n)}} P^*_{\omega_{(n)},n}(T) d(\mu \times \beta^*_{Q,n})(\omega', \omega_{(n)}).$$

So,

$$P^*_{\omega_{(n)},n} = (\mu \times \Pi_{\mathbb{N}})^{J|(I', I_{(n)}) = (\omega', \omega_{(n)})}.$$

It follows that if $f \in L^1(Q)$ then

$$E_{P^*_{\omega_{(n)},n}}(f) = E_{\mu \times \Pi_{\mathbb{N}}}[f \mid (I', I_{(n)}) = (\omega', \omega_{(n)})].$$

when $\mathcal{A}'_{(n)} := (I', I_{(n)})^{-1}(\mathcal{A} \times \mathcal{A}^n)$, we have that $(\mathcal{A}'_{(n)})_n$ is an increasing sequence of sub-$\sigma$-fields of $\mathcal{A} \times \mathcal{A}^{\mathbb{N}}$ such that $\mathcal{A} \times \mathcal{A}^{\mathbb{N}} = \sigma(\cup_n \mathcal{A}'_{(n)})$. According to the martingale convergence theorem of Lévy, if $Y$ is $(\mathcal{A} \times \mathcal{A}^{\mathbb{N}} \times \mathcal{T})$-measurable and $\mu \times \Pi_{\mathbb{N}}$-integrable then

$$E_{\mu \times \Pi_{\mathbb{N}}}(Y | \mathcal{A}'_{(n)})$$

converges $(\mu \times \Pi_{\mathbb{N}})$-a.e. and in $L^1(\mu \times \Pi_{\mathbb{N}})$ to $Y = E_{\mu \times \Pi_{\mathbb{N}}}(Y | \mathcal{A}' \times \mathcal{A}^{\mathbb{N}})$.

Let us consider the $\mu \times \Pi_{\mathbb{N}}$-integrable function

$$Y(\omega', \omega, \theta) := p_\theta(\omega').$$

We shall see that

$$p^{*\,P}_{\omega,\mathbb{N}}(\omega') = E_{\mu \times \Pi_{\mathbb{N}}}(Y \mid (I', I) = (\omega', \omega)). \tag{2}$$

Indeed, given $A' \in \mathcal{A}$ and $A \in \mathcal{A}^{\mathbb{N}}$, we have that

$$\begin{aligned}
\int_{(I',I)^{-1}(A' \times A)} p_\theta(\omega') d(\mu \times \Pi_{\mathbb{N}})(\omega', \omega, \theta) &= \int_A \int_\Theta \int_{A'} p_\theta(\omega') d\mu(\omega') dP^*_{\omega,\mathbb{N}}(\theta) d\beta^*_{Q,\mathbb{N}}(\omega) \\
&= \int_A \int_\Theta P_\theta(A') dP^*_{\omega,\mathbb{N}}(\theta) d\beta_{Q,\mathbb{N}}(\omega) = \int_A P^{*\,P}_{\omega,\mathbb{N}}(A') d\beta^*_{Q,\mathbb{N}}(\omega) \\
&= \int_{A'} \int_A p^{*\,P}_{\omega,\mathbb{N}}(\omega') d\mu(\omega') d\beta^*_{Q,\mathbb{N}}(\omega) = \int_{A' \times A} p^{*\,P}_{\omega,\mathbb{N}}(\omega') d(\mu \times \Pi_{\mathbb{N}})^{(I',I)}(\omega', \omega),
\end{aligned}$$

which proves (2).

Analogously, it can be shown that

$$p^{*\,P}_{\omega_{(n)},n}(\omega') = E_{\mu \times \Pi_{\mathbb{N}}}(Y \mid (I', I_{(n)}) = (\omega', \omega_{(n)})). \tag{3}$$

Hence, it follows from the aforementioned theorem of Lévy that

$$\lim_n p^{*\,P}_{\omega_{(n)},n}(\omega') = p^{*\,P}_{\omega,\mathbb{N}}(\omega'), \quad (\mu \times \Pi_{\mathbb{N}}) - \text{a.e.} \tag{4}$$

and

$$\lim_n \int_{\Omega \times \Omega^{\mathbb{N}} \times \Theta} \left| p^{*\,P}_{\omega_{(n)},n}(\omega') - p^{*\,P}_{\omega,\mathbb{N}}(\omega') \right| d(\mu \times \Pi_{\mathbb{N}})(\omega', \omega, \theta) = 0,$$

i.e.,

$$\lim_n \int_{\Omega^{\mathbb{N}} \times \Theta} \int_\Omega \left| p^{*\,P}_{\omega_{(n)},n}(\omega') - p^{*\,P}_{\omega,\mathbb{N}}(\omega') \right| d\mu(\omega') d\Pi_{\mathbb{N}}(\omega, \theta) = 0. \tag{5}$$

On the other hand, as a consequence of a known theorem of Doob (see Theorem 6.9 and Proposition 6.10 of [4], pp. 129, 130, we have that, for every $\omega' \in \Omega$,

$$\lim_n \int_\Theta p_{\theta'}(\omega') dP^*_{\omega_{(n)},n}(\theta') = p_\theta(\omega'), \quad P_\theta^{\mathbb{N}} - \text{a.e.}$$

for $Q$-almost every $\theta$. Hence

$$\lim_n p^{*\,P}_{\omega_{(n)},n}(\omega') = p_\theta(\omega'), \quad P_\theta^{\mathbb{N}} - \text{a.e.}$$

for $Q$-almost every $\theta$, i.e., given $\omega' \in \Omega$ there exists $T_{\omega'} \in \mathcal{T}$ such that $Q(T_{\omega'}) = 0$ and, $\forall \theta \notin T_{\omega'}$,

$$\lim_n p^{*\,P}_{\omega_{(n)},n}(\omega') = p_\theta(\omega'), \quad P_\theta^{\mathbb{N}} - \text{a.e.}$$

So, for $\theta \notin T_{\omega'}$, there exists $N_{\theta,\omega'} \in \mathcal{A}^{\mathbb{N}}$ such that $P_\theta^{\mathbb{N}}(N_{\theta,\omega'}) = 0$ and

$$\lim_n p^{*\,P}_{\omega_{(n)},n}(\omega') = p_\theta(\omega'), \quad \forall \omega \notin N_{\theta,\omega'}, \forall \theta \notin T_{\omega'}, \forall \omega' \in \Omega.$$

In particular,

$$\lim_n p^{*\,P}_{\omega_{(n)},n}(\omega') = p_\theta(\omega'), \quad \mu \times P_\theta^{\mathbb{N}} - \text{a.e.} \tag{6}$$

From (4) and (6), it follows that $p_\theta(\omega') = p^{*\,P}_{\omega,\mathbb{N}}(\omega')$, $\mu \times P_\theta^{\mathbb{N}} - \text{a.e.}$
From this and (5), it follows that

$$\lim_n \int_{\Omega^{\mathbb{N}} \times \Theta} \int_\Omega \left| p^{*\,P}_{\omega_{(n)},n}(\omega') - p_\theta(\omega') \right| d\mu(\omega') d\Pi_{\mathbb{N}}(\omega,\theta) = 0,$$

i.e., the risk of the Bayes estimator of the density for the $L^1$ loss function goes to 0 when $n \to \infty$.

It follows from this and (1) that

$$\lim_n \int_{\Omega^{\mathbb{N}} \times \Theta} \sup_{A \in \mathcal{A}} \left| P^{*\,P}_{\omega_{(n)},n}(A) - P_\theta(A) \right| d\Pi_{\mathbb{N}}(\omega,\theta) = 0,$$

i.e., the risk of the Bayes estimator of the sampling distribution $P_\theta$ for the variation total loss function goes to 0 when $n \to \infty$.

We ask whether these results remain true for the squared versions of the loss functions. The answer is affirmative because of the following general result: Let $(X_n)$ be a sequence of r.r.v. on a probability space $(\Omega, \mathcal{A}, P)$ such that $\lim_n \int |X_n| dP = 0$. If there exists $a > 0$ such that $|X_n| \leq a$, for all $n$, then $\lim_n \int |X_n|^2 dP = 0$ because

$$0 \leq \int |X_n|^2 dP \leq a \int |X_n| dP \to_n 0.$$

In our case $a = 2$, $P := \Pi_{\mathbb{N}}$ and

$$X_n := \int_\Omega \left| p^{*\,P}_{\omega_{(n)},n}(\omega') - p^{*\,P}_{\omega,\mathbb{N}}(\omega') \right| d\mu(\omega'), \quad \text{or} \quad X_n := \sup_{A \in \mathcal{A}} \left| P^{*\,P}_{\omega_{(n)},n}(A) - P_\theta(A) \right|.$$

So, we have proved the following result.

**Theorem 1.** *Let $(\Omega, \mathcal{A}, \{P_\theta \colon \theta \in (\Theta, \mathcal{T}, Q)\})$ be a Bayesian experiment dominated by a $\sigma$-finite measure $\mu$. Let us assume that $(\Omega, \mathcal{A})$ is a standard Borel space, and that $\Theta$ is a Borel subset of a Polish space and $\mathcal{T}$ is its Borel $\sigma$-field. Assume also that the likelihood function $\mathcal{L}(\omega,\theta) := p_\theta(\omega) = \frac{dP_\theta}{d\mu}(\omega)$ is $\mathcal{A} \times \mathcal{T}$-measurable and the family $\{P_\theta \colon \theta \in \Theta\}$ is identifiable. Then:*

(a) *The posterior predictive density* $p^{*}_{\omega_{(n)},n}{}^{P}$ *is the Bayes estimator of the density* $p_\theta$ *in the product experiment* $(\Omega^n, \mathcal{A}^n, \{P^n_\theta : \theta \in (\Theta, \mathcal{T}, Q)\})$ *for the squared* $L^1$ *loss function. Moreover the risk function converges to 0 for both the* $L^1$ *loss function and the squared* $L^1$ *loss function.*
(b) *The posterior predictive distribution* $P^{*}_{\omega_{(n)},n}{}^{P}$ *is the Bayes estimator of the sampling distribution* $P_\theta$ *in the product experiment* $(\Omega^n, \mathcal{A}^n, \{P^n_\theta : \theta \in (\Theta, \mathcal{T}, Q)\})$ *for the squared variation total loss function. Moreover the risk function converges to 0 for both the variation total loss function and the squared variation total loss function.*
(c) *The posterior predictive density is a strongly consistent estimator of the density* $p_\theta$*, i.e.,*

$$\lim_n p^{*}_{\omega_{(n)},n}{}^{P}(\omega') = p_\theta(\omega'), \quad \mu \times P^{\mathbb{N}}_\theta - a.e.$$

*for Q-almost every* $\theta \in \Theta$.

**Funding:** This research was funded by the Junta de Extremaura (SPAIN) grant number GR21044.

**Institutional Review Board Statement:** Not applicable.

**Informed Consent Statement:** Not applicable.

**Data Availability Statement:** Not applicable.

**Conflicts of Interest:** The author declares no conflict of interest.

## References

1. Nogales, A.G. On Bayesian estimation of densities and sampling distributions: The posterior predictive distribution as the Bayes estimator. *Stat. Neerl.* **2021**, accepted. [CrossRef]
2. Geisser, S. *Predictive Inference: An Introduction*; Chapman & Hall: New York, NY, USA, 1993.
3. Gelman, A.; Carlin, J.B.; Stern, H.S.; Dunson, D.B.; Vehtari, A.; Rubin, D.B. *Bayesian Data Analysis*, 3rd ed.; CRC Press (Taylor & Francis Group): Boca Raton, FL, USA, 2014.
4. Ghosal, S.; Vaart, A.V.D. *Fundamentals of Nonparametric Bayesian Inference*; Cambridge University Press: Cambridge, UK, 2017.
5. Rubin, D.B. Bayesianly justifiable and relevant frequency calculations for the applied statistician. *Ann. Stat.* **1984**, *12*, 1151–1172. [CrossRef]

Σ mathematics

MDPI

*Article*

# Spectral Analysis for Comparing Bitcoin to Currencies and Assets

**Maria Chiara Pocelli [1,†] and Manuel L. Esquível [2,*,†] and Nadezhda P. Krasii [3,†]**

1 Department of Mathematics, School of Industrial and Information Engineering, Politecnico di Milano, Piazza Leonardo da Vinci, 32, 20133 Milano, Italy
2 Department of Mathematics, Centre for Mathematics and Applications, NOVA School of Science and Technology, Quinta da Torre, 2829-516 Caparica, Portugal
3 Department of Higher Mathematics, Faculty of Informatics and Computer Engineering, Don State Technical University, 344003 Rostov-on-Don, Russia
* Correspondence: mle@fct.unl.pt; Tel.: +351-965544623
† These authors contributed equally to this work.

**Abstract:** We present an analysis on variability Bitcoin characteristics that help to quantitatively differentiate Bitcoin from the state-owned traditional currencies and the asset Gold. We provide a detailed study on returns of exchange rates—against the Swiss Franc—of several traditional currencies together with Bitcoin and Gold; for that purpose, we define a distance between currencies by means of the spectral densities of the ARMA models of the returns of the exchange rates, and we present the computed matrix of the distances between the chosen currencies. A statistical analysis of these matrix distances is further proposed, which shows that the distance between Bitcoin and any other currency or Gold is not comparable to any of the distances between currencies or between currencies and Gold and not involving Bitcoin. This result shows that Bitcoin is essentially different from the traditional currencies and from Gold, at least in what concerns the structure of its variance and auto-covariances.

**Keywords:** ARMA modelling; distance between power spectral densities; simulation-based testing; state-backed currencies; gold; exchange rate; bitcoin

**MSC:** 37M10

**Citation:** Pocelli, M.C.; Esquível, M.L.; Krasii, N.P. Spectral Analysis for Comparing Bitcoin to Currencies and Assets. *Mathematics* **2023**, *11*, 1775. https://doi.org/10.3390/math11081775

Academic Editors: Francisco German Badía and María D. Berrade

Received: 15 February 2023
Revised: 27 March 2023
Accepted: 30 March 2023
Published: 7 April 2023



## 1. Introduction

Money, in general, is *a transmitter of value through time and space* (see [1] I.1.19). Money is also a reference for the expression of the exchange value of every commodity (see [1] I.2.22). There are some characteristics of classical forms of money that we must now recall. The usual forms of money are under the control of central banks. These usual forms of money, currencies, have a close relationship with the economies to which the central banks are in charge; Swiss, United States of America, Russian Federation and European Monetary Union, are, respectively, examples of a country, a federation of states, a federation of republics and an economic zone composed of several countries. Thus, the exchange rates of one of these currencies versus the others, tend to vary, in a kind of first-order perturbation, according to the variation of regional economic variables.

The exchange rates also vary as a kind of second-order perturbation attributed to noticeable events—for instance, military instabilities. For these currencies, the monetary mass circulating must be both an equivalent of goods that circulate in the regional economy (to which the currency is connected) and a representation of the value of all the credits that achieve maturity at a given date. In all these credits, one should count even those credits that balance out each other (see [2] p. 135).

Considering a constant intrinsic value of the precious metals—such as silver or gold—and all other goods, we have that, for a usual form of money, the intrinsic value of bank notes decreases if the nominal value increases; this happens in light of the fact that the nominal value of bank notes does not represent the intrinsic value of some precious reference metal, and this may occur, for instance, by means of an increase in the quantity of these bank notes (see [2] pp. 142–143).

The hard connection between a usual form of money and the real economy has been recognized in many important classic economic works. For instance, in the third section of the third chapter of the first part of *Capital*, Karl Marx writes that: *Just as the currency of money, generally considered, is but a reflex of the circulation of commodities, or of the antithetical metamorphoses they undergo, so, too, the velocity of that currency reflects the rapidity with which commodities change their forms. . .*

In addition, concerning the relation between the quantity of money and the speed of the circulation of goods, the author we are quoting says *The total quantity of money functioning during a given period as the circulating medium, is determined, on the one hand, by the sum of the prices of the circulating commodities and, on the other hand, by the rapidity with which the antithetical phases of the metamorphoses follow one another* (see [3]). In more recent times, in the monetarist current of economy, Milton Friedman wrote that *. . .the real quantity of money—the quantity of goods and services that the nominal quantity of money can purchase, or the number of weeks' income to which the nominal quantity of money is equal* (see [4] p. 1).

Bitcoin is a digital currency with many specific characteristics that distinguish it from usual currencies. In order to have a reasonable model for the exchange rate evolution of Bitcoin, some particular attributes should be considered. One of the most relevant characteristics of Bitcoin evolution is volatility (see Figure 1).

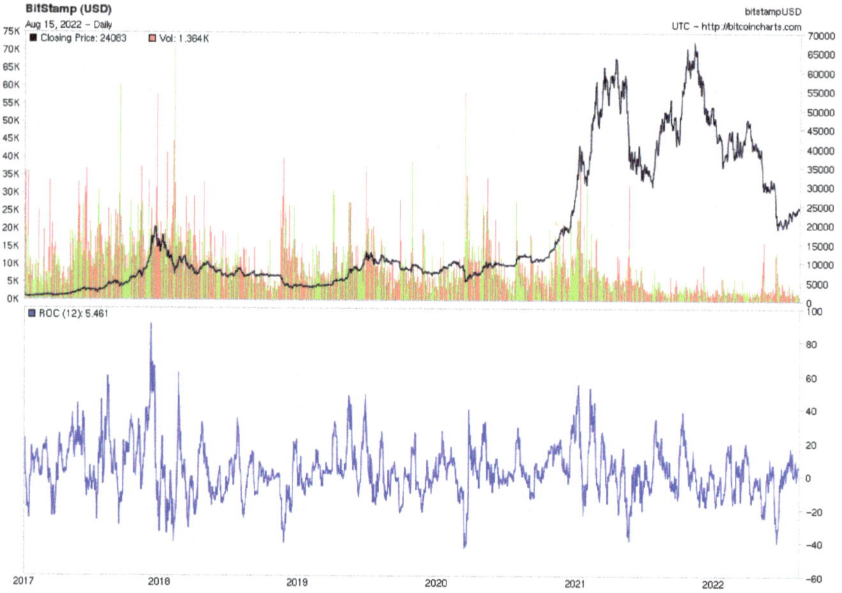


**Figure 1.** Price in US Dollars and the *rate of change evolution* from 2017 to the present.

According to David Yermack, *Bitcoin faces a number of obstacles in becoming a useful unit of account. One problem arises from its extreme volatility,. . .* (see [5] p. 38). A first glimpse into the behaviour of the exchange rate and its variability—in this case, against the US Dollar—is captured in Figure 1 (graphic taken from the bitcoin.org site). Several features of this figure deserve a mention: the significant variability in the period from the middle of 2020 to February 2022 and, on the same period, the reduction in volume and in the rate of change (the lower graphic in blue).

These features certainly have an influence on the variance values that we will recover in the present work since one of our purposes is to study the variability of Bitcoin prices by comparing to the variability of state-owned currencies and a reference asset—Gold. According to Satoshi Nakamoto, the author that is credited for the creation of Bitcoin, . . .*We have proposed a system for electronic transactions without relying on trust.* . . . (see Nakamoto [6] p. 8). Given that it is common sense that the first and most important ingredient of any business is the building of mutual trust, the reality of present day existence of Bitcoin is another aspect that should deserve some analysis.

The market behaviour of Bitcoin has been studied under the perspective of its variability by several authors. In the following, we review some of the contributions that seem more relevant under the perspective of our approach both for the specific theme and for a broad context.

The book chapter [7] is an important review work that reports on the *pairwise comparison of cryptocurrency characteristics with those of fiat currency and hard commodities*, and it . . .*synthesises methods and results from empirical research that investigate the nexus.* One of the remarkable conclusions from the quoted work [8] is that . . .*returns to cryptocurrencies are isolated from returns to currency and commodities*, a result that we also find in our work with great significance. Another conclusion taken from a work using data in the period 2010–2017 (see [9]) is that *Gold is found to be the second most important determinant for the full sample*. . .; this also justifies the choice of Gold in our comparative study.

Comparative behaviours of crypto-currencies have also been studied recently. In [10], the authors compared the long term memory properties of seven cryptocurrencies—Bitcoin, Ethereum, Litecoin, Monero, Stellar, Tron and the EOS token—during and before the COVID-19 period, using high-frequency returns data, to find that *the null hypothesis of true long memory is rejected for all series, implying that the persistence in the high-frequency cryptocurrency returns is not real and might be a spurious one, associated with some regime change during the sample period.* Furthermore, the analysis is complemented with the estimation of the long-run correlation matrix of returns to find that, with the exception of Stellar, *the remaining six crypto returns exhibit significant long-run correlations among each other*, thus, justifying our consideration of only Bitcoin in this work.

The work [11] investigated . . .*the contagious nature of tail events among cryptocurrencies and the mechanism by which tail risk permeates the cryptocurrency markets*. . ., and this was achieved *by constructing a network of tail risk spillovers among the most popular cryptocurrencies and identifying the most important shock-driving and shock-sensitive currencies in the network.*

The work [12] analysed *Bitcoin price volatility from the perspectives of Bitcoin's own and external factors*. . . by means of the structural vector autoregression (SVAR) model, the results showing that *Bitcoin's own factors play fundamental roles in Bitcoin price volatility, and the speculation factors have significant impacts on Bitcoin price volatility.*

Comparative studies on the variances of the US Dollar, Bitcoin and Gold were performed in [13] using both an asymmetric GARCH model with explanatory variables and an exponential GARCH model. The author found that, in the perspective of explaining return, there is . . .*volatility clustering and high volatility persistence similar to gold* and concluded that . . .*bitcoin and gold have similarities when it comes to the volatility of the return*. . .. In the conclusions, it is said that both Bitcoin and Gold seem to react symmetrically to good and bad news but, . . .*the frequency may be higher for bitcoin*. . .

A detailed analysis of the importance of price jumps for Bitcoin is given in [14] showing—by GARCH modelling—that . . .*the role of large movements is found to be stronger in the Bitcoin market than in the markets for crude oil and gold.* A remarkable finding relates the evolution of variance to the occurrence of jumps also showing that the influence of jumps is larger in Bitcoin than in crude or Gold.

The work [15] provides an analysis of the main determinants of Bitcoin prices in a period of roughly 6 years ending in February 2019 using Auto Regressive Distributed Lag time-series model. The findings are on price variation, on one hand, that . . .*macroeconomic and financial determinants... do not have a significant effect in short and long terms* and, on the other hand, that ...*price variation is determined by demand variation*.

Modelling the volatility of currencies and of Bitcoin has been the subject of recent works. In [16], the authors introduced, for a heterogeneous autoregressive model, a new model averaging coefficient estimator with the mean squared error of the coefficient to be minimised, and they provided inference by a double bootstrap since the relevant probability laws are unknown. This inference approach is similar to ours where, instead of bootstrap, we use a Monte Carlo simulation.

The source of any asset value variability is certainly multifactorial. In [17], the authors claim to not take a stand *on the controversial question of what the fundamentals are behind Bitcoin*, and they proceed to show that ...*the bitcoin market is largely like the stock market, with more investors who are more centrally placed on average earning higher returns than others...*

We may conclude that there is a place for the study we now present towards a comparative study of the differences in variability between traditional state supported currencies, the crypto-currency Bitcoin and the asset Gold by means of power spectral distances. Let us briefly describe content and the main contributions of this work.

(i) In Section 2, we present the rationale for the choice of the reference currency against which all other currencies, Bitcoin and Gold are priced, and the choice of the state-backed currencies studied.
(ii) Next, in Section 3, we detail the ARMA process modelling of the returns of the exchange rates.
(iii) Section 4 introduces the distance between currencies and assets as the $L^2$ distance between Power Spectral Densities (PSD) (associated with currencies by means of ARMA modelling of the returns of the exchange rates against a fixed currency) and computes this distance between all pairs of currencies, Bitcoin and Gold. Next, we introduce a statistical test—based on the observed probability distribution of the returns of exchange rates—that allows, in the particular case chosen, to more precisely and firmly analyse the differences between currencies, Bitcoin and Gold.
(iv) In Section 5, we develop a result on the probability law of the distances of PSDs that justifies the empirical results presented in Section 4. These results encompass the case of asymptotically Gaussian-distributed PSD estimators. This result shows that, when considering observed spectral distances as random variables, the law of the distance of these spectral distances has, under assumptions that are verified in our study, a generalised Gamma distribution.
(v) Finally, in Appendix B, we study a variation of the assumption on the normality of returns of exchange rates of currencies that shows that this assumption may be acceptable in a preliminary study of differences between our chosen currencies.

The following are the main contributions of the study:

1. The introduction of the $L^2$ distance between Power Spectral Densities to differentiate the variance and auto-covariance behaviours of currencies, Bitcoin and the asset Gold.
2. The confirmation that an initial grouping of currencies, Bitcoin and Gold, by broad macro-economic criteria, reflects in the grouping driven by the $L^2$ distance between Power Spectral Densities (PSD).
3. The proposal of a statistical test to ascertain the difference of distances between the PSD associated with currencies, Bitcoin and Gold and of a mathematical result that justifies the modelling approaches followed.
4. Theorem 1 giving the probability law of the $L^2$ distance of observed spectral densities under assumptions that are general in the sense that these are assumptions verified with the data analysed in this work.

## 2. Foreign Exchange Markets and the Choice of Currencies and Assets to Study

Foreign Exchange is a form of currency exchange, consisting on the trading of one currency for another (see [18]). A price is associated with each currency pair. This price is the so-called *exchange rate* and it represents the value of a currency with respect to another.

In order to work with exchange rates, a reference currency has to be chosen as well as the currency objects of our analysis. In this section, the choice of these currencies is presented and explained.

### 2.1. On the Choice of the Reference Currency

Although there are hundreds of currencies, only a small number of them make up the vast majority of forex transactions. The most traded in the world are called the *Majors*, and they represent the largest share of the foreign exchange market (around 85%). These are:

- United States dollar (Dollar), USD (United States).
- Euro, EUR (Eurozone).
- Pound Sterling, GBP (United Kingdom).
- Australian dollar, AUD (Australia).
- Canadian dollar, CAD (Canada).
- Swiss franc, CHF (Switzerland).
- Japanese yen, JPY (Japan).

It is reasonable to focus only on this group in order to select our reference currency. The most obvious choice would be the USD or EUR, since they are currently the most active currencies. However, the Global Crisis in 2008 and the COVID-19 crisis have led central banks around the world to roll out quantitative easing (QE) measures. These policies have had large and persistent effects on the Dollar/Euro exchange rate. As a result, investors began to flee to the Swiss franc, which is considered a *safe-haven*, since it offers protection from market shocks.

The dramatic surge of the CHF occurred in 2015, when the Swiss National Bank (SNB) removed the peg of 1.20 francs per euro, since it was no longer sustainable. The Swiss franc has emerged as one of the best alternatives to the US dollar and Euro. The strongpoint of the Swiss franc lies in the size of its related nation, Switzerland. Being a small country has enabled its economic system to become one of the world's most advanced.

Moreover, Switzerland has no deficit, and this makes it self-reliant and stabilizes its currency. The Swiss franc is not backed by gold, meaning that the Swiss National Bank (SNB) can print any amount of currency without any need for a reserve. For all the above reasons, the reference currency chosen for our analysis was the Swiss franc.

### 2.2. On the Choice of Other Currencies and the Asset Gold

A further step was the selection of the other currencies to study with respect to the reference one. The USD is the home denomination of the world's largest economy, the United States, and therefore it must be included among the currencies that we want to analyse. Similarly, all the remaining Majors must be considered.

On the other hand, the group of the greatest emerging economies of the world require special consideration. This group is composed of five countries, namely Brazil, Russia, India, China, South Africa, and it is known by the acronym BRICS. The notion behind the coinage of this acronym was that the BRICS cluster would grow to a size larger than the Majors by 2050, shifting the economic balance of power. That is, the largest global economic powers would no longer belong to the richest countries according to the income per capita. Therefore, the Brazilian real (BRL), the Russian Ruble (RUB), the Indian rupee (INR), the Chinese renminbi (CNY) and the South African rand (ZAR) are included in our analysis.

Likewise, the Israeli new shekel (ILS) has been gaining in strength against major currencies, such as the US dollar and the Euro, due, in large part, to high levels of foreign direct investment and to the strength of the tech sector. For this reason, this currency is also taken into consideration. In addition, the Swedish krona (SEK) and the Norwegian krone (NOK) is examined, as their corresponding countries benefit from a strong economy.

Lastly, it is worthwhile to include the Polish zloty (PLN) to investigate possible ties with USD and EUR.

Finally, the asset gold (Gold) (XAU) is analysed, since it has been considered a highly valuable commodity for millennia acting as a reserve of value. As can be seen in Figure 2, the price evolution of Gold has similarities with the price evolution of Bitcoin—particularly for the most recent dates—leading to the natural question: how do Bitcoin and Gold compare using spectral densities?

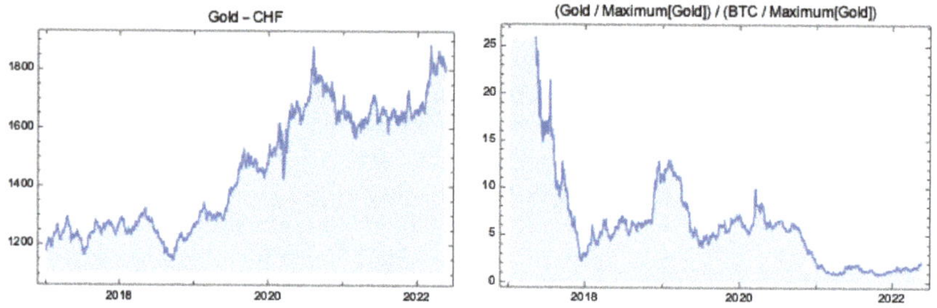


**Figure 2.** Price of Gold from 2017 to the present (left) and ratio of normalised prices of Gold and Bitcoin (right).

Below, a summary of all the currencies considered for this study is shown receded by the indication of the distinctive class of the currency or asset that, by the arguments called in Sections 2.1 and 2.2, justify their inclusion in this study.

- *The Majors*: DOL, EUR, GBP, AUD, CAD and JPY.
- *The BRICS*: BRL, RUB, INR, CNY and ZAR.
- *Independent Currencies*: ILS, NOK, SEK and PLN.
- *Others*: BTC and XAU.

## 3. Time-Series Analysis of the Data

Daily exchange rates against the Swiss franc (CHF) for all the currencies listed above were downloaded from Wolfram Financial Data Services. The study period goes from 1 January 2016 until 20 May 2022 when the effects of the Russian–Ukrainian conflict were not yet large enough to possibly disrupt stationarity. With those data, logarithmic returns were derived as follows:

$$r_t = 100 * \log_{10}\left(\frac{\text{ex\_rate}_t}{\text{ex\_rate}_{t-1}}\right), \quad t = 1, \ldots, \#\text{observations} - 1 \tag{1}$$

Through (1), the time series of logarithmic returns was obtained for each currency. It is advisable to use returns for several reasons: first, to be able to compare different currencies and secondly to analyse dimensionless quantities. In the following Section 3.1, a preliminary analysis of those time series is proposed—keeping in mind the ARMA model application. For further information about the implemented techniques, see [19].

### 3.1. Stationarity Inspection

In order to correctly build the time-series model, it is necessary to first check the stationarity of our data. Here, this is achieved in two ways: statistically, using the augmented Dickey–Fuller test, and visually, looking at the autocorrelation plot of the data.

In the case of DOL/CHF time-series data, for example, the autocorrelation plot (Figure 3) shows that all lags are within the highlighted area in blue. Hence, we may assume stationarity, an assumption confirmed also by the Dickey–Fuller test result (rejection of the null hypothesis that the series is a unit root process). Similarly, stationarity was assessed for all the other currencies.

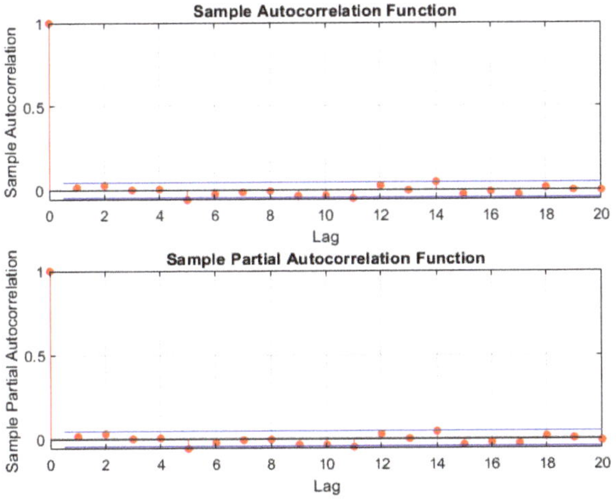


**Figure 3.** Autocorrelation plot of the DOL/CHF time-series data.

### *3.2. ARMA Modelling of the Returns of the Exchange Rates of Currencies against CHF*

Since we assume our time-series data to be stationary, it is possible to model them as ARMA processes. We recall that, given a stationary process X, it is an ARMA(p,q) process if there exist a white noise W, a constant $c$ and parameters $a_1,\dots,a_p$, $b_1,\dots,b_q$ such that ([19] Ch8):

$$\sum_{k=0}^{p} a_k X_{n-k} = c + \sum_{l=0}^{q} b_l W_{n-l}, \quad n \in \mathbb{Z}, \quad a_0, b_0 = 1. \tag{2}$$

Each time series was modelled as ARMA process with varying orders of $p$ and $q$, from 1 to 4, and then the best fit was selected according to the Akaike information criterion (AIC). The results are shown in Table 1. It can be noticed that the variance of almost all the BRICS currencies and of Gold is one order of magnitude greater than the others (10–25% against 1–5%). On top of that, Bitcoin stands out from all the currencies reaching a variance of 279.7%. A more complete analysis of this behaviour is further developed in Section 4 with the use of the spectral density.

**Table 1.** Best-fit ARMA processes for each currency.

| | DOL | EUR | GBP | AUD | CAD | JPY |
|---|---|---|---|---|---|---|
| p | 3 | 3 | 3 | 3 | 4 | 2 |
| q | 3 | 4 | 3 | 3 | 3 | 3 |
| $\sigma^2$ | 0.0277 | 0.0140 | 0.0409 | 0.0450 | 0.0343 | 0.0333 |
| | BRL | RUB | INR | CNY | ZAR | |
| p | 2 | 4 | 2 | 3 | 3 | |
| q | 2 | 4 | 4 | 2 | 4 | |
| $\sigma^2$ | 0.1435 | 0.2514 | 0.0327 | 0.0391 | 0.1339 | |
| | ILS | NOK | SEK | PLN | | |
| p | 3 | 4 | 1 | 4 | | |
| q | 4 | 4 | 1 | 4 | | |
| $\sigma^2$ | 0.0340 | 0.0490 | 0.0290 | 0.0370 | | |
| | BTC | XAU | | | | |
| p | 4 | 4 | | | | |
| q | 4 | 3 | | | | |
| $\sigma^2$ | 2.7970 | 0.1085 | | | | |

The main conclusion that we can draw from this ARMA analysis is that, with the exception of Ruble, Bitcoin and Gold, the assets have variances of the same order of magnitude. Gold and Ruble both have variances one order of magnitude larger than the others assets, and Bitcoin has a variance two orders of magnitude larger than the other assets.

## 4. Comparing Currencies and Assets via the PSDs of Returns of Exchange Rates

In order to further investigate the variance of our time series, an application of spectral properties of ARMA processes is developed in this section (see [20,21] for the basic definitions).

If X is a wide sense stationary process with a summable covariance function, then there exists a function $f_X$ such that the auto-covariance function for the process is given by the formula:

$$R(k) = \mathrm{Cov}(X_n, X_{n+k}) = \int_{[-\pi,\pi]} f_X(\omega) \mathrm{e}^{ik\omega} d\omega, \quad n \in \mathbb{Z} \tag{3}$$

and $f_X$ is called the *power spectral density* (PSD) of the process X (see [20] p. 185). Moreover, if $k = 0$, it is possible to obtain the variance function of the process, which is:

$$R(0) = \mathbb{V}(X_n) = \int_{[-\pi,\pi]} f_X(\omega) d\omega. \tag{4}$$

### 4.1. *Power Spectral Density for the ARMA Process*

In the case of an ARMA process and under the regularity hypothesis (see [20] p. 202), the PSD function is defined as:

$$f_X(\omega) = \frac{\sigma^2}{2\pi} \frac{|Q(\mathrm{e}^{-i\omega})|^2}{|P(\mathrm{e}^{-i\omega})|^2}, \tag{5}$$

where $\mathrm{Q}(z) = \sum_{k=0}^{q} b_k z^k$ and $\mathrm{P}(z) = \sum_{k=0}^{p} a_k z^k$, with $a_k$ and $b_k$ defined in (2). If $z = \mathrm{e}^{-i\omega} = \cos(\omega) - i\sin(\omega)$, the squared moduli of $\mathrm{Q}(z)$ and $\mathrm{P}(z)$ become:

$$\begin{aligned} |\mathrm{Q}(z)|^2 &= \sum_{k=0}^{q} b_k^2 + 2\sum_{l=1}^{q}\sum_{j=0}^{l-1} b_l b_j cos((l-j)\omega) \\ |\mathrm{P}(z)|^2 &= \sum_{k=0}^{p} a_k^2 + 2\sum_{l=1}^{p}\sum_{j=0}^{l-1} a_l a_j cos((l-j)\omega). \end{aligned} \tag{6}$$

Through (5) and (6), it is possible to derive the PSD functions of our currencies, using the parameters obtained from the ARMA modelling. The plots of the computed functions, multiplied by $2\pi$, are shown in Appendix A.

### 4.2. *Distance between Power Spectral Densities*

For the purpose of comparing the obtained PSD functions, the $\mathrm{L}^2([-\pi,\pi])$ distance $d$ is introduced. It is defined as ([20] p. 58):

$$d(f,g) = \left( \int_{[-\pi,\pi]} |f(\omega) - g(\omega)|^2 d\omega \right)^{\frac{1}{2}}, \tag{7}$$

with $f, g \in \mathrm{L}^2([-\pi,\pi])$.

From (7), the distances between our PSD functions are computed, and the results are summarised in the symmetric matrix in Figure 4. The table in Figure 4 shows that the currencies can be divided into three groups:

- A group of currencies for which distances among the elements of the group has order of magnitude equal to −2 (the Majors, the independent ones, INR and CNY).
- Another group of currencies—disjoint from the first group—for which distances among the elements of the group has order of magnitude of −1 (the remaining BRICS and the asset Gold).
- Bitcoin, which has a distance from the other currencies of around 7.

| | DOL | EUR | GBP | AUD | CAD | JPY | BRL | RUB | INR | CNY | ZAR | ILS | NOK | SEK | PLN | BTC | XAU |
|---|---|---|---|---|---|---|---|---|---|---|---|---|---|---|---|---|---|
| **DOL** | 0 | 0.0361 | 0.0378 | 0.0446 | 0.0198 | 0.0179 | 0.2939 | 0.6198 | 0.0194 | 0.0489 | 0.2719 | 0.0226 | 0.0568 | 0.0103 | 0.0293 | 7.1667 | 0.2091 |
| **EUR** | 0.0361 | 0 | 0.0708 | 0.0785 | 0.0522 | 0.0494 | 0.3283 | 0.6522 | 0.0519 | 0.0765 | 0.3066 | 0.0534 | 0.0909 | 0.0388 | 0.0602 | 7.2012 | 0.2429 |
| **GBP** | 0.0378 | 0.0708 | 0 | 0.0173 | 0.0227 | 0.0281 | 0.2607 | 0.5859 | 0.0283 | 0.0469 | 0.2378 | 0.0250 | 0.0255 | 0.0332 | 0.0202 | 7.1318 | 0.1777 |
| **AUD** | 0.0446 | 0.0785 | 0.0173 | 0 | 0.0282 | 0.0319 | 0.2512 | 0.5782 | 0.0349 | 0.0411 | 0.2291 | 0.0300 | 0.0192 | 0.0410 | 0.0244 | 7.1237 | 0.1675 |
| **CAD** | 0.0198 | 0.0522 | 0.0227 | 0.0282 | 0 | 0.0128 | 0.2776 | 0.6044 | 0.0177 | 0.0453 | 0.2553 | 0.0088 | 0.0416 | 0.0146 | 0.0162 | 7.1500 | 0.1930 |
| **JPY** | 0.0179 | 0.0494 | 0.0281 | 0.0319 | 0.0128 | 0 | 0.2799 | 0.6067 | 0.0185 | 0.0392 | 0.2585 | 0.0168 | 0.0451 | 0.0163 | 0.0207 | 7.1534 | 0.1949 |
| **BRL** | 0.2939 | 0.3283 | 0.2607 | 0.2512 | 0.2776 | 0.2799 | 0 | 0.3578 | 0.2809 | 0.2625 | 0.0562 | 0.2778 | 0.2405 | 0.2910 | 0.2708 | 6.8788 | 0.0991 |
| **RUB** | 0.6198 | 0.6522 | 0.5859 | 0.5782 | 0.6044 | 0.6067 | 0.3578 | 0 | 0.6078 | 0.5905 | 0.3783 | 0.6055 | 0.5667 | 0.6165 | 0.5956 | 6.5817 | 0.4380 |
| **INR** | 0.0194 | 0.0519 | 0.0283 | 0.0349 | 0.0177 | 0.0185 | 0.2809 | 0.6078 | 0 | 0.0447 | 0.2583 | 0.0186 | 0.0439 | 0.0195 | 0.0259 | 7.1531 | 0.1969 |
| **CNY** | 0.0489 | 0.0765 | 0.0469 | 0.0411 | 0.0453 | 0.0392 | 0.2625 | 0.5905 | 0.0447 | 0 | 0.2445 | 0.0480 | 0.0487 | 0.0521 | 0.0460 | 7.1374 | 0.1773 |
| **ZAR** | 0.2719 | 0.3066 | 0.2378 | 0.2291 | 0.2553 | 0.2585 | 0.0562 | 0.3783 | 0.2583 | 0.2445 | 0 | 0.2553 | 0.2176 | 0.2686 | 0.2488 | 6.8986 | 0.0905 |
| **ILS** | 0.0226 | 0.0534 | 0.0250 | 0.0300 | 0.0088 | 0.0168 | 0.2778 | 0.6055 | 0.0186 | 0.0480 | 0.2553 | 0 | 0.0431 | 0.0175 | 0.0196 | 7.1499 | 0.1930 |
| **NOK** | 0.0568 | 0.0909 | 0.0255 | 0.0192 | 0.0416 | 0.0451 | 0.2405 | 0.5667 | 0.0439 | 0.0487 | 0.2176 | 0.0431 | 0 | 0.0533 | 0.0379 | 7.1117 | 0.1591 |
| **SEK** | 0.0103 | 0.0388 | 0.0332 | 0.0410 | 0.0146 | 0.0163 | 0.2910 | 0.6165 | 0.0195 | 0.0521 | 0.2686 | 0.0175 | 0.0533 | 0 | 0.0249 | 7.1632 | 0.2066 |
| **PLN** | 0.0293 | 0.0602 | 0.0202 | 0.0244 | 0.0162 | 0.0207 | 0.2708 | 0.5956 | 0.0259 | 0.0460 | 0.2488 | 0.0196 | 0.0379 | 0.0249 | 0 | 7.1425 | 0.1862 |
| **BTC** | 7.1667 | 7.2012 | 7.1318 | 7.1237 | 7.1500 | 7.1534 | 6.8788 | 6.5817 | 7.1531 | 7.1374 | 6.8986 | 7.1499 | 7.1117 | 7.1632 | 7.1425 | 0 | 6.9669 |
| **XAU** | 0.2091 | 0.2429 | 0.1777 | 0.1675 | 0.1930 | 0.1949 | 0.0991 | 0.4380 | 0.1969 | 0.1773 | 0.0905 | 0.1930 | 0.1591 | 0.2066 | 0.1862 | 6.9669 | 0 |

**Figure 4.** Matrix of distances.

This result confirms, in a more precise way, what was previously observed in Section 3.2.

### 4.3. A Statistical Test for Distances between PSDs Associated with Currencies and Assets

To show that the distances between PSD functions are meaningful, we introduce a statistical test procedure illustrated in a particular case. This is a Monte Carlo test procedure as it relies on Monte Carlo simulation of a test statistic in order to obtain its empirical distribution (see [22] or [23]). For the example studied, two currencies the US Dollar and the Euro, are taken. The test is performed in three different ways.

*(a)* If normality of returns—derived from the exchange rates against the reference currency CHF—is assumed a priori (see Appendix B), the sample means $\hat{\mu}_1, \hat{\mu}_2$ and the sample variances $\hat{\sigma}_1^2, \hat{\sigma}_2^2$ of the returns of Dollar and Euro, respectively, are computed. With these values, a simulation of a sample of the returns of the two currencies is implemented, using Monte Carlo method. More precisely, an array of 2000 random numbers is generated from the normal distribution $\mathcal{N}(\hat{\mu}_1, \hat{\sigma}_1^2)$ and from $\mathcal{N}(\hat{\mu}_2, \hat{\sigma}_2^2)$ for Dollar and Euro, respectively. Then, ARMA modelling is executed and spectral density function is calculated for both the simulated returns. Finally, the distance between the computed PSDs is evaluated. This procedure—from the simulation—is repeated 1000 times, obtaining 1000 values of distances. The results are summarised in Figure 5. The red line represents the distance between Dollar and Euro computed using the real returns $d^* = 0.0361$ (row 2, column 1 of the matrix in Figure 4).

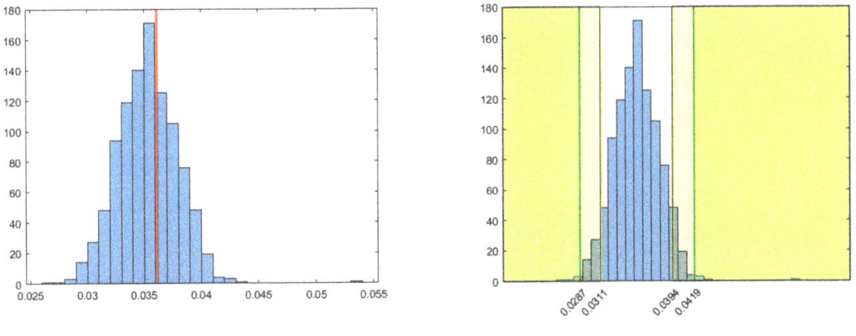


**Figure 5.** Case (a): probability distribution of the distance between Dollar and Euro (**left**) and rejection areas for $\alpha = 0.995$ (green) and $\alpha = 0.95$ (yellow) (**right**).

With those data, it is possible to produce a statistical test with the null hypothesis:

**H**$_0$: *The spectral density of a given currency is either Dollars or Euros.*

Significance levels $\alpha = 0.995, 0.95$ are used. The corresponding empirical quantiles are:

$$q_{0.5\%} = 0.0287 \qquad q_{99.5\%} = 0.0419$$

$$q_{5\%} = 0.0311 \qquad q_{95\%} = 0.0394.$$

The steps for the test are the following:

(i) Consider the distances of a currency $d_{Dol}, d_{Eur}$ from Dollar and Euro, respectively, taken from the matrix in Figure 4.

(ii) If ($d_{Dol} \leq q_{1-\alpha}$ or $d_{Dol} \geq q_\alpha$) and ($d_{Eur} \leq q_{1-\alpha}$ or $d_{Eur} \geq q_\alpha$), then the null hypothesis is rejected (see Figure 5).

*(b)* In order to avoid making assumptions about the distribution of the returns, the empirical cumulative distribution function is considered. This function is computed for both Dollar and Euro returns and 2000 random numbers are generated from it, for the two currencies. Then, the same steps as in Case (a) are repeated. The resulting histogram is shown below in Figure 6.

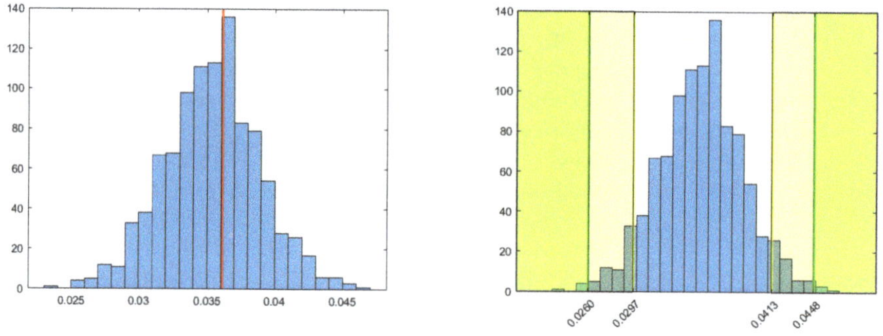


**Figure 6.** Case (b): probability distribution of the distance between Dollar and Euro (**left**) and rejection areas for $\alpha = 0.995$ (green) and $\alpha = 0.95$ (yellow) (**right**).

The new quantiles are given in Formulas (8) and (9), and the new rejection areas are shown in Figure 6.

$$q_{0.5\%} = 0.0260 \qquad q_{99.5\%} = 0.0448 \tag{8}$$

$$q_{5\%} = 0.0297 \qquad q_{95\%} = 0.0413. \tag{9}$$

*(c)* Another nonparametric representation of the probability density function of Dollar and Euro returns can be used, namely the kernel distribution. From this, a simulation is performed, and all the calculations are repeated. The new quantiles are given in Formulas (10) and (11), and the new rejection areas are shown in Figure 7.

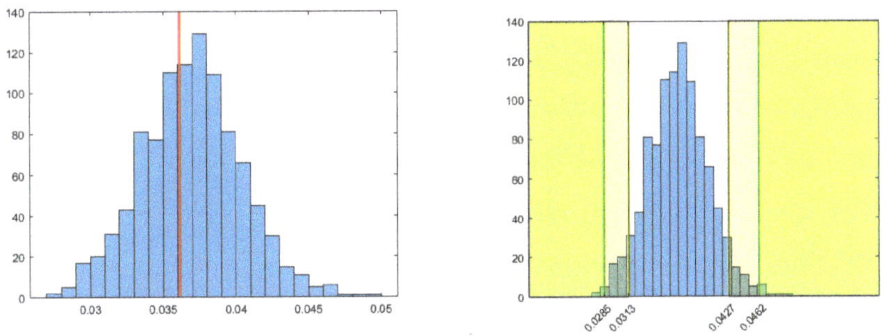


**Figure 7.** Case (c): probability distribution of the distance between Dollar and Euro (**left**) and rejection areas for $\alpha = 0.995$ (green) and $\alpha = 0.95$ (yellow) (**right**).

$$q_{0.5\%} = 0.0285 \qquad q_{99.5\%} = 0.0462 \tag{10}$$

$$q_{5\%} = 0.0313 \qquad q_{95\%} = 0.0427. \tag{11}$$

### 4.4. A Discussion of the Results of the Statistical Tests

From Table 2, it is possible to conclude that it is better to use the ones of case (b) on the left-hand side and case (c) on the right-hand side as rejection areas. This is because the probability distribution of the distance is skewed. The normal approach in case (a) is a direct and quick method for the construction of the probability distribution of the distance.

The so-obtained left quantiles ($q_{0.5\%}$ and $q_{5\%}$) were found to be similar to those of the kernel approach in case (c). Thus, the left tails of case (c) are close to the ones generated in case (a). The reason behind this lies, possibly, in the fact that a default kernel function—which is theoretically optimal for estimating densities for the normal distribution—was used in our computations.

Contrarily, the right quantiles ($q_{99.5\%}$ and $q_{99\%}$) of the normal approach are substantially different from the values obtained using both (b) and (c) approaches. This means that empirical and kernel functions are able to more accurately capture the tail behaviour of the real data returns. The resulting quantiles of the distance distribution might be evidence of this: more extreme values for the real data returns entail more extreme simulated distances. However, the above observations are only possible interpretations of the results and contain questions for further research.

**Table 2.** Quantiles of cases (a), (b) and (c). The values for which it is harder to reject are coloured (the smaller values are on the left of the histogram, and the larger are on the right).

| | $q_{0.5\%}$ | $q_{5\%}$ | $q_{95\%}$ | $q_{99.5\%}$ |
|---|---|---|---|---|
| (a) Normal | 0.0287 | 0.0311 | 0.0394 | 0.0419 |
| (b) Empirical | 0.0260 | 0.0297 | 0.0413 | 0.0448 |
| (c) Kernel | 0.0285 | 0.0313 | 0.0427 | 0.0462 |

Taking into account the quantile values highlighted in Table 2, it is now possible to evaluate, for each currency, whether or not the null hypothesis can be rejected. The table in Figure 8 below displays the results of the test. The distances from Dollar and Euro of the majority of the currencies are in the rejection regions, even for very high levels of significance, meaning that there is a significant statistical separation between these currencies and both USD and EUR, based on the $L^2$-distance. A remarkable observation is that the GBP seems to be close to USD and that SEK seems to be close to EUR; this fact should be the object of further investigation.

| | | $L^2$-distance from DOL | Decision I | | $L^2$-distance from EUR | Decision II | | Decision I&II | |
|---|---|---|---|---|---|---|---|---|---|
| | | | 99.5% | 99% | | 99.5% | 99% | 99.5% | 99% |
| Currencies | GBP | 0.0378 | Support | Support | 0.0708 | Reject | Reject | Support | Support |
| | AUD | 0.0446 | Support | Reject | 0.0785 | Reject | Reject | Support | Reject |
| | CAD | 0.0198 | Reject | Reject | 0.0522 | Reject | Reject | Reject | Reject |
| | JPY | 0.0179 | Reject | Reject | 0.0494 | Reject | Reject | Reject | Reject |
| | BRL | 0.2939 | Reject | Reject | 0.3283 | Reject | Reject | Reject | Reject |
| | RUB | 0.6198 | Reject | Reject | 0.6522 | Reject | Reject | Reject | Reject |
| | INR | 0.0194 | Reject | Reject | 0.0519 | Reject | Reject | Reject | Reject |
| | CNY | 0.0489 | Reject | Reject | 0.0765 | Reject | Reject | Reject | Reject |
| | ZAR | 0.2719 | Reject | Reject | 0.3066 | Reject | Reject | Reject | Reject |
| | ILS | 0.0226 | Reject | Reject | 0.0534 | Reject | Reject | Reject | Reject |
| | NOK | 0.0568 | Reject | Reject | 0.0909 | Reject | Reject | Reject | Reject |
| | SEK | 0.0103 | Reject | Reject | 0.0388 | Support | Support | Support | Support |
| | PLN | 0.0293 | Support | Reject | 0.0602 | Reject | Reject | Support | Reject |
| | BTC | 7.1667 | Reject | Reject | 7.2012 | Reject | Reject | Reject | Reject |
| | XAU | 0.2091 | Reject | Reject | 0.2429 | Reject | Reject | Reject | Reject |

**Figure 8.** Results of the statistical tests.

### *4.5. An Alternative to ARMA Modelling for Comparing Currencies and Assets: The Periodogram*

Instead of computing a PSD function from the ARMA modelling, it is possible to consider an estimation of this function. In particular, in the following, we analyse the periodogram, which is a nonparametric estimate of the power spectral density of a stationary process under regularity assumptions. Its main advantage is that it does not need model fitting as was seen in Section 3. The periodogram is defined as ([20] Ch4.1.2):

$$P(\omega) = \frac{1}{2\pi N}\left|\sum_{n=0}^{N-1} x_n e^{-i\omega n}\right|^2, \quad -\pi \leq \omega \leq \pi, \tag{12}$$

where $x_n$ are the observations and $N$ is the total number of observations. As in (6), it is possible to rewrite the squared modulus of the sum in the following way:

$$\left|\sum_{n=0}^{N-1} x_n e^{-i\omega n}\right|^2 = \sum_{n=0}^{N-1} x_n^2 + 2\sum_{l=1}^{N-1}\sum_{j=0}^{l-1} x_l x_j cos((l-j)\omega) \tag{13}$$

Formulas (12) and (13) were used to compute the periodogram of all the currencies. Once all the periodogram functions are obtained, Formula (7) is applied, in order to find the new matrix of distances (Figure 9). Although the values in Figure 9 are slightly larger than those in Figure 4, it is still possible to divide the currencies in the same three groups previously presented.

| | DOL | EUR | GBP | AUD | CAD | JPY | BRL | RUB | INR | CNY | ZAR | ILS | NOK | SEK | PLN | BTC | XAU |
|---|---|---|---|---|---|---|---|---|---|---|---|---|---|---|---|---|---|
| DOL | 0 | 0.0832 | 0.1265 | 0.1344 | 0.1051 | 0.1065 | 0.4600 | 0.8634 | 0.0946 | 0.1237 | 0.4358 | 0.1070 | 0.1457 | 0.0980 | 0.1176 | 9.9427 | 0.3546 |
| EUR | 0.0832 | 0 | 0.1274 | 0.1399 | 0.1055 | 0.1016 | 0.4808 | 0.8829 | 0.1014 | 0.1296 | 0.4567 | 0.1065 | 0.1494 | 0.0817 | 0.1093 | 9.9673 | 0.3712 |
| GBP | 0.1265 | 0.1274 | 0 | 0.1434 | 0.1268 | 0.1344 | 0.4458 | 0.8373 | 0.1315 | 0.1496 | 0.4203 | 0.1322 | 0.1442 | 0.1280 | 0.1299 | 9.9185 | 0.3411 |
| AUD | 0.1344 | 0.1399 | 0.1434 | 0 | 0.1298 | 0.1415 | 0.4364 | 0.8308 | 0.1373 | 0.1530 | 0.4066 | 0.1377 | 0.1466 | 0.1293 | 0.1380 | 9.9120 | 0.3461 |
| CAD | 0.1051 | 0.1055 | 0.1268 | 0.1298 | 0 | 0.1171 | 0.4481 | 0.8496 | 0.1129 | 0.1299 | 0.4260 | 0.1123 | 0.1419 | 0.1066 | 0.1214 | 9.9304 | 0.3515 |
| JPY | 0.1065 | 0.1016 | 0.1344 | 0.1415 | 0.1171 | 0 | 0.4554 | 0.8563 | 0.1181 | 0.1314 | 0.4329 | 0.1184 | 0.1513 | 0.1085 | 0.1245 | 9.9317 | 0.3503 |
| BRL | 0.4600 | 0.4808 | 0.4458 | 0.4364 | 0.4481 | 0.4554 | 0 | 0.7730 | 0.4496 | 0.4437 | 0.4565 | 0.4519 | 0.4344 | 0.4565 | 0.4455 | 9.7441 | 0.4609 |
| RUB | 0.8634 | 0.8829 | 0.8373 | 0.8308 | 0.8496 | 0.8563 | 0.7730 | 0 | 0.8468 | 0.8427 | 0.7527 | 0.8535 | 0.8246 | 0.8594 | 0.8433 | 9.5536 | 0.7812 |
| INR | 0.0946 | 0.1014 | 0.1315 | 0.1373 | 0.1129 | 0.1181 | 0.4496 | 0.8468 | 0 | 0.1298 | 0.4268 | 0.1128 | 0.1502 | 0.1087 | 0.1210 | 9.9341 | 0.3512 |
| CNY | 0.1237 | 0.1296 | 0.1496 | 0.1530 | 0.1299 | 0.1314 | 0.4437 | 0.8427 | 0.1298 | 0 | 0.4264 | 0.1230 | 0.1604 | 0.1302 | 0.1421 | 9.9200 | 0.3452 |
| ZAR | 0.4358 | 0.4567 | 0.4203 | 0.4066 | 0.4260 | 0.4329 | 0.4565 | 0.7527 | 0.4268 | 0.4264 | 0 | 0.4316 | 0.4071 | 0.4365 | 0.4257 | 9.7588 | 0.4433 |
| ILS | 0.1070 | 0.1065 | 0.1322 | 0.1377 | 0.1123 | 0.1184 | 0.4519 | 0.8535 | 0.1128 | 0.1230 | 0.4316 | 0 | 0.1484 | 0.1077 | 0.1201 | 9.9317 | 0.3486 |
| NOK | 0.1457 | 0.1494 | 0.1442 | 0.1466 | 0.1419 | 0.1513 | 0.4344 | 0.8246 | 0.1502 | 0.1604 | 0.4071 | 0.1484 | 0 | 0.1370 | 0.1429 | 9.9027 | 0.3405 |
| SEK | 0.0980 | 0.0817 | 0.1280 | 0.1293 | 0.1066 | 0.1085 | 0.4565 | 0.8594 | 0.1087 | 0.1302 | 0.4365 | 0.1077 | 0.1370 | 0 | 0.1022 | 9.9374 | 0.3552 |
| PLN | 0.1176 | 0.1093 | 0.1299 | 0.1380 | 0.1214 | 0.1245 | 0.4455 | 0.8433 | 0.1210 | 0.1421 | 0.4257 | 0.1201 | 0.1429 | 0.1022 | 0 | 9.9229 | 0.3489 |
| BTC | 9.9427 | 9.9673 | 9.9185 | 9.9120 | 9.9304 | 9.9317 | 9.7441 | 9.5536 | 9.9341 | 9.9200 | 9.7588 | 9.9317 | 9.9027 | 9.9374 | 9.9229 | 0 | 9.8001 |
| XAU | 0.3546 | 0.3712 | 0.3411 | 0.3461 | 0.3515 | 0.3503 | 0.4609 | 0.7812 | 0.3512 | 0.3452 | 0.4433 | 0.3486 | 0.3405 | 0.3552 | 0.3489 | 9.8001 | 0 |

**Figure 9.** New matrix of distances.

## 5. On the Law of the Distance of Two Spectral Densities

In Section 4.3, we introduced a test for which it was necessary to have the probability distribution of the distance between two spectral densities. In order to consider such a distance as a random variable, we have several options. A first option is to consider the distance computed from the periodogram, such as in Section 4.5. In the case where the returns of the exchange rates may be assumed to be a stationary Gaussian process with zero mean and continuous spectra, the periodogram is known to have the chi-square distribution multiplied by some constant—essentially, a Gamma-distributed random variable (see [21] pp. 264, 270 or [24] p. 485).

In the present case, this option is not advisable since, as seen in Appendix B, the returns of the exchange rates do not satisfy normality assumptions. The results known for the law of the periodogram, not assuming normality of the returns of the exchange rates and in the form proposed in ([25] p. 194) does not seem of utility in our context.

A second option is to assume an ARMA model for the returns of the exchange rates and to inquire about the distribution of the coefficients of the ARMA model. Under regularity assumptions on the noise process, it is known that the coefficients of an ARMA process are asymptotically normal with zero mean and variances given by the spectral density (see [24] p. 482). It is also known that the Whittle-like estimators of the spectral density of a sufficiently regular ARMA process—since such a process is a wide sense stationary time series with an almost everywhere positive density (see [20] p. 226)—are consistent (see [26] p. 351) and asymptotically normal (see [24] p. 539, 540).

We observe that a connection between Gaussian and Whittle's likelihoods is relevant for finite sample estimation; see [27]. From the results just quoted, it may be possible to deduce an asymptotic distribution for the distance of spectral densities. Nevertheless, since we observed good fittings of the actual data to Gamma distributions, we opted to formulate our results, ahead in Theorem 1, by stating directly the natural hypothesis needed instead of resorting to an asymptotic result.

In Section 4, we obtained samples of spectral densities for currencies Dollar US and Euro, let these be, respectively, $f_1(\cdot,\omega)$ and $f_2(\cdot,\omega)$ where, $\Omega$ being the probability space, the dot means that, for every $\omega \in \Omega$ we have two functions given by $t \in [-\pi,+\pi] \mapsto f_1(t,\omega)$ and also by $t \in [-\pi,+\pi] \mapsto f_2(t,\omega)$, which are spectral densities; we recall that these spectral densities are positive, continuous and even functions defined on $[-\pi,+\pi]$.

We suppose that, for each $t \in [-\pi,+\pi]$ fixed, the random variables $f_1(t,\cdot)$ and $f_2(t,\cdot)$ are independent; this hypothesis is implicit in the Monte Carlo simulation procedure used in Section 4. We present, in the following, a result that justifies the computational results found. As a consequence of the construction method given above for the random processes $f_1, f_2$ we have that the map defined by the $L^2$ distance, given by:

$$\begin{aligned}\omega \in \Omega \mapsto d(f_1(\cdot,\omega), f_2(\cdot,\omega))^2 &= \int_{-\pi}^{+\pi} |f_1(t,\omega) - f_2(t,\omega)|^2 dt = \\ &= 2\int_{0}^{+\pi} |f_1(t,\omega) - f_2(t,\omega)|^2 dt \,,\end{aligned}$$

is a random variable. The next result provides a justification for the computational results found. In the following, we will use the parametrisation for $X \frown \Gamma(\alpha,\beta,\gamma,\mu)$, a generalised Gamma-distributed random variable, with parametrisation given for its density $f_X$ by:

$$f_X^{\alpha,\beta,\gamma,\mu}(x) = \begin{cases} \dfrac{\gamma e^{-\left(\frac{x-\mu}{\beta}\right)^{\gamma}} \left(\frac{x-\mu}{\beta}\right)^{\alpha\gamma-1}}{\beta\Gamma(\alpha)} & x > \mu \\ 0 & x \leq \mu \,, \end{cases}$$

depending on parameters $\alpha, \beta, \gamma, \mu$ (see [28] p. 388). As a consequence, we use a parametrisation for $G \frown \Gamma(\alpha, \beta)$, a Gamma-distributed random variable with parameters $\alpha, \beta$, and the following expression for the density $f_G$,

$$f_G^{\alpha,\beta}(x) = \begin{cases} \frac{\beta^{-\alpha} x^{\alpha-1} e^{-\frac{x}{\beta}}}{\Gamma(\alpha)} & x > 0 \\ 0 & x \leq 0 . \end{cases}$$

We observe that $f_X^{\alpha,\beta,1,0} \equiv f_G^{\alpha,\beta}$.

**Theorem 1** (On the probability law of $L^2$ distances of spectral densities). *Consider the following assumptions which are justified by observed computational experiences.*

1. *Assumption A: a Gamma distribution provides a good fit for the random variable $Q_n$ given by:*
$$Q_{k,n}(\omega) := \left|\left(f_1(\pi\frac{k}{2^n}, \omega) - f_2(\pi\frac{k}{2^n}, \omega)\right)\right|^2 \frown \Gamma(\alpha_{k,n}, \beta_{k,n}) ,$$
*with the $\beta_{k,n}$ parameter of the Gamma distribution verifying $0 < \beta_{k,n} \ll 1$.*
2. *Assumption B: for arbitrarily values close to one another $t \neq t'$ in $[-\pi, +\pi]$, the random variables given by:*
$$|f_1(t, \omega) - f_2(t, \omega)| , |f_1(t', \omega) - f_2(t', \omega)|$$
*are independent.*
3. *Assumption C: for $n \geq 1$, we have that, for some constants $\alpha_\infty$ , $0 < \beta_\infty \ll 1$,*
$$\frac{\pi}{2^n} \sum_{k=0}^{2^n} \alpha_{k,n}\beta_{k,n} \approx \alpha_\infty \beta_\infty . \tag{14}$$

*Then, $d(f_1(\cdot, \omega), f_2(\cdot, \omega)) \frown \Gamma(\alpha_\infty, \sqrt{2\beta_\infty}), 2, 0)$, that is, the the random variable $d(f_1(\cdot, \omega)$, $f_2(\cdot, \omega))$ admits a fitting by a generalised Gamma-distributed random variable.*

**Proof.** Consider a standard discretisation numerical procedure that gives an approximation of the integral for large $n$:

$$\int_0^{+\pi} |f_1(t, \omega) - f_2(t, \omega)|^2 dt \approx \sum_{k=0}^{2^n} \frac{\pi}{2^n} \left| f_1(\pi\frac{k}{2^n}, \omega) - f_2(\pi\frac{k}{2^n}, \omega)\right|^2 .$$

By *Assumption A:* , we are bound to find the distribution of the limit of a sum of Gamma-distributed random variables. We use the moment generating function and we determine the limit distribution of:

$$I_n := \sum_{k=0}^{2^n} \frac{\pi}{2^n} \left|\left(f_1(\pi\frac{k}{2^n}, \omega) - f_2(\pi\frac{k}{2^n}, \omega)\right)\right|^2 = \sum_{k=0}^{2^n} \frac{\pi}{2^n} Q_{k,n} .$$

We resort to the moment generating function of a Gamma-distributed random variable $\Gamma(\alpha_n, \beta_n)$ that is, in this case:

$$\varphi_{Q_{k,n}}(t) = \mathbb{E}\left[e^{tQ_{k,n}}\right] = \frac{1}{(1 - \beta_{k,n} t)^{\alpha_{k,n}}} .$$

As a consequence, under *Assumption B*, we have:

$$\varphi_{I_n}(t) = \mathbb{E}\left[e^{\sum_{k=0}^{2^n} \frac{t\pi}{2^n} Q_{k,n}}\right] = \prod_{k=0}^{2^n} \mathbb{E}\left[e^{\frac{t\pi}{2^n} Q_{k,n}}\right] = \prod_{k=0}^{2^n} \varphi_Q(\frac{t\pi}{2^n}) = \prod_{k=0}^{2^n} \frac{1}{(1 - \beta_{k,n} \frac{t\pi}{2^n})^{\alpha_{k,n}}} .$$

Under *Assumption C*, we obtain using $0 < \beta_{k,n} \ll 1$ and $0 < \beta_\infty \ll 1$,

$$\sum_{k=0}^{2^n} \alpha_{k,n} \log\left(1 - \beta_{k,n} \frac{tpi}{2^n}\right) \approx \sum_{k=0}^{2^n} \alpha_{k,n}\beta_{k,n} \frac{t\pi}{2^n} \approx \alpha_\infty \beta_\infty t \approx \alpha_\infty \log(1 - \beta_\infty t)\,,$$

which , in turn, gives, in the limit:

$$\lim_{n \to +\infty} \varphi_{I_n}(t) = \lim_{n \to +\infty} \prod_{k=0}^{2^n} \frac{1}{(1 - \beta_{k,n} \frac{t\pi}{2^n})^{\alpha_{k,n}}} = \frac{1}{(1 - \beta_\infty t)^{\alpha_\infty}}\,.$$

This shows that $d(f_1(\cdot,\omega) - f_2(\cdot,\omega)) = \sqrt{2G(\omega)}$ with $G(\omega) \frown \Gamma(\alpha_\infty, \beta_\infty)$, finally showing that $d(f_1(\cdot,\omega) - f_2(\cdot,\omega))$ admits a fitting by a generalised Gamma-distributed random variable. In fact, we have that, given $f_G$ the density of $G$, the density of $\sqrt{2G(\omega)}$, let it be denoted by $f_{\sqrt{2G(\omega)}}$, is given by $f_{\sqrt{2G(\omega)}}(x) = x f_G(x^2/2)$. This equality, with a simple calculation using densities, shows that if $G \frown \Gamma(\alpha, \beta)$ then $\sqrt{2G(\omega)} \frown \Gamma(\alpha, \sqrt{2\beta}), 2, 0)$, that is, $\sqrt{2G(\omega)}$ admits a fitting by a generalised Gamma distribution as announced. □

**Remark 1** (On the interpretation of *Assumption C*). *Formula* (14) *of Assumption C means that, for all orders $n \geq 1$ of the resolution in the discretisation of the integral, the average of the Gamma distribution parameters for all the discretisation points should be constant. This assumption although with a straightforward interpretation is impossible to be fully verified; nevertheless, it can be verified for values $n \leq n_0$ of the resolution order in the discretisation procedure of the integral, for $n_0 \geq 1$ sufficiently large.*

**Remark 2** (Testing equality of spectral distribution functions in the normal case). *If we could assume the normality of the returns of the exchange rates it would be possible to test the equality of two spectral distribution functions with a simple computation (see [25] p. 198). As already noted this assumption is not valid in our case.*

### 6. Conclusions

The returns of the exchange rates between various currencies and Swiss franc were calculated and modelled as ARMA processes. From this modelling, Power Spectral Densities were computed, and the $L^2$-distance between them was introduced as a measure to compare the volatility behaviour of the returns. The resulting matrix of distances (see the table in Figure 4) clearly shows that there are three main different groups:

- The Majors, the independent ones, INR and CNY.
- The remaining BRICS and gold.
- Bitcoin.

This grouping is similar to the grouping based in macro-economic criteria presented in Section 2, thus, showing that the variance and auto-covariance structure of returns of exchange rates of currencies is tied to the macro-economic properties of the owners of the currencies. Moreover, Bitcoin exhibits an extremely different quantitative behaviour when compared to one of the other currencies, revealing unique volatility properties.

An informed investor aware of the basic principles of *Modern Portfolio Theory*, such as those exposed in [29], has to take into consideration the extreme volatility properties of Bitcoin further revealed in this study. The study of the covariance structure for a portfolio, with similar methods to the one used in this work, can take advantage of modelling with vectorial ARMA processes (see [30]) and in cases where there is the possibility of regime switching VARMA models (see [31]).

An alternative approach presented is to directly estimate the Power Spectral Density with the periodogram, thus, avoiding ARMA modelling. These results add credibility to the ARMA modelling approach as the qualitative conclusions are identical, although the quantitative results in the matrix of distances (see the Table in Figure 9) are less precise. Figure 10 shows a comparison of the two approaches.

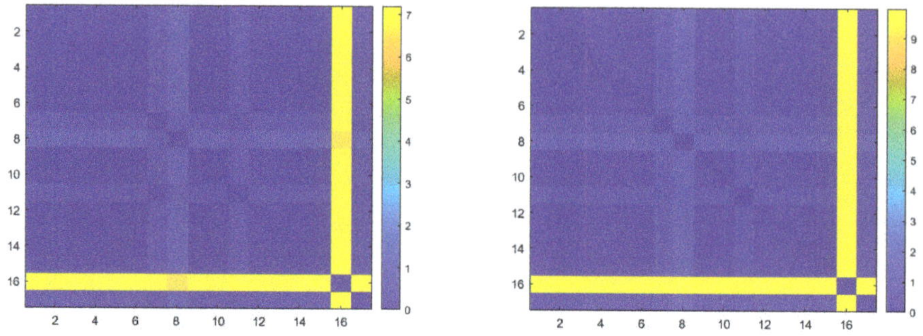


**Figure 10.** Matrices of distances with scaled colours. On the left is the matrix obtained from PSD, and on the right is the matrix obtained from the periodogram.

In both cases, three different groups are clearly detectable, as they exhibit three different shades of colour. Once again, it is noticeable that Bitcoin has standout values (yellow colour). It is also clear that the shades of colour in the graphic corresponding to the use of the PSD in the lefthand side are much more salient that those in the graphic corresponding to the use of the periodogram in the righthand side—also showing a loss of precision attached to the use of the periodogram already noticed in Section 4.5.

Furthermore, a statistical study was introduced. The empirical probability distribution of the $L^2$-distance between the Power Spectral Densities of Dollar and Euro was constructed through performing a Monte Carlo simulation. The results were used to test and validate significant statistical separation between currencies basing on the $L^2$-distance. Furthermore, a formal result was proven, which substantiates the probability distribution assumptions in this work.

As a stationary stochastic process can be characterised by its spectral density, the determination of the distance between the spectral distances introduced in this work is, in fact, a determination of a quantitative distance between (the ARMA models of) the returns of currencies. Furthermore, the statistical test introduced allows for a well-founded discussion of the separation in terms of the distance introduced between currencies and assets.

A natural question for further study is consider ways to obtain information on the joint variation of the returns of two currencies and or assets. A naive starting point may be the fact that, under some regularity assumptions, we can consider the product of ARMA processes (see [32]).

**Author Contributions:** Conceptualization, M.L.E.; methodology, M.L.E.; software, M.C.P. and M.L.E.; validation, M.C.P., M.L.E. and N.P.K.; formal analysis, M.L.E. and N.P.K.; investigation, M.C.P., M.L.E. and N.P.K.; resources, M.C.P., M.L.E. and N.P.K.; data curation, M.C.P.; writing—original draft preparation, M.C.P.; writing—review and editing, M.L.E., M.C.P. and N.P.K.; visualization, M.L.E., M.C.P. and N.P.K.; supervision, M.L.E.; project administration, M.L.E.; funding acquisition, M.L.E. All authors have read and agreed to the published version of the manuscript.

**Funding:** For the second and third authors, this work was partially supported through the project of the Centro de Matemática e Aplicações, UID/MAT/00297/2020, financed by the Fundação para a Ciência e a Tecnologia (Portuguese Foundation for Science and Technology). The APC was by supported by Fidelidade-Companhia de Seguras, S.A.

**Data Availability Statement:** Data for this study was collected with the Mathematica function "FinancialData" from Mathematica (see [33]). Mathematica™ is a Trade Mark from Wolfram Research,

Inc., 100 Trade Center Drive, Champaign, IL 61820-7237, USA. Computations were performed initially with Mathematica and in a second round, for confirmations, with R software (see [34]).

**Acknowledgments:** This work was published with financial support from Fidelidade-Companhia de Seguras, S.A. to which the authors express their warmest acknowledgment. The authors express gratitude to the three referees for their comments, corrections and questions that led to a revised and better version of this work.

**Conflicts of Interest:** The authors declare no conflict of interest.

## Appendix A. Power Spectral Densities

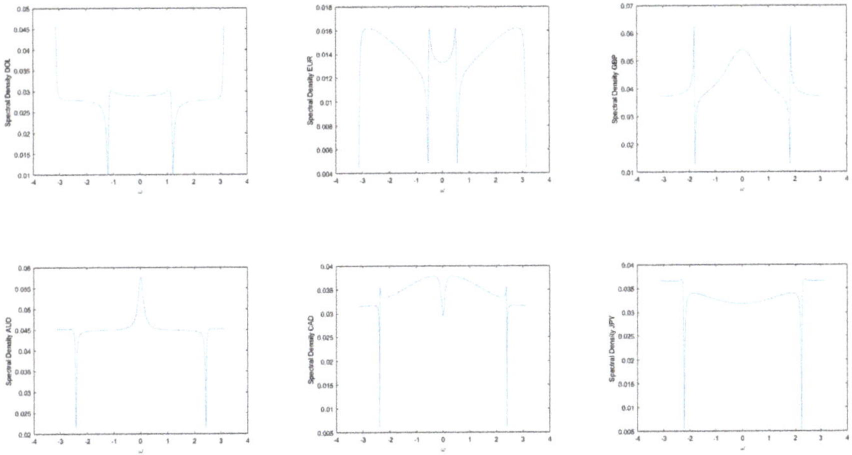

**Figure A1.** Power spectral density functions of the Majors.

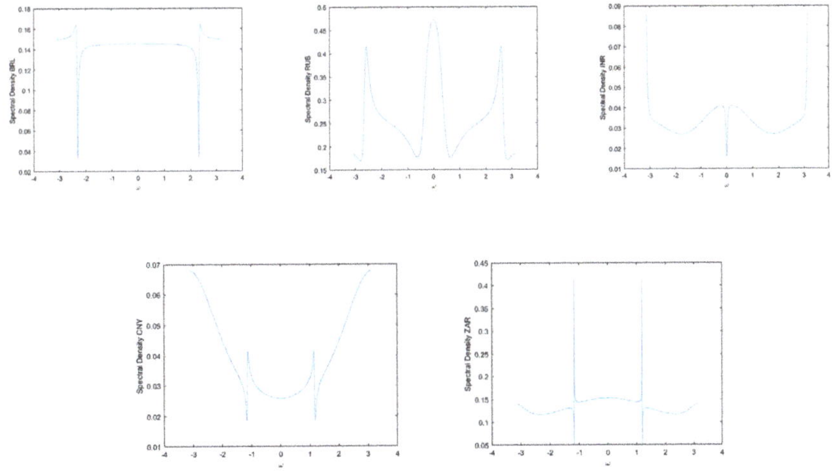

**Figure A2.** Power spectral density functions of the BRICS.

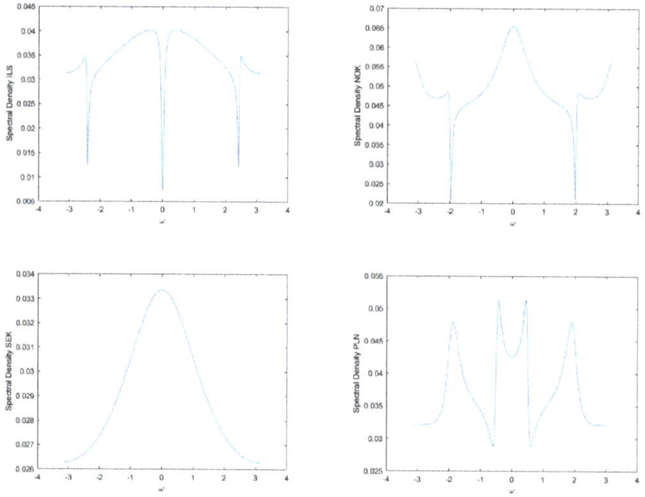


**Figure A3.** Power spectral density functions of the independent currencies.

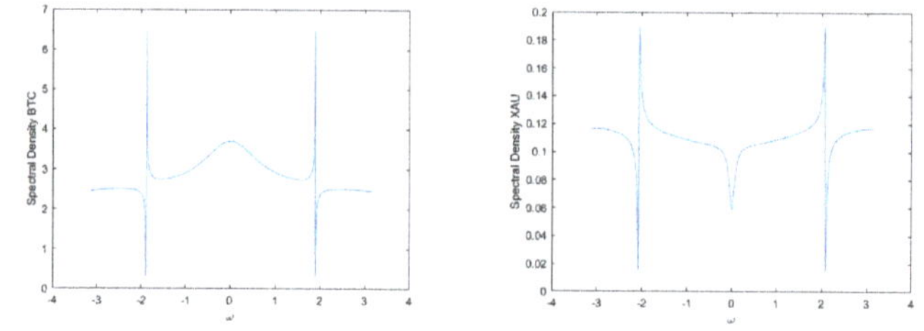


**Figure A4.** Power spectral density functions of Bitcoin and gold.

**Remark A1.** *It is clear that there is very significant information to be drawn from the spectral densities requiring a more sensible tool than the $L^2$ distance used in this work. One of the most remarkable features is the similar location of extrema, particularly in the case of Bitcoin and Gold, which should be placed in parallel with the graphic similarities observed in Figures 1 and 2. We intend to pursue this analysis in future work.*

## Appendix B. Normality of Returns

The Dollar and Euro returns do not satisfy the normality assumptions that result from usual statistical tests. In this section, we present an attempt to transform data in a way so that a normality test is passed.

For both Dollar and Euro, returns $r$ are grouped into sets of 12 elements. The mean of each set is saved in a vector $R$, and then the normality of $R$ is tested and confirmed using the one-sample Kolmogorov–Smirnov test. Its sample mean $\hat{\mu}_R$ and variance $\hat{\sigma}_R^2$ are calculated, and the estimated mean and variance of the returns $r$ correspond to $\hat{\mu}_r = \hat{\mu}_R$ and $\hat{\sigma}_r^2 = 12\hat{\sigma}_R^2$ supposing normality and independence of the elements of $r$.

The new estimated means $\hat{\mu}_1, \hat{\mu}_2$ and variances $\hat{\sigma}_1^2, \hat{\sigma}_2^2$ of Dollar and Euro are obtained as specified above, and computations for the construction of the histogram are performed. The results are summarised in Figure A5. The average of the simulation data is not close to the value $d^*$ (red line), contrarily to the case in Figure 5.

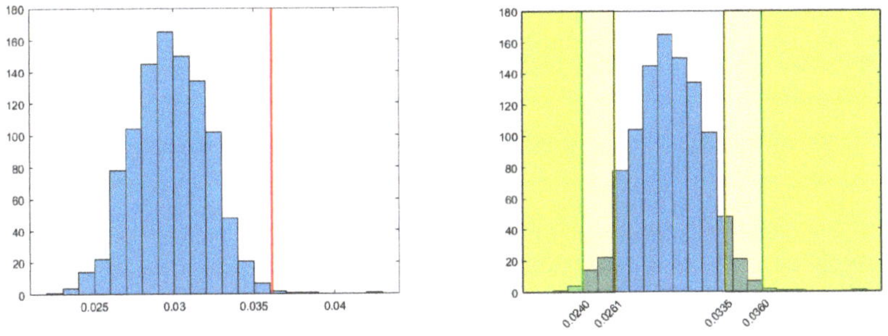


**Figure A5.** New empirical probability distribution of the distance between Dollar and Euro (left) and new rejection areas for $\alpha = 0.995$ (green) and $\alpha = 0.95$ (yellow).

The quantiles for this approach are given in Formulas (A1) and (A2), and the new rejection areas are shown in Figure A5.

$$q_{0.5\%} = 0.0240 \qquad q_{99.5\%} = 0.0360 \tag{A1}$$

$$q_{5\%} = 0.0261 \qquad q_{95\%} = 0.0335 \tag{A2}$$

However, it can be demonstrated that there is no advantage in transforming the data. Indeed, it is possible to produce a statistical test to verify whether or not the mean values of the two histograms in Figures 5 and A5 are the value $d^*$.

The test is performed as follows. Once the mean $\mu$ and the variance $\sigma^2$ of the data visualised in the histogram, are obtained, the value $z = (\mu - d^*)/\sigma$ is computed and compared with the standard normal quantiles:

$$q_{0.5\%} = -2.5758 \qquad q_{99.5\%} = 2.5758$$

$$q_{5\%} = -1.6449 \qquad q_{95\%} = 1.6449.$$

The null hypothesis can be written as:

$$\mathrm{H}_0\colon \mu = z.$$

Figure A6 shows that $\mathrm{H}_0$ is not rejected when normality is assumed a priori. This suggests that, despite Dollar and Euro returns not satisfying normality assumptions, it is possible to derive some results assuming normality.

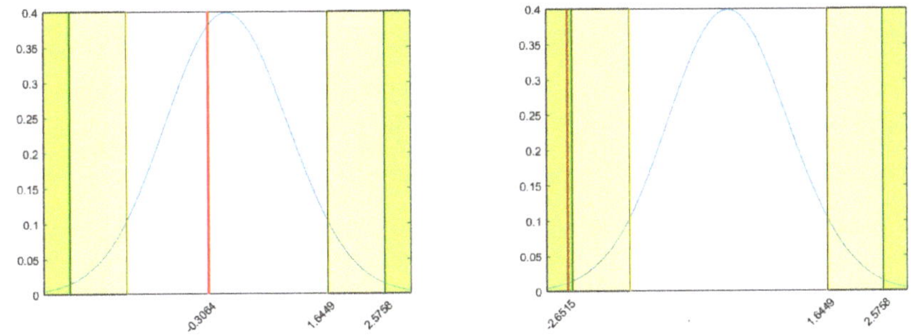


**Figure A6.** Quantiles of the standard normal distribution and the value $z$ (in red). On the (**left**), the case in which normality is assumed a priori. On the (**right**), the case in which data are transformed.

## References


1. von Mises, L. *The Theory of Money and Credit*; Liberty Fund: Indianapolis, Indiana, 1981.
2. Mandel, E. *Traité d'économie Marxiste*; Number vol. 2 in Traité d'économie marxiste; Union Générale d'Éditions; René Julliard: Paris, France, 1962.
3. Marx, K.; Mandel, E.; Fowkes, B. *Capital: A Critique of Political Economy*; Capital, Penguin Books Ltd.: Harmondsworth, UK, 2004.
4. Friedman, M. *The Optimum Quantity of Money*, 1st ed.; Nobel Laureates in Economics; Aldine Transaction: Piscataway, NJ, USA, 1969; p. xii, 296.
5. Yermack, D. Chapter 2—Is Bitcoin a Real Currency? An Economic Appraisal. In *Handbook of Digital Currency*, 1st ed.; Chuen, D.L.K., Ed.; Academic Press: San Diego, CA, USA, 2015; pp. 31–43.
6. Nakamoto, S. Bitcoin: A peer-to-peer electronic cash system. Bitcoin White Paper. Available online: https://bitcoin.org/bitcoin.pdf (accessed on 14 February 2023).
7. Taheri, S.; Mann, J.; McWhirter, A. The Nexus between Cryptocurrencies, Currencies and Commodities: A Primer. In *Cryptofinance*; World Scientific Publishing Co. Pte. Ltd.: Singapore, 2022; Chapter 10, pp. 191–206. [CrossRef]
8. Corbet, S.; Meegan, A.; Larkin, C.; Lucey, B.; Yarovaya, L. Exploring the dynamic relationships between cryptocurrencies and other financial assets. *Econ. Lett.* **2018**, *165*, 28–34. [CrossRef]
9. Panagiotidis, T.; Stengos, T.; Vravosinos, O. On the determinants of bitcoin returns: A LASSO approach. *Financ. Res. Lett.* **2018**, *27*, 235–240. [CrossRef]
10. Assaf, A.; Mokni, K.; Yousaf, I.; Bhandari, A. Long memory in the high frequency cryptocurrency markets using fractal connectivity analysis: The impact of COVID-19. *Res. Int. Bus. Financ.* **2023**, *64*, 101821. [CrossRef]
11. Nguyen, L.H.; Chevapatrakul, T.; Yao, K. Investigating tail-risk dependence in the cryptocurrency markets: A LASSO quantile regression approach. *J. Empir. Financ.* **2020**, *58*, 333–355. [CrossRef]
12. Xu, H.; Xu, X.; Wu, Z.; Guo, H.; Zhang, Y.; Wang, H. A Study on Bitcoin Price Volatility Based on the SVAR Model and Impulse Response Analysis. In *Blockchain and Trustworthy Systems*; Dai, H.N.; Liu, X., Luo, D.X., Xiao, J., Chen, X., Eds.; Springer: Singapore, 2021; pp. 214–225.
13. Dyhrberg, A.H. Bitcoin, gold and the dollar—A GARCH volatility analysis. *Financ. Res. Lett.* **2016**, *16*, 85–92. [CrossRef]
14. Gronwald, M. Is Bitcoin a Commodity? On price jumps, demand shocks, and certainty of supply. *J. Int. Money Financ.* **2019**, *97*, 86–92. [CrossRef]
15. Guizani, S.; Nafti, I.K. The Determinants of Bitcoin Price Volatility: An Investigation With ARDL Model. *Procedia Comput. Sci.* **2019**, *164*, 233–238. [CrossRef]
16. Qiu, Y.; Wang, Z.; Xie, T.; Zhang, X. Forecasting Bitcoin realized volatility by exploiting measurement error under model uncertainty. *J. Empir. Financ.* **2021**, *62*, 179–201. [CrossRef]
17. Tsang, K.P.; Yang, Z. Do connections pay off in the bitcoin market? *J. Empir. Financ.* **2022**, *67*, 1–18. [CrossRef]
18. Lipton, A. *Mathematical Methods for Foreign Exchange*; A Financial Engineer's Approach; World Scientific Publishing Co., Inc.: River Edge, NJ, USA, 2001; p. xxii, 676. [CrossRef]
19. Azencott, R.; Dacunha-Castelle, D. *Series of Irregular Observations*; Springer: New York, NY, USA, 1986.
20. Brémaud, P. *Fourier Analysis and Stochastic Processes*; Springer: Cham, Switzerland, 2014; p. xiii, 385.
21. Koopmans, L.H. The spectral analysis of time series. In *Probability and Mathematical Statistics*, 2nd ed.; Academic Press, Inc.: San Diego, CA, USA, 1995; Volume 22, p. xvi, 366.
22. Dufour, J.M.; Khalaf, L. Monte Carlo Test Methods in Econometrics. In *A Companion to Theoretical Econometrics*; John Wiley & Sons, Ltd.: Hoboken, NJ, USA, 2003; Chapter 23, pp. 494–519. [CrossRef]
23. MacKinnon, J.G. Bootstrap Hypothesis Testing. In *Handbook of Computational Econometrics*; John Wiley & Sons, Ltd.: Hoboken, NJ, USA, 2009; Chapter 6, pp. 183–213. [CrossRef]
24. Anderson, T.W. *The Statistical Analysis of Time Series*; John Wiley & Sons: Hoboken, NJ, USA, 1971.
25. Grenander, U.; Rosenblatt, M. *Statistical Analysis of Stationary Time Series*; John Wiley & Sons: New York, NY, USA; Almqvist & Wiksell: Stockholm, Sweden, 1957; p. 300.
26. Brockwell, P.J.; Davis, R.A. *Time Series: Theory and Methods*; Springer Series in Statistics; Springer: New York, NY, USA, 2006; p. xvi, 577; Reprint of the second (1991) edition.
27. Subba Rao, S.; Yang, J. Reconciling the Gaussian and Whittle likelihood with an application to estimation in the frequency domain. *Ann. Statist.* **2021**, *49*, 2774–2802. [CrossRef]
28. Johnson, N.L.; Kotz, S.; Balakrishnan, N. *Continuous Univariate Distributions*, 2nd ed.; Wiley Series in Probability and Mathematical Statistics: Applied Probability and Statistics; John Wiley & Sons, Inc.: New York, NY, USA, 1994; Volume 1, p. xxii, 756.
29. Benninga, S. *Financial Modeling*, 4th ed.; The MIT Press: Cambridge, MA, USA, 2014; p. xxxi, 1111.
30. Reinsel, G.C. *Elements of Multivariate Time Series Analysis*, 2nd ed.; Springer Series in Statistics; Springer: New York, NY, USA, 1997; p. xviii, 357. [CrossRef]
31. Cavicchioli, M. Spectral density of Markov-switching VARMA models. *Econom. Lett.* **2013**, *121*, 218–220. [CrossRef]
32. Engel, E.M.R.A. A unified approach to the study of sums, products, time-aggregation and other functions of ARMA processes. *J. Time Ser. Anal.* **1984**, *5*, 159–171. [CrossRef]

33. Wolfram Research, Inc. *Mathematica, Version 12.3.1.0*; Wolfram Research, Inc.: Champaign, IL, USA, 2022.
34. R Core Team. *R: A Language and Environment for Statistical Computing*; R Foundation for Statistical Computing: Vienna, Austria, 2021.

mathematics

*Article*

# A Credibility Theory-Based Robust Optimization Model to Hedge Price Uncertainty of DSO with Multiple Transactions

**Li-Peng Shao, Jia-Jia Chen *, Lu-Wen Pan and Zi-Juan Yang**

School of Electrical and Electronic Engineering, Shandong University of Technology, Zibo 255000, China
* Correspondence: jjchen@sdut.edu.cn

**Abstract:** This paper addresses the deregulated electricity market arising in a distribution system with an electricity transaction. Under such an environment, the distribution system operator (DSO) with a distributed generator faces the challenge of electricity price uncertainty in a spot market. In this context, a credibility theory-based robust optimization model with multiple transactions is established to hedge the uncertain spot price of the DSO. Firstly, on the basis of credibility theory, the spot price is taken as a fuzzy variable and a risk aversion-based fuzzy opportunity constraint is proposed. Then, to exploit the resiliency of multiple transactions on hedging against uncertain spot price, the spot market, option contract and bilateral contract integrating power flow constraints are studied, because it is imperative for DSO to consider the operational constraints of the local network in the electricity market. Finally, the clear equivalence class is adopted to transform the risk aversion constraint into a deterministic robust optimization one. Under the premise of considering the expected cost of the DSO, the optimal electricity transaction strategy that maximizes resistance to uncertain spot price is pursued. The rationality and effectiveness of the model are verified with a modified 15-node network. The results show that the introduction of option contracts and bilateral contracts reduces the electricity transaction cost of DSO by USD 28.5. In addition, under the same risk aversion factor, the cost of the proposed model is reduced by USD 195.18 compared with robust optimization, which avoids the over-conservatism of traditional robust optimization.

**Keywords:** price uncertainty; DSO; credibility theory; fuzzy chance constraint; robust optimization

**MSC:** 90-10

**Citation:** Shao, L.-P.; Chen, J.-J.; Pan, L.-W.; Yang, Z.-J. A Credibility Theory-Based Robust Optimization Model to Hedge Price Uncertainty of DSO with Multiple Transactions. *Mathematics* **2022**, *10*, 4420. https://doi.org/10.3390/math10234420

Academic Editors: Francisco German Badía and María D. Berrade

Received: 12 September 2022
Accepted: 21 November 2022
Published: 23 November 2022



## 1. Introduction

The distribution system operator (DSO) is responsible for maintaining the security of supply and power quality through investment, construction and reconfiguration of the existing distribution system [1–3]. With the deepening reform of the electricity market environment, as a stakeholder, DSO with distributed generator (DG) plays an important role in the electricity transaction of the distribution system. That is, DSO purchases electricity in the upper wholesale market to meet customer demand as well as maximization of its utility [4–6]. However, the price in the spot market is characterized by uncertainty due to fluctuations in electricity demand, fuel price and renewable power generation [7,8]. Moreover, the forecast error of the spot price is inevitable [9]. Thus, in order to obtain the optimal electricity transaction and expected utility, DSO has to capture the uncertain spot price from the perspective of risk aversion [10]. In view of this, two main questions need to be answered: how to use a portfolio of electricity purchase transactions to hedge against risk brought by uncertain spot price and how to assess the risk when formulating an optimal electricity transaction strategy under the premise of the expected cost?

### 1.1. Literature Review

For risk decision problems with uncertain electricity price, researchers mainly use three kinds of optimization, including robust optimization [11–15], stochastic optimization [16–20] and fuzzy optimization [21–26]. For instance, in [11], the uncertainty of selling/purchasing price in an electricity market is handled by robust optimization with a polyhedral uncertain set. Accordingly, an economical optimal solution is obtained in consideration of the undesired deviation of the market electricity price from the forecasted one. In [12], an adaptive robust optimization is developed to study the uncertain price in a real-time market. In [13], a maximum–minimum–maximum robust optimization model considering the price deviation in the electricity market is proposed, which improves the robustness of system operation against forecast uncertainty. In [14], the uncertainty of market price is dealt with by the upper deviation of forecast price and the robust electricity trading strategies of risk neutrality and risk aversion are compared. In [15], the uncertainty of the electricity market price is modeled based on robust optimization. In this model, instead of the predicted electricity price, the maximum and minimum amounts of the electricity price are considered. However, robust optimization mainly focuses on the worst-case of an uncertain problem and does not fully investigate the risk preference characteristic of a decision maker [27]. Stochastic optimization is one of the most commonly used methods for managing uncertain price. In [16], by assuming that the uncertain price follows the normal distribution, a scenario generation-based stochastic framework is developed. In this framework, the risk associated with uncertain electricity price is considered through downside risk constraints. In [17], uncertain electricity price is regarded as a random variable and a stochastic optimization model based on the Monte Carlo sampling method is established in microgrid (MG) optimal operation. In [18], a multi-stage stochastic programming method is developed. The bidding strategy in the spot market is described as a Markov decision problem and solved by approximate dual dynamic programming. In [19], the decision-making problem of a retailer under uncertainty is discussed based on stochastic optimization. In [20], the random scenario method is derived to simulate the uncertain spot price and the conditional value at risk is proposed to evaluate the risk of the electricity trading strategy. However, stochastic optimization requires repeated sampling and the solution efficiency is reduced [28].

In addition, the work in [29] states that besides the random feature, the uncertainty also includes the fuzzy feature. Thus, fuzzy optimization, including fuzzy rough set [21], image fuzzy set [22], neutral particle set [23] and so on, has been studied in the operation of a power system over the past few years. In [24], the authors consider the fuzzy feature of uncertain electricity price, in which the fuzzy feature is approximated with a fuzzy number. In [25], a fuzzy set theory-based MG energy management model is established for price uncertainty. In this model, the uncertain electricity price is characterized by triangular fuzzy numbers. In [26], a risk measurement method based on credibility theory is proposed to evaluate the fuzziness of uncertain wind power. However, few studies have addressed the robust power trading model based on credibility theory in view of the uncertainty of spot price in the electricity market.

On the other hand, the existing research on electricity transaction mainly focuses on the discussion of a return model and the formulation of transaction strategy. For example, In [30], the transaction strategy of the power retailer in the spot market is analyzed and the profit model of the retailer under the background of new power reform is discussed. In [31], a deterministic multi-objective optimization model with the goal of profit maximization and peak demand minimization is established to study the short-term decision-making problem of the retailer. In [32], the optimal bidding strategy of an energy hub in the power market is studied under the protection of energy network information privacy. These studies do not take into account the risk assessment of retailers in electricity trading. In [33], a risk decision-making model of electricity transaction with the goal of profit maximization is established. The model analyzes the impact of different electricity transaction combinations on profits from the retailer's point of view. In [34], a risk management model for DSO portfolio with multiple electricity purchase markets is constructed. The impact of different risk appetites on transaction strategy is studied. In [35], the retailer tries to hedge against uncertainty through three trading platforms. The electricity price uncertainty is modeled with the auto regressive integrated moving average method and the retailer's electricity transaction strategy is determined. In [36], based on the portfolio optimization theory, the optimization model of electricity purchase and sale portfolio is constructed to explore the influence of different factors on the purchase and sale risk in the multi-level electricity market. However, in most cases, DSO is not only responsible for trading electricity but also should consider the operational constraints of the distribution system. Therefore, it is necessary to consider network topology as well as power flow constraints of the distribution system when selecting electricity purchase transactions.

Table 1 reports the majority of the studies presented within the last decade; however, most of the existing electricity purchase strategies do not take into account the topological constraints of the network. In addition, to the best of the authors' knowledge of this paper, there are no studies in the literature addressing the robust electricity trading model based on credibility theory in view of the uncertainty of spot price in the electricity market.

**Table 1.** Taxonomy of recent research works.

| Literature | Network Topology Constraint | Deterministic Optimization Model | Risk Assessment Model | Robust Optimization | Stochastic Optimization | Fuzzy Optimization |
|---|---|---|---|---|---|---|
| 11–15 | ✗ | ✗ | ✓ | ✓ | ✗ | ✗ |
| 16–20 | ✗ | ✗ | ✓ | ✗ | ✓ | ✗ |
| 21–26 | ✗ | ✗ | ✓ | ✗ | ✗ | ✓ |
| 30–32 | ✓ | ✓ | ✗ | ✗ | ✗ | ✗ |
| 33–36 | ✗ | ✗ | ✓ | ✗ | ✓ | ✗ |
| The proposed method | ✓ | ✓ | ✓ | ✓ | ✗ | ✓ |

### 1.2. Our Contributions

To address the above issues, this paper develops a risk aversion DSO electricity transaction model based on the credibility theory. The proposed model can help decision makers determine the optimal combination of electricity purchase transactions under an acceptable risk level, considering the uncertain electricity price and power flow constraints when formulating electricity transaction strategy. The main contributions of this paper are as follows:

- Based on credibility theory, a risk aversion-based fuzzy chance constraint model is proposed. In the model, the uncertain spot price is designed as a fuzzy variable and its credibility distribution is derived to assess the uncertain risk. The proposed model optimizes the credibility that the expected objective is met, from which decision makers can assess the risk of transaction strategy.
- Multiple transactions, including the spot market, option contract and bilateral contract, are considered to hedge the risk caused by uncertain price, and the impact of different electricity transaction combinations on DSO cost is analyzed while considering power flow constraints.
- A clear equivalence class method with fuzzy chance constraint is used to transform the proposed model into a deterministic robust optimization model. The effectiveness of the model is verified with a modified 15-node network.

### 1.3. Organization of the Research

The rest of this paper is organized as follows. The credibility function associated with forecast error percentage of spot price is derived in Section 2. The multiple electricity transactions model is established in Section 3. A credibility theory-based robust optimization model to hedge uncertain spot price of DSO with multiple transactions is proposed in Section 4. Case studies and related analysis are introduced in Section 5. Finally, this paper concludes in Section 6.

## 2. Problem Formulation

Fuzzy decision-making is a kind of method to solve problems with fuzzy nature, but the traditional fuzzy decision-making has not established a complete axiomatic system. This leads to unconvincing decision-making conclusions until the credibility theory-based uncertainty measurement is established. It makes up for the disadvantage that possibility measure does not have self-duality [37] and provides a new tool for scholars to study fuzzy decision-making problems. In credibility theory, the credibility measure is developed to describe the credibility of fuzzy events [38]. It holds that events with credibility 1 must occur and events with credibility 0 do not occur, which avoids the decision-making confusion that may be caused by the traditional calculation of membership degree.

The credibility measure can be expressed by the minimum supremum of variable in a fuzzy event set. For any set $A \in \mathfrak{R}$, the credibility measure of fuzzy variable $\xi \in A$ is defined as [39]:

$$\mathrm{Cr}\{\xi \in A\} = \frac{1}{2}\left(\sup_{x \in A} \mu(x) + 1 - \sup_{x \in A^c} \mu(x)\right) \tag{1}$$

where $\sup_{x \in A} \mu(x)$ and $1 - \sup_{x \in A^c} \mu(x)$ denote the possibility measure and necessity measure of $A$, respectively. $A^c$ represents the complement of the set $A$, and $\mu$ is the membership function of the fuzzy variable. The average value of the possibility measure and the necessity measure in Equation (1) is used to ensure the establishment of duality. In addition, the credibility measure satisfies the following four axioms:

***Axiom 1.*** for a non-empty set $\Theta \in \mathfrak{R}$, $\mathrm{Cr}\{\Theta\} = 1$.
***Axiom 2.*** $\mathrm{Cr}\{A\} \leq \mathrm{Cr}\{B\}$ whenever $A \subseteq B \subseteq \Theta$.
***Axiom 3.*** $\mathrm{Cr}\{A\} + \mathrm{Cr}\{A^c\} = 1$ for any event $A \subseteq \Theta$.
***Axiom 4.*** $\mathrm{Cr}\{\cup_i A_i\} = \sup_i \mathrm{Cr}\{A_i\}$ for any collection of events $\{A_i\}$with $\sup_i \mathrm{Cr}\{A_i\} < 0.5$.

In this paper, the uncertain spot price is designed as a fuzzy variable and the credibility distribution function including possibility measure and necessity measure is derived to evaluate the uncertain risk. The uncertain risk measurement model based on credibility theory also satisfies these four axioms.

### *Credibility Distribution Function Associated with Forecast Error Percentage of Spot Price*

In electricity transactions, there are inevitable errors in the forecast of spot price [40]. Assume that the forecast error percentage of spot price is $\varepsilon$ and the mathematical expression is as follows:

$$\varepsilon = \left(\lambda_t^{\mathrm{sm}} - \lambda_t^{\mathrm{sm}\prime}\right) / \lambda_t^{\mathrm{sm}\prime} \tag{2}$$

where $\lambda_t^{\mathrm{sm}}$ and $\lambda_t^{\mathrm{sm}\prime}$ are the actual spot price and the forecast spot price, respectively.

The membership function $\mu$ associated with forecast error percentage of spot price can be expressed as the Cauchy distribution [24]. The uncertain spot price is taken as the fuzzy variable and its mathematical expression can be described as:

$$\mu = \begin{cases} \dfrac{1}{1 + \omega(\varepsilon/E_+)^2}, & \varepsilon > 0 \\ \dfrac{1}{1 + \omega(\varepsilon/E_-)^2}, & \varepsilon \leq 0 \end{cases} \tag{3}$$

where $E_+$ and $E_-$, respectively, represent the statistical average of positive and negative error percentages and $\omega$ is the weighting factor.

After derivation, we can obtain the credibility function of ε:

$$\mathrm{Cr}(\xi \leqslant \varepsilon) = \begin{cases} 1 - \dfrac{1}{2\left[1+\omega(\varepsilon/E_+)^2\right]}, & \varepsilon > 0 \\ \dfrac{1}{2\left[1+\omega(\varepsilon/E_-)^2\right]}, & \varepsilon \leqslant 0 \end{cases} \tag{4}$$

**Proof.** According to Equation (1), for $\varepsilon \in \Re$, the mathematical expression of the credibility measure is

$$\mathrm{Cr}\{\varepsilon\} = \frac{1}{2}\left(\sup_{y\leq\varepsilon}\mu(x) + 1 - \sup_{y>\varepsilon}\mu(x)\right) \tag{5}$$

If $\varepsilon > 0$, we have

$$\begin{aligned} \sup_{y\leq\varepsilon}\mu(y) &= \max\left\{\sup_{0<y\leq\varepsilon}\mu(y), \sup_{y\leq 0}\mu(y)\right\} \\ &= \max\{\mu(0),\mu(0)\} = 1 \end{aligned} \tag{6}$$

and

$$\sup_{y>\varepsilon}\mu(y) = \sup_{y>\varepsilon>0}\frac{1}{1+\omega(y/E_+)^2} = \frac{1}{1+\omega(\varepsilon/E_+)^2} \tag{7}$$

Combining Equations (6) and (7), if $\varepsilon > 0$, we have

$$\mathrm{Cr}(\varepsilon) = 1 - \frac{1}{2\left[1+\omega(\varepsilon/E_+)^2\right]}. \tag{8}$$

If $\varepsilon \leq 0$, we have

$$\sup_{y\leq\varepsilon}\mu(y) = \sup_{y\leq\varepsilon\leq 0}\frac{1}{1+\omega\left(y/(E_-)^2\right)} = \frac{1}{1+\omega\left(\varepsilon/(E_-)^2\right)} \tag{9}$$

and

$$\begin{aligned} \sup_{y>\varepsilon}\mu(y) &= \max\left\{\sup_{y\leqslant\varepsilon\leqslant 0}\mu(y), \sup_{y>0}\mu(y)\right\} \\ &= \max\left\{\sup_{y\leqslant\varepsilon\leqslant 0}\frac{1}{1+\omega\left(y/(E_-)^2\right)}, \sup_{y>0}\frac{1}{1+\omega(y/E_-)^2}\right\} \\ &= \mu(0) = 1. \end{aligned} \tag{10}$$

Combining Equations (9) and (10), if $\varepsilon \leq 0$, we have

$$\mathrm{Cr}(\varepsilon) = \frac{1}{2\left[1+\omega\left(\varepsilon/(E_-)^2\right)\right]}. \tag{11}$$

This completes the proof. □

The credibility and membership functions associated with forecast error percentage of spot price are shown in Figure 1, where $E_+ = 10\%$, $E_- = -10\%$, $\omega = 0.33$ and $\varepsilon \in [-0.5, 0.5]$. From the figure, we can see that the credibility function $\mathrm{Cr}(\xi \leqslant \varepsilon)$ is a monotone increasing function. The value of the credibility distribution function refers to the credibility of the fuzzy variable $\xi$ whose value is less than or equal to $\varepsilon$, which can be compared to the probability distribution function of probability theory.

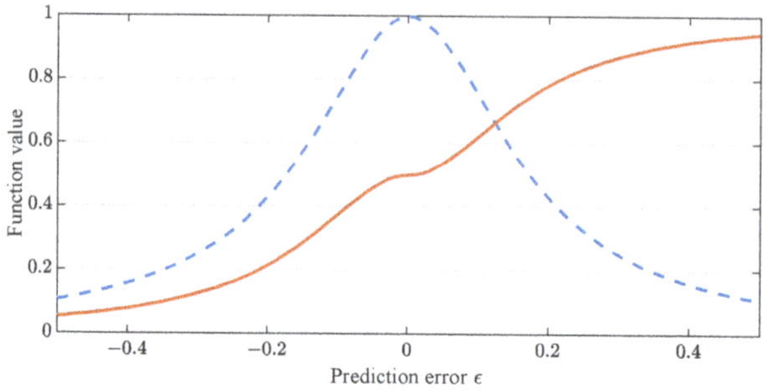


**Figure 1.** Credibility and membership functions associated with forecast error percentage of spot price.

## 3. Multiple Electricity Transaction Model under the Deterministic Spot Price

### 3.1. Objective Function

DSO conducts electricity transaction through the spot market, bilateral contract and option contract. Consider $T$ hour periods and $T_1$ and $T_2$ to be, respectively, the peak and non-peak period sets of power demand, satisfying $T_1 + T_2 = T$. Call option contract is only for $T_1$ and trading volume does not change over time. In addition, suppose there are $N$ bilateral contracts for DSO to choose and the details of the electricity transaction cost are as follows.

(1). The mathematical expression of DSO's cost function $C_{\text{sm}}$ in spot market is as follows:

$$C_{\text{sm}} = \sum_{t \in T} \sum_{b \in B} \left[ \lambda_t^{\text{sm}} p_{t,b}^{\text{sm}} \right] \tag{12}$$

where $b \in B$ is the range of network node. $\lambda_t^{\text{sm}}$ and $p_{t,b}^{\text{sm}}$ are the electricity price and trading volume of DSO in spot market during time $t$, respectively.

(2). The cost function $C_{\text{bc}}$ of DSO in the bilateral contract electricity transaction can be expressed as:

$$C_{\text{bc}} = \sum_{t \in T_1} \sum_{b \in B} \sum_{n \in N} \left[ \lambda_n^{\text{bc}} p_{t,b,n}^{\text{bc}} \right] \tag{13}$$

where $\lambda_n^{\text{bc}}$ is the electricity price with respect to bilateral contract $n$ and $p_{t,b,n}^{\text{bc}}$ is the trading volume of $n$th bilateral contract selected by node $b$ during time $t$.

(3). The cost function $C_{\text{oc}}$ of DSO from the option contract electricity transaction can be calculated as:

$$C_{\text{oc}} = \sum_{t \in T_2} \sum_{b \in B} \left[ \min\{\lambda_{\text{ck}}, \lambda_t^{\text{sm}}\} p_{t,b}^{\text{oc}} + \lambda_0 p_{t,b}^{\text{oc}} \right] \tag{14}$$

where $p_{t,b}^{\text{oc}}$ is the call option contract trading volume of node $b$ during time $t$, $\lambda_{\text{ck}}$ and $\lambda_0$ are the strike price and premium of the call option, respectively. If $\lambda_t^{\text{sm}} > \lambda_{\text{ck}}$, DSO executes the option contract and its option contract purchases electricity at the fixed price; if $\lambda_t^{\text{sm}} < \lambda_{\text{ck}}$, DSO abandons the exercise option and its option contract purchases electricity at the spot market price.

(4). The power generation cost function $C_{\text{dg}}$ of DSO can be expressed as:

$$C_{\text{dg}} = \sum_{t \in T} \sum_{b \in B} \left[ \lambda^{\text{dg}} p_{t,b} \right] \tag{15}$$

where $p_{t,b}$ is the active power output of DG at node $b$ during time $t$ and $\lambda^{dg}$ is the power generation cost price of DG.

The mathematical expression of the cost $C$ of the DSO with the spot market, option contract and bilateral contract in an electricity transaction is as follows:

$$C = C_{sm} + C_{bc} + C_{oc} + C_{dg} \tag{16}$$

*3.2. Constraints*

In order to ensure that the system operates in a safe and reliable environment, the electricity transaction must meet the following constraints.

(1). Active power output constraint of DG:

$$0 \leq p_{t,b} \leq P_{t,b}^{max} \tag{17}$$

where $P_{t,b}^{max}$ is the maximum active power output of DG at node $b$ during time $t$.

(2). Node voltage constraint:

$$v_{t,b}^{min} \leq v_{t,b} \leq v_{t,b}^{max} \tag{18}$$

where $v_{t,b}$ is the square of the voltage at node $b$ during time $t$. $v_{t,b}^{min}$ and $v_{t,b}^{max}$ are the maximum and minimum values of node voltage at node $b$ during time $t$, respectively.

(3). Contract volume constraint for bilateral contract:

$$p_n^{bc,min} s_{b,n} \leq p_{t,b,n}^{bc} \leq p_n^{bc,max} s_{b,n} \tag{19}$$

where $s_{b,n}$ is a binary variable. If node $b$ selects contract $n$, then $s_{b,n} = 1$; otherwise, $s_{b,n} = 0$. $p_n^{bc,min}$, $p_n^{bc,max}$ are the minimum and maximum contract volumes of bilateral contract $n$, respectively.

(4). During time $t$, the total amount of electricity purchased in spot market, bilateral contract and option contract of DSO equals the amount of active power injected from the power grid. Its mathematical expression can be described as:

$$p_{t,b}^{sm} + \sum_{n \in N} p_{t,b,n}^{bc} = P_{t,b}^{grid}, \forall t \in T_1 \tag{20}$$

$$p_{t,b}^{sm} + \sum_{n \in N} p_{t,b,n}^{bc} + p_{t,b}^{oc} = P_{t,b}^{grid}, \forall t \in T_2 \tag{21}$$

where $P_{t,b}^{grid}$ is the amount of active power injected from the power grid at node $b$ during time $t$.

(5). The power flow constraints of the distribution network are as follows:

$$f_{t,l|s(l)=b}^{p} - P_{t,b}^{grid} - \sum_{l|r(l)=b} \left(f_{t,l}^{p} - a_{t,l}R_l\right) - p_{t,b} + D_{t,b}^{p} + G_b v_{t,b} = 0 \tag{22}$$

$$f_{t,l|s(l)=b}^{q} - Q_{t,b}^{grid} - \sum_{l|r(l)=b} \left(f_{t,l}^{q} - a_{t,l}X_l\right) - q_{t,b} + D_{t,b}^{q} - B_b v_{t,b} = 0 \tag{23}$$

$$v_{t,b} - 2\left(R_l f_{t,l}^{p} + X_l f_{t,l}^{q}\right) + a_{t,l}\left(R_l^2 + X_l^2\right) = v_{t,b} \tag{24}$$

$$\left(f_{t,l}^{p} - a_{t,l}R_{t,l}\right)^2 + \left(f_{t,l}^{q} - a_{t,l}X_{t,l}\right)^2 \leq S_{t,l}^2 \tag{25}$$

$$\left(\left(f_{t,l}^{p}\right)^2 + \left(f_{t,l}^{q}\right)^2\right) / a_{t,l} \leq v_{t,b} \tag{26}$$

$$\left(f_{t,l}^{p}\right)^2 + \left(f_{t,l}^{q}\right)^2 \leq S_{t,l}^2 \tag{27}$$

where $l \in L$ is the range of network line. $f^{\mathrm{p}}_{t,l}$, $f^{\mathrm{q}}_{t,l}$ are the active and reactive power flow of line $l$ during time $t$, respectively. $D^{p}_{t,b}$ and $D^{q}_{t,b}$ are the active load and reactive load of node $b$ during time $t$, respectively. $a_{t,l}$ is the square of the current of line $l$ during time $t$. $Q^{\mathrm{grid}}_{t,b}$ is the reactive power injected from the power grid at node $b$ during time $t$. $S^{2}_{t,l}$ is the upper limit of the apparent power of line $l$ during time $t$, and $R_l$, $X_l$, $G_b$ and $B_b$ are the parameters of resistance, reactance, admittance and conductance of distribution network, respectively. $s(l)$ is the power outflow end of line $l$ and $r(l)$ is the power inflow end of line $l$. The balance constraints of active and reactive power are shown in Equations (22) and (23). Equation (24) relates the line flow to the node voltage. Equation (25) represents the apparent power flow limitation of each line transmitting node and Equation (26) is a quadratic curve constraint, which convexes the original non-convex AC OPF problem [41]. Under quite unrestricted assumptions, the rationality of this convexity is proved in [42]. Equation (27) represents the apparent power flow limitation of each line receiving node.

## 4. Robust Optimization Model for DSO Based on Credibility Theory

The forecast error of spot price is inevitable [43]. DSO with different risk preferences needs to hedge the risk caused by forecast error while considering operational cost as well as power flow constraints. Given a certain electricity purchase cost, DSO pursues an electricity transaction strategy that maximizes resistance to the uncertain spot price. In view of this, this paper establishes a credibility theory-based robust optimization model to hedge price uncertainty of DSO with multiple transactions.

$$\max |\varepsilon| \tag{28a}$$

$$\text{s.t.}\begin{cases} \mathrm{Cr}(\max C(\lambda_t^{\mathrm{sm}}, q) \le C_{\mathrm{e}}) \ge \alpha & (28\mathrm{b}) \\ C_{\mathrm{e}} = (1+\sigma)C_0 & (28\mathrm{c}) \\ \lambda_t^{\mathrm{sm}} = (1+\varepsilon)\lambda_t^{\mathrm{sm}\prime} & (28\mathrm{d}) \\ 0 \le \sigma \le 1 & (28\mathrm{e}) \\ 0 \le \alpha \le 1 & (28\mathrm{f}) \\ (17) - (27) & (28\mathrm{g}) \end{cases}$$

where $C_0$ is the minimum cost of DSO when the spot price equals the forecasted spot price. $\sigma$ is the risk aversion factor, which indicates the DSO's aversion to the risk due to the uncertain spot price. $\alpha$ is the credibility index and the physical meaning is equivalent to the probability confidence. Equation (28b) is expressed as the credibility that the actual cost of DSO less than the expected cost is not less than $\alpha$. Equation (28c) represents the expected cost of DSO. When $\sigma$ is larger, expected cost $C_{\mathrm{e}}$ is higher, indicating that DSO has a greater degree of risk aversion. $q$ is the decision variable, which represents the amount of electricity traded by DSO in each market.

Generally, when the actual spot price takes the maximum, the DSO's cost is the highest, so Equation (28b) can be expressed as

$$\mathrm{Cr}\Big( C(\lambda_t^{\mathrm{sm}}, q)|_{\lambda_t^{\mathrm{sm}}=(1+\varepsilon)\lambda_t^{\mathrm{sm}\prime}} \le C_{\mathrm{e}} \Big) \ge \alpha, \quad \varepsilon \ge 0 \tag{29}$$

In view of the fact that the above formula belongs to the fuzzy chance constraint and it is difficult to solve directly, one way to solve the fuzzy chance constraint is to convert it into a clear equivalence class and then use the traditional solving process to calculate the clear equivalence model. According to [44], we can obtain the following theorem:

**Theorem 1.** *Suppose $\xi$ is degenerated into a one-dimensional fuzzy variable and its membership function is $\mu$. If the function $g(\mathbf{x},\xi)$ has the form $g(\mathbf{x},\xi) = h(\mathbf{x}) - \xi$, then $\mathrm{Cr}\{g(\mathbf{x},\xi) \leq 0\} \geq \alpha$, if and only if $h(\mathbf{x}) \leq K_\alpha$, where $\mathbf{x}$ and $g$ are the decision vector and constraint, respectively. Moreover,*

$$K_\alpha = \begin{cases} \sup\Big\{K \mid K = \mu^{-1}(2\alpha)\Big\}, & \alpha < 1/2 \\ \inf\Big\{K \mid K = \mu^{-1}(2(1-\alpha))\Big\}, & \alpha \geq 1/2 \end{cases} \tag{30}$$

When $\varepsilon \geq 0$, $\alpha \geq 1/2$, according to the credibility measure function and the above theorem, the robust optimization model shown in Equation (28) can be expressed as

$$\max K_\alpha \tag{31a}$$

$$\text{s.t.} \begin{cases} C(\lambda_t^{\mathrm{sm}}, q)|_{\lambda_t^{\mathrm{sm}} = (1+K_\alpha)\lambda_t^{\mathrm{sm}\prime}} \leq C_{\mathrm{e}} & (31b) \\ C_{\mathrm{e}} = (1+\sigma)C_0 & (31c) \\ 0 \leq \sigma \leq 1 & (31d) \\ K_\alpha = \mu^{-1}(2(1-\alpha)) \geq 0 & (31e) \\ 1/2 \leq \alpha \leq 1 & (31f) \\ (17)-(27) & (31g) \end{cases}$$

The model considers that the actual spot price fluctuates within a certain range of the predicted spot price. The obtained electricity transaction strategy can ensure that the cost of DSO is less than the expected cost and the credibility is not less than $\alpha$. The solution process of the proposed method is given by Algorithm 1.

**Algorithm 1** Solution process

1: Given system data and forecasted spot price;
2: Considering constraints (17)–(27), calculate (16) to obtain the minimum cost $C_0$ of DSO with predicted spot price;
3: Give DSO risk aversion factor $\sigma$ or expected cost $C_e$;
4: Obtain the membership function associated with forecast error percentage of spot price according to the credibility theory and derive its credibility distribution;
5: By maximizing (28a) and considering constraints (28b)–(28g), a risk measurement model under fuzzy chance constraints is established;
6: Use the clear equivalence class method to transform the above model into a deterministic robust optimization model;
7: Solve the robust optimization model through the SCIP solver and obtain $\varepsilon, \alpha$, $p_{t,b}^{\mathrm{sm}}, p_{t,b}^{\mathrm{oc}}, p_{t,b,n}^{\mathrm{bc}}$.

## 5. Case Analysis

To prove the validity of the proposed model, a modified 15-node distribution network system is selected for numerical study in this paper and the structure of the distribution network system is shown in Figure 2 (the specific parameters are in [45]). Two DGs are set at nodes 1 and 12, respectively. The capacity of each DG is set to 0.15 MW and their power generation cost is USD 30/MWh. The forecast spot price and distribution system load are shown in Figure 3. Suppose that the peak period of electricity consumption is $8:00 \sim 24:00$ and the rest of the period is non-peak period. The call option strike price $\lambda_{\mathrm{ck}}$ = USD 64.3/MWh and the option premium $\lambda_0$ = USD 2.3/MWh. In addition, set the weighting factor $\omega = 0.33$ in the credibility function.

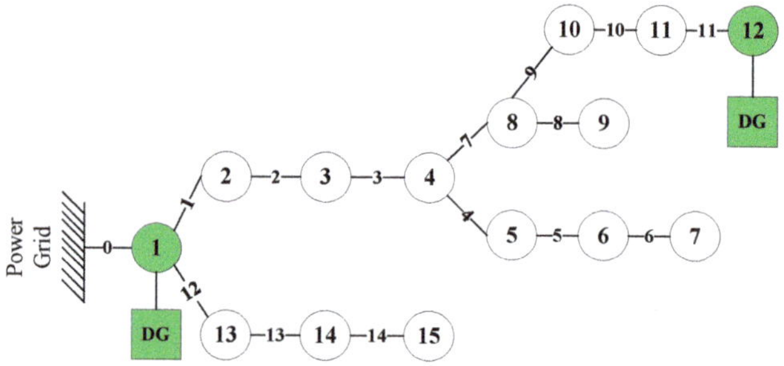


**Figure 2.** The 15-node network structure diagram.

In the competitive power market, the cost of DSO depends on its own power generation and power purchase plan. DSO can purchase electricity through different combinations of spot market, option contract and bilateral contract. Assume that DSO has five bilateral contracts to choose from non-peak and peak periods, respectively. The detailed parameters of the bilateral contract are shown in Table 2. In order to verify the effectiveness of the credibility theory-based robust optimization model to hedge price uncertainty, this paper selects different electricity transaction scenarios. Scenario 1, DSO only purchases electricity through the spot market; scenario 2, DSO purchases electricity through the spot market and option contract; scenario 3, DSO purchases electricity through the spot market, bilateral contract and option contract.

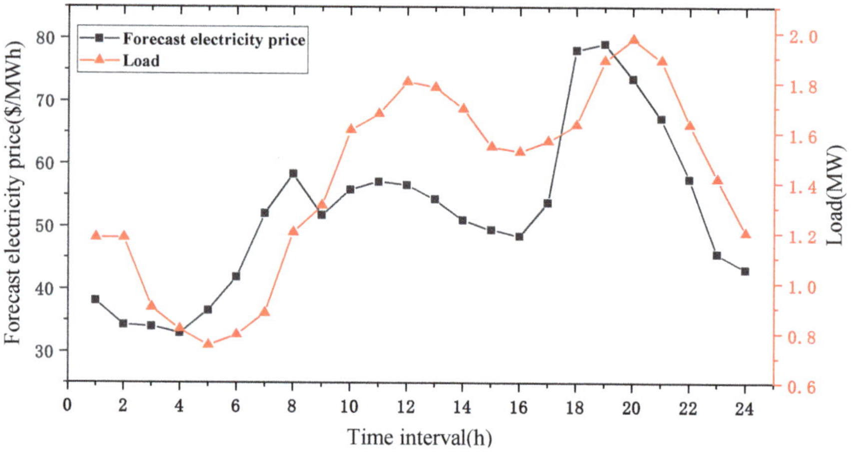


**Figure 3.** Forecast spot price and distribution system load.

**Table 2.** Bilateral contract parameters.

| Contract Number | Period (h) | Min (MW) | Max (MW) | Contract Price (USD/MWh) |
|---|---|---|---|---|
| 1 | Non-peak period | 0.006 | 0.015 | 43.0 |
| 2 | Non-peak period | 0.008 | 0.020 | 42.0 |
| 3 | Non-peak period | 0.010 | 0.025 | 38.0 |
| 4 | Non-peak period | 0.010 | 0.030 | 35.5 |
| 5 | Non-peak period | 0.012 | 0.040 | 33.0 |
| 6 | Peak period | 0.006 | 0.015 | 63.5 |
| 7 | Peak period | 0.008 | 0.020 | 62.0 |
| 8 | Peak period | 0.010 | 0.025 | 59.5 |
| 9 | Peak period | 0.010 | 0.030 | 58.5 |
| 10 | Peak period | 0.012 | 0.040 | 56.0 |

### *5.1. Comparison of Transaction Cost under Deterministic Spot Electricity Price*

First of all, it is assumed that the actual spot price equals the predicted value. The minimum cost of DSO is obtained by solving the deterministic electricity transaction model. The optimal DSO electricity transactions in different scenarios are shown in Figure 4. In scenario 1, DG output is 7.20 WMh, the spot market purchase is 26.48 MWh and the cost of DSO is USD 1684.0. In scenario 2, DG output is 7.20 WMh, the spot market and option contract purchase are 13.70 MWh and 12.78 MWh, respectively, and the cost of DSO is USD 1682.5. In scenario 3, the option contract purchase is 8.09 MWh, the bilateral contract purchase is 6.42 MWh, the DG output is 7.20 MWh, the spot market purchase is 11.96 MWh and the cost of DSO is USD 1655.6. It can be seen that with the increase of transaction form, the electricity purchase cost of DSO gradually decreases.

For scenario 3, DSO's DG output and electricity transaction in spot market, bilateral contract and option contract are shown in Figure 5. As can be seen from the figure, the non-peak period electricity transaction market is mainly in the spot market and bilateral contract and peak period electricity transaction market is mainly in the spot market and option contract. Overall, DG output, bilateral contract, spot market and option contract accounted for 21.4%, 19.1%, 35.5% and 24.0% of the total electricity consumption, respectively. The bilateral contract trading volume of each node is shown in Table 3.We can see that bilateral contract transaction is mainly in nodes 2 and 13. Nodes 2 and 13 choose contracts 3, 4, 5, 7, 8, 9, 10 to trade electricity. This is because these two nodes have a high load demand and multiple bilateral contracts can be selected to meet their own demand. The other nodes with low load demand only choose a bilateral contract to trade electricity during peak and non-peak periods. In addition, since the load demand of node 14 is too small, there is no suitable bilateral contract for it to choose, so it meets its own demand through the spot market and option contract.

**Table 3.** Bilateral contract trading volume of each node.

| Nodes | Contract Number | | | | | | | | | |
|---|---|---|---|---|---|---|---|---|---|---|
| | **1** | **2** | **3** | **4** | **5** | **6** | **7** | **8** | **9** | **10** |
| 1 | - | - | - | - | - | - | - | - | - | - |
| 2 | 0 | 0 | 0.115 | 0.150 | 0.252 | 0 | 0.184 | 0.230 | 0.250 | 0.428 |
| 3 | 0 | 0 | 0 | 0 | 0 | 0 | 0 | 0 | 0 | 0.273 |
| 4 | 0 | 0 | 0 | 0 | 0 | 0 | 0 | 0 | 0 | 0.273 |
| 5 | 0 | 0 | 0 | 0 | 0 | 0 | 0 | 0 | 0.207 | 0 |
| 6 | 0 | 0 | 0 | 0 | 0.112 | 0 | 0 | 0 | 0 | 0.347 |
| 7 | 0 | 0 | 0 | 0 | 0 | 0 | 0 | 0 | 0 | 0.288 |
| 8 | 0 | 0 | 0 | 0 | 0 | 0 | 0 | 0 | 0 | 0.288 |
| 9 | 0 | 0 | 0 | 0.081 | 0 | 0 | 0 | 0 | 0 | 0.301 |
| 10 | 0 | 0 | 0 | 0.080 | 0 | 0 | 0 | 0 | 0 | 0.296 |
| 11 | 0 | 0 | 0 | 0 | 0 | 0 | 0 | 0 | 0 | 0.286 |
| 12 | 0 | 0 | 0 | 0 | 0 | 0 | 0 | 0 | 0 | 0 |
| 13 | 0 | 0 | 0.115 | 0.150 | 0.252 | 0 | 0.184 | 0.230 | 0.250 | 0.428 |
| 14 | 0 | 0 | 0 | 0 | 0 | 0 | 0 | 0 | 0 | 0 |
| 15 | 0 | 0 | 0 | 0.079 | 0 | 0 | 0 | 0 | 0 | 0.292 |

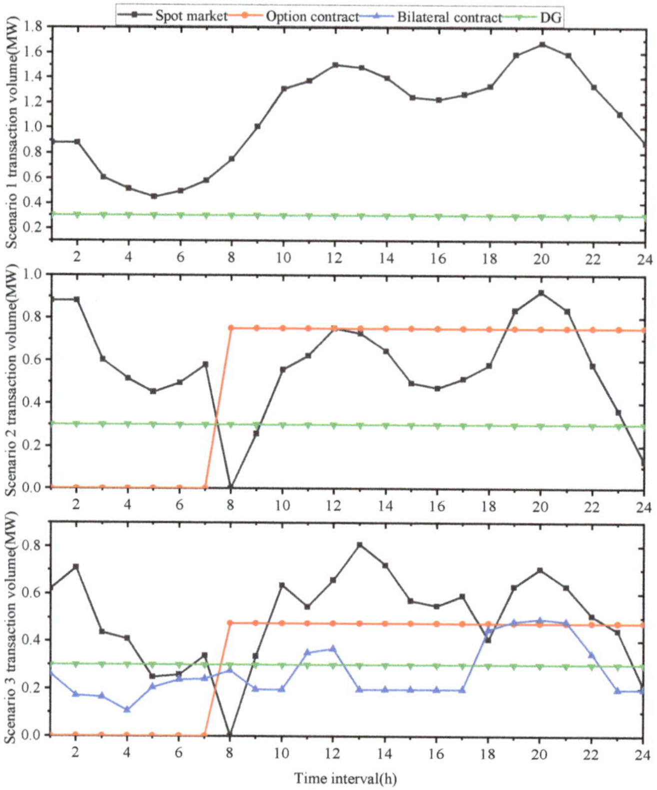


**Figure 4.** DSO electricity transaction strategy in different scenarios.

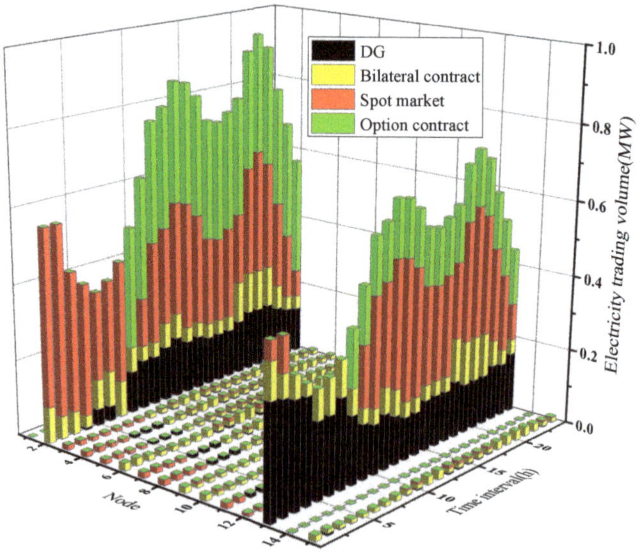


**Figure 5.** DSO electricity trading volume in each market.

### 5.2. Robust Optimization Model to Hedge Price Uncertainty of DSO with Multiple Transactions

Assuming that the risk aversion factor $\sigma$ is 0.1 in scenario 3, the calculated resistible percentage of prediction error is 24.6% and the credibility is 0.83. In this case, if the forecast error percentage of spot price is within the range [0, 24.6%], the cost of DSO is less than or equal to USD 1821.16. If the forecast error percentage of spot price exceeds this range, the actual cost cannot be guaranteed. The electricity transaction strategy of DSO is shown in Figure 6. The credibility associated with the actual cost lower than the expected cost is 0.83, from which the decision maker can assess the risk of the trading strategy.

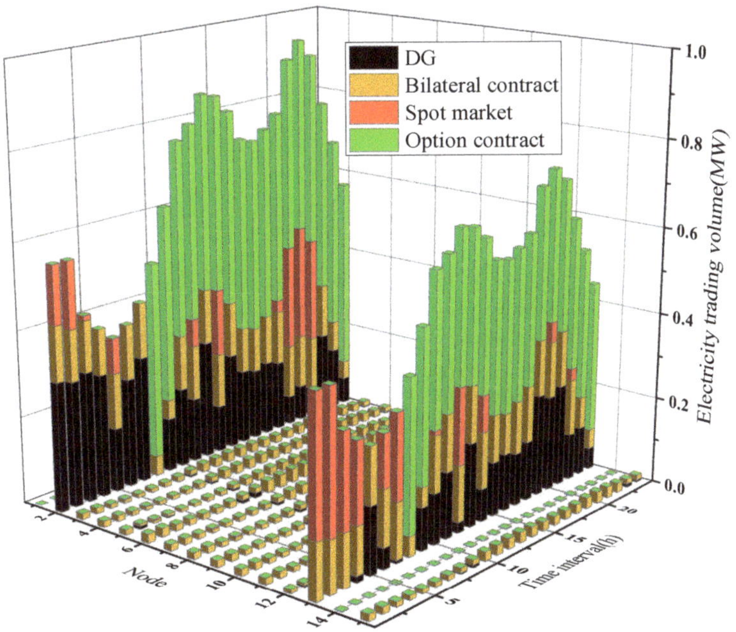


**Figure 6.** Electricity transaction strategy when the risk aversion factor is 0.1.

As can be seen in Figure 6, the load demand of DSO at non-peak period is mainly satisfied through DG output and electricity purchase in spot market, while at peak period it is mainly satisfied through option contract and power purchase in spot market. In 24 h, the option contract purchase is 13.77 MWh, accounting for 40.90%; the bilateral contract purchase is 9.99 MWh, accounting for 29.67%; the DG output is 6.76 MWh, accounting for 20.08%; and the spot market purchase is 3.15 MWh, accounting for 9.35%. Comparing with Figure 5, it can be seen that considering the uncertainty of spot price, the trading volume of the bilateral contract and the option contract increase, the spot market trading volume decreases and the output of DG decreases slightly.

The bilateral contract trading volume of each node under the uncertainty of spot price is shown in Table 4. We can see that the bilateral contract transaction is still mainly in nodes 2 and 13, but they choose contracts 1–10 to trade electricity and other nodes have also increased the trading volume of bilateral contract. Comparing with the electricity purchase strategy in the deterministic environment, it can be found that in order to reduce the risk caused by the uncertainty of the spot price, DSO increases the trading volume of bilateral contract and option contract.

**Table 4.** The bilateral contract transaction value of each node under the uncertainty of spot price.

| Nodes | Contract Number | | | | | | | | | |
|---|---|---|---|---|---|---|---|---|---|---|
| | 1 | 2 | 3 | 4 | 5 | 6 | 7 | 8 | 9 | 10 |
| 1 | - | - | - | - | - | - | - | - | - | - |
| 2 | 0.078 | 0.128 | 0.175 | 0.210 | 0.280 | 0.192 | 0.265 | 0.363 | 0.430 | 0.596 |
| 3 | 0 | 0.077 | 0 | 0 | 0 | 0 | 0 | 0 | 0 | 0.324 |
| 4 | 0 | 0.077 | 0 | 0 | 0 | 0 | 0 | 0 | 0 | 0.324 |
| 5 | 0.056 | 0 | 0 | 0 | 0 | 0 | 0 | 0 | 0.273 | 0 |
| 6 | 0 | 0 | 0 | 0 | 0.115 | 0 | 0 | 0 | 0 | 0.440 |
| 7 | 0 | 0.083 | 0 | 0 | 0 | 0 | 0 | 0 | 0 | 0.349 |
| 8 | 0 | 0.083 | 0 | 0 | 0 | 0 | 0 | 0 | 0 | 0.343 |
| 9 | 0 | 0 | 0 | 0.093 | 0 | 0 | 0 | 0 | 0 | 0.372 |
| 10 | 0 | 0 | 0 | 0.090 | 0 | 0 | 0 | 0 | 0 | 0.356 |
| 11 | 0 | 0.083 | 0 | 0 | 0 | 0 | 0 | 0 | 0 | 0.347 |
| 12 | 0.047 | 0 | 0 | 0 | 0 | 0 | 0.197 | 0 | 0 | 0 |
| 13 | 0.078 | 0.128 | 0.175 | 0.210 | 0.280 | 0.192 | 0.268 | 0.350 | 0.430 | 0.596 |
| 14 | 0 | 0 | 0 | 0 | 0 | 0 | 0 | 0 | 0 | 0 |
| 15 | 0 | 0 | 0 | 0.088 | 0 | 0 | 0 | 0 | 0 | 0.349 |

### 5.3. The Influence of Different Risk Aversion Coefficients of DSO on Electricity Transaction

The curve of electricity transaction strategy with risk aversion factor $\sigma$ is shown in Figure 7. As the value of $\sigma$ increases, the purchase volumes of bilateral contract and option contract increase, the purchase volume in the spot market decreases and DG's output remains basically unchanged. The results show that as the expected cost increases, DSO increases the trading volumes of option contract and fixed-price bilateral contract, while reducing volume in spot market with uncertain price. In this way, the robustness of the electricity transaction strategy is increased.

The changes of robustness and credibility with risk aversion factor in different scenarios are shown in Table 5. It can be seen that the credibility increases as the risk aversion factor increases. This shows that the stronger the risk aversion awareness of DSO, the higher the credibility of the expected goal realization. This is because the greater the risk aversion factor, the higher the expected cost. The robustness factor increases with the increasing of expected cost. This shows that the greater the expected cost of the DSO, the lower the acceptance of risk. The more conservative the electricity purchase strategy, the stronger the ability of the resulting electricity transaction strategy to resist risk.

**Table 5.** The changes of robustness coefficient and credibility with risk aversion factors in different scenarios.

| $\sigma$ | Scenario 1 | | Scenario 2 | | Scenario 3 | |
|---|---|---|---|---|---|---|
| | $\varepsilon$ | Credibility | $\varepsilon$ | Credibility | $\varepsilon$ | Credibility |
| 0 | 0 | 0.50 | 0 | 0.50 | 0 | 0.50 |
| 0.05 | 6% | 0.55 | 7% | 0.57 | 10% | 0.61 |
| 0.1 | 11% | 0.65 | 14% | 0.70 | 25% | 0.83 |

In scenario 1, DSO only trades electricity from the spot market. In the event of a bad price that is not conducive to the transaction, there is no electricity purchase plan that can replace or avoid market transactions and it has to accept the market risk caused by price uncertainty. Therefore, the system robustness of scenario 1 is lower than those of other scenarios.

In scenario 2, DSO purchases electricity through bilateral contract and the spot market. The use of fixed-price bilateral contract to purchase electricity avoids to a certain extent the market risk caused by the uncertainty of spot price.

In scenario 3, DSO conducts electricity transaction through spot market, option contract and bilateral contract. It has more means to actively control electricity purchase cost and possible risk losses through reasonable selection of transaction combination and allocation of electricity purchase ratio.

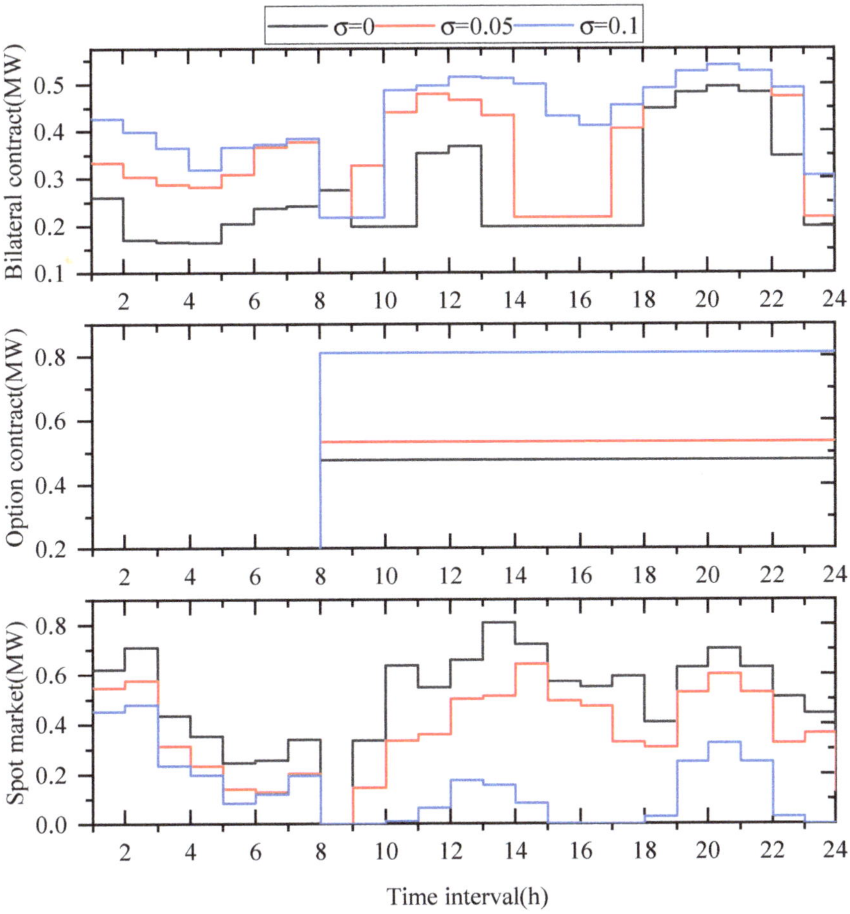


**Figure 7.** The change curve of electric energy trading volume with $\sigma$.

In addition, in order to fully demonstrate the effectiveness of the proposed model in dealing with an uncertain problem, this paper compares the proposed robust optimization model with the robust optimization model (RO) [46] and the stochastic optimization model (SO) [47]. The optimization results obtained by different optimization methods are shown in Table 6.

**Table 6.** Optimization results under different methods.

| | RO | SO | The Proposed Model | | |
|---|---|---|---|---|---|
| | - | - | $\sigma = 0.04$ | $\sigma = 0.05$, | $\sigma = 0.06$ |
| Operation cost | USD 1933.58 | USD 1735.7 | USD 1721.8 | USD 1738.4 | USD 1754.9 |
| Optimization time | 303.3 s | 2310.8 s | 527.5 s | 461.1 s | 694.3 s |

It can be seen from the table that when the risk aversion factor is 0.05, the cost of the proposed model is reduced by 11.2% compared with robust optimization. This is due to the fact that RO is the worst-case cost of uncertain variables and the resulting electricity trading strategy is too conservative. Compared with random optimization, the solution speed is increased by 80.0%. In addition, compared with RO and SO, the proposed model considers the degree of risk aversion of the decision maker and the decision maker can choose the appropriate risk aversion factor according to their ability to bear the risk. In addition, in order for readers to better understand the proposed model, the credibility theory-based robust optimization model for a user is provided in Appendix A.

## 6. Conclusions

Based on the credibility theory, this paper establishes a robust optimization model to hedge price uncertainty of DSO with multiple transactions. This proposed model provides the electricity transaction strategy under different expected cost and the risk-averse DSO achieves the expected goal by rationally allocating the proportion of electricity purchases in different transaction markets. The results of calculation examples show that: (1) Increasing option contract and bilateral contract trading volumes can reduce the electricity transaction cost of DSO by USD 28.5. (2) As the expected cost increases (the degree of risk aversion of DSO increases), DSO will increase the purchase of electricity in option contract and bilateral contract, reduce the trading volume in spot market with uncertain price and increase the robustness of electricity transaction strategy. (3) The proposed robust model takes into account the risk aversion of decision maker and obtains the credibility of the expected goal realization. Compared with random optimization, the solution speed is increased by 80.0%. In addition, under the same risk aversion factor, the cost of the proposed model is reduced by USD 195.18 compared with robust optimization and avoids the over-conservatism of traditional robust optimization. This method provides new tools and ideas for electricity transaction decision maker and risk assessment.

This research work only considers the uncertainty of spot electricity price in electricity transaction. In fact, DSO also faces multiple uncertainties brought by renewable energy and demand. In future research work, we will study how to extend the proposed model to measure the multivariate uncertainty and uncertainty coupling. In order to achieve the goal of energy conservation and emission reduction, the impact of green certificates and carbon emissions trading on electricity trading strategy will be studied in the future.

**Author Contributions:** L.-P.S.: data curation, formal analysis, writing—original draft preparation, validation. J.-J.C.: resources, conceptualization, visualization, formal analysis writing. L.-W.P.: methodology, visualization. Z.-J.Y.: visualization. All authors have read and agreed to the published version of the manuscript.

**Funding:** This research was supported by Shandong Province Natural Science Foundation of China (No. ZR2022ME047).

**Institutional Review Board Statement:** Not applicable.

**Informed Consent Statement:** Not applicable.

**Data Availability Statement:** The data presented in this study are openly available in [45].

**Conflicts of Interest:** The authors report no conflict of interest. The authors alone are responsible for the content and writing of the paper.

## Nomenclature

*Variables* :

| | |
|---|---|
| $\varepsilon$ | forecast error percentage of spot price |
| $\alpha$ | credibility index |
| $\lambda_t^{\mathrm{sm}}$ | actual spot price, USD/MWh |
| $C_{\mathrm{sm}}$ | spot market power purchase cost, USD |
| $C_{\mathrm{bc}}$ | bilateral contract power purchase cost, USD |
| $C_{\mathrm{oc}}$ | option contract power purchase cost, USD |
| $C_{\mathrm{dg}}$ | power generation cost, USD |
| $p_{t,b}^{\mathrm{sm}}$ | trading volume in the spot market, MW |

| | |
|---|---|
| $p_{t,b,n}^{bc}$ | trading volume of $n$th bilateral contract, MW |
| $p_{t,b}^{oc}$ | call option contract trading volume, MW |
| $p_{t,b}$ | active power output of DG, MW |
| $s_{b,n}$ | binary variable |
| *Indexes* : | |
| $b \in B$ | range of network node |
| $l \in L$ | range of network line |
| $t \in T$ | range of time |
| $\lambda_t^{sm\prime}$ | forecast spot price, USD/MWh |
| $\omega$ | weighting factor |
| $E_+, E_-$ | statistical average of positive and negative error percentages |
| $\lambda_n^{bc}$ | electricity price with respect to bilateral contract, USD/MWh |
| $\lambda_{ck}, \lambda_0$ | strike price and premium of the call option, USD/MWh |
| $\lambda^{dg}$ | power generation cost price of DG, USD/MWh |
| $p_{t,b}^{max}$ | maximum active power output of DG, MW |
| $P_{t,b}^{grid}$ | active power injected from the power grid, MW |
| $Q_{t,b}^{grid}$ | reactive power injected from the power grid, MW |
| $a_{t,l}$ | square of the current of line $l$ |
| $S_{t,l}$ | upper limit of the apparent power of line $l$ |
| $s(l)$ | power outflow end of line $l$ |
| $r(l)$ | power inflow end of line $l$ |
| $\sigma$ | risk aversion factor |
| $C_e$ | expected cost of DSO, USD |
| $R_l, X_l$ | resistance and reactance of distribution network |
| $G_b, B_b$ | admittance and conductance of distribution network |
| $p_n^{bc,min}$ | minimum contract volume of bilateral contract, MW |
| $p_n^{bc,max}$ | maximum contract volume of bilateral contract, MW |
| $f_{t,l}^{p}, f_{t,l}^{q}$ | active and reactive power flow |
| $D_{t,b}^{p}, D_{t,b}^{q}$ | active load and reactive load, MW |
| $v_{t,b}^{min}, v_{t,b}^{max}$ | maximum and minimum values of node voltage |

## Appendix A

In this example, we assume that a user needs to buy electricity from the spot market, bilateral contracts, options contracts. The model is as follows:

Determine the optimization model

$$C = \sum_{t \in T}\left[\lambda_t^{sm} p_{t,b}^{sm}\right] + \sum_{t \in T_1}\sum_{n \in N}\left[\lambda_n^{bc} p_{t,b,n}^{bc}\right] + \sum_{t \in T_2}\left[\min\{\lambda_{ck}, \lambda_t^{sm}\} p_{t,b}^{oc} + \lambda_0 p_{t,b}^{oc}\right] \tag{A1}$$

$$p_n^{bc,min} s_n \le p_{t,n}^{bc} \le p_n^{bc,max} s_n \tag{A2}$$

$$p_{t,}^{sm} + \sum_{n \in N} p_{t,n}^{bc} = P_t^{grid}, \forall t \in T_1 \tag{A3}$$

$$p_t^{sm} + \sum_{n \in N} p_{t,n}^{bc} + p_t^{oc} = P_t^{grid}, \forall t \in T_2 \tag{A4}$$

where $\lambda_t^{sm}$ and $p_t^{sm}$ are the electricity price and trading volume of user in spot market during time $t$, respectively. $\lambda_n^{bc}$ is the electricity price with respect to bilateral contract $n$, $p_{t,,n}^{bc}$ is the trading volume of $n$th bilateral contract selected during time $t$. $p_t^{oc}$ is the call option contract trading volume during time $t$, $\lambda_{ck}$ and $\lambda_0$ are the strike price and premium of the call option, respectively. $s_n$ is a binary variable. If user selects contract $n$, then $s_n = 1$, otherwise, $s_n = 0$. Equation (A1) represents the power purchase cost of the user, Equations (A2)–(A4) is the constraint on the user.

The proposed robust optimization model

$$\max|\varepsilon| \tag{A5a}$$

$$\text{s.t.}\begin{cases} \mathrm{Cr}(\max C(\lambda_t^{\mathrm{sm}},q)\le C_\mathrm{e})\ge\alpha & \text{(A5b)}\\ C_\mathrm{e}=(1+\sigma)C_0 & \text{(A5c)}\\ \lambda_t^{\mathrm{sm}}=(1+\varepsilon)\lambda_t^{\mathrm{sm}\prime} & \text{(A5d)}\\ 0\le\sigma\le1 & \text{(A5e)}\\ 0\le\alpha\le1 & \text{(A5f)}\\ (A2)-(A4) & \text{(A5g)} \end{cases}$$

where $C_0$ is the minimum cost of user when the spot price equals the forecasted spot price, $\sigma$ is the risk aversion factor, which indicates the user's aversion to the risk due to the uncertain spot price, $\alpha$ is the credibility index and the physical meaning is equivalent to the probability confidence. Equation (A5b) is expressed as the credibility that the actual cost of user less than the expected cost is not less than $\alpha$. Equation (A5c) represents the expected cost of user. When $\sigma$ is larger, expected cost $C_\mathrm{e}$ is higher, indicating that user has a greater degree of risk aversion. $q$ is the decision variable, which represents the amount of electricity traded by user in each market. When $\varepsilon\ge0$, $\alpha\ge1/2$, according to the credibility measure function and above theorem, the robust optimization model shown in Equation (A5) can be expressed as

$$\max K_\alpha \tag{A6a}$$

$$\text{s.t.}\begin{cases} C(\lambda_t^{\mathrm{sm}},q)|_{\lambda_t^{\mathrm{sm}}=(1+K_\alpha)\lambda_t^{\mathrm{sm}\prime}}\le C_\mathrm{e} & \text{(A6b)}\\ C_\mathrm{e}=(1+\sigma)C_0 & \text{(A6c)}\\ 0\le\sigma\le1 & \text{(A6d)}\\ K_\alpha=\mu^{-1}(2(1-\alpha))\ge0 & \text{(A6e)}\\ 1/2\le\alpha\le1 & \text{(A6f)}\\ (A2)-(A4) & \text{(A6g)} \end{cases}$$

## References


1. Johansson, P.; Vendel, M.; Nuur, C. Integrating distributed energy resources in electricity distribution systems: An explorative study of challenges facing DSOs in Sweden. *Util. Policy* **2020**, *67*, 101117. [CrossRef]
2. Tsaousoglou, G.; Giraldo, J.S.; Pinson, P.; Paterakis, N.G. Mechanism design for fair and efficient dso flexibility markets. *IEEE Trans. Smart Grid* **2021**, *12*, 2249–2260. [CrossRef]
3. Villanueva-Rosario, J.A.; Santos-García, F.; Aybar-Mejía, M.E.; Mendoza-Araya, P.; Molina-García, A. Coordinated ancillary services, market participation and communication of multi-microgrids: A review. *Appl. Energy* **2022**, *308*, 118332. [CrossRef]
4. Su, H.; Peng, X.; Liu, H.; Quan, H.; Wu, K.; Chen, Z. Multi-Step-Ahead Electricity Price Forecasting Based on Temporal Graph Convolutional Network. *Mathematics* **2022**, *10*, 2366. [CrossRef]
5. Xiang, D.; Wei, E. A general sensitivity analysis approach for demand response optimizations. *IEEE Trans. Netw. Sci. Eng.* **2020**, *8*, 40–52. [CrossRef]
6. Yang, S.; Tan, Z.; Liu, Z.; Lin, H.; Ju, L.; Zhou, F.; Li, J. A multi-objective stochastic optimization model for electricity retailers with energy storage system considering uncertainty and demand response. *J. Clean. Prod.* **2020**, *277*, 124017. [CrossRef]
7. Zhao, H.; Guo, S. Uncertain interval forecasting for combined electricity-heat-cooling-gas loads in the integrated energy system based on multi-task learning and multi-kernel extreme learning machine. *Mathematics* **2021**, *9*, 1645. [CrossRef]
8. Li, Y.; Ding, Y.; Liu, Y.; Yang, T.; Wang, P.; Wang, J.; Yao, W. Dense Skip Attention based Deep Learning for Day-Ahead Electricity Price Forecasting. *IEEE Trans. Power Syst.* **2022**. [CrossRef]
9. Shafiee, S.; Zareipour, H.; Knight, A.M. Developing bidding and offering curves of a price-maker energy storage facility based on robust optimization. *IEEE Trans. Smart Grid* **2017**, *10*, 650–660. [CrossRef]
10. Rodriguez, D.E.; Trespalacios, A.; Galeano, D. Risk transfer in an electricity market. *Mathematics* **2021**, *9*, 2661. [CrossRef]
11. Nazari-Heris, M.; Mohammadi-Ivatloo, B.; Gharehpetian, G.B.; Shahidehpour, M. Robust short-term scheduling of integrated heat and power microgrids. *IEEE Syst. J.* **2018**, *13*, 3295–3303. [CrossRef]
12. Gholami, A.; Shekari, T.; Grijalva, S. Proactive management of microgrids for resiliency enhancement: An adaptive robust approach. *IEEE Trans. Sustain. Energy* **2017**, *10*, 470–480. [CrossRef]

13. Najafi, A.; Pourakbari-Kasmaei, M.; Jasinski, M.; Lehtonen, M.; Leonowicz, Z. A max–min–max robust optimization model for multi-carrier energy systems integrated with power to gas storage system. *J. Energy Storage* **2022**, *48*, 103933. [CrossRef]
14. Nojavan, S.; Nourollahi, R.; Pashaei-Didani, H.; Zare, K. Uncertainty-based electricity procurement by retailer using robust optimization approach in the presence of demand response exchange. *Int. J. Electr. Power Energy Syst.* **2019**, *105*, 237–248. [CrossRef]
15. Nojavan, S.; Najafi-Ghalelou, A.; Majidi, M.; Zare, K. Optimal bidding and offering strategies of merchant compressed air energy storage in deregulated electricity market using robust optimization approach. *Energy* **2018**, *142*, 250–257. [CrossRef]
16. Yu, D.; Ebadi, A.G.; Jermsittiparsert, K.; Jabarullah, N.H.; Vasiljeva, M.V.; Nojavan, S. Risk-constrained stochastic optimization of a concentrating solar power plant. *IEEE Trans. Sustain. Energy* **2019**, *11*, 1464–1472. [CrossRef]
17. Shuai, H.; Fang, J.; Ai, X.; Tang, Y.; Wen, J.; He, H. Stochastic optimization of economic dispatch for microgrid based on approximate dynamic programming. *IEEE Trans. Smart Grid* **2018**, *10*, 2440–2452. [CrossRef]
18. Wozabal, D.; Rameseder, G. Optimal bidding of a virtual power plant on the Spanish day-ahead and intraday market for electricity. *Eur. J. Oper. Res.* **2020**, *280*, 639–655. [CrossRef]
19. Charwand, M.; Gitizadeh, M.; Siano, P. A new active portfolio risk management for an electricity retailer based on a drawdown risk preference. *Energy* **2017**, *118*, 387–398. [CrossRef]
20. Wang, K.; Zhu, Z.; Guo, Z. Optimal Day-Ahead Decision-Making Scheduling of Multiple Interruptible Load Schemes for Retailer With Price Uncertainties. *IEEE Access* **2021**, *9*, 102251–102263. [CrossRef]
21. Yu, B.; Guo, L.; Li, Q. A characterization of novel rough fuzzy sets of information systems and their application in decision making. *Expert Syst. Appl.* **2019**, *122*, 253–261. [CrossRef]
22. Si, A.; Das, S.; Kar, S. An approach to rank picture fuzzy numbers for decision making problems. *Decis. Making Appl. Manag. Eng.* **2019**, *2*, 54–64. [CrossRef]
23. Solis, A.R.; Panoutsos, G. Granular computing neural-fuzzy modelling: A neutrosophic approach. *Appl. Soft Comput.* **2013**, *13*, 4010–4021. [CrossRef]
24. Yan, H.; Luh, P.B. A fuzzy optimization-based method for integrated power system scheduling and inter-utility power transaction with uncertainties. *IEEE Trans. Power Syst.* **1997**, *12*, 756–763.
25. Moradi, M.H.; Eskandari, M. A hybrid method for simultaneous optimization of DG capacity and operational strategy in microgrids considering uncertainty in electricity price forecasting. *Renew. Energy* **2014**, *68*, 697–714. [CrossRef]
26. Chen, J.; Qi, B.; Rong, Z.; Peng, K.; Zhao, Y.; Zhang, X. Multi-energy coordinated microgrid scheduling with integrated demand response for flexibility improvement. *Energy* **2021**, *217*, 119387. [CrossRef]
27. Zhao, P.; Gu, C.; Huo, D.; Shen, Y.; Hernando-Gil, I. Two-stage distributionally robust optimization for energy hub systems. *IEEE Trans. Ind. Inform.* **2019**, *16*, 3460–3469. [CrossRef]
28. Zare, A.; Chung, C.; Zhan, J.; Faried, S.O. A distributionally robust chance-constrained MILP model for multistage distribution system planning with uncertain renewables and loads. *IEEE Trans. Power Syst.* **2018**, *33*, 5248–5262. [CrossRef]
29. Lacagnina, V.; Pecorella, A. A stochastic soft constraints fuzzy model for a portfolio selection problem. *Fuzzy Sets Syst.* **2006**, *157*, 1317–1327. [CrossRef]
30. Peng, X.; Tao, X. Cooperative game of electricity retailers in China's spot electricity market. *Energy* **2018**, *145*, 152–170. [CrossRef]
31. Ghazvini, M.A.F.; Soares, J.; Horta, N.; Neves, R.; Castro, R.; Vale, Z. A multi-objective model for scheduling of short-term incentive-based demand response programs offered by electricity retailers. *Appl. Energy* **2015**, *151*, 102–118. [CrossRef]
32. Li, R.; Wei, W.; Mei, S.; Hu, Q.; Wu, Q. Participation of an energy hub in electricity and heat distribution markets: An MPEC approach. *IEEE Trans. Smart Grid* **2018**, *10*, 3641–3653. [CrossRef]
33. Sun, B.; Wang, F.; Xie, J.; Sun, X. Electricity Retailer trading portfolio optimization considering risk assessment in Chinese electricity market. *Electr. Power Syst. Res.* **2021**, *190*, 106833. [CrossRef]
34. Soroudi, A.; Ehsan, M. IGDT based robust decision making tool for DNOs in load procurement under severe uncertainty. *IEEE Trans. Smart Grid* **2012**, *4*, 886–895. [CrossRef]
35. Golmohamadi, H.; Keypour, R. Stochastic optimization for retailers with distributed wind generation considering demand response. *J. Mod. Power Syst. Clean Energy* **2018**, *6*, 733–748. [CrossRef]
36. Yu, X.; Sun, Y. Trading risk control model of electricity retailers in multi-level power market of China. *Energy Sci. Eng.* **2019**, *7*, 2756–2767. [CrossRef]
37. Zhou, J.; Li, X.; Pedrycz, W. Mean-semi-entropy models of fuzzy portfolio selection. *IEEE Trans. Fuzzy Syst.* **2016**, *24*, 1627–1636. [CrossRef]
38. Gao, J.; Chen, J.; Qi, B.; Zhao, Y.; Peng, K.; Zhang, X. A cost-effective two-stage optimization model for microgrid planning and scheduling with compressed air energy storage and preventive maintenance. *Int. J. Electr. Power Energy Syst.* **2021**, *125*, 106547. [CrossRef]
39. Liu, B. A survey of credibility theory. *Fuzzy Optim. Decis. Mak.* **2006**, *5*, 387–408. [CrossRef]
40. Pinhão, M.; Fonseca, M.; Covas, R. Electricity Spot Price Forecast by Modelling Supply and Demand Curve. *Mathematics* **2022**, *10*, 2012. [CrossRef]
41. Farivar, M.; Low, S.H. Branch flow model: Relaxations and convexification—Part I. *IEEE Trans. Power Syst.* **2013**, *28*, 2554–2564. [CrossRef]

42. Low, S.H. Convex relaxation of optimal power flow—Part II: Exactness. *IEEE Trans. Control. Netw. Syst.* **2014**, *1*, 177–189. [CrossRef]
43. Jahangir, H.; Tayarani, H.; Baghali, S.; Ahmadian, A.; Elkamel, A.; Golkar, M.A.; Castilla, M. A novel electricity price forecasting approach based on dimension reduction strategy and rough artificial neural networks. *IEEE Trans. Ind. Inform.* **2019**, *16*, 2369–2381. [CrossRef]
44. Lu, M. On crisp equivalents and solutions of fuzzy programming with different chance measures. *Information-Yamaguchi* **2003**, *6*, 125–134.
45. Kim, J.; Dvorkin, Y. A P2P-dominant distribution system architecture. *IEEE Trans. Power Syst.* **2019**, *35*, 2716–2725. [CrossRef]
46. Baringo, L.; Conejo, A.J. Offering strategy via robust optimization. *IEEE Trans. Power Syst.* **2010**, *26*, 1418–1425. [CrossRef]
47. Mei, F.; Zhang, J.; Lu, J.; Lu, J.; Jiang, Y.; Gu, J.; Yu, K.; Gan, L. Stochastic optimal operation model for a distributed integrated energy system based on multiple-scenario simulations. *Energy* **2021**, *219*, 119629. [CrossRef]

*mathematics* MDPI

*Article*

# Economic Performance and Stock Market Integration in BRICS and G7 Countries: An Application with Quantile Panel Data and Random Coefficients Modeling

José Clemente Jacinto Ferreira [1], Ana Paula Matias Gama [2], Luiz Paulo Fávero [3], Ricardo Goulart Serra [4], Patrícia Belfiore [5], Igor Pinheiro de Araújo Costa [6,*] and Marcos dos Santos [7]

1 Department of Management and Economics, Universidade da Beira Interior, 2635-434 Rio de Mouro, Portugal
2 Department of Management and Economics, Universidade da Beira Interior, 6200-209 Covilhã, Portugal
3 School of Economics, Business and Accounting, University of São Paulo, Cidade Universitária, São Paulo 05508-900, SP, Brazil
4 INSPER and FECAP, Vila Olímpia 04546-042, SP, Brazil
5 Engineering, Modeling and Applied Social Science Center, Federal University of ABC, São Bernardo do Campo 09606-045, SP, Brazil
6 Operational Research Department, Naval Systems Analysis Centre (CASNAV), Rio de Janeiro 20091-000, RJ, Brazil
7 Systems and Computing Department, Military Institute of Engineering (IME), Urca 22290-270, RJ, Brazil
* Correspondence: costa_igor@id.uff.br

**Citation:** Ferreira, J.C.J.; Gama, A.P.M.; Fávero, L.P.; Serra, R.G.; Belfiore, P.; Costa, I.P.d.A.; Santos, M.d. Economic Performance and Stock Market Integration in BRICS and G7 Countries: An Application with Quantile Panel Data and Random Coefficients Modeling. *Mathematics* **2022**, *10*, 4013. https://doi.org/10.3390/math10214013

Academic Editors: Francisco German Badía and María D. Berrade

Received: 24 September 2022
Accepted: 21 October 2022
Published: 28 October 2022



**Abstract:** The interest in studies aimed at understanding the integration of the stock market with the economic performance of countries has been growing in recent years, perhaps driven by the recent economic crises faced by the world. Although several studies on the topic have been carried out, the results are still far from a meaningful conclusion. In this sense, this paper considered the dual objective of investigating whether there is significant variance in the economic performance of developed and emerging markets' countries and whether the global risk factors are statistically significant in explaining the variations in their future economic performance over time. From a sample of (i) gross domestic products from BRICS and G7 countries (total of twelve countries), and (ii) returns of the risk factors of developed and emerging stock markets for the period 1993 to 2019, we applied longitudinal regression modeling for five distinct percentiles, and random coefficients modeling (RCM) with repeated measures. We found that risk factors explain the future economic performance, there is significant variation in economic performance over time among countries, and the temporal variation in the random effects of intercepts can be explained by RCM. The results of this study confirm that stock markets follow an integration process and that moderately integrated markets may have the same risk factors. Furthermore, considering that risk factors are related to future GDP growth, they act as proxies for unidentified state variables.

**Keywords:** GDP growth; BRICS and G7; five-factor asset pricing model; panel data; quantile models; random coefficient models

**MSC:** 60-11

## 1. Introduction

Emerging markets have long been a challenge to finance [1], and there has been extensive debate about the relationship between the real economy and stock market performance, especially in the context of emerging markets [2]. As a result of recent global economic crises such as the COVID-19 pandemic, research interest in the field of market integration has increased considerably in the last decade [3]. According to [4], financial integration intensifies during sovereign debt crises, being mainly driven by macroeconomic variables, market capitalization, political uncertainty and technological developments. In view of the process of integrating stock markets at the regional and global levels, an increasing number of studies on asset pricing have been carried out in developed markets [5–8] and emerging markets [9–12]. Many studies use multifactor models such as those of [13,14], in which diversified portfolios of stocks are formed based on characteristics such as size (SMB, small minus big), book-to-market index (HML, high minus low), operating profit (RMW, robust minus weak) and investment (CMA, conservative minus aggressive). These portfolios produce risk and return different, from market beta risk (MKT), and reflect unidentified state variables consistent with Merton's intertemporal capital asset pricing model (ICAPM) [15], such as [13,14,16]. In general, empirical evidence indicates that multi-factor models present positive risk premiums and better explain the variation of expected returns than the single-factor model, capital asset pricing model (CAPM) and there is segmentation between developed and emerging stock markets.

Fama [17] and Aylward and Glen [18] verified a positive and statistically significant relationship between returns on stock market portfolios and the future economic growth of the United States and of twenty-three countries with developed and emerging stock markets, respectively. Liew and Vassalou [19], motivated by [17,18], using data from ten developed stock market countries (Australia, Canada, France, Germany, Italy, Japan, Netherlands, Switzerland, United Kingdom and United States), demonstrated returns on the SMB and HML risk factors considered in [13] contain information about future GDP growth. SMB and HML are related to changes in the set of investment opportunities, and act as substitutes for two sources of the real economy's risk, consistent with the ICAPM state variables.

Although empirical evidence suggests that variations in expected returns reflect business cycle exposures [19–22], and that a considerable part of the risk and return of domestic stock markets can be attributed to the co-movement and interdependence of regional and global stock markets [6,7,23,24], given the integration process of stock markets and the real economy, few studies have analyzed the relationship between future domestic economic growth and risk factors of a global nature from a temporal perspective that allows us to investigate whether there is variability in economic performance between different countries and whether risk factors of a global nature help to explain the variations in economic performance between different countries.

The size risk factor (SMB) of [14] represents the average of three elementary risk factors formed from diversified portfolios of stocks grouped in (i) size and book-to-market (B/M) ($SMB_{B/M}$, difference between returns of diversified portfolios of stocks of small and large companies with high and low B/M ratio), (ii) size and operating income ($SMB_{OP}$, difference between returns of diversified portfolios of stocks of small and large companies with high and low operating income) and (iii) size and investment ($SMB_{INV}$, difference between the returns of diversified portfolios of stocks of small and large companies with low and high investment). The decomposition of the SMB risk factor into three elementary risk factors makes it possible to explore the three dimensions of systematic risk of size effect, through the magnitude and sign of the respective risk premiums and offers a new understanding of the behavior of each return parcel in the average SMB premium, and, in our study, its relationship to future economic growth.

Although many studies have been carried out in different regions and countries that analyzed the influence of bank financing or the stock market on economic growth, the findings are still far from meaningful conclusions [25]. Our study seeks to fill this gap in the literature by proposing a new model in terms of variables, aggregating the elementary risk factors of SMB ($SMB_{B/M}$, $SMB_{OP}$ and $SMB_{INV}$) in explaining the future economic growth in addition to methodological differences to consider (i) the asymmetric distribution of the GDP growth rate and (ii) the heterogeneity of GDP growth rates between developed and emerging countries.

The present study has the dual objective of investigating whether the global risk factors considered in [14] are statistically significant to explain the variations in countries' future economic performance over time, measured by the growth rate of the gross domestic product (GDP), and whether there is significant variance in the economic performance of developed and emerging markets' countries. To achieve these objectives, we applied panel data and random-coefficient models to a sample of developed (G7: Germany, Canada, United States, France, Italy, Japan, United Kingdom) and emerging (BRICS: South Africa, Brazil, China, India, and Russia) countries, considering their GDP data and the return of global risk factors in the period from 1993 to 2019.

The first objective is to analyze whether the global risk factors of developed and emerging stock markets considered in [14], including the decomposed SMB factor in its elementary risk factors ($SMB_{B/M}$, $SMB_{OP}$ and $SMB_{INV}$), capture information that helps to explain the variation in future economic performance, represented by GDP of 12 analyzed countries (G7 and BRICS). We estimate longitudinal regression models for panel data, using the quantile regression technique for the percentiles 0.05; 0.25; 0.50; 0.75; and 0.95 to accomplish this objective.

The second objective is to analyze whether there is significant variance in the economic performance of BRICS and G7 countries over time, and across countries over time, and whether the global, developed and emerging stock market risk factors from [14] help to explain variation in future economic performance over time. We estimate a two-level model with repeated measures to accomplish this objective.

The present study is structured in six sections. Section 2 presents the literature review; Section 3 presents the methodologies and the hypothesis; Section 4 presents the description of the data, followed by the analysis and discussion of the results in Section 5, and finally, the conclusion is drawn in Section 6.

## 2. Literature Review

Research on financial development and economic growth has been growing comprehensively for a long time in the theoretical and empirical literature [25]. Fama and French [5–7] observed that moderately integrated stock markets may have the same risk factors that reflect important dimensions of systematic risk in returns not priced by market beta risk, which condition future investment opportunities.

Positive and statistically significant relationships between the return of the stocks of the market portfolio and the future economic growth of the United States, and of twenty-three countries of developed and emerging stock markets were verified by [17,18], respectively. Motivated by them, Liew and Vassalou [19] were pioneers in demonstrating that the returns of the SMB and HML risk factors considered in [13] are related to changes in the set of investment opportunities and act as substitutes for two sources of the real economy's risk, consistent with the ICAPM state variables. The authors estimated simple and multiple regression models, with data on the returns of domestic risk factors and the GDP growth rate from 1978 to 1996 for ten developed countries (Germany, Australia, Canada, United States, France, Netherlands, Italy, Japan, United Kingdom and Switzerland). They found that the risk factors SMB and HML independently present positive and statistically significant relationships with the future GDP growth rate. Additionally, each risk factor, SMB and HML, in the presence of the MKT risk factor, maintains the positive relationship and magnitude of the regression coefficient.

Several studies followed [19], such as:

(1) Neves and Leal [26] verified a positive relationship between the SMB and HML risk factors and the future economic growth of Brazil for the period from 1986 to 2001.
(2) Font-Belaire and Grau-Grau [27] provided evidence on the positive and statistically significant relationship between future GDP growth and the SMB risk factor of the Spanish market during the period from 1995 to 2000.
(3) Hanhardt and Ansotegui [28] used data from 1990 to 2008 and found that the SMB risk factor has an explanatory capacity for the future economic growth of the Euro Zone.
(4) Fajardo and Fialho [29], using Brazilian market data from 1995 to 2008, observed that the risk factor SMB and HML are positively related to economic growth and negatively related to inflation.

(5) Liu and Di Iorio [30] provided evidence of the explanatory power of SMB and HML risk factors in predicting future Australian economic growth for the period 1993 to 2010.
(6) Boamah [31] confirmed the ability of [13] in predicting the economic growth of South Africa for the period 1996 to 2016.
(7) Ali, He and Jiang [32] reported that the MKT and SMB risk factors help to predict the future economic growth of Pakistan in the period 2002 to 2016.

Although the empirical evidence is supports [13] in relation to the CAPM, in capturing the expected return, Fama and French [14] extended the model from three to five risk factors that outperform the model of three factors in describing average returns. For this purpose, the authors added the (i) operating profit factor (RMW) that results from the difference between the returns on diversified portfolios of stocks of companies with high and low operating profits and (ii) the investment factor (CMA) that results from the difference between the returns of diversified portfolios of stocks of companies with low and high investment. In this context, Lalwani and Chakraborty [33], using data from the period 1992 to 2017, analyzed the ability of [14] to explain the future economic growth of five developed countries (Australia, United States, Canada, Japan and the United Kingdom) and four emerging countries (China, South Korea, India and Taiwan). The authors observed that in the presence of MKT, the additional risk factors (SMB, HML, RMW and CMA) remained positive and statistically significant for Canada, the United Kingdom, South Korea, and India, respectively.

In view of the process of integrating the stock markets, Ferreira and Gama [34], using data from the period from 1991 to 2018, confirmed the evidence that the risk factors of a regional nature considered in [14] help to predict the future economic growth of six developed markets namely, Germany, Canada, the United States, France, Hong Kong and Singapore. Ferreira et al. [35] reported that global risk factors capture information that helps explain the future economic performance of each emerging BRICS country (South Africa, Brazil, China, India and Russia).

*Economic Performance and Stock Market's Integration*

Regarding the integration between stock market and economic performance, the academic literature has several studies. Bekaert and Harvey [1] explored the financial effects of market integration as well as the impact on the real economy and presented results on political risk and liberalization, the volatility of capital flows and the performance of investments in emerging markets.

Tripathi and Seth [2] examined causal relationships between stock market performance and macroeconomic variables in India. The authors used various statistical approaches to data analysis and found that there is a significant correlation between stock market variables and macroeconomic factors, with the exception of the exchange rate.

Sehgal et al. [36] studied the dynamic nature of stock market integration in some Asian countries. The authors used the Copula GARCH models to study the intertemporal process of stock market integration and found that fiscal position, stock market performance, external position, governance and trade linkages appear to be the fundamental drivers of the integration of the stock market in that region.

Saji [3] analyzed the dynamics of price integration among Asian financial markets during the post-2008 financial crisis period. The authors analyzed monthly stock index data from five Asian economies from April 2009 to March 2020. The results did not yield any conclusive evidence of long-term relationships between stock markets. According to the authors, the asymmetric pattern of price behavior of Asian markets has important implications for the price efficiency of domestic markets and offers arbitrage potential for global investors to optimize returns through market diversification in a long-term perspective.

Olubiyi [37] assessed the relationship between economic integration and stock market performance in Nigeria alongside its main trading partners. The author found a negative relationship between US stock price and trade integration with Nigeria. The study made it possible to verify sectors that positively drive the Nigerian stock market, which could be prioritized by the country's trade policies.

Chukwuma et al. [38] carried out a study to demonstrate how forensic accounting can be used to predict future financial performance. The authors used OLS data analysis, unit root test and cointegration analysis. The results obtained revealed that forensic accounting indicators are statistically significant and have a significant positive impact on the growth of financial performance.

Jamil et al. [39] examined the impact of corporate social responsibility, leverage on assets and company age on the performance of organizations. The study considered the OLS model to estimate the impact and the use of the robustness factor so that the result was reliable. The results showed that sustainable corporate social responsibility is the main factor that enhances the company's performance.

Abdelkafi et al. [40] investigated the dynamic relationship between pandemics and government actions, such as government response rates and economic support packages. The authors used a panel dataset to analyze the effect of government actions on stock market returns. The empirical results showed the harmful effect of the COVID-19 pandemic on stock prices, hence the risk-adverse behavior of investors.

According to [25], several studies have been carried out in different regions and countries, analyzing the influence of banking or stock market finance on economic growth. However, the results are still far from a meaningful conclusion. Therefore, our study proposes a deeper and more detailed analysis of the topic. The methodology proposed in this article presents a new model in terms of variables, adding the elementary risk factors of SMB ($SMB_{B/M}$, $SMB_{OP}$ and $SMB_{INV}$) in explaining the future economic growth; besides methodological differences to consider (i) the asymmetric distribution of the GDP growth rate and (ii) the heterogeneity of GDP growth rates between developed and emerging countries.

## 3. Methodology

Given the process of integration of stock markets, this study analyzes, based on a longitudinal quantile regression model and a two-level model with repeated measures, whether the risk factors MKT, SMB, HML, RMW and CMA considered in [14], as well as the three elementary risk factors ($SMBB_{/M}$, SMBOP and $SMB_{INV}$) of the SMB risk, capture information that helps to explain the differences in GDP growth rates for a total of twelve countries composed of G7 developed countries (Germany, Canada, United States, France, Italy, Japan and United Kingdom) and BRICS emerging countries (South Africa, Brazil, China, India and Russia) and whether these differences occur over time.

Thus, the longitudinal regression models for long panel data are estimated using the quantile regression technique for the percentiles 0.05; 0.25; 0.50; 0.75; and 0.95. The percentiles 0.05 and 0.25 represent the lowest growth rates, the percentile 0.50 denotes median growth rate; and the percentiles 0.75 and 0.95 represent the highest growth rates. For the purpose of comparing the magnitudes and signs of the coefficients, regression models are estimated by Pooled Ordinary Least Squares (POLS). Two-level model with repeated measures is estimated to verify whether there is variance in the economic performance over time, and between countries over time, explained by the risk factors of [14] model.

We chose a sample that includes countries from different continents and sub-regions that, in the set of all developed and emerging stock market countries, according to the Morgan Stanley Capital International (MSCI) classification, represent the countries with high economic development (G7) and high potential for economic development (BRICS). We chose methodologies that considers: (i) that the statistical distribution of the dependent variable—GDP growth rate presents an asymmetric distribution, in addition, the error terms of the regression models do not show adherence to normality, which allows exploring the different behaviors for the different percentiles of the conditional distribution, not observable in the regression models to the mean estimated by the ordinary least squares (OLS) method, and (ii) the technological development focused on computer science and analysis software of data offers new approaches to panel data that allows estimating not only parameters by fixed effects, but also investigating the interaction between individual explanatory variables and the random effects of intercept and slope [41] whose models estimate parameters that present the best fit between actual and predicted values.

*Hypothesis*

Following the proposed objectives, using panel data, this study:

(1) First explores the relationship between the global risk factors MKT, SMB, HML, RMW and CMA, as well as the three elementary risk factors ($SMB_{B/M}$, $SMB_{OP}$ and $SMB_{INV}$) of the SMB, considered in the five-factor model by Fama and French (2015) and the future economic performance of the BRICS and G7 countries.

(2) In the second moment, this study analyses (i) if there are significant differences, over the years, in the economic performance of the G7 and BRICS countries, as well as (ii) if these differences can be explained by the global risk factors of the model developed by [14].

The studies that analyzed the relationship between future economic growth and the risk factors of the models [13,14], such as [28,34,35], attested that such risk factors, of regional and global nature, individually or in association with each other, help to predict future domestic economic growth. The risk factors of a global nature of the developed and emerging stock markets will be used to test the following investigation hypotheses:

**Hypothesis 1.** *The global risk factors of [14] asset pricing model, individually or in association with each other, explain the variability in future economic growth in BRICS and G7 countries.*

**Hypothesis 2.** *There is significant variability in the economic growth rates of BRICS and G7 countries over time.*

**Hypothesis 3.** *There is significant variability in the economic growth rates of BRICS and G7 countries over time across countries.*

**Hypothesis 4.** *The economic growth rates of BRICS and G7 countries follow a linear trend over time, and there are differences in this trend between countries.*

**Hypothesis 5.** *The global risk factors of [14] asset pricing model help to explain the variability in the future economic growth rate over time.*

**Hypothesis 6.** *Elementary size-effect risk factors associated with market beta risk help to explain the variability in the rate of future economic growth over time.*

In order to answer the first objective, simple and multiple quantile regression models are estimated [35]. The analysis was carried out in three stages. The first stage consists of the estimation of eight simple regression models, having each of the risk factors as an explanatory variable, to assess whether the return in period $t-1$ of each of the risk factors individually explains the variability between the percentiles of the annual economic performance, measured by the logarithmic growth rate of GDP for the twelve countries under analysis. Equation (1) represents this first stage.

$$GDP_{i,t} = \alpha_i + \beta_{ij} Factor_{ij,t-1} + \varepsilon_{i,t},\ j = 1, 2, \ldots, 8. \quad (1)$$

where, $GDP_{i,t}$ denotes the growth rate of the Gross Domestic Product of each observation in the sample for period t, calculated logarithmically; Factor represents the returns of each of the five (MKT, SMB, HML, RMW and CMA) and three elementary risk factors ($SMB_{B/M}$, $SMB_{OP}$ and $SMB_{INV}$) in the previous period $(t-1)$ of each observation; and $\varepsilon_{i,t}$ represents the error terms.

The second stage consists of estimating three multiple regression models, with two explanatory variables represented by the Equation (2), which includes the MKT risk factor and each elementary risk factor of the size effect (SMB).

$$GDP_{i,t} = \alpha_i + \beta_1 MKT_{i,t-1} + \beta_2 Factor_{i,t-1} + \varepsilon_{i,t} \tag{2}$$

$Factor_{i,t-1} \in \{SMB_{B/M,i,t-1}, SMB_{OP,i,t-1}, SMB_{INV,i,t-1}\}$.

where, $MKT_{it-1}$ represents the market returns in the previous period (t − 1) of each observation; and Factor represents the global market returns of each of the three elementary risk factors, $SMBB_{/M}$, $SMB_{OP}$ and $SMB_{INV}$ in the previous period (t − 1) of each observation.

The third stage consists of estimating a multiple regression model represented by the Equation (3), which includes the five risk factors of [14] model.

$$GDP_{i,t} = \alpha_i + \beta_1 MKT_{i,t-1} + \beta_2 SMB_{i,t-1} + \beta_3 HML_{i,t-1} + \beta_4 RMW_{i,t-1} + \beta_5 CMA_{i,t-1} + \varepsilon_{i,t} \tag{3}$$

The estimates of the regression models by OLS are made using the statistical software Gretl version 2021d. The estimates of the simple and multiple quantile regression models offer results that allow us to reject or not the investigation hypothesis (H1), thus concluding the first objective.

The second objective is to verify whether there is variability in the economic performance of the countries under analysis over time, and between countries over time, explained by risk factors. Thus, random coefficients models are estimated for two-level data with repeated measures, in which the nesting of the data will be characterized by the presence of repeated measures, that is, the existence of temporal evolution in the behavior of GDP growth rates, following the procedures by [41–43].

Random coefficients models represent a generalization of regression methods, which allow estimating the parameters of the fixed effects component (intercept and slopes) and, simultaneously, estimating parameters of random effects of intercepts and slopes of different subgroups of the sample, given certain individual and group characteristics [41–43].

In this study, a two-level model with repeated measures is applied, where the same observation is evaluated in more than one period. The two levels of analysis are formulated in two sub-models that represent, respectively, individual variability in the economic performance of countries over time (level 1) and variability in economic performance (represented by the GDP growth rate) between countries (level 2).

Based on [41–43], the models to be estimated follow the step-up strategy procedure, which consists, at first, of analyzing the variance decomposition from the definition of a null model with repeated measures (to access the existence of temporal evolution of the distribution of the dependent variable) which is characterized by the absence of explanatory variables and presents estimates of the parameters of fixed and random effects, of which the variance component between the two levels (variance in time and between countries) provides an intraclass correlation index that measures the proportion of total variance that is due to levels 1 and 2, and serves as a comparison for the estimates of conditional models (models with explanatory variables).

In this sequence, models with random intercepts and a model with intercepts and random slopes are estimated. The comparison of the performance of the estimations is based on the restricted likelihood ratio test—Log restricted-likelihood, obtained by the difference of the logarithms of the two restricted likelihood functions. Finally, from the identification of the random character of the error terms (intercept or intercept and slope) the complete model is formulated with the inclusion of explanatory variables of level 2. The final model must be estimated according to the statistical significance of the explanatory variables that result of the complete model. For this study, given the absence of level 2 data, the analysis of the complete model focuses only on the interaction between level 1 risk factors and level 2 random effects, to capture any contextual heterogeneities. Thus, in order to obtain the best estimator, random coefficients models will be estimated without the explanatory variables in the fixed effects component, however, with random slopes precisely in the temporal evolution.

Thus, the null model to be estimated is expressed in the Equation (6).

Level 1 (Repeated Measure) of the null model is expressed in Equation (4):

$$GDP_{t,i} = \beta_{0i} + r_{t,i}, \qquad r_{t,i} \sim N(0,\ \sigma_i^2) \tag{4}$$

where, t = 1, 2, ... , $T_i$ (years) and i = 1, 2, ... , n (countries); $\beta_{0i}$ denotes the expected (average) GDP growth rate of country i in year 1; and $\sigma^2$ is the variance "within" the country.

Level 2 (Country) of the null model is expressed in Equation (5):

$$\beta_{0i} = \gamma_{00} + u_{0i} \qquad u_{0i} \sim N(0,\ \tau_{0i}) \tag{5}$$

where, $\gamma_{00}$ is the general average of GDP growth rates; $\tau_{0i}$ is the variance between expected GDP growth rates of each country.

Thus, the null model (combining Equations (4) and (5)) is expressed in Equation (6):

$$GDP_{t,i} = \gamma_{00} + u_{0i} + r_{t,i} \tag{6}$$

Given the existence of two proportions of variance ($\sigma^2$ and $\tau_{00}$), the level 2 intraclass correlation index ($\rho$), which measures the relationship between the idiosyncratic and group error terms, is calculated according to Equation (7).

$$\rho = \frac{\tau_{00}}{\tau_{00} + \sigma^2} \tag{7}$$

The intraclass correlation coefficient ($\rho$) varies between 0 and 1. A null value means that there was no variance of individuals between the level 2 groups (country), so estimates from random coefficients models are not appropriate; and a positive value indicates the presence of at least one statistically significant error term of level 2, therefore the estimations of regression parameters by OLS are not adequate [41,43], and a random coefficients model should be adopted. To this end, the likelihood ratio test (LR test) is analyzed in order to verify whether the error terms of the variance components of the random effects of intercepts ($\tau_{00}$) are statistically different from zero.

The null model allows that hypotheses 2 and 3 to be tested. If the investigation hypotheses (H2) and (H3) are statistically supported, for the verification of the hypothesis (H4), two random coefficients models are estimated that include a trend component, variation over time at level 1.

The first model, represented by Equation (10) considers only random intercept effects.

Level 1 (Repeated Measure) is expressed in Equation (8):

$$GDP_{t,i} = \beta_{0i} + \beta_{1i} YEAR_{t,i} + r_{t,i} \qquad r_{t,i} \sim N(0,\ \sigma_i^2) \tag{8}$$

where, $\beta_{1i}$ is the country i GDP growth rate; e $YEAR_{ti}$ is the explanatory variable of level 1, which represents the repeated measure of the temporal variable. A repeated measure is defined by the temporal evolution within the multilevel panel.

Level 2 (Country) is expressed in Equation (9):

$$\beta_{0i} = \gamma_{00} + u_{0i} \qquad \beta_{1i} = \gamma_{10} \qquad u_{0i} \sim N(0,\ \tau_{0i}) \tag{9}$$

where, $\gamma_{10}$ is the overall average of expected GDP growth rates.

Thus, the random intercept model (combining Equations (8) and (9)) is expressed in Equation (10):

$$GDP_{t,i} = \gamma_{00} + \gamma_{10i} YEAR_{t,i} + u_{0i} + r_{t,i} \tag{10}$$

The second model, represented by the Equation (13), includes the random effects of the slopes, therefore, considering the random effects of intercepts and slopes.

Level 1 (Repeated Measure) is expressed in Equation (11):

$$GDP_{t,i} = \beta_{0i} + \beta_{1i}YEAR_{t,i} + r_{t,i}, \qquad r_{t,i} \sim N\left(0,\ \sigma_i^2\right) \tag{11}$$

Level 2 (Country) is expressed in Equation (12):

$$\beta_{0i} = \gamma_{00} + u_{0i} \qquad \beta_{1i} = \gamma_{10} + u_{1i} \qquad u_{0i} \sim N(0,\ \tau_{00}) \qquad u_{1i} \sim N(0,\ \tau_{11}) \tag{12}$$

where, $\tau_{11}$, variance between expected growth rates across countries.

Thus, the random intercept and slope model (combining Equations (11) and (12)) is expressed in Equation (13a):

$$GDP_{t,i} = \gamma_{00} + \gamma_{10i}YEAR_{t,i} + u_{0i} + u_{1i}YEAR_{t,i} + r_{t,i} \tag{13a}$$

Given the existence of three proportions of variance ($\sigma^2$, $\tau_{00}$ and $\tau_{11}$), the level 2 intraclass correlation index ($\rho$) is calculated according to Equation (13b).

$$\rho = \frac{\tau_{00} + \tau_{11}}{\tau_{00} + \tau_{11} + \sigma^2} \tag{13b}$$

The best fit between the estimates of the models with random intercepts and with random intercepts and slopes is given by the result of the restricted-likelihood ratio test (Log restricted-likelihood), obtained by the difference of the logarithms of the two restricted likelihood functions.

Once the randomness of the error terms has been identified, that is, a model with only random intercepts, or a model with random intercepts and slopes is selected, which supports the research hypothesis (H4), a complete model is proposed that includes the interaction between the risk factors and the random effects of intercepts and slopes at level 2, for the verification of the investigation hypothesis (H5), as represented in the Equations (14) and (15).

Level 1 (Repeated Measure) is expressed in Equation (14):

$$GDP_{t,i} = \beta_{0i} + \beta_{1i}YEAR_{t,i} + \beta_{2i}MKT_{t,i-1} + \beta_{3i}SMB_{t,i-1} + \beta_{4i}HML_{t,i-1} + \beta_{5i}RMW_{t,i-1} + \beta_{6i}CMA_{t,i-1} + r_{t,i} \tag{14}$$

Level 2 (Country) is expressed in Equation (15):

$$\begin{gathered}\beta_{0i} = \gamma_{00} + u_{0i} \quad \beta_{1i} = \gamma_{10} + u_{1i} \quad \beta_{2i} = \gamma_{20} + u_{2i} \quad \beta_{3i} = \gamma_{30} + u_{3i} \quad \beta_{4i} = \gamma_{40} + u_{4i} \\ \beta_{5i} = \gamma_{50} + u_{5i} \quad \beta_{6i} = \gamma_{60} + u_{6i}\end{gathered} \tag{15}$$

To answer the research hypothesis (H6), a complete model will be estimated, represented by the (i) Equations (16) and (19), (ii) Equations (17) and (19) and (iii) Equations (18) and (19), respectively, (i) considering the elementary risk factor B/M of the size risk factor: size B/M ($SMBB_{/M}$), (ii) considering the elementary risk factor operating profit of the size risk factor: size operating profit ($SMB_{OP}$) and (iii) considering the elementary risk factor investment of the size risk factor: size investment ($SMB_{INV}$). This formulation is discussed by [24,38]. Level 1 (Repeated Measure) are expressed in Equations (16)–(18):

Considering size B/M (Equation (16)):

$$\mathbf{GDP_{t,i}=\beta_{0i}+\beta_{1i}YEAR_{t,i}} + \mathbf{\beta_{2i}MKT_{t,i-1}+\beta_{3i}SMB_{B/M,t,i-1}+r_{t,i}} \tag{16}$$

Considering size operating profit (Equation (17)):

$$GDP_{t,i} = \beta_{0i} + \beta_{1i}YEAR_{t,i} + \beta_{2i}MKT_{t,i-1} + \beta_{3i}SMB_{OP,t,i-1} + r_{t,i} \tag{17}$$

Considering size investment (Equation (18)):

$$GDP_{t,i} = \beta_{0i} + \beta_{1i}YEAR_{t,i} + \beta_{2i}MKT_{t,i-1} + \beta_{3i}SMB_{INV,t,i-1} + r_{t,i} \tag{18}$$

Level 2 (Country) is expressed in Equation (19):

$$\beta_{0i} = \gamma_{00} + u_{0i}\ \beta_{1i} = \gamma_{10} + u_{1i}\ \beta_{2i} = \gamma_{20} + u_{2i}\ \beta_{3i} = \gamma_{30} + u_{3i} \tag{19}$$

The composition of the final complete model will be done through the stepwise procedure, which consists of the step-by-step inclusion of each explanatory variable, in which a statistical significance of 10% is assumed [41]. This formulation is discussed by [24,38].

The fixed effects parameters and the error terms variances of the random effects component of the random coefficients model are estimated by the maximum likelihood method that produces the z test, to measure statistical significance of the fixed effect component and, Wald's z test, to measure the variance component of random effects. Model estimations are obtained using SPSS 22 and Stata 14 statistical software.

Table 1 presents the research hypotheses as well as the methods to be used for their validation.

**Table 1.** Research hypotheses and methodologies for their validation.

| Research Hypotheses | Methodology |
| --- | --- |
| H1: The global risk factors of [14] asset pricing model, individually or in association with each other, explain the variability in future economic growth in BRICS and G7 countries. | Quantile regression modeling for longitudinal repeated measures data<br>Longitudinal models of simple and multiple regression, with five explanatory variables, the risk factors of [14] model |
| H2: There is significant variability in the economic growth rates of BRICS and G7 countries over time. | Random coefficients modeling<br>Null Model |
| H3: There is significant variability in the economic growth rates of BRICS and G7 countries over time across countries. | |
| H4: The economic growth rates of BRICS and G7 countries follow a linear trend over time, and there are differences in this trend between countries. | Random coefficients modeling<br>Linear trend model with random intercept effects<br>Linear trend model with random intercept and slope effects |
| H5: The global risk factors of [14] asset pricing model help to explain the variability in the future economic growth rate over time. | Random coefficients modeling<br>Full model—Linear trend model with random effects and interaction of explanatory variables at level 1, risk factors, from [14] model and the random effects of slope at level 2 in order to capture differences in rates of economic growth of each country |
| H6: Elementary size-effect risk factors associated with market beta risk help to explain the variability in the rate of future economic growth over time. | |

Table 2 summarizes the variables definitions and the expected relationships to the output variable according to the literature review.

The confirmation of a positive relationship between future economic growth and risk factors supports the arguments of [13,14,16] that risk factors obtained from company characteristics reflect proxies of variables of unidentified states that produce non-diversifiable risks in returns not estimated by the CAPM and represent innovations that affect the set of future investment opportunities, in the context of the ICAPM, and have three implications: (1) in the face of the risk-based explanation, there is a dual function of the asset pricing models, that is, they act as (1.i) instruments for analyzing the company's cost of capital and the investment portfolio management, and (1.ii) auxiliary indicator for forecasting economic growth, which, according to [19], in periods of expected economic growth the shares of small companies, with high B/M ratios and operating profit and with low investment index are better able to prosper than the stocks of large companies, with low B/M ratios and operating income and with high investment ratio, so when the market signals that the business cycle is unfavorable, investors seek to hold stock portfolios with good growth opportunities and a low debt ratio, (2) they act as substitutes for sources of risk in the real economy and (3) in view of the integrating process, moderately integrated markets [5,6,14], selectively offers complementary information to investors for decision making on the selection and formation of the investment portfolio.

**Table 2.** Variables definition and the expected relationship according to the literature review.

| Variables | Variable Definition | Expected Signal | Reference |
|---|---|---|---|
| | Dependent Variable | | |
| Economic performance (GDP) | GDP growth rate | | [19,26–35] |
| | Independent Variables—Stock market risk factor | | |
| Market beta risk factor (MKT) | Difference between the market portfolio rate of return and the risk-free rate | Positive | [19,26–35] |
| Size B/M ($SMB_{B/M}$) [13] | Difference between the returns of diversified portfolios of stocks of small and large companies with high and low B/M ratio | Positive | [19,26–34] |
| Size operating profit ($SMB_{OP}$) [14] | Difference between returns of diversified portfolios of stocks of small and large companies with high and low operating income | Positive | N.A. |
| Size investment ($SMB_{INV}$) [14] | Difference between the returns of diversified portfolios of stocks of small and large companies with low and high investment | Positive | N.A. |
| Size (SMB) [14] | Difference between the returns of diversified portfolios of stocks of small and large companies | Positive | [33–35] |
| B/M ratio (HML) | Difference between the returns of diversified portfolios of high and low B/M ratio stocks | Positive | [19,26–35] |
| Operating profitability (RMW) | Difference between returns on diversified portfolios of stocks of companies with high and low operating income | Positive | [33–35] |
| Investment (CMA) | Difference between returns on diversified portfolios of stocks of low and high investment companies | Positive | [33–35] |

## 4. Data

### *4.1. Sample*

For the present study, historical series of annual data valued in US dollars were collected for the period between January 1993 and December 2019 referring to the Gross Domestic Product (GDP), at constant prices and base year 2010, from a total of twelve countries among developed (Germany, Canada, United States, France, Italy, Japan and United Kingdom) and emerging (South Africa, Brazil, China, India and Russia), according to Morgan Stanley Capital International (MSCI) classification, extracted from the World Bank database; and global risk factor returns for developed and emerging stock markets, obtained from the Kenneth French database.

### *4.2. Univariate Analysis*

Table 3 presents the descriptive statistics of the variance decomposition of the variables, dependent (GDP growth rate) and explanatory (risk factors of developed and emerging countries), for a data structure in a balanced longitudinal panel with 26 periods, year (from 1994 to 2019, GDP; 1993 to 2018, risk factors), and for each of the 12 countries under analysis, totaling 312 observations.

Given the panel data structure of the sample under analysis, overall (general), within (variation over time for a given individual) and between (variation between individuals) variances are reported.

**Table 3.** Descriptive statistics—Decomposition of variance.

| Variable | | Mean | Std Deviation | Minimum | Maximum | Observations | |
|---|---|---|---|---|---|---|---|
| GDP | Overall | 0.02827 | 0.03243 | −0.13433 | 0.13305 | N.T = | 312 |
| | Between | | 0.02350 | 0.00734 | 0.08780 | N = | 12 |
| | Within | | 0.02332 | −0.12599 | 0.10365 | T = | 26 |
| MKT | Overall | 0.08472 | 0.26108 | −0.55360 | 0.86370 | N.T = | 312 |
| | Between | | 0.01842 | 0.06982 | 0.10560 | N = | 12 |
| | Within | | 0.26048 | −0.57447 | 0.84283 | T = | 26 |
| SMB | Overall | 0.02072 | 0.09402 | −0.17240 | 0.44850 | N.T = | 312 |
| | Between | | 0.00573 | 0.01608 | 0.02721 | N = | 12 |
| | Within | | 0.09386 | −0.16777 | 0.44201 | T = | 26 |
| $SMB_{B/M}$ | Overall | 0.00741 | 0.09019 | −0.17730 | 0.34440 | N.T = | 312 |
| | Between | | 0.00077 | 0.00679 | 0.00828 | N = | 12 |
| | Within | | 0.09019 | −0.17668 | 0.34353 | T = | 26 |
| $SMB_{OP}$ | Overall | 0.03244 | 0.09265 | −0.16873 | 0.43013 | N.T = | 312 |
| | Between | | 0.00734 | 0.02651 | 0.04075 | N = | 12 |
| | Within | | 0.09238 | −0.16280 | 0.42182 | T = | 26 |
| $SMB_{INV}$ | Overall | 0.02230 | 0.10512 | −0.18020 | 0.57103 | N.T = | 312 |
| | Between | | 0.00907 | 0.01497 | 0.03258 | N = | 12 |
| | Within | | 0.10476 | −0.17286 | 0.56076 | T = | 26 |
| HML | Overall | 0.06319 | 0.14011 | −0.30320 | 0.50870 | N.T = | 312 |
| | Between | | 0.03347 | 0.03611 | 0.10111 | N = | 12 |
| | Within | | 0.13638 | −0.27612 | 0.47078 | T = | 26 |
| RMW | Overall | 0.02801 | 0.09050 | −0.51730 | 0.12860 | N.T = | 312 |
| | Between | | 0.01633 | 0.00951 | 0.04122 | N = | 12 |
| | Within | | 0.08914 | −0.49881 | 0.13839 | T = | 26 |
| CMA | Overall | 0.03167 | 0.09953 | −0.26800 | 0.30940 | N.T = | 312 |
| | Between | | 0.01144 | 0.02242 | 0.04463 | N = | 12 |
| | Within | | 0.09892 | −0.25874 | 0.29644 | T = | 26 |

Obs.: N.T: total observations; N: number of countries; T: number of periods.

For the dependent variable, GDP growth rate, the variation between countries (between effect) is slightly higher than the variation over time for a given country (within effect), which indicates the existence of variation in economic performance between the countries. With respect to the explanatory variables, the risk factors showed greater variation over time (within effect) than between individuals (between effect). The minimum and maximum values, respectively, indicate that the economic performance (GDP) of the between effect was in the range from 0.734% to 8.78%, and in relation to the performance of the within effect, the it was in the range from −12.599% to 10.365%.

## 5. Multivariate Analysis

### *5.1. Quantile Regression Analysis*

This section analyzes the relationship between risk factors and GDP in twelve developed and emerging countries that are part of G7 (Germany, Canada, the United States, France, Italy, Japan and the United Kingdom) and BRICS (South Africa, Brazil, China, India and Russia), through the estimation of linear longitudinal regression models for long panel data, using the quantile regression technique for the percentiles 0.05; 0.25; 0.50; 0.75; and 0.95. For the purpose of comparing the magnitudes and signs of the parameters, the POLS regression model is also used. Thereafter, beginning at Table 4, the existence of variation in economic performance is analyzed, through the decomposition of the variance, based on random coefficients modeling.

**Table 4.** Simple and multiple regression estimates.

| | **Model** | | **Pooled OLS** | **Quantile Regression** | | | | |
|---|---|---|---|---|---|---|---|---|
| | | | | **0.05** | **0.25** | **0.50** | **0.75** | **0.95** |
| Panel A: $GDP_{i,t} = \alpha + \beta Fator_{i,t-1} + \varepsilon_{i,t}$ | | | | | | | | |
| 1 | MKT | Coef | 0.036 *** | 0.079 *** | 0.045 *** | 0.038 *** | 0.037 *** | 0.019 ** |
| | | SE | 0.006 | 0.011 | 0.003 | 0.004 | 0.011 | 0.008 |
| 2 | SMB | Coef | 0.020 | 0.124 * | 0.042 ** | 0.036 ** | 0.015 | 0.089 ** |
| | | SE | 0.019 | 0.067 | 0.016 | 0.016 | 0.024 | 0.039 |
| 3 | HML | Coef | 0.032 | 0.079 ** | 0.020 * | 0.036 *** | 0.045 *** | 0.088 *** |
| | | SE | 0.013 | 0.035 | 0.010 | 0.010 | 0.016 | 0.018 |
| 4 | RMW | Coef | −0.037 | 0.190 ** | −0.035 ** | −0.052 *** | −0.098 *** | −0.071 |
| | | SE | 0.020 | 0.082 | 0.015 | 0.014 | 0.031 | 0.045 |
| 5 | CMA | Coef | −0.019 | −0.168 *** | −0.029 ** | −0.016 | 0.004 | 0.035 |
| | | SE | 0.018 | 0.028 | 0.014 | 0.014 | 0.021 | 0.049 |
| 6 | $SMB_{B/M}$ | Coef | 0.013 | 0.122 | 0.033 * | 0.030 ** | −0.010 | 0.048 * |
| | | SE | 0.020 | 0.084 | 0.019 | 0.015 | 0.021 | 0.026 |
| 7 | $SMB_{OP}$ | Coef | 0.027 | 0.133 ** | 0.044 *** | 0.034 ** | 0.026 | 0.099 *** |
| | | SE | 0.019 | 0.064 | 0.016 | 0.017 | 0.023 | 0.021 |
| 8 | $SMB_{INV}$ | Coef | 0.018 | −0.095 | 0.034 ** | 0.033 ** | 0.018 | 0.074 *** |
| | | SE | 0.017 | 0.062 | 0.012 | 0.015 | 0.021 | 0.021 |
| Panel B: $GDP_{i,t} = \alpha_i + \beta_1 MKT_{i,t-1} + \beta_2 Fator_{i,t-1} + \varepsilon_{i,t}$ | | | | | | | | |
| 9 | MKT | Coef | 0.039 *** | 0.081 *** | 0.045 *** | 0.040 *** | 0.043 *** | 0.017 * |
| | | SE | 0.007 | 0.011 | 0.004 | 0.005 | 0.011 | 0.009 |
| | $SMB_{B/M}$ | Coef | −0.025 | −0.045 | −0.010 | −0.009 | −0.029 | 0.014 |
| | | SE | 0.020 | 0.033 | 0.010 | 0.015 | 0.032 | 0.025 |
| 10 | MKT | Coef | 0.037 *** | 0.08 1 *** | 0.045 *** | 0.037 *** | 0.036 *** | 0.005 |
| | | SE | 0.007 | 0.014 | 0.004 | 0.005 | 0.012 | 0.008 |
| | $SMB_{OP}$ | Coef | −0.010 | −0.039 | 0.000 | 0.016 | −0.012 | 0.089 *** |
| | | SE | 0.020 | 0.039 | 0.011 | 0.014 | 0.033 | 0.023 |
| | Model | | Pooled OLS | Quantile regression | | | | |
| | | | | 0.05 | 0.25 | 0.50 | 0.75 | 0.95 |
| 11 | MKT | Coef | 0.039 *** | 0.083 *** | 0.044 *** | 0.038 *** | 0.039 *** | 0.009 |
| | | SE | 0.007 | 0.011 | 0.004 | 0.006 | 0.011 | 0.018 |
| | $SMB_{INV}$ | Coef | −0.019 | −0.033 | −0.005 | 0.008 | −0.013 | 0.056 |
| | | SE | 0.018 | 0.027 | 0.009 | 0.014 | 0.026 | 0.044 |
| Panel C: $GDP_{i,t} = \alpha_i + \beta_1 MKT_{i,t-1} + \beta_2 SMB_{i,t-1} + \beta_3 HML_{i,t-1} + \beta_4 RMW_{i,t-1} + \beta_5 CMA_{i,t-1} + \varepsilon_{i,t}$ | | | | | | | | |
| 12 | MKT | Coef | 0.039 *** | 0.089 *** | 0.049 *** | 0.046 *** | 0.025 *** | 0.007 *** |
| | | SE | 0.008 | 0.015 | 0.004 | 0.008 | 0.010 | 0.002 |
| | SMB | Coef | −0.017 | 0.035 | −0.016 | −0.001 | −0.025 | 0.107 *** |
| | | SE | 0.023 | 0.041 | 0.012 | 0.023 | 0.026 | 0.005 |
| | HML | Coef | 0.038 *** | 0.019 | 0.026 *** | 0.039 ** | 0.055 *** | 0.050 *** |
| | | SE | 0.017 | 0.029 | 0.009 | 0.016 | 0.019 | 0.003 |
| | RMW | Coef | 0.037 | 0.235 *** | 0.016 | 0.028 | −0.044 | 0.020 *** |
| | | SE | 0.028 | 0.048 | 0.014 | 0.027 | 0.031 | 0.006 |
| | CMA | Coef | −0.017 | 0.039 | 0.004 | −0.025 | −0.028 | 0.067 *** |
| | | SE | 0.023 | 0.040 | 0.012 | 0.022 | 0.025 | 0.005 |

Obs.: Coef: coefficient; SE, standard error; ***, **, *, $p < 1\%$, 5% and 10%.

Through Panel A of Table 4, it is observed that the estimates obtained by the simple quantile regression, represented by the Equation 1, indicate that all models presented a positive and statistically significant relationship, at least in one of the five percentiles under analysis, except model 5, estimated with the explanatory variable CMA. The magnitude of the coefficients varied between 1.9% (MKT—0.95 percentile) and 7.9% (MKT—0.05 percentile); 3.6% (SMB—0.50 percentile) and 12.4% (SMB—0.05 percentile); 2% (HML—0.25 percentile) and 8.8% (HML—0.95 percentile); −9.8% (RMW—0.75 percentile) and 19% (RMW—0.05 percentile);

3% (SMBB/M—0.50 percentile) and 4.8% ($SMB_{B/M}$—0.95 percentile); 3.4% ($SMB_{OP}$—0.50 percentile) and 13.3% ($SMB_{OP}$—0.05 percentile); and between 3.3% ($SMB_{INV}$—0.50th percentile) and 7.4% ($SMB_{INV}$—0.95 percentile), compared to the mean value of 3.6% (MKT), the only statistical significant coefficient (at the 5% level) of the POLS estimation.

Regarding the results of multiple quantile regression, with two explanatory variables composed of (i) each elemental risk factor of size effect associated with the (ii) beta market risk, represented by the Equation 2 (Panel B of Table 4), it can be seen that differently from the negative mean values of POLS estimation, in the presence of the MKT risk factor, the coefficients estimated by the risk factors $SMB_{B/M}$, $SMB_{OP}$ and S $SMB_{INV}$ present themselves positive at least in one percentile of the entire conditional distribution of economic performance. Within the five percentiles under analysis, $SMB_{OP}$ presented a positive and statistically significant coefficient with a magnitude of 8.9% ($SMB_{OP}$—0.95 percentile). The risk factor $SMB_{INV}$ showed positive and statistically significant coefficients between the 0.86 (6.83%) and 0.99 (9.85%) percentiles, as illustrated in Figure 1.

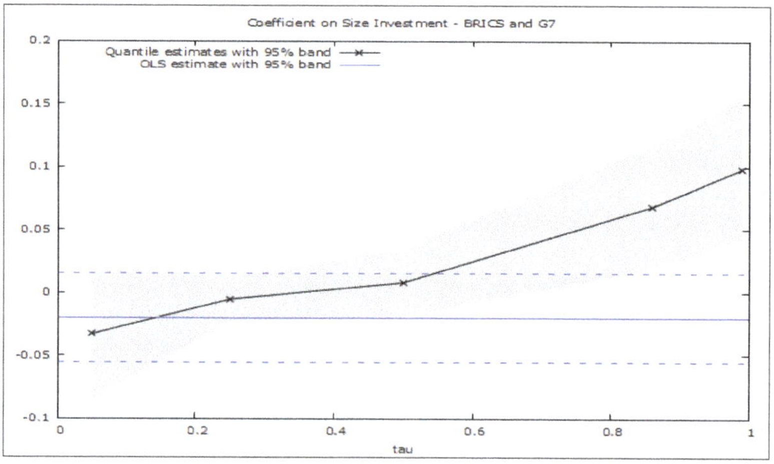


**Figure 1.** Performance of the $SMB_{INV}$ risk factor on the percentiles and conditional average of the GDP growth rate of the BRICS and G7 countries.

Figure 1 illustrates the individual performance of the risk factor $SMB_{INV}$, on the conditional quantile distribution, as well as the estimation by OLS, of the GDP growth rate of BRICS and G7 countries. The vertical and horizontal lines show, respectively, the risk factor coefficients and the percentiles (tau) from 0 to 1. The solid blue line represents the estimated mean coefficient obtained through OLS, and the dotted blue lines the respective confidence intervals at 95%. The shaded area represents the confidence intervals of the parameters obtained through the estimation of the quantile regression models, with the black line being the average estimation of the parameters for each of the percentiles under analysis. Thus, through Figure 1, it can be seen that for the conditional performance to the risk factors MKT and $SMB_{INV}$, ceteris paribus, the positive coefficients were observed between the percentiles 0.43 and 0.58, 0.63 and 0.66, and between 0.84 and 0.99, however, statistically significant values were estimated between the 0.86 and 0.99 percentiles, as illustrated in Figure 1.

Regarding the multiple quantile regression model, with five explanatory variables being the global risk factors of developed and emerging countries considered in the asset pricing model of [14], represented by the Equation (3), it can be noted in Panel C of Table 4, with statistical significance at the 5% level, that risk factors help to explain the variation in the future economic performance of BRICS and G7 countries, at least in one percentile of the conditional distribution of GDP growth rates. Ceteris paribus, the MKT risk factor remained the central element of the explanation for the variability of economic growth in the five percentiles under analysis, with the magnitude of the coefficients varying between 2.5% (MKT—0.75 percentile) and 8.9% (MKT—0.05 percentile), compared to the mean value of 3.9% (MKT) of statistical significance, at the 5% level, obtained through the POLS estimation.

The SMB and CMA factors, respectively, showed positive and statistically significant coefficients, in one percentile, with magnitudes of 10.7% (SMB—0.95 percentile) and 6.7% (CMA—0.95 percentile), and the risk factors, respectively, RMW and HML, showed positive coefficients of statistical significance at two and four percentiles, respectively, ranging between 2% (RMW—0.95 percentile) and 23.7% (RMW—0.05 percentile), and between 2.6% (HML—0.25 percentile) and 5.5% (HML—0.50 percentile), compared to the mean value of 3.8% for HML, of statistical significance at the 5% level. As a consequence, the results presented here support the observations of [19] on the ability of risk factors to predict future economic growth, and in line with the study by [35] sheds light on the performance of global risk factors of developed and emerging equity markets in forecasting domestic economic performance, given the process of integration of stock markets. Based on the above, the research hypothesis (H1) is supported.

As noted by [41,44,45], the main utility of longitudinal data modeling is the fact that it allows the analysis of possible differences in the performance behaviors of individuals over time. However, without the effect of the panel structure on the data, the parameter estimators can be analyzed through OLS estimation, considering individual time series regression models. Thus, for the purpose of comparing the magnitudes and signs of the coefficients of the explanatory variables, Table A1 in Appendix A presents, for each country under analysis, the parameter estimates of six linear models of simple and multiple regression, with two explanatory variables being (i) each elemental risk factor of size effect associated with (ii) market beta risk, for time series data, using the quantile regression technique for the percentiles 0.05; 0.25; 0.50; 0.75; and 0.95.

For the purpose of comparing the magnitudes and signs of the parameters, the OLS regression model is also used. For the models estimated by OLS that showed autocorrelation and heteroscedasticity of residuals, the robust estimators of [46,47] were applied, which, although they do not correct the standard error, adjust the significance bands for the estimation, eventually, of more parsimonious models. Through Panel A of Table A1 in Appendix A, it is observed that for the estimates obtained by the simple quantile regression, the three models presented a positive and statistically significant relationship, at least in one of the five percentiles under analysis, of all countries, except for South Africa ($SMB_{OP}$), Brazil ($SMB_{B/M}$ and $SMB_{OP}$) and Russia ($SMB_{B/M}$, $SMB_{OP}$ and $SMB_{INV}$).

For the three models, the asymmetry of the GDP growth rate vis-à-vis the explanatory variable varied between 2.9% (India, $SMB_{INV}$—0.75 percentile) and 29.6% (Canada, $SMB_{B/M}$—0.05 percentile), compared to the mean value of 7.8% (Japan, $SMB_{B/M}$) of statistical significance, at the 5% level of estimation by OLS. However, beyond the five percentiles under analysis, the risk factors $SMB_{B/M}$ and $SM_{BOP}$, showed a positive and statistically significant relationship to explain future economic performance, at least in one quantile for South Africa, 10.1% ($SMB_{OP}$—percentile 0.01) and for Brazil, 10.4% ($SMB_{B/M}$—percentile 0.30) and 16.8% ($SMB_{OP}$—percentile 0.80), as illustrated in Figures A1–A3 in Appendix A. In general, within the five percentiles under analysis, for the three risk factors, the positive coefficients of statistical significance and with high magnitude were in the percentiles below the median, with a variation between 3.3% (India, $SMB_{B/M}$,—0.75th percentile) and 29.6% (Canada, $SMB_{B/M}$—0.05 percentile), 3% (India, $SMB_{OP}$—0.75th percentile) and 29.4% (Canada, $SMB_{OP}$—0.05 percentile), and 2.9% (India, $SMB_{INV}$—0.05 percentile) and 27.5% (Canada, $SMB_{INV}$—0.05 percentile), for $SMB_{B/M}$, $SMB_{OP}$ and $SMB_{INV}$, respectively.

Regarding the results of three multiple quantile regression models (Panel B of Table A1 in Appendix A), with two explanatory variables, as expected, it can be seen that within the five percentiles under analysis, in the presence of the MKT risk factor, the elementary risk factors $SMB_{B/M}$, $SMB_{OP}$ and $SMB_{INV}$ remained positive at least in percentile of the conditional distribution of economic performance of all countries under analysis, except for South Africa, Brazil, United Kingdom and Russia ($SMB_{B/M}$ and $SMB_{INV}$). Thus, ceteris paribus, the magnitude of the positive and statistically significant coefficients of the risk factors, respectively, $SMB_{B/M}$, $SMB_{OP}$ and $SMB_{INV}$, varied between 2.4% (India, $SMB_{B/M}$—0.95 percentile) and 9.4% (China, $SMB_{B/M}$—0.25 percentile), 3.1% (India, $SMB_{OP}$—0.95 percentile) and 9% (Italy, $SMB_{OP}$—0.05 percentile), and 3% (India, $SMB_{INV}$—0.95 percentile) and 8.2% (Italy, $SMB_{INV}$—0.05 percentile), compared to the mean values of 4.8% ($SMB_{OP}$, Japan) and 4.5% ($SMB_{INV}$, China) of statistical significance at the 10% level, obtained through the estimation by OLS.

However, beyond the five percentiles under analysis, the risk factors $SMB_{B/M}$, $SMB_{OP}$ and $SMB_{INV}$, respectively, showed a positive and statistically significant relationship to explain future economic performance, in a South African percentile, 2.1% ($SMB_{B/M}$—0.01 percentile) and 2% ($SMB_{OP}$—0.01 percentile), Brazil, 3.9% ($SMB_{OP}$—0.12 percentile) and 3.1% ($SMB_{INV}$—0.13 percentile), and United Kingdom, 2% ($SMB_{OP}$—0.01 percentile).

Thereafter, Table A2 in Appendix B, presents the results of each of the seven linear longitudinal regression models for long panel data, through the estimation of fixed effects, random effects, POLS, fixed effects with AR(1) error terms, random effects with AR(1) error terms, POLS with AR(1) error terms, and model with GLS (General Least Squares) estimation method with AR(1) error terms. It can be noted that the estimated parameters vary between models.

In general, it is observed that the fixed effects, random effects and POLS models present slightly higher standard errors compared to those obtained by the respective AR(1) error term models. The estimations with the GLS method are the most adequate, the parameters have slightly lower standard errors compared to those obtained by the other models. All risk factors showed positive coefficients in at least four models, except for CMA. The MKT risk factor was statistically significant in all models. With the exception of SMB and CMA risk factors, all risk factors showed statistical significance (in positive coefficients) in at least three models. The Hausman test applied to fixed and random effects models with AR(1) error terms support the null hypothesis that regression models with random effects provide consistent estimators of the parameters.

All these complementary analyses based on tables and figures in Appendices A and B, also support hypothesis (H1).

### 5.2. Random Coefficients Modeling

The existence of heterogeneity of within and between effects on economic performance between BRICS and G7 countries, according to the results presented in Table 3 on the variance decomposition, offers an opportunity through random coefficients modeling to investigate whether in fact there is significant variability, over time, in the economic growth rates of BRICS and G7 countries and whether this variability occurs between countries as a function of risk factors, considering the random variability of intercepts and slopes. As a consequence, the research hypotheses (H2, H3, H4, H5 and H6) stated will be verified. Table 5 presents the estimates of the two-level random coefficients models (Level 1: time or repeated measure and Level 2: country) with repeated measures, for a balanced panel data structure with 26 annual periods (from 1994 to 2019) for each of the countries under analysis, totaling 312 observations.

Table 5 presents the estimated results for the null model, without any explanatory variable, represented by the Equation 6. This estimate aims to analyze the existence or not of variability of error terms and the decomposition of variance between levels. If the intraclass correlation is different from zero, OLS estimates do not offer the best estimator of statistical significance other than zero, which justifies the application of random coefficients modeling [41–43].

**Table 5.** Variance Decomposition—Null Model.

| Fixed Effect | Coefficient | Std Error | z |
|---|---|---|---|
| Global Mean—GDP | 0.028 *** | 0.007 | 4.17 |
| Random Effect | Variance Components (%) | Std Error (%) | z |
| Level 1 (time)<br>Temporal Variation ($r_{ti}$) | 0.056 *** | 0.005 | 12.25 |
| Level 2 (country)<br>Country Variation—Intercept ($u_{0i}$) | 0.053 ** | 0.024 | 2.25 |
| Variance Decomposition | % per Level | | |
| Level 1 (time) | 51.512 | | |
| Level 2 (country) | 48.488 | | |
| LR test vs. OLS | 158.32 *** | | |
| Log restricted-likelihood | 701.36 | | |

Obs.: ***; ** $p < 1\%$ and 5%.

Through the analysis of the results presented in Table 5, there are significant differences in economic performance (GDP growth rates) between BRICS and G7 countries and these differences also occur over time, that is, in the period of 1994 to 2019. The parameter of the fixed effects component (global mean of expected economic performances, $\gamma_{00}$) and the estimates of the variance component of the error terms (rti and u0i) different from zero, at a significance level of 5%, which is why random coefficients modeling is justified. Regarding the coefficients of random effects, the variance decomposition indicates that 51.512% (z = 12.25; $p < 0.01$) of the variability in economic performance was due to the temporal evolution in each country, however, 48.488% (z = 2.25; $p < 0.05$) of the total variance of economic performance is due to differences between countries.

The result of the likelihood ratio test (LR test; LR test = 158.32; $p$ $X^2 = 0.00 < 0.01$), which compares the robustness of the estimate (in terms of values expected) of random coefficients model in relation to linear regression by OLS (LR test vs. OLS), indicates that at the significance level of 5%, the random intercepts are not equal to zero, thus proving that for the repeated measures data for the analyzed period, estimation of a linear regression model by OLS, which produces only fixed effects coefficients, is not the most indicated. The null model results support the research hypotheses (H2) and (H3).

With the verification of the existence of significant variances in economic performance (i) over time, and (ii) over time, between countries, a temporal explanatory variable, YEAR at level 1, is included according to the proposed model, represented by the Equation (10). This model seeks to analyze whether the variable corresponding to time (linear trend) is statistically significant to explain the temporal variability in performance.

Table 6 presents the results of the linear trend model with random intercept effects.

Through the analysis of Table 6, it can be seen that with the inclusion of the explanatory variable of linear trend, YEAR at level 1, the parameters of intercept fixed effects, global mean of GDP (z = 4.88, $p < 0.01$) and the global means of the rates of change of GDP growth (parameter of the linear trend variable, YEAR; z = −2.85; $p < 0.05$) are statistically different from zero, at the significance level of 5%. The random intercept coefficients ($\sigma 2 = 0.055\%$; z = 12.23; $p < 0.01$; $\tau 00 = 0.053\%$; z = 2.26, $p < 0.05$) are statistical significant, at 5% significance level. Indeed, the intraclass correlation ($\rho$) indicates that 50.9% of the variance is due to the time evolution in each country and 49.1% of the total variance in economic performance is due to differences between countries.

There is a slight increase in the proportion of the variance component of the level 2 intercept in relation to the null model ($\rho$ = 48.488%).The result of the likelihood ratio test (LR test = 161.46; $p$ $X^2 = 0.00 < 0.01$) at a significance level of 5%, indicates the rejection of the null hypothesis that the intercepts of random effects are equal to zero, so the random coefficients model with repeated measures offers better estimates than the linear fit model by OLS.

**Table 6.** Variance Decomposition—Linear Trend Model with Random Intercepts Effects.

| **Fixed Effect** | **Coefficient** | **Std Error** | **z** |
|---|---|---|---|
| Global Mean—GDP | 0.035 *** | 0.007 | 4.88 |
| YEAR | −0.001 *** | $1.77 \times 10^{-4}$ | −2.85 |
| Random Effect | Variance Component (%) | Std Error (%) | z |
| Level 1 (time) | | | |
| Temporal Variation ($r_{ti}$) | 0.055 *** | 0.005 | 12.23 |
| Level 2 (country) | | | |
| Country Variation—Intercept ($u_{0i}$) | 0.053 ** | 0.024 | 2.26 |
| Variance Decomposition | % per Level | | |
| Level 1 (time) | 50.900 | | |
| Level 2 (country) | 49.100 | | |
| LR test vs. OLS | 161.46 *** | | |
| Log restricted-likelihood | 697.67 | | |

Obs.: ***, ** $p < 1\%$ and 5%.

Table 7 presents the expected values of the random effects temporal intercept terms for the economic performance (GDP) of the twelve countries under analysis. These results are illustrated in Figure 2.

**Table 7.** Expected Values of Intercepts of Random Effects by Country Estimated by the Linear Trend Model of Explanatory Variable Level 1—YEAR.

| **Country** | **Random Intercept** | **Country** | **Random Intercept** |
|---|---|---|---|
| Brazil | −0.00412 | Italy | −0.02012 |
| Canada | −0.00366 | Japan | −0.01827 |
| China | 0.05725 | Russia | −0.00802 |
| France | −0.01126 | South Africa | −0.00216 |
| Germany | −0.01361 | UK | −0.00654 |
| India | 0.03371 | United States | −0.00319 |

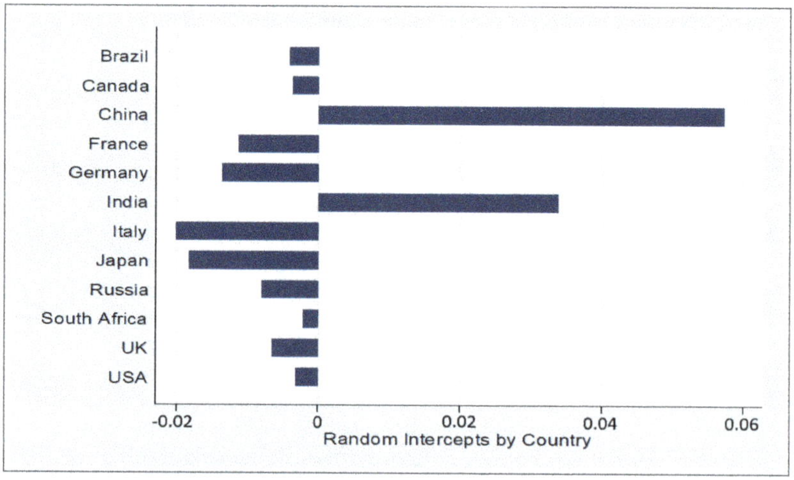


**Figure 2.** Expected values of intercepts of random effects by country estimated by the linear trend model of explanatory variable level 1—YEAR.

The expected error terms of random intercepts for the GDP of the same country do not vary over time, however, they vary between the GDP of each country, so, according to [41–43], it establishes the existence of an intercept for each country. Through the analysis of Table 7 and Figure 2, it can be seen that, on average, the initial economic performance dependent on the explanatory variable YEAR was of in the range from −2.012% (Italy) to 5.725% (China). Two countries, China and India, presented positive random temporal intercept terms, with a minimum magnitude of 3.371% (India).

Table 8 presents the results of the linear trend model with random effects of intercepts and slopes, represented by the Equation (13a).

**Table 8.** Variance Decomposition—Linear Trend Model with Random Intercepts and Slopes Effects.

| Fixed Effect | Coefficient | Std Error | z |
|---|---|---|---|
| Global Mean—GDP | 0.035 *** | 0.007 | 4.86 |
| YEAR | −0.001 *** | $1.941 \times 10^{-4}$ | −2.60 |
| Random Effect | Variance Component (%) | Std Error (%) | z |
| Level 1 (time) | | | |
| Temporal variance ($r_{ti}$) | 0.055 *** | 0.005 | 11.96 |
| Level 2 (country) | | | |
| Country Variance—Intercept ($u_{0i}$) | 0.054 ** | 0.024 | 2.20 |
| Country Variance—Slope ($u_{1i}$) | $7.9 \times 10^{-8}$ | $1.78 \times 10^{-7}$ | 0.44 |
| Variance Decomposition | % per Level | | |
| Level 1 (time) | 50.411 | | |
| Level 2 (country) | 49.589 | | |
| LR test vs. OLS | 161.71 *** | | |
| Log restricted-likelihood | 697.79 | $X^2$ | $p$ |
| LR test—Random Intercept Model vs. Random Intercept and Slope Model | | 0.26 | 0.61 |

Obs.: ***, ** $p < 1\%$ and 5%.

The statistical results support that for the analyzed period, there were no significant variances of slopes in economic performance over time between different countries. It is observed that the estimates of the fixed effects parameters (global means of the intercept, $\gamma_{00} = 0.035$), the global mean of the GDP growth rate ($\gamma_{10} = -0.001$) and of the residual variance ($\sigma^2 = 0.055$) in the model with intercept and random slopes do not differ from those obtained in the model with only random intercepts (see Table 6), because the variance component of the random slope terms (u1i) has statistical significance ($z = 0.44$; $p > 0.05$) equal to zero. In fact, the result of the likelihood ratio test, applied to compare the estimates of linear trend models with random intercepts (Log restricted-likelihood = 697.67) and with random intercepts and slopes (Log restricted-likelihood = 697.79), indicates that the values obtained by the difference of the logarithms of the two restricted likelihood functions (LR test = −0.26; $p$ $X^2 = 0.61 > 0.05$) of the models are statistically equal, so that a linear trend model with only random intercepts is the most suitable.

From the analysis made through Tables 6 and 8, it is concluded that the investigation hypothesis (H4) is supported.

With the identification of the random character of the error terms (linear trend of random intercept), a final complete model of linear trend will be built, with the inclusion of explanatory variables at level 1, the risk factors considered in [14], where the interaction between level 1 and the random effects of slopes, at level 2, allows to capture the differences in GDP growth rates of each country, and offers the best fit model.

Of the five risk factors in [14], only the MKT and RMW risk factors showed statistical significance, at the 10% level, to explain the variation in GDP growth rates in BRICS and G7 countries. Thus, Table 9 presents the results of the final complete linear trend model with the inclusion of two risk factors MKT and RMW in the fixed effects component that capture the intercept random effects at level 2, represented by the Equation (20).

$$GDP_{t,i} = \gamma_{00} + \gamma_{10i}YEAR_{t,i} + \gamma_{11i}MKT_{t,i-1} + \gamma_{12i}RMW_{t,i-1} + u_{0i} + r_{t,i} \quad (20)$$

**Table 9.** Decomposition of variance—Linear Trend Model with Random Intercepts and MKT and RMW Explanatory Variables, Which Captures the Level 2 Random Effects—Final Complete Model.

| **Fixed Effect** | **Coefficient** | **Std Error** | **z** |
|---|---|---|---|
| Global Mean—GDP | 0.030 *** | 0.007 | 4.24 |
| YEAR | −0.001 *** | $1.627 \times 10^{-4}$ | −3.40 |
| MKT | 0.043 *** | 0.005 | 7.98 |
| RMW | 0.059 *** | 0.016 | 3.69 |
| Random Effect | Variance Component (%) | Std Error (%) | z |
| Level 1 (time) | | | |
| Temporal variance ($r_{ti}$) | 0.046 *** | 0.004 | 12.19 |
| Level 2 (country) | | | |
| Country variance—Intercept ($u_{0i}$) | 0.054 ** | 0.024 | 2.27 |
| Variance Decomposition | % per Level | | |
| Level 1 (time) | 45.807 | | |
| Level 2 (country) | 54.193 | | |
| LR test vs. OLS | 188.51 *** | | |
| Log restricted-likelihood | 719.15 | | |

Obs.: ***, ** $p < 1\%$ and 5%.

However, a random coefficients model without the MKT and RMW risk factors in the fixed effects component, yet, with level 2 random slopes in the temporal evolution, presents the best estimators. The estimates of this model, represented by the Equation (21), are presented in Table 10.

$$GDP_{t,i} = \gamma_{00} + \gamma_{10i} YEAR_{t,i} + u_{0i} + u_{1i} MKT_{t,i-1} + u_{2i} RMW_{t,i-1} + r_{t,i} \quad (21)$$

**Table 10.** Decomposition of Variance—Linear Trend Model with Random Intercepts Without the Risk Factors MKT and RMW in the Fixed Effects Component, yet, with Random Slopes in the Temporal Evolution.

| **Fixed Effect** | **Coefficient** | **Std Error** | **z** |
|---|---|---|---|
| Global Mean—GDP | 0.032 *** | 0.008 | 4.21 |
| Global mean GDP growth rate ($\gamma_{10}$) | −0.001 *** | $1.465 \times 10^{-4}$ | −3.79 |
| Random Effect | Variance Component (%) | Std Error (%) | z |
| Level 1 | | | |
| Temporal variance ($r_{ti}$) | 0.037 *** | 0.003 | 11.71 |
| Level 2 | | | |
| Country Variance—Intercept ($u_{0i}$) | 0.062 ** | 0.027 | 2.28 |
| Country Variance—Slope MKT ($u_{1i}$) | 0.243 ** | 0.115 | 2.11 |
| Country Variance—Slope RMW ($u_{1i}$) | 1.018 ** | 0.487 | 2.09 |
| Variance Decomposition | % per Level | | |
| Level 1 (time) | 2.699 | | |
| Level 2 (country) | 97.301 | | |
| LR test vs. OLS | 234.60 *** | | |
| Log restricted-likelihood | 734.24 | | |

Obs.: ***, ** $p < 1\%$ and 5%.

From the analysis of Tables 9 and 10, it can be seen that the parameters of fixed effects and of the random coefficients of intercepts, present statistical significance different from zero, at a significance level of 5%. The global mean of economic performance (GDP) was adjusted to 3%. The explanatory variables of level 1, MKT ($z = 7.98$, $p < 0.01$) and RMW ($z = 3.69$, $p < 0.01$), showed positive coefficients and predicted an increase in performance economic growth between countries of 4.3% and 5.9%.

The variance decomposition between levels indicates that 45.807% ($z = 12.19$, $p < 0.01$), against 2.695% ($z = 11.71$, $p < 0.01$), of the model without the risk factors MKT and RMW in the fixed effects component of the variability of economic performance is due to the temporal evolution in each country, however, a significant portion of variance in the order of 54.193% (z = 2.27, $p < 0.05$), against 97.301% (z = 2.09, $p < 0.05$) of the model without the MKT and RMW risk factors in the fixed effects component, is due to differences in economic performance between countries.

The result of the likelihood ratio test (LR test = 188.51, $p\ X^2 = 0.00 < 0.01$ against LR test = 234.60, $p\ X^2 = 0.00 < 0.01$) indicates statistical significance, at the level of 5%, suggesting that the intercepts of random effects are in fact different from zero, so that the estimates of a linear regression model by OLS are discarded, however, a model without the explanatory variables MKT and RMW in the fixed effects, but in the random effects of slopes produces estimates with less distortions, as illustrated in Figure 3, which complements the result of the LR test, and illustrates the superiority of the random coefficients model with repeated measures in relation to the regression model estimated by OLS.

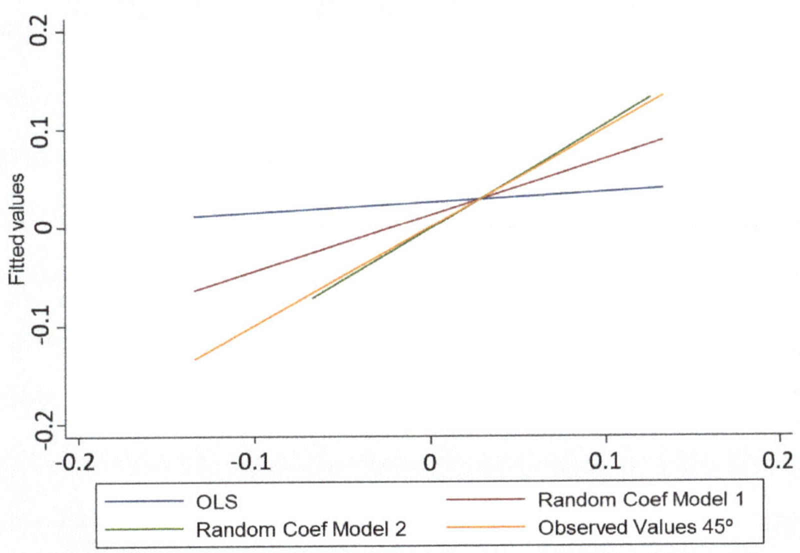


**Figure 3.** Values predicted by OLS and random coefficients vs. observed values of economic performance.

Indeed, it compares the predicted values of future economic performance estimated by the random coefficients modeling with the predicted values estimated by OLS, using the same explanatory variables in the fixed effects components (YEAR, MKT and RMW) and with observed real values of economic performance, represented by the sample GDP growth rates.

As shown in Figure 3, the yellow line at 45° indicates the observed values of the economic performance of each of the countries in the sample, in each of the analyzed periods. The red line indicates the values estimated by the random coefficients model, considering the explanatory variables YEAR, MKT and RMW in the fixed effects component, the green line indicates the values estimated by the random coefficients model without the explanatory variables MKT and RMW in the component of fixed effects, however, with random slopes of MKT and RMW precisely in the temporal evolution. Finally, the blue line denotes the fixed effects estimates of the multiple regression model by OLS.

It is found that, in relation to the OLS regression model, the random coefficients model, with a linear trend with explanatory variables YEAR, MKT and RMW and with random intercepts at level 2, presents a better adjustment in capturing random contexts of intercepts, however, it does not outperforms the random coefficients model with random slopes that presents less distortions in the adjustments of the expected values.

Table 11 presents the expected values of the random effects intercept terms, considering the linear trend models with explanatory variables YEAR, MKT and RMW in the fixed effects component, and without the explanatory variables, MKT and RMW in the fixed effects component, however, on the random effects of level 2 slopes on temporal evolution. The magnitudes and signs of the expected values of intercepts and random slopes, respectively, are illustrated in Figures 4 and 5.

**Table 11.** Expected Values of Intercepts of Random Effects by Country Estimated by Linear Trend Models of Explanatory Variables YEAR, MKT and RMW in the Fixed Effects Component and without MKT and RMW in the Fixed Effects Component, but rather in the Random Effects of the Slopes.

| Country | Random Intercept | | Random Slope | |
|---|---|---|---|---|
| | YEAR MKT RMW as Fixed Effect Components | YEAR as Fixed Effect Components | MKT | RMW |
| Brazil | −0.00397 | −0.00557 | 0.04922 | 0.01287 |
| Canada | −0.00382 | −0.00105 | 0.04290 | −0.04448 |
| China | 0.05784 | 0.06062 | 0.01705 | −0.03760 |
| France | −0.01147 | −0.01059 | 0.03852 | 0.00791 |
| Germany | −0.01384 | −0.01564 | 0.06489 | 0.02938 |
| India | 0.03413 | 0.03878 | −0.00447 | −0.02460 |
| Italy | −0.02040 | −0.01977 | 0.04492 | 0.00136 |
| Japan | −0.01853 | −0.01873 | 0.04975 | 0.01434 |
| Russia | −0.00790 | −0.01492 | 0.07647 | 0.28924 |
| South Africa | −0.00200 | −0.00177 | 0.02975 | 0.03371 |
| UK | −0.00671 | −0.00730 | 0.04081 | 0.04156 |
| USA | −0.00334 | −0.00405 | 0.04767 | 0.03408 |

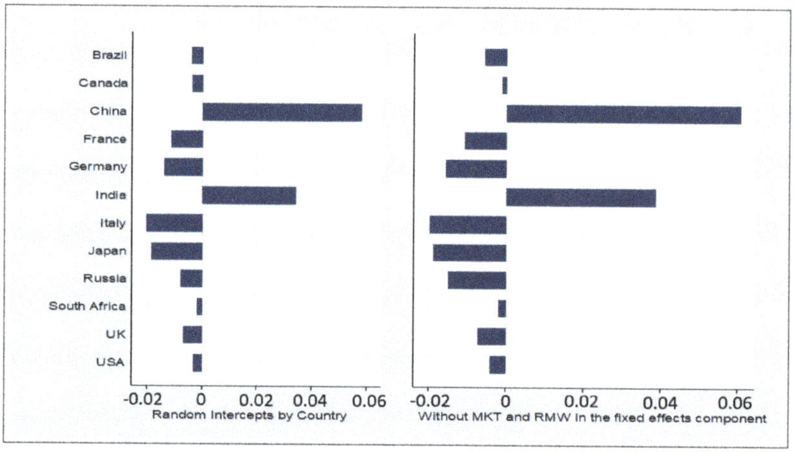


**Figure 4.** Expected values of random effects intercepts by country estimated by the linear trend model with and without the explanatory variables MKT and RMW in the fixed effects component.

Through the analysis of Table 11 and of Figure 4, it is found that considering the variables YEAR, MKT and RMW in the fixed effects component, the expected average of economic performance between countries varied between −2.040% and −1.977 (Italy), and 5.784% and 6.062% (China). Two countries, China and India preserved the terms of positive temporal intercepts, however, the minimum magnitude was adjusted to 3.413% (India), as illustrated in Figure 4.

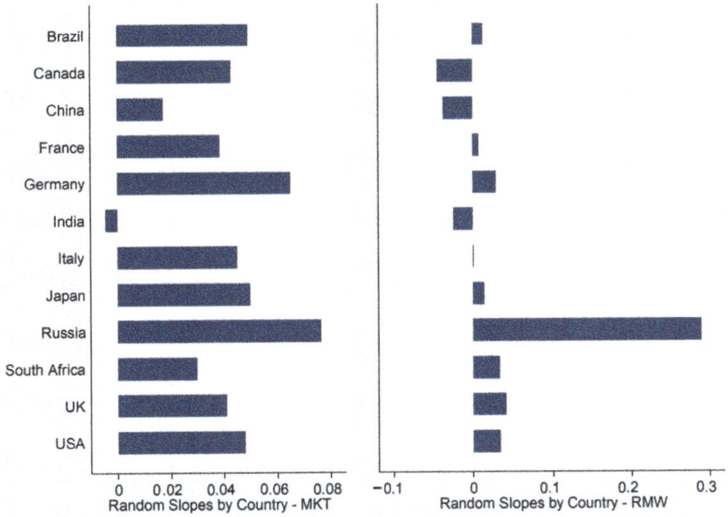


**Figure 5.** Expected values of random effects slopes by country estimated by the risk factors MKT and RMW for the linear trend model only with the explanatory variable YEAR in the fixed effects component.

Regarding the random slopes, through the analysis of Table 11 and of Figure 5, it is found that the expected average of economic performance between countries, considering the explanatory variables, respectively, MKT and RMW in the random effects component was of the order of −0.447% and −2.46% (India) to 7.647% and 28.924% (Russia). For the MKT risk factor, eleven countries, South Africa, Germany, Brazil, Canada, China, the United States, France, Italy, Japan, the United Kingdom and Russia presented positive slope terms, with a minimum magnitude of 1.705% (China). Regarding the RMW risk factor, nine countries, South Africa, Germany, Brazil, the United States, France, Italy, Japan, the United Kingdom and Russia, presented positive slope terms, with a minimum magnitude adjusted to 0.136% (Italy), as illustrated in Figure 5.

From the analysis made through Tables 10 and 11, it is concluded that the investigation hypothesis (H5) is supported.

Table 12 presents the decomposition of the variance between levels of three random coefficients models with three explanatory variables, YEAR, MKT and one of the three elementary risk factor ($SMB_{B/M}$, $SMB_{OP}$ and $SMB_{INV}$). Panel A, B and C, respectively, correspond to the final complete model YEAR, MKT and $SMB_{B/M}$, YEAR, MKT and $SMB_{OP}$ and YEAR, MKT and $SMB_{B/M}$, represented by the Equations (22)–(24).

$$GDP_{t,i} = \gamma_{00} + \gamma_{10i}ANO_{t,i} + \gamma_{11i}MKT_{t,i-1} + \gamma_{12i}SMB_{B/M,\ t,i-1} + u_{0i} + r_{t,i} \quad (22)$$

$$GDP_{t,i} = \gamma_{00} + \gamma_{10i}ANO_{t,i} + \gamma_{11i}MKT_{t,i-1} + \gamma_{12i}SMB_{OP,t,i-1} + u_{0i} + r_{t,i} \quad (23)$$

$$GDP_{t,i} = \gamma_{00} + \gamma_{10i}ANO_{t,i} + \gamma_{11i}MKT_{t,i-1} + \gamma_{12i}SMB_{INV,t,i-1} + u_{0i} + r_{t,i} \quad (24)$$

From the analysis of Table 12, which presents the results of the linear trend model with random intercept effects, it can be seen that the fixed effect parameters and the random intercept coefficients have a statistical significance different from zero. Although the parameters of the variables $SMB_{B/M}$, $SMB_{OP}$ and $SMB_{INV}$ showed a negative sign due to the presence of the other explanatory variables (YEAR and MKT), the correlation between economic performance and each elemental risk factor is positive, as seen in Table 4. The global mean (intercept) of economic performance was adjusted to 3.2% (Panel A), 3.3% (Panel B) and 3.3% (Panel C). The market beta risk factor of the three models, respectively, MKT (z = 7.22; $p < 0.01$, panel A), MKT (z = 7.16; $p < 0.05$, panel B) and MKT (z = 7.54; $p < 0.01$, panel C), showed positive coefficients and predicted an increase in economic performance of 3.6%, 3.6% and 3.8%, ceteris paribus.

**Table 12.** Decomposition of variance—Linear Trend Model with Random Intercepts and Explanatory Variables that Capture Level 2 Random Effects—Final Complete Model.

| Panel A | | | | Panel B | | | | Panel C | | | |
|---|---|---|---|---|---|---|---|---|---|---|---|
| **Fixed Effect** | **Coef** | **SE** | **z** | **Fixed Effect** | **Coef** | **SE** | **z** | **Fixed Effect** | **Coef** | **SE** | **z** |
| Global Mean (Gm)—GDP | 0.032 *** | 0.007 | 4.57 | Gm GDP | 0.033 *** | 0.007 | 4.65 | Gm GDP | 0.033 *** | 0.007 | 4.68 |
| YEAR | −0.001 *** | $1.64 \times 10^{-4}$ | −3.07 | YEAR | −0.001 *** | $1.66 \times 10^{-4}$ | −3.13 | YEAR | −0.001 *** | $1.65 \times 10^{-4}$ | −3.33 |
| MKT | 0.036 *** | 0.005 | 7.22 | MKT | 0.036 *** | 0.005 | 7.16 | MKT | 0.038 *** | 0.005 | 7.54 |
| $SMB_{B/M}$ | −0.028 * | 0.015 | 1.92 | $SMB_{OP}$ | −0.026 * | 0.014 | −1.79 | $SMB_{INV}$ | −0.035 ** | 0.013 | 2.73 |
| Random Effect | VC (%) | SE (%) | z | | VC (%) | SE (%) | z | | VC (%) | SE (%) | z |
| Level 1 (time) Temporal Variance ($r_{ti}$) | 0.047 *** | 0.004 | 12.19 | | 0.047 *** | 0.004 | 12.20 | | 0.047 *** | 0.004 | 12.19 |
| Level 2 (country) Country Variance—Intercept ($u_{0i}$) | 0.052 *** | 0.025 | 2.27 | | 0.052 *** | 0.023 | 2.27 | | 0.052 *** | 0.023 | 2.27 |
| Variance Decomposition | % per Level | | | | % per Level | | | | per Level | | |
| Level 1 (time) | 47.738 | | | | 47.551 | | | | 47.066 | | |
| Level 2 (country) | 52.262 | | | | 52.449 | | | | 52.934 | | |
| LR test vs. OLS | 178.57 *** | | | | 179.51 *** | | | | 182.29 *** | | |
| Log restricted-likelihood | 714.24 | | | | 713.99 | | | | 715.97 | | |

Obs.: Gm: global mean; Coef: coefficient; VC: variance component; SE: standard error; ***, **, * $p < 1\%$, 5% and 10%.

The decomposition of the variance between levels indicates that 47.738% (z = 12.19; $p < 0.01$), 47.551% (z = 12.2; $p < 0.01$) and 47.066% (z = 12.19; $p < 0.01$) of the variability of economic performance is due to the temporal evolution in each country, however, a significant portion of variance of 52.262% (z = 2.27; $p < 0.01$), 52.449% (z = 2.27; $p < 0.01$) and 52.934% (z = 2.78; $p < 0.01$) is due to the difference in economic performance between countries. It is observed that the coefficients of the three models present equal performance to explain the differences in random intercepts in economic growth. The result of the likelihood ratio test (LR test = 178.57; $p < 0.01$), for Panel A, (LR test = 179.51; $p < 0.01$), for Panel B, and for Panel C (LR test = 182.29; $p < 0.01$) indicates statistical significance, at the 5% level, and supports the evidence that the intercepts of random effects are in fact different from zero, therefore discarding the estimates of a linear regression model by OLS.

Table 13 presents the expected values of the intercept terms of random effects of the economic performance of each of the twelve countries, estimated by the final complete model. Panels A, B and C, respectively, present the expected values of the intercept terms estimated with the explanatory variables YEAR, MKT and $SMB_{B/M}$, YEAR, MKT and $SMB_{OP}$, and YEAR, MKT and $SMB_{INV}$.

Through the analysis of Table 13, it can be seen that the variation of the expected average of economic performance between countries was of the order of −1.971% (Italy) to 5.681% (China), Panel A, −1.985% (Italy) to 5.701% (China), Panel B and −1.993% (Italy) to 5.714% (China), Panel C. Two countries, India and China kept positive temporal intercepts, however, the minimum magnitude was adjusted to 3.315% (India), Panel A, 3.335% (India), Panel B and 3.347% (India), Panel C.

As expected, the results presented in Tables 12 and 13 attest that, for the analyzed period, the economic performance of BRICS and G7 countries follows a linear trend over time and there are significant differences in random intercepts between countries. Size effect elementary risk factors $SMB_{B/M}$, $SMB_{OP}$ and $SMB_{INV}$ help to explain the variability in the future economic growth rate over time, so the research hypothesis (H6) is supported.

**Table 13.** Expected Values of Intercepts of Random Effects by Country Estimated by the Linear Trend Model with Explanatory Variables Regional Risk Factors Associated with the Final Complete Model.

| Country | Panel A Independent Variable YEAR MKT $SMB_{B/M}$ | Panel B Independent Variable YEAR MKT $SMB_{OP}$ | Panel C Independent Variable YEAR MKT $SMB_{INV}$ |
|---|---|---|---|
| Brazil | −0.00484 | −0.00466 | −0.00457 |
| Canada | −0.00318 | −0.00331 | −0.00338 |
| China | 0.05681 | 0.05701 | 0.05714 |
| France | −0.01081 | −0.01094 | −0.01102 |
| Germany | −0.01317 | −0.01330 | −0.01338 |
| India | 0.03315 | 0.03335 | 0.03347 |
| Italy | −0.01971 | −0.01985 | −0.01993 |
| Japan | −0.01785 | −0.01798 | −0.01807 |
| Russia | −0.00876 | −0.00858 | −0.00849 |
| South Africa | −0.00288 | −0.00270 | −0.00260 |
| UK | −0.00606 | −0.00620 | −0.00627 |
| USA | −0.00270 | −0.00283 | −0.00290 |

## 6. Conclusions

In this study, in view of the integrating process of stock markets at the regional and global level, we explore the existence of variability in GDP growth rates, and the explanatory power of global risk factors of developed and emerging stock markets of [14] model as an indicator of the change in economic growth of a total of twelve countries, developed G7 countries and emerging BRICS countries, using GDP data and risk factor returns for a 26-year period, from 1993 to 2019.

The results show that global risk factors, from developed and emerging markets, considered in [14] help to explain the differences in GDP growth rates of the analyzed countries (developed from G7 and emerging from the BRICS). They also show that the temporal variation of the random effects of the intercepts can be explained by random coefficients models formed by a set of two risk factors: (i) MKT and RMW, (ii) MKT and $SMB_{B/M}$; (iii) MKT and $SMB_{OP}$, and (iv) MKT and $SMB_{INV}$.

The univariate analysis of the descriptive statistics of the decomposition of the variance of the return of the risk factors allowed to verify that all the risk factors presented positive average returns. The three elementary risk factors of the size effect ($SMB_{B/M}$, $SMB_{OP}$ and $SMB_{INV}$) contributed positively to the average size risk premium; $SMB_{B/M}$ and $SMB_{OP}$, respectively, presented the lowest and highest average value of premiums. Risk factors showed greater variation over time than between countries. The variation in the GDP growth rate between countries was slightly greater than the variation over time. This result was confirmed through multivariate analysis, considering longitudinal quantile regression modeling for panel data that evaluated the existence of differences in future economic performance explained by global risk factors, as well as random coefficients modeling with repeated measures, which sought to investigate the existence of differences in economic performance across countries and over time, and the reasons for such differences.

The results obtained support that for the analyzed period, there are significant differences in the behavior of the conditional asymmetric distribution of the GDP growth rate, explained by the returns of the global risk factors of [14]. Like [19], we report that the market risk factors, $SMB_{B/M}$, $SMB_{OP}$ e $SMB_{INV}$, SMB, HML, RMW and CMA individually, contain information about the future GDP growth variability, and jointly, the predictive capacity of these risk factors is independent of the information contained in the market risk factor beta.

By decomposing the variance through the estimation of a null model, it was possible to attest that economic performance follows a linear trend over analyzed period, there is significant variability in economic performance, over time, and between countries, 48% of the total variability of the GDP growth rate is due to the existence of differences between countries. For the analyzed period, the temporal variation of random effects of intercepts can be explained by four random coefficients models formed by a set of two explanatory variables, the fundamental risk factors, respectively, (i) MKT e RMW, (ii) MKT e $SMB_{B/M}$; (iii) MKT e $SMB_{OP}$, and (iv) MKT and $SMB_{INV}$, which explain approximately 54%, 52%, 52% and 53% of the total variability in the future GDP growth rate of BRICS and G7 countries.

The results of this study confirm that stock markets follow an integration process, and support the arguments of [5–7] that moderately integrated markets may have the same risk factors, and just like [13,14,16,19], since risk factors are related to future GDP growth, they act as proxies for unidentified state variables, consistent with the ICAPM pricing model of [15].

Given that the total country-effect GDP growth rate variability was considerable and variations in expected returns reflect business cycle exposures [20–22], a study that includes macroeconomic factors of each country provides a new understanding of the performance of economic growth in the face of elementary risk factors of the size effect, $SMB_{B/M}$, $SMB_{OP}$ and $SMB_{INV}$.

Future studies may address the influence of other types of market besides stocks on the economic performance of countries. In addition, these studies can estimate such relationships by other statistical techniques to enable the comparison of results between different models.

**Author Contributions:** Conceptualization: J.C.J.F., A.P.M.G. and L.P.F.; methodology: J.C.J.F., L.P.F. and R.G.S.; software: J.C.J.F., A.P.M.G. and P.B.; validation: L.P.F., R.G.S. and P.B.; writing—original draft preparation: J.C.J.F., A.P.M.G., R.G.S. and L.P.F.; writing—review and editing: I.P.d.A.C. and M.d.S.; supervision: L.P.F. All authors have read and agreed to the published version of the manuscript.

**Funding:** This research received no external funding.

**Data Availability Statement:** Not applicable, the study does not report any data.

**Conflicts of Interest:** The authors declare no conflict of interest.

## Appendix A

Table A1 presents the estimates of three simple and multiple quantile regression models for the percentiles 0.05; 0.25; 0.50; 0.75; and 0.95, having as explanatory variables the market beta risk factors, MKT and the elementary size effects $SMB_{B/M}$, $SMB_{OP}$ and $SMB_{INV}$, represented by the Equations (1) (Panel A) and (2) (Panel B).

**Table A1.** Simple and Multiple Regression Estimates with Two Explanatory Variables Risk Factors MKT, $SMB_{B/M}$, $SMB_{OP}$ and $SMB_{INV}$.

| Model | | | OLS | Quantile Regression | | | | |
|---|---|---|---|---|---|---|---|---|
| | | | | 0.05 | 0.25 | 0.50 | 0.75 | 0.95 |
| Panel A: $GDP_{it} = \alpha + \beta Factor_{it-1} + \varepsilon_{i,t}$ | | | | | | | | |
| Brazil | | | | | | | | |
| 1 | $SMB_{B/M}$ | Coef | 0.045 | −0.215 ** | −0.044 *** | 0.084 | 0.040 | 0.061 |
| | | SE | 0.048 | 0.075 | 0.015 | 0.058 | 0.062 | 0.046 |
| 2 | $SMB_{OP}$ | Coef | 0.071 ** | −0.269 *** | 0.071 | 0.082 | 0.033 | 0.073 |
| | | SE | 0.034 | 0.018 | 0.066 | 0.050 | 0.058 | 0.055 |
| 3 | $SMB_{INV}$ | Coef | 0.057 ** | −0.274 *** | 0.076 | 0.047 | 0.025 | 0.069 ** |
| | | SE | 0.021 | 0.020 | 0.050 | 0.050 | 0.049 | 0.032 |

**Table A1.** *Cont.*

| Model | | | OLS | Quantile Regression | | | | |
|---|---|---|---|---|---|---|---|---|
| | | | | **0.05** | **0.25** | **0.50** | **0.75** | **0.95** |
| | | | | Canada | | | | |
| 1 | $SMB_{B/M}$ | Coef<br>SE | 0.075<br>0.049 | 0.296 **<br>0.104 | 0.099 ***<br>0.023 | 0.065<br>0.043 | 0.056<br>0.067 | −0.111 ***<br>0.010 |
| 2 | $SMB_{OP}$ | Coef<br>SE | 0.062<br>0.049 | 0.294 **<br>0.142 | 0.096 ***<br>0.027 | 0.066 **<br>0.027 | 0.037<br>0.030 | −0.114 **<br>0.049 |
| 3 | $SMB_{INV}$ | Coef<br>SE | 0.064<br>0.049 | 0.275 *<br>0.163 | 0.089 **<br>0.031 | 0.110 ***<br>0.027 | 0.040<br>0.050 | −0.081 *<br>0.044 |
| | | | | China | | | | |
| 1 | $SMB_{B/M}$ | Coef<br>SE | 0.060 *<br>0.032 | 0.054 ***<br>0.013 | 0.044<br>0.033 | 0.107 **<br>0.038 | 0.072<br>0.045 | 0.009<br>0.113 |
| 2 | $SMB_{OP}$ | Coef<br>SE | 0.075 ***<br>0.019 | 0.060 ***<br>0.014 | 0.113 **<br>0.050 | 0.098 ***<br>0.031 | 0.058<br>0.042 | 0.007<br>0.108 |
| 3 | $SMB_{INV}$ | Coef<br>SE | 0.066 ***<br>0.011 | 0.059 ***<br>0.019 | 0.086 ***<br>0.027 | 0.066 **<br>0.028 | 0.050<br>0.036 | 0.005<br>0.069 |
| | | | | France | | | | |
| 1 | $SMB_{B/M}$ | Coef<br>SE | 0.016<br>0.035 | 0.122 ***<br>0.015 | 0.089 ***<br>0.006 | 0.041 *<br>0.023 | 0.002<br>0.014 | 0.011<br>0.043 |
| 2 | $SMB_{OP}$ | Coef<br>SE | 0.048<br>0.036 | 0.213 ***<br>0.051 | 0.064 **<br>0.026 | 0.030<br>0.022 | −0.016<br>0.022 | −0.021<br>0.052 |
| 3 | $SMB_{INV}$ | Coef<br>SE | 0.005<br>0.035 | 0.034 ***<br>0.004 | 0.073 ***<br>0.014 | 0.041 **<br>0.015 | −0.015<br>0.018 | −0.019<br>0.054 |
| | | | | Germany | | | | |
| 1 | $SMB_{B/M}$ | Coef<br>SE | 0.043<br>0.044 | 0.116 ***<br>0.039 | 0.023<br>0.032 | 0.060 *<br>0.033 | 0.034<br>0.029 | 0.076 ***<br>0.004 |
| 2 | $SMB_{OP}$ | Coef<br>SE | 0.026<br>0.043 | 0.202 ***<br>0.057 | −0.005<br>0.042 | −0.018<br>0.040 | 0.031<br>0.041 | 0.077 ***<br>0.007 |
| 3 | $SMB_{INV}$ | Coef<br>SE | 0.039<br>0.029 | 0.057<br>0.036 | 0.029<br>0.021 | 0.023<br>0.017 | 0.025<br>0.024 | 0.078 ***<br>0.019 |
| | | | | India | | | | |
| 1 | $SMB_{B/M}$ | Coef<br>SE | 0.018<br>0.034 | 0.014<br>0.061 | 0.039<br>0.063 | 0.031<br>0.025 | 0.033 ***<br>0.005 | 0.039 **<br>0.016 |
| 2 | $SMB_{OP}$ | Coef<br>SE | 0.010<br>0.033 | 0.030<br>0.060 | 0.038<br>0.085 | −0.017<br>0.019 | 0.030 ***<br>0.008 | 0.076 ***<br>0.013 |
| 3 | $SMB_{INV}$ | Coef<br>SE | 0.016<br>0.026 | 0.023<br>0.048 | 0.026<br>0.056 | −0.013<br>0.014 | 0.029 ***<br>0.005 | 0.077 ***<br>0.005 |
| | | | | Italy | | | | |
| 1 | $SMB_{B/M}$ | Coef<br>SE | 0.045<br>0.034 | 0.167 ***<br>0.054 | 0.073 ***<br>0.019 | 0.007<br>0.035 | −0.001<br>0.018 | 0.064 **<br>0.025 |
| 2 | $SMB_{OP}$ | Coef<br>SE | 0.034<br>0.035 | 0.175 ***<br>0.031 | 0.071 **<br>0.026 | 0.007<br>0.038 | −0.001<br>0.013 | −0.066 ***<br>0.013 |
| 3 | $SMB_{INV}$ | Coef<br>SE | 0.033<br>0.033 | 0.150 ***<br>0.045 | 0.064 *<br>0.036 | 0.006<br>0.032 | −0.001<br>0.018 | 0.064 **<br>0.028 |

**Table A1.** *Cont.*

| | Model | | OLS | Quantile Regression | | | | |
|---|---|---|---|---|---|---|---|---|
| | | | | **0.05** | **0.25** | **0.50** | **0.75** | **0.95** |
| | | | | Japan | | | | |
| 1 | $SMB_{B/M}$ | Coef<br>SE | 0.078 *<br>0.039 | 0.049 *<br>0.025 | 0.079 **<br>0.034 | 0.062 **<br>0.024 | 0.070 **<br>0.027 | 0.088 **<br>0.031 |
| 2 | $SMB_{OP}$ | Coef<br>SE | 0.066<br>0.039 | 0.224 ***<br>0.047 | 0.085 ***<br>0.015 | 0.059 *<br>0.034 | 0.022<br>0.027 | 0.074 ***<br>0.026 |
| 3 | $SMB_{INV}$ | Coef<br>SE | 0.064<br>0.039 | 0.053<br>0.035 | 0.081 ***<br>0.016 | 0.054<br>0.033 | 0.057<br>0.059 | 0.088 ***<br>0.025 |
| | | | | Russia | | | | |
| 1 | $SMB_{B/M}$ | Coef<br>SE | −0.234 **<br>0.104 | −0.185<br>0.193 | −0.360 **<br>0.134 | −0.316 *<br>0.160 | −0.094<br>0.109 | −0.284 ***<br>0.012 |
| 2 | $SMB_{OP}$ | Coef<br>SE | −0.179<br>0.105 | −0.169<br>0.163 | −0.320 ***<br>0.132 | −0.145<br>0.137 | −0.102<br>0.102 | −0.225 ***<br>0.026 |
| 3 | $SMB_{INV}$ | Coef<br>SE | −0.191 **<br>0.078 | −0.133<br>0.124 | −0.240 **<br>0.084 | −0.137<br>0.095 | −0.106<br>0.066 | −0.152 ***<br>0.026 |
| | | | | South Africa | | | | |
| 1 | $SMB_{B/M}$ | Coef<br>SE | 0.010<br>0.026 | 0.105 *<br>0.063 | 0.053<br>0.046 | 0.012<br>0.032 | −0.026<br>0.035 | 0.019<br>0.023 |
| 2 | $SMB_{OP}$ | Coef<br>SE | 0.026<br>0.023 | 0.080<br>0.071 | 0.047<br>0.062 | 0.011<br>0.033 | −0.022<br>0.040 | −0.050<br>0.051 |
| 3 | $SMB_{INV}$ | Coef<br>SE | 0.016<br>0.015 | 0.056 **<br>0.021 | 0.036<br>0.053 | 0.008<br>0.026 | −0.015<br>0.030 | 0.082 ***<br>0.010 |
| | | | | United Kingdom | | | | |
| 1 | $SMB_{B/M}$ | Coef<br>SE | 0.012<br>0.032 | 0.090 ***<br>0.027 | 0.030<br>0.040 | −0.002<br>0.026 | −0.009<br>0.046 | −0.001<br>0.013 |
| 2 | $SMB_{OP}$ | Coef<br>SE | 0.022<br>0.035 | 0.089 ***<br>0.018 | 0.031**<br>0.011 | −0.002<br>0.019 | −0.008<br>0.038 | 0.008<br>0.010 |
| 3 | $SMB_{INV}$ | Coef<br>SE | 0.015<br>0.033 | 0.082 **<br>0.034 | 0.029<br>0.023 | −0.002<br>0.027 | −0.020<br>0.028 | 0.007<br>0.024 |
| | | | | United States | | | | |
| 1 | $SMB_{B/M}$ | Coef<br>SE | 0.012<br>0.043 | 0.084 ***<br>0.015 | 0.056 **<br>0.024 | 0.051 ***<br>0.016 | −0.022<br>0.018 | −0.021 ***<br>0.005 |
| 2 | $SMB_{OP}$ | Coef<br>SE | 0.001<br>0.045 | 0.214 ***<br>0.023 | −0.009<br>0.022 | 0.031<br>0.033 | −0.035<br>0.045 | −0.024 **<br>0.011 |
| 3 | $SMB_{INV}$ | Coef<br>SE | −0.001<br>0.044 | 0.089 **<br>0.035 | −0.011<br>0.040 | 0.041<br>0.030 | −0.035<br>0.043 | −0.022 ***<br>0.006 |
| | | | | Panel B: $GDP_{i,t} = \alpha + \beta_1 MKT_{i,t-1} + \beta_2 Fator_{it-1} + \varepsilon_{i,t}$ | | | | |
| | | | | Brazil | | | | |
| 4 | MKT | Coef<br>SE | 0.052 ***<br>0.010 | 0.121 ***<br>0.018 | 0.050 ***<br>0.010 | 0.048 ***<br>0.010 | 0.051 ***<br>0.005 | 0.033 ***<br>0.004 |
| | $SMB_{B/M}$ | Coef<br>SE | −0.021<br>0.034 | −0.053<br>0.064 | −0.011<br>0.037 | −0.038<br>0.036 | 0.010<br>0.017 | −0.023<br>0.027 |
| 5 | MKT | Coef<br>SE | 0.053 ***<br>0.011 | 0.124 ***<br>0.022 | 0.050 ***<br>0.009 | 0.048 ***<br>0.011 | 0.050 ***<br>0.005 | 0.036 **<br>0.013 |
| | $SMB_{OP}$ | Coef<br>SE | −0.021<br>0.032 | −0.050<br>0.076 | −0.010<br>0.032 | −0.031<br>0.031 | 0.013<br>0.018 | −0.029<br>0.046 |

**Table A1.** *Cont.*

| Model | | | OLS | Quantile Regression | | | | |
|---|---|---|---|---|---|---|---|---|
| | | | | 0.05 | 0.25 | 0.50 | 0.75 | 0.95 |
| 6 | MKT | Coef | 0.052 *** | 0.095 *** | 0.049 *** | 0.047 *** | 0.050 *** | 0.035 ** |
| | | SE | 0.010 | 0.013 | 0.009 | 0.009 | 0.008 | 0.012 |
| | $SMB_{INV}$ | Coef | −0.011 | −0.015 | −0.006 | −0.023 | 0.013 | −0.030 |
| | | SE | 0.020 | 0.036 | 0.025 | 0.026 | 0.021 | 0.034 |
| | | | | Canada | | | | |
| 4 | MKT | Coef | 0.051 ** | 0.072 *** | 0.063 *** | 0.020 | 0.021 ** | 0.049 *** |
| | | SE | 0.024 | 0.010 | 0.011 | 0.021 | 0.009 | 0.003 |
| | $SMB_{B/M}$ | Coef | 0.037 | 0.050 ** | 0.031 | 0.052 | 0.056 ** | −0.133 *** |
| | | SE | 0.049 | 0.021 | 0.023 | 0.044 | 0.019 | 0.005 |
| 5 | MKT | Coef | 0.054 ** | 0.073 *** | 0.061 *** | 0.018 | 0.031 | 0.033 ** |
| | | SE | 0.023 | 0.009 | 0.007 | 0.015 | 0.024 | 0.011 |
| | $SMB_{OP}$ | Coef | 0.045 | 0.046 ** | 0.034 ** | 0.054 * | 0.058 | −0.115 *** |
| | | SE | 0.046 | 0.018 | 0.014 | 0.031 | 0.049 | 0.023 |
| 6 | MKT | Coef | 0.054 ** | 0.075 *** | 0.057 *** | 0.017 | 0.029 | 0.040 *** |
| | | SE | 0.046 | 0.008 | 0.019 | 0.018 | 0.027 | 0.009 |
| | $SMB_{INV}$ | Coef | 0.043 | 0.039 ** | 0.033 | 0.058 | 0.059 | −0.124 *** |
| | | SE | 0.046 | 0.017 | 0.039 | 0.037 | 0.056 | 0.019 |
| | | | | China | | | | |
| 4 | MKT | Coef | 0.021 ** | 0.032 *** | 0.021 *** | 0.026 | 0.010 | 0.052 *** |
| | | SE | 0.009 | 0.003 | 0.007 | 0.018 | 0.019 | 0.013 |
| | $SMB_{B/M}$ | Coef | 0.034 | 0.085 *** | 0.094 *** | 0.026 | 0.048 | −0.111 ** |
| | | SE | 0.031 | 0.010 | 0.024 | 0.063 | 0.067 | 0.046 |
| 5 | MKT | Coef | 0.018 * | 0.027 *** | 0.021 ** | 0.005 | 0.012 | 0.057 *** |
| | | SE | 0.010 | 0.001 | 0.009 | 0.010 | 0.024 | 0.013 |
| | $SMB_{OP}$ | Coef | 0.044 | 0.087 *** | 0.086 *** | 0.089 ** | 0.033 | −0.104 ** |
| | | SE | 0.032 | 0.003 | 0.030 | 0.034 | 0.083 | 0.045 |
| 6 | MKT | Coef | 0.016 * | 0.023 *** | 0.026 *** | 0.012 | 0.006 | 0.057 *** |
| | | SE | 0.009 | 0.003 | 0.005 | 0.008 | 0.017 | 0.006 |
| | $SMB_{INV}$ | Coef | 0.045 ** | 0.068 *** | 0.054 *** | 0.055 ** | 0.039 | −0.079 *** |
| | | SE | 0.018 | 0.007 | 0.013 | 0.022 | 0.047 | 0.017 |
| | | | | France | | | | |
| 4 | MKT | Coef | 0.049 ** | 0.051 *** | 0.015 | 0.035 *** | 0.041 *** | 0.050 *** |
| | | SE | 0.018 | 0.014 | 0.010 | 0.011 | 0.008 | 0.011 |
| | $SMB_{B/M}$ | Coef | −0.020 | 0.074 ** | 0.066 *** | −0.012 | −0.038 ** | −0.016 |
| | | SE | 0.026 | 0.028 | 0.020 | 0.023 | 0.017 | 0.023 |
| 5 | MKT | Coef | 0.046 *** | 0.051 *** | 0.023 * | 0.035 *** | 0.036 *** | 0.042 *** |
| | | SE | 0.016 | 0.003 | 0.012 | 0.011 | 0.005 | 0.004 |
| | $SMB_{OP}$ | Coef | −0.010 | 0.072 *** | 0.049 * | −0.013 | −0.034 *** | −0.021 ** |
| | | SE | 0.027 | 0.006 | 0.024 | 0.022 | 0.011 | 0.009 |
| 6 | MKT | Coef | 0.047 *** | 0.053 *** | 0.024 * | 0.035 *** | 0.038 *** | 0.043 *** |
| | | SE | 0.017 | 0.011 | 0.013 | 0.012 | 0.007 | 0.004 |
| | $SMB_{INV}$ | Coef | −0.014 | 0.064 *** | 0.048 * | −0.012 | −0.033 ** | −0.021 ** |
| | | SE | 0.026 | 0.021 | 0.026 | 0.024 | 0.014 | 0.009 |

**Table A1.** *Cont.*

| Model | | | OLS | Quantile Regression | | | | |
|---|---|---|---|---|---|---|---|---|
| | | | | **0.05** | **0.25** | **0.50** | **0.75** | **0.95** |
| | | | | Germany | | | | |
| 4 | MKT | Coef<br>SE | 0.076 ***<br>0.026 | 0.106 ***<br>0.008 | 0.047 ***<br>0.014 | 0.068 ***<br>0.006 | 0.056 **<br>0.024 | 0.044 ***<br>0.013 |
| | $SMB_{B/M}$ | Coef<br>SE | −0.013<br>0.029 | −0.057 ***<br>0.017 | −0.044<br>0.029 | −0.012<br>0.013 | 0.030<br>0.049 | 0.074 **<br>0.026 |
| 5 | MKT | Coef<br>SE | 0.070 ***<br>0.024 | 0.107 ***<br>0.010 | 0.041 ***<br>0.008 | 0.066 ***<br>0.012 | 0.046 ***<br>0.007 | 0.069 ***<br>0.008 |
| | $SMB_{OP}$ | Coef<br>SE | 0.033<br>0.023 | −0.058 ***<br>0.019 | −0.040 **<br>0.017 | −0.009<br>0.023 | 0.052 ***<br>0.015 | 0.077 ***<br>0.015 |
| 6 | MKT | Coef<br>SE | 0.075 ***<br>0.025 | 0.106 ***<br>0.012 | 0.043 ***<br>0.011 | 0.067 ***<br>0.016 | 0.050 ***<br>0.012 | 0.066 ***<br>0.003 |
| | $SMB_{INV}$ | Coef<br>SE | −0.008<br>0.029 | −0.053 **<br>0.024 | −0.035<br>0.022 | −0.010<br>0.033 | 0.039<br>0.024 | 0.077 ***<br>0.007 |
| | | | | India | | | | |
| 4 | MKT | Coef<br>SE | −0.003<br>0.010 | −0.016 ***<br>0.004 | −0.002<br>0.031 | −0.011<br>0.008 | 0.001<br>0.001 | −0.004<br>0.004 |
| | $SMB_{B/M}$ | Coef<br>SE | 0.022<br>0.037 | 0.024<br>0.015 | 0.049<br>0.113 | 0.021<br>0.031 | 0.031 ***<br>0.009 | 0.024 *<br>0.013 |
| 5 | MKT | Coef<br>SE | −0.002<br>0.011 | −0.018 ***<br>0.005 | 0.013<br>0.016 | −0.012<br>0.012 | 0.001<br>0.005 | −0.006 *<br>0.003 |
| | $SMB_{OP}$ | Coef<br>SE | 0.014<br>0.039 | −0.020<br>0.016 | −0.046<br>0.057 | 0.011<br>0.043 | 0.028<br>0.018 | 0.031 **<br>0.011 |
| 6 | MKT | Coef<br>SE | −0.004<br>0.011 | −0.014<br>0.011 | −0.016<br>0.026 | −0.012<br>0.012 | −0.001<br>0.002 | −0.007 *<br>0.003 |
| | $SMB_{INV}$ | Coef<br>SE | 0.022<br>0.029 | 0.037<br>0.031 | 0.046<br>0.072 | 0.009<br>0.033 | 0.031 ***<br>0.006 | 0.030 ***<br>0.009 |
| | | | | Italy | | | | |
| 4 | MKT | Coef<br>SE | 0.053 **<br>0.027 | 0.062 ***<br>0.019 | 0.030 **<br>0.011 | 0.031 **<br>0.014 | 0.045 ***<br>0.014 | 0.002<br>0.018 |
| | $SMB_{B/M}$ | Coef<br>SE | 0.006<br>0.027 | 0.087 **<br>0.038 | 0.005<br>0.023 | −0.019<br>0.029 | −0.005<br>0.029 | 0.063 *<br>0.037 |
| 5 | MKT | Coef<br>SE | 0.053 *<br>0.025 | 0.061 ***<br>0.018 | 0.019<br>0.012 | 0.031 **<br>0.012 | 0.035 **<br>0.013 | 0.040 *<br>0.021 |
| | $SMB_{OP}$ | Coef<br>SE | 0.017<br>0.027 | 0.090 **<br>0.036 | 0.056 **<br>0.024 | −0.014<br>0.024 | −0.001<br>0.026 | −0.013<br>0.042 |
| 6 | MKT | Coef<br>SE | 0.053 **<br>0.025 | 0.061 ***<br>0.020 | 0.029 **<br>0.010 | 0.031 **<br>0.012 | 0.035 ***<br>0.012 | 0.041 *<br>0.020 |
| | $SMB_{INV}$ | Coef<br>SE | 0.011<br>0.026 | 0.082 *<br>0.040 | 0.004<br>0.021 | −0.015<br>0.024 | −0.001<br>0.023 | −0.027<br>0.041 |
| | | | | Japan | | | | |
| 4 | MKT | Coef<br>SE | 0.051 *<br>0.028 | 0.081 ***<br>0.018 | 0.013<br>0.022 | 0.021<br>0.015 | 0.029 *<br>0.014 | 0.050 ***<br>0.008 |
| | $SMB_{B/M}$ | Coef<br>SE | 0.040<br>0.031 | 0.060<br>0.038 | 0.074<br>0.045 | 0.033<br>0.031 | 0.074 **<br>0.029 | 0.010<br>0.016 |

**Table A1.** *Cont.*

| | Model | | OLS | Quantile Regression | | | | |
|---|---|---|---|---|---|---|---|---|
| | | | | 0.05 | 0.25 | 0.50 | 0.75 | 0.95 |
| 5 | MKT | Coef | 0.054 ** | 0.081 *** | 0.023 * | 0.036 *** | 0.040 | 0.052 *** |
| | | SE | 0.025 | 0.004 | 0.013 | 0.016 | 0.025 | 0.014 |
| | $SMB_{OP}$ | Coef | 0.048 * | 0.059 *** | 0.075 ** | 0.001 | 0.059 | 0.007 |
| | | SE | 0.026 | 0.008 | 0.026 | 0.032 | 0.051 | 0.028 |
| 6 | MKT | Coef | 0.054 ** | 0.082 *** | 0.017 *** | 0.035 *** | 0.034 *** | 0.041 *** |
| | | SE | 0.026 | 0.007 | 0.003 | 0.006 | 0.005 | 0.011 |
| | $SMB_{INV}$ | Coef | 0.042 | 0.052 *** | 0.072 *** | 0.001 | 0.067 *** | 0.024 |
| | | SE | 0.028 | 0.014 | 0.006 | 0.012 | 0.011 | 0.022 |
| | | | | Russia | | | | |
| 4 | MKT | Coef | 0.057 * | 0.129 *** | 0.110 *** | 0.055 ** | 0.035 | 0.037 *** |
| | | SE | 0.031 | 0.038 | 0.026 | 0.026 | 0.025 | 0.003 |
| | $SMB_{B/M}$ | Coef | −0.306 ** | −0.504 *** | −0.204 ** | −0.148 | −0.250 ** | −0.017 |
| | | SE | 0.141 | 0.139 | 0.092 | 0.092 | 0.089 | 0.012 |
| 5 | MKT | Coef | 0.070 ** | 0.125 *** | 0.137 ** | 0.079 * | 0.023 | 0.046 ** |
| | | SE | 0.031 | 0.003 | 0.054 | 0.045 | 0.017 | 0.017 |
| | $SMB_{OP}$ | Coef | −0.302 * | −0.449 *** | −0.277 | −0.129 | −0.171 *** | 0.100 * |
| | | SE | 0.152 | 0.009 | 0.189 | 0.159 | 0.058 | 0.059 |
| 6 | MKT | Coef | 0.078 ** | 0.127 *** | 0.125 *** | 0.072 *** | 0.039 ** | 0.027 |
| | | SE | 0.029 | 0.013 | 0.042 | 0.025 | 0.016 | 0.021 |
| | $SMB_{INV}$ | Coef | −0.294 *** | −0.338 *** | −0.404 *** | −0.209 *** | −0.231 *** | −0.120 * |
| | | SE | 0.079 | 0.037 | 0.115 | 0.068 | 0.045 | 0.059 |
| | | | | South Africa | | | | |
| 4 | MKT | Coef | 0.028 *** | 0.027 *** | 0.035 ** | 0.018 * | 0.024 * | 0.040 *** |
| | | SE | 0.009 | 0.004 | 0.016 | 0.009 | 0.015 | 0.003 |
| | $SMB_{B/M}$ | Coef | −0.025 | 0.021 | −0.025 | −0.038 | −0.075 | −0.106 *** |
| | | SE | 0.029 | 0.016 | 0.059 | 0.032 | 0.052 | 0.012 |
| 5 | MKT | Coef | 0.029 *** | 0.027 *** | 0.030 *** | 0.019 * | 0.038 *** | 0.042 *** |
| | | SE | 0.010 | 0.005 | 0.007 | 0.011 | 0.005 | 0.004 |
| | $SMB_{OP}$ | Coef | −0.024 | 0.020 | −0.011 | −0.035 | −0.098 *** | −0.065 *** |
| | | SE | 0.034 | 0.019 | 0.024 | 0.038 | 0.018 | 0.013 |
| 6 | MKT | Coef | 0.029 *** | 0.027 *** | 0.044 *** | 0.019 * | 0.035 *** | 0.049 *** |
| | | SE | 0.009 | 0.006 | 0.010 | 0.010 | 0.012 | 0.002 |
| | $SMB_{INV}$ | Coef | −0.023 | 0.015 | −0.033 | −0.023 | −0.065 * | −0.082 *** |
| | | SE | 0.021 | 0.016 | 0.029 | 0.029 | 0.032 | 0.006 |
| | | | | United Kingdom | | | | |
| 4 | MKT | Coef | 0.047 | 0.085 *** | 0.040 ** | 0.011 | 0.010 | 0.016 * |
| | | SE | 0.031 | 0.001 | 0.014 | 0.014 | 0.020 | 0.009 |
| | $MB_{B/M}$ | Coef | −0.022 | −0.002 | −0.043 | −0.016 | −0.009 | −0.017 |
| | | SE | 0.027 | 0.001 | 0.029 | 0.029 | 0.042 | 0.018 |
| 5 | MKT | Coef | 0.042 | 0.085 *** | 0.029 *** | 0.007 | 0.007 | 0.014 ** |
| | | SE | 0.029 | 0.000 | 0.005 | 0.016 | 0.013 | 0.006 |
| | $SMB_{OP}$ | Coef | 0.008 | −0.001 | −0.014 | 0.008 | −0.008 | 0.002 |
| | | SE | 0.031 | 0.001 | 0.009 | 0.033 | 0.027 | 0.012 |
| 6 | MKT | Coef | 0.043 | 0.085 *** | 0.030 *** | 0.002 | 0.008 | 0.014 |
| | | SE | 0.030 | 0.002 | 0.005 | 0.014 | 0.013 | 0.009 |
| | $SMB_{INV}$ | Coef | −0.003 | −0.002 | −0.014 | −0.003 | −0.008 | 0.002 |
| | | SE | 0.029 | 0.005 | 0.009 | 0.028 | 0.027 | 0.018 |

**Table A1.** *Cont.*

| Model | | | OLS | Quantile Regression | | | | |
|---|---|---|---|---|---|---|---|---|
| | | | | 0.05 | 0.25 | 0.50 | 0.75 | 0.95 |
| United States | | | | | | | | |
| 4 | MKT | Coef | 0.057 *** | 0.058 *** | 0.031 | 0.052 *** | 0.055 *** | 0.040 *** |
| | | SE | 0.018 | 0.017 | 0.025 | 0.021 | 0.014 | 0.002 |
| | $MB_{B/M}$ | Coef | −0.030 | 0.058 * | 0.008 | −0.033 | −0.047 | −0.069 *** |
| | | SE | 0.035 | 0.035 | 0.052 | 0.044 | 0.029 | 0.005 |
| 5 | MKT | Coef | 0.053 *** | 0.059 *** | 0.035 *** | 0.053 *** | 0.044 *** | 0.029 *** |
| | | SE | 0.017 | 0.010 | 0.006 | 0.011 | 0.014 | 0.006 |
| | $SMB_{OP}$ | Coef | −0.017 | 0.058 *** | 0.041 *** | −0.034 | −0.047 | −0.029 ** |
| | | SE | 0.036 | 0.019 | 0.011 | 0.022 | 0.028 | 0.013 |
| 6 | MKT | Coef | 0.054 *** | 0.061 *** | 0.033 | 0.052 *** | 0.048 *** | 0.031 *** |
| | | SE | 0.017 | 0.015 | 0.020 | 0.018 | 0.006 | 0.007 |
| | $SMB_{INV}$ | Coef | −0.023 | 0.061 * | 0.044 | −0.028 | −0.045 *** | −0.029 ** |
| | | SE | 0.034 | 0.031 | 0.041 | 0.036 | 0.012 | 0.013 |

Obs.: Coef, coefficient; SE, standard error; ***, **, *, $p < 1\%$, 5% and 10%.

Figures A1–A3 respectively, illustrate the individual performance of the risk factors SMBOP, SMBB/M and SMBOP on the conditional quantile distribution, as well as the estimation by OLS, of the GDP growth rate of South Africa, Brazil and Brazil.

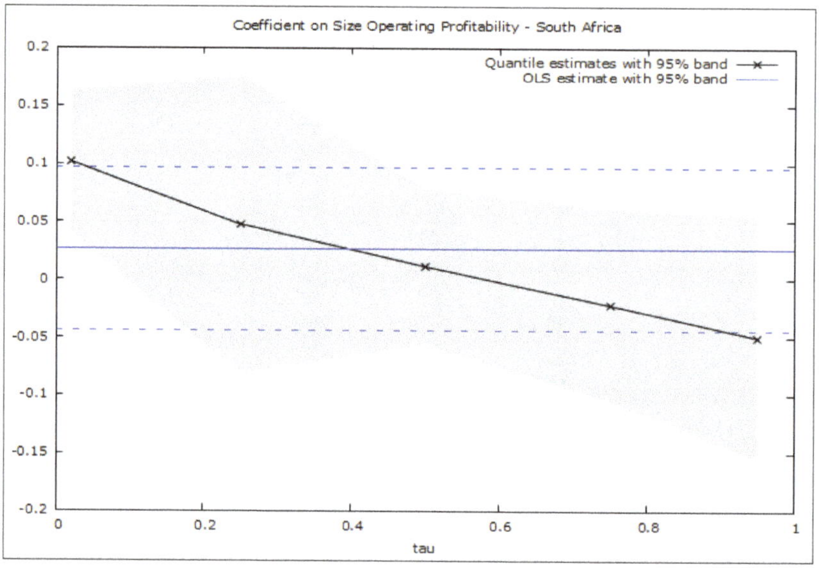


**Figure A1.** Performance of the $SMB_{OP}$ risk factor on the percentiles and conditional average of South Africa's GDP growth rate.

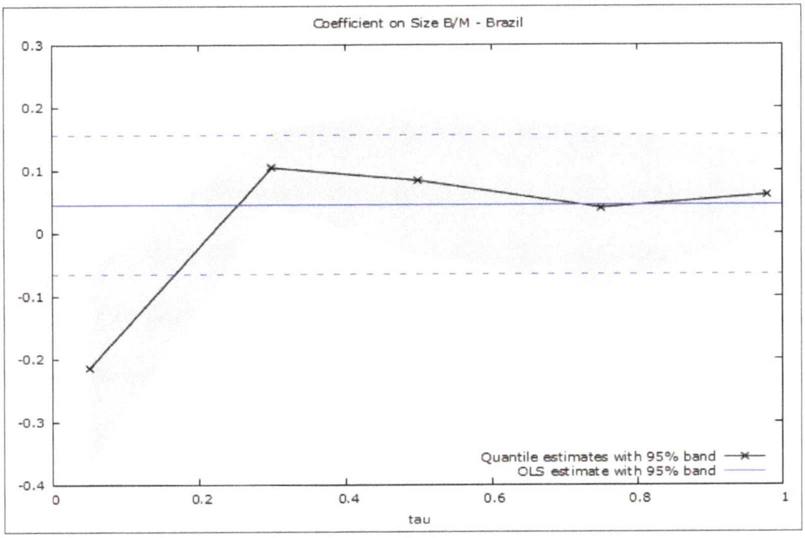


**Figure A2.** Performance of the $SMB_{B/M}$ risk factor on the percentiles and conditional average of Brazil's GDP growth rate.

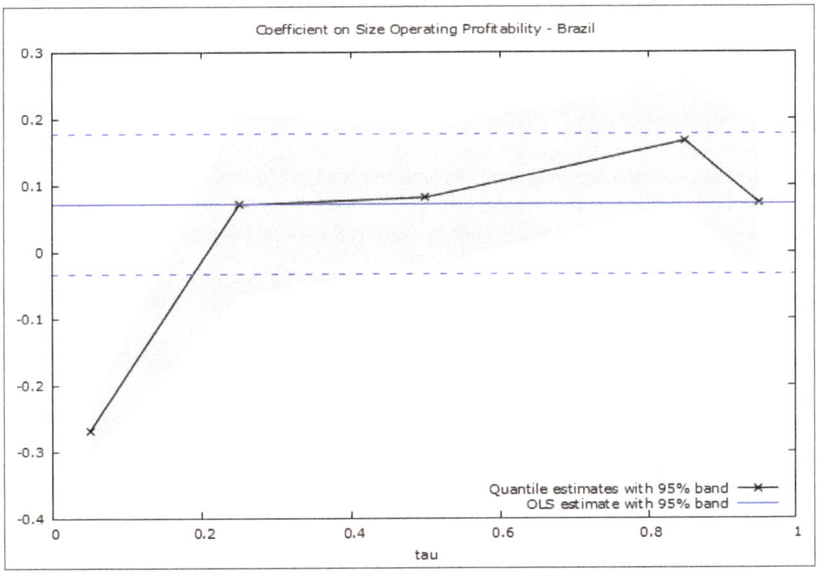


**Figure A3.** Performance of the $SMB_{OP}$ risk factor on the percentiles and conditional average of Brazil's GDP growth rate.

## Appendix B

In order to compare the parameters, Table A2 presents the results of the estimations of seven longitudinal long-panel multiple regression models, with five explanatory variables, the risk factors considered in the Fama and French (2015) model, estimated by: (1) fixed effects, (2) random effects, (3) Pooled by OLS, and considering the existence of first order serial correlation in terms of AR(1) error (4) fixed effect, (5) random effects models, (6) Pooled by OLS and (7) GLS (General Least Squares) method.

**Table A2.** Long-Panel Data Model Multiple Regression Estimates.

| Model | | | Fixed Effect | Random Effect | Pooled OLS | Fixed Effect AR(1) | Random Effect AR(1) | Pooled OLS AR(1) | GLS AR(1) |
|---|---|---|---|---|---|---|---|---|---|
| $GDP_{it} = \alpha_i + \beta_1 MKT_{i,t-1} + \beta_2 SMB_{i,t-1} + \beta_3 HML_{i,t-1} + \beta_4 RMW_{i,t-1} + \beta_5 CMA_{i,t-1} + \varepsilon_{i,t}$ | | | | | | | | | |
| 6 | MKT | Coef | 0.04051 *** | 0.04048 *** | 0.03990 *** | 0.03094 *** | 0.03137 *** | 0.03029 *** | 0.02637 *** |
| | | SE | 0.00597 | 0.00602 | 0.00849 | 0.00413 | 0.00451 | 0.00676 | 0.00393 |
| | SMB | Coef | −0.00548 | −0.00605 | −0.01693 | 0.01129 | 0.00311 | 0.00427 | 0.00358 |
| | | SE | 0.01642 | 0.01654 | 0.02328 | 0.01546 | 0.01637 | 0.02512 | 0.01441 |
| | HML | Coef | 0.02024 * | 0.02115 * | 0.03849 ** | 0.00587 | 0.00429 | 0.00501 | −0.00154 |
| | | SE | 0.01183 | 0.01191 | 0.01662 | 0.00925 | 0.01003 | 0.01518 | 0.00927 |
| | RMW | Coef | 0.05789 *** | 0.05683 *** | 0.03655 | 0.02665 | 0.04323 ** | 0.03629 | 0.02464 * |
| | | SE | 0.01946 | 0.01960 | 0.02750 | 0.01726 | 0.01697 | 0.02547 | 0.01484 |
| | CMA | Coef | −0.01730 | −0.01728 | −0.01691 | −0.02660 *** | −0.02651 ** | −0.02744 | −0.02289 ** |
| | | SE | 0.01586 | 0.01597 | 0.02254 | 0.01164 | 0.01274 | 0.01878 | 0.01036 |
| | Cons | Coef | 0.02260 *** | 0.02259 *** | 0.02232 *** | 0.02558 *** | 0.02479 *** | 0.02488 *** | 0.02597 *** |
| | | SE | 0.00178 | 0.00588 | 0.00253 | 0.00119 | 0.00666 | 0.00434 | 0.00295 |

Obs.: Cons: constant; Coef: coefficient; SE, standard error; ***, **, *, $p < 1\%$, 5% and 10%.

## References

1. Bekaert, G.; Harvey, C.R. Emerging Markets Finance. *J. Empir. Financ.* **2003**, *10*, 3–55. [CrossRef]
2. Tripathi, V.; Seth, R. Stock Market Performance and Macroeconomic Factors: The Study of Indian Equity Market. *Glob. Bus. Rev.* **2014**, *15*, 291–316. [CrossRef]
3. Saji, T.G. Asian Stock Market Integration after the Global Financial Crisis: An ARDL Bound Testing Approach. *Manag. Financ.* **2021**, *47*, 1651–1671. [CrossRef]
4. Nardo, M.; Ossola, E.; Papanagiotou, E. Financial Integration in the EU28 Equity Markets: Measures and Drivers. *J. Financ. Mark.* **2022**, *57*, 100633. [CrossRef]
5. Fama, E.F.; French, K.R. Value versus Growth: The International Evidence. *J. Financ.* **1998**, *53*, 1975–1999. [CrossRef]
6. Fama, E.F.; French, K.R. Size, Value, and Momentum in International Stock Returns. *J. Financ. Econ.* **2012**, *105*, 457–472. [CrossRef]
7. Fama, E.F.; French, K.R. International Tests of a Five-Factor Asset Pricing Model. *J. Financ. Econ.* **2017**, *123*, 441–463. [CrossRef]
8. Cakici, N. The Five-Factor Fama-French Model: International Evidence. Available online: https://papers.ssrn.com/sol3/papers.cfm?abstract_id=2601662 (accessed on 1 September 2020).
9. Cakici, N.; Fabozzi, F.J.; Tan, S. Size, Value, and Momentum in Emerging Market Stock Returns. *Emerg. Mark. Rev.* **2013**, *16*, 46–65. [CrossRef]
10. Leite, A.L.; Klotzle, M.C.; Pinto, A.C.F.; da Silva, A.F. Size, Value, Profitability, and Investment: Evidence from Emerging Markets. *Emerg. Mark. Rev.* **2018**, *36*, 45–59. [CrossRef]
11. Hanauer, M.X.; Lauterbach, J.G. The Cross-Section of Emerging Market Stock Returns. *Emerg. Mark. Rev.* **2019**, *38*, 265–286. [CrossRef]
12. Tenorio, F.M.; Dos Santos, M.; Gomes, C.F.S.; Araujo, J.D.C.; De Almeida, G.P. THOR 2 Method: An Efficient Instrument in Situations Where There Is Uncertainty or Lack of Data. *IEEE Access* **2021**, *9*, 161794–161805. [CrossRef]
13. Fama, E.F.; French, K.R. Common Risk Factors in the Returns on Stocks and Bonds. *J. Financ. Econ.* **1993**, *33*, 3–56. [CrossRef]
14. Fama, E.F.; French, K.R. A Five-Factor Asset Pricing Model. *J. Financ. Econ.* **2015**, *116*, 1–22. [CrossRef]
15. Merton, R.C. An Intertemporal Capital Asset Pricing Model. *Econometrica* **1973**, *41*, 867–887. [CrossRef]
16. Fama, E.F.; French, K.R. The Capital Asset Pricing Model: Theory and Evidence. *J. Econ. Perspect.* **2004**, *18*, 25–46. [CrossRef]
17. Fama, E.F. Stock Returns, Real Activity, Inflation, and Money. *Am. Econ. Rev.* **1981**, *71*, 545–565.
18. Aylward, A.; Glen, J. Some International Evidence on Stock Prices as Leading Indicators of Economic Activity. *Appl. Financ. Econ.* **2000**, *10*, 1–14. [CrossRef]
19. Liew, J.; Vassalou, M. Can Book-to-Market, Size and Momentum Be Risk Factors That Predict Economic Growth? *J. Financ. Econ.* **2000**, *57*, 221–245. [CrossRef]
20. Chan, K.C.; Chen, N. Structural and Return Characteristics of Small and Large Firms. *J. Financ.* **1991**, *46*, 1467–1484. [CrossRef]
21. Burmeister, E.; Roll, R.; Ross, S.A. Using Macroeconomic Factors to Control Portfolio Risk. *Pract. Guide Factor Model.* **2003**, *9*, 1–27.
22. Kassimatis, K. Size, Book to Market and Momentum Effects in the Australian Stock Market. *Aust. J. Manag.* **2008**, *33*, 145–168. [CrossRef]
23. Brooks, R.; Del Negro, M. Country versus Region Effects in International Stock Returns. *J. Portf. Manag.* **2005**, *31*, 67–72. [CrossRef]
24. Lehkonen, H. Stock Market Integration and the Global Financial Crisis. *Rev. Financ.* **2015**, *19*, 2039–2094. [CrossRef]

25. Bibi, R. Sumaira the Effect of Financial Development on Economic Growth: Evidence from South Asian Developing Countries. *J. Environ. Sci. Econ.* **2022**, *1*, 1–17. [CrossRef]
26. Das Neves, M.B.E.; Leal, R.P.C. Existe Relação Entre o Crescimento do PIB Brasileiro e os Efeitos Tamanho, Valor e Momento. *Encontro Nac. ANPAD* **2003**, *17*, 1–16.
27. Font-Belaire, B.; Grau-Grau, A.J. Los Factores Tamaño, Book-to-Market y Momentum en el Mercado de Capitales Español: Explicaciones Racionales y Efecto en la Formación del Precio. *Span. J. Financ. Account. Rev. Española Financ. Contab.* **2007**, *36*, 509–535.
28. Hanhardt, A.; Ansotegui Olcoz, C. Do the Fama and French Factors Proxy for State Variables That Predict Macroeconomic Growth in the Eurozone? Available online: https://papers.ssrn.com/sol3/papers.cfm?abstract_id=1098225 (accessed on 11 October 2019).
29. Fajardo, J.; Fialho, M.L. Fama-French Three Factors, Business Cycles and Inflation in Brazil. Available online: https://papers.ssrn.com/sol3/papers.cfm?abstract_id=1969481 (accessed on 1 April 2022).
30. Liu, B.; Di Iorio, A. Do the Asset Pricing Factors Predict Future Economy Growth? An Australian Study. *Eur. Financ. Manag. Assoc.* **2013**, 1–33. Available online: http://ro.uow.edu.au/cgi/viewcontent.cgi?article=2046&context=buspapers (accessed on 28 August 2019).
31. Boamah, N.A. Robustness of the Carhart Four-Factor and the Fama-French Three-Factor Models on the South African Stock Market. *Rev. Account. Financ.* **2015**, *14*, 413–430. [CrossRef]
32. Ali, F.; He, R.; Jiang, Y. Size, Value and Business Cycle Variables. The Three-Factor Model and Future Economic Growth: Evidence from an Emerging Market. *Economies* **2018**, *6*, 14. [CrossRef]
33. Lalwani, V.; Chakraborty, M. Asset Pricing Factors and Future Economic Growth. *Econ. Lett.* **2018**, *168*, 151–154. [CrossRef]
34. Ferreira, J.C.J.; Gama, A.P.M. The Relationship between the Factors of Risk in Asset Evaluation Models and Future Economic Growth: Evidence from Three Regional Markets. *J. Spat. Organ. Dyn.* **2020**, *8*, 300–319.
35. Ferreira, J.C.J.; Gama, A.P.M.; Fávero, L.P.; Costa, R. O Modelo de 5-Fatores de Fama-French e o Crescimento Econômico Futuro: Evidências em Mercados Emergentes. *Rev. Contab. UFBA* **2021**, *15*, e2101. [CrossRef]
36. Sehgal, S.; Pandey, P.; Deisting, F. Stock Market Integration Dynamics and Its Determinants in the East Asian Economic Community Region. *J. Quant. Econ.* **2018**, *16*, 389–425. [CrossRef]
37. Olubiyi, E.A. Economic Integration and Stock Market Development: Evidence from Nigeria. *Int. Trade J.* **2021**, 1–24. [CrossRef]
38. Chukwuma, O.V.; Ugwu, J.I.; Babalola, D.S. Application of Forensic Accounting in Predicting the Financial Performance Growth of MTN Mobile Communication in Nigeria. *J. Environ. Sci. Econ.* **2022**, *1*, 67–76. [CrossRef]
39. Jamil, M.N.; Rasheed, A.; Mukhtar, Z. Corporate Social Responsibility Impacts Sustainable Organizational Growth (Firm Performance): An Empirical Analysis of Pakistan Stock Exchange-Listed Firms. *J. Environ. Sci. Econ.* **2022**, *1*, 25–29. [CrossRef]
40. Abdelkafi, I.; Ben Romdhane, Y.; Loukil, S.; Zaarour, F. Covid-19 Impact on Latin and Asian Stock Markets. *Manag. Financ.* **2022**. *ahead-of-print*. [CrossRef]
41. Fávero, L.P.; Belfiore, P. *Manual de Análise de Dados: Estatística e Modelagem Multivariada com Excel®, SPSS® e Stata®*; Elsevier Brasil: Rio de Janeiro, Brazil, 2017; ISBN 8535285059.
42. Fávero, L.P.; Belfiore, P.; da Silva, F.L.; Chan, B.L. *Análise de Dados: Modelagem Multivariada Para Tomada de Decisões*; Elsevier Brasil: Rio de Janeiro, Brazil, 2009.
43. Hair Jr, J.F.; Fávero, L.P. Multilevel Modeling for Longitudinal Data: Concepts and Applications. *RAUSP Manag. J.* **2019**, *54*, 459–489. [CrossRef]
44. Islam, N. Growth Empirics: A Panel Data Approach. *Q. J. Econ.* **1995**, *110*, 1127–1170. [CrossRef]
45. Fávero, L.P.L. Dados em Painel em Contabilidade e Finanças: Teoria e Aplicação. *BBR-Braz. Bus. Rev.* **2013**, *10*, 131–156.
46. Newey, W.K.; West, K.D. A Simple, Positive Semi-Definite, Heteroskedasticity and Autocorrelationconsistent Covariance Matrix. *Econometrica* **1987**, *55*, 703–708. [CrossRef]
47. White, H. A Heteroskedasticity-Consistent Covariance Matrix Estimator and a Direct Test for Heteroskedasticity. *Econom. J. Econom. Soc.* **1980**, *48*, 817–838. [CrossRef]

mathematics

MDPI

Article

# Quantile Regression with a New Exponentiated Odd Log-Logistic Weibull Distribution

Gabriela M. Rodrigues [1,†], Edwin M. M. Ortega [1,*,†], Gauss M. Cordeiro [2,†] and Roberto Vila [3,†]

1 Department of Exact Sciences, University of São Paulo, Piracicaba 13418-900, Brazil
2 Department of Statistics, Federal University of Pernambuco, Recife 50670-901, Brazil
3 Department of Statistics, University of Brasilia, Brasilia 70910-900, Brazil
* Correspondence: edwin@usp.br
† These authors contributed equally to this work.

**Abstract:** We define a new quantile regression model based on a reparameterized exponentiated odd log-logistic Weibull distribution, and obtain some of its structural properties. It includes as sub-models some known regression models that can be utilized in many areas. The maximum likelihood method is adopted to estimate the parameters, and several simulations are performed to study the finite sample properties of the maximum likelihood estimators. The applicability of the proposed regression model is well justified by means of a gastric carcinoma dataset.

**Keywords:** censored data; hazard function; odd log-logistic Weibull; statistical reparameterization; survival function

**MSC:** 62G08; 62N02; 62E15

**Citation:** Rodrigues, G.M.; Ortega, E.M.M.; Cordeiro, G.M.; Vila, R. Quantile Regression with a New Exponentiated Odd Log-Logistic Weibull Distribution. *Mathematics* **2023**, *11*, 1518. https://doi.org/10.3390/math11061518

Academic Editors: Francisco German Badía and María D. Berrade

Received: 13 February 2023
Revised: 15 March 2023
Accepted: 17 March 2023
Published: 21 March 2023



## 1. Introduction

For survival data, the outcome variable is usually the time until the occurrence of an event of interest. A common characteristic of this type of data is the presence of censoring, that is, when the event of interest is not observed for some subjects before the study is finished. Furthermore, this variable depends on one or more explanatory variables (covariables), which have characteristics of the sample under study. Cox's proportional hazards and accelerated failure time (AFT) models are two common tools in time-to-event modeling. The first class of models has the strong assumption of proportional risks, which is often invalid, so the effects of the covariables on the risk function are examined which can lead to difficult interpretations. The second class assumes that an association exists between the predictors and the survival time, permitting a direct interpretation of the effects of the covariables on lifetimes.

Nevertheless, these methods can fail to capture the heterogeneity of the effects of the covariables. In this respect, the quantile regression (QR) (Koenker and Bassett [1]) can be an alternative to these models, enabling evaluation of the heterogeneous effects of the predictors via analysis of different quantiles. This method involves modeling the quantiles of the survival time and links them to the covariables, providing some advantages, such as:

- Possible identification and inference under the heterogeneous effects of the covariables for different quantiles, thus supplying more complete information about the covariables and more flexibly controlling for the heterogeneity caused by them;
- Flexibility regarding the assumption of proportional risks;
- Provision of a direct interpretation of the results, that is, between the survival time and the covariables of interest;
- Possible analysis of different quantiles, allowing identification of the different effects of the covariables on individuals with different risks; and
- Robustness with respect to outliers in the regression models.

Originally, the QR methods are based on minimizing weighted absolute residuals [1] without any probability distribution, and the estimation of the parameters occurs by means of linear programming algorithms.

Although this approach is very flexible, some challenges such as: (i) the quantile crossing, that is, when two or more estimated quantile curves cross or overlap, causing difficulty in interpretability; and (ii) the drawback of the inability to apply parametric inference tools led to the search for other methods. Regarding the quantile crossing problem, we can verify alternative methods, such as: semiparametric models [2], the support vector (SV) regression approach [3], and a joint quantile estimation approach [4,5]. The weighted absolute residuals estimators coincide with the maximum likelihood estimators (MLEs), when the response follows a skewed Laplace distribution, so the initial association of a continuous distribution to the QR models was based on it (Koenker and Machado [6]).

In the context of censored data, an extensive bibliography can be mentioned, for example: Peng and Huang [7] developed a QR approach for survival data subject to conditionally independent censoring, Wang and Wang [8] proposed a locally weighted censored QR approach following the redistribution-of-mass idea and employed a local reweighing scheme. Zarean et al. [9] used the censored QR for determining overall survival and risk factors in esophageal cancer. Yang [10] presented a new approach for censored QR estimation, and Du et al. [11] developed estimation procedures for partially linear QR models, where some of the responses were censored by another random variable. Further, Xue et al. [12] addressed these limitations by using both simulated examples and data from National Wilms Tumor clinical trials to illustrate proper interpretation of the censored QR model and the differences and advantages of the model compared to the Cox proportional hazard model. Hong et al. [13] provided a practical guide for using QR for right-censored outcome data with covariates of low or high dimensionality, and De Backer et al. [14] studied a novel approach for the estimation of quantiles when facing potential right-censoring of the responses. Recently, De Backer et al. [15] investigated a new procedure for estimating a linear QR with possibly right-censored responses; Qiu et al. [16] considered the QR model for survival data with missing censoring indicators; Yazdani et al. [17] introduced the QR approach for modelling failure time and investigated the covariate effects for different quantiles; Peng [18] provided a comprehensive review of statistical methods for performing QR with different types of survival data; Hsu et al. [19] studied regression models for interval censored data using quantile coefficient functions via a set of parametric basis functions; He et al. [20] provided a unified analysis of the smoothed sequential estimator and its penalized counterpart for increasing dimensions in censored QR; and Wei [21] introduced a discussion about QR for censored data in haematopoietic cell transplant research. Note that all these articles cited in the QR with censored data did not use parametric models or use the skewed Laplace distribution (see [17]), whose estimators coincide.

Subsequently, other distributions were proposed by re-parameterizing them in terms of the quantile function (qf). Recent papers involving models for non-censored data based on other distributions can be mentioned: log-extended exponential-geometric [22]; Birnbaum–Saunders [23,24]; discrete generalized half-normal [25]; transmuted unit-Rayleigh [26]; unit-Burr-XII [27]; unit-Chen [28]; log-symmetric [29]; arcsecant hyperbolic Weibull [30]; and Dagum and Singh–Maddala [31] distributions. However, there is a relative lack in the literature of models for censored data in the parametric context: generalized Gompertz [32] and skew-t [33].

It is well known that the hazard rate function can assume different forms, which has led to the proposal of a large number of new distributions with the purpose of obtaining greater flexibility of data modeling, for example, Ref. [34]. In this sense, we introduce a QR regression model based on a reparameterized, exponentiated, odd log-logistic Weibull (EOLLW) distribution. It has two extra shape parameters, thus enabling the modeling of different forms of hazard rate functions, as well as data with positive or negative symmetric or asymmetric bimodal shapes, making it an alternative to the mixture models commonly used in the presence of bimodality. Another important feature of the new QR model is that it has as special cases: the exponentiated Weibull and odd log-logistic Weibull QR models. A detailed discussion of the theoretical foundations is given in analysis of survival data with concrete applications. The maximum likelihood method is adopted, and several simulations evaluate the behavior of these estimators under some scenarios. Additionally, we show that the model can establish functional relations of the covariables with other parameters, including scale and kurtosis, besides the quantile parameter.

The paper is structured as follows. Section 2 introduces a reparametrization of the EOLLW distribution based on quantiles. Section 3 addresses some mathematical properties. The proposed QR regression model, and some classic inference methods to estimate the parameters are addressed in Section 4. Some simulations are reported in Section 5. Section 6 provides a real application for the new regression model. Section 7 ends with a brief conclusion.

## 2. The Reparameterized EOLLW Distribution

Let $G(x;\boldsymbol{\eta})$ be a parent cumulative distribution function (cdf) and $g(x;\boldsymbol{\eta}) = \mathrm{d}G(x;\boldsymbol{\eta})/\mathrm{d}x$ be its associated probability density function (pdf), both functions of a parameter vector $\boldsymbol{\eta}$. The cdf of the exponentiated odd log-logistic (EOLL-G) family is given by (Alizadeh et al. [35]) (for $x \in \mathbb{R}$)

$$F(x;\nu,\lambda,\boldsymbol{\eta}) = \frac{G(x;\boldsymbol{\eta})^{\nu\lambda}}{\{G(x;\boldsymbol{\eta})^{\nu} + [1-G(x;\boldsymbol{\eta})]^{\nu}\}^{\lambda}}, \tag{1}$$

where $\nu > 0$ and $\lambda > 0$ are two extra shape parameters.

The pdf corresponding to Equation (1) has the form

$$f(x;\nu,\lambda,\boldsymbol{\eta}) = \frac{\nu\,\lambda\, g(x;\boldsymbol{\eta})\, G(x;\boldsymbol{\eta})^{\nu\lambda-1}[1-G(x;\boldsymbol{\eta})]^{\nu-1}}{\{G(x;\boldsymbol{\eta})^{\nu} + [1-G(x;\boldsymbol{\eta})]^{\nu}\}^{\lambda+1}}. \tag{2}$$

Henceforth, let $X \sim$ EOLL-G$(\nu,\lambda,\boldsymbol{\eta})$ be a random variable with density function (2).

The EOLL-G family reduces to the OLL-G class when $\lambda = 1$ (Gleaton and Lynch [36]), and to the exponentiated (Exp-G) family (Mudholkar et al., [37]) when $\nu = 1$. Clearly, it becomes the parent $G(x;\boldsymbol{\eta})$ when $\nu = \lambda = 1$.

The EOLLW distribution is defined from (2) by taking the parent Weibull

$$G(x;\gamma,\sigma) = 1-\exp\left[-\left(\frac{x}{\gamma}\right)^{\sigma}\right] \quad \text{and} \quad g(x;\gamma,\sigma) = \frac{\sigma}{\gamma^{\sigma}}\,x^{\sigma-1}\exp\left[-\left(\frac{x}{\gamma}\right)^{\sigma}\right], \quad x>0, \tag{3}$$

respectively, where $\boldsymbol{\eta} = (\gamma,\sigma)$, $\gamma > 0$ is a scale parameter, and $\sigma > 0$ is a shape parameter.

The cdf of the random variable $X \sim \text{EOLLW}(\nu,\lambda,\gamma,\sigma)$ follows from Equations (1) and (3)

$$F(x;\nu,\lambda,\gamma,\sigma) = \frac{\{1-\exp\left[-(\frac{x}{\gamma})^{\sigma}\right]\}^{\nu\lambda}}{\left[\{1-\exp\left[-(\frac{x}{\gamma})^{\sigma}\right]\}^{\nu} + \{\exp\left[-(\frac{x}{\gamma})^{\sigma}\right]\}^{\nu}\right]^{\lambda}}, \quad x>0. \tag{4}$$

Based on Equations (2) and (3), the pdf of $X$ becomes

$$f(x;\nu,\lambda,\gamma,\sigma) = \frac{\nu\,\lambda\,\sigma\,x^{\sigma-1}\,\{\exp\left[-(\frac{x}{\gamma})^{\sigma}\right]\}^{\nu}\,\{1-\exp\left[-(\frac{x}{\gamma})^{\sigma}\right]\}^{\nu\lambda-1}}{\gamma^{\sigma}\left[\{1-\exp\left[-(\frac{x}{\gamma})^{\sigma}\right]\}^{\nu} + \{\exp\left[-(\frac{x}{\gamma})^{\sigma}\right]\}^{\nu}\right]^{\lambda+1}}, \quad x>0. \tag{5}$$

The hazard rate function corresponding to (5) is $h(x;\nu,\lambda,\gamma,\sigma) = f(x;\nu,\lambda,\gamma,\sigma)/[1-F(x;\nu,\lambda,\gamma,\sigma)]$.

By inverting (1), the qf of $X$ reduces to

$$x = Q(q) = Q_W\left\{\frac{q^{1/(\nu\lambda)}}{q^{1/(\nu\lambda)} + (1-q^{1/\lambda})^{1/\nu}}\right\}, \quad 0<q<1, \tag{6}$$

where $Q_W(q) = G^{-1}(p;\gamma,\sigma)$ $(p \in (0,1))$ is the qf of the Weibull distribution, namely

$$G^{-1}(p;\gamma,\sigma) = \gamma[-\log(1-p)]^{1/\sigma}. \quad (7)$$

Thus, we rewrite the $\tau$th quantile (6) as

$$x = Q(q) = \gamma\left\{-\log\left[\frac{(1-q^{1/\lambda})^{1/\nu}}{q^{1/(\nu\lambda)} + (1-q^{1/\lambda})^{1/\nu}}\right]\right\}^{1/\sigma}. \quad (8)$$

We can easily obtain the quartiles: first quartile (Q(0.25)), median (Q(0.5)), and third quartile (Q(0.75)).

We define a reparametrization of the pdf (5) as a function of the $\tau$th quantile (6), where the scale $\gamma$ becomes

$$\gamma = \mu\left\{-\log\left[\frac{(1-\tau^{1/\lambda})^{1/\nu}}{\tau^{1/(\nu\lambda)} + (1-\tau^{\frac{1}{\lambda}})^{1/\nu}}\right]\right\}^{-1/\sigma}, \quad (9)$$

$\mu > 0$ is the location, and $\tau \in (0,1)$th is the quantile of $X$ (assumed known).

By substituting (9) into Equation (4), the reparameterized cdf of $X$ reduces to

$$F(x;\nu,\lambda,\mu,\sigma) = \frac{\left[1-\exp\left\{-w(\frac{x}{\mu})^{\sigma}\right\}\right]^{\nu\lambda}}{\left\{\left[1-\exp\left\{-w(\frac{x}{\mu})^{\sigma}\right\}\right]^{\nu} + \left[\exp\left\{-w(\frac{x}{\mu})^{\sigma}\right\}\right]^{\nu}\right\}^{\lambda}}, \quad (10)$$

where $w(\tau,\lambda,\nu) = -\log\left\{(1-\tau^{\frac{1}{\lambda}})^{1/\nu}/[\tau^{1/(\nu\lambda)} + (1-\tau^{1/\lambda})^{1/\nu}]\right\}$.

By simple differentiation, the reparameterized pdf of $X$ has the form

$$f(x;\nu,\lambda,\mu,\sigma) = \frac{\nu\,\lambda\,\sigma\,x^{\sigma-1}\,w\,\exp\left\{-w(\frac{x}{\mu})^{\sigma}\right\}^{\nu}\left[1-\exp\left\{-w(\frac{x}{\mu})^{\sigma}\right\}\right]^{\nu\lambda-1}}{\mu^{\sigma}\left\{\left[1-\exp\left\{-w(\frac{x}{\mu})^{\sigma}\right\}\right]^{\nu} + \left[\exp\left\{-w(\frac{x}{\mu})^{\sigma}\right\}\right]^{\nu}\right\}^{\lambda+1}}. \quad (11)$$

Henceforth, we redefine $X \sim \mathrm{EOLLW}(\nu,\lambda,\mu,\sigma,\tau)$ as a random variable with pdf (11), where $\tau \in (0,1)$ is fixed. Figure 1 displays plots of the pdf of $X$ for some $\tau$ values, thus showing its asymmetry and bimodality.

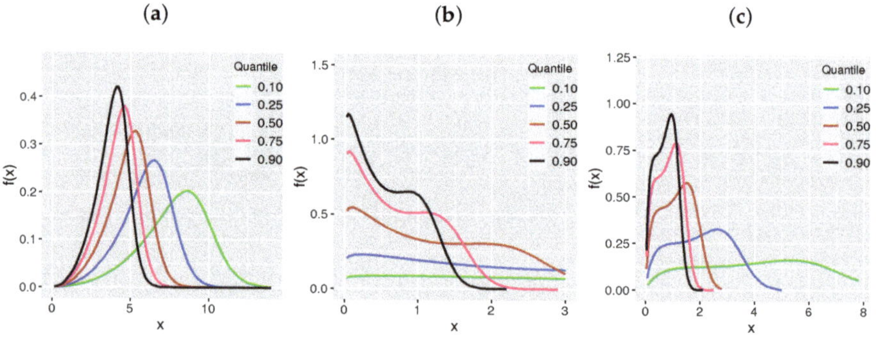


**Figure 1.** Plots of the pdf of $X$ for some $\tau$ values: (**a**) $\nu$ = 2, $\lambda$ = 0.4, $\mu$ = 5, $\sigma$ = 4, (**b**) $\nu$ = 0.4, $\lambda$ = 0.90, $\mu$ = 1.2, $\sigma$ = 3, (**c**) $\nu$ = 0.4, $\lambda$ = 1.5, $\mu$ = 1.2, $\sigma$ = 2.9.

The qf of $X$ is obtained by replacing (9) in Equation (8)

$$x = Q(q) = \mu\left[\log\left(\frac{(1-q^{1/\lambda})^{1/\nu}}{q^{1/(\nu\lambda)}+(1-q^{1/\lambda})^{1/\nu}}\right)\Big/\log\left(\frac{(1-\tau^{1/\lambda})^{1/\nu}}{\tau^{1/(\nu\lambda)}+(1-\tau^{1/\lambda})^{1/\nu}}\right)\right]^{1/\sigma}, \quad 0 < q < 1. \quad (12)$$

**3. Structural Properties**

Some known properties of the reparameterized EOLLW distribution are given below:

(A) Equation (11) gives $\lim_{x\to\infty} f(x;\nu,\lambda,\gamma,\sigma) = 0$. Furthermore (Rodrigues et al. [38]),

$$\lim_{x\to 0^+} f(x;\nu,\lambda,\gamma,\sigma) = \begin{cases} \infty, & \nu\lambda < 1/\sigma, \\ w/\mu^{\sigma}, & \nu\lambda = 1/\sigma, \\ 0, & \nu\lambda > 1/\sigma, \end{cases}$$

where $w(\tau,\lambda,\nu)$ is defined in Section 2.

(B) The point $(x, f(x))$ is called a critical point of $f$ if $x$ is in the domain of $f$, and either $f'(x) = 0$ or $f'(x)$ do not exist. Since $f$ in (11) is differentiable, $f'(x)$ always exists in its domain. Differentiating $f(x)$ in (11) and setting it equal to zero, its critical points are the roots of (Rodrigues et al. [38])

$$\frac{T''(x)}{[T'(x)]^2} = \frac{(\nu+1)T^{\nu}(x) + (1-\nu\lambda)}{T(x)[1+T^{\nu}(x)]}, \tag{13}$$

where $T(x) = G(x)\,[1-G(x)]^{-1}$, $T'(x) = g(x)\,[1-G(x)]^{-2}$, $T''(x) = g'(x)\,[1-G(x)]^{-2} + 2g^2(x)\,[1-G(x)]^{-3}$, and $g(x)$ and $G(x)$ are given in (3). Every critical point where $f$ reaches a maximum (resp., minimum) value is called the mode (resp., minimum point). Using the intermediate value theorem, it is simple to verify that, for $\nu\lambda > 1/\sigma$, Equation (13) has at least one root in $(0,\infty)$ (see Appendix A).

(C) If $\sigma = 1$ and $\nu > 0$ is an integer, the pdf of $X$ is (Rodrigues et al. [38])

1. decreasing or decreasing–increasing–decreasing for $\nu\lambda < 1$;
2. unimodal for $\nu\lambda \geqslant 1$.

Note that Figure 1a ($\nu = 2, \lambda = 0.4$) shows the unimodality of the OELLW pdf when $\nu\lambda < 1$ and $\sigma = 4 > 1$. We emphasize that the values of the parameters in Figure 1a do not satisfy the hypothesis of the result C(2), so it does not contradict this one.

(D) For $0 < \nu \leqslant 1$, the pdf of $X$ is (Rodrigues et al. [38])

1. decreasing or decreasing–increasing–decreasing for $\nu\lambda < \sigma^{-1}$;
2. decreasing or uni/bimodal or decreasing–increasing–decreasing for $\nu\lambda = \sigma^{-1}$.

(E) If $X \sim$ EOLLW$(\nu,\lambda,\gamma,\sigma)$ and $0 < \nu \leqslant 1$, the pdf of $X$ is uni- or bimodal for $\nu\lambda > \sigma^{-1}$ (Rodrigues et al. [38]).
Note that Figure 1b ($\nu = 0.4, \lambda = 0.90$) and Figure 1c ($\nu = 0.4, \lambda = 1.5$) are consistent with this result, because bimodality is obtained and $\nu\lambda > \sigma^{-1}$ is satisfied for both cases.

(F) If $D$ has the Type I Dagum distribution (Dagum [39]), say $D \sim$ DAGUM$(\nu, 1, \lambda)$, the cdf of $X \sim$ EOLL-G$(\nu,\lambda,\gamma,\sigma)$ in (10) can be written as

$$F(x;\nu,\lambda,\mu,\sigma) = \mathbb{P}[D \leqslant T(x)] = \mathbb{P}\left[G^{-1}\left(\frac{D}{1+D};\boldsymbol{\eta}\right) \leqslant x\right]. \tag{14}$$

Consequently,

$$X = G^{-1}\left(\frac{D}{1+D}\right)$$

is a stochastic representation for $X$.

(G) The cdf (10) satisfies the identity

$$F(x) = \mathbb{P}\left[G^{-1}\left(\frac{1}{1+B}\right) \geqslant x\right],$$

where $B = 1/D$, $D \sim$ DAGUM$(\nu, 1, \lambda)$ and $G(x)$ is as given in Item (B).

(H) We write $\mathcal{A} = \{(\nu, \lambda) \in (0, \infty)^2 : (1+\nu)t^{2\nu} + \nu^2(1+\lambda)t^{\nu+1} + [\nu^2(1+\lambda) + \nu(1-\lambda) + 2]t^{\nu} + (1-\nu\lambda) > 0,\ \forall t > 0\}$ (see Rodrigues et al. [38]).

1. If $(\nu, \lambda) \in \mathcal{A}$ and $\sigma = 1$, the hrf of $X$ is increasing.
2. Let $\nu^2(1+\lambda) + \nu(1-\lambda) + 2 \geqslant 0$, $\nu\lambda > 1$, and $\nu > 0$ be an integer. For example, take the $\nu \geqslant 1$ integer and $\lambda > \nu^{-1}$.
   (a) If there exists $0 < x^* < \nu/\gamma$ such that $h'(x^*) = 0$, the hrf of $X$ has a bathtub (BT) shape.
   (b) If there does not exist $0 < x^* < \nu/\gamma$ such that $h'(x^*) = 0$, the hrf of $X$ is increasing.
3. Let $\nu^2 + 3\nu - 1 > 0$, $\nu\lambda = 1$, and $\nu > 0$ be an integer. For example, take $0 < \nu < (\sqrt{13} - 3)/2$ and $\lambda > nu^{-1}$. Under the conditions of Item (a) [Item (b)], the hrf of $X$ has a BT (increasing) shape.

(I) The EOLLW density transitions from heavy-tailed to light-tailed (Rodrigues et al. [38]).

### 3.1. Other Properties

#### 3.1.1. Existence of Moments

The tail of the density of $X$ follows from (14),

$$\mathbb{P}(X \geqslant x) = \mathbb{P}[D \geqslant T(x)], \quad D \sim \text{DAGUM}(\nu, 1, \lambda),$$

where $T(x) = \exp[(x/\gamma)^\sigma] - 1$. Markov's inequality gives

$$\mathbb{P}[D \geqslant T(x)] \leqslant \frac{\mathbb{E}(D)}{T(x)} = \frac{\lambda\Gamma(1-\frac{1}{\nu})\Gamma(1+\frac{1}{\nu})}{T(x)}, \quad \nu > 1.$$

Hence,

$$\mathbb{P}(X \geqslant x) \leqslant \frac{\lambda\Gamma(1-\frac{1}{\nu})\Gamma(1+\frac{1}{\nu})}{T(x)}, \quad \nu > 1. \tag{15}$$

Having an upper bound on the tail of the distribution, we proceed to bound the moments of $X$. This will prove its existence.

Based on the known formula $\mathbb{E}(X^p) = p\int_0^\infty x^{p-1}\,\mathbb{P}(X \geqslant x)\mathrm{d}x$ (for $X \geqslant 0$ and $p > 0$), the inequality holds:

$$\begin{aligned}\mathbb{E}(X^p) &\overset{(15)}{\leqslant} p\lambda\Gamma\Big(1-\frac{1}{\nu}\Big)\Gamma\Big(1+\frac{1}{\nu}\Big)\int_0^\infty \frac{x^{p-1}}{T(x)}\mathrm{d}x, \quad p > 0, \nu > 1,\\ &= p\lambda\Gamma\Big(1-\frac{1}{\nu}\Big)\Gamma\Big(1+\frac{1}{\nu}\Big)\frac{\gamma^p}{\sigma}\int_0^\infty \frac{y^{(p/\sigma)-1}}{\exp(y)-1}\mathrm{d}y,\end{aligned}$$

where $y = \exp[(x/\gamma)^\sigma]$.

From the Riemann zeta function $\zeta(s) = \sum_{n=1}^\infty n^{-s} = [\Gamma(s)]^{-1}\int_0^\infty z^{s-1}[\exp(z)-1]^{-1}\mathrm{d}z$, $\mathrm{Re}(s) > 1$, where $\Gamma(s) = \int_0^\infty x^{s-1}\,\mathrm{e}^{-x}\mathrm{d}x$ is the gamma function, we obtain

$$\mathbb{E}(X^p) \leqslant \frac{p\lambda\gamma^p}{\sigma}\Gamma\Big(1-\frac{1}{\nu}\Big)\Gamma\Big(1+\frac{1}{\nu}\Big)\Gamma\Big(\frac{p}{\sigma}\Big)\zeta\Big(\frac{p}{\sigma}\Big) < \infty, \quad p > \sigma.$$

Thus, for $\nu > 1$ and $p > \sigma$, the existence of the $p$th moment of $X$ (for any $p > 0$) is guaranteed.

### 3.1.2. Gini's Mean Difference

Given the random variables $X_1, \cdots, X_n$, the Gini mean difference (GMD) is defined as

$$\mathrm{GMD}_n = \frac{1}{\binom{n}{2}} \sum_{1\leqslant i<j\leqslant n} \mathbb{E}(|X_i - X_j|), \tag{16}$$

provided the involved expectations exist. The GMD is a very useful measure of variability in the presence of non-normality.

(a) If $X_1, \cdots, X_n$ is a sequence of independent and identically distributed (iid) random variables, the classical GMD (La Haye and Zizler [40]) is $\mathrm{GMD} = \mathbb{E}(|X_1 - X_2|)$. From Proposition 3 of Vila et al. [41], the GMD for a random sample $X_1, \cdots, X_n$ of the EOLLW model is

$$\mathrm{GMD} = \int_0^1 (2u-1) F_{X_1}^{-1}(u)\mathrm{d}u, \tag{17}$$

where

$$F_{X_1}^{-1}(u) = \mu \left[ \ln\left( \frac{(1-u^{1/\lambda})^{1/\nu}}{u^{1/(\nu\lambda)} + (1-u^{1/\lambda})^{1/\nu}} \right) \Big/ \ln\left( \frac{(1-\tau^{1/\lambda})^{1/\nu}}{\tau^{1/(\nu\lambda)} + (1-\tau^{1/\lambda})^{1/\nu}} \right) \right]^{1/\sigma}.$$

Note that analytically, the GMD (17) for the OELLW model is difficult to obtain. Vila et al. [41] provided the following upper bound $(2/\sqrt{3})\sqrt{\mathrm{Var}(X_1)}$ for the GMD.

(b) If $X \sim \mathrm{EOLLW}(\nu_i, \lambda_i, \gamma_i, \sigma_i)$, and $X_1, \cdots, X_n$ is a sample not necessarily independent nor identically distributed, the following inequality for the GMD (16) follows from Vila et al. [41]

$$\mathrm{GMD}_n \leqslant \frac{1}{\binom{n}{2}} \sum_{1\leqslant i<j\leqslant n} \left[ \sqrt{(\sqrt{\mathrm{Var}(X_i)} - \sqrt{\mathrm{Var}(X_j)}\rho_{i,j})^2 + \mathrm{Var}(X_j)(1-\rho_{i,j}^2)} + |\varsigma| \right],$$

where $\varsigma = \mathbb{E}(X_i) - \mathbb{E}(X_j)$ and $\rho_{i,j} = \mathrm{Corr}(X_i, X_j)$, for $i, j = 1, \ldots, n$.

Under constraints $\nu_i > 1$ and $\sigma_i < 1$, the moments of $X_i \sim \mathrm{EOLLW}(\nu_i, \lambda_i, \gamma_i, \sigma_i)$ $(i = 1, \ldots, n)$ always exist (see Section 3.1.1). Then, the mean $\mathbb{E}(X_i)$, variance $\mathrm{Var}(X_i)$, and correlations $\rho_{i,j} = \mathrm{Corr}(X_i, X_j)$ (for $i, j = 1, \ldots, n$) also exist. Hence, for both cases (a) and (b), we can deduce non-trivial upper bounds (then its existence) of the GMD for the EOLLW model.

## 4. The EOLLW QR Model for Censored Data

A new regression model is defined from the reparametrized EOLLW density (11), and two systematic components for the parameters $\mu_i$ and $\sigma_i$ (for $i = 1, \ldots, n$)

$$\mu_i(\tau) = \exp\left\{ \mathbf{v}_i^\top \boldsymbol{\beta}_1(\tau) \right\} \quad \text{and} \quad \sigma_i(\tau) = \exp\left\{ \mathbf{v}_i^\top \boldsymbol{\beta}_2(\tau) \right\}, \tag{18}$$

where $\boldsymbol{\beta}_1(\tau) = (\beta_{10}, \beta_{11}, \cdots, \beta_{1p})^\top$ and $\boldsymbol{\beta}_2(\tau) = (\beta_{20}, \beta_{21}, \cdots, \beta_{2p})^\top$ are unknown parameter vectors, and $\mathbf{v}_i^\top = (v_{i1}, \cdots, v_{ip})$ is the explanatory variable vector. Thus, the heteroscedasticity is modeled via $\sigma$.

The EOLLW QR model is defined by Equations (11) and (18), where $\nu$ and $\lambda$ are unknown constants, and it has as special models:

- Rhe exponentiated Weibull (EW) QR model for $\nu = 1$;
- the odd log-logistic Weibull (OLLW) QR model for $\lambda = 1$;
- and the Weibull QR model for $\nu = \lambda = 1$.

Consider a sample $(x_1, \delta_1, \mathbf{v}_1), \cdots, (x_n, \delta_n, \mathbf{v}_n)$ of independent observations, where each random response is defined by $x_i = \min\{X_i, C_i\}$, $\delta_i = I_{X_i \leq C_i}$ (censoring indicator), where $I(\cdot)$ denotes the indicator function. We consider non-informative censoring and the observed lifetimes and censoring times are independent given $\mathbf{v}_i$. Let $F$ and $C$ be the sets of individuals for which $x_i$ is the lifetime or censoring time, respectively. Conventional likelihood estimation techniques can be applied here. The log-likelihood function for the vector $\boldsymbol{\theta} = (\boldsymbol{\beta}_1^\top(\tau), \boldsymbol{\beta}_2^\top(\tau), \nu, \lambda)^\top$ from model (18) has the form

$$\ell(\boldsymbol{\theta}) = \sum_{i \in F} \ell_i(\boldsymbol{\theta}) + \sum_{i \in C} \ell_i^{(c)}(\boldsymbol{\theta}),$$

where $\ell_i(\boldsymbol{\theta}) = \log[f(x_i)]$, $\ell_i^{(c)}(\boldsymbol{\theta}) = \log[S(x_i)]$, $f(x_i)$ is the density (11), $S(x_i) = 1 - F(x_i)$ is the survival function, and $F(x_i)$ is the cdf (10) of $X_i$. The total log-likelihood function for $\boldsymbol{\theta}$ can be expressed as

$$\begin{aligned} \ell(\boldsymbol{\theta}) \;=\;& r^\dagger \log(\nu\,\lambda\,w) + \sum_{i \in F} \log[\sigma_i(\tau)] + \sum_{i \in F} [\sigma_i(\tau) - 1] \log(x_i) + \nu \sum_{i \in F} \log(u_i) + \\ & (\nu\,\lambda - 1) \sum_{i \in F} \log(1 - u_i) - \sum_{i \in F} \sigma_i(\tau) \log[\mu_i(\tau)] - \\ & (\lambda + 1) \sum_{i \in F} \log[(1 - u_i)^\nu + u_i^\nu] + \sum_{i \in C} \log\left[1 - \frac{(1 - u_i)^{\nu\,\lambda}}{[(1 - u_i)^\nu + u_i^\nu]^\lambda}\right], \end{aligned} \tag{19}$$

where

$$w(\nu, \lambda, \tau) = -\log\left(\frac{(1 - \tau^{\frac{1}{\lambda}})^{\frac{1}{\nu}}}{\tau^{\frac{1}{\nu\lambda}} + (1 - \tau^{\frac{1}{\lambda}})^{\frac{1}{\nu}}}\right), \qquad u_i = \exp\left\{-w(\nu, \lambda, \tau)\left[\frac{x_i}{\mu_i(\tau)}\right]^{\sigma_i(\tau)}\right\},$$

and $r^\dagger$ is the number of uncensored observations (failures).

The `gamlss` package in `R` [42] is used to find the maximum likelihood estimate $\widehat{\boldsymbol{\theta}}$ of $\boldsymbol{\theta}$. This package comes from the general class of generalized additive models for location, scale and shape (GAMLSS) (Rigby and Stasinopoulos [43]). These models allow all parameters of a distribution to be modeled as a function of covariates, such as non-parametric, parametric and/or additive smooth functions. Furthermore, they do not have the restriction that the response distribution belongs to a given family such as the exponential family. The package basically has two algorithms: `CG` (Cole and Green [44]) and `RS` (Rigby and Stasinopoulos [43]), whose acronyms come from the names of the authors. These algorithms are stable and do not require precise initial values to guarantee convergence. For this reason, we work with the `RS` algorithm with initial values for $\boldsymbol{\beta}_1(\tau)$ and $\boldsymbol{\beta}_2(\tau)$ obtained from the fitted Weibull QR model ($\nu = \lambda = 2$). Compared to the `CG` algorithm, `RS` is faster for larger datasets and does not use the expected value of cross derivatives, which can be useful when these values are equal to zero. For more details of the algorithms, see [43].

The codes for the reparametric EOLLW distribution in the GAMLSS framework are available at https://github.com/gabrielamrodrigues/EOLLW_quantiles (accessed on 10 February 2023). Following this approach, different regression models can be constructed by incorporating non-parametric smoothing functions, random effects, or other additive terms to the predictors.

Under conditions that are fulfilled for the parameter vector $\boldsymbol{\theta}$ in the interior of the parameter space but not on the boundary, the asymptotic distribution of $\sqrt{n}(\widehat{\boldsymbol{\theta}} - \boldsymbol{\theta})$ is multivariate normal $N_{2p+2}(0, K(\boldsymbol{\theta})^{-1})$, where $K(\boldsymbol{\theta})$ is the information matrix. The asymptotic covariance matrix $K(\boldsymbol{\theta})^{-1}$ of $\widehat{\boldsymbol{\theta}}$ can be approximated by the inverse of the $(2p+2) \times (2p+2)$ observed information matrix $-\ddot{\mathbf{L}}(\boldsymbol{\theta})$. The approximate multivariate normal distribution $N_{2p+2}(0, -\ddot{\mathbf{L}}(\boldsymbol{\theta})^{-1})$ for $\widehat{\boldsymbol{\theta}}$ can be used in the classical way to construct approximate confidence regions for some parameters in $\boldsymbol{\theta}$.

We can use the likelihood ratio (LR) statistic for comparing some sub-models with the EOLLW QR model. We consider the partition $\boldsymbol{\theta} = (\boldsymbol{\theta}_1^T, \boldsymbol{\theta}_2^T)^T$, where $\boldsymbol{\theta}_1$ is the subset of parameters of interest and $\boldsymbol{\theta}_2$ is the subset of remaining parameters. The LR statistic for testing the null hypothesis $H_0 : \boldsymbol{\theta}_1 = \boldsymbol{\theta}_1^{(0)}$ versus the alternative hypothesis $H_1 : \boldsymbol{\theta}_1 \neq \boldsymbol{\theta}_1^{(0)}$ is given by $w^* = 2\{\ell(\widehat{\boldsymbol{\theta}}) - \ell(\widetilde{\boldsymbol{\theta}})\}$, where $\widetilde{\boldsymbol{\theta}}$ and $\widehat{\boldsymbol{\theta}}$ are the estimates under the null and alternative hypotheses, respectively. The statistic $w$ is asymptotically (as $n \to \infty$) distributed as $\chi^2_k$, where $k$ is the dimension of the subset of parameters $\boldsymbol{\theta}_1$ of interest.

The standard maximum likelihood techniques can be adopted for the proposed regression, such as the quantile residuals ($qr_i$) (Dunn and Smyth [45]), namely

$$qr_i = \Phi^{-1}\left\{\frac{(1-\hat{u}_i)^{\hat{\nu}\hat{\lambda}}}{[(1-\hat{u}_i)^{\hat{\nu}} + \hat{u}_i^{\hat{\nu}}]^{\hat{\lambda}}}\right\}, \tag{20}$$

where

$$\hat{u}_i = \exp\left\{-\hat{w}(\hat{\nu},\hat{\lambda},\tau)\left[\frac{x_i}{\hat{\mu}_i(\tau)}\right]^{\hat{\sigma}_i(\tau)}\right\}, \qquad \hat{w}(\hat{\nu},\hat{\lambda},\hat{\tau}) = -\log\left(\frac{(1-\hat{\tau}^{\frac{1}{\hat{\lambda}}})^{\frac{1}{\hat{\nu}}}}{\hat{\tau}^{\frac{1}{\hat{\nu}\hat{\lambda}}} + (1-\hat{\tau}^{\frac{1}{\hat{\lambda}}})^{\frac{1}{\hat{\nu}}}}\right),$$

$$\hat{\mu}_i(\tau) = \exp\left\{\mathbf{v}_i^\top \widehat{\boldsymbol{\beta}}_1(\tau)\right\}, \qquad \hat{\sigma}_i(\tau) = \exp\left\{\mathbf{v}_i^\top \widehat{\boldsymbol{\beta}}_2(\tau)\right\},$$

and $\Phi(\cdot)^{-1}$ is the inverse cumulative standard normal distribution.

## 5. Simulation Study

A simulation study is carried out to verify the accuracy of the MLEs in the EOLLW QR model for the quartiles $\tau = 0.25, 0.50$ and $0.75$, and approximate censoring percentages 0%, 10% and 50%. Just one covariate $v_1 \sim$Binomial $(1, 0.5)$ is included in the systematic components:

$$\mu_i = \exp(\beta_{10} + \beta_{11}v_{1i}), \quad \sigma_i = \exp(\beta_{20} + \beta_{21}v_{1i}), \quad \nu_i = \exp(\beta_{30}), \quad \text{and} \quad \lambda_i = \exp(\beta_{40}),$$

For each combination, $N = 1000$ replicas of sizes $n = 100, 300$ and $500$ are generated. The true values used are: $\beta_{10} = 1.5$, $\beta_{11} = -1.32$, $\beta_{20} = 0.5$, $\beta_{21} = 0.2$, $\beta_{30} = 1.1$ and $\beta_{40} = 1.4$.

The inverse transformation method is used to generate the lifetimes $x_1, \cdots, x_n$ from the EOLLW$(\mu_i, \sigma_i, \nu, \lambda, \tau)$ distribution, and the censoring times $c_1, \cdots, c_n$ are determined from a uniform distribution $(0, k)$, where $k$ controls the censoring percentages. For each scenario, the Average Estimates (AEs), Biases and Mean Square Errors (MSEs) of the MLEs are calculated from:

$$\text{AE}(\hat{\boldsymbol{\theta}}) = \frac{1}{N}\sum_{i=1}^{N}\hat{\theta}_i, \quad \text{Bias}(\hat{\boldsymbol{\theta}}) = \frac{1}{N}\sum_{i=1}^{N}(\hat{\theta}_i - \theta_i), \quad \text{MSE}(\hat{\boldsymbol{\theta}}) = \frac{1}{N}\sum_{i=1}^{N}(\hat{\theta}_i - \theta_i)^2, \tag{21}$$

where $\hat{\boldsymbol{\theta}}^\top = (\hat{\beta}_{10}, \hat{\beta}_{11}, \hat{\beta}_{20}, \hat{\beta}_{21}, \hat{\beta}_{30}, \hat{\beta}_{40})$. The software R is used and Algorithm 1 presents the simulation steps.

Tables 1–3 report the findings. For all scenarios, the AEs converge to the true parameter values, and the biases and MSEs decrease when $n$ increases. These facts indicate that the consistency of the estimators hold. In addition, this behavior is verified even for high censoring percentages. We also found the empirical coverage probabilities (CPs) corresponding to the 95% confidence intervals calculated from the simulations. Table 4 reports CPs values which approach to the nominal level.

**Algorithm 1:** Simulation study

**Input:** $\tau$: quantile
  $n$: sample size
  $\beta_{10}, \beta_{11}, \beta_{20}, \beta_{21}, \beta_{30}, \beta_{40}$: parameter initial values
  $k$: controls censoring percentage
  $n.par$: number of parameters
  $r$: number of replicates
$theta$ = matrix(0, $r$, $n.par$)
$i = 1$
**while** $i \leq r$ **do**
  $v_{1i} \sim$ Binomial $(n, 1, 0.5)$
  $\mu_i = \exp(\beta_{10} + \beta_{11} v_{1i})$
  $\sigma_i = \exp(\beta_{20} + \beta_{21} v_{1i})$
  $\nu_i = \exp(\beta_{30})$
  $\lambda_i = \exp(\beta_{40})$
  $x_i^* \sim$ EOLLW $(n, \mu_i, \sigma_i, \nu_i, \lambda_i, \tau)$ from Equation (12)
  $c_i \sim$ Uniform $(n, 0, k)$
  $\delta$= vector of zeros
  $x$= vector of zeros
  **if** $c_i \leq x_i^*$ **then**
    $x_i = c_i$
    $\delta_i = 0$
  **else**
    $x_i = x_i^*$
    $\delta_i = 1$
  **end**
  Fit the model
  **if** *Model converges* **then**
    $theta[i,]$ = Parameter estimates
    $i = i + 1$
  **else**
    $i = i$
  **end**
**end**
Calculate AEs, BIASES and MSEs from Equation (21).

**Table 1.** Simulation results from the fitted EOLLW QR model for $\tau = 0.25$.

| % | $\theta$ | True Value | $n$ = 100 | | | $n$ = 300 | | | $n$ = 500 | | |
|---|---|---|---|---|---|---|---|---|---|---|---|
| | | | **AEs** | **Biases** | **MSEs** | **AEs** | **Biases** | **MSEs** | **AEs** | **Biases** | **MSEs** |
| 0% | $\beta_{10}$ | 1.50 | 1.5017 | 0.0017 | 0.0006 | 1.5010 | 0.0010 | 0.0002 | 1.5015 | 0.0015 | 0.0001 |
| | $\beta_{11}$ | −1.32 | −1.3208 | −0.0008 | 0.0009 | −1.3195 | 0.0005 | 0.0003 | −1.3204 | −0.0004 | 0.0002 |
| | $\beta_{20}$ | 0.50 | 0.4713 | −0.0287 | 0.3744 | 0.4689 | −0.0311 | 0.0811 | 0.4661 | −0.0339 | 0.0647 |
| | $\beta_{21}$ | 0.20 | 0.2026 | 0.0026 | 0.0232 | 0.1983 | −0.0017 | 0.0072 | 0.1996 | −0.0004 | 0.0043 |
| | $\beta_{30}$ | 1.10 | 0.9322 | −0.1678 | 0.6286 | 1.1410 | 0.0410 | 0.1523 | 1.1606 | 0.0606 | 0.1208 |
| | $\beta_{40}$ | 1.40 | 2.1725 | 0.7725 | 2.2507 | 1.3820 | −0.0180 | 0.2594 | 1.3228 | −0.0772 | 0.1726 |
| 10% | $\beta_{10}$ | 1.50 | 1.5019 | 0.0019 | 0.0006 | 1.5007 | 0.0007 | 0.0002 | 1.5012 | 0.0012 | 0.0001 |
| | $\beta_{11}$ | −1.32 | −1.3213 | −0.0013 | 0.0010 | −1.3199 | 0.0001 | 0.0003 | −1.3205 | -0.0005 | 0.0002 |
| | $\beta_{20}$ | 0.50 | 0.5107 | 0.0107 | 0.3516 | 0.4687 | −0.0313 | 0.0775 | 0.4664 | −0.0336 | 0.0663 |
| | $\beta_{21}$ | 0.20 | 0.1998 | −0.0002 | 0.0251 | 0.1992 | −0.0008 | 0.0080 | 0.1955 | −0.0045 | 0.0046 |
| | $\beta_{30}$ | 1.10 | 0.8796 | −0.2204 | 0.6288 | 1.1319 | 0.0319 | 0.1517 | 1.1640 | 0.0640 | 0.1210 |
| | $\beta_{40}$ | 1.40 | 2.1030 | 0.7030 | 1.7695 | 1.4245 | 0.0245 | 0.3137 | 1.3198 | −0.0802 | 0.1713 |

**Table 1.** *Cont.*

| % | $\theta$ | True Value | $n$ = 100 | | | $n$ = 300 | | | $n$ = 500 | | |
|---|---|---|---|---|---|---|---|---|---|---|---|
| | | | AEs | Biases | MSEs | AEs | Biases | MSEs | AEs | Biases | MSEs |
| 50% | $\beta_{10}$ | 1.50 | 1.5083 | 0.0083 | 0.0024 | 1.5015 | 0.0015 | 0.0006 | 1.5005 | 0.0005 | 0.0003 |
| | $\beta_{11}$ | −1.32 | −1.3262 | −0.0062 | 0.0029 | −1.3208 | −0.0008 | 0.0007 | −1.3202 | −0.0002 | 0.0004 |
| | $\beta_{20}$ | 0.50 | 0.7797 | 0.2797 | 0.3705 | 0.5016 | 0.0016 | 0.1765 | 0.4869 | −0.0131 | 0.0922 |
| | $\beta_{21}$ | 0.20 | 0.1276 | −0.0724 | 0.0767 | 0.1830 | −0.0170 | 0.0197 | 0.1865 | −0.0135 | 0.0127 |
| | $\beta_{30}$ | 1.10 | 0.5845 | −0.5155 | 0.6681 | 1.0430 | −0.0570 | 0.3344 | 1.1165 | 0.0165 | 0.1563 |
| | $\beta_{40}$ | 1.40 | 2.1757 | 0.7757 | 1.6396 | 1.6131 | 0.2131 | 0.6815 | 1.4305 | 0.0305 | 0.2805 |

**Table 2.** Simulation results from the fitted EOLLW QR model for $\tau = 0.50$.

| % | $\theta$ | True Value | $n$ = 100 | | | $n$ = 300 | | | $n$ = 500 | | |
|---|---|---|---|---|---|---|---|---|---|---|---|
| | | | AEs | Biases | MSEs | AEs | Biases | MSEs | AEs | Biases | MSEs |
| 0% | $\beta_{10}$ | 1.50 | 1.5018 | 0.0018 | 0.0005 | 1.5007 | 0.0007 | 0.0002 | 1.5010 | 0.0010 | 0.0001 |
| | $\beta_{11}$ | −1.32 | −1.3213 | −0.0013 | 0.0008 | −1.3197 | 0.0003 | 0.0003 | −1.3205 | −0.0005 | 0.0002 |
| | $\beta_{20}$ | 0.50 | 0.5026 | 0.0026 | 0.3890 | 0.4834 | −0.0166 | 0.0697 | 0.4664 | −0.0336 | 0.0700 |
| | $\beta_{21}$ | 0.20 | 0.2076 | 0.0076 | 0.0202 | 0.2042 | 0.0042 | 0.0066 | 0.2006 | 0.0006 | 0.0039 |
| | $\beta_{30}$ | 1.10 | 0.9111 | −0.1889 | 0.6434 | 1.1457 | 0.0457 | 0.1317 | 1.1694 | 0.0694 | 0.1291 |
| | $\beta_{40}$ | 1.40 | 2.1463 | 0.7463 | 2.2571 | 1.3320 | −0.0680 | 0.2332 | 1.3050 | −0.0950 | 0.1874 |
| 10% | $\beta_{10}$ | 1.50 | 1.5016 | 0.0016 | 0.0007 | 1.5004 | 0.0004 | 0.0002 | 1.5005 | 0.0005 | 0.0001 |
| | $\beta_{11}$ | −1.32 | −1.3203 | −0.0003 | 0.0010 | −1.3197 | 0.0003 | 0.0004 | −1.3200 | −0.0000 | 0.0002 |
| | $\beta_{20}$ | 0.50 | 0.5788 | 0.0788 | 0.2982 | 0.4814 | −0.0186 | 0.0787 | 0.4676 | −0.0324 | 0.0666 |
| | $\beta_{21}$ | 0.20 | 0.2037 | 0.0037 | 0.0236 | 0.2032 | 0.0032 | 0.0082 | 0.1994 | −0.0006 | 0.0046 |
| | $\beta_{30}$ | 1.10 | 0.8421 | −0.2579 | 0.5646 | 1.1418 | 0.0418 | 0.1473 | 1.1686 | 0.0686 | 0.1223 |
| | $\beta_{40}$ | 1.40 | 1.9985 | 0.5985 | 1.5804 | 1.3647 | −0.0353 | 0.2598 | 1.3109 | −0.0891 | 0.1954 |
| 50% | $\beta_{10}$ | 1.50 | 1.5040 | 0.0040 | 0.0033 | 1.4995 | −0.0005 | 0.0007 | 1.4996 | −0.0004 | 0.0004 |
| | $\beta_{11}$ | −1.32 | −1.3213 | −0.0013 | 0.0036 | −1.3185 | 0.0015 | 0.0008 | −1.3191 | 0.0009 | 0.0005 |
| | $\beta_{20}$ | 0.50 | 0.8284 | 0.3284 | 0.4059 | 0.5002 | 0.0002 | 0.2775 | 0.4885 | −0.0115 | 0.1185 |
| | $\beta_{21}$ | 0.20 | 0.1409 | −0.0591 | 0.0730 | 0.1852 | −0.0148 | 0.0195 | 0.1931 | −0.0069 | 0.0127 |
| | $\beta_{30}$ | 1.10 | 0.5795 | −0.5205 | 0.6660 | 1.0593 | −0.0407 | 0.4554 | 1.1395 | 0.0395 | 0.1775 |
| | $\beta_{40}$ | 1.40 | 2.0447 | 0.6447 | 1.4838 | 1.5840 | 0.1840 | 0.6743 | 1.3576 | −0.0424 | 0.2460 |

**Table 3.** Simulation results from the fitted EOLLW QR model for $\tau = 0.75$.

| % | $\theta$ | True Value | $n$ = 100 | | | $n$ = 300 | | | $n$ = 500 | | |
|---|---|---|---|---|---|---|---|---|---|---|---|
| | | | AEs | Biases | MSEs | AEs | Biases | MSEs | AEs | Biases | MSEs |
| 0% | $\beta_{10}$ | 1.50 | 1.4978 | −0.0022 | 0.0006 | 1.4974 | −0.0026 | 0.0002 | 1.4982 | −0.0018 | 0.0001 |
| | $\beta_{11}$ | −1.32 | −1.3202 | −0.0002 | 0.0011 | −1.3189 | 0.0011 | 0.0004 | −1.3200 | −0.0000 | 0.0002 |
| | $\beta_{20}$ | 0.50 | 0.4999 | −0.0001 | 0.4778 | 0.5031 | 0.0031 | 0.0630 | 0.4692 | −0.0308 | 0.0629 |
| | $\beta_{21}$ | 0.20 | 0.2057 | 0.0057 | 0.0187 | 0.1994 | −0.0006 | 0.0064 | 0.2003 | 0.0003 | 0.0038 |
| | $\beta_{30}$ | 1.10 | 0.9645 | −0.1355 | 0.7290 | 1.1483 | 0.0483 | 0.1149 | 1.1851 | 0.0851 | 0.1136 |
| | $\beta_{40}$ | 1.40 | 2.0572 | 0.6572 | 2.0673 | 1.3201 | −0.0799 | 0.2256 | 1.2860 | −0.1140 | 0.1613 |
| 10% | $\beta_{10}$ | 1.50 | 1.4968 | −0.0032 | 0.0008 | 1.4973 | −0.0027 | 0.0003 | 1.4981 | −0.0019 | 0.0002 |
| | $\beta_{11}$ | −1.32 | −1.3207 | −0.0007 | 0.0011 | −1.3192 | 0.0008 | 0.0004 | −1.3200 | −0.0000 | 0.0003 |
| | $\beta_{20}$ | 0.50 | 0.5707 | 0.0707 | 0.3092 | 0.5012 | 0.0012 | 0.0666 | 0.4817 | −0.0183 | 0.0553 |
| | $\beta_{21}$ | 0.20 | 0.2045 | 0.0045 | 0.0233 | 0.2046 | 0.0046 | 0.0069 | 0.2004 | 0.0004 | 0.0043 |
| | $\beta_{30}$ | 1.10 | 0.9004 | −0.1996 | 0.5399 | 1.1452 | 0.0452 | 0.1179 | 1.1760 | 0.0760 | 0.0991 |
| | $\beta_{40}$ | 1.40 | 1.9765 | 0.5765 | 1.7309 | 1.3391 | −0.0609 | 0.2326 | 1.2787 | −0.1213 | 0.1641 |

**Table 3.** *Cont.*

| % | $\theta$ | True Value | $n$ = 100 | | | $n$ = 300 | | | $n$ = 500 | | |
|---|---|---|---|---|---|---|---|---|---|---|---|
| | | | AEs | Biases | MSEs | AEs | Biases | MSEs | AEs | Biases | MSEs |
| 50% | $\beta_{10}$ | 1.50 | 1.4909 | −0.0091 | 0.0037 | 1.4949 | −0.0051 | 0.0010 | 1.4953 | −0.0047 | 0.0007 |
| | $\beta_{11}$ | −1.32 | −1.3134 | 0.0066 | 0.0043 | −1.3177 | 0.0023 | 0.0011 | −1.3172 | 0.0028 | 0.0007 |
| | $\beta_{20}$ | 0.50 | 0.8283 | 0.3283 | 0.5621 | 0.5214 | 0.0214 | 0.2210 | 0.5234 | 0.0234 | 0.0790 |
| | $\beta_{21}$ | 0.20 | 0.1300 | −0.0700 | 0.0778 | 0.1920 | −0.0080 | 0.0184 | 0.1904 | −0.0096 | 0.0120 |
| | $\beta_{30}$ | 1.10 | 0.6175 | −0.4825 | 0.8154 | 1.0842 | −0.0158 | 0.3476 | 1.1419 | 0.0419 | 0.1129 |
| | $\beta_{40}$ | 1.40 | 2.0680 | 0.6680 | 1.6198 | 1.5014 | 0.1014 | 0.6340 | 1.3051 | −0.0949 | 0.1893 |

**Table 4.** CPs for the 95% nominal level from the fitted EOLLW QR regression model when $\tau = 0.25$, 0.50 and 0.75 and approximate censoring percentages 0%, 10% and 50%.

| $\tau$ | $\theta$ | 0% ($n$) | | | 10% ($n$) | | | 50% ($n$) | | |
|---|---|---|---|---|---|---|---|---|---|---|
| | | (100) | (300) | (500) | (100) | (300) | (500) | (100) | (300) | (500) |
| 0.25 | $\beta_{10}$ | 0.939 | 0.946 | 0.957 | 0.948 | 0.951 | 0.947 | 0.922 | 0.949 | 0.953 |
| | $\beta_{11}$ | 0.954 | 0.949 | 0.959 | 0.946 | 0.942 | 0.966 | 0.937 | 0.951 | 0.946 |
| | $\beta_{20}$ | 0.973 | 0.974 | 0.965 | 0.972 | 0.981 | 0.969 | 0.962 | 0.975 | 0.981 |
| | $\beta_{21}$ | 0.948 | 0.955 | 0.956 | 0.946 | 0.957 | 0.954 | 0.937 | 0.961 | 0.954 |
| | $\beta_{30}$ | 0.980 | 1.000 | 1.000 | 0.978 | 0.998 | 1.000 | 0.954 | 0.981 | 0.993 |
| | $\beta_{40}$ | 0.990 | 0.999 | 0.991 | 0.993 | 0.999 | 0.993 | 0.996 | 0.998 | 1.000 |
| 0.50 | $\beta_{10}$ | 0.950 | 0.947 | 0.952 | 0.940 | 0.935 | 0.951 | 0.907 | 0.939 | 0.968 |
| | $\beta_{11}$ | 0.950 | 0.939 | 0.956 | 0.947 | 0.937 | 0.950 | 0.913 | 0.933 | 0.996 |
| | $\beta_{20}$ | 0.969 | 0.972 | 0.959 | 0.955 | 0.977 | 0.962 | 0.959 | 0.975 | 0.973 |
| | $\beta_{21}$ | 0.959 | 0.967 | 0.964 | 0.953 | 0.948 | 0.957 | 0.945 | 0.956 | 0.998 |
| | $\beta_{30}$ | 0.986 | 0.999 | 1.000 | 0.970 | 0.999 | 1.000 | 0.941 | 0.976 | 0.995 |
| | $\beta_{40}$ | 0.986 | 0.999 | 0.987 | 0.995 | 0.999 | 0.995 | 0.995 | 0.996 | 0.989 |
| 0.75 | $\beta_{10}$ | 0.950 | 0.956 | 0.963 | 0.941 | 0.959 | 0.958 | 0.895 | 0.955 | 0.938 |
| | $\beta_{11}$ | 0.946 | 0.956 | 0.959 | 0.954 | 0.958 | 0.963 | 0.914 | 0.964 | 0.949 |
| | $\beta_{20}$ | 0.952 | 0.968 | 0.966 | 0.952 | 0.974 | 0.969 | 0.939 | 0.972 | 0.991 |
| | $\beta_{21}$ | 0.968 | 0.969 | 0.965 | 0.962 | 0.968 | 0.968 | 0.936 | 0.970 | 0.959 |
| | $\beta_{30}$ | 0.980 | 0.999 | 1.000 | 0.979 | 1.000 | 1.000 | 0.952 | 0.987 | 0.996 |
| | $\beta_{40}$ | 0.980 | 0.999 | 0.989 | 0.991 | 0.998 | 0.996 | 0.986 | 0.993 | 0.999 |

## 6. Application to Gastric Cancer Data

Gastric cancer is the 5th most common cancer worldwide. There are more than one million new cases of this cancer every year, and it ranked as the 2nd leading cause of mortality from cancer in the world. We consider a survival dataset of patients suffering from gastric adenocarcinoma treated by surgery at Helsinki University Hospital in Finland [46] (available at https://doi.org/10.5061/dryad.hb62394, accessed on 29 November 2022 [47]), which contains 301 individuals with approximate censoring of 60%. Here we consider two covariables. The first corresponds to the classification of Lauren (Figure 2a). Various pathological classifications of the disease exist, but that of Lauren is the most common. Originally developed in the 1960s, the classification system adopted cell structural components to separate the patients in three types: well differentiated (non-cardia/intestinal), poorly differentiated (cardia/diffuse), and mixed disease [48]. Based on histology, the two leading types of gastric cancer are diffuse and intestinal [49]. These two types are reflected in the dataset. The second covariable corresponds to the presence of distant metastasis (M1 disease) (Figure 2b). Many patients diagnosed with gastric cancer present distant metastasis, implying a very poor prognosis, generally indicating prophylactic rather than curative treatment ([50,51]). The objective here is to verify the effects of the covariables in different quantiles, so as to obtain a more complete view of this dataset. Table 5 gives a descriptive summary, which includes the mean times, median times and times for the first and third quartiles. We can observe differences for the Lauren classification covariate: between the quantiles, the average time, and the Lauren 1 and Lauren 2 levels. However, we note subtle differences for the presence of distant metastases covariate. Then, the variables considered are ($i = 1, \ldots, 301$):

- $x_i$ survival time (in years);
- cens$_i$: censoring indicator (0 = censored, 1 = observed);
- $v_{1i}$: Lauren classification (1 = intestinal, 2 = diffuse), defined by a dummy variable (0 = intestinal, 1 = diffuse);
- $v_{2i}$: Presence of distant metastases (pm) (1 = yes, 0 = no)

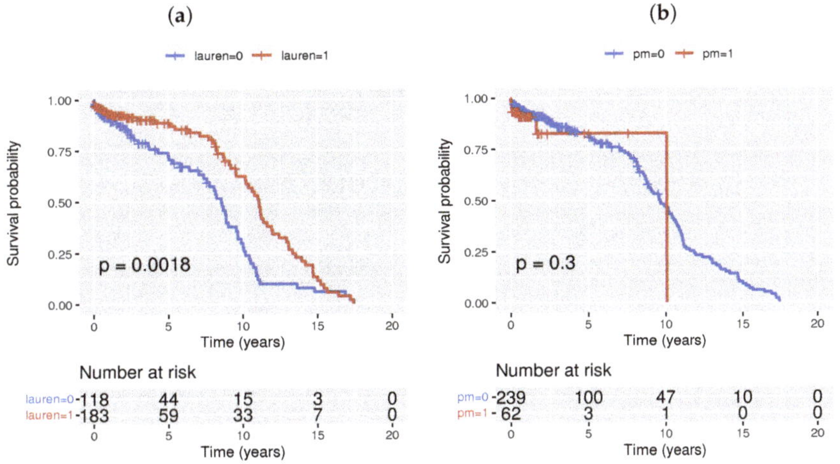


**Figure 2.** Kaplan-Meier survival curves for gastric cancer data: (**a**) Lauren classification; (**b**) Presence of distant metastases.

**Table 5.** Descriptive analysis of gastric cancer data.

| | 0.25 | 0.50 | 0.75 | Mean |
|---|---|---|---|---|
| Lauren 1 | 4.33 | 8.57 | 10.18 | 7.73 |
| Lauren 2 | 8.32 | 11.08 | 13.30 | 10.39 |
| Pm 0 | 7.15 | 9.66 | 11.90 | 9.24 |
| Pm 1 | 10.06 | 10.06 | 10.06 | 8.48 |

*Regression Model*

We compare the EOLLW QR model with the nested OLLW, Exp-W and Weibull models under three systematic components:

$$\mathcal{M}_0 = \begin{cases} \mu(\tau) = \exp[\beta_{10}(\tau)] \\ \sigma_i(\tau) = \exp[\beta_{20}(\tau)]; \end{cases}$$
$$\mathcal{M}_1 = \begin{cases} \mu(\tau) = \mu(\tau) = \exp[\beta_{10}(\tau) + \beta_{11}(\tau)v_{1i} + \beta_{12}(\tau)v_{2i}] \\ \sigma_i(\tau) = \exp[\beta_{20}(\tau)]; \end{cases}$$
$$\mathcal{M}_2 = \begin{cases} \mu(\tau) = \exp[\beta_{10}(\tau) + \beta_{11}(\tau)v_{1i} + \beta_{12}(\tau)v_{2i}] \\ \sigma_i(\tau) = \exp[\beta_{20}(\tau) + \beta_{21}(\tau)v_{1i} + \beta_{22}(\tau)v_{2i}]. \end{cases}$$

We consider the following quantiles: $\tau = 0.10, 0.25, 0.50, 0.75$ and $0.90$. Table 6 reports the Akaike information criterion (AIC) values for the fitted QR regression models. The EOLLW QR model under structure $\mathcal{M}_2$ gives the lowest values for these quantiles.

**Table 6.** AIC values for some fitted QR models to gastric cancer data.

| Model | | $\tau$ | | | | |
|---|---|---|---|---|---|---|
| | | **0.10** | **0.25** | **0.50** | **0.75** | **0.90** |
| $\mathcal{M}_0$ | EOLLW | 755.3104 | 760.6965 | 755.1712 | 755.1715 | 755.1759 |
| | OLLW | 773.1060 | 773.1021 | 773.1010 | 773.1017 | 773.1011 |
| | Exp-W | 759.9144 | 759.0376 | 758.4132 | 757.2295 | 757.9724 |
| | Weibull | 813.5743 | 813.5743 | 813.5744 | 813.5744 | 813.5746 |
| $\mathcal{M}_1$ | EOLLW | 755.2259 | 755.1844 | 755.1742 | 755.1753 | 755.1778 |
| | OLLW | 774.2566 | 774.2433 | 774.2239 | 774.2288 | 774.2294 |
| | Exp-W | 762.3150 | 761.8464 | 761.2808 | 760.9295 | 938.5430 |
| | Weibull | 811.0754 | 811.0752 | 811.0754 | 811.0755 | 811.0756 |
| $\mathcal{M}_2$ | EOLLW | **750.3085** | **750.1898** | **750.1712** | **750.1812** | **750.1930** |
| | OLLW | 769.1151 | 769.1514 | 769.2313 | 769.2891 | 769.3191 |
| | Exp-W | 755.8550 | 755.7825 | 755.7881 | 755.8164 | 768.3938 |
| | Weibull | 797.4298 | 797.4352 | 797.4666 | 797.5064 | 797.5421 |

Table 7 gives three likelihood ratio (LR) statistics ($p$-values in parentheses), thus indicating that the EOLLW QR model under structure $\mathcal{M}_2$ is better than the others. Thus, we can consider this model as the predictive model.

**Table 7.** LR statistics for the ELLOW QR model under structure $\mathcal{M}_2$ and some $\tau$ values for the gastric cancer data.

| Models | Hypotheses | $\tau$ | | | | |
|---|---|---|---|---|---|---|
| | | **0.10** | **0.25** | **0.50** | **0.75** | **0.90** |
| EOLLW vs. OLLW | $H_0 : \lambda = 1$ vs. $H_1 : H_0$ is false | 20.80(<0.001) | 20.95(<0.001) | 21.06(<0.001) | 21.10(<0.001) | 21.12(<0.001) |
| EOLLW vs. Exp-W | $H_0 : \nu = 1$ vs. $H_1 : H_0$ is false | 7.54(0.006) | 7.58(0.005) | 7.61(0.005) | 7.63(0.005) | 20.20(<0.001) |
| EOLLW vs. Weibull | $H_0 : \lambda = \nu = 1$ vs. $H_1 : H_0$ is false | 51.12(<0.001) | 51.24(<0.001) | 51.29(<0.001) | 51.28(<0.001) | 51.34(<0.001) |

Figure 3 displays the MLEs and the corresponding confidence intervals along with the interval $[0.01, 0.99]$, and Table 8 gives the MLEs and their standard errors (SEs) for the quantiles $\tau = 0.10, 0.25, 0.50, 0.75$ and 0.90 at the significance level of 5%. The following facts can be mentioned:

- The effect of the Lauren classification 2 in comparison with 1 is decreasing along the quantiles and its confidence interval shows significant estimates for all quantiles. These results corroborate with those point quantiles reported in Table 8.
- The effect of the presence of distant metastasis is rising along the quantiles. Its confidence interval includes zero in the interval $[0.25, 0.75)$, thus indicating that the covariable is not significant for these quantiles. These results can be noted by the non-significant $p$-values for $\tau = 0.25$ and 0.50.
- For the parameters $\beta_{21}$ and $\beta_{22}$, the estimates are significant for both quantiles, thus indicating that those covariables influence the variability of the survival times.
- The estimates corresponding to the shape parameters $\beta_{30}$ and $\beta_{40}$ are also significant for all quantiles.

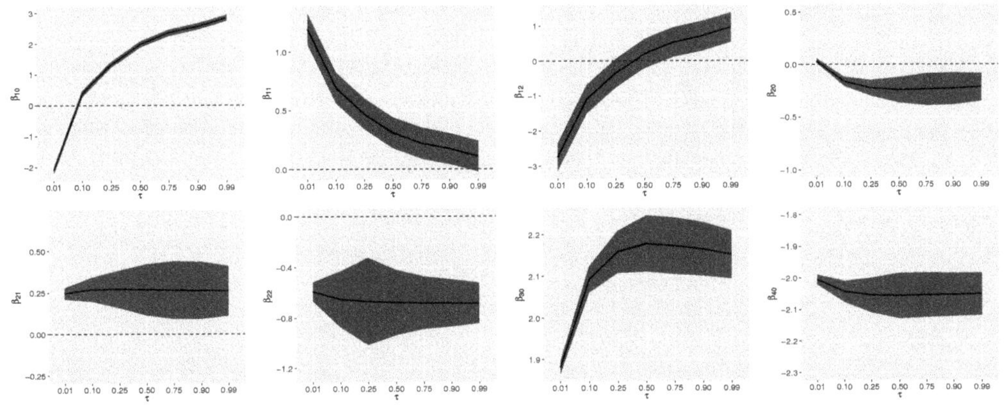

**Figure 3.** Point estimates and 95% confidence intervals for the parameters versus $\tau$ from the fitted ELLOW QR model under structure $\mathcal{M}_2$ for the gastric cancer data.

**Table 8.** Estimation findings from the ELLOW QR model under structure $\mathcal{M}_2$ and $\tau$ = 0.10, 0.25, 0.50, 0.75 and 0.90 for the current data.

| $\tau$ | $\theta$ | MLEs | SEs | *p*-Values |
|---|---|---|---|---|
| 0.10 | $\beta_{10}$ | 0.372 | 0.050 | <0.01 |
| | $\beta_{11}$ | 0.691 | 0.066 | <0.01 |
| | $\beta_{12}$ | −1.100 | 0.206 | <0.01 |
| | $\beta_{20}$ | −0.165 | 0.022 | <0.01 |
| | $\beta_{21}$ | 0.269 | 0.036 | <0.01 |
| | $\beta_{22}$ | −0.652 | 0.113 | <0.01 |
| | $\beta_{30}$ | 2.092 | 0.016 | <0.01 |
| | $\beta_{40}$ | −2.043 | 0.017 | <0.01 |
| 0.25 | $\beta_{10}$ | 1.322 | 0.050 | <0.01 |
| | $\beta_{11}$ | 0.468 | 0.066 | <0.01 |
| | $\beta_{12}$ | −0.350 | 0.210 | 0.096 |
| | $\beta_{20}$ | −0.226 | 0.037 | <0.01 |
| | $\beta_{21}$ | 0.271 | 0.057 | <0.01 |
| | $\beta_{22}$ | −0.670 | 0.176 | <0.01 |
| | $\beta_{30}$ | 2.159 | 0.026 | <0.01 |
| | $\beta_{40}$ | −2.054 | 0.028 | <0.01 |
| 0.50 | $\beta_{10}$ | 1.990 | 0.050 | <0.01 |
| | $\beta_{11}$ | 0.308 | 0.066 | <0.01 |
| | $\beta_{12}$ | 0.211 | 0.212 | 0.320 |
| | $\beta_{20}$ | −0.245 | 0.061 | <0.01 |
| | $\beta_{21}$ | 0.269 | 0.078 | <0.01 |
| | $\beta_{22}$ | −0.679 | 0.131 | <0.01 |
| | $\beta_{30}$ | 2.178 | 0.034 | <0.01 |
| | $\beta_{40}$ | −2.056 | 0.037 | <0.01 |
| 0.75 | $\beta_{10}$ | 2.362 | 0.050 | <0.01 |
| | $\beta_{11}$ | 0.220 | 0.066 | <0.01 |
| | $\beta_{12}$ | 0.533 | 0.213 | 0.013 |
| | $\beta_{20}$ | −0.239 | 0.077 | <0.01 |
| | $\beta_{21}$ | 0.266 | 0.088 | <0.01 |
| | $\beta_{22}$ | −0.682 | 0.105 | <0.01 |
| | $\beta_{30}$ | 2.172 | 0.034 | <0.01 |
| | $\beta_{40}$ | −2.054 | 0.036 | <0.01 |
| 0.90 | $\beta_{10}$ | 2.565 | 0.050 | <0.010 |
| | $\beta_{11}$ | 0.172 | 0.066 | 0.010 |
| | $\beta_{12}$ | 0.710 | 0.213 | <0.01 |
| | $\beta_{20}$ | −0.231 | 0.077 | <0.01 |
| | $\beta_{21}$ | 0.264 | 0.087 | <0.01 |
| | $\beta_{22}$ | −0.684 | 0.094 | <0.01 |
| | $\beta_{30}$ | 2.165 | 0.033 | <0.01 |
| | $\beta_{40}$ | −2.053 | 0.034 | <0.01 |

*Residual Analysis*

Figures 4–8 provide the normal probability plots of the $qr_i$'s in Equation (20) under structure $\mathcal{M}_2$ for some quantiles. They reveal that the EOLLW QR model is the best among the fitted models. Further, they approximately follow a standard normal distribution, thus indicating adequate fits. Figure 9 shows the index plot of the $qr_i$'s for the EOLLW QR model under structure $\mathcal{M}_2$. There are few points outside the interval $[-3,3]$ for both quantiles, and a random pattern around zero which show that these models are very adequate to the current data.

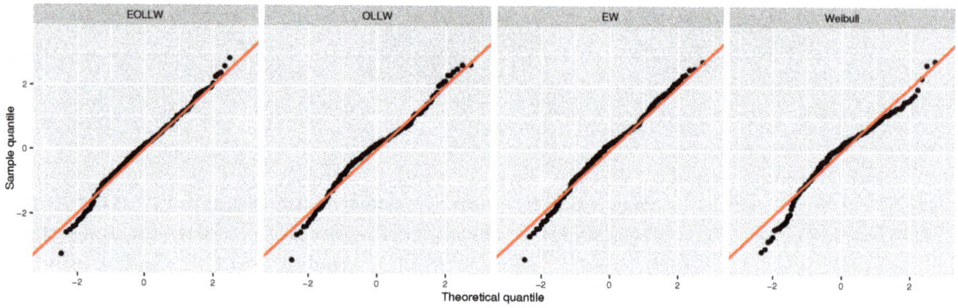


**Figure 4.** QQ plots for $qr_i$'s from some fitted regression models under structure $\mathcal{M}_2$ and $\tau = 0.10$.

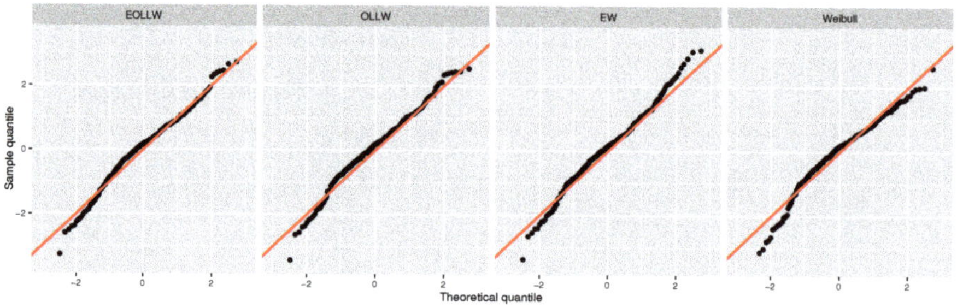


**Figure 5.** QQ plots for the $qr_i$'s from some fitted regression models under structure $\mathcal{M}_2$ and $\tau = 0.25$.

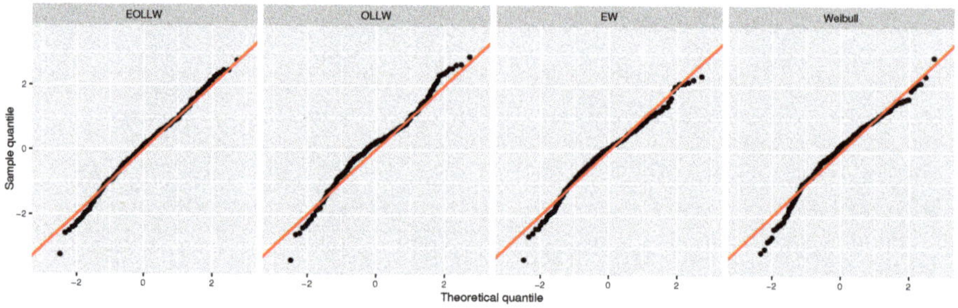


**Figure 6.** QQ plots for the $qr_i$'s from some fitted regression models under structure $\mathcal{M}_2$ and $\tau = 0.50$.

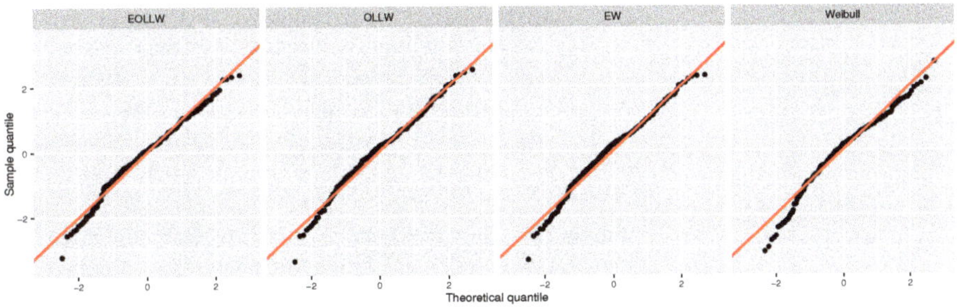


**Figure 7.** QQ plots for the $qr_i$'s from some regression models under structure $\mathcal{M}_2$ and $\tau = 0.75$.

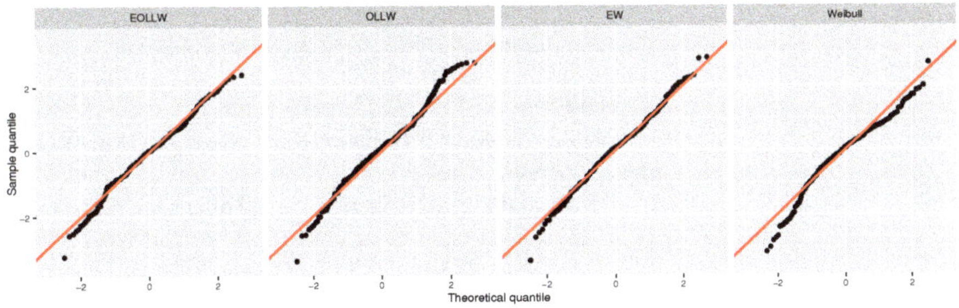


**Figure 8.** QQ plots for the $qr_i$'s from some regression models under structure $\mathcal{M}_2$ and $\tau = 0.90$.

(a) (b) (c) (d) (e)

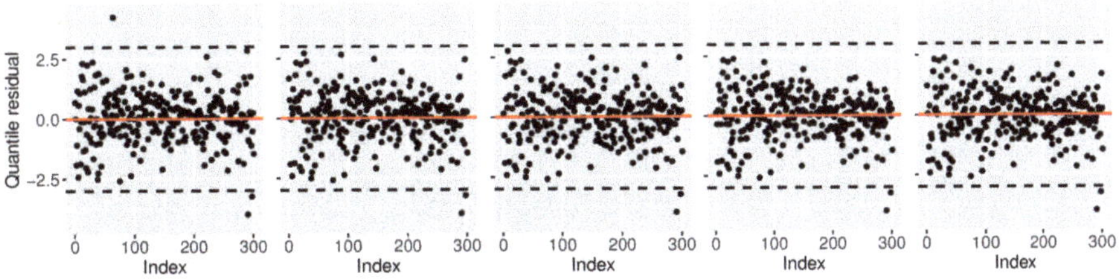


**Figure 9.** Index plots for the $qr_i$'s from some regression models under structure $\mathcal{M}_2$: (**a**) $\tau = 0.10$; (**b**) $\tau = 0.25$; (**c**) $\tau = 0.50$; (**d**) $\tau = 0.75$; (**e**) $\tau = 0.90$.

## 7. Concluding Remarks

We introduced a new quantile regression model for censored data based on the reparametrization of the exponentiated log-logistic odd Weibull (EOLLW) distribution in terms of quantiles with two systematic components. We presented some mathematical properties of the reparametrized EOLLW distribution. The proposed quantile regression model is an important extension of other regression models and can be a valuable addition to the survival analysis area. The new regression model also serves as a good alternative for the analysis of lifetime data and may be more flexible than the exponentiated Weibull, odd log-logistic Weibull and Weibull models. Several simulations were performed for different parameter settings, sample sizes and censoring percentages, to assess the accuracy of the maximum likelihood estimators. The usefulness of the new model was also proved by means of a gastric cancer dataset.

**Author Contributions:** Conceptualization, G.M.R., E.M.M.O., G.M.C., R.V.; methodology, G.M.R., E.M.M.O., G.M.C., R.V.; software, G.M.R., E.M.M.O., G.M.C., R.V.; validation, G.M.R., E.M.M.O., G.M.C., R.V.; formal analysis, G.M.R., E.M.M.O., G.M.C., R.V.; investigation, G.M.R., E.M.M.O., G.M.C., R.V.; data curation, G.M.R., E.M.M.O., G.M.C., R.V.; writing—original draft preparation, G.M.R., E.M.M.O., G.M.C., R.V.; writing—review and editing, G.M.R., E.M.M.O., G.M.C., R.V.; visualization, G.M.R., E.M.M.O., G.M.C., R.V.; supervision, G.M.R., E.M.M.O., G.M.C., R.V. All authors have read and agreed to the current version of the manuscript.

**Funding:** This study was financed in part by the Coordenação de Aperfeiçoamento de Pessoal de Nível Superior–Brasil (CAPES) (Finance Code 001).

**Informed Consent Statement:** Not applicable.

**Data Availability Statement:** The dataset was obtained from https://doi.org/10.5061/dryad.hb62394. We also made the data available at https://github.com/gabrielamrodrigues/EOLLW_quantiles.

**Conflicts of Interest:** The authors declare no conflict of interest.

## Appendix A

Here, for the EOLLW model, we verify (11), Equation (13) has at least one zero under the restriction $\nu\lambda > 1/\sigma$.

Indeed, if $G(x;\gamma,\sigma)$ and $g(x;\gamma,\sigma)$ are as in (3), Equation (13) can be written as

$$\mathcal{L}(z) \equiv \left(2 - \frac{1}{\sigma}\right)\left[\frac{1 - \exp(-z)}{z}\right] - \nu\,\frac{[\exp(z) - 1]^{\nu} - \lambda}{[\exp(z) - 1]^{\nu} + 1} - 1 = 0, \quad \text{where } z = \left(\frac{x}{\gamma}\right)^{\sigma}.$$

L'Hospital's rule gives

$$\lim_{z \to 0^+} \mathcal{L}(z) = \left(2 - \frac{1}{\sigma}\right) - \nu(-\lambda) - 1 = 1 + \nu\lambda - \frac{1}{\sigma} > 0$$

and

$$\lim_{z \to \infty} \mathcal{L}(z) = -(\nu + 1) < 0,$$

since $\nu\lambda > 1/\sigma$. Further, $\mathcal{L}$ is continuous in $(0,\infty)$, and by the intermediate value theorem, there is a $c \in (0,\infty)$ such that $\mathcal{L}(c) = 0$. In other words, Equation (13) has at least one zero if $\nu\lambda > 1/\sigma$.

## References

1. Koenker, R.; Bassett, G., Jr. Regression quantiles. *Econometrica* **1978**, *46*, 33–50. [CrossRef]
2. Gijbels, I.; Karim, R.; Verhasselt, A. Semiparametric quantile regression using family of quantile-based asymmetric densities. *Comput. Stat. Data Anal.* **2021**, *157*, 107–129. [CrossRef]
3. Takeuchi, I.; Furuhashi, T. Non-crossing quantile regressions by SVM. *Int. Jt. Conf. Neural Netw.* **2004**, *1*, 401–406.
4. Das, K.; Krzywinski, M.; Altman, N. Quantile regression. *Nat. Methods* **2019**, *16*, 451–452. [CrossRef] [PubMed]
5. Liu, Y.; Wu, Y. Simultaneous multiple non-crossing quantile regression estimation using kernel constraints. *J. Non Parametr. Stat.* **2011**, *23*, 415–437. [CrossRef]
6. Koenker, R.; Machado, J.A.F. Goodness of fit and related inference processes for quantile regression. *J. Am. Stat. Assoc.* **1999**, *94*, 1296–1310. [CrossRef]
7. Peng, L.; Huang, Y. Survival analysis with quantile regression models. *J. Am. Stat. Assoc.* **2008**, *103*, 637–649. [CrossRef]
8. Wang, H.J.; Wang, L. Locally weighted censored quantile regression. *J. Am. Stat. Assoc.* **2009**, *104*, 1117–1128. [CrossRef]
9. Zarean, E.; Mahmoudi, M.; Azimi, T.; Amini, P. Determining overall survival and risk factors in esophageal cancer using censored quantile regression. *Asian Pac. J. Cancer Prev.* **2018**, *19*, 3081–3086. [CrossRef]
10. Yang, X.; Narisetty, N.N.; He, X. A new approach to censored quantile regression estimation. *J. Comput. Graph. Stat.* **2018**, *27*, 417–425. [CrossRef]
11. Du, J.; Zhang, Z.; Xu, D. Estimation for the censored partially linear quantile regression models. *Commun. Stat. Simul. Comput.* **2018**, *47*, 2393–2408. [CrossRef]
12. Xue, X.; Xie, X.; Strickler, H.D. A censored quantile regression approach for the analysis of time to event data. *Stat. Methods Med. Res.* **2018**, *27*, 955–965. [CrossRef] [PubMed]

13. Hong, H.G.; Christiani, D.C.; Li, Y. Quantile regression for survival data in modern cancer research: Expanding statistical tools for precision medicine. *Precis. Clin. Med.* **2019**, *2*, 90–99. [CrossRef] [PubMed]
14. De Backer, M.; Ghouch, A.E.; Van Keilegom, I. An adapted loss function for censored quantile regression. *J. Am. Stat. Assoc.* **2019**, *114*, 1126–1137. [CrossRef]
15. De Backer, M.; El Ghouch, A.; Van Keilegom, I. Linear censored quantile regression: A novel minimum-distance approach. *Scand. J. Stat.* **2020**, *47*, 1275–1306. [CrossRef]
16. Qiu, Z.; Ma, H.; Chen, J.; Dinse, G.E. Quantile regression models for survival data with missing censoring indicators. *Stat. Methods Med. Res.* **2021**, *30*, 1320–1331. [CrossRef]
17. Yazdani, A.; Yaseri, M.; Haghighat, S.; Kaviani, A.; Zeraati, H. The comparison of censored quantile regression methods in prognosis factors of breast cancer survival. *Sci. Rep.* **2021**, *11*, 18268. [CrossRef]
18. Peng, L. Quantile regression for survival data. *Annu. Rev. Stat. Appl.* **2021**, *8*, 413–437. [CrossRef]
19. Hsu, C.Y.; Wen, C.C.; Chen, Y.H. Quantile function regression analysis for interval censored data, with application to salary survey data. *Jpn. J. Stat. Data Sci.* **2021**, *4*, 999–1018. [CrossRef]
20. He, X.; Pan, X.; Tan, K.M.; Zhou, W.X. Scalable estimation and inference for censored quantile regression process. *Ann. Stat.* **2022**, *50*, 2899–2924. [CrossRef]
21. Wei, B. Quantile regression for censored data in haematopoietic cell transplant research. *Bone Marrow Transplant.* **2022**, *57*, 853–856. [CrossRef] [PubMed]
22. Jodrá, P.; Jiménez-Gamero, M.D. A quantile regression model for bounded responses based on the exponential-geometric distribution. *Revstat Stat. J.* **2020**, *18*, 415–436.
23. Sánchez, L.; Leiva, V.; Galea, M.; Saulo, H. Birnbaum-Saunders quantile regression and its diagnostics with application to economic data. *Appl. Stoch. Model. Bus. Ind.* **2020**, *37*, 53–73. [CrossRef]
24. Sánchez, L.; Leiva, V.; Galea, M.; Saulo, H. Birnbaum-Saunders quantile regression models with application to spatial data. *Mathematics* **2020**, *8*, 1000. [CrossRef]
25. Gallardo,D.I.; Gómez-Déniz, E.; Gómez, H.W. Discrete generalized half-normal distribution with applications in quantile regression. *SORT* **2020**, *44*, 265–284
26. Korkmaz, M.C.; Chesneau, C.; Korkmaz, Z.S. Transmuted unit Rayleigh quantile regression model: Alternative to beta and Kumaraswamy quantile regression models. *Sci. Bull.* **2021**, *83*, 149–159.
27. Korkmaz, M.M.; Chesneau, C. On the unit Burr-XII distribution with the quantile regression modeling and applications. *Comput. Appl. Math.* **2021**, *40*, 2–26. [CrossRef]
28. Korkmaz, M.Ç.; Altun, E.; Chesneau, C.; Yousof, H.M. On the unit-Chen distribution with associated quantile regression and applications. *Math. Slovaca* **2022**, *72*, 765–786. [CrossRef]
29. Saulo, H.; Dasilva, A.; Leiva, V.; de la Fuente-Mella, L.S. Log-symmetric quantile regression models. *Stat. Neerl.* **2022**, *76*, 124–163. [CrossRef]
30. Korkmaz, M.C.; Chesneau, C.; Korkmaz, Z.Z.S. A new alternative quantile regression model for the bounded response with educational measurements applications of OECD countries. *J. Appl. Stat.* **2023**, *50*, 131–154. [CrossRef]
31. Saulo, H.; Vila, R.; Borges, G.V.; Bourguignon, M.; Leiva, V.; Marchant, C. Modeling Income Data via New Parametric Quantile Regressions: Formulation, Computational Statistics, and pplication. *Mathematics* **2023**, *11*, 448. [CrossRef]
32. Rodrigues, A.; Borges, P.; Santos, B. A Defective Cure Rate Quantile Regression Model for Male Breast Cancer Data. 2021. Preprint. Available online: https://arxiv.org/abs/2105.03699 (accessed on 19 December 2022).
33. Morales, C.E.G.; Lachos, V.H.; Bourguignon, M. A skew-t quantile regression for censored and missing data. *Stat* **2021**, *10*, e379.
34. Ozel, G.; Alizadeh, M.; Cakmakyapan, S.; Hamedani, G.G.; Ortega, E.M.; Cancho, V.G. The odd log-logistic Lindley Poisson model for lifetime data. *Commun. -Stat.-Simul. Comput.* **2017**, *46*, 6513–6537. [CrossRef]
35. Alizadeh, M.; Tahmasebi, S.; Haghbin, H. The exponentiated odd log-logistic family of distributions: Properties and applications. *J. Stat. Model. Theory Appl.* **2020**, *1*, 29–52.
36. Gleaton, J.U.; Lynch, J.D. Properties of generalized log-logistic families of lifetime distributions. *J. Probab. Stat. Sci.* **2006**, *4*, 51–64.
37. Mudholkar, G.S.; Srivastava, D.K.; Kollia, G. A generalization of the Weibull distribution with application to the analysis of survival data. *J. Am. Stat. Assoc.* **1996**, *91*, 1575–1583. [CrossRef]
38. Rodrigues, G.M.; Vila, R.; Ortega, E.M.M.; Cordeiro, G.M.; Serra, V. New Results and Regression Model for the Exponentiated Odd Log-Logistic Weibull Family of Distributions with Applications. 2022. Preprint. Available online: https://arxiv.org/abs/2203.14189 (accessed on 7 February 2023).
39. Dagum, C. A model of income distribution and the conditions of existence of moments of finite order. *Bull. Int. Stat. Inst.* **1975**, *46*, 199–205.
40. La Haye, R.; Zizler, P. The Gini mean difference and variance. *Metron* **2019**, *77*, 43–52. [CrossRef]
41. Vila, R.; Balakrishnan, N.; Saulo, H. An Upper Bound and a Characterization for GINI's Mean Difference Based on Correlated Random Variables. 2023. Preprint. Available online: https://arxiv.org/abs/2301.07229 (accessed on 7 February 2023).
42. R Core Team. *R: A Language and Environment for Statistical Computing*; R Foundation for Statistical Computing: Vienna, Austria, 2022.
43. Rigby, R.A.; Stasinopoulos, D.M. Generalized additive models for location, scale and shape. *J. R. Stat. Soc. Ser. (Appl. Stat.)* **2005**, *54*, 507–554. [CrossRef]

44. Cole, T.J.; Green, P.J. Smoothing reference centile curves: The LMS method and penalized likelihood. *Stat. Med.* **1992**, *11*, 1305–1319. [CrossRef]
45. Dunn, P.; Smyth, G. Randomized quantile residuals. *J. Comput. Graph. Stat.* **1996**, *5*, 236–44.
46. Kasurinen, A.; Tervahartiala, T.; Laitinen, A.; Kokkola, A.; Sorsa, T.; Böckelman, C.; Haglund, C. High serum MMP-14 predicts worse survival in gastric cancer. *PLoS ONE* **2018**, *13*, e0208800. [CrossRef] [PubMed]
47. Kasurinen, A.; Tervahartiala, T.; Laitinen, A.; Kokkola, A.; Sorsa, T.; Böckelman, C.; Haglund, C. Data from: High Serum MMP-14 Predicts Worse Survival in Gastric Cancer. Available online: https://doi.org/10.5061/dryad.hb62394 (accessed on 29 November 2022).
48. Chen, Y.C.; Fang, W.L.; Wang, R.F.; Liu, C.A.; Yang, M.H.; Lo S.S.; Wu, C.W.; Li, A.F.; Shyr, Y.M.; ; Huang, K.H. Clinico pathological variation of Lauren classification in gastric cancer. *Pathol. Oncol. Res.* **2016**, *22*, 197–202. [CrossRef]
49. Lauren, P. The two histologic main types of gastric carcinoma: Diffuse and so-called intestinal type carcinoma. An attempt at a histoclinicalclassification. *Acta Parhol. Microbid. Scan.* **1965**, *64*, 31–49. [CrossRef] [PubMed]
50. Dixon, M.; Mahar, A.L.; Helyer, L.K.; Vasilevska-Ristovska, J.; Law, C.; Coburn, N.G. Prognostic factors in metastatic gastric cancer: Results of a population-based, retrospective cohort study in Ontario. *Gastric Cancer* **2016**, *19*, 150–159. [CrossRef]
51. Kwee, R.M.; Kwee, T.C. Modern imaging techniques for preoperative detection of distant metastases in gastric cancer. *World J. Gastroenterol. WJG* **2015**, *21*, 10502–10509. [CrossRef]

mathematics

MDPI

Article

# On the Residual Lifetime and Inactivity Time in Mixtures

**Francisco Germán Badía *,† and María Dolores Berrade †**

Departamento de Metodos Estadísticos, Escuela de Ingeniería y Arquitectura, Universidad de Zaragoza, 50018 Zaragoza, Spain

* Correspondence: gbadia@unizar.es

† These authors contributed equally to this work.

**Abstract:** In this paper we study the aging characteristics in mixtures of distributions, providing characterizations for their derivatives that explain the smooth behavior of the mixture. The classical preservation results for the reversed hazard rate, mean residual life and mean inactivity time are derived under a different approach than in previous studies. We focus on the variance of both the residual life and inactivity time in mixtures, obtaining some preservation properties. We also state conditions for weak and strong bending properties for the variance of the residual life and the inactivity time in mixtures.

**Keywords:** mixture; residual life variance; inactivity time variance; aging class; bending property

**MSC:** 62N05; 60E15; 60K10

**Citation:** Badía, F.G.; Berrade, M.D. On the Residual Lifetime and Inactivity Time in Mixtures. *Mathematics* **2022**, *10*, 2795. https://doi.org/10.3390/math10152795

Academic Editor: Tzong-Ru Tsai

Received: 14 June 2022
Accepted: 4 August 2022
Published: 6 August 2022



## 1. Introduction

Systems fail due to age, and the way this process occurs is described by the aging characteristics. The failure rate, indicating the proneness to failure, and the residual life measuring the remaining time span of a system that has not yet failed, are traditionally used as indicators of the system state. Therefore they can be used to assess the appropriateness of carrying out some types of preventive maintenance. It can be observed that both the failure rate and the residual life are calculated at a given time $x$ for individuals or units that have survived up to $x$, and thus we can define them as "forward age characteristics" since they reflect, respectively, the probability of failure in the imminent future and the random time from $x$ until it occurs.

Sometimes the research subject of interest emerges when the failure has already occurred. For example, when a failure is unrevealed, that is, it is detected only by inspection, the maintainer would like to estimate the probability that it occurred sometime between two consecutive inspections if, for example, he suspects that failures are induced by inspections [1], or he may wish to estimate the losses incurred up to a given moment due to the downtime. This aspect is also particularly relevant in epidemiological studies when people are diagnosed as being infected by a virus and a retrospective analysis is required [2].

Given a non-negative random variable $X$, the reversed hazard rate $q_X(x)$ and the inactivity time $\nu_X(x)$ provide information for this type of analysis. Both can be interpreted as "backward age characteristics" since they are defined conditionally for a failure that has occurred in $[0, x]$. Thus, $q_X(x)dx$ is interpreted in [3] as the conditional probability of failure for an object in $(x - dx, x]$, whereas the inactivity time represents the time elapsed from the failure until $x$. Both concepts are relevant for maintenance models if a downtime cost is assumed. When dealing with people diagnosed with a disease, they represent the probability of having been infected just before the infection is detected and the period from infection to detection, respectively. The connection between the two characteristics is studied in [4]. In this study, we aim at shedding light on both the expectation and variance of the residual life and inactivity time.

Often the time to failure of a system is described by a mixture of distributions. This is so, for example, when there is a subpopulation of "bad" units mixed with the normal ones. Studies of aging characteristics in mixtures lead to actual applications in maintenance modeling. The work in [5] uses a mixture to model the case of progressive wear in metal cutting tools when a proportion of the supply is affected by hidden defects. The mixing random variable is usually an unobserved random variable (frailty) representing, for example, users with different levels of expertise or the changing environmental conditions under which the system operates. The frailty is used to introduce random effects to account for such heterogeneities caused by distinct risks when there are no observable covariates.

An amazing outcome is that the aging characteristics are observed to improve in mixed populations compared to those corresponding to the distributions in the mixture. The best known preservation property is that mixtures of DFR (decreasing failure rate) populations are also DFR. In addition, a bending behavior is observed for some mixtures of IFR populations, which are first increasing and then asymptotically DFR [6]. This means that mixtures tend to transform a positive aging of the failure rate into a negative one. The research in [7] illustrates this property with a number of actual examples ranging from social issues (divorce) to entomology (mortality in fruit flies) and health (mortality due to cancer). In doing so, the author develops a nice intuition regarding the meaning of frailty and its effects.

Regarding the reversed hazard rate, mean residual life and mean inactivity time, the following properties are preserved by mixtures: increasing reversed hazard [8], increasing mean residual life [9] and decreasing mean inactivity time [8]. All these properties imply that the system reliability increases with time and therefore preventive maintenance at the beginning of the useful life may be profitable, to prevent early failures [10]. The bending properties imply that the aging characteristics in a mixture of populations take greater values than the mean value of the corresponding aging characteristics of the subpopulations in the mixture. Therefore, the study of bending properties provides additional insight into condition-based maintenance.

The residual life variance and inactivity time variance are useful in many areas of statistics, including biometry, actuarial science and reliability theory. In addition, there is an increasing interest in the study of the corresponding stochastic orders and their associated aging classes at a fixed time. A number of papers [11–22] contain relevant results on this issue. Recent research concerning stochastic orders of discrete random variables can be found in [23].

The preservation of the increasing residual life variance under mixtures was addressed in [24]. As far as we know, a similar study for the decreasing inactivity time variance has not yet been undertaken. In this paper, the corresponding preservation properties are derived, generalizing the property in [24], since we relax the assumptions.

Our description of the residual life variance and inactivity time variance follows the approach in [25] for the failure rate and that in [26] for the reversed hazard rate in mixtures. Both studies present a Bayesian perspective, based on the conditional distribution of the frailty given the data, which is different from that in [2–4,6–8,11–24]. Hence, the frailty cannot be observed but it can be updated. Highlighting the differences between this work and previous research, we must also point out that the authors in [2,7] provide data-driven properties, whereas this paper focuses on theoretical results with pending applicability in empirical studies.

The bending properties of the failure rate in mixtures were originally studied in [25]. The authors in [27] extended this analysis to the reversed hazard rate, mean residual life and mean inactivity time. The properties of mixtures under the proportional reversed hazard rate were considered in [28]. Recently, the discrete case of the reversed hazard rate was studied in [29].

This paper is organized as follows. Notation, basic results and the representation assumed for mixtures are presented in Section 2. Section 3 is devoted to the preservation of aging characteristics under mixtures, whereas the bending properties are the central topic of Section 4. Section 5 contains the main conclusions of this paper.

## 2. Preliminaries

In what follows, we present the basics of aging properties, mixtures and stochastic orders. Almost all of these have been obtained in previous research, and therefore the corresponding proofs can be found in the cited references. For the readability of the results without extending the section with known results, some of them are developed in more detail in Appendix A. The following notation is used throughout the paper.

A random variable $X$ ($X > 0$) can be specified in different ways. The more popular ways are the density function $f_X$, the cumulative distribution function $F_X(x) = P(X \leq x)$, the reliability or survival function $\overline{F}_X(x) = P(X > x)$ and the hazard rate $r_X(x)$, defined as follows:

$$r_X(x) = \lim_{\Delta x \to 0} \frac{P(x \leq X < x + \Delta | X > x)}{\Delta x} = \frac{f(x)}{\overline{F}_X(x)}.$$

Observe that $r_X(x)\Delta x = \frac{f(x)\Delta x}{\overline{F}_X(x)}$ can be interpreted as the probability of imminent failure in $[x, x + \Delta x)$.

The reversed hazard rate $q_X(x)$, defined below, is another aging characteristic:

$$q_X(x) = \lim_{\Delta x \to 0} \frac{P(x - \Delta x < X \leq x | X \leq x)}{\Delta x} = \frac{f_X(x)}{F_X(x)}.$$

It follows that $q_X(x)\Delta x = \frac{f_X(x)\Delta x}{F_X(x)}$ is the probability that the failure has just occurred when time $x$ arrives. Consider, for example, that a tumor is diagnosed at $x$, then $q_X(x)\Delta x$ is the probability that tumor appeared during the time $(x - \Delta x, x]$. An important result states that there exists no non-negative random variable with support in $(0, \infty)$ having an increasing reversed hazard rate function [3]. From a practical point of view, this makes perfect sense. Observe that if such a variable were possible, then under the previous context a tumor diagnosed at time $x_1$ would be less likely to be formed in $(x_1 - \Delta x_1, x_1]$ than in $(x_2 - \Delta x_2, x_2]$ in the case where the diagnosis time is $x_2$ with $x_2 > x_1$ . In other words, the longer the time until the tumor is detected, the greater the probability that it had just occurred and, thus, the lower the time elapsed since then. This contradicts actual knowledge of this disease, which points to early detection as one of the keys for cure. The importance of the reversed hazard rate in the estimation of the survival function under left-censored observations was highlighted in [2,3].

The residual life and inactivity time are random variables closely related to the hazard rate and reversed hazard rate, respectively. Thus, the residual life of a unit that has survived up to $x$ is the remaining life until the unit fails, that is, $X - x | X > x$. $P(X - x > t | X > x)$ is the probability that such a unit survives $t$ additional units of time. This is important for maintenance scheduling since the larger the previous probability for a given $t$, the less urgent the replacement of the system.

The inactivity time refers to the elapsed time from failure on condition that it occurred before a given time $x$, $x - X | X \leq x$. The importance of this variable appears, for example, if we wish to obtain information about the time since a tumor appeared when it is diagnosed at $x$. Now, $P(x - X > t | X \leq x)$ determines the probability that the tumor was formed more than $t$ units ago. Therefore a high probability is an adverse result, since the more likely it has remained hidden, the lower the chance of recovery. Both the expectation and the variance of the random variables are always relevant, and so we focus on the the mean residual life $m_X(x) = E[X - x | X > x]$, the mean inactivity time $\nu_X(x) = E[x - X | X \leq x]$, the residual life variance $\sigma_X^2(x) = Var[X - x | X > x]$ and the inactivity time variance $\overline{\sigma}_X^2(x) = Var[x - X | X \leq x]$. The hazard rate and the mean residual life are dual functions; when the former increases, the latter decreases. The reversed hazard rate and the mean inactivity time are coupled in the same way.

$Z$ denotes the frailty random variable, and we assume without loss of generality that it is a continuous non-negative random variable with probability density function (pdf) $\pi(z)$. In addition, $X^*$ represents the mixture of random variables and $X^*|Z = z$ is the distribution of the mixture given that the conditions take a particular value $z$, that is, if $Z = z$.

At this point, we must highlight a crucial difference in $Z$ when the reversed hazard rate and inactivity time are under study. The analysis in [7] concerning the heterogeneity of individuals sheds light on the effect of non-susceptible subgroups, that is, those people either immune to or cured of an illness. The time to failure of long-term survivors is represented by a defective distribution [30]. In [31], the concept of resilience is used as an alternative to frailty when the survival function increases with the mixing random variable. Therefore, and for estimation purposes, the possibility of immune persons in that particular problem cannot be neglected. However, in the case of the reversed hazard rate and inactivity time, this situation no longer applies. Observe that both are "backward age characteristics" and hence are defined once the event has occurred. It follows that non-susceptible (immune) individuals make no sense when both measures are involved, and hence the distributions for the frailty cannot include defective distributions.

The aging characteristics of the population in the mixture conditional to a given value of the frailty $Z = z$ are represented by $F(x,z)$ (distribution function), $\overline{F}(x,z)$ (reliability function), $f(x,z)$ (density function), $r(x,z)$ (failure rate), $q(x,z)$ (reversed hazard rate), $m(x,z)$ (mean residual time), $v(x,z)$ (mean inactivity time), $\sigma^2(x,z)$ (residual life variance) and $\overline{\sigma}^2(x,z)$ (inactivity time variance). The corresponding aging characteristics of the mixture are, respectively, denoted by $F^*(x)$, $\overline{F}^*(x)$, $f^*(x)$, $r^*(x)$, $q^*(x)$, $m^*(x)$, $v^*(x)$, $\sigma^{*2}(x)$ and $\overline{\sigma}^{*2}(x)$.

The comparison between random variables emerges naturally in reliability or survival analysis. For example, does the disease-free time increase under a new treatment? Are two vaccines equally effective? Does the interval between failures in a machine depend on the working conditions? Stochastic orders answer questions like these.

$X$ is less or equal than $Y$ ($X \leq Y$) under a specific stochastic order if the corresponding properties given in the following hold:

- Usual stochastic order *(st)*:
  $\overline{F}_X(x) \leq \overline{F}_Y(x)$. Equivalently, $E[h(X)] \leq E[h(Y)]$ for an increasing function $h$;
- Hazard rate order *(hr)*: $r_X(x) \geq r_Y(x)$;
- Reversed hazard rate order *(rhr)*: $q_X(x) \leq q_Y(x)$;
- Likelihood ratio order *(lr)*: $f_X(y)f_Y(x) \leq f_X(x)f_Y(y)$, $x \leq y$;
- Mean residual life order *(mrl)*: $m_X(x) \leq m_Y(x)$;
- Residual life variance order *(rlv)*: $\sigma^2_X(x) \leq \sigma^2_Y(x)$;
- Mean inactivity time order *(mit)*: $v_X(x) \geq v_Y(x)$;
- Inactivity time variance order *(itv)*: $\overline{\sigma}^2_X(x) \geq \overline{\sigma}^2_Y(x)$;

given that $x, y$ are in the support set of $X$ and $Y$.

Note that $X \leq Y$ under all the previous stochastic orders except for the *rlv*, indicates that $X$ is worse than $Y$ in different senses: a greater hazard rate or a smaller mean residual life. A lower reversed hazard rate, and therefore a larger mean inactivity time, also represent worse conditions.

Some of the previous properties are stronger than others. A thorough study of this subject can be found in [32–34]. The chain of implications between orders is well known, and these results are shown in Appendix A.

Since the frailty is used to reflect different operating conditions in a system or biological heterogeneity between individuals [7], then it is relevant to analyze its effect on the aging characteristics. As an alternative to models with covariates, the following definitions aim at describing the effect of these unobservable variations.

**Remark 1.** *$X^*|Z = z$ is increasing in $z$ under a particular order if, for all $z_1 < z_2$, the corresponding properties below hold:*

- *Usual stochastic order:* $\overline{F}(x,z_1) \leq \overline{F}(x,z_2)$*;*
- *Hazard rate order:* $r(x,z_1) \geq r(x,z_2)$*;*
- *Reversed hazard rate order:* $q(x,z_1) \leq q(x,z_2)$*;*
- *Mean residual life order:* $m(x,z_1) \leq m(x,z_2)$*;*
- *Mean inactivity time order:* $\nu(x,z_1) \geq \nu(x,z_2)$*;*
- *Residual life variance order:* $\sigma^2(x,z_1) \leq \sigma^2(x,z_2)$*;*
- *Inactivity variance time order:* $\overline{\sigma}^2(x,z_1) \geq \overline{\sigma}^2(x,z_2)$*.*

*Therefore, an increasing $z$ implies a beneficial effect of the frailty, since all the aging characteristics reveal an improvement in the system with the exception of the residual life variance.*

*Given the chain of implications in Appendix A, if the failure rate $r(x,z)$ is decreasing in $z$, then $\overline{F}(x,z)$, $m(x,z)$ and $\sigma^2(x,z)$ are increasing in $z$, and if $q(x,z)$ is increasing in $z$, then $F(x,z)$, $\nu(x,z)$ and $\overline{\sigma}^2(x,z)$ are decreasing in $z$.*

The following property is relevant for the forthcoming results. Its proof can be found in [35,36].

**Lemma 1.** *Let $X$ be a random variable and $h(x)$, $g(x)$ two real functions.*

*(a)* *If both $h(x)$ and $g(x)$ are simultaneously increasing or decreasing, then*

$$Cov(h(X), g(X)) \geq 0,$$

*(b)* *If $h(x)$ is increasing and $g(x)$ is decreasing, then*

$$Cov(h(X), g(X)) \leq 0.$$

The conditions for Lemma 1 to hold are relaxed in the next result in Remark 2.

**Remark 2.** *Case (a) [(b)] follows, provided that $(h(x) - h(y))(g(x) - g(y)) \geq [\leq] 0$ for all $x$ and $y$ in the support of $X$.*

*Observe that*

$$\begin{aligned}&(h(x) - h(y))(g(x) - g(y)) \geq [\leq]\, 0 \Leftrightarrow \\ &(h(x) - h(y))(g(x) - g(y))f_X(x)f_X(y) \geq [\leq]\, 0\end{aligned}$$

*where $f_X$ is the density function of $X$. Therefore, the condition in Lemma 1 is verified:*

$$\int_0^\infty \int_0^\infty (h(x) - h(y))(g(x) - g(y))f_X(x)f_X(y)dxdy = 2Cov(h(X), g(X)).$$

*Hence, $h(x)$ and $g(x)$ having the same monotonicity behavior is a sufficient but not a necessary condition for Lemma 1 to hold.*

Models with covariates are basically concerned with estimating risks or predicting new values under different observable conditions. Hence, there is no uncertainty about the latter. In contrast, frailty models allow the variation caused by unobserved environments to be taken into account, and therefore a Bayesian analysis emerges as a natural way to study the frailty distribution once the data are observed [37]. Thus, right-censored and left-censored data can provide relevant information about the frailty. This is considered next.

The pdfs of the conditional distributions $Z|X^* > x$ and $Z|X^* \leq x$ are given as follows:

$$f_{Z|X^*>x}(z) = \frac{\overline{F}(x,z)\pi(z)}{\int_0^\infty \overline{F}(x,z)\pi(z)dz}, \quad z \geq 0 \tag{1}$$

and

$$f_{Z|X^*\leq x}(z) = \frac{F(x,z)\pi(z)}{\int_0^\infty F(x,z)\pi(z)dz}, \quad z \geq 0 \tag{2}$$

Similar formulae for the the conditional reliability and the cumulative failure rate can also be obtained. The corresponding expressions are derived in Appendix B.

The expressions below for the mixture failure rate and reversed hazard rate can be found, respectively, in [25,26].

$$r^*(x) = E[r(x,Z)|X^* > x], \quad q^*(x) = E[q(x,Z)|X^* \leq x]. \tag{3}$$

By using the same techniques as in [25,26], the following identities for the mean residual life and mean inactivity time in mixtures can be derived:

$$m^*(x) = E[m(x,Z)|X^* > x], \quad \nu^*(x) = E[\nu(x,Z)|X^* \leq x]. \tag{4}$$

The expressions in (3) and (4) not only provide nice representations of the aging characteristics of the mixture but will also be useful in forthcoming results.

Given a random variable $X$ with a distribution function $F_X(x)$ and $x$ such that $F_X(x) > 0$ and $\overline{F}_X(x) > 0$, the following definitions apply:

The mean residual life is

$$m_X(x) = E[X - x|X > x] = \frac{\int_x^\infty \overline{F}_X(y)dy}{\overline{F}_X(x)}. \tag{5}$$

The residual life variance is

$$\sigma_X^2(x) = Var[X - x|X > x] = 2\frac{\int_x^\infty \int_y^\infty \overline{F}_X(u)dudy}{\overline{F}_X(x)} - m_X^2(x). \tag{6}$$

The mean inactivity time is

$$\nu_X(x) = E[x - X|X \leq x] = \frac{\int_0^x F_X(y)dy}{F_X(x)}. \tag{7}$$

The inactivity time variance is

$$\overline{\sigma}_X^2(x) = Var[x - X|X \leq x] = 2\frac{\int_0^x \int_0^y F_X(u)dudy}{F_X(x)} - \nu_X^2(x). \tag{8}$$

These representations are repeatedly used in this paper and, although they are well known, we derive them for the mean residual life and residual life variance in Appendix C, aiming at producing a self-contained text. We omit the proofs corresponding to the mean inactivity time and inactivity time variance since they are similar.

The main properties of the mean residual lifetime (inactivity time) and the residual life (inactivity time) variance can be found in the references mentioned in the Introduction. Next, we focus on their monotonicity properties, which are determinant in maintenance decision-making.

A random variable $X$ shows increasing (decreasing) residual life variance if $\sigma_X^2(x)$ is increasing (decreasing) in $x$. Similar definitions regarding $\overline{\sigma}_X^2(x)$ lead to the class increasing (decreasing) inactivity time variance.

Next, well-known relations between the aging characteristics are recalled:

$$r_X(x) = \frac{\frac{dm_X(x)}{dx} + 1}{m_X(x)}. \tag{9}$$

$$q_X(x) = \frac{1 - \frac{d\nu_X(x)}{dx}}{\nu_X(x)}. \tag{10}$$

$$\frac{d\sigma_X^2(x)}{dx} = r_X(x)(\sigma_X^2(x) - m_X^2(x)). \tag{11}$$

$$\frac{d\overline{\sigma}_X^2(x)}{dx} = q_X(x)(\nu_X^2(x) - \overline{\sigma}_X^2(x)). \tag{12}$$

In the next remark, conditions for the monotonicity of the aging characteristics are stated.

**Remark 3.** *From (11), increasing (decreasing) residual life variance is equivalent to*

$$\sigma_X^2(x) \geq (\leq) m_X^2(x)$$

*for all $x$.*

*From (12), decreasing (increasing) residual life variance is equivalent to*

$$\overline{\sigma}_X^2(x) \geq (\leq) \nu_X^2(x)$$

*for all $x$.*

The following lemma contains the key representations for the residual life variance and inactivity time variance of the mixture.

**Lemma 2.**

$$\sigma^{*2}(x) = E[\sigma^2(x,Z)|X^* > x] + Var[m(x,Z)|X^* > x]; \tag{13}$$
$$\overline{\sigma}^{*2}(x) = E[\overline{\sigma}^2(x,Z)|X^* \leq x] + Var[\nu(x,Z)|X^* \leq x]. \tag{14}$$

**Proof of Lemma 2.** From (6), it follows that

$$\begin{aligned}
\sigma^{*2}(x) &= 2\frac{\int_x^\infty \int_y^\infty \overline{F}^*(u)dudy}{\overline{F}^*(x)} - m^{*2}(x) \\
&= \int_0^\infty \frac{2\int_x^\infty \int_y^\infty \overline{F}(u,z)dudy\pi(z)dz}{\int_0^\infty \overline{F}(x,z)\pi(z)dz} - m^{*2}(x) \\
&= \int_0^\infty \left( \frac{2\int_x^\infty \int_y^\infty \overline{F}(u,z)dudy}{\overline{F}(x,z)} - m^2(x,z) \right) f_{Z|X^*>x}(z)dz \\
&+ \int_0^\infty m^2(x,z) f_{Z|X^*>x}(z)dz - \left( \int_0^\infty m(x,z) f_{Z|X^*>x}(z)dz \right)^2 \\
&= \int_0^\infty \sigma^2(x,z) f_{Z|X^*>x}(z)dz + \int_0^\infty m^2(x,z) f_{Z|X^*>x}(z)dz - \left( \int_0^\infty m(x,z) f_{Z|X^*>x}(z)dz \right)^2.
\end{aligned}$$

From (8), we have

$$\begin{aligned}
\overline{\sigma}^{*2}(x) &= 2\frac{\int_0^x \int_0^y F^*(u)dudy}{F^*(x)} - \nu^{*2}(x) \\
&= \int_0^\infty \frac{2\int_0^x \int_0^y F(u,z)dudy\pi(z)dz}{\int_0^\infty F(x,z)\pi(z)dz} - \nu^{*2}(x) \\
&= \int_0^\infty \overline{\sigma}^2(x,z) f_{Z|X^*\leq x}(z)dz + \int_0^\infty \nu^2(x,z) f_{Z|X^*\leq x}(z)dz - \left( \int_0^\infty \nu(x,z) f_{Z|X\leq x}(z)dz \right)^2.
\end{aligned}$$

□

## 3. Preservation of Aging Classes under Mixtures

When defining a maintenance policy, the monotonicity of the failure rate plays a central role. If it is an increasing function, preventive replacement can be carried out, avoiding the cost derived from failure, which is usually higher than that incurred due to the replacement itself. However, it is well known that the optimum replacement time is infinite in the case of non-increasing failure rates as the exponential. This is so, either for revealed failures [38] or unrevealed failures, when inspections to detect them are free from false-negative outcomes [39]. The recent work carried out in [40] introduces a more general concept, i.e., the deviation cost per unit time between replacement and failure, so that age replacement policies can be valid for the exponential distribution. The forthcoming results aim at studying the aging in frailty models.

The analysis in [8] provides bounds for $\frac{dq^*(x)}{dx}$ and $\frac{dv^*(x)}{dx}$, whereas the corresponding ones for $\frac{dr^*(x)}{dx}$ and $\frac{dm^*(x)}{dx}$ can be found in [41]. These results indicate that the change in the aging characteristic in the mixture is not completely arbitrary but is under control of both the distributions in the mixture and the frailty. Theorem 1 contains more precise expressions, since they are new representations of the derivatives of the aging characteristic in the mixture. Moreover, these results provide the exact difference between the derivative of the aging characteristics of the mixture and the conditional expectation of the derivatives of the aging characteristic corresponding to the distributions in the mixture given the updated frailty. Hence, they constitute a formal approach to the improvement observed in mixtures of populations compared with individuals.

**Theorem 1.** *The following properties hold, provided the derivatives exist and can be interchanged with the corresponding integrals.*

*(a)*

$$\frac{dr^*(x)}{dx} = E\left[\frac{dr(x,Z)}{dx}|X^* > x\right] - Var(r(x,Z)|X^* > x)$$

*(b)*

$$\frac{dq^*(x)}{dx} = E\left[\frac{dq(x,Z)}{dx}|X^* \leq x\right] + Var(q(x,Z)|X^* \leq x)$$

*(c)*

$$\frac{dm^*(x)}{dx} = E\left[\frac{dm(x,Z)}{dx}|X^* > x\right] - Cov(r(x,Z), m(x,Z)|X^* > x)$$

*(d)*

$$\frac{dv^*(x)}{dx} = E\left[\frac{dv(x,Z)}{dx}|X^* \leq x\right] + Cov(v(x,z), q(x,z)|X^* \leq x)$$

**Proof of Theorem 1.** The result in *(a)* has been proven in [42].

*(b)* Straightforward derivatives in (1) and (2) lead, respectively, to

$$\frac{df_{Z|X^*>x}(z)}{dx} = f_{Z|X^*>x}(z)(-r(x,z) + r^*(x)) \quad (15)$$

$$\frac{df_{Z|X^*\leq x}(z)}{dx} = f_{Z|X^*\leq x}(z)(q(x,z) - q^*(x)) \quad (16)$$

Taking the derivative in the expression of the reversed hazard rate in (3), and given the assumption of possible exchange between the derivative and the integral, it follows that

$$\frac{dq^*(x)}{dx} = \int_0^\infty \frac{dq(x,z)}{dx} f_{Z|X^*\leq x}(z)dz + \int_0^\infty q(x,z)\frac{df_{Z|X^*\leq x}(z)}{dx}dz,$$

and then, based on (16), *(b)* is proven.

Consider now the derivatives in (4), again with the corresponding assumption of possible exchange with the integrals. Then,

$$\frac{dm^*(x)}{dx} = \int_0^\infty \frac{dm(x,z)}{dx} f_{Z|X^*>x}(z)dz + \int_0^\infty m(x,z)\frac{df_{Z|X^*>x}(z)}{dx}dz \quad (17)$$

$$\frac{dv^*(x)}{dx} = \int_0^\infty \frac{dv(x,z)}{dx} f_{Z|X^*\leq x}(z)dz + \int_0^\infty v(x,z)\frac{df_{Z|X^*\leq x}(z)}{dx}dz \quad (18)$$

The results in *(c)* and *(d)* follow from (15) and (16), respectively. □

In the case that the individuals in the mixture present a deteriorating state with time expressed as $r_X(x)$ increases, $q_X(x)$ decreases, $m_X(x)$ decreases or $\nu_X(x)$ increases, then the second term on the right-hand side in (a)–(d) is, respectively, negative, positive, positive or negative. Therefore, the mixture presents a smoother behavior than the distributions that compound the mixture. When individuals with increasing failure rate are mixed, the effect is that the derivative of the failure rate of the mixture is below the mean of the derivatives, and therefore a decreasing behavior could even be observed given the negative term on the right-hand side of the equality in (a). Similar comments apply for individuals with a decreasing reversed hazard rate, decreasing mean residual life or increasing inactivity time. In all the cases, the derivative in the mixture is below the mean of the derivatives, and reversed behaviors can also occur. This explains the noticeable improvement in the mixture compared with the distributions therein.

The preservation under mixtures of the classes decreasing hazard rate, increasing reversed hazard rate, increasing mean residual life and decreasing mean inactivity time are known properties. The next corollary presents them as a straightforward consequence of Theorem 1.

**Corollary 1.**

(a) *Preservation, under mixtures of both the decreasing failure rate and the increasing reversed hazard rate [8], follows from Theorem 1 (a) and (b), respectively.*

(b) *Preservation of the increasing mean residual life holds, provided that the term on the right-hand side of Theorem 1 (c) is positive. Consider $z_1 \leq z_2$ in the support of the frailty Z and the roots of the equation $r(y,z_1) - r(y,z_2) = 0$. Then, for a given x, there exist two roots $y_0$ and $y_1$ ($y_0 \leq y_1$) of the previous equation such that $x \in [y_0, y_1]$ and $r(y,z_1) - r(y,z_2)$ are non-negative or non-positive in $[y_0, y_1]$.*
*Let us assume that $r(y,z_1) - r(y,z_2) \leq 0$. We define the failure rates $\lambda_1(x)$, $\lambda_2(x)$ as follows:*

$$\lambda_1(y) = \begin{cases} r(y,z_1), & y_0 \leq y \leq y_1 \\ r(y_1,z_1), & y > y_1 \end{cases}$$

$$\lambda_2(y) = \begin{cases} r(y,z_2), & y_0 \leq y \leq y_1 \\ r(y_1,z_2), & y > y_1 \end{cases}$$

*Observe that the assumption $r(y,z_1) - r(y,z_2) \leq 0$ leads to $\lambda_1(y) \leq \lambda_2(y)$. In addition, $\lambda_1(y)$ and $\lambda_2(y)$ are constant values for $y \geq y_1$, with $\lambda_1(y) = \lambda_2(y)$. Denoting by $X_1$ and $X_2$ the random variables with failure rates $\lambda_1(y)$ and $\lambda_2(y)$, respectively, then, $X_1 \geq_{hr} X_2$.*

*Consider next the mean residual lives $m_1(y)$ and $m_2(y)$ such that $m_1(y) = m(y,z_1)$ and $m_2(y) = m(y,z_2)$ for $y \in [y_0, y_1]$, and taking the constant values indicated below, otherwise:*

$$\begin{cases} m_1(y) = m_2(y) = \frac{1}{r(y_0,z_1)}, & y \leq y_0 \\ m_1(y) = m_2(y) = \frac{1}{r(y_1,z_1)}, & y \geq y_1 \end{cases}$$

*From (9), it follows that the mean residual life of $X_i$ is $m_i(x)$, $i = 1,2$, and Remark 1 implies $X_1 \geq_{mrl} X_2$. Therefore, $(r(x,z_1) - r(x,z_2))(m(x,z_1) - m(x,z_2)) \leq 0$, and then $Cov(r(x,Z), m(x,Z)) \leq 0$ follows from both Lemma 1 and Remark 2.*
*A similar proof applies when $r(y,z_1) - r(y,z_2) \geq 0$. If so, $X_1 \leq_{hr} X_2$ and $X_1 \leq_{mrl} X_2$.*

(c) *The preservation of decreasing mean inactivity time under mixtures [8] can also be derived from Theorem 1 (d), once the second term on the right side of (d) is proven to be negative, using a similar strategy to the previous one in (b). Now, when defining the mean inactivity times, $v_1(y)$ and $v_2(y)$, we assume $v_1(y) = v_2(y)$ for $y \leq y_0$. The remaining details are omitted for brevity.*

The preservation results under mixtures are considered to be important properties, given their practical relevance, for example in maintenance modeling. The next theorem generalizes the preservation results, since the assumption of non-crossing distributions in the mixture appearing in previous research has been dropped.

**Theorem 2.** *Distributions with increasing (decreasing) residual life (inactivity time) variance distributions are preserved under mixtures.*

**Proof of Theorem 2.** The result is proved for the residual life variance. Since the variance is non-negative, by Equation (13) we have that

$$\sigma^{*2}(x) \geq E[\sigma^2(x,Z)|X^* > x] \geq E[m^2(x,Z)|X^* > x] \geq E^2[m(x,Z)|X^* > x] = m^*(x)^2$$

where the second inequality follows given that $\sigma^2(x,z)$ is increasing in $x$ (see Remark 3) and the third inequality is derived from Jensen's inequality applied to the convex function $x^2$. Therefore, the claim is proven by Remark 3. The details for the inactivity time variance are omitted, since the result is obtained by using a similar series of inequalities as in (14) and Remark 3. □

## 4. Bending Properties

When dealing with a random variable, its expectation and variance are usually considered to be key values. This is so because it is enlightening to know its average behavior and whether an observation lies far from the mean, becoming an outlier. In addition, in order to obtain good estimators of both the mean and the variance, only a large enough sample is required. This idea also applies for mixtures. Let $X$ be a random variable with $L = (r_X, q_X, m_X, \sigma_X^2, v_X, \overline{\sigma}_X^2)$ being an specific aging characteristic of $X$. A bending property for a mixture of distributions $(\{\overline{F}(x,z)\})$ with frailty $Z$ is a comparison between the mixture aging characteristic $L^*(x)$ and its mean value $L_E(x) = E[L(x,Z)]$. Previous studies state that $L_E(x)$ retains the monotonicity conditions of the mixture $L^*(x)$ ([25]). In [27], bending properties for the mean residual life and mean inactivity time are studied. In what follows, we extend this analysis to the residual lifetime variance and inactivity time variance.

Regarding the residual life (inactivity time) variance, the following properties are defined:

- The weak bending up property if $\sigma^{*2}(x) \geq \sigma_E^2(x)$ $(\overline{\sigma}^{*2}(x) \geq \overline{\sigma}_E^2(x))$.
- The strong bending up property if $\sigma^{*2}(x) - \sigma_E^2(x)$ $(\overline{\sigma}^{*2}(x) - \overline{\sigma}_E^2(x))$ is increasing (decreasing) in $x$.

Observe that under both definitions, the variability of the residual life and inactivity time of the mixture is larger than in the individuals. Large residual lives are associated with long-term survivors and small ones with those corresponding to high failure rates. Regarding the inactivity time in failed units, a proportion of them will have just entered the failed state at the moment it is detected, whereas the failure will have remained undiscovered for longer periods in other cases. Thus, the previous definitions follow the idea that when considering the overall data, strong individuals are mixed with weak ones. They also give a theoretical support for the interpretation in [43] regarding the reversal of increasing failure rates under mixtures. The authors in [43] state that the long-term survivors, although they represent a small proportion of the pooled data, determine the behavior of the failure rate in the long run, resembling outliers in a regression analysis.

**Theorem 3.** *In the case of a mixture of distributions* $\{\overline{F}(x,z)\}$ *with frailty* $Z$*, the following properties apply:*

(a) *If* $\overline{F}(x,z)$ *is increasing (decreasing) in* $z$ *and* $\sigma^2(x,z)$ *is increasing (decreasing) in* $z$*, then the weak bending up property holds for the residual lifetime variance.*
(b) *If* $\overline{F}(x,z)$ *is increasing (decreasing) in* $z$ *and* $\overline{\sigma}^2(x,z)$ *is decreasing (increasing) in* $z$*, then the weak bending up property holds for the inactivity time variance.*

**Proof of Theorem 3.**

(a) The following inequalities apply:

$$\sigma^{*2}(x) \geq E[\sigma^2(x,Z)|X^* > x] \geq E[\sigma^2(x,Z)]$$

where the first inequality is derived by (13). The following steps lead to the second inequality:

1. From (1), we have that $\frac{\overline{F}(x,z)}{\int_0^\infty \overline{F}(x,z)\pi(z)dz} = \frac{f_{Z|X^*>x}(z)}{\pi(z)}$. Since the left-hand side of this equality is assumed to be increasing (decreasing) in $z$, so is the term on the right-hand side.
2. From the previous point and $z_1 \leq z_2$, it follows that

$$f_{Z|X^*>x}(z_1)\pi(z_2) \leq (\geq) f_{Z|X^*>x}(z_2)\pi(z_2)$$

and thus, $Z|X^* > x \geq_{\text{lr}} (\leq_{\text{lr}}) Z$.
3. The implications in Remark 1 (which follow the chain in Appendix A) imply that $Z|X^* > x \geq_{\text{st}} (\leq_{\text{st}}) Z$.
4. The equivalent definition for the usual stochastic order when the expectation for an increasing function is considered, leads to the second inequality, since $\sigma^2(x,z)$ is assumed to be increasing (decreasing) in $z$.

(b) The following inequalities hold:

$$\overline{\sigma}^{*2}(x) \geq E[\overline{\sigma}^2(x,Z)|X^* \leq x] \geq E[\overline{\sigma}^2(x,Z)]$$

The result in (14) leads to the first inequality. The steps to prove the second one are as follows:

1. From (2), we have that $\frac{F(x,z)}{\int_0^\infty F(x,z)\pi(z)dz} = \frac{f_{Z|X^*\leq x}(z)}{\pi(z)}$. Since the left-hand side of this equality is assumed to be decreasing (increasing) in $z$, so is the term on the right-hand side.
2. From the previous point and $z_1 \leq z_2$, it follows that

$$f_{Z|X^*\leq x}(z_1)\pi(z_2) \geq (\leq) f_{Z|X^*\leq x}(z_2)\pi(z_2)$$

and thus $Z|X^* \leq x \leq_{\text{lr}} (\geq_{\text{lr}}) Z$.
3. The implications in Remark 1 (which follow the chain in Appendix A) imply that $Z|X^* \leq x \leq_{\text{st}} (\geq_{\text{st}}) Z$.
4. The assumption that $\overline{\sigma}^2(x,z)$ is decreasing (increasing) leads to the second inequality.

□

The results in Theorem 3 are consistent with the negative aging that mixtures tend to show. In case (a), if $\overline{F}(x,z)$ is increasing in $z$, then the larger $Z$ is, the better the effect on the survival function. The situation is just the opposite if $\overline{F}(x,z)$ is decreasing in $z$. In both cases, the distributions for which the random effect $Z$ is good correspond to a long-term survivor. According to [7], $Z$ represents a biological advantage or an individual propensity, and with the assumptions in Theorem 3, these individuals also present the greatest variance. Therefore it makes perfect sense that the variance of the residual life of the mixture is greater than the mean of the variances.

In case (b), if the values of $Z$ corresponding to the shortest survival times are also those with larger inactivity time variances, then the variance of the inactivity time of the mixture is greater than the mean of the variances. Following the interpretation in [43], the mixture shows the effect of outliers.

In the last result, we revisit the proportional mean residual life model [44]. This is an alternative to Cox's proportional hazard model for describing the effect of the frailty. A mixture of distributions $\{\overline{F}(x,z)\}$ with the frailty random variable $Z$ follows the proportional mean residual life if the mean residual life of the mixture when $Z = z$, $m(x,z)$ verifies:

$$m(x,z) = z m_X(x), \quad 0 < z \leq 1$$

where $m_X(x)$ is a baseline mean residual life.

If we assume that $m_X(x)$ accounts for the mean residual life when the system operates under "normal" conditions, the proportional mean residual life is useful for representing more adverse environments that accelerate the failure. The function $m(x,z)$ is increasing with $z$, and so a higher value of the frailty implies a better operating condition for the system.

The failure rate of the mixture conditional to $Z = z$ is derived from (9) as

$$r(x,z) = r_X(x) + \frac{1-z}{z}\frac{1}{m_X(x)} \tag{19}$$

where $r(x,z)$ is decreasing with $z$.

The mean residual life of the mixture is

$$m^*(x) = E[Z|X^* > x] m_X(x) \tag{20}$$

The next theorem states the conditions where there is an increasing difference between the variance of the residual life of the mixture and the average variance of the residual lives of the subpopulations. In other words, the effect of the frailty is stronger with time. The outlier subpopulations tend to appear more different from the rest of the distributions as the time increases.

**Theorem 4.** *Consider a mixture of distributions $\{\overline{F}(x,z)\}$ satisfying the proportional mean residual life. If $m_X(x)$ is an increasing function, then the strong bending up property holds for the residual lifetime variance.*

**Proof of Theorem 4.** By Equation (13) we have

$$\sigma^{*2}(x) - E[\sigma^2(x,Z)] = \int_0^\infty \sigma^2(x,z) f_{Z|X^*>x}(z)dz - E[\sigma^2(x,Z)]$$
$$+ \int_0^\infty m^2(x,z) f_{Z|X^*>x}(z)dz - \left(\int_0^\infty m(x,z) f_{Z|X^*>x}(z)dz\right)^2.$$

The derivative with respect to $x$ in the foregoing expression can be written as follows after exchanging the derivative and integral and taking into account the result in (15):

$$
\begin{aligned}
& \int_0^\infty \frac{d\sigma^2(x,z)}{dx} f_{Z|X^*>x}(z)dz - E\left[\frac{d\sigma^2(x,Z)}{dx}\right] + \int_0^\infty \sigma^2(x,z)\frac{df_{Z|X^*>x}(z)}{dx}dz \\
+ \; & 2\int_0^\infty m(x,z)\frac{dm(x,z)}{dx} f_{Z|X^*>x}(z)dz + \int_0^\infty m^2(x,z)\frac{df_{Z|X^*>x}(z)dz}{dx} \\
- \; & 2\int_0^\infty m(x,z) f_{Z|X^*>x}(z)dz\left(\int_0^\infty \frac{dm(x,z)}{dx} f_{Z|X^*>x}(z)dz + \int_0^\infty m(x,z)\frac{df_{Z|X^*>x}(z)}{dx}dz\right) \\
= \; & \int_0^\infty \frac{d\sigma^2(x,z)}{dx} f_{Z|X^*>x}(z)dz - E\left[\frac{d\sigma^2(x,Z)}{dx}\right] \\
+ \; & \int_0^\infty (\sigma^2(x,z) + m^2(x,z))(r^*(x) - r(x,z)) f_{Z|X^*>x}(z)dz \\
+ \; & 2\int_0^\infty m(x,z)\frac{dm(x,z)}{dx} f_{Z|X^*>x}(z)dz \\
- \; & 2m^*(x)\int_0^\infty \left(\frac{dm(x,z)}{dx} + m(x,z)(r^*(x) - r(x,z))\right) f_{Z|X^*>x}(z)dz \\
= \; & E\left[\frac{d\sigma^2(x,Z)}{dx}|X^* > x\right] - E\left[\frac{d\sigma^2(x,Z)}{dx}\right] && (21) \\
- \; & Cov\left(r(x,Z), \sigma^2(x,Z) + m^2(x,Z)|X^* > x\right) && (22) \\
+ \; & 2Cov\left(m(x,Z), \frac{dm(x,Z)}{dx}|X^* > x\right) && (23) \\
+ \; & 2m^*(x)Cov(r(x,Z), m(x,Z)|X^* > x). && (24)
\end{aligned}
$$

The following steps aim at checking that all the previous terms are positive.

We must take into account the fact that that $\frac{d\sigma^2(x,z)}{dx}$ is increasing in $z$. The proof is in Remark A2 in Appendix C.

Equation (21) is non-negative.

According to the assumptions, $r(x,z)$ is decreasing in $z$. Then, from Remark 1, it follows that $\overline{F}(x,z)$ is increasing in $z$ and so is $\frac{f_{Z|X^*>x}(z)}{\pi(z)}$, following the same algebra as that in step 1 of Theorem 3 (a). Hence, $Z|X^* > x \geq_{\text{st}} Z$, which in addition to $\frac{d\sigma^2(x,z)}{dx}$ being increasing in $z$ implies the positiveness of the term.

With the assumption that $m_X(x)$ is increasing, Equation (23) is also non-negative:

$$
\begin{aligned}
& 2Cov\left(m(x,Z), \frac{dm(x,Z)}{dx}|X^* > x\right) = 2m_X(x)\frac{dm_X(x)}{dx}Cov(Z,Z) = \\
& 2m_X(x)\frac{dm_X(x)}{dx}Var[Z|X^* > x].
\end{aligned}
$$

The expressions in (22) and (24) can be alternatively expressed as:

$$
\begin{aligned}
& -Cov\left(r(x,Z), \sigma^2(x,Z) - m^2(x,Z)|X^* > x\right) - 2Cov\left(r(x,Z), m^2(x,Z)|X^* > x\right) \\
& +2m^*(x)Cov(r(x,Z), m(x,Z)|X^* > x).
\end{aligned}
$$

Next, we focus on the right-hand side of the first term, $A(z) = \sigma^2(x,Z) - m^2(x,Z)$, which is increasing in $z$. The proof is in Remark A3 in Appendix C. Since $r(x,z)$ is decreasing with $z$, Lemma 1 implies that

$$
-Cov\left(r(x,Z), \sigma^2(x,Z) - m^2(x,Z)|X^* > x\right) > 0.
$$

The remaining two terms verify

$$
\begin{aligned}
& -2Cov(r(x,Z), m^2(x,Z)|X^* > x) + 2m^*(x)Cov(r(x,Z), m(x,Z)|X^* > x) \\
= \;& -2Cov\left(r(x) + \frac{1-Z}{Z}\frac{1}{m_X(x)}, Z^2 m_X^2(x)|X^* > x\right) \\
& +2m_X(x)E[Z|X^* > x]Cov\left(r(x) + \frac{1-Z}{Z}\frac{1}{m_X(x)}, Zm(x)|X^* > x\right) \\
= \;& -2m_X(x)Cov\left(\frac{1-Z}{Z}, Z^2|X^* > x\right) + 2m_X(x)E[Z|X^* > x]Cov\left(\frac{1-Z}{Z}, Z\right) \\
= \;& 2m_X(x)\left(E\left[\frac{1-Z}{Z}|X^* > x\right]E[Z^2|X^* > x] - E[Z(1-Z)|X^* > x]\right) \\
+ \;& 2m_X(x)\left(E[Z|X^* > x]E[1-Z|X^* > x] - E^2[Z|X^* > x]E\left[\frac{1-Z}{Z}|X^* > x\right]\right) \\
= \;& 2\left(E\left[\frac{1-Z}{Z}|X^* > x\right]Var[Z|X^* > x] - Cov(Z, 1-Z|X^* > x])\right).
\end{aligned}
$$

$E\left[\frac{1-Z}{Z}|X^* > x\right]$ is positive since it is the expectation of a positive random variable. According to Lemma 1, $Cov(Z, 1-Z|X^* > x) < 0$. Given the positiveness of all the terms, then $\sigma^{*2}(x) - \sigma_E^2(x)$ is increasing and the strong bending up property holds. □

**Example 1.** *Consider the proportional mean residual life $m(x,z) = zm_X(x)$, where $m_X(x)$ is a baseline mean residual life and $0 < z \leq 1$. The relation in (19) implies that $r(x,z)$ is decreasing in $z$ and $\overline{F}(x,z)$ and $\sigma^2(x,z)$ are also increasing (Remark 1). Therefore, the assumptions in Theorem 3 (a) hold and so does the weak bending up property for the residual life variance, when the assumption that $m_X(x)$ is increasing is dropped.*

**Example 2.**

$$m(x,z) = z(1+x), \quad 0 < z \leq 1, \quad x \geq 0.$$

*In this case*

$$\overline{F}(x,z) = (1+x)^{-\left(\frac{1}{z}+1\right)}, \quad 0 < z \leq 1, \quad x \geq 0.$$

*Straightforward algebra yields*

$$\sigma^2(x,z) = (x+1)^2 z^2 \frac{1+z}{1-z}, \quad 0 < z < 1, \quad x \geq 0.$$

*As the baseline mean residual life $(1+x)$ is increasing, conditions for both the weak and strong bending up property in the case of the residual life variance are fulfilled. We assume now that the frailty $Z$ follows a beta distribution with parameters $a$, $b > 0$. The corresponding density function is*

$$f_Z(z) = \frac{1}{B(a,b)} z^{a-1}(1-z)^{b-1}, \quad 0 < z < 1$$

*where $B(a,b)$ is the standard beta function. Thus,*

$$f_{Z|X^*>x}(z) = \frac{(1+x)^{-\left(\frac{1}{z}+1\right)} z^{a-1}(1-z)^{b-1}}{\int_0^1 (1+x)^{-\left(\frac{1}{v}+1\right)} v^{a-1}(1-v)^{b-1} dv}.$$

*It follows that*

$$E[\sigma^2(x,Z)] = (x+1)^2 \int_0^1 z^2 \frac{1+z}{1-z} \frac{1}{B(a,b)} z^{a-1}(1-z)^{b-1} dz$$

*and*

$$\begin{aligned}\sigma^{*2}(x) &= E[\sigma^2(x,Z)|X^* > x] + Var[(1+x)Z|X^* > x] \\ &= (x+1)^2 \int_0^1 z^2 \frac{1+z}{1-z} \frac{(1+x)^{-\left(\frac{1}{z}+1\right)} z^{a-1}(1-z)^{b-1}}{\int_0^1 (1+x)^{-\left(\frac{1}{v}+1\right)} v^{a-1}(1-v)^{b-1} dv} \\ &+ (x+1)^2 \left( \int_0^1 z^2 f_{Z|X^*>x}(z) dz - \left( \int_0^1 z f_{Z|X^*>x}(z) dz \right)^2 \right).\end{aligned}$$

*Figure 1 represents $\sigma^{*2}(x) - E[\sigma^2(x,Z)]$ with Z following a beta random variable under different values of a and b, with $m(x,z) = z(1+x)$. The function $\sigma^{*2}(x) - E[\sigma^2(x,Z)]$ is non-negative and therefore the weak bending up property is verified. Furthermore, the strong bending up property also holds, since $\sigma^{*2}(x) - E[\sigma^2(x,Z)]$ is increasing.*

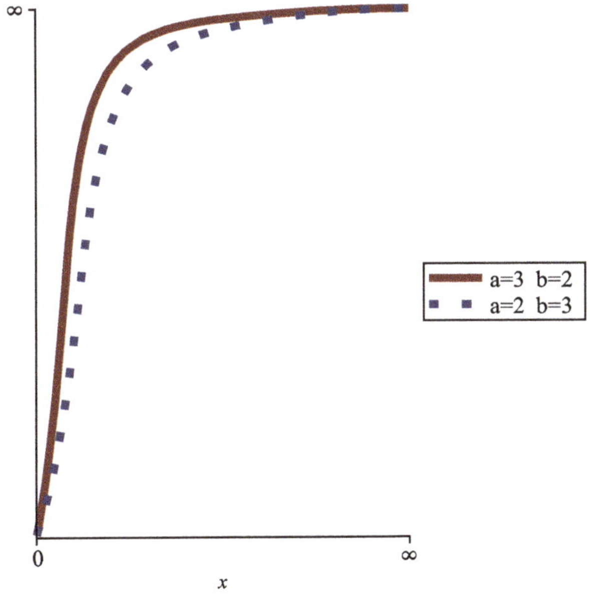


**Figure 1.** The difference against time between the residual life variance of the mixture and the average variance of the residual lives of the subpopulations, $\sigma^*(x) - E[\sigma^2(x,Z)]$. The mixture follows the mean proportional residual life model with the baseline $m_X(x) = 1 + x$, and Z is a beta random variable with parameters $a$ and $b$.

## 5. Conclusions

The study of the residual lifetime and inactivity time in mixtures is crucial in reliability, since the behavior of the former has implications in maintenance modeling and the latter in retrospective analysis. When systems are affected by a changing environment but there are no observable covariates, the changes are described by a random variable (frailty), and mixtures emerge to describe the time to failure of the whole population.

This paper focused on the residual life and inactivity time of a non-negative random variable, representing a time to failure. The former is useful for maintenance purposes, to decide whether to replace a non-failed system. The latter provides information in retrospective studies, such as when a disease is detected and the time elapsed since the person was infected is relevant to understanding the infection process and even determining contacts with high risks of exposure.

Aging properties are used to describe and summarize random variables. In this paper, we analyzed the residual life variance and inactivity time, in contrast to previous papers dealing with the corresponding expectations. The results were obtained by using the approach in [25,26], based on the conditional distribution of the frailty. In so doing, we provided new representations of the residual life variance and inactivity time variance, extending the preservation of the classes increasing residual life variance and decreasing inactivity time variance for an arbitrary mixture.

We provided new characterizations for the derivatives of the aging characteristics in mixtures in terms of the expectations of the corresponding derivatives of the distributions in the mixture which, in turn, included the information from the data. The results provided in this paper explain the improvement of the aging characteristics with time in actual systems affected by random effects. When the distributions present a decreasing reliability, the mixture shows smoother changes with less adverse aging than the mean of the distributions in the mixture.

This paper was also concerned with bending properties for comparing the residual time variance and the inactivity time variance of the mixture with the corresponding means of the residual time variances and inactivity time variances of the distributions therein. The former are greater when subpopulations that are more different from the rest due to the frailty match those with larger variances. This effect of strong components determining the behavior of the mixture has been reported many times in both theoretical and empirical studies. Some authors refer to them as outliers.

Regarding forthcoming work, this methodology based on the conditional distribution of the frailty seems to be a promising way to obtain new bending properties involving, for example, the inactivity time variance. Once we have data at hand, the verification of these properties via actual problems would enhance the interest of this research. At present, the use of simulations seems likely to be more affordable in the near future.

**Author Contributions:** Conceptualization, F.G.B. and M.D.B.; methodology, F.G.B.; validation, F.G.B. and M.D.B.; formal analysis, F.G.B.; investigation, F.G.B. and M.D.B.; writing—original draft preparation, F.G.B. and M.D.B.; writing—review and editing, F.G.B. and M.D.B.; visualization, F.G.B. and M.D.B.; supervision, F.G.B.; project administration, F.G.B.; funding acquisition, F.G.B. and M.D.B. All authors have read and agreed to the published version of the manuscript.

**Funding:** The work of both authors was supported by the Spanish Ministry of Economy and Competitiveness under Project PGC2018-094964-B-100 (MINECO-FEDER).

**Acknowledgments:** The authors thank the three anonymous referees for their thoughtful comments, which improved this paper.

**Conflicts of Interest:** The authors declare no conflict of interest.

## Appendix A

The chain of implications between stochastic orders is as follows:

$$\begin{array}{ccccccc}
 & & & & \text{mrl} & \longrightarrow & \text{rlv} \\
 & & \text{hr} & \begin{array}{c}\nearrow \\ \searrow\end{array} & & & \\
\text{lr} & \begin{array}{c}\nearrow \\ \searrow\end{array} & & & \text{st} & & \\
 & & \text{rhr} & \begin{array}{c}\nearrow \\ \searrow\end{array} & & & \\
 & & & & \text{mit} & \longrightarrow & \text{itv}
\end{array}$$

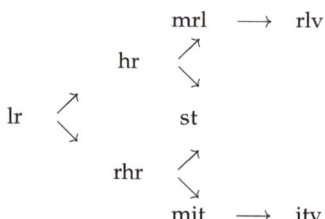

In this chain of implications, the stronger the stochastic order, the closer its position to the left-hand side. Observe that the likelihood ratio order is the strongest condition, whereas the residual life variance and inactivity time variance are the weakest ones. In addition, when two orders are connected by an arrow, it means that if two random variables present the stochastic order on the left, then they also verify the order indicated by the arrowhead. The reverse implication does not necessarily hold. When two stochastic orders are not connected, each of them can hold, independently of the other.

$X \leq_{lr} Y$ implies that given two values, for example two survival times $x$ and $y$ with $x \leq y$, it is more likely that the larger value $y$ belongs to the population $Y$ and the smaller value $x$ to $X$ than the other way around. Hence, when $X$ and $Y$ represent times to failure, the latter constitutes the tough group and the other two conditions follow: $X \leq_{hr} Y$ and $X \leq_{rhr} Y$. Therefore, $X$ presents a higher failure rate than $Y$ and a lower reversed hazard rate. Thus, when a failure or a disease is detected, the probability that it has just occurred is lower in the weaker population $X$. If $X \leq_{hr} Y$, then an item from population $X$ has a lower chance of remaining without failure from a given time $x$ onward than another item belonging to $Y$, provided that neither of them had failed at $t$. Hence, $X \leq_{mrl} Y$. In a similar way, $X \leq_{rhr} Y$ implies that when a disease is revealed, it is more likely that group $Y$ was infected later than $X$, and thus $X \leq_{mit} Y$.

## Appendix B

Next, some aging properties of the frailty, conditional to data, are provided.

The conditional reliability function is:

$$\bar{F}_{Z|X^*>x}(z) = P(Z \geq z|X^* > x) = \int_z^\infty f_{Z|X^*>x}(t)dt = \frac{\int_z^\infty \overline{F}(x,t)\pi(t)dt}{\int_0^\infty \overline{F}(x,t)\pi(t)dt}, \quad z \geq 0$$

where the last equality was obtained after (1).

The conditional failure rate is:

$$r_{Z|X^*>x}(z) = \frac{f_{Z|X^*>x}(z)}{\bar{F}_{Z|X^*>x}(z)} = \frac{\overline{F}(x,z)\pi(z)}{\int_z^\infty \overline{F}(x,t)\pi(t)dt}.$$

The conditional cumulative failure rate is:

$$\Delta_{Z|X^*>x}(z) = \int_0^z r_{Z|X^*>x}(t)dt = \int_0^z \frac{\overline{F}(x,t)\pi(t)dt}{\int_t^\infty \overline{F}(x,u)\pi(u)du}.$$

## Appendix C

The expectations of the residual residual life and its square are:

$$E[X-x, X>x] = \\ \int_x^\infty (t-x)f_X(t)dt = -(t-x)\bar{F}_X(t)|_x^\infty + \int_x^\infty \bar{F}_X(t)dt = \int_x^\infty \bar{F}_X(t)dt.$$

The previous result is derived by using integration by parts with $(t-x) = u$ and $dv = f_X(t)dt$. Therefore,

$$m_X(x) = \frac{\int_x^\infty \bar{F}_X(y)dy}{\bar{F}_X(x)}$$

$$E[(X-x)^2, X>x] = \\ \int_x^\infty (t-x)^2 f_X(t)dt = -(t-x)^2\bar{F}_X(t)|_x^\infty + 2\int_x^\infty (t-x)\bar{F}_X(t)dt = 2\int_x^\infty (t-x)\bar{F}_X(t)dt$$

where a new integration by parts with $(t-x)^2 = u$ and $dv = f_X(t)dt$ has been applied.

$$2\int_x^\infty (t-x)\bar{F}_X(t)dt = 2\int_x^\infty \left(\int_x^t du\right)\bar{F}_X(t)dt = 2\int_x^\infty \int_u^\infty \bar{F}_X(t)dtdu.$$

The last integral is obtained using Fubini's theorem. Hence,

$$\sigma_X^2(x) = 2\frac{\int_x^\infty \int_y^\infty \overline{F}_X(u)dudy}{\overline{F}_X(x)} - m_X^2(x)$$

The next remarks are used in the proof of Theorem 4.

**Remark A1.** *The failure rate, $r(x,z)$ and the reliability function $\bar{F}(x,z)$ verify*

$$\bar{F}(x,z) = e^{-\int_0^x r(u,z)du}$$

**Remark A2.** *Under the proportional mean residual life $m(x,z) = zm_X(x)$, with $m_X(x)$ as an increasing function, then $\frac{d\sigma^2(x,z)}{dx}$ is increasing in $z$.*

Consider the proportional mean residual life $m(x,z) = zm_X(x)$, where $m_X(x)$ is a baseline mean residual life and $0 < z \leq 1$. Following (6) we obtain

$$\begin{aligned}
\sigma^2(x,z) &= \frac{2\int_x^\infty \int_y^\infty \overline{F}(u,z)dudy}{\overline{F}(x,z)} - m^2(x,z) \\
&= \frac{2\int_x^\infty \overline{F}(y,z)m(y,z)dy}{\overline{F}(x,z)} - m^2(x,z) \\
&= \frac{2\int_x^\infty \overline{F}(y,z)(m(y,z) - m(x,z))dy}{\overline{F}(x,z)} + m^2(x,z)
\end{aligned}$$

where the last equality follows from (5).

Combining the previous identity and (11), we obtain

$$\begin{aligned}
\frac{d\sigma^2(x,z)}{dx} &= r(x,z)(\sigma^2(x,z) - m^2(x,z)) = \left(zr_X(x) + (1-z)\frac{1}{m_X(x)}\right) \\
&\times \; 2\int_x^\infty (m_X(y) - m_X(x))e^{-\int_x^y r(u,z)du}dy.
\end{aligned}$$

Given the formula in (9), the derivative of the foregoing expression with respect to $z$ is

$$\begin{aligned}
&\frac{\frac{dm_X(x)}{dx}}{m_X(x)^2}2\int_x^\infty (m_X(y) - m_X(x))e^{-\int_x^y r(u,z)du}dy \\
&- (zr_X(x) + (1-z)\frac{1}{m_X(x)})2\int_x^\infty (m_X(y) - m_X(x))\int_x^y \left(\frac{dr(u,z)}{dz}du\right)e^{-\int_x^y r(u,z)du}dy \geq 0.
\end{aligned}$$

The first term is non-negative since $m_X(x)$ is increasing. The second term is also non-negative because $r(x,z)$ decreasing in $z$ results in $\frac{dr(u,z)}{dz}$ being negative. Hence, $\frac{d\sigma^2(x,z)}{dx}$ is increasing in $z$.

**Remark A3.** *Under the proportional mean residual life $m(x,z) = zm_X(x)$, where $m_X(x)$ is an increasing function, then $A(z) = \sigma^2(x,Z) - m^2(x,Z)$ is an increasing function.*

From Remark A2, we can write

$$\begin{aligned}
A(z) = \sigma^2(x,z) - m^2(x,z) = \frac{2\int_x^\infty \overline{F}(y,z)(m(y,z) - m(x,z))dy}{\overline{F}(x,z)} \\
= 2z\int_x^\infty e^{-\int_x^y r(u,z)du}(m_X(y) - m_X(x))dy.
\end{aligned}$$

The last term in the previous formula is obtained by using the expression of the proportional mean residual life together with the relation between $r(x,z)$ and $\bar{F}(x,z)$ given in Remark A1. In addition, $A(z)$ is increasing in $z$, since $(m_X(y) - m_X(x))$ is a positive term and $r(x,z)$ is decreasing in $z$. Both result in $A(z)$ being increasing in $z$.

## References


1. Flage, R. A delay time model with imperfect and failure-inducing inspections. *Reliab. Eng. Syst. Saf.* **2014**, *124*, 1–12. [CrossRef]
2. Kalbfleisch, J.D.; Lawless, J.F. Inference based on retrospective ascertainment: An analysis of the data on transfusion-related AIDS. *J. Am. Stat. Assoc.* **1989**, *84*, 360–372. [CrossRef]
3. Block,H.W.; Savits, T.H.; Singh, H. The Reversed Hazard Rate Function. *Probab. Eng. Inf. Sci.* **1998**, *12*, 69–90. [CrossRef]
4. Finkelstein, M.S. On the reversed hazard rate. *Reliab. Eng. Syst. Saf.* **2002**, *78*, 71–75. [CrossRef]
5. Vagnorius, Z.; Rausand, M.; Sørby, K. Determining optimal replacement time for metal cutting tools. *Eur. J. Oper. Res.* **2010**, *206*, 407–416. [CrossRef]
6. Block, H.W.; Li, Y.; Savits, T.H. Initial and final behavior of failure rate functions for mixtures and functions. *J. Appl. Probab.* **2003**, *40*, 721–740. [CrossRef]
7. Aalen, O.O. Effects of frailty in survival analysis. *Stat. Methods. Med. Res.* **1994**, *3*, 227–243. [CrossRef]
8. Badía, F.G.; Berrade, M.D. On the reversed hazard rate and mean inactivity time of mixtures. In *Advances in Mathematical Modeling for Reliability*; Bedford, T., Quigley, J., Walls, L., Alkali, B., Daneshkhah, A., Hardman, G., Eds.; IOS Press: Glasgow, UK, 2007; pp. 103–110.
9. Haines, L.; Singpurwalla, N.Z. Some contributions to the stochastic characterization of wear. In *Reliability and Biometry: Statistical Analysis of Lifelenght*; Proschan, F., Serfling, R.J., Eds.; Society for Industrial and Applied Mathematics: Philadelphfia, PA, USA, 1974; pp. 47–80.
10. Zhang, M.; Ye, Z.; Xie, M. A condition-based maintenance strategy for heterogeneous populations. *Comput. Ind. Eng.* **2014**, *77*, 103–114. [CrossRef]
11. Launer, R.L. Inequalities for NBUE and NWUE life distributions. *Oper. Res.***1984**, *32*, 660–667. [CrossRef]
12. Gupta, R.C. On the monotonic properties of the residual variance and their applications in reliability. *J. Stat. Plan. Inference* **1987**, *16*, 329–335. [CrossRef]
13. Gupta, R.C.; Kirmani, S.N.U.A.; Launer, R.L. On life distributions having monotone residual variance. *Probab. Eng. Inf. Sci.* **1987**, *1*, 299–307. [CrossRef]
14. Kanjo, A.I. Asymptotic test for monotone variance residual life. *Arab J. Math. Sci.* **1996**, *1*, 65–75.
15. Nanda, A.K.; Singh, H.; Misra, N.; Paul, P. Reliability properties of reversed residual lifetime. *Commun. Stat. Theory Methods* **2003**, *32*, 2031–2042. [CrossRef]
16. Abu-Youssef, S.E. Nonparametric test for monotone variance residual life class of life distributions with hypothesis testing applications. *Appl. Math. Comput.* **2004**, *158*, 817–826. [CrossRef]
17. Gupta, R.C. Variance residual life function in reliability studies. *METRON Int. J. Stat.* **2006**, *LXIV*, 343–355.
18. Kundu, C.; Nanda, A.K. Some reliability properties of the inactivity time. *Commun. Stat. Theory Methods* **2010**, *39*, 899–911. [CrossRef]
19. Mahdy, M. Characterization and preservations of the variance inactivity time ordering and the increasing variance inactivity time class. *J. Adv. Res.* **2012**, *32*, 29–34. [CrossRef]
20. Kayid, M.; Izadkhah, S. Some new results about the variance inactivity time ordering with applications. *Appl. Math. Model.* **2016**, *40*, 3832–3842. [CrossRef]
21. Patra, A.; Kundu, C. Stochastic comparisons and ageing properties of RLRT (ITRT) based on variance residual life. *Commun. Stat. Theory Methods* **2022**, *51*, 4276–4295. [CrossRef]
22. Patra, A.; Kundu, C. Stochastic comparisons and ageing properties of residual lifetime mixture models. *Math. Methods Oper. Res.* **2021**, *94*, 123–143. [CrossRef]
23. Belzunce, F.; , Martínez-Riquelme, C.; Pereda, M. Sufficient conditions for some stochastic orders of discrete random variables with applications in reliability. *Mathematics* **2022**, *10*, 147. [CrossRef]
24. Stoyanov, J.; Al-Sadi, M.H.M. Properties of Classes of Life Distribution Based on the Conditional Variance. *J. Appl. Probab.* **2004**, *41*, 953–960. [CrossRef]
25. Finkelstein, M.S.; Esaulova, V. On Mixture Failure Rates Ordering. *Commun. Stat. Theory Methods* **2006**, *35*, 1943–1955. [CrossRef]
26. Li, X.; Da, G.; Zhao, P. On reversed hazard rate in general mixture models. *Stat. Probab. Lett.* **2010**, *80*, 654–661. [CrossRef]
27. Badía, F.G.; Cha, J.H. On bending (down and up) property of reliability measures in mixtures. *Metrika* **2017**, *80*, 455–482. [CrossRef]
28. Li, X.; Li, Z. A mixture model of proportional reversed hazard rate. *Commun. Stat. Theory Methods* **2008**, *37*, 2953–2963. [CrossRef]
29. Lee, H. Mixture discrete reversed hazard rate and its main properties. *Commun. Stat. Theory Methods* **2022**. [CrossRef]
30. Feller, W. *An Introduction to Probability Theory and Its Applications*, 3rd ed.; Wiley: New York, NY, USA, 1968; Volume 1.
31. Misra, N.; Francis, J. Relative ageing in frailty and resilience models. *Metrika* **2020**, *83*, 171–196. [CrossRef]
32. Muller, A.; Shanthikumar, J.G. *Comparison Methods for Stochastic Models and Risks*; Wiley: New York, NY, USA, 2002.
33. Nair, N.U.; Sankaran, P.G.; Balakrishnan, N. *Stochastic Orders in Reliability: In Quantile Based Reliability Analysis. Statistics for Industry and Technology*; Birkhäuser: New York, NY, USA, 2013.

34. Shaked, M.; Shanthikumar, J.G. *Stochastic Orders*; Springer: New York, NY, USA, 2007.
35. Cuadras, C.M. On the covariance between functions. *J. Multivar. Anal.* **2002**, *81*, 19–27. [CrossRef]
36. Joe, H. *Multivariate Models and Dependence Concepts*; Chapman and Hall: London, UK, 1997.
37. Cha, J.H.; Finkelstein, M. On ageing concepts for repairable items from heterogeneous populations. *IEEE Trans. Reliab.* **2016**, *65*, 1864–1870. [CrossRef]
38. Barlow, R. E.; Proschan, F. *Mathematical Theory of Reliability*; Wiley: Hoboken, NJ, USA, 1965.
39. Berrade, M.D.; Scarf, P.A.; Cavalcante, C.A.V. Some insights into the effect of maintenance quality for a protection system. *IEEE Trans. Reliab.* **2015**, *64*, 661–672. [CrossRef]
40. Zhao, X.; Li, B.; Mizutani, S.; Nakagawa, T. A revisit of age-based replacement models with exponential failure distributions. *IEEE Trans. Reliab.* **2021**. [CrossRef]
41. Badía, F.G.; Berrade, M.D.; Campos, C.A.; Navascués, M.A. On the behavior of aging characteristic in mixtures. *Probab. Eng. Inf. Sci.* **2001**, *15*, 83–94. [CrossRef]
42. Finkelstein, M.S.; Esaulova, V. Modeling a failure rate for a mixture of distributions functions. *Probab. Eng. Inf. Sci.* **2001**, *15*, 383–400. [CrossRef]
43. Gurland, J.; Sethuraman, J. Reversal of increasing failure fates when pooling failure data. *Tecnometrics* **1994**, *36*, 416–418.
44. Rezaei, M.; Gholizadeh, V. On proportional mean residual life model. *Commun. Stat. Theory Methods* **2015**, *44*, 4263–4277. [CrossRef]

mathematics

MDPI

Article

# A Preventive Replacement Policy for a System Subject to Bivariate Generalized Polya Failure Process

**Hyunju Lee [1], Ji Hwan Cha [2,*] and Maxim Finkelstein [3,4]**

1 Department of Statistics, Hankuk University of Foreign Studies, Yongin 17035, Korea; hyunjlee@hufs.ac.kr
2 Department of Statistics, Ewha Womans University, Seoul 03760, Korea
3 Department of Mathematical Statistics, University of the Free State, Bloemfontein 9300, South Africa; finkelm@ufs.ac.za
4 Department of Management Science, University of Strathclyde, Glasgow G1 1XQ, UK
* Correspondence: jhcha@ewha.ac.kr

**Abstract:** Numerous studies on preventive maintenance of minimally repaired systems with statistically independent components have been reported in reliability literature. However, in practice, the repair can be worse-than-minimal and the components of a system can be statistically dependent. The existing literature does not cover this important in-practice setting. Therefore, our paper is the first to deal with these issues by modeling dependence in the bivariate set up when a system consists of two dependent parts. We employ the bivariate generalized Polya process to model the corresponding failure and repair process. Relevant stochastic properties of this process have been obtained in order to propose and further discuss the new optimal bivariate preventive maintenance policy with two decision parameters: age and operational history. Moreover, introducing these two parameters in the considered context is also a new feature of the study. Under the proposed policy, the long-run average cost rate is derived and the optimal replacement policies are investigated. Detailed numerical examples illustrate our findings and show the potential efficiency of the obtained results in practice.

**Keywords:** dependent failure process; bivariate generalized Polya process; dependent worse-than-minimal repair process; optimal replacement policy

**MSC:** 90B25; 60K10

**Citation:** Lee, H.; Cha, J.H.; Finkelstein, M. A Preventive Replacement Policy for a System Subject to Bivariate Generalized Polya Failure Process. *Mathematics* **2022**, *10*, 1833. https://doi.org/10.3390/math10111833

Academic Editor: Tadashi Dohi

Received: 14 April 2022
Accepted: 23 May 2022
Published: 26 May 2022



## 1. Introduction

Preventive maintenance (PM) is usually performed on degrading systems in order to decrease the probabilities of failures during operation that can result in substantial losses. As the cost of the PM is smaller than that of a repair upon failure (also taking into account the additional losses due to failures), the corresponding cost-wise optimization problems can be formulated and solved. In this way, an optimal PM time can be obtained that minimizes, e.g., the corresponding cost rate. Thousands of papers devoted to different PM problems and several books entirely dealing with this important in-practice problem have been published in recent decades (see, e.g., the following influential monographs: [1–3]).

There have been numerous studies on PM models, where various counting processes are used to model the corresponding failure/repair process. Until now, most of these studies were focused on univariate counting processes of failure/repair such as the nonhomogeneous Poisson process (NHPP) or the renewal process (see [4–9] to name a few). For instance, in [4], it was assumed that the failure process follows the NHPP, which means that the corresponding repair type is a minimal repair. In [5], a system subject to two types of failures (minor and catastrophic failures) and repairs (minimal and perfect repairs) was considered for the maintenance optimization. Thus, from the process point of view, it corresponds to the combination of an NHPP and a renewal process.

The well-known minimal repair assumption holds when the corresponding system is composed of a large number of statistically independent components. Hence, its failure rate (FR) 'is practically unchanged' after the replacement of the failed component by a new one. However, in real life, the remaining non-failed components are often affected by the failure of a component in a system because it causes additional stress or damage to them. This eventually results in a worse-than-minimal repair of a system as the states of the non-failed components after the minimal repair of the failed component can be 'worse' than just before the failure. Some relevant examples of this situation are as follows ([10–12]):

(i) The failure of a still wire cable in a bridge or in an elevator instantaneously increases the stress on the remaining cables and leads to some damages.
(ii) For a multi-engine airplane, the failure of an engine during flight instantaneously causes increased stress on the non-failed engines.
(iii) A failure of a pump in a multi-pump hydraulic control system instantly increases the pressure for each non-failed pump.

Recently, as a generalization of the NHPP, a new counting process (called the generalized Polya process (GPP)) has been defined and applied for modeling the univariate failure/repair processes [13]. It is important to note that, under the GPP model, the repair is worse-than-minimal (GPP repair), which makes this process an effective tool for modeling the corresponding optimal PM policies in this case. Specifically, in [12], two periodic PM models were considered and some properties of the optimal policies assuming the GPP repair process were studied. Furthermore, Ref. [14] proposed a generalized replacement policy that already considers the operational history of a system.

The forgoing applies to univariate counting processes, whereas stochastically dependent multivariate series of events arise in many contexts. For some examples in reliability applications, finance, and economics, see [15–18]. Ref. [17] suggested a general theoretical framework for the multivariate counting process. Recently, new classes of multivariate counting processes have been developed in the literature (see [19–21]). Specifically, in [20], the multivariate generalized Polya process (MVGPP) with mathematically tractable properties was defined.

However, to the best of our knowledge, applications of multivariate processes to maintenance models has not yet been developed in the literature. Therefore, in this paper, assuming that the failure process follows the bivariate generalized Polya process (BVGPP) developed in [20], we propose and discuss a new bivariate preventive maintenance policy based on two 'parameters': age and operational history. As in [14], where the failure process was univariate, we show the superiority of the proposed policy compared with the original age-based replacement policy for the BVGPP.

In accordance with the foregoing discussion, we want to concisely emphasize the motivation and the novelty of our study:

- Motivation: Most systems in real life have dependent components, whereas the existing literature does not cover this aspect. Moreover, to the best of our knowledge, until now there have been no studies that consider the PM models with worse-than-minimal repair in multicomponent systems (that also often occurs in practice).
- Novelty: We employ the bivariate generalized Polya process to model the corresponding failure and repair process. This modeling approach was not considered in the literature so far. Some new stochastic properties of the process are derived and the corresponding optimal bivariate preventive maintenance policy with two decision parameters (age and operational history) is proposed. The latter is another novel feature of the study. Thus, development and application of the new mathematical models for modeling PM with the worse-than-minimal repair can be considered as the main contribution of the paper.

The structure of the paper is as follows: In Section 2, we introduce some preliminary results on the bivariate generalized Polya process (BVGPP) and the related repair process. In Section 3, we develop a bivariate preventive replacement policy assuming the BVGPP failure process and derive the corresponding long-run expected cost rate. In Section 4, we discuss the optimal policy for providing results of an illustrative numerical example. Finally, in Section 5, concluding remarks are given.

## 2. Preliminaries

In this section, we briefly review the definition of the bivariate generalized Polya process (BVGPP) and of some of its basic properties to be used in this paper. For this, we first need to recall the definition of the univariate generalized Polya process (GPP) via the concept of stochastic intensity. Note that, for an orderly (regular) counting process $\{N(t),\ t \geq 0\}$ and its past history $H_{t-} \equiv \{N(u),\ 0 \leq u < t\}$, the stochastic intensity is defined as (see, e.g., [13,22]),

$$\lambda_t = \lim_{\Delta t \to 0} \frac{P(N(t, t+\Delta t) = 1 | H_{t-})}{\Delta t} = \lim_{\Delta t \to 0} \frac{E[N(t, t+\Delta t) | H_{t-}]}{\Delta t},$$

where $N(t_1, t_2), t_1 < t_2$, is the number of events in $[t_1, t_2)$. In the following definitions, $\lambda(t)$ is a non-negative deterministic function.

**Definition 1 (Generalized Polya Process (GPP) [13]).** *Let $\{N(t),\ t \geq 0\}$ be an orderly counting process and*

(i) $N(0) = 0$;
(ii) $\lambda_t = (\alpha N(t-) + \beta)\lambda(t)$,

*then it is called the Generalized Polya Process (GPP) with the corresponding parameter set $(\lambda(t), \alpha, \beta)$, $\alpha \geq 0$, $\beta > 0$.*

As stated in [13], the GPP with $(\lambda(t), \alpha = 0, \beta = 1)$ reduces to the NHPP, and thus, the GPP is a generalization of the NHPP. Based on the GPP, and assuming that the repair times are negligible, Ref. [13] has defined a new type of imperfect repair for a system with the baseline (prior to the first repair) failure rate $\beta\lambda(t)$, which was called the 'GPP repair'.

**Definition 2 (GPP Repair).** *If $\{N(t),\ t \geq 0\}$, where $N(t)$ is the number of failures of the system in $(0, t]$, is the GPP with $(\lambda(t), \alpha, \beta)$, then we say that the corresponding repair is the 'GPP repair' with the parameters $\alpha, \beta > 0$.*

Accordingly, the corresponding stochastic intensity is given by

$$\lambda_t = (\alpha N(t-) + \beta)\lambda(t) \tag{1}$$

Note that according to Definition 2 and Equation (1), the failure rate prior to the first failure starts from $\beta\lambda(t)$, which is called the baseline failure rate. From Equation (1), it is clear that the failure rate after each failure/repair is larger than that before it. Thus, due to GPP repair, the reliability performance of the system after failure/repair becomes worse. In general, in the definition of the GPP repair, the parameter $\beta$ can be set $\beta = 1$ because the stochastic intensity in Equation (1) can be written as

$$\lambda_t = (\frac{\alpha}{\beta} N(t-) + 1)\beta\lambda(t) = (\alpha' N(t-) + 1)\varphi(t),$$

with $\alpha' = \frac{\alpha}{\beta}$ and $\varphi(t) = \beta\lambda(t)$. However, for a convenient description of the bivariate failure process, we follow Definition 2 throughout this paper.

Let $\{\mathbf{N}(t),\ t \geq 0\}$, where $\mathbf{N}(t) = (N_1(t), N_2(t))$, be a bivariate counting process and define the corresponding 'pooled' point process $\{M(t),\ t \geq 0\}$, where $M(t) = N_1(t) + N_2(t)$. The marginal point processes $\{N_i(t),\ t \geq 0\}$, for convenience, will be called type $i$ point process, $i = 1, 2$, respectively. Furthermore, the events from type $i$ point process $\{N_i(t),\ t \geq 0\}$ will also be called type $i$ events. For a regular multivariate process $\{\mathbf{N}(t),\ t \geq 0\}$, let $H_{Pt-} \equiv \{M(u), 0 \leq u < t\}$ be the history of the pooled process in $[0, t)$, i.e., the set of all point events in $[0, t)$. Observe that $H_{Pt-}$ can equivalently be defined in terms of $M(t-)$ and the sequential arrival points of the events $0 \le S_1 \le S_2 \le \cdots \le S_{M(t-)} < t$ in $[0, t)$, where $M(t-)$ is the total number of events in $[0, t)$ and $S_i$ is the time from 0 until the arrival of the $i$th event in $[0, t)$ of the pooled process $\{M(t),\ t \ge 0\}$. Similarly, define the marginal histories of the marginal processes $H_{i,t-} \equiv \{N_i(u), 0 \le u < t\}, i = 1, 2$.

As with the case of univariate point processes, the most convenient general description of the multivariate point processes can be achieved through the stochastic intensities approach. Accord ingly, the 'regular bivariate process' can be specified by

$$\lambda_{1t} \equiv \lim_{\Delta t \to 0} \frac{P(N_1(t, t + \Delta t) = 1 | H_{1,t-}; H_{2,t-})}{\Delta t},$$

$$\lambda_{2t} = \lim_{\Delta t \to 0} \frac{P(N_2(t, t + \Delta t) = 1 | H_{1,t-}; H_{2,t-})}{\Delta t},$$

where $N_i(t_1, t_2),\ t_1 < t_2$, denotes the number of events in $[t_1, t_2),\ i = 1, 2$, respectively (see [17]). According to [20], the BVGPP denoted further by BVGPP $(\lambda_1(t), \lambda_2(t), \alpha, \beta)$, is defined as follows. In the following definition, $\lambda_i(t), i = 1, 2$, are non-negative deterministic functions.

**Definition 3 (Bivariate generalized Polya process (BVGPP)).** *A bivariate counting process $\{\mathbf{N}(t),\ t \ge 0\}$ is called the bivariate generalized Polya process (BVGPP) with the set of parameters $(\lambda_1(t), \lambda_2(t), \alpha, \beta)$, $\lambda_i(t) \ge 0$ for all $t \ge 0,\ i = 1, 2,\ \alpha \ge 0,\ \beta > 0$, if*

(i) $N_1(0) = 0,\ N_2(0) = 0$;
(ii) $\lambda_{1t} = (\alpha(N_1(t-) + N_2(t-)) + \beta)\lambda_1(t)$;
(iii) $\lambda_{2t} = (\alpha(N_1(t-) + N_2(t-)) + \beta)\lambda_2(t)$.

Conditions (ii) and (iii) in Definition 3 specify the dependence structure of the process in a fully intuitive way. That is, the occurrences of any type of events in the previous interval increase the occurrence probabilities of both types of events in the next interval. This type of dependency in a bivariate point process can be frequently observed in practice (see our examples in the Introduction).

Similar to the univariate counting process, a new type of dependent failure and repair process is defined based on the BVGPP in Definition 3, which is called 'dependent worse-than-minimal repair process (DWMRP)' [20]. Suppose that a system is composed of two parts (part 1 and part 2) having respective failure rates $\beta\lambda_i(t),\ i = 1, 2$. Under the DWMRP, the reliability performances of both parts after a repair of any part are worse than before the failure, which can be observed in reliability practice.

We will define now the concept of 'thinning' ([20,23]) for our further discussion and to provide some important properties of the BVGPP.

**Definition 4 ($p(t)$-thinning).** *Let $\{N(t), t \ge 0\}$ be a univariate point process and denote it by $\left\{N_{p(\cdot)}(t), t \ge 0\right\}$ the point process obtained by retaining (in the same location) every point of the process with probability $p(t)$ and deleting it with probability $q(t) = 1 - p(t)$, independently of everything else. Denote by $\left\{N_{q(\cdot)}(t), t \ge 0\right\}$ the point process constructed by the deleted points. Then the processes $\left\{N_{p(\cdot)}(t), t \ge 0\right\}$ and $\left\{N_{q(\cdot)}(t), t \ge 0\right\}$ are the $p(t)$-thinning of $\{N(t), t \ge 0\}$.*

*Denote: $\lambda(t) = \lambda_1(t) + \lambda_2(t)$, $\Lambda(t) = \int_0^t \lambda(x)dx$ and $p_i(t) = \lambda_i(t)/\lambda(t), i = 1, 2$.*

**Proposition 1.** *Let $\{N(t), t \ge 0\}$ be the BVGPP $(\lambda_1(t), \lambda_2(t), \alpha, \beta)$. Then*

(i) *$\{M(t), t \ge 0\}$ is GPP $(\lambda(t), \alpha, \beta)$.*

(ii) *The process* $\{\mathbf{N}(t),\ t \geq 0\}$ *is constructed by* $p_1(t)$*-thinning of* $\{M(t), t \geq 0\}$ *as* $\left\{(M_{p_1(\cdot)}(t),\ M_{p_2(\cdot)}(t)),\ t \geq 0\right\}$.

(iii) *The marginal processes* $\{N_i(t), t \geq 0\}$ *are GPP* $(\gamma_i(t), \alpha, \beta)$*, where*

$$\gamma_i(t) = \frac{\lambda_i(t)\exp\left\{\alpha\int_0^t \lambda_1(x) + \lambda_2(x)dx\right\}}{\alpha\int_0^t \lambda_i(v)\exp\left\{\alpha\int_0^v \lambda_1(x) + \lambda_2(x)dx\right\}dv + 1},\ i = 1,2.$$

See [20] for the proof of Proposition 1. The following proposition presents the joint distribution of number of events ([20]).

**Proposition 2.** *Let* $t > 0$*. It holds that*

$$\begin{aligned} &P(N_i(t) = n_i, i = 1,2) \\ &= \tfrac{\Gamma(\beta/\alpha+n_1+n_2)}{\Gamma(\beta/\alpha)n_1!n_2!}\left(\alpha\int_0^t \lambda_1(x)\exp\{-\alpha[\Lambda(t) - \Lambda(x)]\}dx\right)^{n_1}\left(\alpha\int_0^t \lambda_2(x)\exp\{-\alpha[\Lambda(t) - \Lambda(x)]\}dx\right)^{n_2} \\ &\times(\exp\{-\alpha\Lambda(T)\})^{\beta/\alpha}. \end{aligned}$$

## 3. Bivariate Preventive Replacement Policy

We will now develop a new preventive replacement policy for a repairable deteriorating system which is composed of two statistically dependent parts. It should be noted that the PM models based on the univariate counting processes were only considered in the literature previously. Denote by $N_i(t)$, $i = 1,2$, the number of failures in part 1 and part 2 until time $t$, respectively. Under the BVGPP failure/repair process, we assume that $\{\mathbf{N}(t),\ t \geq 0\}$, where $\mathbf{N}(t) = (N_1(t), N_2(t))$, follows BVGPP $(\lambda_1(t), \lambda_2(t), \alpha, \beta)$. As mentioned before, under the BVGPP (or DWMRP), the reliability performances of 'both parts' deteriorate on each failure of any of the two parts, as the corresponding stochastic intensities in Definition 3 'count' the overall number of events, i.e., $N_1(t-) + N_2(t-)$. Therefore, it could be reasonable to suggest the preventive replacement policy based on $N_1(t) + N_2(t)$ for the BVGPP $(\lambda_1(t), \lambda_2(t), \alpha, \beta)$ failure/repair process. Recall that $S_N$ $(N = 1,2,\ldots)$ denotes the arrival times in the pooled point process $\{M(t),\ t \geq 0\}$.

### 3.1. Bivariate Preventive Replacement Policy

The system is replaced at time $T(T > 0)$ or at $S_N$ $(N = 1,2,\ldots)$ after its inception into operation (or last replacement), whichever occurs first, and it undergoes the BVGPP repairs at failures between replacements. The times for repairs and replacements are negligible.

Let us denote, by $c(N,T)$, the corresponding long-run expected cost rate function. Let $c_{GPP}^{(i)}$ be the cost incurred by a BVGPP repair performed on the failure of part $i$, $i = 1,2$, and $c_r$ be the cost of system's replacement. To derive the cost rate function, we need some preliminary lemmas. In the following, denote by $N_{GP}^{(i)}$, $i = 1,2$, the total number of BVGPP repairs of part $i$ in a renewal cycle (between replacements).

**Lemma 1.** *Conditional expectations* $E(N_{GP}^{(i)}|S_N \leq T)$*, i = 1,2, are given by*

$$\begin{aligned} E(N_{GP}^{(i)}|S_N \leq T) &= \int_0^T\left\{(N-1)\tfrac{\alpha\int_0^t \lambda_i(x)\exp\{\alpha\Lambda(x)\}dx}{\exp\{\alpha\Lambda(t)\}-1} + \tfrac{\lambda_i(t)}{\lambda(t)}\right\} \\ &\times\tfrac{\Gamma(\beta/\alpha+N-1)}{\Gamma(\beta/\alpha)(N-1)!}(1-\exp\{-\alpha\Lambda(t)\})^{N-1}\exp\{-\beta\Lambda(t)\}((N-1)\alpha+\beta)\lambda(t)dt\cdot\tfrac{1}{P(S_N \leq T)}, i = 1,2. \end{aligned}$$

**Proof.** In this proof, we derive just $E(N_{GP}^{(1)}|S_N \leq T)$, whereas $E(N_{GP}^{(2)}|S_N \leq T)$ can be obtained 'symmetrically'. Observe that

$$E(N_{GP}^{(1)}|S_N \leq T) = \int_0^T E(N_{GP}^{(1)}|S_N \leq T, S_N = t) f_{(S_N|S_N \leq T)}(t)dt, \tag{2}$$

where $f_{(S_N|S_N \leq T)}(t)$ is the conditional pdf of $(S_N|S_N \leq T)$ given by

$$\begin{aligned} f_{(S_N|S_N \leq T)}(t) &= \tfrac{f_{S_N}(t)}{P(S_N \leq T)} \\ &= \tfrac{\Gamma(\beta/\alpha+N-1)}{\Gamma(\beta/\alpha)(N-1)!}(1-\exp\{-\alpha\Lambda(t)\})^{N-1}\exp\{-\beta\Lambda(t)\}((N-1)\alpha+\beta)\lambda(t) \cdot \tfrac{1}{P(S_N \leq T)}. \end{aligned}$$

Furthermore,

$$\begin{aligned} E(N_{GP}^{(1)}|S_N \leq T, S_N = t) &= E(N_{GP}^{(1)}|S_N = t, I_N = 1)P(I_N = 1|S_N = t) \\ &+ E(N_{GP}^{(1)}|S_N = t, I_N = 2)P(I_N = 2|S_N = t), \end{aligned} \tag{3}$$

where $I_N = i$, $i = 1,2$, if the failure at time $S_N$ occurs in part $i$, respectively. From Proposition 1-(ii),

$$P(I_N = i|S_N = t) = \lambda_i(t)/\lambda(t), \; i = 1,2, \tag{4}$$

and $E(N_{GP}^{(1)}|S_N = t, I_N = 1)$ can be represented as

$$E(N_{GP}^{(1)}|S_N = t, I_N = 1) = \sum_{n_1=1}^{N} n_1 P(N_{GP}^{(1)} = n_1|S_N = t, I_N = 1) = \sum_{n_1=1}^{N} n_1 \frac{f_{(N_{GP}^{(1)}, S_N, I_N)}(n_1, t, 1)}{f_{(S_N, I_N)}(t, 1)}$$

where $f_{(S_N,I_N)}(t,1)$ is the joint distribution of $(S_N = t, I_N = 1)$ and $f_{(N_{GP}^{(1)}, S_N, I_N)}(n_1, t, 1)$ is that of $(N_{GP}^{(1)} = n_1, S_N = t, I_N = 1)$, given by

$$\begin{aligned} &f_{(S_N,I_N)}(t,1) \\ &= \tfrac{\Gamma(\beta/\alpha+N-1)}{\Gamma(\beta/\alpha)(N-1)!}(1-\exp\{-\alpha\Lambda(t)\})^{N-1}\exp\{-\beta\Lambda(t)\}((N-1)\alpha+\beta)\lambda(t)\tfrac{\lambda_1(t)}{\lambda(t)}, \end{aligned}$$

and

$$\begin{aligned} &f_{(N_{GP}^{(1)}, S_N, I_N)}(n_1, t, 1) \\ &= \lim_{\Delta t \to 0} \tfrac{1}{\Delta t} P(N_1(t-) = n_1 - 1,\, N_2(t-) = N - n_1, t \leq S_N < t + \Delta t, I_N = 1) \\ &= P(N_1(t-) = n_1 - 1,\, N_2(t-) = N - n_1) \\ &\times \lim_{\Delta t \to 0} \tfrac{1}{\Delta t} P(t \leq S_N < t + \Delta t, I_N = 1|N_1(t-) = n_1 - 1,\, N_2(t-) = N - n_1) \\ &= \tfrac{\Gamma(\beta/\alpha+N-1)}{\Gamma(\beta/\alpha)(n_1-1)!(N-n_1)!}\left(\alpha\int_0^t \lambda_1(x)\exp\{-\alpha[\Lambda(t)-\Lambda(x)]\}dx\right)^{n_1-1} \\ &\times \left(\alpha\int_0^t \lambda_2(x)\exp\{-\alpha[\Lambda(t)-\Lambda(x)]\}dx\right)^{N-n_1}\exp\{-\alpha\Lambda(t)\}^{\beta/\alpha} \\ &\times ((N-1)\alpha+\beta)\lambda(t)\tfrac{\lambda_1(t)}{\lambda(t)}. \end{aligned}$$

Therefore, we have

$$\begin{aligned} &P(N_{GP}^{(1)} = n_1|S_N = t, I_N = 1) \\ &= \tfrac{(N-1)!}{(n_1-1)!(N-n_1)!}\left(\alpha\int_0^t \lambda_1(x)\exp\{-\alpha[\Lambda(t)-\Lambda(x)]\}dx\right)^{n_1-1}\left(\alpha\int_0^t \lambda_2(x)\exp\{-\alpha[\Lambda(t)-\Lambda(x)]\}dx\right)^{N-n_1} \\ &/(1-\exp\{-\alpha\Lambda(t)\})^{N-1} \\ &= \tfrac{(N-1)!}{(n_1-1)!(N-n_1)!}\left(\tfrac{\alpha\int_0^t \lambda_1(x)\exp\{-\alpha[\Lambda(t)-\Lambda(x)]\}dx}{1-\exp\{-\alpha\Lambda(t)\}}\right)^{n_1-1}\left(\tfrac{\alpha\int_0^t \lambda_2(x)\exp\{-\alpha[\Lambda(t)-\Lambda(x)]\}dx}{1-\exp\{-\alpha\Lambda(t)\}}\right)^{N-n_1} \\ &= \tfrac{(N-1)!}{(n_1-1)!(N-n_1)!}\left(\tfrac{\alpha\int_0^t \lambda_1(x)\exp\{\alpha\Lambda(x)\}dx}{\exp\{\alpha\Lambda(t)\}-1}\right)^{n_1-1}\left(\tfrac{\alpha\int_0^t \lambda_2(x)\exp\{\alpha\Lambda(x)\}dx}{\exp\{\alpha\Lambda(t)\}-1}\right)^{N-n_1}, \; n_1 = 1,2,\ldots,N. \end{aligned}$$

Let $L \equiv N_{GP}^{(1)} - 1$. Then, the conditional distribution of $P(L = m | S_N = t, I_N = 1)$, $m = 0, 1, 2, \ldots, N-1$, is

$$P(L = m | S_N = t, I_N = 1) = P(N_{GP}^{(1)} = m + 1 | S_N = t, I_N = 1)$$
$$= \frac{(N-1)!}{m!(N-1-m)!} \left( \frac{\alpha \int_0^t \lambda_1(x) \exp\{\alpha \Lambda(x)\} dx}{\exp\{\alpha \Lambda(t)\} - 1} \right)^m \left( \frac{\alpha \int_0^t \lambda_2(x) \exp\{\alpha \Lambda(x)\} dx}{\exp\{\alpha \Lambda(t)\} - 1} \right)^{N-1-m},$$

$m = 0, 1, 2, \ldots, N-1$, which is the Binomial distribution with parameters $N-1$ and $\frac{\alpha \int_0^t \lambda_1(x) \exp\{\alpha \Lambda(x)\} dx}{\exp\{\alpha \Lambda(t)\} - 1}$. Accordingly, $E(N_{GP}^{(1)} | S_N = t, I_N = 1)$ is given by

$$E(N_{GP}^{(1)} | S_N = t, I_N = 1) = E(L + 1 | S_N = t, I_N = 1)$$
$$= (N-1) \frac{\alpha \int_0^t \lambda_1(x) \exp\{\alpha \Lambda(x)\} dx}{\exp\{\alpha \Lambda(t)\} - 1} + 1.$$

In a similar way,

$$f_{(S_N, I_N)}(t, 2)$$
$$= \frac{\Gamma(\beta/\alpha + N - 1)}{\Gamma(\beta/\alpha)(N-1)!} (1 - \exp\{-\alpha \Lambda(t)\})^{N-1} \exp\{-\beta \Lambda(t)\} ((N-1)\alpha + \beta) \lambda(t) \frac{\lambda_2(t)}{\lambda(t)},$$

and

$$f_{(N_{GP}^{(1)}, S_N, I_N)}(n_1, t, 2)$$
$$= \lim_{\Delta t \to 0} \frac{1}{\Delta t} P(N_1(t-) = n_1,\ N_2(t-) = N - 1 - n_1, t \le S_N < t + \Delta t, I_N = 2)$$
$$= P(N_1(t-) = n_1,\ N_2(t-) = N - 1 - n_1)$$
$$\times \lim_{\Delta t \to 0} \frac{1}{\Delta t} P(t \le S_N < t + \Delta t, I_N = 2 | N_1(t-) = n_1,\ N_2(t-) = N - 1 - n_1)$$
$$= \frac{\Gamma(\beta/\alpha + N - 1)}{\Gamma(\beta/\alpha) n_1! (N-1-n_1)!} \left( \alpha \int_0^t \lambda_1(x) \exp\{-\alpha [\Lambda(t) - \Lambda(x)]\} dx \right)^{n_1}$$
$$\times \left( \alpha \int_0^t \lambda_2(x) \exp\{-\alpha [\Lambda(t) - \Lambda(x)]\} dx \right)^{N-1-n_1} \exp\{-\alpha \Lambda(t)\}^{\beta/\alpha}$$
$$\times ((N-1)\alpha + \beta) \lambda(t) \frac{\lambda_2(t)}{\lambda(t)}.$$

Thus,

$$P(N_{GP}^{(1)} = n_1 | S_N = t, I_N = 2)$$
$$= \frac{(N-1)!}{n_1!(N-1-n_1)!} \left( \frac{\alpha \int_0^t \lambda_1(x) \exp\{\alpha \Lambda(x)\} dx}{\exp\{\alpha \Lambda(t)\} - 1} \right)^{n_1} \left( \frac{\alpha \int_0^t \lambda_2(x) \exp\{\alpha \Lambda(x)\} dx}{\exp\{\alpha \Lambda(t)\} - 1} \right)^{N-1-n_1},$$

$n_1 = 0, 1, \ldots, N-1$, and

$$E(N_{GP}^{(1)} | S_N = t, I_N = 2) = (N-1) \frac{\alpha \int_0^t \lambda_1(x) \exp\{\alpha \Lambda(x)\} dx}{\exp\{\alpha \Lambda(t)\} - 1}.$$

From Equations (3) and (4),

$$E(N_{GP}^{(1)} | S_N \le T, S_N = t) = \left\{ (N-1) \frac{\alpha \int_0^t \lambda_1(x) \exp\{\alpha \Lambda(x)\} dx}{\exp\{\alpha \Lambda(t)\} - 1} \right\} \left( \frac{\lambda_1(t)}{\lambda(t)} + \frac{\lambda_2(t)}{\lambda(t)} \right) + \frac{\lambda_1(t)}{\lambda(t)}$$
$$= (N-1) \frac{\alpha \int_0^t \lambda_1(x) \exp\{\alpha \Lambda(x)\} dx}{\exp\{\alpha \Lambda(t)\} - 1} + \frac{\lambda_1(t)}{\lambda(t)},$$

and from Equation (2),

$$E(N_{GP}^{(1)} | S_N \le T) = \int_0^T \left\{ (N-1) \frac{\alpha \int_0^t \lambda_1(x) \exp\{\alpha \Lambda(x)\} dx}{\exp\{\alpha \Lambda(t)\} - 1} + \frac{\lambda_1(t)}{\lambda(t)} \right\}$$
$$\times \frac{\Gamma(\beta/\alpha + N - 1)}{\Gamma(\beta/\alpha)(N-1)!} (1 - \exp\{-\alpha \Lambda(t)\})^{N-1} \exp\{-\beta \Lambda(t)\} ((N-1)\alpha + \beta) \lambda(t) dt \cdot \frac{1}{P(S_N \le T)}.$$

□

**Lemma 2.** *$E(N_{GP}^{(i)})$ and $i = 1, 2$, are given by*

$$\begin{aligned} E(N_{GP}^{(1)}) &= \int_0^T \left\{ (N-1) \frac{\alpha \int_0^t \lambda_1(x) \exp\{\alpha\Lambda(x)\} dx}{\exp\{\alpha\Lambda(t)\} - 1} + \frac{\lambda_1(t)}{\lambda(t)} \right\} \\ &\times \frac{\Gamma(\beta/\alpha + N - 1)}{\Gamma(\beta/\alpha)(N-1)!} (1 - \exp\{-\alpha\Lambda(t)\})^{N-1} \exp\{-\beta\Lambda(t)\}((N-1)\alpha + \beta)\lambda(t) dt \\ &+ \sum_{j=0}^{N-1} \sum_{k=0}^{N-1-j} j \cdot \frac{\Gamma(\beta/\alpha + j + k)}{\Gamma(\beta/\alpha) j! k!} \left( \alpha \int_0^T \lambda_1(x) \exp\{-\alpha[\Lambda(T) - \Lambda(x)]\} dx \right)^j \\ &\times \left( \alpha \int_0^T \lambda_2(x) \exp\{-\alpha[\Lambda(T) - \Lambda(x)]\} dx \right)^k (\exp\{-\alpha\Lambda(T)\})^{\beta/\alpha}, \end{aligned} \tag{5}$$

and

$$\begin{aligned} E(N_{GP}^{(2)}) &= \int_0^T \left\{ (N-1) \frac{\alpha \int_0^t \lambda_2(x) \exp\{\alpha\Lambda(x)\} dx}{\exp\{\alpha\Lambda(t)\} - 1} + \frac{\lambda_2(t)}{\lambda(t)} \right\} \\ &\times \frac{\Gamma(\beta/\alpha + N - 1)}{\Gamma(\beta/\alpha)(N-1)!} (1 - \exp\{-\alpha\Lambda(t)\})^{N-1} \exp\{-\beta\Lambda(t)\}((N-1)\alpha + \beta)\lambda(t) dt \\ &+ \sum_{j=0}^{N-1} \sum_{k=0}^{N-1-j} j \cdot \frac{\Gamma(\beta/\alpha + j + k)}{\Gamma(\beta/\alpha) j! k!} \left( \alpha \int_0^T \lambda_2(x) \exp\{-\alpha[\Lambda(T) - \Lambda(x)]\} dx \right)^j \\ &\times \left( \alpha \int_0^T \lambda_1(x) \exp\{-\alpha[\Lambda(T) - \Lambda(x)]\} dx \right)^k (\exp\{-\alpha\Lambda(T)\})^{\beta/\alpha}. \end{aligned} \tag{6}$$

**Proof.** Observe that, using Proposition 2,

$$\begin{aligned} &E(N_{GP}^{(1)} | S_N > T) = E(N_1(T) | M(T) \le N-1) \\ &= \sum_{j=0}^{N-1} j P(N_1(T) = j | M(T) \le N-1) = \sum_{j=0}^{N-1} j \frac{P(N_1(T) = j, N_2(T) \le N-1-j)}{P(M(T) \le N-1)} \\ &= \sum_{j=0}^{N-1} \sum_{k=0}^{N-1-j} j \cdot \frac{\Gamma(\beta/\alpha + j + k)}{\Gamma(\beta/\alpha) j! k!} \left( \alpha \int_0^T \lambda_1(x) \exp\{-\alpha[\Lambda(T) - \Lambda(x)]\} dx \right)^j \\ &\times \left( \alpha \int_0^T \lambda_2(x) \exp\{-\alpha[\Lambda(T) - \Lambda(x)]\} dx \right)^k (\exp\{-\alpha\Lambda(T)\})^{\beta/\alpha} \cdot \frac{1}{P(S_N > T)}. \end{aligned}$$

Therefore, using the result in Lemma 1, we have

$$\begin{aligned} E(N_{GP}^{(1)}) &= E(N_{GP}^{(1)} | S_N \le T) P(S_N \le T) + E(N_{GP}^{(1)} | S_N > T) P(S_N > T) \\ &= \int_0^T \left\{ (N-1) \frac{\alpha \int_0^t \lambda_1(x) \exp\{\alpha\Lambda(x)\} dx}{\exp\{\alpha\Lambda(t)\} - 1} + \frac{\lambda_1(t)}{\lambda(t)} \right\} \\ &\times \frac{\Gamma(\beta/\alpha + N - 1)}{\Gamma(\beta/\alpha)(N-1)!} (1 - \exp\{-\alpha\Lambda(t)\})^{N-1} \exp\{-\beta\Lambda(t)\}((N-1)\alpha + \beta)\lambda(t) dt \\ &+ \sum_{j=0}^{N-1} \sum_{k=0}^{N-1-j} j \cdot \frac{\Gamma(\beta/\alpha + j + k)}{\Gamma(\beta/\alpha) j! k!} \left( \alpha \int_0^T \lambda_1(x) \exp\{-\alpha[\Lambda(T) - \Lambda(x)]\} dx \right)^j \\ &\times \left( \alpha \int_0^T \lambda_2(x) \exp\{-\alpha[\Lambda(T) - \Lambda(x)]\} dx \right)^k (\exp\{-\alpha\Lambda(T)\})^{\beta/\alpha}, \end{aligned}$$

and symmetrically, $E(N_{GP}^{(2)})$ can be derived as

$$\begin{aligned} E(N_{GP}^{(2)}) &= E(N_{GP}^{(2)} | S_N \le T) P(S_N \le T) + E(N_{GP}^{(2)} | S_N > T) P(S_N > T) \\ &= \int_0^T \left\{ (N-1) \frac{\alpha \int_0^t \lambda_2(x) \exp\{\alpha\Lambda(x)\} dx}{\exp\{\alpha\Lambda(t)\} - 1} + \frac{\lambda_2(t)}{\lambda(t)} \right\} \\ &\times \frac{\Gamma(\beta/\alpha + N - 1)}{\Gamma(\beta/\alpha)(N-1)!} (1 - \exp\{-\alpha\Lambda(t)\})^{N-1} \exp\{-\beta\Lambda(t)\}((N-1)\alpha + \beta)\lambda(t) dt \\ &+ \sum_{j=0}^{N-1} \sum_{k=0}^{N-1-j} j \cdot \frac{\Gamma(\beta/\alpha + j + k)}{\Gamma(\beta/\alpha) j! k!} \left( \alpha \int_0^T \lambda_2(x) \exp\{-\alpha[\Lambda(T) - \Lambda(x)]\} dx \right)^j \\ &\times \left( \alpha \int_0^T \lambda_1(x) \exp\{-\alpha[\Lambda(T) - \Lambda(x)]\} dx \right)^k (\exp\{-\alpha\Lambda(T)\})^{\beta/\alpha}. \end{aligned}$$

□

In the following theorem, we derive the corresponding expected cost rate function $c(N,T)$, which is, as usual, defined as the expected cost on a renewal cycle over the expected length of this cycle.

**Theorem 1.** *The cost rate function $c(N,T)$ is given by*

$$c(N,T) = \frac{\left(c_{GPP}^{(1)}E[N_{GP}^{(1)}] + c_{GPP}^{(2)}E[N_{GP}^{(2)}] + c_r\right)}{\int\limits_0^T \sum\limits_{j=0}^{N-1} \frac{\Gamma(\beta/\alpha+j)}{\Gamma(\beta/\alpha)j!}(1-\exp\{-\alpha\Lambda(t)\})^j(\exp\{-\alpha\Lambda(t)\})^{\frac{\beta}{\alpha}}\,dt}, N = 1,2,\ldots,\ T > 0, \quad (7)$$

*where $E[N_{GP}^{(i)}]$,$i = 1,2$, are given by Equations (5) and (6), respectively.*

**Proof.** Observe that the expected length of one renewal cycle is $E[\min(S_N,T)]$. Then, by the Renewal Reward Theorem ([23]) the long-run expected cost rate function $c(N,T)$ is defined as

$$c(N,T) = \frac{c_{GPP}^{(1)}E[N_{GP}^{(1)}] + c_{GPP}^{(2)}E[N_{GP}^{(2)}] + c_r}{E[\min(S_N,T)]}. \quad (8)$$

From Proposition 1-(i), the expected length of a cycle, $E[\min(S_N,T)]$, is given as follows:

$$\begin{aligned} E[\min(S_N,T)] &= \int\limits_0^T P(\min(S_N,T) > t)\,dt = \int\limits_0^T P(S_N > t)\,dt = \int\limits_0^T P(M(t) \le N-1)\,dt \\ &= \int\limits_0^T \sum\limits_{j=0}^{N-1} \frac{\Gamma(\beta/\alpha+j)}{\Gamma(\beta/\alpha)j!}(1-\exp\{-\alpha\Lambda(t)\})^j(\exp\{-\alpha\Lambda(t)\})^{\frac{\beta}{\alpha}}\,dt. \end{aligned} \quad (9)$$

Eventually, using Lemma 2, Equations (8) and (9), the long-run expected cost rate function $c(N,T)$ is given by Equation (7). □

It is important to compare the proposed bivariate policy (age or the occurrence of the $N$-th event in the corresponding BVGGP, whichever comes first) with the conventional ordinary age-based replacement policy at age $T_A$ ($T_A > 0$). Thus, the number of GPP repairs are not considered as an additional parameter in this simplified policy. The corresponding expected cost rate (denoted by $c_A(T_A)$) can be obtained as

$$c_A(T_A) = \frac{\frac{\beta}{\alpha}\left\{c_{GPP}^{(1)}\int_0^{T_A}\alpha\lambda_1(x)\exp(\alpha\Lambda(x))dx + c_{GPP}^{(2)}\int_0^{T_A}\alpha\lambda_2(x)\exp(\alpha\Lambda(x))dx\right\} + c_r}{T_A}. \quad (10)$$

Observe that Equation (10) can be directly derived from Theorem 1 by setting $N = \infty$, i.e., $c_A(T_A) = \lim\limits_{N\to\infty} c(N,T_A)$. In addition, we can see that when $c_{GPP}^{(1)} = c_{GPP}^{(2)} = c_{GPP}$, the expected cost rate $c_A(T_A)$ in Equation (10) is equal to that in [13]:

$$c*_A(T_A) = \frac{c_{GPP}\beta\{\exp(\alpha\Lambda(T_A)) - 1\}/\alpha + c_r}{T_A}$$

*3.2. Optimal PM*

We can now formulate the optimal PM problem for the described setting. Thus, the optimal vector $(N^*,T^*)$ should be obtained such that

$$c(N^*,T^*) = \min_{T>0,N=1,2,\ldots}c(N,T).$$

To find $(N^*,T^*)$, the two-stage procedure will be applied. At the first step, for a fixed $N$, we find $T^*(N)$ such that

$$c(N,T^*(N)) = \min_{T>0}c(N,T).$$

At the second step, we search for $N^*$ such that

$$c(N^*, T^*(N^*)) = \min_{N=1,2,\ldots} c(N, T^*(N)).$$

Then, the optimal maintenance policy parameters are given by $(N^*, T^*(N^*))$.

The expression for $c(N, T)$ obtained in Theorem 1 is extremely cumbersome and its analytical analysis of the optimal solution is practically impossible. Therefore, in the next section, we will illustrate our findings numerically. Note that, from general considerations, it is clear that the optimal policy proposed in this study should result in a smaller (not larger) optimal expected cost rate than for the case defined by Equation (10). The numerical study of the next section among other findings illustrates this claim as well.

## 4. Numerical Illustration and Discussion

Following the optimization procedure stated above, we conduct numerical studies for illustration. Suppose that two parts of the system has the following baseline intensities: $\lambda_1(t) = 0.25\,(t+2)$ and $\lambda_2(t) = 0.5\,(t+2)$. Let the repair and replacement costs are given by $c_{GPP}^{(1)} = 5$, $c_{GPP}^{(2)} = 10$, and $c_r = 100$, respectively. Then, for instance, for $\alpha = \beta = 1$, the optimal values are obtained as $(N^*, T^*) = (5,\ 3.9801)$ and the corresponding minimal cost rate is $c(N^*, T^*) = 130.8159$.

In what follows, assume $\beta = 1$, which is a natural assumption in defining the BVGGP that describes the failure/repair process. Then the optimal preventive maintenance policy $(N^*, T^*)$ and the corresponding cost rate $c(N^*, T^*)$ for different values $c_{GPP}^{(1)}$, $c_{GPP}^{(2)}$, and $\alpha$ are given in Tables 1 and 2 for $c_r = 80$ and $c_r = 100$, respectively. From these tables, we can observe that as the degree of the GPP repair increases (i.e., $\alpha$ increases) and as each GPP repair cost incurred by the failure of each part increases (i.e., $c_{GPP}^{(i)}$ increases), the mean time until replacement, $E[\min(S_{N^*}, T^*)]$, decreases; that is, the system should be replaced earlier. Moreover, it can be seen that as the replacement cost $c_r$ gets larger, the mean time until replacement, $E[\min(S_{N^*}, T^*)]$, increases.

To compare the cost rates of the two policies, $c(N^*, T^*)$ and $c_A({T_A}^*)$ (see our discussion at the end of Section 3), we introduce the following index:

$$\Delta(\%) = \frac{c_A(T_A^*) - c(N^*, T^*)}{c_A(T_A^*)} \times 100\,\%$$

which indicates the relative difference between the minimum cost rate of the two maintenance policies. A larger $\Delta\,(\%)$ means that the *proposed policy* has priority over the conventional age-based replacement policy from the cost-rate-minimization point of view. The optimal conventional maintenance policy ${T_A}^*$ and the corresponding cost rates $c_A({T_A}^*)$ under different combinations of $c_r$, $c_{GPP}^{(1)}$, $c_{GPP}^{(2)}$, and $\alpha$ are summarized in Table 3. From Tables 1–3, we can see that under all combinations $c_r$, $c_{GPP}^{(1)}$, $c_{GPP}^{(2)}$, and $\alpha$, the cost rate for the proposed policy is relatively smaller than that for the original one having the values of $\Delta\,(\%)$ in a range of (10%, 20%). This means that there exists a meaningful difference between the two maintenance policies in terms of the expected cost rate. Table 3 shows that the difference between the two minimum cost rates decreases as $\alpha$ increases.

**Table 1.** The optimal $(N^*, T^*)$ and $c(N^*, T^*)$ for different values of $\alpha$ and $c_{GPP}^{(i)}, i = 1, 2$ $(c_r = 80)$.

| | $c_{GPP}^{(1)}$ | $c_{GPP}^{(2)}$ | $N^*$ | $T^*$ | $E[\min(S_{N^*}, T^*)]$ | $c(N^*, T^*)$ |
|---|---|---|---|---|---|---|
| $\alpha = 0.1$ | 1 | 1 | 43 | 5.167063 | 4.839603 | 24.613510 |
| | | 5 | 25 | 3.570791 | 3.515909 | 40.370606 |
| | | 10 | 22 | 2.917147 | 2.907530 | 54.556764 |
| | 5 | 1 | 29 | 4.090193 | 3.966627 | 33.444139 |
| | | 5 | 23 | 3.245566 | 3.217194 | 46.421183 |
| | | 10 | 22 | 2.757668 | 2.753356 | 59.567110 |
| | 10 | 1 | 24 | 3.481198 | 3.429802 | 41.947039 |
| | | 5 | 22 | 2.963350 | 2.951428 | 53.259190 |
| | | 10 | 22 | 2.598863 | 2.597111 | 65.502361 |
| $\alpha = 0.5$ | 1 | 1 | 27 | 3.813358 | 2.381693 | 44.905501 |
| | | 5 | 12 | 2.643918 | 1.847879 | 66.290938 |
| | | 10 | 10 | 1.944151 | 1.622081 | 84.952145 |
| | 5 | 1 | 16 | 2.983852 | 2.046325 | 57.014955 |
| | | 5 | 12 | 2.148094 | 1.77202 | 74.384448 |
| | | 10 | 10 | 1.771289 | 1.556203 | 91.553627 |
| | 10 | 1 | 12 | 2.480472 | 1.832928 | 68.366798 |
| | | 5 | 10 | 1.998873 | 1.638653 | 83.243218 |
| | | 10 | 9 | 1.683485 | 1.475049 | 99.086616 |
| $\alpha = 1.0$ | 1 | 1 | 23 | 4.458552 | 1.694946 | 60.768793 |
| | | 5 | 10 | 3.085826 | 1.365100 | 85.423285 |
| | | 10 | 7 | 2.371505 | 1.204417 | 106.546497 |
| | 5 | 1 | 13 | 3.641256 | 1.473804 | 74.858730 |
| | | 5 | 8 | 2.904525 | 1.268782 | 94.502131 |
| | | 10 | 6 | 2.364720 | 1.134614 | 114.03389 |
| | 10 | 1 | 9 | 3.205668 | 1.320562 | 87.817809 |
| | | 5 | 7 | 2.499525 | 1.206568 | 104.632805 |
| | | 10 | 6 | 1.960038 | 1.120323 | 122.666147 |

**Table 2.** The optimal $(N^*, T^*)$ and $c(N^*, T^*)$ for different values of $\alpha$ and $c_{GPP}^{(i)}, i = 1, 2$ $(c_r = 100)$.

| | $c_{GPP}^{(1)}$ | $c_{GPP}^{(2)}$ | $N^*$ | $T^*$ | $E[\min(S_{N^*}, T^*)]$ | $c(N^*, T^*)$ |
|---|---|---|---|---|---|---|
| $\alpha = 0.1$ | 1 | 1 | 48 | 5.485968 | 5.062683 | 28.648590 |
| | | 5 | 27 | 3.817166 | 3.737695 | 45.883026 |
| | | 10 | 23 | 3.129246 | 3.111605 | 61.198240 |
| | 5 | 1 | 32 | 4.357206 | 4.196250 | 38.343312 |
| | | 5 | 24 | 3.481181 | 3.429788 | 52.433799 |
| | | 10 | 22 | 2.963349 | 2.951427 | 66.573986 |
| | 10 | 1 | 26 | 3.722206 | 3.649914 | 47.592342 |
| | | 5 | 23 | 3.178678 | 3.156975 | 59.803276 |
| | | 10 | 22 | 2.794272 | 2.789043 | 72.923917 |
| $\alpha = 0.5$ | 1 | 1 | 31 | 4.078488 | 2.464836 | 53.138310 |
| | | 5 | 14 | 2.779690 | 1.953065 | 76.74202 |
| | | 10 | 12 | 2.014106 | 1.730446 | 97.289067 |
| | 5 | 1 | 18 | 3.240933 | 2.127228 | 66.583640 |
| | | 5 | 12 | 2.480472 | 1.832928 | 85.458497 |
| | | 10 | 10 | 1.998873 | 1.638653 | 104.054023 |
| | 10 | 1 | 13 | 2.757591 | 1.905457 | 79.035012 |
| | | 5 | 12 | 2.069472 | 1.749067 | 95.393134 |
| | | 10 | 10 | 1.808951 | 1.572418 | 112.421272 |

**Table 2.** *Cont.*

| | $c_{GPP}^{(1)}$ | $c_{GPP}^{(2)}$ | $N^*$ | $T^*$ | $E[\min(S_{N^*},T^*)]$ | $c(N^*,T^*)$ |
|---|---|---|---|---|---|---|
| $\alpha = 1.0$ | 1 | 1 | 27 | 4.639853 | 1.754148 | 72.399750 |
| | | 5 | 11 | 3.501533 | 1.405433 | 99.841511 |
| | | 10 | 8 | 2.563363 | 1.266254 | 122.837466 |
| | 5 | 1 | 15 | 3.878627 | 1.530984 | 88.176667 |
| | | 5 | 9 | 3.205668 | 1.320562 | 109.772261 |
| | | 10 | 7 | 2.499525 | 1.206568 | 130.791007 |
| | 10 | 1 | 11 | 3.176349 | 1.405078 | 102.448963 |
| | | 5 | 8 | 2.704431 | 1.267669 | 120.746421 |
| | | 10 | 7 | 2.06428 | 1.193740 | 140.30300 |

**Table 3.** The optimal $T_A{}^*$, $c(T_A{}^*)$, and $\Delta(\%)$ for different values of $\alpha$ and $c_{GPP}^{(i)}, i = 1,2$ ($c_r = 80$ and $c_r = 100$).

| | $c_{GPP}^{(1)}$ | $c_{GPP}^{(2)}$ | $c_r$=80 | | | $c_r$=100 | | |
|---|---|---|---|---|---|---|---|---|
| | | | $T_A{}^*$ | $c(T_A{}^*)$ | $\Delta(\%)$ | $T_A{}^*$ | $c(T_A{}^*)$ | $\Delta(\%)$ |
| $\alpha = 0.1$ | 1 | 1 | 4.792556 | 24.73827 | 0.504320 | 5.022464 | 28.81093 | 0.563467 |
| | | 5 | 3.497507 | 40.41667 | 0.113973 | 3.712159 | 45.96080 | 0.169218 |
| | | 10 | 2.902790 | 54.56740 | 0.019491 | 3.102907 | 61.22304 | 0.040508 |
| | 5 | 1 | 3.936392 | 33.52346 | 0.236613 | 4.158405 | 38.46142 | 0.307082 |
| | | 5 | 3.206681 | 46.44719 | 0.055993 | 3.414981 | 52.48364 | 0.094965 |
| | | 10 | 2.750663 | 59.57278 | 0.009518 | 2.946040 | 66.58946 | 0.023238 |
| | 10 | 1 | 3.414981 | 41.98691 | 0.094961 | 3.627975 | 47.66229 | 0.146758 |
| | | 5 | 2.946040 | 53.27157 | 0.023239 | 3.147431 | 59.83133 | 0.046888 |
| | | 10 | 2.595846 | 65.50489 | 0.003861 | 2.785933 | 72.93223 | 0.011398 |
| $\alpha = 0.5$ | 1 | 1 | 2.280309 | 47.06474 | 4.587806 | 2.370803 | 55.65973 | 4.530062 |
| | | 5 | 1.75982 | 69.16807 | 4.159625 | 1.847788 | 80.2483 | 4.304914 |
| | | 10 | 1.510966 | 87.83091 | 3.277622 | 1.595671 | 100.6977 | 3.385016 |
| | 5 | 1 | 1.938804 | 59.70407 | 4.470884 | 2.028205 | 69.78078 | 4.568952 |
| | | 5 | 1.639218 | 77.22535 | 3.678717 | 1.725783 | 89.10439 | 4.09171 |
| | | 10 | 1.445795 | 94.25774 | 2.86885 | 1.529378 | 107.693 | 3.379028 |
| | 10 | 1 | 1.725783 | 71.28351 | 4.091706 | 1.813389 | 82.57799 | 4.290463 |
| | | 5 | 1.529378 | 86.15439 | 3.379018 | 1.614373 | 98.86931 | 3.51593 |
| | | 10 | 1.378737 | 101.7853 | 2.651349 | 1.460969 | 115.8614 | 2.969175 |
| $\alpha = 1.0$ | 1 | 1 | 1.550914 | 67.21102 | 9.585075 | 1.609079 | 79.86217 | 9.344124 |
| | | 5 | 1.215585 | 95.30571 | 10.36918 | 1.272421 | 111.3726 | 10.35361 |
| | | 10 | 1.05409 | 118.2154 | 9.870882 | 1.109187 | 136.6934 | 10.13651 |
| | 5 | 1 | 1.33114 | 83.43543 | 10.27925 | 1.388719 | 98.13309 | 10.14577 |
| | | 5 | 1.137439 | 105.2673 | 10.22651 | 1.193554 | 122.416 | 10.3285 |
| | | 10 | 1.011592 | 125.9852 | 9.486281 | 1.06608 | 145.2245 | 9.938745 |
| | 10 | 1 | 1.193554 | 97.93283 | 10.32853 | 1.250203 | 114.2905 | 10.36091 |
| | | 5 | 1.06608 | 116.1796 | 9.938746 | 1.121332 | 134.4538 | 10.19486 |
| | | 10 | 0.967724 | 135.0222 | 9.151127 | 1.021496 | 155.117 | 9.55021 |

The graphs for the optimal $N^*$ and $T^*$ with respect to the value of $\alpha$ are given in Figures 1 and 2. As $c_{GPP}^{(1)}$ or $c_{GPP}^{(2)}$ increases, the system should be replaced earlier and thus the corresponding curves are ordered. As $\alpha$ increases, the mean length of the renewal cycle $E[\min(S_{N^*}, T^*)]$ should be smaller and thus $N^*$ and $T^*$ initially decreases. However, when $\alpha$ is larger, the replacement should be made mainly based on the number of failures $N^*$ (this follows from the form of stochastic intensities in Definition 3) and the role of $T^*$ should be weaker. Due to this effect, $T^*$ is increasing when $\alpha$ is increasing.

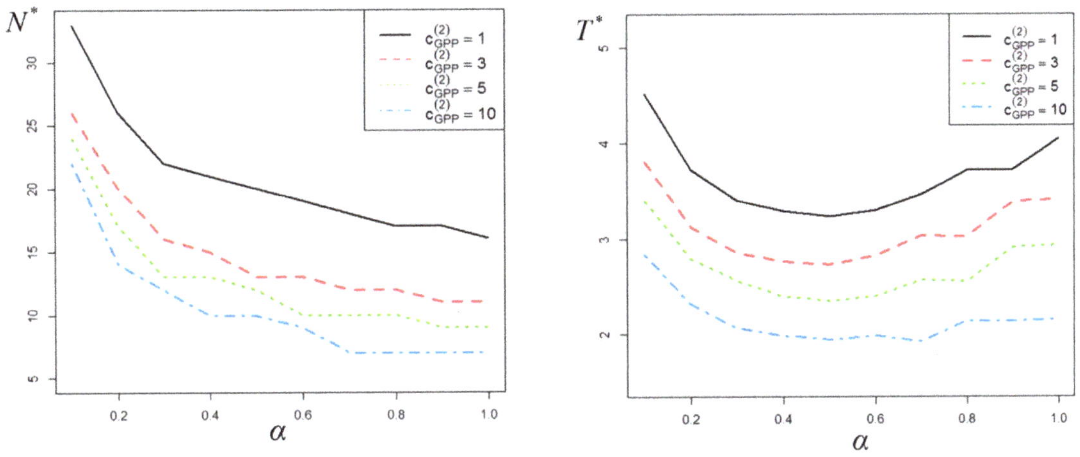


**Figure 1.** Optimal values $N^*$ and $T^*$ for different values of $\alpha$ and $c_{GPP}^{(2)}$ when $\beta = 1$, $c_r = 80$, $c_{GPP}^{(1)} = 3$ (fixed).

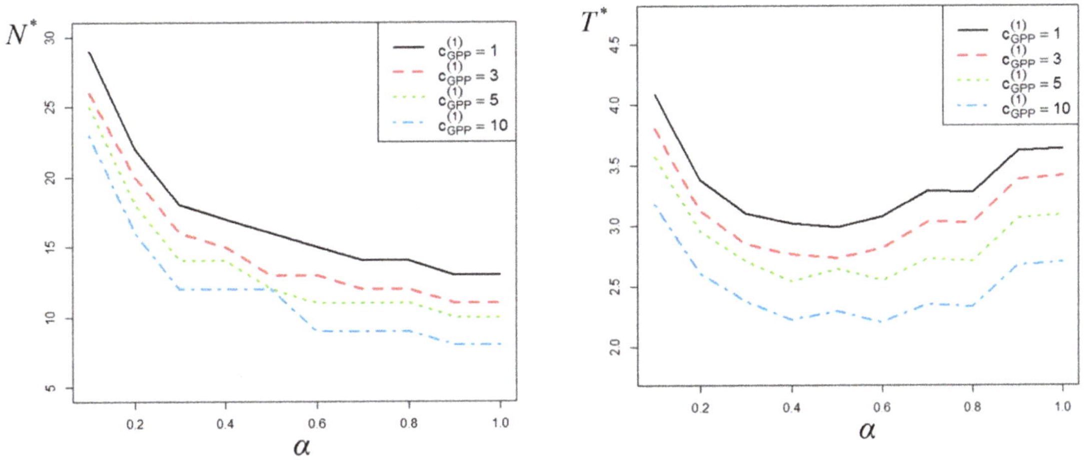


**Figure 2.** Optimal values $N^*$ and $T^*$ for different values of $\alpha$ and $c_{GPP}^{(1)}$ when $\beta = 1, c_r = 80, c_{GPP}^{(2)} = 3$ (fixed).

In Figure 3, the minimum expected cost rates of the two policies for different values of $\alpha$ are presented. The superiority of the proposed replacement policy is clearly seen.

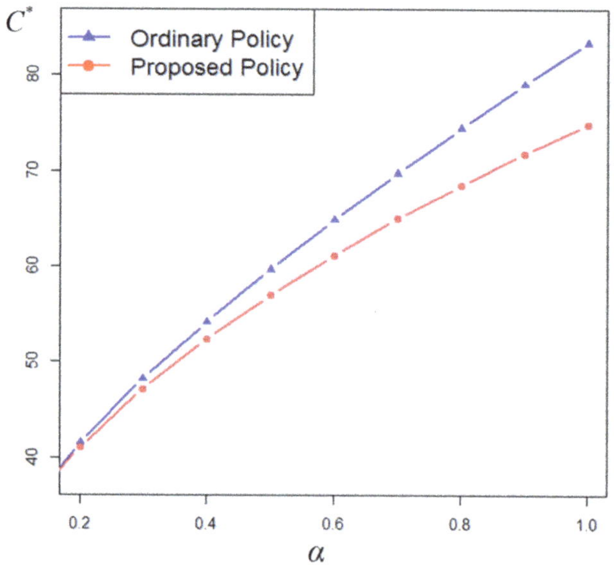


**Figure 3.** The minimum cost rates of the two policies for different values of $\alpha$ when $c_{GPP}^{(1)} = 1$, $c_{GPP}^{(2)} = 3$, and $c_r = 80$.

## 5. Concluding Remarks

In reliability modeling and analysis, the assumption of independence of components in a system is usually made for simplicity and convenience of stochastic description. However, most often, the failures in two or more parts in a system are statistically dependent. Furthermore, in practice, a failure of one part in a system often causes additional stress or damage to the remaining parts, which results in a worse condition of a system than it had just prior this failure. Even a minimal repair of the failed component results in a worse-than-minimal repair of a system in this case.

To model the described practical setting, we employ the bivariate generalized Polya process, which corresponds to the dependent worse-than-minimal repair process. Under these assumptions, a new bivariate preventive maintenance policy based on two parameters (age and operational history) has been proposed and discussed. The corresponding long-run average cost rate has been derived and the optimal replacement policies are investigated and illustrated numerically.

Our mathematical study has a clear practical application in the field of the PM modeling. Along with optimal maintenance, in the future research, the proposed concept of dependent worse-than-minimal repair processes could be used also for describing other reliability properties of repairable systems, such as stationary and non-stationary availability.

As far as we know, our study is the first to apply the dependent bivariate or multivariate counting processes to modeling the multivariate failure processes for stochastic description of repairable systems. Some new stochastic properties of these processes have been derived and the corresponding optimal bivariate preventive maintenance policy with two decision parameters (age and operational history) has been proposed. The latter is another novel feature of the study. Thus, development and application of the new mathematical models for modeling PM with the worse-than-minimal repair can be considered as the main contribution of the paper.

The developed approach and obtained results provide the tools for more adequate stochastic description of real systems with dependent components and worse-than-minimal repair. Neglecting these real-life properties can result in substantial discrepancies in reliability estimates and PM schedules of systems, along with higher costs of maintenance.

The implications of some assumptions in the study should be also addressed in future research. In the multivariate setting, it is also interesting to consider the case when some components undergo minimal repair, whereas others undergo worse-than-minimal repair.

**Author Contributions:** Investigation and Numerical Study, H.L.; Methodology, J.H.C.; Supervision, M.F. All authors have read and agreed to the published version of the manuscript.

**Funding:** The work of the first author was supported by Hankuk University of Foreign Studies Research Fund of 2022 and the National Research Foundation of Korea (NRF) grant funded by the Korea Government (Ministry of Science of ICT) (no. 2021R1F1A1048037). The work of the second author was also supported by Basic Science Research Program through the National Research Foundation of Korea (NRF) funded by the Ministry of Education (grant no. 2019R1A6A1A11051177).

**Institutional Review Board Statement:** Not applicable.

**Informed Consent Statement:** Not applicable.

**Data Availability Statement:** Not applicable.

**Acknowledgments:** The authors thank the reviewers for helpful comments and advice.

**Conflicts of Interest:** The authors declare no conflict of interest.

## References

1. Gertsbakh, I. *Reliability Theory with Applications to Preventive Maintenance*; Springer: Berlin/Heidelberg, Germany, 2005.
2. Nakagawa, T. *Maintenance Theory of Reliability*; Springer: London, UK, 2005.
3. Wang, H.; Pham, H. *Reliability and Optimal Maintenance*; Springer: London, UK, 2006.
4. Barlow, R.E.; Hunter, L. Optimum preventive maintenance policies. *Oper. Res.* **1960**, *8*, 90–100. [CrossRef]
5. Beichelt, F. A generalized block replacement policy. *IEEE Trans. Reliab.* **1981**, *30*, 171–172. [CrossRef]
6. Jhang, J.P.; Sheu, S.H. Opportunity-based age replacement policy with minimal repair. *Reliab. Eng. Syst. Saf.* **1999**, *64*, 339–344. [CrossRef]
7. Makabe, H.; Morimura, H. On some preventive maintenance policies. *J. Oper. Res. Soc. Jpn.* **1963**, *6*, 17–47.
8. Sheu, S.H.; Griffith, W.S.; Nakagawa, T. Extended optimal replacement model with random minimal repair cost. *Eur. J. Oper. Res.* **1995**, *85*, 636–649. [CrossRef]
9. El-Damcese, M.A. Suggested procedure for preventive maintenance policy. *Microelectron. Reliab.* **1997**, *37*, 1173–1177. [CrossRef]
10. Høyland, A.; Rausand, M. *System Reliability Theory: Models and Statistical Methods*; John Wiley & Sons: Hoboken, NJ, USA, 1994.
11. Jeong, J.S. Failure mechanism and reliability test method for USB interface circuitry on CPUs for mobile devices. *Microelectron. Reliab.* **2012**, *52*, 2014–2018. [CrossRef]
12. Lee, H.; Cha, J.H. New stochastic models for preventive maintenance and maintenance optimization. *Eur. J. Oper. Res.* **2016**, *255*, 80–90. [CrossRef]
13. Cha, J.H. Characterization of the generalized Polya process and its applications. *Adv. Appl. Probab.* **2014**, *46*, 1148–1171. [CrossRef]
14. Lee, H.; Cha, J.H. A bivariate optimal replacement policy for a system subject to a generalized failure and repair process. *Appl. Stoch. Models Bus. Ind.* **2019**, *35*, 637–650. [CrossRef]
15. Allen, F.; Gale, D. Financial contagion. *J. Political Econ.* **2000**, *108*, 1–34. [CrossRef]
16. Bowsher, C.G. Modelling security market events in continuous time: Intensity based, multivariate point process models. *J. Econ.* **2007**, *141*, 876–912. [CrossRef]
17. Cox, D.R.; Lewis, P.A.W. Multivariate point processes. In *Proceedings of the Berkeley Symposium on Mathematical Statistics and Probability*; University of California Press: Berkeley, CA, USA, 1972; Volume III, pp. 401–448.
18. Partrat, C. Compound model for two dependent kinds of claim. *Insur. Math. Econ.* **1994**, *15*, 219–231. [CrossRef]
19. Cha, J.H.; Badia, F.G. On a multivariate generalized Polya process without regularity property. *Probab. Eng. Inf. Sci.* **2020**, *34*, 484–506. [CrossRef]
20. Cha, J.H.; Giorgio, M. On a class of multivariate counting processes. *Adv. Appl. Probab.* **2016**, *48*, 443–462. [CrossRef]
21. Cha, J.H.; Giorgio, M. A new class of multivariate counting processes and its characterization. *Stoch. Int. J. Probab. Stoch. Process.* **2019**, *91*, 383–406. [CrossRef]
22. Aven, T.; Jensen, U. *Stochastic Models in Reliability*; Springer: New York, NY, USA, 1999.
23. Ross, S. *Stochastic Processes*; John Wiley & Sons: New York, NY, USA, 1996.

mathematics

MDPI

Article

# Statistical Analysis of the Lifetime Distribution with Bathtub-Shaped Hazard Function under Lagged-Effect Step-Stress Model

Zihui Zhang and Wenhao Gui *

Department of Mathematics, Beijing Jiaotong University, Beijing 100044, China; 19271285@bjtu.edu.cn
* Correspondence: whgui@bjtu.edu.cn

**Abstract:** In survival analysis, applying stress is often used to accelerate an experiment. Stress can be discontinuous, and the step-stress model is applied widely due to its flexibility. However, in reality, when new stress is applied, it often does not take effect immediately, but there will be a lagged effect. Under the lagged-effect step-stress model, the statistical inference of the Chen distribution is discussed. The Chen distribution is an important life distribution as its risk function is bathtub-shaped with certain parameters. In this paper, the maximum likelihood estimators are presented and the Newton–Raphson algorithm is used. According to the form of risk function under this model, the explicit expressions of least squares estimators are obtained. The calculation methods of asymptotic confidence intervals and coverage probabilities are proposed by using the observed Fisher matrix. Finally, to evaluate the performance of the above estimation methods, a Monte Carlo simulation study is provided.

**Keywords:** bathtub-shaped; lagged effect; step-stress; maximum likelihood estimators; least squares estimators; asymptotic confidence intervals; Monte Carlo simulation

**Citation:** Zhang, Z.; Gui, W. Statistical Analysis of the Lifetime Distribution with Bathtub-Shaped Hazard Function under Lagged-Effect Step-Stress Model. *Mathematics* **2022**, *10*, 674. https://doi.org/10.3390/math10050674

Academic Editors: Francisco German Badía and María D. Berrade

Received: 3 February 2022
Accepted: 19 February 2022
Published: 22 February 2022



## 1. Introduction

### 1.1. Chen Distribution

In survival analysis, hazard function plays an important role in studying the life phenomenon of a product. For many products, their failure rates decrease first, then keep at a constant level, and increase finally. Such failure rate is like a bathtub, and this life distribution is widely used in electronic, machinery, and medical fields. For example, some drugs do not work well for children and the elderly, but they work well for middle-aged people. In other words, the failure rate of drugs is relatively high in childhood but gradually decreases with age. Then, the failure rate remains low in middle age for some time and eventually increases with age. One of the life distributions with such hazard function is the Chen distribution, which was first proposed by ref.[1]. It is a two-parameter lifetime distribution with the bathtub-shaped or increasing hazard function and can model the real data well.

Ref. [1] proposed confidence intervals and joint confidence regions for the Chen distribution's parameters under Type-II censoring. Ref. [2] investigated a simple method to conduct the statistical test and obtain the exact confidence interval of the Chen distribution's shape parameter, which can also be applied to models under Type-II right censoring. Based on Type-II right-censored samples of the Chen distribution, ref. [3] later discussed several test statistics for an exact hypothesis test concerning the shape parameter. Ref. [4] obtained the point estimations and interval estimations for the parameters under a Type-II censored model. Ref. [5] proposed an extended maximum spacing method to estimate parameters of the Chen distribution. Under hybrid censoring, ref. [6] discussed the maximum likelihood estimations and several asymptotic confidence intervals. They also used the Lindley method, and the Tierney and Kadane method, to calculate Bayes estimates. Based on the Chen distribution, ref. [7] analyzed the stress–strength reliability under progressive Type-II censoring and generalized it to the proportional hazard family. Under progressively censored samples of the Chen distribution, ref. [8] discussed maximum likelihood estimates, different Bayes estimates, asymptotic confidence intervals, and prediction intervals. Based on data from the Chen distribution, ref. [9] developed simplified forms of the single moments and covariances. The estimates of the shape parameters as well as the prediction of the records are also proposed.

A Chen (Chen($\beta$,$\lambda$)) random variable $T$ with two positive parameters $\beta$ ($\geq$0) and $\lambda$ ($\geq$0) has the following probability density function (pdf):

$$f(t;\beta,\lambda) = \lambda\beta t^{\beta-1}e^{t^{\beta}}\exp\left\{\lambda\left(1-e^{t^{\beta}}\right)\right\}, \quad t>0. \tag{1}$$

The cumulative distribution function and the survival function are, respectively, given by:

$$F(t;\beta,\lambda) = 1-\exp\left\{\lambda\left(1-e^{t^{\beta}}\right)\right\}, \quad t>0. \tag{2}$$

$$S(t;\beta,\lambda) = 1-F(t;\beta,\lambda) = \exp\left\{\lambda\left(1-e^{t^{\beta}}\right)\right\}, \quad t>0. \tag{3}$$

Accordingly, the hazard function is:

$$h(t;\beta,\lambda) = \frac{f(t;\beta,\lambda)}{S(t;\beta,\lambda)} = \lambda\beta t^{\beta-1}e^{t^{\beta}}, \quad t>0. \tag{4}$$

The shape of the pdf varies with the parameters and the characteristics are summarized as follows: (1) If $0<\beta<1$: the pdf will decrease throughout or decrease first and then increase when $0<\lambda<1$; the pdf will decrease throughout when $\lambda\geq 1$. (2) If $\beta=1$: the pdf will be unimodal when $0<\lambda<1$; the pdf will decrease throughout when $\lambda\geq 1$. (3) If $\beta>1$: the pdf will always be unimodal no matter which value $\lambda$ takes. Different plots of pdf are shown in Figures 1–4, respectively.

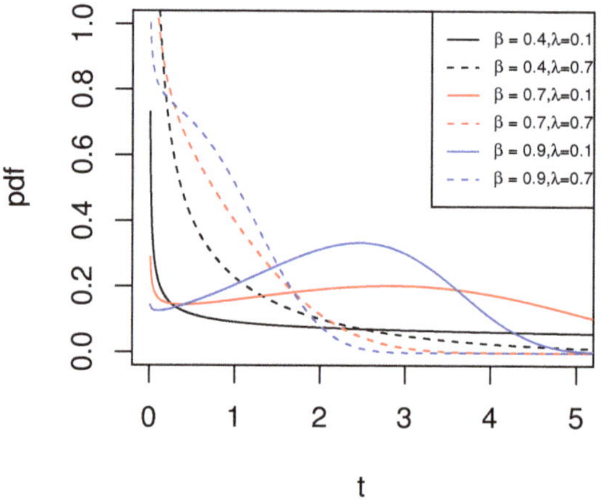


**Figure 1.** pdf of Chen($t;\beta,\lambda$), $0<\beta<1$.

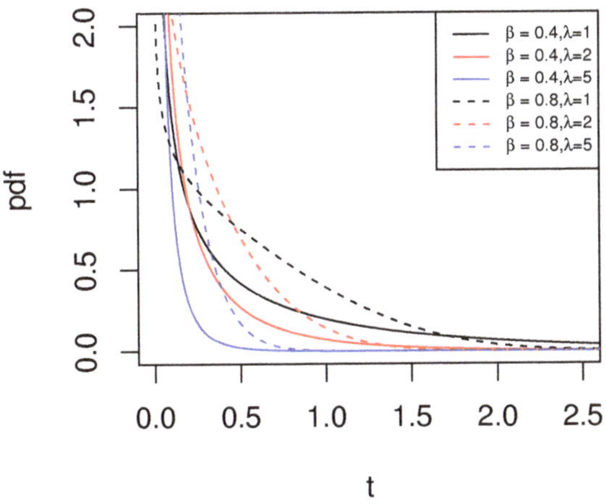


**Figure 2.** pdf of $\mathrm{Chen}(t;\beta,\lambda), 0<\beta<1$.

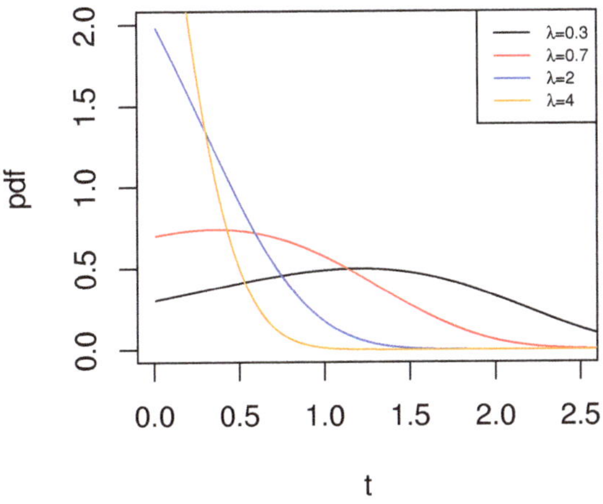


**Figure 3.** pdf of $\mathrm{Chen}(t;\beta,\lambda)$, $\beta=1$.

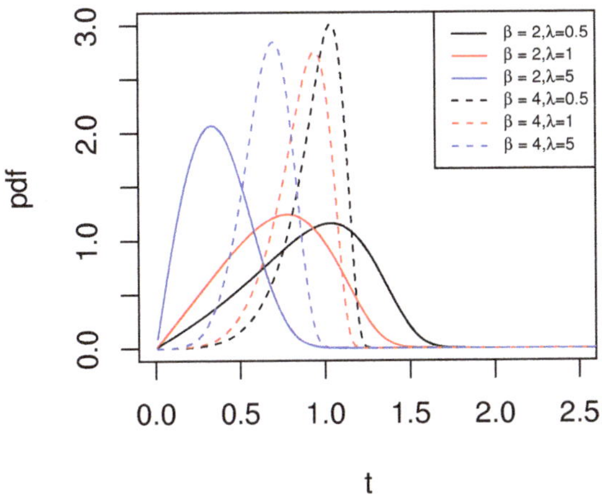


**Figure 4.** pdf of $\mathrm{Chen}(t;\beta,\lambda)$, $\beta>1$.

Take the derivative of $h(t;\beta,\lambda)$ with respect to $t$, then $h'(t;\beta,\lambda) = \lambda\beta t^{\beta-2}e^{t^\beta}[(\beta-1) + \beta t^\beta]$. Thus, the hazard function shows different shapes when $\beta$ differs and the properties are as follows: (1) The hazard function is bathtub-shaped when $0 < \beta < 1$. (2) The hazard function increases throughout when $\beta \geq 1$. The corresponding plots are shown in Figures 5 and 6, respectively.

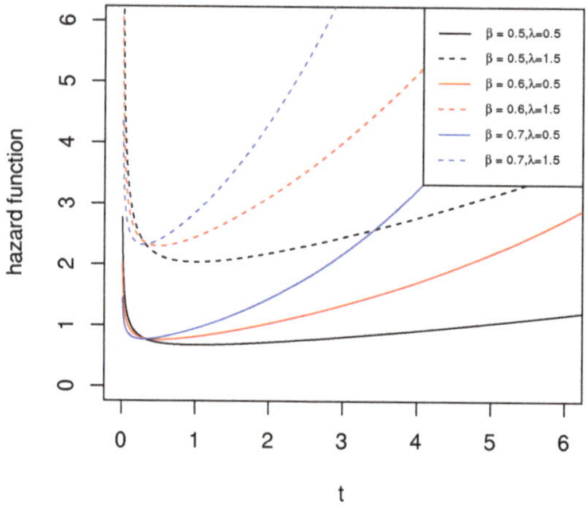


**Figure 5.** $h(t;\beta,\lambda)$, $0 < \beta < 1$.

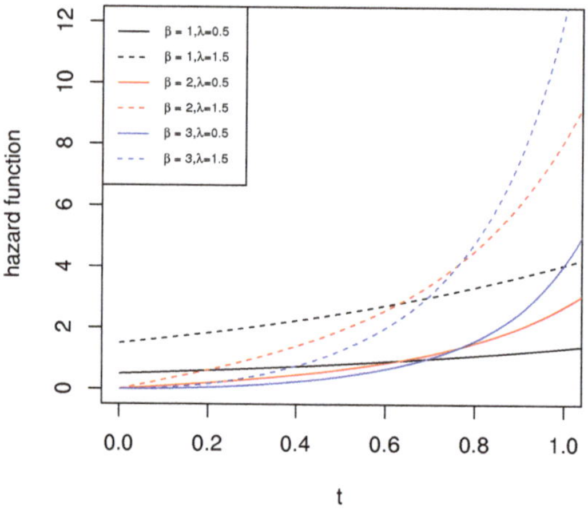


**Figure 6.** $h(t;\beta,\lambda)$, $\beta \geq 1$.

*1.2. Step-Stress Model with Lagged Effect*

Nowadays, due to the development of science and technology, the life of a product is getting longer and longer, and waiting for the product to fail will cause a great waste of time and manpower. Therefore, some measures need to be taken to accelerate product failure. Applying stress is a common means to accelerate the experiment in life test and reliability analysis, which can reduce time waste and other related costs. Stress can be voltage, temperature, oxygen, etc. There are three common stress-application schemes: constant-stress model, step-stress model, and progressive-stress model. Under the constant-stress model, the stress remains unchanged until the products fail. The increase in stress in the progressive-stress model is linear and continuous. In the step-stress model, the stress can be changed, but it does not have to be changed continuously, and sudden change is allowed. In this paper, a simple step-stress model is considered: at first, the initial stress level lasts for some time, and then at a given time, the stress level increases and remains unchanged until all products fail.

The cumulative exposure model (CEM) is a commonly used step-stress model, which assumes that the remaining life of the product is only associated with the cumulative exposure experienced previously and current stress. Ref. [10] first proposed the concept of the cumulative exposure model. Ref. [11] used the CEM to analyze step-stress data of the Weibull distribution and presented the maximum likelihood estimation and interval estimation under this method. Ref. [12] then presented the optimum scheme of the model, including the optimum duration of the first stress, the optimum proportion failing, and the asymptotic variance. Ref. [13] took into account the multiplier effect of stress, calculating the maximum likelihood estimation of the Weibull family of functions and the Fisher information matrix. Under CEM, ref. [14] discussed the maximum likelihood estimation and interval estimations of the exponential distribution with Type-I hybrid censoring. Ref. [15] later considered the Type-II censoring and independent competing risks in the model. Ref. [16] proposed the optimal life tests of the Weibull distribution using the Bayesian method under the model and used two algorithms to optimize it. Under CEM, Ref. [17] discussed the maximum likelihood estimation of the Weibull distribution with Type-I progressive hybrid censoring. Based on Type-II progressive hybrid censoring, Ref. [18] discussed statistical inference and optimal design on a step-stress partially accelerated life test for a hybrid system in the presence of masked data.

Although the CEM is widely used, ref. [19] pointed out that the hazard function is discontinuous when the stress level changes. That is, the impact of stress change is instantaneous. In reality, when the stress level changes, it often does not take effect immediately, but there exists a lag period. The CEM is unreasonable and inappropriate in this case. To solve this problem, the cumulative risk model (CRM) is proposed, which takes into account the lagged effect. In this model, the risk function is continuous, and it is supposed that the lagged effect causes a linear risk function in the intermediate period, which is more consistent with reality. Ref. [19] first proposed the concept of the cumulative risk model, and discussed the maximum likelihood estimation and least squares estimation of the model under exponential distribution. Ref. [20] combined the CRM with the degradation test model for data analysis. Ref. [21] took into account competing risks under the exponential distribution. In addition to calculating the maximum likelihood estimation, it also used three methods to calculate the confidence interval and coverage probabilities. Ref. [22] later extended this model to the Weibull distribution, and took the competing risks into account. Under masked data, ref. [23] also introduced competing risks based on the CRM. Ref. [24] applied the CRM to fuzzy lifetime data. Ref. [25] calculated the maximum likelihood estimation, the least square estimation, and Bayesian estimation under a Weibull cumulative risk model.

Many studies on the step-stress model consider the CEM, but the CRM is more in line with reality. In addition, most of the existing research on the CRM only involves the exponential distribution or Weibull distribution. From the point of view of the hazard function, although the Weibull distribution is widely used in survival and reliability analysis, its hazard function can only be monotonic or constant. Compared with the Weibull distribution, the Chen distribution has a hazard function that can not only be monotonous but also show the shape of the bathtub, which is important in practical fields. Statistical analysis based on the Chen distribution can make applications of the CRM deeper and wider. In this article, the Chen distribution and step-stress with lagged effect model are both considered, which is of great significance in theory and practice.

It is assumed that lifetime under the initial stress level obeys the Chen distribution. The stress level changes at $\tau_1$, which starts to take effect at $\tau_2$ due to the lagged effect, and the parameters of the Chen distribution change at $\tau_2$ as well. From $\tau_1$ to $\tau_2$, the hazard functions under these two stress levels are connected by a linear function.

The rest of the paper is arranged as follows. Some basic calculations and derivations of the model are shown in Section 2. In Section 3, the maximum likelihood estimation and least square estimation under the CRM are given. In Section 4, the asymptotic confidence intervals and coverage probabilities are discussed by using the large sample theory. To evaluate the performance of the estimators, the simulation results are presented in Section 5. Section 6 considers a special case where only one parameter changes when stress level changes. Section 7 is the summary of the article.

## 2. Model Description

Assume that the lifetime under the initial stress obeys Chen$(\beta_1, \lambda_1)$. The new stress is applied at $\tau_1$, and it starts to take effect at $\tau_2$ ($\tau_1$ and $\tau_2$ are known). The lifetime under the new stress obeys Chen$(\beta_2, \lambda_2)$. From $\tau_1$ to $\tau_2$, the hazard function is linear and denoted as $a + bt$ (here, $a$ and $b$ are parameters).

The Chen hazard functions under the initial stress level and the second level are:

$$h_1(t) = \lambda_1 \beta_1 t^{\beta_1 - 1} e^{t^{\beta_1}}, \quad t > 0, \tag{5}$$

$$h_2(t) = \lambda_2 \beta_2 t^{\beta_2 - 1} e^{t^{\beta_2}}, \quad t > 0. \tag{6}$$

Under the CRM, the hazard function is given by:

$$h(t) = \begin{cases} \lambda_1 \beta_1 t^{\beta_1 - 1} e^{t^{\beta_1}}, & 0 < t < \tau_1 \\ a + bt, & \tau_1 \le t < \tau_2 . \\ \lambda_2 \beta_2 t^{\beta_2 - 1} e^{t^{\beta_2}}, & t \ge \tau_2 \end{cases} \tag{7}$$

Note that when $\tau_1 = \tau_2$, the hazard function $h_0(t)$ can be written as follows, which is the hazard function of the CEM as well:

$$h_0(t) = \begin{cases} \lambda_1 \beta_1 t^{\beta_1 - 1} e^{t^{\beta_1}}, & 0 < t < \tau_1 \\ \lambda_2 \beta_2 t^{\beta_2 - 1} e^{t^{\beta_2}}, & t \ge \tau_1 \end{cases} \tag{8}$$

In the CRM, we assume that $\tau_1 \neq \tau_2$.

To make sure that the hazard function is continuous at $\tau_1$ and $\tau_2$, the following equations must be satisfied:

$$\begin{cases} \lambda_1 \beta_1 {\tau_1}^{\beta_1 - 1} e^{\tau_1^{\beta_1}} = a + b\tau_1 \\ \lambda_2 \beta_2 {\tau_2}^{\beta_2 - 1} e^{\tau_2^{\beta_2}} = a + b\tau_2 \end{cases} \tag{9}$$

According to (9), $\lambda_1$ and $\lambda_2$ can be solved as:

$$\begin{cases} \lambda_1 = \dfrac{(a + b\tau_1) e^{-\tau_1^{\beta_1}}}{\beta_1 {\tau_1}^{\beta_1 - 1}} \\ \lambda_2 = \dfrac{(a + b\tau_2) e^{-\tau_2^{\beta_2}}}{\beta_2 {\tau_2}^{\beta_2 - 1}} \end{cases}. \tag{10}$$

The cumulative hazard function $H(t)$ under the model can be obtained by using the formula $H(t) = \int_0^t h(x)dx$ and replacing the parameters $\lambda_1$ and $\lambda_2$ according to (10).

$$H(t) = \begin{cases} \frac{(a+b\tau_1)e^{-\tau_1^{\beta_1}}}{\beta_1\tau_1{}^{\beta_1-1}}(e^{t^{\beta_1}}-1), & 0 < t < \tau_1 \\ \frac{(a+b\tau_1)e^{-\tau_1^{\beta_1}}}{\beta_1\tau_1{}^{\beta_1-1}}(e^{\tau_1^{\beta_1}}-1) + a(t-\tau_1) + \frac{b}{2}(t^2-\tau_1^2), & \tau_1 \le t < \tau_2 \\ \frac{(a+b\tau_1)e^{-\tau_1^{\beta_1}}}{\beta_1\tau_1{}^{\beta_1-1}}(e^{\tau_1^{\beta_1}}-1) + a(\tau_2-\tau_1) + \frac{b}{2}(\tau_2^2-\tau_1^2) & \\ +\frac{(a+b\tau_2)e^{-\tau_2^{\beta_2}}}{\beta_2\tau_2{}^{\beta_2-1}}(e^{t^{\beta_2}}-e^{\tau_2^{\beta_2}}), & t \ge \tau_2 \end{cases} \quad (11)$$

The survival function $S(t)$ under the model can be given as follows by the formula $S(t) = e^{-H(t)}$:

$$S(t) = \begin{cases} \exp\left\{-\frac{(a+b\tau_1)e^{-\tau_1^{\beta_1}}}{\beta_1\tau_1{}^{\beta_1-1}}(e^{t^{\beta_1}}-1)\right\}, & 0 < t < \tau_1 \\ \exp\left\{-\frac{(a+b\tau_1)e^{-\tau_1^{\beta_1}}}{\beta_1\tau_1{}^{\beta_1-1}}(e^{\tau_1^{\beta_1}}-1) - a(t-\tau_1) - \frac{b}{2}(t^2-\tau_1^2)\right\}, & \tau_1 \le t < \tau_2 \\ \exp\left\{-\frac{(a+b\tau_1)e^{-\tau_1^{\beta_1}}}{\beta_1\tau_1{}^{\beta_1-1}}(e^{\tau_1^{\beta_1}}-1) - a(\tau_2-\tau_1) - \frac{b}{2}(\tau_2^2-\tau_1^2)\right\} & \\ \times\exp\left\{-\frac{(a+b\tau_2)e^{-\tau_2^{\beta_2}}}{\beta_2\tau_2{}^{\beta_2-1}}(e^{t^{\beta_2}}-e^{\tau_2^{\beta_2}})\right\}, & t \ge \tau_2 \end{cases} \quad (12)$$

According to the formula $f(t) = h(t)S(t)$, the probability density function $f(t)$ of the lifetime under the CRM is as follows:

$$f(t) = \begin{cases} \frac{(a+b\tau_1)e^{-\tau_1^{\beta_1}}}{\tau_1{}^{\beta_1-1}}t^{\beta_1-1}e^{t^{\beta_1}}\exp\left\{-\frac{(a+b\tau_1)e^{-\tau_1^{\beta_1}}}{\beta_1\tau_1{}^{\beta_1-1}}(e^{t^{\beta_1}}-1)\right\}, & 0 < t < \tau_1 \\ (a+bt)\exp\left\{-\frac{(a+b\tau_1)e^{-\tau_1^{\beta_1}}}{\beta_1\tau_1{}^{\beta_1-1}}(e^{\tau_1^{\beta_1}}-1) - a(t-\tau_1) - \frac{b}{2}(t^2-\tau_1^2)\right\}, & \tau_1 \le t < \tau_2 \\ \frac{(a+b\tau_2)e^{-\tau_2^{\beta_2}}}{\tau_2{}^{\beta_2-1}}t^{\beta_2-1}e^{t^{\beta_2}}\exp\left\{-\frac{(a+b\tau_1)e^{-\tau_1^{\beta_1}}}{\beta_1\tau_1{}^{\beta_1-1}}(e^{\tau_1^{\beta_1}}-1) - a(\tau_2-\tau_1) - \frac{b}{2}(\tau_2^2-\tau_1^2)\right\} & \\ \times\exp\left\{-\frac{(a+b\tau_2)e^{-\tau_2^{\beta_2}}}{\beta_2\tau_2{}^{\beta_2-1}}(e^{t^{\beta_2}}-e^{\tau_2^{\beta_2}})\right\}, & t \ge \tau_2 \end{cases} \quad (13)$$

Thus, the corresponding cumulative distribution function $F(t)$ under the CRM is obtained by:

$$F(t) = \begin{cases} 1 - \exp\left\{ -\frac{(a+b\tau_1)e^{-\tau_1^{\beta_1}}}{\beta_1 \tau_1{}^{\beta_1 - 1}} (e^{t^{\beta_1}} - 1) \right\}, & 0 < t < \tau_1 \\ 1 - \exp\left\{ -\frac{(a+b\tau_1)e^{-\tau_1^{\beta_1}}}{\beta_1 \tau_1{}^{\beta_1 - 1}} (e^{\tau_1^{\beta_1}} - 1) - a(t - \tau_1) - \frac{b}{2}(t^2 - \tau_1^2) \right\}, & \tau_1 \le t < \tau_2 \\ 1 - \exp\left\{ -\frac{(a+b\tau_1)e^{-\tau_1^{\beta_1}}}{\beta_1 \tau_1{}^{\beta_1 - 1}} (e^{\tau_1^{\beta_1}} - 1) - a(\tau_2 - \tau_1) - \frac{b}{2}(\tau_2^2 - \tau_1^2) \right\} \\ \quad \times \exp\left\{ -\frac{(a+b\tau_2)e^{-\tau_2^{\beta_2}}}{\beta_2 \tau_2{}^{\beta_2 - 1}} (e^{t^{\beta_2}} - e^{\tau_2^{\beta_2}}) \right\}, & t \ge \tau_2 \end{cases} . \tag{14}$$

Based on the above analysis, the estimations of the parameters can be given in the following section.

## 3. Point Estimation

### *3.1. Maximum Likelihood Estimation*

Assume that $t_1, t_2, \cdots, t_n$ are the failure times under the model. Among them, $n_1$ products fail during the first stress application (before $\tau_1$), $n_2$ products fail in the lag period (from $\tau_1$ to $\tau_2$), $n_3$ products fail during the second stress application (after $\tau_2$), and $n_1 + n_2 + n_3 = n$.

The maximum likelihood estimation method (MLE) is a classical point estimation method and is widely used in estimating parameters. According to the theory of maximum likelihood estimation, the likelihood function can be written as follows. Denote it as $L(\beta_1, \beta_2, a, b)$.

$$L(\beta_1, \beta_2, a, b) = \prod_{i=1}^{n} f(t_i) \tag{15}$$

Plug (13) into (15), and the likelihood function can be expressed as:

$$\begin{aligned} L(\beta_1, \beta_2, a, b) = & \prod_{i=1}^{n_1} \left[ \frac{(a + b\tau_1)e^{-\tau_1^{\beta_1}}}{\tau_1{}^{\beta_1 - 1}} t_i{}^{\beta_1 - 1} e^{t_i^{\beta_1}} \exp\left\{ -\frac{(a + b\tau_1)e^{-\tau_1^{\beta_1}}}{\beta_1 \tau_1{}^{\beta_1 - 1}} (e^{t_i^{\beta_1}} - 1) \right\} \right] \\ & \times \prod_{i=n_1+1}^{n_1+n_2} \left[ (a + bt_i) \exp\left\{ -\frac{(a + b\tau_1)e^{-\tau_1^{\beta_1}}}{\beta_1 \tau_1{}^{\beta_1 - 1}} (e^{\tau_1^{\beta_1}} - 1) - a(t_i - \tau_1) - \frac{b}{2}(t_i^2 - \tau_1^2) \right\} \right] \\ & \times \prod_{i=n_1+n_2+1}^{n} \left[ \frac{(a + b\tau_2)e^{-\tau_2^{\beta_2}}}{\tau_2{}^{\beta_2 - 1}} t_i{}^{\beta_2 - 1} e^{t^{\beta_2}} \exp\left\{ -a(\tau_2 - \tau_1) - \frac{b}{2}(\tau_2^2 - \tau_1^2) \right\} \right. \\ & \left. \times \exp\left\{ -\frac{(a + b\tau_1)e^{-\tau_1^{\beta_1}}}{\beta_1 \tau_1{}^{\beta_1 - 1}} (e^{\tau_1^{\beta_1}} - 1) - \frac{(a + b\tau_2)e^{-\tau_2^{\beta_2}}}{\beta_2 \tau_2{}^{\beta_2 - 1}} (e^{t_i^{\beta_2}} - e^{\tau_2^{\beta_2}}) \right\} \right]. \end{aligned} \tag{16}$$

Based on the form of $L(\beta_1, \beta_2, a, b)$, it can be seen that when $n_2 = 0, n_1 = 0$ or $n_2 = 0, n_3 = 0$, the maximum likelihood estimates (MLEs) do not exist. In the following, it is assumed that $n_i > 0$.

The log-likelihood function $l(\beta_1, \beta_2, a, b)$ is given by:

$$
\begin{aligned}
l(\beta_1,\beta_2,a,b) =& \ln L(\beta_1,\beta_2,a,b) \\
=& n_1\left[\ln(a+b\tau_1)-{\tau_1}^{\beta_1}\right]+(\beta_1-1)\sum_{i=1}^{n_1}\ln(\frac{t_i}{\tau_1})+\sum_{i=1}^{n_1}{t_i}^{\beta_1}-\frac{(a+b\tau_1)e^{-\tau_1^{\beta_1}}}{\beta_1{\tau_1}^{\beta_1-1}}\sum_{i=1}^{n_1}(e^{t_i^{\beta_1}}-1) \\
&+\sum_{i=n_1+1}^{n_1+n_2}\ln(a+bt_i)-(n_2+n_3)\frac{(a+b\tau_1)e^{-\tau_1^{\beta_1}}}{\beta_1{\tau_1}^{\beta_1-1}}(e^{{\tau_1}^{\beta_1}}-1)-a\sum_{i=n_1+1}^{n_1+n_2}(t_i-\tau_1) \\
&-\frac{b}{2}\sum_{i=n_1+1}^{n_1+n_2}(t_i^2-\tau_1^2)+n_3\left[\ln(a+b\tau_2)-{\tau_2}^{\beta_2}\right]+(\beta_2-1)\sum_{i=n_1+n_2+1}^{n}\ln(\frac{t_i}{\tau_1})+\sum_{i=n_1+n_2+1}^{n}{t_i}^{\beta_2} \\
&-a(\tau_2-\tau_1)n_3-\frac{b}{2}(\tau_2^2-\tau_1^2)n_3-\frac{(a+b\tau_2)e^{-\tau_2^{\beta_2}}}{\beta_2{\tau_2}^{\beta_2-1}}\sum_{i=n_1+n_2+1}^{n}(e^{t_i^{\beta_2}}-e^{\tau_2^{\beta_2}}).
\end{aligned}
\tag{17}
$$

In order to maximize the $l(\beta_1,\beta_2,a,b)$, take partial derivatives in (17) with respect to $\beta_1$, $\beta_2$, $a$, and $b$. The results are as follows:

$$
\begin{aligned}
\frac{\partial l(\beta_1,\beta_2,a,b)}{\partial\beta_1} =& -\frac{(a+b\tau_1)e^{-\tau_1^{\beta_1}}}{\beta_1{\tau_1}^{\beta_1-1}}\Bigg\{-(\frac{1}{\beta_1}+\ln\tau_1+\tau_1^{\beta_1}\ln\tau_1)\Big[\sum_{i=1}^{n_1}(e^{t_i^{\beta_1}}-1)+(n_2+n_3)(e^{{\tau_1}^{\beta_1}}-1)\Big] \\
&+(n_2+n_3)(e^{{\tau_1}^{\beta_1}}{\tau_1}^{\beta_1}\ln\tau_1)+\sum_{i=1}^{n_1}e^{t_i^{\beta_1}}t_i^{\beta_1}\ln t_i\Bigg\}-n_1\tau_1^{\beta_1}\ln\tau_1+\sum_{i=1}^{n_1}\ln(\frac{t_i}{\tau_1}) \\
&+\sum_{i=1}^{n_1}{t_i}^{\beta_1}\ln t_i,
\end{aligned}
\tag{18}
$$

$$
\begin{aligned}
\frac{\partial l(\beta_1,\beta_2,a,b)}{\partial\beta_2} =& -\frac{(a+b\tau_2)e^{-\tau_2^{\beta_2}}}{\beta_2{\tau_2}^{\beta_2-1}}\Bigg\{-(\frac{1}{\beta_2}+\ln\tau_2+\tau_2^{\beta_2}\ln\tau_2)\Big[\sum_{i=n_1+n_2+1}^{n}(e^{t_i^{\beta_2}}-e^{\tau_2^{\beta_2}})\Big] \\
&+\sum_{i=n_1+n_2+1}^{n}(e^{t_i^{\beta_2}}t_i^{\beta_2}\ln t_i-e^{\tau_2^{\beta_2}}\tau_2^{\beta_2}\ln\tau_2)\Bigg\}-n_3\tau_2^{\beta_2}\ln\tau_2+\sum_{i=n_1+n_2+1}^{n}\ln(\frac{t_i}{\tau_1}) \\
&+\sum_{i=n_1+n_2+1}^{n}{t_i}^{\beta_2}\ln t_i,
\end{aligned}
\tag{19}
$$

$$
\begin{aligned}
\frac{\partial l(\beta_1,\beta_2,a,b)}{\partial a} =& \frac{n_1}{a+b\tau_1}-\frac{e^{-\tau_1^{\beta_1}}}{\beta_1{\tau_1}^{\beta_1-1}}\Big[\sum_{i=1}^{n_1}(e^{t_i^{\beta_1}}-1)+(n_2+n_3)(e^{{\tau_1}^{\beta_1}}-1)\Big]+\sum_{i=n_1+1}^{n_1+n_2}\frac{1}{a+bt_i} \\
&-\sum_{i=n_1+1}^{n_1+n_2}(t_i-t_1)+\frac{n_3}{a+b\tau_2}-(\tau_2-\tau_1)n_3-\frac{e^{-\tau_2^{\beta_2}}}{\beta_2{\tau_2}^{\beta_2-1}}\sum_{i=n_1+n_2+1}^{n}(e^{t_i^{\beta_2}}-e^{\tau_2^{\beta_2}}),
\end{aligned}
\tag{20}
$$

$$
\begin{aligned}
\frac{\partial l(\beta_1,\beta_2,a,b)}{\partial b} =& \frac{n_1\tau_1}{a+b\tau_1}-\frac{e^{-\tau_1^{\beta_1}}}{\beta_1{\tau_1}^{\beta_1-2}}\Big[\sum_{i=1}^{n_1}(e^{t_i^{\beta_1}}-1)+(n_2+n_3)(e^{{\tau_1}^{\beta_1}}-1)\Big]+\sum_{i=n_1+1}^{n_1+n_2}\frac{t_i}{a+bt_i} \\
&-\frac{1}{2}\sum_{i=n_1+1}^{n_1+n_2}(t_i^2-t_1^2)+\frac{n_3\tau_2}{a+b\tau_2}-\frac{1}{2}(\tau_2^2-\tau_1^2)n_3-\frac{e^{-\tau_2^{\beta_2}}}{\beta_2{\tau_2}^{\beta_2-2}}\sum_{i=n_1+n_2+1}^{n}(e^{t_i^{\beta_2}}-e^{\tau_2^{\beta_2}}).
\end{aligned}
\tag{21}
$$

By making the above functions equal to 0 simultaneously, the maximum likelihood estimates of $\beta_1$, $\beta_2$, $a$, and $b$ can be solved. However, explicit solutions cannot be given because the forms of the equations are complex and nonlinear. Therefore, some numerical techniques, such as the Newton–Raphson algorithm, can be used to calculate approximate estimates of parameters. This can be realized by using the *optim* function in R software.

### 3.2. Least Squares Estimation

Observing the form of cumulative hazard function (11), we notice that it is a linear function of $a$ and $b$ when assuming other parameters are known. As a result, least squares estimation (LSE) can be used to estimate $a$ and $b$.

For a dataset size of $n$, if we estimate the probability of the $i$-th failure time by its relative frequency, using the non-parametric estimation, the fitted cumulative density function $\hat{F}(t_i)$ can be obtained by:

$$\hat{F}(t_i) = \hat{P}(t \leq t_i) = \frac{i-1}{n}. \tag{22}$$

According to the formula $H(t) = -\ln(1 - F(t))$, the fitted cumulative hazard function $\hat{H}(t_i)$ is:

$$\hat{H}(t_i) = \ln(\frac{n}{n-i+1}). \tag{23}$$

Based on the above analysis, when the parameters $\beta_1$ and $\beta_2$ are known, the least squares estimates of $a, b$ can be obtained by minimizing the least squares distance between $H(t)$ and $\hat{H}(t)$. Denote the least squares distance function as $Q(a,b)$, and it is given by:

$$\begin{aligned} Q(a,b) &= \sum_{i=1}^{n}(H(t_i) - \hat{H}(t_i)) \\ &= \sum_{i=1}^{n_1}[(k_1a + k_2b)(e^{t_i^{\beta_1}} - 1) - \ln(\frac{n}{n-i+1})]^2 \\ &+ \sum_{i=n_1+1}^{n_1+n_2}[(k_1a + k_2b)(e^{\tau_1^{\beta_1}} - 1) + a(t_i - \tau_1) + \frac{b}{2}(t_i^2 - \tau_1^2) - \ln(\frac{n}{n-i+1})]^2 \\ &+ \sum_{i=n_1+n_2+1}^{n}[(k_1a + k_2b)(e^{\tau_1^{\beta_1}} - 1) + a(\tau_2 - \tau_1) + \frac{b}{2}(\tau_2^2 - \tau_1^2) + (k_3a + k_4b)(e^{t^{\beta_2}} - e^{\tau_2^{\beta_2}}) \\ &\quad - \ln(\frac{n}{n-i+1})]^2 \end{aligned} \tag{24}$$

where:

$$k_1 = \frac{1}{e^{\tau_1^{\beta_1}}\beta_1\tau_1^{\beta_1-1}},\ k_2 = \frac{1}{e^{\tau_1^{\beta_1}}\beta_1\tau_1^{\beta_1-2}},\ k_3 = \frac{1}{e^{\tau_2^{\beta_2}}\beta_2\tau_2^{\beta_2-1}},\ k_4 = \frac{1}{e^{\tau_2^{\beta_2}}\beta_2\tau_2^{\beta_2-2}}. \tag{25}$$

For the given $\beta_1$ and $\beta_2$, the analytic expression of least square estimates $\hat{a}(\beta_1, \beta_2)$ and $\hat{b}(\beta_1, \beta_2)$ can be obtained by taking the derivative of $Q(a,b)$. The results are as follows:

$$\begin{aligned} \hat{a}(\beta_1, \beta_2) &= \frac{B_1C_2 - B_2C_1}{A_1B_2 - B_1^2} \\ \hat{b}(\beta_1, \beta_2) &= \frac{B_1C_1 - A_1C_2}{A_1B_2 - B_1^2} \end{aligned} \tag{26}$$

where $A_1, B_1, C_1, B_2$, and $C_2$ are concerned with $\beta_1, \beta_2, a, b, \tau_1, \tau_2, t_i$ and are shown specifically in the Appendix A.

Note that if $\beta_1$ and $\beta_2$ are assumed to be unknown, we can plug $\hat{a}(\beta_1, \beta_2)$ and $\hat{b}(\beta_1, \beta_2)$ into the log-likelihood function $l(\beta_1, \beta_2, a, b)$. Thus, the log-likelihood function is only concerned with $\beta_1$ and $\beta_2$ (denote it as $l(\beta_1, \beta_2)$), which makes it more conducive to calculate the maximum likelihood estimates. By maximizing $l(\beta_1, \beta_2)$, the estimates of $\beta_1$ and $\beta_2$ can be obtained. Using (10) and (26), the estimates of $\lambda_1, \lambda_2, a$, and $b$ can be calculated as well.

The least squares estimates (LSEs) of the parameters calculated in this section can also be used as the initial iterative values when calculating the maximum likelihood estimates in the previous section.

## 4. Interval Estimation

### 4.1. Observed Fisher Information Matrix

Based on the large-sample theory, when the sample size $n$ is large enough, the inverse of the Fisher information matrix can be used as the approximation of the variance–covariance matrix. Denote the Fisher information matrix as $I$.

$$I = E\begin{pmatrix} -\frac{\partial^2 l}{\partial a^2} & -\frac{\partial^2 l}{\partial a \partial b} & -\frac{\partial^2 l}{\partial a \partial \beta_1} & -\frac{\partial^2 l}{\partial a \partial \beta_2} \\ -\frac{\partial^2 l}{\partial b \partial a} & -\frac{\partial^2 l}{\partial b^2} & -\frac{\partial^2 l}{\partial b \partial \beta_1} & -\frac{\partial^2 l}{\partial b \partial \beta_2} \\ -\frac{\partial^2 l}{\partial \beta_1 \partial a} & -\frac{\partial^2 l}{\partial \beta_1 \partial b} & -\frac{\partial^2 l}{\partial \beta_1^2} & -\frac{\partial^2 l}{\partial \beta_1 \partial \beta_2} \\ -\frac{\partial^2 l}{\partial \beta_2 \partial a} & -\frac{\partial^2 l}{\partial \beta_2 \partial b} & -\frac{\partial^2 l}{\partial \beta_2 \partial \beta_1} & -\frac{\partial^2 l}{\partial \beta_2^2} \end{pmatrix} \quad (27)$$

The specific elements of $I$ are provided in the Appendix A.

Since it is difficult to calculate the above expectations, the observed Fisher information matrix is often used as a substitute for the Fisher matrix, which does not take expectations but takes the parameter values as the maximum likelihood estimates. Denote it as $O$.

$$O = \begin{pmatrix} -\frac{\partial^2 l}{\partial a^2} & -\frac{\partial^2 l}{\partial a \partial b} & -\frac{\partial^2 l}{\partial a \partial \beta_1} & -\frac{\partial^2 l}{\partial a \partial \beta_2} \\ -\frac{\partial^2 l}{\partial b \partial a} & -\frac{\partial^2 l}{\partial b^2} & -\frac{\partial^2 l}{\partial b \partial \beta_1} & -\frac{\partial^2 l}{\partial b \partial \beta_2} \\ -\frac{\partial^2 l}{\partial \beta_1 \partial a} & -\frac{\partial^2 l}{\partial \beta_1 \partial b} & -\frac{\partial^2 l}{\partial \beta_1^2} & -\frac{\partial^2 l}{\partial \beta_1 \partial \beta_2} \\ -\frac{\partial^2 l}{\partial \beta_2 \partial a} & -\frac{\partial^2 l}{\partial \beta_2 \partial b} & -\frac{\partial^2 l}{\partial \beta_2 \partial \beta_1} & -\frac{\partial^2 l}{\partial \beta_2^2} \end{pmatrix}_{|a=\hat{a},b=\hat{b},\beta_1=\hat{\beta}_1,\beta_2=\hat{\beta}_2} \quad (28)$$

Therefore, the approximated variance–covariance matrix of $\hat{a}, \hat{b}, \hat{\beta}_1$, and $\hat{\beta}_2$ is given by:

$$\begin{pmatrix} \hat{Var}(\hat{a}) & \hat{Cov}(\hat{a},\hat{b}) & \hat{Cov}(\hat{a},\hat{\beta}_1) & \hat{Cov}(\hat{a},\hat{\beta}_2) \\ \hat{Cov}(\hat{b},\hat{a}) & \hat{Var}(\hat{b}) & \hat{Cov}(\hat{b},\hat{\beta}_1) & \hat{Cov}(\hat{b},\hat{\beta}_2) \\ \hat{Cov}(\hat{\beta}_1,\hat{a}) & \hat{Cov}(\hat{\beta}_1,\hat{b}) & \hat{Var}(\hat{\beta}_1) & \hat{Cov}(\hat{\beta}_1,\hat{\beta}_2) \\ \hat{Cov}(\hat{\beta}_2,\hat{a}) & \hat{Cov}(\hat{\beta}_2,\hat{b}) & \hat{Cov}(\hat{\beta}_2,\hat{\beta}_1) & \hat{Var}(\hat{\beta}_2) \end{pmatrix} = O^{-1}. \quad (29)$$

As the maximum likelihood estimators have asymptotic normality under regularity condition, it can be known that $(\hat{a}, \hat{b}, \hat{\beta}_1, \hat{\beta}_2)$ obeys the quaternion normal distribution approximately. Its mean vector is $(a, b, \beta_2, \beta_2)$ and the variance–covariance matrix is $O^{-1}$. Based on the above analysis, the asymptotic confidence intervals of $\hat{a}, \hat{b}, \hat{\beta}_1$, and $\hat{\beta}_2$ can also be calculated. In the next section, the specific implementation steps and the calculation method of coverage probabilities are given.

### 4.2. Asymptotic Confidence Interval

When given a set of initial parameters $\beta_1, \beta_2, \lambda_1$, and $\lambda_2$, the following steps can generate sample data and compute the confidence intervals and coverage probabilities.

Step 1: Generate $n$ random numbers that are independent and identically distributed in a Uniform distribution $U(0,1)$. Then, invert $F(t)$ in (14) to generate the survival time $t_i$. The corresponding function is as follows:

$$t_i = \begin{cases} \left[\ln\left(1 - \frac{\beta_1 \tau_1^{\beta_1 - 1} \ln(1-u_i)}{(a+b\tau_1)e^{-\tau_1^{\beta_1}}}\right)\right]^{\frac{1}{\beta_1}}, & 0 < u_i < F(\tau_1) \\ \frac{-a + \sqrt{a^2 - 2b[\ln(1-u_i) + \frac{(a+b\tau_1)e^{-\tau_1^{\beta_1}}}{\beta_1 \tau_1^{\beta_1 - 1}}(e^{\tau_1^{\beta_1}} - 1) - a\tau_1 - \frac{b}{2}\tau_1^2]}}{b} & F(\tau_1) \le u_i < F(\tau_2) \\ \left[\ln\left(e^{-\tau_2^{\beta_2}} - \frac{\ln(1-u_i) + \frac{(a+b\tau_1)e^{-\tau_1^{\beta_1}}}{\beta_1 \tau_1^{\beta_1 - 1}}(e^{\tau_1^{\beta_1}} - 1) + a(\tau_2 - \tau_1) + \frac{b}{2}(\tau_2^2 - \tau_1^2) - \ln(1-u_i)}{(a+b\tau_2)e^{-\tau_2^{\beta_2}}} \beta_2 \tau_2^{\beta_2 - 1}\right)\right]^{\frac{1}{\beta_2}} & u_i \ge F(\tau_2) \end{cases} \quad (30)$$

Step 2: Use the data $t_i$ generated from *Step* 1 and the log-likelihood function (17) to calculate the MLEs of $a$, $b$, $\beta_1$, and $\beta_2$. Denote them as $\hat{a}$, $\hat{b}$, $\hat{\beta}_1$, and $\hat{\beta}_2$. Calculate the MLEs of $\lambda_1$ and $\lambda_2$ via the equation (10) and denote them as $\hat{\lambda}_1$ and $\hat{\lambda}_2$.

Step 3: Use the data $t_i$ generated from *Step* 1 and the MLEs from *Step* 2 to calculate the observed Fisher information matrix $O$.

Step 4: Invert $O$ matrix to calculate the asymptotic variance–covariance matrix, and denote it as $A$. Obtain the asymptotic variance of $\beta_1$ and $\beta_2$ as $\hat{var}(\hat{\beta}_1)$ and $\hat{var}(\hat{\beta}_2)$.

Step 5: Based on the theory of the Delta method ([26]), the asymptotic variance of $\hat{\lambda}_1$ and $\hat{\lambda}_2$ can be calculated using the following equations:

$$\begin{aligned} \hat{var}(\hat{\lambda}_1) &= C_1 A C_1^T \\ \hat{var}(\hat{\lambda}_2) &= C_2 A C_2^T \end{aligned} \quad (31)$$

where:

$$\begin{aligned} C_1 &= \left(\frac{\partial \lambda_1(a,b,\beta_1)}{\partial a}, \frac{\partial \lambda_1(a,b,\beta_1)}{\partial b}, \frac{\partial \lambda_1(a,b,\beta_1)}{\partial \beta_1}, \ 0 \ \right) \\ C_2 &= \left(\frac{\partial \lambda_2(a,b,\beta_2)}{\partial a}, \frac{\partial \lambda_2(a,b,\beta_2)}{\partial b}, \ 0 \ , \frac{\partial \lambda_2(a,b,\beta_2)}{\partial \beta_2}\right) \end{aligned} \quad (32)$$

$C_1^T$ and $C_2^T$ are the transpose matrices of $C_1$ and $C_2$, respectively. Further, the specific expressions of $C_1$ and $C_2$ are shown in the Appendix A.

*Step* 6: The lower and upper bounds of the $100(1-\alpha)\%$ confidence intervals for $\beta_1, \beta_2, \lambda_1, \lambda_2$ are given by:

$$\begin{aligned} \hat{\beta}_i^L &= \min\{\hat{\beta}_i - u_{\frac{\alpha}{2}}\sqrt{\hat{var}(\hat{\beta}_i)}, 0\} \quad \hat{\beta}_i^U = \hat{\beta}_i + u_{\frac{\alpha}{2}}\sqrt{\hat{var}(\hat{\beta}_i)}, \quad i = 1,2 \\ \hat{\lambda}_i^L &= \min\{\hat{\lambda}_i - u_{\frac{\alpha}{2}}\sqrt{\hat{var}(\hat{\lambda}_i)}, 0\} \quad \hat{\lambda}_i^U = \hat{\lambda}_i + u_{\frac{\alpha}{2}}\sqrt{\hat{var}(\hat{\lambda}_i)}, \quad i = 1,2 \end{aligned} \quad (33)$$

where $u_q$ is the $q$-quantile of a standardized normal distribution.

Step 7: Repeat the foregoing steps 999 times to obtain the coverage probabilities as CPrs.

$$CPr(\beta_1) = \sum_{j=1}^{999} \frac{I(\hat{\beta}_{1j}^L < \beta_1 < \hat{\beta}_{1j}^U)}{999} \quad (34)$$

where $I(\hat{\beta}_{1j}^L < \beta_1 < \hat{\beta}_{1j}^U)$ is the indicator function. $\hat{\beta}_{1j}^L$ and $\hat{\beta}_{1j}^U$ are the $j$-th results of the $\beta_1'$ lower and upper bounds of the $100(1-\alpha)\%$ confidence intervals.

In the same way, we can obtain the CPrs of $\beta_2, \lambda_1$, and $\lambda_2$.

## 5. Simulation Results and Analysis

In this section, the simulation results under different sample sizes ($n$) and different parameters are presented using the method given in the previous section with the R program.

The simulation results of the MLEs, LSEs, 95% and 99% confidence intervals, and the corresponding coverage probabilities are given by Monte Carlo simulations, which evaluate the performance of the estimation methods. By comparing the mean, bias, and mean square error of MLEs and LSEs, the advantages and disadvantages of the two methods are compared.

Based on the characteristics of the Chen distribution's hazard function, different parameters are chosen to generate random numbers, and the results are listed in Tables 1–4. The results include the mean, bias, mean square error (MSE), lower bounds ($LB_{95\%}$), upper bounds ($UB_{95\%}$), and coverage probabilities ($CPr_{95\%}$) of 95% confidence interval and lower bounds ($LB_{99\%}$), upper bounds ($UB_{99\%}$), and coverage probabilities ($CPr_{99\%}$) of 99% confidence intervals.

Table 1 shows the simulation results when the hazard functions under the two stresses are both bathtub-shaped with $n = 50, n = 100, n = 200$.

**Table 1.** The results of MLEs, LSEs, interval estimates, and CPrs when $\beta_1 = 0.7, \beta_2 = 0.9, \lambda_1 = 0.5016, \lambda_2 = 1.0015, \tau_1 = 0.5, \tau_2 = 1, a = -0.85, b = 3.3$.

| $n$ | Par | Method | Mean | Bias | MSE | $LB_{95\%}$ | $UB_{95\%}$ | $CPr_{95\%}$ | $LB_{99\%}$ | $UB_{99\%}$ | $CPr_{99\%}$ |
|---|---|---|---|---|---|---|---|---|---|---|---|
| 50 | $\lambda_1$ | MLE | 0.5469 | 0.0454 | 0.0247 | 0.2580 | 0.8359 | 0.944 | 0.1666 | 0.9273 | 0.984 |
| | | LSE | 0.5165 | 0.0149 | 0.0173 | | | | | | |
| | $\lambda_2$ | MLE | 1.0326 | 0.0311 | 0.1454 | 0 | 2.5273 | 0.964 | 0 | 3.0001 | 0.981 |
| | | LSE | 0.6894 | −0.3121 | 0.0137 | | | | | | |
| | $\beta_1$ | MLE | 0.7597 | 0.0597 | 0.0473 | 0.3832 | 1.1362 | 0.947 | 0.2641 | 1.2553 | 0.988 |
| | | LSE | 0.7294 | 0.0294 | 0.0191 | | | | | | |
| | $\beta_2$ | MLE | 1.1487 | 0.2487 | 0.2595 | 0.2605 | 2.0368 | 0.901 | -0.0204 | 2.3178 | 0.964 |
| | | LSE | 1.1840 | 0.2840 | 0.0512 | | | | | | |
| 100 | $\lambda_1$ | MLE | 0.5181 | 0.0165 | 0.0102 | 0.3220 | 0.7142 | 0.948 | 0.2599 | 0.7762 | 0.993 |
| | | LSE | 0.5286 | 0.0270 | 0.0089 | | | | | | |
| | $\lambda_2$ | MLE | 1.1001 | 0.0986 | 1.6755 | 0.1456 | 2.0545 | 0.953 | 0 | 2.3564 | 0.984 |
| | | LSE | 0.7872 | −0.2143 | 0.0114 | | | | | | |
| | $\beta_1$ | MLE | 0.7238 | 0.0238 | 0.0178 | 0.4708 | 0.9768 | 0.951 | 0.3907 | 1.0568 | 0.988 |
| | | LSE | 0.7327 | 0.0327 | 0.0095 | | | | | | |
| | $\beta_2$ | MLE | 1.0009 | 0.1009 | 0.1027 | 0.4122 | 1.5896 | 0.917 | 0.2259 | 1.7758 | 0.970 |
| | | LSE | 1.0530 | 0.1530 | 0.0117 | | | | | | |
| 200 | $\lambda_1$ | MLE | 0.5108 | 0.0092 | 0.0047 | 0.3736 | 0.6480 | 0.960 | 0.3302 | 0.6914 | 0.992 |
| | | LSE | 0.5171 | 0.0155 | 0.0049 | | | | | | |
| | $\lambda_2$ | MLE | 0.9841 | −0.0173 | 0.1017 | 0.3514 | 1.6168 | 0.969 | 0.1512 | 1.8170 | 0.995 |
| | | LSE | 0.8632 | −0.1382 | 0.0072 | | | | | | |
| | $\beta_1$ | MLE | 0.7143 | 0.0143 | 0.0089 | 0.5382 | 0.8904 | 0.953 | 0.4825 | 0.9462 | 0.988 |
| | | LSE | 0.7210 | 0.0210 | 0.0041 | | | | | | |
| | $\beta_2$ | MLE | 0.9707 | 0.0707 | 0.0439 | 0.5673 | 1.3740 | 0.930 | 0.4397 | 1.5016 | 0.977 |
| | | LSE | 0.9881 | 0.0881 | 0.0046 | | | | | | |

Table 2 shows the simulation results when the distributions under the two stress levels are the same as those in Table 1, but the lag time ($\tau_2 - \tau_1$) is shortened.

Table 3 shows the simulation results when the hazard functions under the two different stresses both increase monotonically with $n = 50, n = 100, n = 200$.

**Table 2.** The results of MLEs, LSEs, interval estimates, and CPrs when $\beta_1 = 0.7, \beta_2 = 0.9, \lambda_1 = 0.5016, \lambda_2 = 1.0015, \tau_1 = 0.5, \tau_2 = 0.7, a = -2.0235, b = 5.6470$.

| $n$ | $Par$ | $Method$ | $Mean$ | $Bias$ | $MSE$ | $LB_{95\%}$ | $UB_{95\%}$ | $CPr_{95\%}$ | $LB_{99\%}$ | $UB_{99\%}$ | $CPr_{99\%}$ |
|---|---|---|---|---|---|---|---|---|---|---|---|
| 50 | $\lambda_1$ | MLE | 0.5406 | 0.0390 | 0.0278 | 0.2367 | 0.8444 | 0.947 | 0.1406 | 0.9406 | 0.981 |
| | | LSE | 0.5392 | 0.0376 | 0.0221 | | | | | | |
| | $\lambda_2$ | MLE | 1.0617 | 0.0602 | 0.3453 | 0.2177 | 1.9056 | 0.955 | 0 | 2.1726 | 0.988 |
| | | LSE | 0.8517 | −0.1498 | 0.0387 | | | | | | |
| | $\beta_1$ | MLE | 0.7529 | 0.0529 | 0.0489 | 0.3675 | 1.1382 | 0.944 | 0.2456 | 1.2602 | 0.979 |
| | | LSE | 0.7409 | 0.0409 | 0.0194 | | | | | | |
| | $\beta_2$ | MLE | 1.0346 | 0.1346 | 0.1296 | 0.3951 | 1.6742 | 0.930 | 0.1928 | 1.8765 | 0.983 |
| | | LSE | 1.0550 | 0.1550 | 0.0041 | | | | | | |
| 100 | $\lambda_1$ | MLE | 0.5205 | 0.0189 | 0.0130 | 0.3122 | 0.7288 | 0.931 | 0.2464 | 0.7947 | 0.981 |
| | | LSE | 0.5247 | 0.0231 | 0.0124 | | | | | | |
| | $\lambda_2$ | MLE | 1.0101 | 0.0086 | 0.1397 | 0.4483 | 1.5719 | 0.953 | 0.2706 | 1.7496 | 0.984 |
| | | LSE | 0.8970 | −0.1044 | 0.0212 | | | | | | |
| | $\beta_1$ | MLE | 0.7259 | 0.0259 | 0.0189 | 0.4647 | 0.9872 | 0.952 | 0.3820 | 1.0698 | 0.990 |
| | | LSE | 0.7302 | 0.0302 | 0.0107 | | | | | | |
| | $\beta_2$ | MLE | 0.9733 | 0.0733 | 0.0555 | 0.5470 | 1.3996 | 0.927 | 0.4122 | 1.5345 | 0.978 |
| | | LSE | 0.9928 | 0.0928 | 0.0012 | | | | | | |
| 200 | $\lambda_1$ | MLE | 0.5099 | 0.0083 | 0.0058 | 0.3649 | 0.6549 | 0.949 | 0.3191 | 0.7007 | 0.987 |
| | | LSE | 0.5235 | 0.0219 | 0.0063 | | | | | | |
| | $\lambda_2$ | MLE | 1.0059 | 0.0044 | 0.0406 | 0.6175 | 1.3943 | 0.953 | 0.4946 | 1.5172 | 0.992 |
| | | LSE | 0.9280 | −0.0735 | 0.0124 | | | | | | |
| | $\beta_1$ | MLE | 0.7135 | 0.0135 | 0.0086 | 0.5323 | 0.8947 | 0.949 | 0.4750 | 0.9520 | 0.988 |
| | | LSE | 0.7201 | 0.0201 | 0.0047 | | | | | | |
| | $\beta_2$ | MLE | 0.9285 | 0.0285 | 0.0225 | 0.6366 | 1.2204 | 0.948 | 0.5442 | 1.3128 | 0.992 |
| | | LSE | 0.9569 | 0.0569 | 0.0041 | | | | | | |

Table 4 shows the simulation results when the hazard function under the first stress level is bathtub-shaped and in the second stress level is monotonically increasing with $n = 50, n = 100, n = 200$.

**Table 3.** The results of MLEs, LSEs, interval estimates, and CPrs when $\beta_1 = 1, \beta_2 = 1.2, \lambda_1 = 0.7642, \lambda_2 = 1.1061, \tau_1 = 0.4, \tau_2 = 0.6, a = -0.7, b = 4.6$.

| $n$ | $Par$ | $Method$ | $Mean$ | $Bias$ | $MSE$ | $LB_{95\%}$ | $UB_{95\%}$ | $CPr_{95\%}$ | $LB_{99\%}$ | $UB_{99\%}$ | $CPr_{99\%}$ |
|---|---|---|---|---|---|---|---|---|---|---|---|
| 50 | $\lambda_1$ | MLE | 0.9009 | 0.1367 | 0.2990 | 0.2552 | 1.5466 | 0.940 | 0.0509 | 1.7509 | 0.987 |
| | | LSE | 0.8342 | 0.0700 | 0.0793 | | | | | | |
| | $\lambda_2$ | MLE | 1.1245 | 0.0185 | 0.1404 | 0.4643 | 1.7848 | 0.938 | 0.2554 | 1.9937 | 0.978 |
| | | LSE | 1.0138 | −0.0923 | 0.0563 | | | | | | |
| | $\beta_1$ | MLE | 1.0870 | 0.0870 | 0.1224 | 0.5168 | 1.6572 | 0.944 | 0.3364 | 1.8376 | 0.982 |
| | | LSE | 1.0527 | 0.0527 | 0.0511 | | | | | | |
| | $\beta_2$ | MLE | 1.3984 | 0.1984 | 0.2188 | 0.5822 | 2.2146 | 0.940 | 0.324 | 2.4727 | 0.989 |
| | | LSE | 1.3959 | 0.1959 | 0.0055 | | | | | | |

**Table 3.** *Cont.*

| $n$ | $Par$ | $Method$ | $Mean$ | $Bias$ | $MSE$ | $LB_{95\%}$ | $UB_{95\%}$ | $CPr_{95\%}$ | $LB_{99\%}$ | $UB_{99\%}$ | $CPr_{99\%}$ |
|---|---|---|---|---|---|---|---|---|---|---|---|
| 100 | $\lambda_1$ | MLE | 0.8139 | 0.0497 | 0.0504 | 0.3951 | 1.2326 | 0.950 | 0.2627 | 1.3651 | 0.988 |
| | | LSE | 0.8284 | 0.0643 | 0.0451 | | | | | | |
| | $\lambda_2$ | MLE | 1.1094 | 0.0033 | 0.0576 | 0.6578 | 1.5613 | 0.942 | 0.5152 | 1.7038 | 0.984 |
| | | LSE | 1.0331 | −0.0730 | 0.0343 | | | | | | |
| | $\beta_1$ | MLE | 1.0354 | 0.0354 | 0.0390 | 0.6529 | 1.4179 | 0.955 | 0.5319 | 1.5389 | 0.988 |
| | | LSE | 1.0504 | 0.0504 | 0.0249 | | | | | | |
| | $\beta_2$ | MLE | 1.2926 | 0.0926 | 0.0779 | 0.7531 | 1.8323 | 0.951 | 0.5823 | 2.003 | 0.989 |
| | | LSE | 1.3152 | 0.1152 | 0.0015 | | | | | | |
| 200 | $\lambda_1$ | MLE | 0.7859 | 0.0217 | 0.0208 | 0.4976 | 1.0741 | 0.957 | 0.4064 | 1.1653 | 0.994 |
| | | LSE | 0.8156 | 0.0514 | 0.0219 | | | | | | |
| | $\lambda_2$ | MLE | 1.1142 | 0.0082 | 0.0290 | 0.7977 | 1.4307 | 0.947 | 0.6976 | 1.5309 | 0.987 |
| | | LSE | 1.0520 | −0.0541 | 0.0170 | | | | | | |
| | $\beta_1$ | MLE | 1.0168 | 0.0168 | 0.0184 | 0.7512 | 1.2823 | 0.963 | 0.6672 | 1.3664 | 0.993 |
| | | LSE | 1.0339 | 0.0339 | 0.0122 | | | | | | |
| | $\beta_2$ | MLE | 1.2398 | 0.0398 | 0.0382 | 0.8716 | 1.6081 | 0.949 | 0.7551 | 1.7246 | 0.992 |
| | | LSE | 1.2693 | 0.0693 | 0.0005 | | | | | | |

**Table 4.** The results of MLEs, LSEs, interval estimates, and CPrs when $\beta_1 = 0.8, \beta_2 = 1.2, \lambda_1 = 0.3679$, $\lambda_2 = 0.0802, \tau_1 = 1, \tau_2 = 2, a = 0.5, b = 0.3$.

| $n$ | $Par$ | $Method$ | $Mean$ | $Bias$ | $MSE$ | $LB_{95\%}$ | $UB_{95\%}$ | $CPr_{95\%}$ | $LB_{99\%}$ | $UB_{99\%}$ | $CPr_{99\%}$ |
|---|---|---|---|---|---|---|---|---|---|---|---|
| 50 | $\lambda_1$ | MLE | 0.3705 | 0.0027 | 0.0048 | 0.2254 | 0.5157 | 0.977 | 0.1795 | 0.5616 | 0.996 |
| | | LSE | 0.3761 | 0.0082 | 0.0061 | | | | | | |
| | $\lambda_2$ | MLE | 0.0295 | −0.0508 | 0.5604 | 0 | 0.2688 | 0.981 | 0 | 0.3445 | 0.994 |
| | | LSE | 0.0426 | −0.0376 | 0.0001 | | | | | | |
| | $\beta_1$ | MLE | 0.8371 | 0.0371 | 0.0278 | 0.5147 | 1.1595 | 0.954 | 0.4127 | 1.2615 | 0.990 |
| | | LSE | 0.8159 | 0.0159 | 0.0105 | | | | | | |
| | $\beta_2$ | MLE | 1.3156 | 0.1156 | 0.0826 | 0.7707 | 1.8606 | 0.871 | 0.5984 | 2.0329 | 0.936 |
| | | LSE | 1.3586 | 0.1586 | 0.0133 | | | | | | |
| 100 | $\lambda_1$ | MLE | 0.3715 | 0.0036 | 0.0024 | 0.2717 | 0.4714 | 0.972 | 0.2401 | 0.5029 | 0.991 |
| | | LSE | 0.3737 | 0.0058 | 0.0031 | | | | | | |
| | $\lambda_2$ | MLE | 0.0908 | 0.0106 | 0.0077 | 0 | 0.2173 | 0.969 | 0 | 0.2573 | 0.993 |
| | | LSE | 0.0552 | −0.0250 | 0.0001 | | | | | | |
| | $\beta_1$ | MLE | 0.8204 | 0.0204 | 0.0141 | 0.5984 | 1.0424 | 0.943 | 0.5282 | 1.1126 | 0.995 |
| | | LSE | 0.8161 | 0.0161 | 0.0052 | | | | | | |
| | $\beta_2$ | MLE | 1.2495 | 0.0495 | 0.0363 | 0.8793 | 1.6197 | 0.923 | 0.7622 | 1.7368 | 0.969 |
| | | LSE | 1.2895 | 0.0895 | 0.0035 | | | | | | |
| 200 | $\lambda_1$ | MLE | 0.3711 | 0.0032 | 0.0012 | 0.3016 | 0.4405 | 0.965 | 0.2796 | 0.4625 | 0.994 |
| | | LSE | 0.3709 | 0.0030 | 0.0015 | | | | | | |
| | $\lambda_2$ | MLE | 0.0791 | −0.0011 | 0.0019 | 0 | 0.1625 | 0.965 | 0 | 0.1889 | 0.997 |
| | | LSE | 0.0635 | −0.0167 | 0.0001 | | | | | | |
| | $\beta_1$ | MLE | 0.8058 | 0.0058 | 0.0060 | 0.6519 | 0.9596 | 0.956 | 0.6033 | 1.0083 | 0.993 |
| | | LSE | 0.8101 | 0.0101 | 0.0026 | | | | | | |
| | $\beta_2$ | MLE | 1.2360 | 0.0360 | 0.0161 | 0.9859 | 1.4861 | 0.915 | 0.9068 | 1.5652 | 0.971 |
| | | LSE | 1.2551 | 0.0551 | 0.0014 | | | | | | |

Based on Tables 1–4, some conclusions are summarized as follows.

(1) No matter which values the parameters take, the estimated values are close to the real values, and mostly the bias and mean square errors decrease with the increase in sample size, which shows that the two estimations are effective.

(2) From the perspective of bias, the results of LSE are generally better than MLE when $n = 50$; the results of MLE are generally better than LSE when $n = 100$ and $n = 200$. This means that LSE is preferred when the sample size is small, while MLE is preferred when the sample size is large.

(3) Under different parameters, the mean square errors of LSEs are generally less than that of MLEs, and the advantage of LSE in the mean square errors is more obvious when the sample size $n$ is small.

(4) In terms of the asymptotic confidence intervals, generally, the coverage probabilities of the 95% are close to 95%, and the coverage probabilities of the 99% are close to 99%, which verifies the correctness of the methods. The coverage probabilities are closer to 1-$\alpha$ with the increase in the sample size, which means the asymptotic confidence intervals will be more precise when the sample size is larger.

(5) In general, the estimations perform better when the hazard function under the first stress is bathtub-shaped and under the second stress is monotonically increasing. The coverage probabilities fit better when the risk function is monotonically increasing under both stress levels.

(6) Comparing Tables 1 and 2, it can be seen that when the lagged-effect time is shortened, the mean square errors of MLEs and LSEs both increase under the small sample size.

## 6. A Special Case

Since the parameter $\beta$ determines whether the shape of the hazard function is a bathtub shape or not and, in many cases, the stress does not change the shape of the hazard function, a special case will be discussed below.

When assuming that parameter $\beta_1$ is equal to parameter $\beta_2$ and denoting them as $\beta$, the model becomes the following form.

The hazard functions under the two stresses are:

$$h_1(t) = \lambda_1 \beta t^{\beta-1} e^{t^\beta}, \quad t > 0, \tag{35}$$

$$h_2(t) = \lambda_2 \beta t^{\beta-1} e^{t^\beta}, \quad t > 0. \tag{36}$$

Under the CRM, the hazard function is obtained by:

$$h(t) = \begin{cases} \lambda_1 \beta t^{\beta-1} e^{t^\beta}, & 0 < t < \tau_1 \\ a + bt \quad , & \tau_1 \le t < \tau_2 \\ \lambda_2 \beta t^{\beta-1} e^{t^\beta}, & t \ge \tau_2 \end{cases} \tag{37}$$

Replace parameters $\lambda_1$ and $\lambda_2$ with $a$ and $b$, and the cumulative hazard function $H(t)$ under the model is:

$$H(t) = \begin{cases} \frac{(a+b\tau_1)e^{-\tau_1^\beta}}{\beta \tau_1{}^{\beta-1}}(e^{t^\beta} - 1), & 0 < t < \tau_1 \\ \frac{(a+b\tau_1)e^{-\tau_1^\beta}}{\beta \tau_1{}^{\beta-1}}(e^{\tau_1^\beta} - 1) + a(t-\tau_1) + \frac{b}{2}(t^2 - \tau_1^2), & \tau_1 \le t < \tau_2 \\ \frac{(a+b\tau_1)e^{-\tau_1^\beta}}{\beta \tau_1{}^{\beta-1}}(e^{\tau_1^\beta} - 1) + a(\tau_2 - \tau) + \frac{b}{2}(\tau_2^2 - \tau_1^2) \\ \quad + \frac{(a+b\tau_2)e^{-\tau_2^\beta}}{\beta \tau_2{}^{\beta-1}}(e^{t^\beta} - e^{\tau_2^\beta}), & t \ge \tau_2 \end{cases} \tag{38}$$

The survival function $S(t)$ under the model is:

$$S(t)=\begin{cases}\exp\left\{-\frac{(a+b\tau_1)e^{-\tau_1^\beta}}{\beta\tau_1{}^{\beta-1}}(e^{t\beta}-1)\right\}, & 0<t<\tau_1\\ \exp\left\{-\frac{(a+b\tau_1)e^{-\tau_1^\beta}}{\beta\tau_1{}^{\beta-1}}(e^{\tau_1^\beta}-1)-a(t-\tau_1)-\frac{b}{2}(t^2-\tau_1^2)\right\}, & \tau_1\le t<\tau_2\\ \exp\left\{-\frac{(a+b\tau_1)e^{-\tau_1^\beta}}{\beta\tau_1{}^{\beta_1-1}}(e^{\tau_1^\beta}-1)-a(\tau_2-\tau_1)-\frac{b}{2}(\tau_2^2-\tau_1^2)\right\}\\ \quad\times\exp\left\{-\frac{(a+b\tau_2)e^{-\tau_2^\beta}}{\beta\tau_2{}^{\beta-1}}(e^{t\beta}-e^{\tau_2^\beta})\right\}, & t\ge\tau_2\end{cases} \tag{39}$$

The probability density function $f(t)$ of the lifetime is as follows:

$$f(t)=\begin{cases}\frac{(a+b\tau_1)e^{-\tau_1^\beta}}{\tau_1{}^{\beta-1}}t^{\beta-1}e^{t\beta}\exp\left\{-\frac{(a+b\tau_1)e^{-\tau_1^\beta}}{\beta\tau_1{}^{\beta-1}}(e^{t\beta}-1)\right\}, & 0<t<\tau_1\\ (a+bt)\exp\left\{-\frac{(a+b\tau_1)e^{-\tau_1^\beta}}{\beta\tau_1{}^{\beta-1}}(e^{\tau_1^\beta}-1)-a(t-\tau_1)-\frac{b}{2}(t^2-\tau_1^2)\right\}, & \tau_1\le t<\tau_2\\ \frac{(a+b\tau_2)e^{-\tau_2^\beta}}{\tau_2{}^{\beta-1}}t^{\beta-1}e^{t\beta}\exp\left\{-\frac{(a+b\tau_1)e^{-\tau_1^\beta}}{\beta_1\tau_1{}^{\beta-1}}(e^{\tau_1^\beta}-1)-a(\tau_2-\tau_1)-\frac{b}{2}(\tau_2^2-\tau_1^2)\right\}\\ \quad\times\exp\left\{-\frac{(a+b\tau_2)e^{-\tau_2^\beta}}{\beta\tau_2{}^{\beta-1}}(e^{t\beta}-e^{\tau_2^\beta})\right\}, & t\ge\tau_2\end{cases} \tag{40}$$

The corresponding cumulative distribution function $F(t)$ is given by:

$$F(t)=\begin{cases}1-\exp\left\{-\frac{(a+b\tau_1)e^{-\tau_1^\beta}}{\beta\tau_1{}^{\beta-1}}(e^{t\beta}-1)\right\}, & 0<t<\tau_1\\ 1-\exp\left\{-\frac{(a+b\tau_1)e^{-\tau_1^\beta}}{\beta\tau_1{}^{\beta-1}}(e^{\tau_1^\beta}-1)-a(t-\tau_1)-\frac{b}{2}(t^2-\tau_1^2)\right\}, & \tau_1\le t<\tau_2\\ 1-\exp\left\{-\frac{(a+b\tau_1)e^{-\tau_1^\beta}}{\beta\tau_1{}^{\beta-1}}(e^{\tau_1^\beta}-1)-a(\tau_2-\tau_1)-\frac{b}{2}(\tau_2^2-\tau_1^2)\right\}\\ \quad\times\exp\left\{-\frac{(a+b\tau_2)e^{-\tau_2^\beta}}{\beta\tau_2{}^{\beta-1}}(e^{t\beta}-e^{\tau_2^\beta})\right\}, & t\ge\tau_2\end{cases} \tag{41}$$

Accordingly, the log-likelihood function $l(\beta,a,b)$ can be written as:

$$
\begin{aligned}
l(\beta,a,b) =& n_1\left[\ln(a+b\tau_1)-\tau_1{}^{\beta}\right]+\sum_{i=n_1+1}^{n_1+n_2}\ln(a+bt_i)+n_3\left[\ln(a+b\tau_2)-\tau_2{}^{\beta}\right] \\
&+(\beta-1)[\sum_{i=1}^{n_1}\ln(\frac{t_i}{\tau_1})+\sum_{i=n_1+n_2+1}^{n}\ln(\frac{t_i}{\tau_1})]+\sum_{i=1}^{n_1}t_i{}^{\beta}+\sum_{i=n_1+n_2+1}^{n}t_i{}^{\beta} \\
&-a[\sum_{i=n_1+1}^{n_1+n_2}(t_i-\tau_1)+(\tau_2-\tau_1)n_3]-\frac{b}{2}[\sum_{i=n_1+1}^{n_1+n_2}(t_i^2-\tau_1^2)+(\tau_2^2-\tau_1^2)n_3] \\
&-\frac{(a+b\tau_1)e^{-\tau_1^{\beta}}}{\beta\tau_1{}^{\beta-1}}[\sum_{i=1}^{n_1}(e^{t_i^{\beta}}-1)+(n_2+n_3)+(e^{\tau_1{}^{\beta}}-1)] \\
&-\frac{(a+b\tau_2)e^{-\tau_2^{\beta}}}{\beta\tau_2{}^{\beta-1}}\sum_{i=n_1+n_2+1}^{n}(e^{t_i^{\beta}}-e^{\tau_2^{\beta}})
\end{aligned}
\tag{42}
$$

Other relevant parameter estimations can also be obtained. The corresponding methods are similar to those of previous sections and the specific steps are omitted.

## 7. Conclusions

In this paper, the parameter estimations and the statistical inference of the Chen distribution under the step-stress model with lagged effect are studied. Maximum likelihood estimation is used for point estimation, and the Newton–Raphson algorithm is used when solving the nonlinear equations. Based on the unique linear form of risk function under CRM, another point estimation is obtained based on the large sample theory and the least squares estimation method. Different from maximum likelihood estimation, it gives the specific expressions of $a$, $b$ for the given $\beta_1, \beta_2$. Moreover, using the observed Fisher matrix and the asymptotic normality of the maximum likelihood estimators, a method to construct the asymptotic confidence interval and coverage probabilities is provided. The performance of those estimation methods is evaluated by Monte Carlo simulation. It can be seen from the simulation results that the accuracy of the two point estimations is different when parameters or sample sizes change, which may be due to distinct forms of the Chen distribution's risk functions.

The bathtub-shaped hazard function of the Chen distribution is of great significance in real life. The step-stress model is practical in survival analysis and the lagged effect makes it more consistent with reality. This paper can also be further extended by considering competing risks or a censoring scheme.

**Author Contributions:** Investigation, Z.Z.; Supervision, W.G. All authors have read and agreed to the published version of the manuscript.

**Funding:** This research was supported by Project 202210004002 which was supported by National Training Program of Innovation and Entrepreneurship for Undergraduates.

**Institutional Review Board Statement:** Not applicable.

**Informed Consent Statement:** Not applicable.

**Data Availability Statement:** Not applicable.

**Conflicts of Interest:** The authors declare no conflict of interest.

## Appendix A

*Appendix A.1. The Expressions of $\hat{a}(\beta_1, \beta_2)$ and $\hat{b}(\beta_1, \beta_2)$*

$$\begin{aligned}\hat{a}(\beta_1, \beta_2) &= \frac{B_1C_2 - B_2C_1}{A_1B_2 - B_1^2} \\ \hat{b}(\beta_1, \beta_2) &= \frac{B_1C_1 - A_1C_2}{A_1B_2 - B_1^2}\end{aligned} \tag{A1}$$

where:

$$\begin{aligned}
A_1 =& \sum_{i=1}^{n_1}[k_1(e^{t_i^{\beta_1}} - 1)]^2 + \sum_{i=n_1+1}^{n_1+n_2}[k_1(e^{\tau_1^{\beta_1}} - 1) + (t_i - \tau_1)]^2 \\
&+ \sum_{i=n_1+n_2+1}^{n}[k_1(e^{\tau_1^{\beta_1}} - 1) + (\tau_2 - \tau_1) + k_3(e^{t^{\beta_2}} - e^{\tau_2^{\beta_2}})]^2 \\
B_1 =& \sum_{i=1}^{n_1} k_1k_2(e^{t_i^{\beta_1}} - 1)^2 + \sum_{i=n_1+1}^{n_1+n_2}[k_1(e^{\tau_1^{\beta_1}} - 1) + (t_i - \tau_1)][k_2(e^{\tau_1^{\beta_1}} - 1) + \frac{1}{2}(t_i^2 - \tau_1^2)] \\
&+ \sum_{i=n_1+n_2+1}^{n}[k_1(e^{\tau_1^{\beta_1}} - 1) + (\tau_2 - \tau_1) + k_3(e^{t^{\beta_2}} - e^{\tau_2^{\beta_2}})][k_2(e^{\tau_1^{\beta_1}} - 1) + \frac{1}{2}(\tau_2^2 - \tau_1^2) + k_4(e^{t^{\beta_2}} - e^{\tau_2^{\beta_2}})] \\
C_1 =& -\sum_{i=1}^{n_1}[ln(\frac{n}{n-i+1})k_1(e^{t_i^{\beta_1}} - 1)] - \sum_{i=n_1+1}^{n_1+n_2} ln(\frac{n}{n-i+1})[k_1(e^{\tau_1^{\beta_1}} - 1) + (t_i - \tau_1)] \\
&- \sum_{i=n_1+n_2+1}^{n} ln(\frac{n}{n-i+1})[k_1(e^{\tau_1^{\beta_1}} - 1) + (\tau_2 - \tau_1) + k_3(e^{t^{\beta_2}} - e^{\tau_2^{\beta_2}})] \\
B_2 =& \sum_{i=1}^{n_1}[k_2(e^{t_i^{\beta_1}} - 1)]^2 + \sum_{i=n_1+1}^{n_1+n_2}[k_2(e^{\tau_1^{\beta_1}} - 1) + \frac{1}{2}(t_i^2 - \tau_1^2)]^2 \\
&+ \sum_{i=n_1+n_2+1}^{n}[k_2(e^{\tau_1^{\beta_1}} - 1) + \frac{1}{2}(\tau_2^2 - \tau_1^2) + k_4(e^{t^{\beta_2}} - e^{\tau_2^{\beta_2}})]^2 \\
C_2 =& -\sum_{i=1}^{n_1}[ln(\frac{n}{n-i+1})k_2(e^{t_i^{\beta_1}} - 1)] - \sum_{i=n_1+1}^{n_1+n_2} ln(\frac{n}{n-i+1})[k_2(e^{\tau_1^{\beta_1}} - 1) + \frac{1}{2}(t_i^2 - \tau_1^2)] \\
&- \sum_{i=n_1+n_2+1}^{n} ln(\frac{n}{n-i+1})[k_2(e^{\tau_1^{\beta_1}} - 1) + \frac{1}{2}(\tau_2^2 - \tau_1^2) + k_4(e^{t^{\beta_2}} - e^{\tau_2^{\beta_2}})]
\end{aligned} \tag{A2}$$

*Appendix A.2. The Specific Elements of I*

$$\frac{\partial^2 l}{\partial a^2} = -\frac{n_1}{(a+b\tau_1)^2} - \sum_{i=n_1+1}^{n_1+n_2} \frac{1}{(a+bt_i)^2} - \frac{n_3}{(a+b\tau_2)^2}$$

$$\frac{\partial^2 l}{\partial b^2} = -\frac{n_1 \tau_1^2}{(a+b\tau_1)^2} - \sum_{i=n_1+1}^{n_1+n_2} \frac{t_i^2}{(a+bt_i)^2} - \frac{n_3 \tau_2^2}{(a+b\tau_2)^2}$$

$$\begin{aligned}
\frac{\partial^2 l}{\partial \beta_1^2} = & - n_1 \tau_1^{\beta_1} (\ln \tau_1)^2 + \sum_{i=1}^{n_1} t_i{}^{\beta_1} (\ln t_i)^2 \\
& + \frac{(a+b\tau_1)e^{-\tau_1^{\beta_1}}}{\beta_1 \tau_1{}^{\beta_1 - 1}} \left(\frac{1}{\beta_1} + \ln \tau_1 + \tau_1^{\beta_1} \ln \tau_1\right) \Bigg\{ -\left(\frac{1}{\beta_1} + \ln \tau_1 + \tau_1^{\beta_1} \ln \tau_1\right) \Big[ \sum_{i=1}^{n_1} (e^{t_i^{\beta_1}} - 1) \\
& + (n_2 + n_3)(e^{\tau_1{}^{\beta_1}} - 1) \Big] + (n_2 + n_3)(e^{\tau_1{}^{\beta_1}} \tau_1{}^{\beta_1} \ln \tau_1) + \sum_{i=1}^{n_1} e^{t_i^{\beta_1}} t_i^{\beta_1} \ln t_i \Bigg\} \\
& - \frac{(a+b\tau_1)e^{-\tau_1^{\beta_1}}}{\beta_1 \tau_1{}^{\beta_1 - 1}} \Bigg\{ \left(\frac{1}{(\beta_1)^2} - \tau_1^{\beta_1} (\ln \tau_1)^2\right) \Big[ \sum_{i=1}^{n_1} (e^{t_i^{\beta_1}} - 1) + (n_2 + n_3)(e^{\tau_1{}^{\beta_1}} - 1) \Big] \\
& - \left(\frac{1}{\beta_1} + \ln \tau_1 + \tau_1^{\beta_1} \ln \tau_1\right) \Big[ \sum_{i=1}^{n_1} e^{t_i^{\beta_1}} t_i^{\beta_1} \ln t_i + (n_2 + n_3)(e^{\tau_1{}^{\beta_1}} \tau_1^{\beta_1} \ln \tau_1) \Big] \\
& \Big[ (n_2 + n_3) e^{\tau_1{}^{\beta_1}} \tau_1^{\beta_1} (\ln \tau_1)^2 (\tau_1^{\beta_1} + 1) \Big] + \sum_{i=1}^{n_1} e^{t_i^{\beta_1}} t_i^{\beta_1} (\ln t_i)^2 (t_i^{\beta_1} + 1) \Bigg\}
\end{aligned} \tag{A3}$$

$$\begin{aligned}
\frac{\partial^2 l}{\partial \beta_2^2} = & - n_3 \tau_2^{\beta_2} (\ln \tau_1)^2 + \sum_{i=n_1+n_2+1}^{n} t_i{}^{\beta_2} (\ln t_i)^2 \\
& + \frac{(a+b\tau_2)e^{-\tau_2^{\beta_2}}}{\beta_2 \tau_2{}^{\beta_2 - 1}} \left(\frac{1}{\beta_2} + \ln \tau_2 + \tau_2^{\beta_2} \ln \tau_2\right) \Bigg\{ -\left(\frac{1}{\beta_2} + \ln \tau_2 + \tau_2^{\beta_2} \ln \tau_2\right) \Big[ \sum_{i=n_1+n2+1}^{n} (e^{t_i^{\beta_2}} - e^{\tau_2^{\beta_2}}) \Big] \\
& + \sum_{i=1}^{n_1} (e^{t_i^{\beta_2}} t_i^{\beta_2} \ln t_i - e^{\tau_2^{\beta_2}} \tau_2^{\beta_2} \ln \tau_2) \Bigg\} \\
& - \frac{(a+b\tau_2)e^{-\tau_2^{\beta_2}}}{\beta_2 \tau_2{}^{\beta_2 - 1}} \Bigg\{ \left(\frac{1}{\beta_2^2} - \tau_2^{\beta_2} \ln \tau_2\right) \Big[ \sum_{i=n_1+n_2+1}^{n} (e^{t_i^{\beta_2}} - e^{\tau_2^{\beta_2}}) \Big] \\
& - \left(\frac{1}{\beta_2} + \ln \tau_2 + \tau_2^{\beta_2} \ln \tau_2\right) \Big[ \sum_{i=n_1+n_2+1}^{n} (e^{t_i^{\beta_2}} t_i^{\beta_2} \ln t_i - e^{\tau_2^{\beta_2}} \tau_2^{\beta_2} \ln \tau_2) \\
& \sum_{i=n_1+n_2+1}^{n} \Big[ e^{t_i^{\beta_2}} t_i^{\beta_2} (\ln t_i)^2 (t_i^{\beta_2} + 1) - e^{\tau_2^{\beta_2}} \tau_2^{\beta_2} (\ln \tau_2)^2 (\tau_2^{\beta_2} + 1) \Big] \Bigg\}
\end{aligned}$$

$$\frac{\partial^2 l}{\partial a \partial b} = \frac{\partial^2 l}{\partial b \partial a} = -\frac{n_1 \tau_1}{(a+b\tau_1)^2} - \sum_{i=n_1+1}^{n_1+n_2} \frac{t_i}{(a+bt_i)^2} - \frac{n_3 \tau_2}{(a+b\tau_2)^2}$$

$$\begin{aligned}
\frac{\partial^2 l}{\partial a \partial \beta_1} = \frac{\partial^2 l}{\partial \beta_1 \partial a} &= -\frac{(a+b\tau_1)e^{-\tau_1^{\beta_1}}}{\beta_1 \tau_1{}^{\beta_1-1}} \Bigg\{ -(\frac{1}{\beta_1} + \ln\tau_1 + \tau_1^{\beta_1}\ln\tau_1)[\sum_{i=1}^{n_1}(e^{t_i^{\beta_1}} - 1) + (n_2+n_3)(e^{\tau_1{}^{\beta_1}} - 1)] \\
&\quad + (n_2+n_3)(e^{\tau_1{}^{\beta_1}} \tau_1{}^{\beta_1} \ln\tau_1) + \sum_{i=1}^{n_1} e^{t_i^{\beta_1}} t_i^{\beta_1} \ln t_i \Bigg\} \\
\frac{\partial^2 l}{\partial a \partial \beta_2} = \frac{\partial^2 l}{\partial \beta_2 \partial a} &= -\frac{(a+b\tau_2)e^{-\tau_2^{\beta_2}}}{\beta_2 \tau_2{}^{\beta_2-1}} \Bigg\{ -(\frac{1}{\beta_2} + \ln\tau_2 + \tau_2^{\beta_2}\ln\tau_2)[\sum_{i=n_1+n_2+1}^{n}(e^{t_i^{\beta_2}} - e^{\tau_2^{\beta_2}})] \\
&\quad + \sum_{i=n_1+n_2+1}^{n}(e^{t_i^{\beta_2}} t_i^{\beta_2} \ln t_i - e^{\tau_2^{\beta_2}} \tau_2^{\beta_2} \ln\tau_2) \Bigg\} \\
\frac{\partial^2 l}{\partial b \partial \beta_1} = \frac{\partial^2 l}{\partial \beta_1 \partial b} &= -\frac{(a+b\tau_1)e^{-\tau_1^{\beta_1}}}{\beta_1 \tau_1{}^{\beta_1-2}} \Bigg\{ -(\frac{1}{\beta_1} + \ln\tau_1 + \tau_1^{\beta_1}\ln\tau_1)[\sum_{i=1}^{n_1}(e^{t_i^{\beta_1}} - 1) + (n_2+n_3)(e^{\tau_1{}^{\beta_1}} - 1)] \\
&\quad + (n_2+n_3)(e^{\tau_1{}^{\beta_1}} \tau_1{}^{\beta_1} \ln\tau_1) + \sum_{i=1}^{n_1} e^{t_i^{\beta_1}} t_i^{\beta_1} \ln t_i \Bigg\} \\
\frac{\partial^2 l}{\partial b \partial \beta_2} = \frac{\partial^2 l}{\partial \beta_2 \partial b} &= -\frac{(a+b\tau_2)e^{-\tau_2^{\beta_2}}}{\beta_2 \tau_2{}^{\beta_2-2}} \Bigg\{ -(\frac{1}{\beta_2} + \ln\tau_2 + \tau_2^{\beta_2}\ln\tau_2)[\sum_{i=n_1+n_2+1}^{n}(e^{t_i^{\beta_2}} - e^{\tau_2^{\beta_2}})] \\
&\quad + \sum_{i=n_1+n_2+1}^{n}(e^{t_i^{\beta_2}} t_i^{\beta_2} \ln t_i - e^{\tau_2^{\beta_2}} \tau_2^{\beta_2} \ln\tau_2) \Bigg\} \\
\frac{\partial^2 l}{\partial \beta_1 \partial \beta_2} = \frac{\partial^2 l}{\partial \beta_2 \partial \beta_1} &= 0
\end{aligned} \tag{A4}$$

*Appendix A.3. The Expression of $C_1$ and $C_2$*

$$\begin{aligned}
C_1 &= (\frac{\partial \lambda_1(a,b,\beta_1)}{\partial a}, \frac{\partial \lambda_1(a,b,\beta_1)}{\partial b}, \frac{\partial \lambda_1(a,b,\beta_1)}{\partial \beta_1}, \ 0 \ ) \\
C_2 &= (\frac{\partial \lambda_2(a,b,\beta_2)}{\partial a}, \frac{\partial \lambda_2(a,b,\beta_2)}{\partial b}, \ 0 \ , \frac{\partial \lambda_2(a,b,\beta_2)}{\partial \beta_2})
\end{aligned} \tag{A5}$$

where:

$$
\begin{aligned}
\lambda_1(a,b,\beta_1) &= \frac{(a+b\tau_1)e^{-\tau_1^{\beta_1}}}{\beta_1\tau_1{}^{\beta_1-1}} \\
\lambda_2(a,b,\beta_2) &= \frac{(a+b\tau_2)e^{-\tau_2^{\beta_2}}}{\beta_2\tau_2{}^{\beta_2-1}} \\
\frac{\partial\lambda_1(a,b,\beta_1)}{\partial a} &= \frac{e^{-\tau_1^{\beta_1}}}{\beta_1\tau_1{}^{\beta_1-1}} \\
\frac{\partial\lambda_1(a,b,\beta_1)}{\partial b} &= \frac{\tau_1 e^{-\tau_1^{\beta_1}}}{\beta_1\tau_1{}^{\beta_1-1}} \\
\frac{\partial\lambda_1(a,b,\beta_1)}{\partial\beta_1} &= -\frac{(a+b\tau_1)}{(\beta_1\tau_1{}^{\beta_1-1}e^{\tau_1^{\beta_1}})^2}e^{\tau_1^{\beta_1}}\tau_1{}^{\beta_1-1}(1+\beta_1 ln\tau_1+\beta_1\tau_1{}^{\beta_1}ln\tau_1) \\
\frac{\partial\lambda_2(a,b,\beta_2)}{\partial a} &= \frac{e^{-\tau_2^{\beta_2}}}{\beta_2\tau_2{}^{\beta_2-1}} \\
\frac{\partial\lambda_2(a,b,\beta_2)}{\partial b} &= \frac{\tau_2 e^{-\tau_2^{\beta_2}}}{\beta_2\tau_2{}^{\beta_2-1}} \\
\frac{\partial\lambda_2(a,b,\beta_2)}{\partial\beta_2} &= -\frac{(a+b\tau_2)}{(\beta_2\tau_2{}^{\beta_2-1}e^{\tau_2^{\beta_2}})^2}e^{\tau_2^{\beta_2}}\tau_2{}^{\beta_2-1}(1+\beta_2 ln\tau_2+\beta_2\tau_2{}^{\beta_2}ln\tau_2)
\end{aligned} \tag{A6}
$$

## References


1. Chen, Z. A new two-parameter lifetime distribution with bathtub shape or increasing failure rate function. *Stat. Probab. Lett.* **2000**, *49*, 155–161. [CrossRef]
2. Wu, J.-W.; Lu, H.-L.; Chen, C.-H.; Wu, C.-H. Statistical inference about the shape parameter of the new two-parameter bathtub-shaped lifetime distribution. *Qual. Reliab. Eng. Int.* **2004**, *20*, 607–616. [CrossRef]
3. Wu, S.; Wu, C.-C.; Lin, H.-M. The exact hypothesis test for the shape parameter of a new two-parameter distribution with the bathtub shape or increasing failure rate function under progressive censoring with random removals. *J. Stat. Comput. Simul.* **2009**, *79*, 1015–1042. [CrossRef]
4. Wang, R.; Sha, N.; Gu, B.; Xu, X. Statistical analysis of a Weibull extension with bathtub-shaped failure rate function. *Adv. Stat.* **2014**, *2014*, 304724. [CrossRef]
5. Jiang, R. A new bathtub curve model with a finite support. *Reliab. Eng. Syst. Saf.* **2013**, *119*, 44–51. [CrossRef]
6. Rastogi, M.K.; Tripathi, Y.M. Estimation using hybrid censored data from a two-parameter distribution with bathtub shape. *Comput. Stat. Data Anal.* **2013**, *67*, 268–281. [CrossRef]
7. Shoaee, S.; Khorram, E. Stress-strength reliability of a two-parameter bathtub-shaped lifetime distribution based on progressively censored samples. *Commun. Stat.-Theory Methods* **2015**, *44*, 5306–5328. [CrossRef]
8. Kayal, T.; Tripathi, Y.; Singh, D.P.; Rastogi, M. Estimation and prediction for Chen distribution with bathtub shape under progressive censoring. *J. Stat. Comput. Simul.* **2016**, *87*, 348–366. [CrossRef]
9. Raqab, M.; Bdair, O.; Al-Aboud, F. Inference for the two-parameter bathtub-shaped distribution based on record data. *Metrika* **2018**, *81*, 229–253. [CrossRef]
10. Sedyakin, N. On one physical principle in reliability theory. *Tech. Cybern.* **1966**, *3*, 80–87.
11. Nelson, W. Accelerated life testing—Step-stress models and data analyses. *IEEE Trans. Reliab.* **1980**, *29*, 103–108. [CrossRef]
12. Miller, R.; Nelson, W. Optimum simple step-stress plans for accelerated life testing. *IEEE Trans. Reliab.* **1983**, *32*, 59–65. [CrossRef]
13. Bhattacharyya, G.K.; Zanzawi, S. A tampered failure rate model for step-stress accelerated life test. *Commun. Stat.-Theory Methods* **1989**, *18*, 1627–1643. [CrossRef]
14. Balakrishnan, N.; Xie, Q. Exact inference for a simple step-stress model with Type-I hybrid censored data from the Exponential distribution. *J. Stat. Plan. Inference* **2007**, *137*, 3268–3290. [CrossRef]
15. Balakrishnan, N.; Han, D. Exact inference for a simple step-stress model with competing risks for failure from exponential distribution under Type-II censoring. *J. Stat. Plan. Inference* **2008**, *138*, 4172–4186. [CrossRef]
16. Yuan, T.; Liu, X. Planning simple step-stress accelerated life tests using Bayesian methods. *IEEE Trans. Reliab.* **2012**, *61*, 254–263. [CrossRef]
17. Ismail, A.A. Statistical inference for a step-stress partially-accelerated life test model with an adaptive Type-I progressively hybrid censored data from Weibull distribution. *Stat. Pap.* **2016**, *57*, 271–301. [CrossRef]
18. Shi, X.; Lu, P.; Shi, Y. Inference and optimal design on step-stress partially accelerated life test for hybrid system with masked data. *J. Syst. Eng. Electron.* **2018**, *29*, 1089–1100.

19. Kannan, N.; Kundu, D.; Balakrishnan, N. *Survival Models for Step-Stress Experiments with Lagged Effects*; Chapter Advances in Degradation Modeling; Birkhäuser: Boston, MA, USA, 2010; pp. 355–369.
20. Yao, J.; Luo, R. Step-stress accelerated degradation test model of storage life based on lagged effect for electronic products. In *The 19th International Conference on Industrial Engineering and Engineering Management*; Qi, E., Shen, J., Dou, R., Eds.; Springer: Berlin/Heidelberg, Germany, 2013; pp. 541–550.
21. Beltrami, J. Exponential competing risk step-stress model with lagged effect. *Int. J. Math. Stat.* **2015**, *16*, 1–24.
22. Beltrami, J. Weibull lagged effect step-stress model with competing risks. *Commun. Stat.-Theory Methods* **2016**, *46*, 5419–5442. [CrossRef]
23. Huang, W.; Zhou, J.; Ning, J. Competing risks model for step-stress experiments under lagged effects with masked data. *J. Inf. Comput. Sci.* **2015**, *12*, 495–502. [CrossRef]
24. Shafiq, M.; Atif, M. On the survival models for step-stress experiments based on fuzzy life time data. *Qual. Quant.* **2017**, *51*, 79–91. [CrossRef]
25. Kannan, N.; Kundu, D. Weibull step-stress model with a lagged effect. *Am. J. Math. Manag. Sci.* **2018**, *37*, 33–50. [CrossRef]
26. Hong, H.; Li, J. The numerical delta method. *J. Econom.* **2018**, *206*, 379–394. [CrossRef]

mathematics

MDPI

*Article*

# A Geologic-Actuarial Approach for Insuring the Extraction Tasks of Non-Renewable Resources by One and Two Agents

**Rigoberto Real-Miranda *,† and José Daniel López-Barrientos †**

Facultad de Ciencias Actuariales, Universidad Anáhuac México, Av. Universidad Anáhuac 46, Naucalpan de Juárez 52786, Mexico; daniel.lopez@anahuac.mx

* Correspondence: rigoberto.realm@anahuac.mx

† These authors contributed equally to this work.

**Abstract:** This work uses classic stochastic dynamic programming techniques to determine the equivalence premium that each of two extraction agents of a non-renewable natural resource must pay to an insurer to cover the risk that the extraction pore explodes. We use statistical and geological methods to calibrate the time-until-failure distribution of extraction status for each agent and couple a simple approximation scheme with the actuarial standard of Bühlmann's recommendations to charge the extracting agents a variance premium, while the insurer earns a return on its investment at risk. We test our analytical results through Monte Carlo simulations to verify that the probability of ruin does not exceed a certain predetermined level.

**Keywords:** extraction game for two agents; time-until-failure; hazard rates; vertical pressure gradient; Bühlmann recommendations for premium calculation

**MSC:** 90C39; 91A12; 91B16

**Citation:** Real-Miranda, R.; López-Barrientos, J.D. A Geologic-Actuarial Approach for Insuring the Extraction Tasks of Non-Renewable Resources by One and Two Agents. *Mathematics* **2022**, *10*, 2242. https://doi.org/10.3390/math10132242

Academic Editors: Francisco German Badía and María D. Berrade

Received: 10 June 2022
Accepted: 22 June 2022
Published: 26 June 2022



## 1. Introduction

In late 2020, Lloyd's of London announced plans to stop selling insurance to some types of fossil fuel companies by 2030. Indeed, several insurance companies are expected to follow Lloyd's lead. In addition to the damage that the extraction work causes to the environment, and the subsequent social and governmental pressure to which the extractive fossil fuel industry is subject, the decision of the insurance industry is due to the fact that, during the last thirty years, insurers have lost approximately sixty billion dollars in this sector alone, while losses in all other sectors amount to only thirty million dollars. See [1]. Despite this, it is not clear that the governments of the world (for example, that of Mexico) are prepared to stop investing in the fossil fuel industry, nor that the companies in this field are ready to face it on their own. In any case, the very high value of a single loss related to oil platforms and the short term that the insurance industry has determined to stop its exposure to these risks, gives a paramount importance to the problem of valuation of insurance premia for the members of the actuarial community.

Broadly speaking, what insurance companies generally do is allocate capital using historical data and other factors to calculate the right mix of aggressive and conservative risks, and try to balance frequency and severity. However, these risk estimates are *not* made based on geological or geophysical technical considerations, and therefore, the calculation of premia and benefits does not take into account the geological conditions of the area where a well will be drilled.

The risk we will be studying in this work is that the well explodes during drilling. Approached correctly, and based on seismic and statistical data, it is possible for insurance companies to capitalize on the risk—at least—until 2030. Indeed, with the seismic data from the extraction zone, it is possible to invoke the results presented in [2] to calculate the pore pressure. This data, together with the statistical information on the behavior of the wells in the area, will help us estimate the parameters of the probability distribution of the time until this event occurs while the well is being drilled.

In the actuarial field, it is well known that if the probability of the loss occurring turns out to be low, the insurance company could charge a very competitive and differentiable premium in the market. If, on the other hand, the probability of an explosion turns out to be too high, the insurer could decline to insure the well, reducing the financial risk considerably, for its own benefit.

The works [3,4] use the principle of dynamic programming to show that, when the utility function of an agent extracting a non-renewable resource (for example, oil) is logarithmic, then a kind of equivalence principle (see p. 2 and Example 6.1.1 in [5]), namely

$$x - u^*(t,x) \cdot \bar{a}_t = 0, \tag{1}$$

where $x$ is the resource level available for extraction, $u^*(t,x)$ is the optimal control for the extraction agent at time $t$ when the resource level is $x$, and $\bar{a}_t$ is a contingent annuity valued at zero interest and payable continuously issued in favor of the agent when the resource has been extracted for $t$ years. In fact, in [6] a detailed analysis is made of the behavior of the funding reserves for a single agent when the downtime follows the Gamma, Weibull and Chen distributions.

Moreover, if instead of considering a single agent, we consider two, and for $i = 1, 2$, the $i$-th extractor receives a prize of $c_i$ if it continues extracting resources at the time the other one has stopped, then ([4], Theorem 3) gives us that we can replace (1), by the relation

$$x - u_i^*(t,x) \cdot \left( \bar{a}_{[t]_1:[t]_2} + c_i \bar{A}_{[t]_i:\overset{1}{[t]_{-i}}} \right) = 0, \tag{2}$$

where $\bar{a}_{[t]_1:[t]_2}$ is a joint lives contingent annuity and $\bar{A}_{[t]_i:\overset{1}{[t]_{-i}}}$ represents a contingent function that pays a monetary unit to the $i$-th extractor when the $-i$-th leaves the system. Note that here we make use of the standard nomenclatures of selection in actuarial calculus, and of game theory to refer to the players. Especially when mentioning the $-i$-th player: that is, not the $i$-th.

This research paper presents a statistical and geological calibration of the distribution of the time-until-failure of the extraction status of each agent, studies the fund that the insurer must set up to cover the insurance costs of both extractors, and analyzes the sufficiency of the fund from the point of view of the actuarial standard of the variance premium (at the down level), and of the standard deviation premium (at the top level) to pay dividends to insurers. Finally, we test the results obtained analytically through Monte Carlo simulations to verify that the probability of ruin does not exceed a certain predetermined level (see [7]).

To guarantee that the relationships (1) and (2) hold, the calculations are performed with random variables belonging to the exponential family (see [8], Chapter VII.4.4), and are replicable up to the point where the statistical considerations on the extractors in an area satisfy this condition. The work [5] is all about the computation of equivalence premia and their derivations. In this text, all the random variables under study belong to the exponential family. We aim at following its approach to use (1) and (2) with Gamma, Weibull and Chen distributions. In this work, we base the geological analysis on the presentation provided by [9] to estimate the vertical pressure gradient in the oil well.

The rest of the paper is divided as follows. The next section presents the technical preliminaries of our work, while Section 3 presents the application of [2] to calibrate the parameters of the distributions used to model the time-until-failure of the extraction status. Section 4 uses Bühlmann's recommendations (see [10]) and a simple numerical scheme to calculate a premium payable by each agent such that the insurer earns dividends for its foray into the business of insuring the extraction of non-renewable resources. Section 5 shows the use of the Monte Carlo simulation technique used in [7] to test the theory exposed throughout the document. Finally, Section 6 is devoted to presenting our conclusions.

## 2. Mathematical and Actuarial Preliminaries

We begin our study by describing the problem of our interest and presenting the elementary definitions to which we will refer in the following.

Let us consider the conflict control process in the extraction of a non-renewable resource in which two participants are involved (to avoid monotony, we will use the terms participants, players, extracting agents, extractors or agents). We will assume that both agents are present in the system at the beginning of time (We can study the case in which the agents decide when they start extracting oil. The paper [3] does it like this.).

We use the model presented in ([11], Chapter 10.3) to describe the dynamics of resource consumption, according to which,

$$\dot{x}(t) = -u_1(t) - u_2(t), \text{con } x(t_0) = x_0, \tag{3}$$

where $x(t)$ is the amount of resource available at time $t \geq 0$, $u_i(t)$ is the extraction rate of the $i$-th agent at time $t$, $x_0$ is the initial amount of the resource, and $i = 1, 2$.

Let $\mathcal{G}(x_0)$ be a differential game whose system satisfies the Assumptions 1 and 2 described below.

**Assumption 1.**

(a) *Both players act simultaneously and start the game at some initial time $t_0$ from state $x_0$.*
(b) *The players' control variables are their respective rates of extraction at each moment, namely $u_1, u_2 : [0; \infty] \to \mathcal{U}$, where $\mathcal{U}$ is a compact subset of $[0; \infty]$.*
(c) *The system dynamics is given by (3).*

The system (3) reflects the nonrenewability of the resource because, according to Assumption 1(b), $x(\cdot)$ does not increase.

In this work, we will assume that the extraction of the $i$-th agent stops at a random moment $\tau_i$ for $i = 1, 2$, and that when this happens, the other player continues to extract the resource until attaining its own stopping time (which can happen when the resource is exhausted). We know that $\tau_i$ is a stopping time because the event $\{\tau_i = t\}$ depends only on the story of the stock level up to time $t$ (see [12], p. 253).

**Assumption 2.**

(a) *The stopping times of each agent are pairwise independent.*
(b) *The stopping times belong to the exponential family (cf. [13], Appendices A.2–A.4 and [8], VII.4.4). That is, if $F_{\tau_i}(\cdot)$ is the distribution function of the stopping timpe of the i-th player, then*

$$F_{\tau_i}(t) = 1 - \exp\left(-\int_0^t \lambda_i(s)\mathrm{d}s\right), \tag{4}$$

*where $\lambda_i(\cdot)$ is the failure (hazard) rate of the i-th agent for $i = 1, 2$.*

**Definition 1.** *The random variable for the time-until-failure of the first extracting agent is defined as $\tau := \min\{\tau_1, \tau_2\}$.*

Assumptions 1 and 2 give us a way to characterize the distribution function of $\tau$ using [14], Chapter 16.3 and [5], Chapter 9.3 through the relation:

$$F_\tau(t) = 1 - (1 - F_{\tau_1}(t))(1 - F_{\tau_2}(t)) = 1 - \exp\left(-\int_0^t (\lambda_1(s) + \lambda_2(s))\mathrm{d}s\right). \tag{5}$$

Let $u_1$ and $u_2$ be the controllers that the agents can apply. Define the performance index of the $i$-th agent as

$$
\begin{aligned}
K_i(x_0,u_1,u_2) &= \mathbb{E}_{x_0}^{u_1,u_2}\left[\int_0^{\tau_i} h_i(x(t),u_1(t),u_2(t))\mathrm{d}t\cdot\chi_{\{\tau_i\le\tau_j\}}\right] && (6)\\
&+\mathbb{E}_{x_0}^{u_1,u_2}\left[\int_0^{\tau_j} h_i(x(t),u_1(t),u_2(t))\mathrm{d}t\cdot\chi_{\{\tau_i>\tau_j\}}\right] && (7)\\
&+\mathbb{E}_{x_0}^{u_1,u_2}\left[\Psi_i(x(\tau))\cdot\chi_{\{\tau_i>\tau_j\}}\right], && (8)
\end{aligned}
$$

for $i=1,2$, where $\mathbb{E}_{x_0}^{u_1,u_2}[\cdot]$ represents the conditional expectation of $\cdot$, given that (3) starts at $x_0$, and the players use controllers $u_1$ and $u_2$; $\chi_{\mathcal{A}}$ is the indicator function of the event $\mathcal{A}$; and $h_i$ and $\Psi_i$ are running and terminal utility functions, respectively.

**Remark 1.** *As is to be expected, the performance index $K_i(x_0,u_1,u_2)$ reflects the total payoff that the i-th agent will obtain for the duration of the joint extraction tasks. In particular, $\chi_{\{\tau_i\le\tau_j\}}$ in (6) means that if the i-th agent leaves the system before the j-th ($i,j=1,2$, $i\neq j$) does, then he will receive—on the average—the total reward $\mathbb{E}_{x_0}^{u_1,u_2}\left[\int_0^{\tau_i} h_i(x(t),u_1(t),u_2(t))\mathrm{d}t\right]$. If, on the other hand, the j-th agent leaves the system before the i-th does, then the i-th participant will receive the reward $\mathbb{E}_{x_0}^{u_1,u_2}\left[\int_0^{\tau_j} h_i(x(t),u_1(t),u_2(t))\mathrm{d}t\right]$ specified in (7), plus the terminal reward $\mathbb{E}_{x_0}^{u_1,u_2}[\Psi_i(x(\tau))]$, referred to in (8).*

Naturally, we are interested in modelling the situation in which each player wishes to maximize its own performance index. To this end, we use the traditional definition of a Nash equilibrium.

**Definition 2.** *For $i=1,2$, let $\Pi^i$ be the set of measurable controllers (in Lebesgue's sense) $u_i:[0;\infty[\to[0;x_0]$. We say that a pair of strategies $(u_1^*,u_2^*)\in\Pi^1\times\Pi^2$ is optimal for the differential game $\mathcal{G}(x_0)$ if such a pair is a* Nash equilibrium. *That is,*

$$
\begin{aligned}
K_1(x_0,u_1^*,u_2^*) &\ge K_1(x_0,u_1,u_2^*) \text{ for all } u_1\in\Pi^1 \text{ and}\\
K_2(x_0,u_1^*,u_2^*) &\ge K_2(x_0,u_1^*,u_2) \text{ for all } u_2\in\Pi^2.
\end{aligned}
$$

Proposition 1 in [4] proves that, if $\int_0^t h_i(x^*(s),u_1^*(s),u_2^*(s))\mathrm{d}s<\infty$ for all $t>0$ (where $x^*(s)$ represents the trajectory that (3) follows when the strategies referred by Definition 2 are used) and under our hypotheses, the optimal expected payment for each player is

$$
\begin{aligned}
&K_i(x_0,u_1^*,u_2^*)\\
=&\int_0^\infty h_i(x^*(s),u_1^*(s),u_2^*(s))(1-F_\tau(s))+\Psi_i(x^*(s))f_{\tau_j}(s)(1-F_{\tau_i}(s))\mathrm{d}s,
\end{aligned}
$$

where $f_{\tau_j}(\cdot)$ is a density function for $\tau_j$. Moreover, Theorem 1 in [4] uses common stochastic dynamic programming techniques to see that if a single agent exploits a well of a nonrenewable resource and its utility function is of logarithmic type, i.e., $h(x,u)=\ln u$, then, the optimal controller for such agent is of a closed-loop form (In fact, what ([4], Theorem 1) proves is the particular case where the random variable $\tau$ follows Weibull's or Chen's law. However, it is not difficult to extend that exact same proof to the general case where the distribution meets (4) in Asssumption 2).

$$
u^*(t,x)=\frac{x}{\bar{a}_t}. \tag{9}
$$

Here,

$$
\bar{a}_t:=\int_0^\infty\frac{1-F_\tau(t+s)}{1-F_\tau(t)}\mathrm{d}s, \tag{10}
$$

that is, $\bar{a}_t$ represents the classic contingent annuity from actuarial mathematics for life contingencies (with zero interest rate).

The expression (9) invites us to relate it to the net level premium referred to in any basic text on actuarial mathematics (such as Chapter 6 in [5]), as well as to establish expressions such as (1). Moreover, Theorem 3 in [4] considers the case of two participants that we study in this work, and proves that if the players' running utility functions are logarithmic (i.e., $h_i(x, u_i) = \ln u_i$ for $i = 1, 2$), and the terminal payoff function of the $i$-th player is

$$\Psi_i(x(t \wedge \tau)) = c_i \ln(x(t \wedge \tau)) = c_i \ln(x) \cdot \chi_{\{\tau \leq t\}},$$

where $c_i$ is a known non-negative constant, for $i = 1, 2$, then

$$u_i^*(t, x) = \frac{x}{\bar{a}_{[t]_1:[t]_2} + c_i \bar{A}_{[t]_i:\overset{1}{[t]}_{-i}}}. \tag{11}$$

Here, if $i = 1$, then $-i = 2$ and vice versa; $\bar{a}_{[t]_1:[t]_2} = \int_0^\infty \frac{1-F_\tau(t+s)}{1-F_\tau(t)} \mathrm{d}s$ (with $\tau$ as in (5)) and $\bar{A}_{[t]_i:\overset{1}{[t]}_{-i}} = \int_0^\infty \frac{1-F_\tau(t+s)}{1-F_\tau(t)} \lambda_{-i}(t+s) \mathrm{d}s$. From (11), it is possible to establish relationships as that in (2) to devise a model to insure the extraction tasks of both agents. In both cases, the utility functions of the extracting agents are logarithmic, the benefit is $x$, and under a variant of the classic actuarial equivalence principle, the net level premia will be given by (9) and (11).

Going down the road to review the feasibility of insuring single-agent extraction and conducting the corresponding reserve analysis based on the results of [5], Chapter 7, the conclusion that the reader will eventually achieve will be in the style of Section 3 in [6]. This will lead you to use (9) to define the prospective loss random variable:

$${}_tL := x^*(w + \tau) \cdot v^{\tau - t} - u^*(w, x^*) \cdot \bar{a}_{\overline{\tau - t|}}, \tag{12}$$

where $w$ is the moment of issue of the policy, $x^*$ represents the trajectory that solves (3) (for the case of a single player) when the optimal control (9) is used, $v^z$ is the $z$ period discount factor of compound interest and $\bar{a}_{\overline{z|}}$ is a certain annuity for $z$ periods.

**Remark 2.** *Although (12) expressly refers to the discount factor and the certain annuity, we maintain the approach used in our previous calculations, and we will take an interest rate of zero. The reason we have used these financial symbols is that we want to keep the presentation as close as possible to the study of the theory of life contingencies from the classic acturial perspective. We recognize, however, that doing this might look redundant.*

*Negative Reserves?*

We compute the mathematical reserve ${}_t\bar{V}(\bar{A}_{x(w)}) := \mathbb{E}[{}_tL | \tau > t]$ by finding the conditional distribution of the future lifetime $t$ for a "life" selected at $(w)$, given it has survived until $t > t_0$. With this in mind, we assume—as usual—that $T(w + t) = [T(w) - t | T(w) > t]$ and we prove that

$${}_t\bar{V}(\bar{A}_{x(w)}) = \bar{A}_{x(w+t)} - \frac{\bar{A}_{x(w)}}{x(w)} \frac{x(w)}{\bar{a}_w} \bar{a}_{w+t} = \bar{A}_{x(w+t)} - \frac{\bar{A}_{x(w)}}{x(w)} u^*(w, x) \, \bar{a}_{w+t}. \tag{13}$$

(The details that lead from (12) to (13) can be found in Sectionn 3.3 of [6].) To fix ideas, let us consider only those probability distributions that meet Assumption 2(b) and whose hazard rate functions are of the form of Figure 1, so that they are a nice fit for the time-until-failure of the extracting agent (see [15], Chapter 1).

A plausible interpretation of Figure 1 is that, as time goes by, the failure rate goes from being a decreasing function, to being a more or less constant funtion, and eventually, it becomes an increasing function. In this section we present our analyses on Gamma, Weibull and Chen random variables. We start by presenting the corresponding definitions to contribute to the self-containedness of our work. However, the proofs that the corresponding failure rates look like the one in Figure 1 for certain choices of the parameters should be looked for in [4] (see the Remark 3 below).

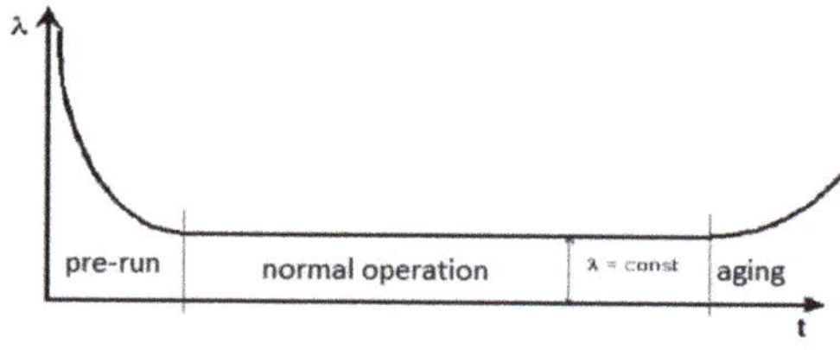


**Figure 1.** Observe that the hazard rate $\mu(t)$ resembles a bathtub. Source: [4,15].

**Definition 3** (Cf. [13], A.3.2.1). *We say that a random variable $\tau$ with support on $]0;\infty[$ follows the* Gamma law *with parameters of shape $\alpha > 0$ and scale $\theta > 0$ if the distribution function of $\tau$ is $F(t) = \int_0^t f(s)\mathrm{d}s$, where $f$ is a density function given by*

$$f(t) = \frac{t^{\alpha-1}\exp(-\frac{t}{\theta})}{\theta^{\alpha}\Gamma(\alpha)} \text{ for } t > 0 \text{ and } \Gamma(\alpha) := \int_0^{\infty} x^{\alpha-1}\mathrm{e}^{-x}\mathrm{d}x.$$

*The hazard rate of Gamma distribution is given by*

$$\mu(t) = \frac{t^{\alpha-1}\mathrm{e}^{-t}}{\Gamma(\alpha) - \Gamma_t(\alpha)} \text{ for } t \geq 0 \text{ and } \Gamma_t(\alpha) := \int_0^{t} x^{\alpha-1}\mathrm{e}^{-x}\mathrm{d}x.$$

*In this case, we will write $\tau \sim \Gamma(\alpha,\theta)$.*

**Definition 4** (See [13], A.3.2.3). *We say that a random variable $\tau$ with support on $[0;\infty]$ follows* Weibull's law *with parameters of shape $\alpha > 0$ and scale $\theta > 0$ if the distribution function of $\tau$ is*

$$F(t) = 1 - \exp\left(-\left(\frac{t}{\theta}\right)^{\alpha}\right) \text{ for } t > 0.$$

*The corresponding hazard rate is*

$$\mu(t) = \frac{\alpha}{\theta}t^{\alpha-1} \text{ for } t > 0.$$

*In this case, we will write $\tau \sim \mathrm{Weibull}(\alpha,\theta)$.*

**Definition 5** (Cf. [16]). *We say that a random variable $\tau$ with support in $[0;\infty]$ follows* Chen's law *with parameters $\alpha > 0$ and $\lambda > 0$, if the distribution function of $\tau$ is*

$$F(t) = 1 - \exp\left(\lambda \cdot \left(1 - \mathrm{e}^{t^{\alpha}}\right)\right) \text{ for } t > 0.$$

*The corresponding hazard rate is*

$$\mu(t) = \alpha\lambda t^{\alpha-1}\exp(t^{\alpha}) \text{ for } t > 0.$$

*In this case, we will write $\tau \sim \mathrm{Chen}(\alpha,\lambda)$.*

**Remark 3.** *For the random variables of Definitions 3–5, it is true that if the shape parameter $\alpha < 1$, then the lifetime modelled by $\tau$ is in prime conditions; if $\alpha = 1$, then the failure rate $\mu(t)$ is* more or less *constant; and if $\alpha > 1$, the machinery is at an aging stage. See the details in [4].*

For the case where $\tau \sim \Gamma(\alpha,\theta)$, the mathematical reserve is obtained by substituting the expressions cited in the Definition 3 in (10), and the resulting ones, in (13) (technical details can be read in Section 3.3 in [6]). See Figure 2.

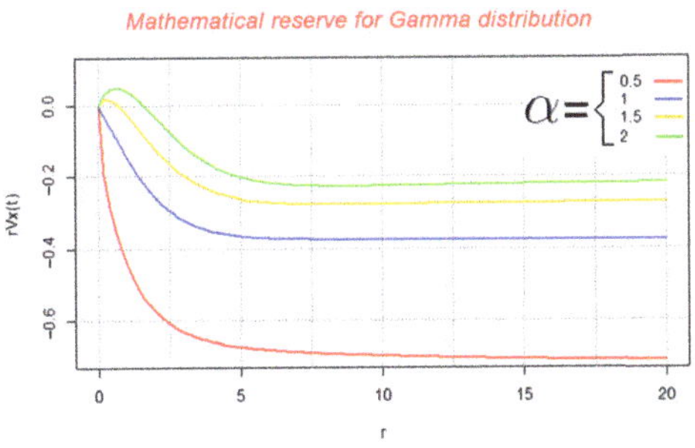


**Figure 2.** Mathematical reserve ${}_t\bar{V}(x(0))$, for Gamma distribution with parameters $\theta = 1$, and $\alpha = 0.5, 1.0, 1.5, 2.0$.

For the case where $\tau \sim \text{Weibull}(\alpha, \theta)$, the mathematical reserve is obtained by substituting the expressions cited in the Definition 4 in (10), and the resulting ones, in (13) (technical details can be seen in section 3.3 on [6]). See Figure 3.

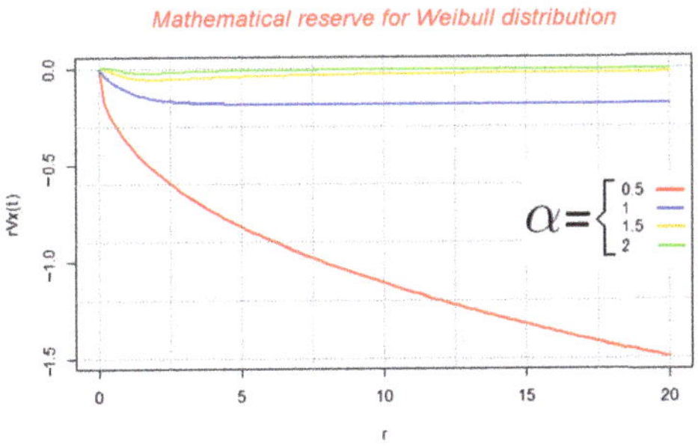


**Figure 3.** Mathematical reserve ${}_t\bar{V}(x(0))$, for Weibull distribution with parameters $\theta = 1$ and $\alpha = 0.5, 1.0, 1.5, 2.0$.

For the case where $\tau \sim \text{Chen}(\alpha, \lambda)$, the mathematical reserve is obtained by substituting the expressions cited in the Definition 5 in (10), and the resulting ones, in (13) (technical details can be found in Section 4.2 on [6]). See Figure 4.

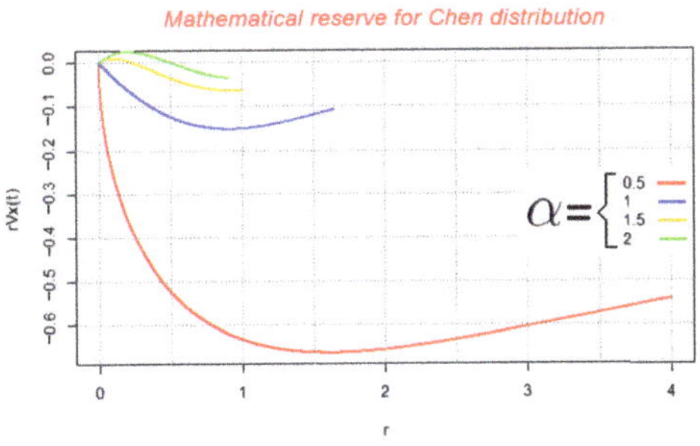


**Figure 4.** Mathematical reserve ${}_t\bar{V}(x(0))$, for Chen distribution with parameters $\theta = 1$ and $\alpha = 0.5$, $1.0, 1.5, 2.0$.

**Remark 4.** *Section 7.3 in [5] mentions that, in most applications, mathematical reserves are positive. However, there is no theoretical support that guarantees it. In fact, Figures 2–4 would represent a reliable counterexample to any result that affirms that the reserves must be positive. It is also important to note that the values that we assign to the shape parameter $\alpha$ in each of the studied* *cases correspond to different periods of operation of the extraction tool (see [15], Chapter 1): from the period in which the machinery is new ($\alpha < 1$), passing through the period of normal operation ($\alpha = 1$), and until reaching the decay period ($\alpha > 1$). Two things are noteworthy.*

- *The scale parameter $\theta$ remains unchanged in all calculations. What would happen if we used a more* ad hoc *parameter to the extractive industry of non-renewable resources?*
- *It might be worth reviewing what happens when* not *charging only the "equivalence premium" (We enclose these words in quotation marks because, in reality, it is not an equivalence premium. Recall that this case occurs when the utility function of the policyholder is linear (see [5], Example 6.1.1). However, we do know that, from Doob's Submartingale Convergence Theorem (see Theorem (1) in [12], Chapter 12.3) and the notes in Section D.1.1 in [17], the bankruptcy is a certain event if the insurer does not charge more than the equivalency premium.) in exchange for insurance protection. Is it possible to charge an amount that guarantees a profit for whoever insures all the extractors?*

  *Sections 3 and 4 deal with the first and second points just noted, respectively.*

## 3. A Realistic Scaling Parameter for the Weibull Distribution in the Gulf of Mexico

In this section we use common geological tools to estimate the pressure of the pore in which drilling is to be carried out, in order to use it as a parameter to calculate an a priori probability distribution that is suitable for modeling the times until the failure of the agents. With these data at hand, it would be feasible to complement the observations gathered from experience with some Bayesian technique to estimate a posteriori distribution for these variables (for example, the [18] study presents an interesting comparison between three of these techniques in a forestry context). To the best of our knowledge, this proposal is new and therefore not applied in the actuarial field.

Geophysicists know that before drilling a deepwater pore to extract oil, it is necessary to estimate the internal pressure by processing seismic reflection data. Failing to do this has consequences that can be fatal (not to mention extremely costly). We consider it natural to use the vertical pressure gradient in deep water to calibrate the distribution of time to failure of the extracting agent.

Let $h$ be the depth below the ocean floor (measured in meters). Having measured the seismic velocity with sufficient precision, it is possible to conclude the process of estimating the pressure gradient $p(h)$ (measured in $\frac{\mathrm{Pa}}{\mathrm{m}}$) by applying some function that transforms it into the pore pressure of our interest. The most commonly used methods in the industry are:

- That of Bowers (cf. [9]):

$$p(h) = \frac{\mathrm{d}}{\mathrm{d}h}\left[g\int_0^h \rho(z)\mathrm{d}z - \sqrt[B]{\frac{v(h)-v_0}{A}}\right] \tag{14}$$

where $g = 9.8067\ \frac{\mathrm{m}}{\mathrm{s}^2}$ is the acceleration of gravity on Earth, $\rho$ is the density (measured in $\frac{\mathrm{kg}}{\mathrm{m}^3}$) of the sediment, $v(h)$ is the velocity (measured in $\frac{\mathrm{m}}{\mathrm{s}}$) of the sediments $h$ meters below the sea floor and $v_0$ is the velocity of the unconsolidated sediments saturated with liquid. The parameters $A$ and $B$ are artificial and describe the variation in speed when the differential voltage increases; and in the Gulf of Mexico they take values of $A = 28.3711$ and $B = 0.6207$ (see [19]). In fact, in the Gulf of Mexico, the normally pressurized sediment velocity varies linearly, satisfying $v(h) = v_0 + k \cdot h$, where $k$ is measured in $\frac{1}{\mathrm{s}}$, represents the vertical velocity gradient and, in that region, satisfies $k \in [0.6; 1]$ (see [2,20,21]). With this simplification, (14) reduces to

$$\begin{aligned} p(h) &= \frac{\mathrm{d}}{\mathrm{d}h}\left[9.8067\int_0^h \rho(z)\mathrm{d}z - \sqrt[B]{\frac{k\cdot h}{A}}\right] \\ &= 9.8067\rho(h) - \frac{1}{B}\sqrt[B]{\frac{k}{A}}\,h^{\frac{1-B}{B}}. \end{aligned} \tag{15}$$

- And that of Eaton (cf. [22]):

$$p(h) = \frac{\mathrm{d}}{\mathrm{d}h}\left[g\int_0^h \rho(z)\mathrm{d}z - \sigma_{\mathcal{N}}(h)\left(\frac{v(h)}{v_{\mathcal{N}}(h)}\right)^n\right], \tag{16}$$

where $\sigma_{\mathcal{N}}(h)$ is the normal vertical differential stress of the sediment—that is, without the action of man—at $h$ meters below the seafloor (measured in Pa) and $v_{\mathcal{N}}(h)$ is the normal seismic velocity $h$ meters below the sea floor. The exponent $n$ has no units, and describes the sensitivity of the seismic velocity to the stress differential, and in the Gulf of Mexico it is common to take $n = 3$ (see [19]).

As we have already stated in Section 2, it is proven that if the failure rate of a random variable is shaped like a bathtub (such as Gamma, Weibull and Chen), then it is adequate to model the time-until-failure (explosion or exhaustion) of an extracting agent. However, papers like [4,6] simplify the task of modeling by considering that one of the parameters is unitary. Our intention is to use (15) or (16) to replace this unrealistic data by the multiplicative inverse of the pore pressure even when data on interval velocities are not available. In the latter case, geology specialists (cf. [2,19]) propose taking a sample of $N$ pressures in wells reasonably close to the one whose pressure is to be estimated, and taking an estimator of the pressure $\tilde{p}(h)$ such that the sample mean squared error statistic

$$\frac{1}{N}\sum_{i=1}^{N}(p_i(h) - \tilde{p}(h))^2$$

is minimal. This approach is very attractive for those who have been trained in statistical techniques, but it is also very convenient for use in the insurance industry, since it validates the investigation of the pressure data in the pores surrounding the one to be insured.

To fix ideas, we will use parameter estimates which are valid for the Gulf of Mexico in Bowers' method. According to [23], the average density of the sediment in the Gulf of Mexico satisfies the empirical relationship

$$\rho(h) = 1953.1638 + 1.95538406399448h^{0.6}. \tag{17}$$

Inserting $A = 28.3711$, $B = 0.6207$, $k = 0.6$ and the density (17) in (15), we obtain Table 1 and Figure 5.

**Table 1.** Estimated values of the pressure gradient.

| $h$ (in m) | 0 | 500 | 1000 | 1500 | 2000 | 2500 | 3000 |
|---|---|---|---|---|---|---|---|
| $p(h)$ (in $\frac{\text{kPa}}{\text{m}}$) | 19.15 | 19.95 | 20.36 | 20.70 | 20.99 | 21.25 | 21.49 |

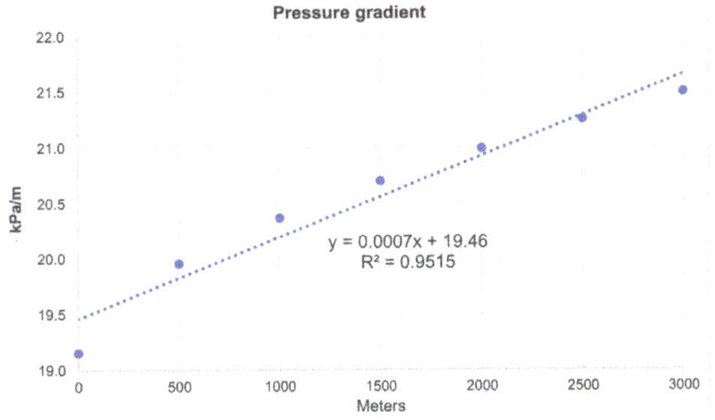


**Figure 5.** Pressure gradient estimates from depth.

Observe that, in spite of the fact that relation (15) is clearly non-linear, we can execute a linear regression with the obtained points:

$$\hat{p}(h) = 0.0007h + 19.46. \tag{18}$$

This yields a statistic $R^2$ of 95.15%, and what is more important: it provides us with a linear estimation method for the pressure in a suboceanic oil extraction well in the Gulf of Mexico.

With this in mind, we can assume that the time-until-failure (measured in years) of an extracting agent is modeled by $\tau \sim \text{Weibull}\left(\alpha, \frac{1}{p(h)}\right)$. In Table 2 we display the probability that the agent leaves the extractive work before a month has passed by. That is,

$$\mathbb{P}\left(\tau \leq \frac{1}{12}\right) = 1 - \exp\left(-\left(\frac{p(h)}{12}\right)^{\alpha}\right),$$

with $\alpha = 0.5, 1, 1.5, 2$; and $h = 0.500, 1000, 1500, 2000, 2500, 3000$.

**Table 2.** Probability that the agent leaves the extractive tasks before a month has passed by.

| | | $\theta$ | | | | | | |
|---|---|---|---|---|---|---|---|---|
| | | $\frac{1}{19.15}$ | $\frac{1}{19.95}$ | $\frac{1}{20.36}$ | $\frac{1}{20.69}$ | $\frac{1}{20.98}$ | $\frac{1}{21.25}$ | $\frac{1}{21.49}$ |
| $\alpha$ | 0.5 | 71.73% | 72.46% | 72.82% | 73.11% | 73.35% | 73.57% | 73.77% |
| | 1 | 79.73% | 81.04% | 81.68% | 82.18% | 82.60% | 82.98% | 83.32% |
| | 1.5 | 86.69% | 88.28% | 89.04% | 89.62% | 90.10% | 90.53% | 90.90% |
| | 2 | 92.17% | 93.70% | 94.39% | 94.89% | 95.31% | 95.65% | 95.96% |

Recall Remark 3. Note that as the extraction equipment ages (that is, as the shape parameter $\alpha$ grows), the chances of explosion increase even over a horizon as short as that of one month. On the other hand, note that as the depth $h$, and therefore the vertical pressure gradient $p(h)$ increases, the probability of an accident occurring also increases. A valid criticism that the parameterizations we show deserve is that the chances of experiencing a loss may seem too great. However, to study the cause of the large losses that insurers have experienced in the past (documented in [1]), we need to get exactly this effect on the probabilities. In any case, we invite the reader to review the computational tool (available here: https://keisan.casio.com/exec/system/1180573175 (accessed on 23 May 2022)) to form their own judgment and reach their own conclusions.

## 4. A Numeric Approximation to the Bühlmann Model to Insure Two Agents

We borrow the theory presented in, for example [24], Chapter 5.2 to study an insurance model for the mining activities of two agents that includes charging each agent a (variance) premium and obtaining a dividend payment on the capital with which the portfolio is insured.

The algorithm to accomplish this has two steps and first appeared in [10]. It assumes that the decision makers set the probability of ruin at the level $\varepsilon$ (for it acceptable to them) and the percentage that they want to obtain as a dividend $q \in [0;1]$ of the capital $w$ that they contribute. The first step is for the decision makers to calculate the capital needed to cover a risk $S$:

$$w = \sqrt{\text{var}[S]}\sqrt{\frac{|\ln \varepsilon|}{2q}}. \tag{19}$$

The second step is for the decision maker to calculate the variance premium that each policyholder must pay in exchange for agreeing to cover the risk $X_i$:

$$r_i = \mathbb{E}[X_i] + \frac{|\ln \varepsilon|}{w}\text{var}[X_i]. \tag{20}$$

If a single insurer commits to insure the activities of the two extractive agents immersed in the differential game $\mathcal{G}(x_0)$ described in Section 2, then, by (2), such company will face the risk of paying $x(\tau)$ to each of the agents.

It is worth noting that although, by its nature, the game $\mathcal{G}(x_0)$ should pay only the player who remains extracting oil, it is possible that both players will have to leave the system due to the same incident.

### 4.1. Weibull Failure Times

It should be clear that $X_i = x(\tau)$, where $\tau$ is the random variable from Definition 1; and that $S = 2x(\tau)$. So $\tau = \min\{\tau_1, \tau_2\}$ and $\tau_i \sim \text{Weibull}\left(\alpha_i, \frac{1}{p}\right)$, with $p \equiv p(h)$ for $i = 1, 2$. The reason for which we take the same pressure for each agent is that we implicitly assume that they use the same well to extract the resource. Note, however, that the shape parameters are not necessarily equal to each other. In this way we take into account the technological differences between the participants.

In order to find the capital $w$ referred to in (19), we must compute $\text{var}[S] = 4\text{var}[x(\tau)]$. This requires discovering the functional form of $x(t)$. Inserting (11) into (3) and solving the resulting differential equation gives us the random variable we seek to specify the benefit:

$$x(\tau) = x_0 \exp\left( -\int_0^\tau \frac{1}{\bar{a}_{[t]_1:[t]_2} + c_1 \bar{A}^1_{[t]_1:[t]_2}} + \frac{1}{\bar{a}_{[t]_1:[t]_2} + c_2 \bar{A}^1_{[t]_1:[t]_2}} \mathrm{d}t \right). \tag{21}$$

To simplify the work, we will only solve the particular case in which the terminal reward for both players is null, that is, $c_1 = 0 = c_2$. With this in mind, (21) reduces to

$$x(\tau) \quad = \quad x_0 \exp\left( -2 \int_0^\tau \frac{1}{\bar{a}_{[t]_1:[t]_2}} \mathrm{d}t \right),$$

and using (5), we turn it into

$$\begin{aligned} x(\tau) &= x_0 \exp\left( -2 \int_0^\tau \frac{(1 - F_{\tau_1}(t))(1 - F_{\tau_2}(t))}{\int_0^\infty (1 - F_{\tau_1}(t+s))(1 - F_{\tau_2}(t+s)) \mathrm{d}s} \mathrm{d}t \right) \\ &= x_0 \exp\left( -2 \int_0^\tau \frac{\exp(-(tp)^{\alpha_1}) \exp(-(tp)^{\alpha_2})}{\int_0^\infty \exp(-[(t+s)p]^{\alpha_1}) \exp(-[(t+s)p]^{\alpha_2}) \mathrm{d}s} \mathrm{d}t \right) \\ &= x_0 \exp\left( -2 \int_0^\tau \frac{\exp(-(p^{\alpha_1} t^{\alpha_1} + p^{\alpha_2} t^{\alpha_2}))}{\int_0^\infty \exp(-(p^{\alpha_1}(t+s)^{\alpha_1} + p^{\alpha_2}(t+s)^{\alpha_2})) \mathrm{d}s} \mathrm{d}t \right) \\ &= x_0 \exp\left( -2 \int_0^\tau \frac{1}{\int_0^\infty \exp(-p^{\alpha_1}((t+s)^{\alpha_1} - t^{\alpha_1}) - p^{\alpha_2}((t+s)^{\alpha_2} - t^{\alpha_2})) \mathrm{d}s} \mathrm{d}t \right). \end{aligned} \tag{22}$$

The second equality arose from substituting Weibull's distribution function specified in the Definition 4 into (22). On the other hand, the integral in the denominator of the last expression depends absolutely on the values that we assign to the shape parameters of each agent.

With the aim of illustrating the result, we consider that the technology of the first agent is obsolete (that is, $\alpha_1 = 2$) and that the second agent is in the period of normal operation of its machinery (thus, $\alpha_2 = 1$). Also, we assume that they are drilling at a depth of 771.4285714 m below the sea floor of the Gulf of Mexico, and we use the regression line (18) so that $\hat{p} = 20 \, \frac{\text{kPa}}{\text{m}}$. This gives us that

$$\begin{aligned} &\int_0^\infty \exp(-p^{\alpha_1}((t+s)^{\alpha_1} - t^{\alpha_1}) - p^{\alpha_2}((t+s)^{\alpha_2} - t^{\alpha_2})) \mathrm{d}s \\ = \; &\frac{1}{20} \exp\left( \left( 20t + \frac{1}{2} \right)^2 \right) \int_{20t + \frac{1}{2}}^\infty \mathrm{e}^{-z^2} \mathrm{d}z \end{aligned}$$

$$= \frac{1}{40}\sqrt{\pi}\exp\left(\left(20t+\frac{1}{2}\right)^2\right)\left(2\Phi\left[\sqrt{2}\left(20t+\frac{1}{2}\right)\right]-1\right),$$

where, as usual, $\Phi(z)$ represents the probability that a standard Normal random variable does not exceed $z$. This gives us that

$$x(\tau) = x_0 \exp\left(-\frac{80}{\sqrt{\pi}}\int_0^{\tau}\frac{\exp\left(-\left(20t+\frac{1}{2}\right)^2\right)}{2\Phi\left[\sqrt{2}\left(20t+\frac{1}{2}\right)\right]-1}dt\right).$$

Below we show some points of this trajectory, together with the corresponding densities. Note that, thanks to (5), it is easy to obtain the expression that corresponds to a density for $\tau$:

$$f_\tau(t) = \left(\alpha_1 p^{\alpha_1} t^{\alpha_1-1} + \alpha_2 p^{\alpha_2} t^{\alpha_2-1}\right)\exp(-p^{\alpha_1}t^{\alpha_1} - p^{\alpha_2}t^{\alpha_2}) \text{ for } t > 0. \quad (23)$$

We make an equidistant partition of the interval $[0; T]$ with 10,000 subintervals. In Table 3 we show only a subset of the first 2600 realizations of $x$, since the significance of the figures in the third and fourth columns is negligible. However, the resource has not been depleted at this point, as it largely depends on the initial value assigned to $x_0$, which for the purpose of illustrating this example will be taken as equal to one.

**Table 3.** Values of $x(t)$ and $f(t)$.

| $\ell$ | $t_\ell$ | $x(t_\ell)$ | $f_\tau(t_\ell)$ |
|---|---|---|---|
| 1 | 0 | $1x_0$ | 20 |
| 2 | 0.0001 | $0.99269x_0$ | 20.0398 |
| 3 | 0.0002 | $0.985421x_0$ | 20.0792 |
| 4 | 0.0003 | $0.978194x_0$ | 20.1182 |
| 5 | 0.0004 | $0.971008x_0$ | 20.1568 |
| 6 | 0.0005 | $0.963862x_0$ | 20.1950 |
| 7 | 0.0006 | $0.956758x_0$ | 20.2328 |
| 8 | 0.0007 | $0.949694x_0$ | 20.2702 |
| 9 | 0.0008 | $0.942671x_0$ | 20.3072 |
| 10 | 0.0009 | $0.935689x_0$ | 20.3438 |
| 11 | 0.001 | $0.928746x_0$ | 20.3800 |
| 12 | 0.0011 | $0.921844x_0$ | 20.4158 |
| 13 | 0.0012 | $0.914982x_0$ | 20.4512 |
| 14 | 0.0013 | $0.90816x_0$ | 20.4862 |
| 15 | 0.0014 | $0.901378x_0$ | 20.5207 |
| ⋮ | ⋮ | ⋮ | ⋮ |
| 2597 | 0.2596 | $2.9958 \times 10^{-30}x_0$ | $2.4845 \times 10^{-12}$ |
| 2598 | 0.2597 | $2.8605 \times 10^{-30}x_0$ | $2.4294 \times 10^{-12}$ |
| 2599 | 0.2598 | $2.7312 \times 10^{-30}x_0$ | $2.3756 \times 10^{-12}$ |
| 2600 | 0.2599 | $2.6078 \times 10^{-30}x_0$ | $2.3228 \times 10^{-12}$ |
| ⋮ | ⋮ | ⋮ | ⋮ |

Since the random variable $x(\tau)$ is a function of $\tau$, we can use the law of the unconscious statistician and the data in the table to find a discrete approximation of $\mathbb{E}[x(\tau)]$. To this end, define the step size $\Delta_\ell$ as the forward difference $\Delta_\ell := t_{\ell+1} - t_\ell$. Thus,

$$\mathbb{E}[x(\tau)] \approx \sum_{\ell=1}^{2600} x(t_\ell)\cdot f_\tau(t_\ell)\cdot\Delta_\ell = 0.24161871x_0.$$

Similarly, it is possible to approximate

$$\text{var}[x(\tau)] = \mathbb{E}\left[(x(\tau))^2\right] - (\mathbb{E}[x(\tau)])^2 \approx 0.07379422x_0^2.$$

According to (19), the capital that the insurer needs to invest to obtain a return of $q$ is $w \approx 0.54330185x_0\sqrt{\frac{|\ln\varepsilon|}{2q}}$, and the premium that the $i$-th agent must pay according to (20), is $r_i = 0.24161871x_0 + 0.07379422x_0^2\frac{|\ln\varepsilon|}{w}$ for $i = 1,2$. To illustrate this result, we will take $x_0 = 1$ in the appropriate units, a 5% probability of ruin, and a 10% dividend. Thus,

$$w = 2.1027018 \text{ and } r_i = 0.3467538 \text{ for } i = 1,2.$$

It is important to note that, since the initial oil reserve is unitary, our result indicates that each extractor must make a considerably large payment (compared to the equivalence premium, since $r_i$ is 30.31% larger than $\mathbb{E}[x(\tau)]$) to become creditor to the benefit in the event of an accident. On the other hand, this is the effect achieved by calibrating the distribution of $\tau = \min\{\tau_1, \tau_2\}$ with the parameters indicated in our example.

On the other hand, note that the assumption that the terminal rewards are zero implies that the premia that each of the agents pays are identical. An economic interpretation of this is that the agents that extract resources on the same platform certainly compete to maximize their own benefit, but they collaborate with each other for the good of their own businesses. In our case, the first agent has obsolete technology and the second has equipment in normal operating conditions, but both pay the same premium.

### 4.2. Gamma Failure Times

In this section we will carry out the same exercise as in the former, but now considering that the extraction tasks are of two agents whose respective failure times follow the Gamma distribution.

To find the capital $\omega$, we will first calculate the functional form of $x(\tau)$ according to (22). For this reason, in order to illustrate our result, we will consider the same parameters used for the Weibull distribution, that is, that the technology of the first agent is obsolete ($\alpha_1 = 2$), while that of the second is in normal mode of operation ($\alpha_2 = 1$); plus $\hat{p} = 20\ \frac{\text{kPa}}{\text{m}}$. Thus, the distribution functions for $\tau_1$ and $\tau_2$ are given by:

$$\begin{aligned} F_{\tau_1}(t) &= 1 - (1+20t)\mathrm{e}^{-20t}, \\ F_{\tau_2}(t) &= 1 - \mathrm{e}^{-20t}. \end{aligned}$$

The distribution function of $\tau$ is:

$$F_\tau(t) = \int_0^\infty (1 - F_{\tau_1}(t+s))(1 - F_{\tau_2}(t+s))\mathrm{d}s \quad = \quad \frac{1}{80}(3+40t)\mathrm{e}^{-20t}.$$

Then

$$x(\tau) = x_0\frac{1}{9}(3+40\tau)\mathrm{e}^{-80\tau}.$$

With the definition of $x(\tau)$ we can find $\mathbb{E}[x(\tau)]$ and $\mathrm{var}[x(\tau)]$ and, from (5), obtain the expression of the density function of $\tau$:

$$f_\tau(t) = 40(1+20t)\mathrm{e}^{-40t} - 20\mathrm{e}^{-40t} \text{ for } t > 0.$$

So, an analogous procedure to the one given by Table 3 now gives us $\mathbb{E}[x(\tau)] = 0.29218107x_0$ and $\mathrm{var}[x(\tau)] = 0.081871704x_0^2$.

Now, if we consider that $x_0 = 1$, a probability of ruin of 5%, and a dividend of 10%; (19) yields that the initial capital that the insurer needs to invest to obtain this return, and the premium that the $i$-th agent must pay, according to (20), are, respectively

$$\omega = 2.214794372 \text{ and } r_i = 0.402920789 \text{ for } i = 1,2.$$

In this case, the result indicates that each extractor must pay 38% more than the equivalence premium, $\mathbb{E}[x(\tau)]$. This premium may be perceived as high, however, when compared to the 44% that must be paid when failure times obey the Weibull law, it is not so high. Furthermore, given that the lifetime of the pore using the Weibull distribution is less lower than the same statistic using Gamma's law, it is natural that the premium is cheaper, since ultimately the time to failure is smaller. The following table shows the calculations of the initial capital, the Bühlmann premium and the equivalence premium in both cases.

If we compare the initial capital and the premium that each agent must pay for both distributions under study, we find that assuming a Gamma distribution makes the insurance more expensive. Therefore, if the company considers that the time until failure of the extraction of the resource follows this distribution, it should have an initial capital 5% higher than that required for the Weibull distribution. The same occurs with the premium that each agent must pay, since it would be 16% higher, while the equivalence premium is 21% higher.

A plausible conclusion from the above is that the choice of extraction pore lifetime distribution can lead to more expensive insurance. For this reason it is very important to decide on this with absolute care.

## 5. Monte Carlo Simulation for the Wealth Process

We dedicate this section to verifying that the Bühlmann model generates a prorated payoff scheme across the horizon that results in a probability of ruin consistent with the one used to obtain $r_i$ and $\omega$. As the results shown in Table 4 we are given that Weibull insurance is less onerous, we focus on the assumption that failure times follow Weibull's law, for this purpose we will use the approach proposed in [7].

**Table 4.** Comparison of Bühlmann's schemas.

| | $\omega$ | $r_i$ | $\mathbb{E}[x(\tau)]$ |
|---|---|---|---|
| Weibull | 2.102701805 | 0.346753803 | 0.24161871 |
| Gamma | 2.214794372 | 0.402920789 | 0.29218107 |
| $\frac{\text{Gamma}}{\text{Weibull}}$ | 1.0533088 | 1.1619794 | 1.2092651 |

According to the results of Section 4, for an insurer to agree to cover the risk of the two extractive agents whose failure times follow Weibull's law without falling into insolvency, it must charge each of them a premium of at least $r_i = 0.3467538$ for $i = 1.2$, and have an initial capital of $\omega = 2.1027018$. Under these conditions, the Bühlmann model guarantees that the insurer's probability of ruin will not be greater than $\varepsilon = 5\%$.

### *5.1. Simulation*

Next, we will see through a Monte Carlo simulation the behavior of wealth, assuming that both, the premium and the initial capital are fixed.

Define $W_0 = \omega$ as the initial wealth. Next, let us denote the observed richness in the following time interval as

$$W_k = W_{k-1} - \Delta t \cdot 10\% W_0 + \Delta t \cdot 2\pi - 2N_0, \text{ with } k = 1, 2, \ldots,$$

where $\pi$ denotes the premium that each of the two agents will have to pay in exchange for the insurance; $(N_{k-1} : k = 1, 2, \ldots)$ is a sequence of random variables that indicate the payment of the claim, or a null amount; and $\Delta t$ is the step size in our simulation. Note that we consider that, in the event of a loss, the company will pay both agents. We also assume that at each moment, the company receives a dividend of $\Delta t \cdot 10\% W_0$.

Let us recall that, in Table 3, the time horizon considered to evaluate the functions $f_\tau(t_\ell)$ and $x(t_\ell)$ was $0 \le t \le 0.2599$ (because, for higher values of $t$, the values of both functions are of the order $10^{-12}$ and lower, and we decided to discard them from our analysis). Similarly, by (23), the density function for $\tau$ is given by

$$f_\tau(t) = (2 \cdot 20^2 t + 20)\mathrm{e}^{-(20^2 t^2 + 20t)}$$

and the distribution function is:

$$F_\tau(t) = 1 - \mathrm{e}^{-(20^2 t^2 + 20t)}.$$

Let $u := F_\tau(t)$. Due to the monotony of $F_\tau(t)$, calculate its inverse:

$$t = \sqrt{-\frac{1}{20^2}\ln(1-u) + \left(\frac{1}{2\cdot 20}\right)^2} - \frac{1}{2\cdot 20}, \tag{24}$$

where $u \sim U(0,1)$. To apply the inverse transformation method, we take a (pseudo) random sample of size $n$ from the Uniform distribution on $[0;1]$: $\{u_1,\ldots,u_n\}$. For each $u_j$, $j = 1,\ldots,n$, we apply the inverse transformation method using the expression (24). With this, we obtain $t_1,\ldots,t_n$ different, and each one represents the time in which the failure of one of the agents occurs. For each $t_j$, $j = 1,\ldots,n$, we build a trajectory for the wealth. It is important to mention that the difference between the various trajectories that we simulate is the moment of failure. The other elements remain identical in each one because both, the payment of the premium and that of the dividends, remain invariant over time.

In this way, the trajectory of wealth is given by:

$$\begin{aligned}
W_0 &= \omega,\\
W_1 &= W_0 - \Delta t\cdot 10\% W_0 + \Delta t\cdot 2\pi - 2N_0,\\
W_2 &= W_1 - \Delta t\cdot 10\% W_0 + \Delta t\cdot 2\pi - 2N_1,\\
&\vdots\\
W_k &= W_{k-1} - \Delta t\cdot 10\% W_0 + \Delta t\cdot 2\pi - 2N_{k-1},
\end{aligned} \tag{25}$$

where $\Delta t = 0.0001$, and $W_0$ corresponds to the time $t_0 = 0$; $W_1$, at $t_1 = t_0 + \Delta t = 0.0001$; $W_2$, at $t_2 = t_1 + \Delta t = 0.0002$; $W_\ell$, a $t_\ell = t_{\ell-1} + \Delta t$; and so on, until obtaining the wealth $W_k$ in the time $t_k$, which represents the moment in which the failure of the agents occurs. Thus, $N_\ell = 0$ if $t_\ell \neq t_k$, and $N_\ell = x(t_\ell)$ otherwise. That is, when $t_\ell \geq t_k$, then $N_\ell = x(t_k)$, the path ends and benefits are paid to both agents.

In (25) the coefficient $\Delta t$ represents the apportionment of dividend and premium payments over the horizon.

The above process is done for each of the $n$ random numbers.

In Figure 6 five Monte Carlo simulations of wealth and failure are presented, for 100 random numbers each. In this case, the colour of the lines is useful to appreciate each trajectory, but it does not represent anything in particular.

As can be seen, the greatest losses that can be obtained, derived from an accident, occur when the start of the extraction of the resource is recent, and the payment that the company must make to both agents, in the event of an accident, is reduced as time progresses. The above makes sense because we assume that the benefit obtained is determined by the extraction dynamics, which is a decreasing function over time.

It is important to note that in the graphs, the wealth obtained is accumulated in the line that is perceived as almost horizontal, while the "vertical" lines are the values of the benefit paid to the agents. As we have said, the payoff function is decreasing over the horizon.

Likewise, in these graphs it is observed that none of them crosses zero, which indicates that the company will never go bankrupt at the time of failure with the premium and initial capital considered.

The above is easy to see because for $t = 0$, $x(t) = 1$, which is the maximum value of the benefit that can be granted, also, this is when the initial capital $W_0 = 2.1027$ is contributed. For $t = 0.0001$, $x(t) = 0.9927$ and wealth $W_1 = W_0 - \Delta t\cdot 10\% W_0 + \Delta t\cdot 2\pi - 2N_0 = 2.10275 - 2\cdot 0.9927 = 0.11737$. As time grows, $W_t$ also grows, however, since $x(t)$ is a decreasing function, in the event of a claim, the amount to be paid is decreasing.

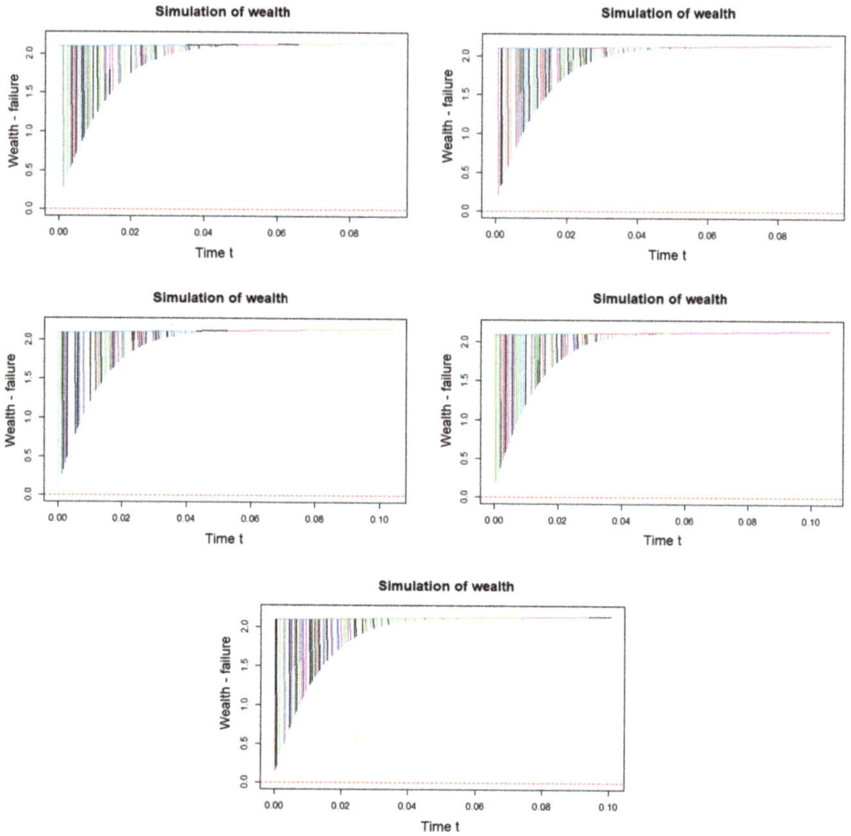


**Figure 6.** Monte Carlo simulations of wealth, for an initial wealth of $\omega = 2.1027018$ and a premium of $\pi = 0.3467538$.

## 5.2. *Probability of Ruin*

Next, we will use the procedure described in the previous section to approximate the company's probability of ruin, by generating a considerable number of Monte Carlo simulations. For this purpose, we will use the Law of large numbers. That is, if we have a sequence of independent and identically distributed random variables $\phi_1, \phi_2, \ldots$ with common mean, $\mu$, and if we consider that

$$\bar{\phi} := \frac{\phi_1 + \phi_2 + \ldots + \phi_m}{m}$$

then, for very large $m$ and for any positive number $\varepsilon$,

$$\mathbb{P}(|\bar{\phi}_m - \mu| > \varepsilon) \to 0.$$

To perform the Monte Carlo simulations, we will start by taking $m = 10{,}000$, which is the number of times that we will apply the simulation procedure seen in Section 5.1. This will yield the approximation of the probability of ruin $\bar{\phi}$ we seek.

As a starting point, we will take the initial values obtained in Section 3, that is, an initial capital of $\omega = 2.1027018$, and a premium of $r_i = 0.3467538$ for $i = 1.2$. In this case, the probability of ruin turned out to be equal to zero, $\bar{\phi} = 0\%$. The above makes sense because the initial capital is $W_0 = 2.1027$, while the maximum value of profit, $x(t)$, occurs when $t = 0$; so if the loss occurred at time zero, the company would have to pay $2 \cdot x(t) = 2 \cdot x_0 = 2$.

Likewise, we wonder what would happen if we set the value of the initial capital $\omega = 2.1027018$, and take different values of the premium that each agent has to pay, that is, $r_i = 0.3, 0.4, 0.5$ for $i = 1, 2$. In all these cases, something similar to the previous paragraph was concluded, since it was observed that the probability of ruin obtained was equal to zero. This is because the premium is prorated over the horizon, so it practically does not affect the evolution of wealth, $W_t$.

Now we consider the opposite: we will fix the initial value of the premium, $r_i = 0.3467538$ for $i = 1, 2$, to vary the value of the initial capital, we will take the values $\omega = 1.5, 1.65, 1.7$. In these cases, we obtained considerable differences, since the probabilities of ruin turn out to be non-zero. Furthermore, we note that the probability of ruin increases as the initial capital decreases, since for $\omega = 1.7$, the probability of ruin was $\bar{\phi} = 4.3\%$; for $\omega = 1.65$, the probability of ruin was close to $\bar{\phi} = 5.2\%$; and, for $\omega = 1.5$, the probability of ruin reached a value of $\bar{\phi} = 7.8\%$.

To complete this analysis, we reviewed what happens when we alternate the rest of the starting capital and premium values, and including $\omega = 1.95$; so we consider the cross between the values of $\omega = 1.5, 1.65, 1.7, 1.95$ with $r_i = 0.3, 0.4, 0.5$ for $i = 1, 2$. Table 5 shows the complete results of these crosses, where the first column indicates the premium; and the first line, the initial capital. As we have said before, the probability of ruin increases when the initial capital decreases. However, by varying the value of the premium, we observe that the probability of ruin is invariant, that is, it has no impact in leading the company to ruin.

**Table 5.** Probabilities of ruin for several values of $\omega$ and $\pi$.

| $\pi$ = Premium | $\omega = 1.5$ | $\omega = 1.65$ | $\omega = 1.7$ | $\omega = 1.95$ | $\omega = 2.102701805$ |
|---|---|---|---|---|---|
| 0.3 | 7.8% | 5.2% | 4.3% | 0.7% | 0.0% |
| 0.346753803 | 7.8% | 5.2% | 4.3% | 0.7% | 0.0% |
| 0.4 | 7.8% | 5.2% | 4.3% | 0.7% | 0.0% |
| 0.5 | 7.8% | 5.2% | 4.3% | 0.7% | 0.0% |

It follows from our simulations that, in general, in order for the probability of ruin to be positive, it suffices that the condition $\omega_0 < 2 \cdot x(t_0) = 2 \cdot x_0$ is satisfied, regardless of the value of the premium $\pi$ or of $x_0$, and as the initial capital is smaller, the probability of ruin for the company will be greater. On the contrary, if we want to prevent the company from eventually going bankrupt, then $\omega_0 \geq 2 \cdot x_0$ must happen, and this guarantees that the probability of ruin is zero.

## 6. Conclusions

This work represents an effort to combine techniques from the disciplines of mathematics, geology, stochastic games, and life and non-life actuarial mathematics. We believe that a multidisciplinary approach such as the one we present can lead to a reinvention of the way insurers understand the market for risks that are inherent to the extractive industry.

We have managed to pose the problem of competition between two agents to extract oil in deep waters from the point of view of game theory, and based on the results of [4], present the analysis of the resulting reserves as if it were of the elementary principle of equivalence of the classical actuarial calculation. In this work, we have based our developments on the results presented in [6], and we have verified first-hand the mathematical results that affirm that the risk is not insurable if only the "equivalence premium" is charged.

Subsequently, we use elementary tools in geology and statistics to propose a method to calibrate one of the probability distributions typically used to model the time to failure of extractors. Here, the articles [2,9,19] were a source of inspiration for our results. Finally, we use all the machinery developed in the body of the work to extend Bühlmann's model to calculate premia that allow the insurer to cover the risk, while obtaining a dividend for its foray into the non-renewable resource extraction market.

We consider that it is possible to study an extension of the results presented here using Insurance Optimization Theorems by applying deductibles (as in [5], Theorem 1.5.1 and [24], Theorem 1.4.3) or coinsurance (as in [24], Chapter 5.5) and thus re-estimate premia at the base and portfolio levels. Another possibility for future work is to test the results obtained analytically through Monte Carlo simulations to verify that the probability of ruin does not exceed the value $\varepsilon$ cited in the Section 4. To do this, we believe we can build on the approach presented in [7]. Finally, we believe that we will dedicate further work to calibrate the other two distributions of the time until the failure of the extractor presented in the Definitions 3 and 5.

**Author Contributions:** Conceptualization, software, validation, formal analysis and data curation are due to R.R.-M. and J.D.L.-B. The original draft preparation is due to J.D.L.-B. The work of writing—review, and editing was performed by R.R.-M. Visualization, supervision, project administration and funding acquisition are due to J.D.L.-B. All authors have read and agreed to the published version of the manuscript.

**Funding:** This research was funded by Universidad Anáhuac México, whom also covered the APC in full.

**Institutional Review Board Statement:** Not applicable.

**Informed Consent Statement:** Not applicable.

**Conflicts of Interest:** The authors declare no conflict of interest.

## References


1. Johansmeyer, T. How the Insurance Industry Could Bring Down Fossil Fuels. *Harvard Business Review*, 27 May 2021. Available online: https://hbr.org/2021/05/how-the-insurance-industry-could-bring-down-fossil-fuels (accessed on 26 April 2022).
2. Sayers, C.; Johnson, G.; Denyer, G. Predrill pore-pressure prediction using seismic data. *Geophysics* **2002**, *67*, 1286–1292. [CrossRef]
3. Gromova, E.V.; López-Barrientos, J.D. A Differential Game Model for The Extraction of Nonrenewable Resources with Random Initial Times—The Cooperative and Competitive Cases. *Int. Game Theory Rev.* **2016**, *18*, 1640004. [CrossRef]
4. López-Barrientos, J.D.; Gromova, E.V.; Miroshnichenko, E.S. Resource Exploitation in a Stochastic Horizon under Two Parametric Interpretations. *Mathematics* **2020**, *8*, 1081. [CrossRef]
5. Bowers, N.; Gerber, H.; Hickman, J.; Jones, D.; Nesbitt, C. *Actuarial Mathematics*; The Society of Actuaries: Schaumburg, IL, USA, 1997.
6. Real-Miranda, R.; López-Barrientos, J.D. Reserva Matemática Actuarial para la extracción de recursos no-renovables a partir de variables de pérdida no-negativas. *Rev. Electrón. Comun. Trab. ASEPUMA* **2022**, *in press*. Available online: https://www.dropbox.com/s/1wmel6a8eddmrwf/2021.12.29_ReservasMatem%C3%A1ticasActuariales.pdf?dl=0 (accessed on 28 April 2022).
7. Cano-Ramos, A.E.; López-Barrientos, J.D. ¿¡Te lo aseguro! o ¡te lo apuesto!? He ahí el dilema… *Miscelánea Mat.* **2022**, *72*, 1–20. [CrossRef]
8. Mood, A.M.; Graybill, F.A.; Boes, D.C. *Introduction to the Theory of Statistics*, 3rd ed.; McGraw-Hill: New York, NY, USA, 1974; pp. 312–314.
9. Bowers, G. Pore pressure estimation from velocity data: Accounting for pore pressure mechanisms besides undercompaction. *SPE Drill. Complet.* **1995**, *10*, 89–95. [CrossRef]
10. Bühlmann, H. Premium Calculation from Top Down. *ASTIN Bull.* **1985**, *15*, 89–101. [CrossRef]
11. Dockner, E.; Jørgensen, S.; van Long, N.; Sorger, G. *Differential Games in Economics and Management Science*; Cambridge University Press: Cambridge, UK, 2000.
12. Grimmett, G.; Stirzaker, D. *Probability and Random Processes*; Oxford Science Publications: Oxford, UK, 1994.
13. Klugman, S.; Panjer, H.; Willmot, G. *Loss Models: From Data to Decisions*; John Wiley and Sons: Hoboken, NJ, USA, 2019.
14. Promislow, D. *Fundamentals of Actuarial Mathematics*, 3rd ed.; John Wiley and Sons: Hoboken, NJ, USA, 2011.
15. Henley, E.; Kumamoto, H. *Probabilistic Risk Assessment: Reliability Engineering, Design, and Analysis*; IEEE Press: New York, NY, USA, 1992.
16. Chen, Z. A new two-parameter lifetime distribution with bathtub shape or increasing failure rate function. *Stat. Probab. Lett.* **2000**, *49*, 155–161. [CrossRef]
17. Schmidli, H. *Stochastic Controls in Insurance*; Springer: London, UK, 2008.
18. Lei, Y. Evaluation of three methods for estimating the Weibull distribution parameters of Chinese pine (*Pinus tabulaeformis*). *J. For. Sci.* **2008**, *54*, 566–571. [CrossRef]
19. Sayers, C.; den Boer, L.; Nagy, Z.; Hooyman, P.; Ward, V. Pore pressure in the Gulf of Mexico: Seeing ahead of the bit. *World Oil* **2005**, *55*, 55–58.
20. Slotnick, M. On seismic computation with applications. *Geophysics* **1936**, *1*, 9–22. [CrossRef]

21. Xu, Y.; Gardner, G.; MacDonald, J. Some effects of velocity variation on AVO and its interpretation. *Geophysics* **1993**, *58*, 1297–1300. [CrossRef]
22. Eaton, B. The equation for geopressure prediction from well logs. *SPE* **1975**, *5544*, 2–4.
23. Traugott, M. Pore/fracture pressure determinations in deep water. *World Oil Deep. Technol. Spec. Suppl.* **1997**, *8*, 68–70.
24. Kaas, R.; Goovaerts, M.; Dhaene, J.; Denuit, M. *Actuarial Risk Theory Using R*; Springer: Berlin/Heidelberg, Germany, 2008.

MDPI
St. Alban-Anlage 66
4052 Basel
Switzerland
www.mdpi.com

*Mathematics* Editorial Office
E-mail: mathematics@mdpi.com
www.mdpi.com/journal/mathematics

www.ingramcontent.com/pod-product-compliance
Lightning Source LLC
LaVergne TN
LVHW070231100526
838202LV00015B/2117
* 9 7 8 3 0 3 6 5 8 8 5 2 0 *